MARTIN LUTHER.
1483-1546.
This one man brought about the Reformation
and was the father of Protestantism. He also
translated the Bible from Latin into German, and
his version is the accepted text for all editions in
that language.

SUNDAY HALF HOURS
WITH GREAT PREACHERS

THE GREATEST SERMONS BY THE GREATEST
PREACHERS OF THE CHRISTIAN FAITH IN ALL AGES.

A SERMON FOR
EVERY SUNDAY IN THE YEAR

EDITED BY

REV. JESSE LYMAN HURLBUT, D.D.,

AUTHOR OF

"Hurlbut's Story of the Bible," "Hurlbut's Bible Lessons," "Studies in Old
Testament History," "Revised Normal Lessons," "Studies in the
Four Gospels," former editor of the "International Sun-
day-school Lessons," etc., etc.

PROFUSELY ILLUSTRATED.

THE JOHN C. WINSTON CO.
<small>CHICAGO</small>   <small>PHILADELPHIA</small>   <small>TORONTO</small>

PREFACE

Among the potent forces that have molded the Christian civilization during the last twenty centuries, the pulpit must be regarded not as one of the least, but as one of the greatest. The deepest and highest elements of the human nature are alike connected with religion, or the relation of man to the Unseen; and these are the influences affecting the characters, and the forces directed by the preaching of the gospel.

The preaching of St. Paul transformed Christianity from a national and narrow sect into a religion for the world; and uncounted millions since have received an impulse from his words. The discourses of St. Augustine cast the Pauline doctrine into molds that have shaped not only the beliefs but the lives as well, of some of the greatest men in modern times. The impassioned oratory of Peter the Hermit, in the eleventh century set all Europe on fire, and sent millions to wrest the Holy Sepulchre from the hands of the Moslem. The preaching of Martin Luther made a new world of northern Europe. The sermons of Whitefield caused tears to wash the grimy countenances of ten thousand coal-miners, and those of John Wesley emptied the churches and filled the open fields with worshipers. The America of to-day would not be what it is, but for the preaching of Jonathan Edwards and Timothy Dwight, and Henry Ward Beecher, and Phillips Brooks.

There are some in our age who tell us that the pulpit has been shorn of its powers; and that the newspaper now sits upon its throne. But to-day there are in every great city of our land ministers whose words will outweigh any editorial; and the village pastor certainly outranks in scholarship, ability, and personal influence the village editor.

It is surely a valuable service, to bring together in one volume for convenient reference, many of the masterpieces of preaching in all ages. This volume represents a careful sifting from many sources of the great sermons from those of St. Augustine to the present day. It contains fifty-two discourses, one for each Sunday of the year, rep-

PREFACE

resenting the great preachers of Asia and Africa in Chrysostom and Augustine, of Germany and France in Luther and Massillon, of England, in many preachers from Hugh Latimer to Alexander Maclaren, and America, from Jonathan Edwards, to some of the younger men who fill with such power the pulpits of New York and Chicago.

With each sermon is given a biographical sketch of the preacher, and a brief critical estimate of his style and his power. These with the many portraits, will aid in bringing the reader into something of an acquaintance with these masters of assemblies.

This work was originally published in 1871, under the same title, and with the same plan, ably wrought out by the Rev. M. Laird Simons, to whose labors the present editor is greatly indebted. In a generation, however, the perspective changes, and some men who were once deemed great are less prominent to-day, while new figures come to the front; so that nearly half of the sermons in this volume are different from those in the earlier edition. The accompanying sketches have also been re-written, and for the greater part are new. Wherever practicable, each Sermon is a verbatim reprint from the standard edition of each author's works, thus preserving the individuality of punctuation, capitals, etc. An exception has been made to this rule by substituting modern usage in place of antiquated spelling, and by modifying the inordinate use of capitals in the case of *Who* and *Himself,* when applied to the Deity. Never has the slightest liberty been taken to prune or expunge any sentiment expressed, as such action would have been a gross violation of personal rights; yet several times, because of extreme length, slight omissions have been made of matter local in interest, or otherwise irrelevant. In the seventeenth century people enjoyed sermons hours in length; and it has been found necessary to omit certain portions from the discourses of these divines, while giving every endeavor to preserve the peculiar flavor of their individuality.

In its new form this book, which has already served a generation in the nineteenth century, is sent forth with the prayer that it may become a blessing to many in the twentieth century.

JESSE LYMAN HURLBUT.

September, 1907.

TABLE OF CONTENTS

LIST OF AUTHORS, THEIR DATES AND TITLES OF SER-
MONS, ARRANGED IN CHRONOLOGICAL ORDER.

X

JEAN BAPTISTE MASSILLON

1663–1742

*"And many lepers were in Israel in the time of Eliseus the prophet;
and none of them was cleansed, saving Naaman the Syrian."—Luke
iv. 27.*

XI

JONATHAN EDWARDS

1703–1758

*"To fill up their sins alway; for the wrath is to come upon them
to the uttermost."— 1 Thess. ii. 16.*

XII

JOHN WESLEY

1703–1791

"Not as the Transgression, so is the Free Gift."—Romans v. 15.

XIII

GEORGE WHITEFIELD

1714–1770

*"They have healed also the hurt of the daughter of my people slightly,
saying, peace, peace, when there is no peace."—Jeremiah vi. 14.*

XIV

ROWLAND HILL

1744–1833

*"This month shall be unto you the beginning of months; it shall be
the first month of the year to you."—Exodus xii. 2.*

XV

TIMOTHY DWIGHT

1752–1817

*"O Lord, I know that the way of man is not in himself: it is not in
man that walketh to direct his steps."—Jeremiah x. 23.*

Page.

CONTENTS

I

JOHN CHRYSOSTOM

347–407

THE name of this great church-father, preacher and reformer was John; and the title of "Chrysostomos" or "the golden-mouthed," was not bestowed upon him until after his death; but it has become practically the only name by which he is known; and it befits him as the most eloquent and powerful preacher of Christianity in five centuries. He was born at Antioch in Syria, about 347 A. D.; the precise date of his birth being unknown. During his youth, like Augustine in a different land at about the same time, he stood at poise between the pagan and Christian religions; and like Augustine, was led to embrace the gospel of Christ by the influence of his mother, Anthusa. After his baptism, when he was twenty-one years old, he maintained for several years an ascetic life of great severity. In 386 he was ordained a priest; and his passionate earnestness in preaching at Antioch drew the attention of the prime-minister of the Emperor Arcadius, who called him to Constantinople and caused him to be made Bishop. But John as Bishop of Constantinople preached with such vehemence against the sins of his age, the corruptions of the court and the church, and undertook such radical reforms, that he was more than once sent into banishment to remote places, where his influence, it was thought, would be narrowed. But from his seclusion he wrote such strong letters and treatises as to arouse at once the people in his behalf and the rulers in church and state against him. He died in 407 A. D., while on his way to a distant place of exile. His last words were, "God be praised for everything!" He was regarded by his friends as a martyr; and so deep and enduring was the feeling throughout the empire, that thirty years after his death, the Emperor Theodosius II caused his body to be brought to Constantinople and interred with the highest honors. His writings were many; but the most valuable of them are his Homilies — or sermons — on the New Testament and the Psalms. They show us the highest type of preaching in the earlier centuries of the church after the apostolic age.

FOOLISHNESS OF THE CROSS CONQUERING.

" For the preaching of the Cross is to them that perish foolishness; but to us which are saved it is the power of God. For it is written, I will destroy the wisdom of the wise, and will bring to nothing the understanding of the prudent. Where is the wise? Where is the Scribe? Where is the disputer of this world?"— 1 Cor. i. 18–20.

To the sick and broken-spirited even wholesome meats are unpleasant, friends and relations burdensome; who are oftentimes not even recognised, but are rather accounted intruders. Much like this often is the case of those who are perishing in their souls. For the things which tend to salvation they know not; and those who are careful about them they consider to be troublesome. Now this ensues not from the nature of the thing, but from their disease. And just what the insane do, hating those who take care of them, and ever after reviling them, the same is the case with unbelievers also. But as in the case of the former, they who are insulted then more than ever compassionate them, and weep, taking this as the worst symptom of the disease in its intense form, when they know not their best friends; so also in the case of the Gentiles let us act; yea more than for our wives let us wail over them, because they know not the common salvation. For not so dearly ought a man to love his wife as we should love all mankind, and draw them over unto salvation; be a man a Gentile, or be he what he may. For these then let us weep; for " the preaching of the Cross is to them foolishness," being itself Wisdom and Power. " For," saith he, " the preaching of the Cross to them that perish is foolishness."

For since it was likely that they, the Cross being derided by the Greeks, would resist and contend by aid of that wisdom, which came (forsooth) of themselves, as being disturbed by the expressions of the Greeks; Paul comforting them saith, Think it not strange and unaccountable, which is taking place. This is the nature of that which we now treat of, to have them that perish fail in acknowledging its power.

For they are besides themselves, and behave as madmen; and so they rail and are disgusted at the medicines which bring health.

But what sayest thou, O man? Christ became a slave for thee, "having taken the form of a slave," and was crucified, and rose again. And when thou oughtest to adore Him risen for this and admire His loving-kindness; because what neither father, nor friend, nor son, did for thee, all this the Lord wrought, for thee, the enemy and offender — when, I say, thou oughtest to admire Him for these things, callest thou that foolishness, which is full of so great wisdom? Well, it is nothing wonderful; for it is a mark of them that perish not to recognise the things which lead to salvation. Be not troubled therefore, for it is no strange nor unaccountable event, that things truly great are mocked at by those who are beside themselves. Now such as are in this mind you cannot convince by human wisdom. Yea, if you want so to convince them, you do but the contrary. For the things which transcend reasoning require faith alone. Thus, should we set about convincing men by reasonings, how God became man, and entered into the Virgin's womb, and not commit the matter unto faith, they will but deride the more. Therefore they who inquire by reasonings, these are they who perish.

And why speak I of God? for in regard of created things, should we do this, great derision will ensue. For suppose a man, wishing to make out all things by reasoning; and let him try by thy discourse to convince himself how we see the light; and do thou try to convince him by reasoning. Nay, thou canst not: for if thou sayest that it suffices to see by opening the eyes, thou hast not expressed the manner, but the fact. For " why see we not," one will say, " by our hearing, and with our eyes hear? And why hear we not with the nostril, and with the hearing smell? " If then, he being in doubt about these things, and we unable to give the explanation of them, he is to begin laughing, shall not we rather laugh him to scorn? " For since both have their origin from one brain, since the two members are near neighbors to each other, why can they not do the same work? " Now we shall not be able to state the cause, nor the method of the unspeakable and curious operation; and should we make the attempt, we shall be laughed to scorn. Wherefore, leaving this unto God's power and boundless wisdom, let us be silent.

Just so with regard to the things of God; should we desire to explain them by the wisdom which is from without, great derision will ensue, not from their infirmity, but from the folly of men. For the great things of all no language can explain.

Now observe: when I say, " He was crucified; " the Greek saith, " And how can this be reasonable? Himself He helped not when undergoing crucifixion and sore trial at the moment of the Cross: how then after these things did He rise again and help others? For if He had been able, before death was the proper time." (For this the Jews actually said.) " But He who helped not himself, how helped He others? There is no reason in it," saith he. True, O man, for indeed it is above reason; and unspeakable is the power of the Cross. For that being actually in the midst of horrors, He should have shown Himself above all horrors; and being in the enemy's hold should have overcome; this cometh of Infinite Power. For as in the case of the Three Children, their not entering the furnace would not have been so astonishing, as that having entered in they trampled upon the fire; — and in the case of Jonah, it was a greater thing by far, after he had been swallowed by the fish, to suffer no harm from the monster, than if he had not been swallowed at all;— so also in regard to Christ; His not dying would not have been so inconceivable, as that being dead He should loose the bands of death. Say not then, " why did He not help Himself on the Cross? " for He was hastening on to close conflict with death himself. He descended not from the Cross, not because He could not, but because He would not. For Him whom the tyranny of death restrained not, how could the nails of the Cross restrain?

But these things, though known to us, are not so as yet to the unbelievers. Wherefore he said, that " the preaching of the Cross is to them that perish foolishness; but to us who are saved it is the power of God. For it is written, I will destroy the wisdom of the wise, and the understanding of the prudent will I bring to nothing." Nothing from himself which might give offence, does he advance up to this point; but first he comes to the testimony of the Scripture, and then, furnished with boldness from thence, adopts more vehement words and saith,

Ver. 20, 21. " Hath not God made foolish the wisdom of this world? Where is the wise? Where the Scribe? Where the disputer of this world? Hath not God made foolish the wisdom of this world? For after that, by the wisdom of God, the world by wisdom knew not God, it pleased God, by the foolishness of preaching, to save them that believe." Having said, " It is written, I will destroy the wisdom of the wise," he subjoins the demonstration from facts, saying, " Where is the wise? where the Scribe? " at the same time glancing at both Gentiles and Jews. For what sort of philosopher, which among those who have studied logic, which of those knowing in Jewish matters, hath saved us, and made known the truth? Not one. It was the Fishermen's work, the whole of it.

Having then inferred what he had in view, and brought down their pride, and said, " Hath not God made foolish the wisdom of this world? " he states the reason also, why these things were so done. " For after that by the wisdom of God," saith he, " the world by wisdom knew not God," the Cross appeared. Now what means, " by the wisdom of God? " The wisdom apparent in those works, whereby it was His will to make Himself known. For to this end did He frame them, and frame them such as they are, that by a sort of proportion, from the things which are seen, admiration of the Maker might be learned. Is the heaven great, and the earth boundless? Wonder then at Him who made them. For this heaven, great as it is, not only was made by Him, but made with ease; and that boundless earth too, was brought into being even as if it had been nothing. Wherefore of the former He saith, " The works of Thy fingers are the heavens; " and concerning the earth, " Who hath made the earth as it were nothing." Since then by this wisdom the world was unwilling to acknowledge God, He employed what seemed to be foolishness, i. e. the Gospel, to persuade men; not by reasonings, but by faith. It remains that where God's wisdom is, there is no longer need of man's. For before, to infer that He who made the world, such and so great, must in all reason be a God possessed of a certain uncontrollable, unspeakable power; and by these means to apprehend Him; — this was the part of human wisdom. But now we need no more reasonings, but faith alone. For to believe on Him that was crucified and buried, and to be most fully persuaded that this person Himself both rose again, and sat down on high; this needeth not wisdom, nor reasonings, but faith. For the Apostles themselves came in not by wisdom, but by faith, and surpassed the heathen wise men in wisdom and loftiness, and that so much the more, by how much to raise disputings is less than to receive by faith the things of God. For this transcends all human understanding.

But how hath He " destroyed wisdom? " Being made known to us by Paul and others like him, He hath shown it to be unprofitable. For towards receiving the evangelical proclamation, neither is the wise profited at all by wisdom, nor the unlearned injured at all by ignorance. But if one may speak somewhat even wonderful, ignorance rather than wisdom is a condition suitable for that impression, and more easily dealt with. For the shepherd and the rustic will more quickly receive this, once for all repressing all doubting thoughts, and delivering himself to the Lord. In this way then He hath destroyed wisdom. For since she first cast herself down, she is ever after useful for nothing. Thus when she ought to have displayed her proper powers, and by the works to have seen the Lord, she would not. Wherefore though she were now willing to introduce herself, she is not able. For the matter is not of that kind: this way of knowing God being far greater than the other. You see then, faith and simplicity are needed, and this we should seek everywhere, and prefer it before the wisdom which is from without. For "God," saith he, "hath made wisdom foolish."

But what is "He hath made foolish?" He hath shown it foolish in regard of receiving the faith. For since they prided themselves on it, He lost no time in exposing it. For what sort of wisdom is it, when it cannot discover the chief of things that are good? He caused her therefore to appear foolish, after she had first convicted herself. For if when discoveries might have been made by reasoning, she proved nothing, now when things proceed on a larger scale, how will she be able to accomplish aught? now when there is need of faith alone, and not of acuteness? You see then, God hath shown her to be foolish.

It was His good pleasure too by the foolishness of the Gospel to save; foolishness, I say, not real, but appearing to be such. For that which is more wonderful yet is His having prevailed by bringing in, not another such wisdom more abundant than the first, but what seemed to be foolishness. He cast out Plato, for example, not by means of another philosopher of more skill, but by an unlearned fisherman. For thus the defeat became greater, and the victory more splendid.

Ver. 22-24. Next, to show the power of the Cross, he saith, "For the Jews require a sign, and the Greeks seek after wisdom: but we preach Christ crucified, unto the Jews a stumbling-block, and unto the Greeks foolishness; but unto them which are called, both Jews and Greeks, Christ the Power of God, and the Wisdom of God."

Vast is the import of the things here spoken! For he means to say how by contraries God hath overcome, and how the Gospel is not of man. What he saith is something of this sort. When, saith he, we say unto the Jews, Believe; they answer, Raise the dead, Heal the demoniacs, Show unto us signs. But instead thereof what say we? That He was crucified, and died, who is preached. And this is enough, not only to fail in drawing over the unwilling, but utterly to drive away those even who are willing. Nevertheless, it drives not away, but attracts, and holds fast, and overcomes.

Again; the Greeks demand of us a rhetorical style, and the acuteness of sophistry. But we to these also preach the Cross: and that which in the case of the Jews is deemed to be of weakness, this in the case of the Greeks is foolishness. Wherefore, when we not only fail in producing what they demand, but also produce the very opposites of their demand; (for the Cross has not merely no appearance of being a sign sought out by reasoning, but even the very annihilation of a sign; — is not merely deemed no proof of power, but a conviction of weakness; — not merely no display of wisdom, but a ground for surmising foolishness) ; — when therefore they who seek for signs and wisdom not only receive not the things which they ask, but even hear the contrary to what they desire, and then by means of contraries are persuaded; — how is not the power of Him that is preached unspeakable? As if to some one tempest-tost and longing for a haven, you were to show not a haven but another wilder portion of the sea, and so could make him follow with thankfulness! Or as if a physician could attract to himself the man that was wounded and in need of remedies, by promising to cure him not with drugs, but with burning of him again! For this is a result of great power indeed. So also the Apostles prevailed, not simply by a sign, but even by a thing which seemed contrary to all the known signs. Which thing also Christ did in the case of the blind man. For when He would heal him, He restored him by a thing which increased the blindness: i. e. He put on clay. As then by means of clay He healed the blind man, so also by means of the Cross hath He brought the world to Himself. That certainly was adding an offence, not taking an offence away. So did He also in the Creation, working out things by their contraries. With sand, for instance, He walled in the sea, having made the weak a bridle to the strong. He placed the earth upon water, having taken order that the heavy and the dense might be borne on the soft and fluid. By means of the Prophets again with a small piece of wood He raised up iron from the bottom. In like manner also with the Cross He hath drawn the world to Himself. For as the water beareth up the earth, so also the Cross beareth up the world. You see now, it is proof of great power and wisdom, to

convince by means of the things which tell directly against us. Thus
the Cross seems to be matter of offence; and yet far from scandalizing, it
even attracts.

Ver. 25. All these things, therefore, Paul bearing in mind, and
being struck with astonishment, said, that "the foolishness of God is
wiser than men, and the weakness of God is stronger than men;" in
relation to the Cross, speaking of a folly and weakness, not real but
apparent. For he is answering with respect unto the other party's
opinion. For that which philosophers were not able by means of reasoning to accomplish, this, what seemed to be foolishness did excellently
well. Which then is the wiser, he that persuadeth the many or but
few, I should say, no one? He who persuadeth concerning the greatest
points, or about matters which are nothing? What great labors did
Plato endure, and his followers, discoursing to us about a line, and an
angle, and a point, and about numbers even and odd, and equal unto
one another and unequal, and such-like spiderwebs (for indeed those
webs are not more useless to man's life, than were these subjects):
and without doing good to any one great or small by their means, so
he made an end of his life. How greatly did he labor, endeavoring to
show that the soul is immortal! and even as he came he went away,
having spoken nothing with certainty, nor persuaded any hearer. But
the Cross wrought persuasion by means of unlearned men; yea it persuaded even the whole world: and not about common things, but in
discourse of God and the godliness which is according to truth, and the
evangelical way of life, and the judgment of the things to come. And
of all men it made philosophers: the very rustics, the utterly unlearned.
Behold how "the foolishness of God is wiser than men," and "the
weakness stronger!" How, *stronger?* Because it overran the whole
world, and took all by main force, and while men were endeavoring by
ten thousands to quench the name of the Crucified, the contrary came
to pass: that flourished and increased more and more, but they perished
and wasted away; and the living, in war with the dead, had no power.
So that when the Greek calls me foolish, he shows himself exceedingly
above measure foolish: since I who am esteemed by him a fool, evidently
appear wiser than the wise. When he calleth me weak, then he showeth
himself to be weaker. For the noble things which publicans and fishermen were able to effect by the grace of God, these, philosophers, and
rhetoricians, and tyrants, and in short the whole world, running ten
thousand ways here and there, could not even form a notion of. For

what did not the Cross introduce? The doctrine concerning the Immortality of the Soul; that concerning the Resurrection of the Body; that concerning the contempt of things present; that concerning the desire of things future. Yea, Angels it hath made of men, and all, everywhere, practice self-denial, and show forth all kinds of fortitude.

But among them also, it will be said, many have been found contemners of death. Tell me who? was it he who drank the hemlock? But if thou wilt, I can bring forward ten thousand such from within the Church. For had it been lawful when persecution befell them to drink hemlock and depart, all had become more famous than he. And besides, he drank when he was not at liberty to drink or not to drink; but willing or against his will he must have undergone it: no effect surely of fortitude, but of necessity, and nothing more. For even robbers and man-slayers, having fallen under the condemnation of their judges, have suffered things more grievous. But with us it is all quite the contrary. For not against their will did the martyrs endure, but of their will, and being at liberty not to suffer; showing forth fortitude harder than all adamant. This then you see is no great wonder, that he whom I was mentioning drank hemlock, it being no longer in his power not to drink, and also when he had arrived at a very great age. For when he dispised life he stated himself to be seventy years old; if this can be called despising. For I for my part could not affirm it: nor, what is more, can any one else. But show me some one enduring firm in torments for godliness' sake, as I show thee ten thousand everywhere in the world. Who, while his nails were tearing out, nobly endured? Who, while his joints were wrenching asunder? Who, while his body was enduring spoil, member by member? or his head? Who, while his bones were being heaved out by levers? Who, while placed without intermission upon frying-pans? Who, when thrown into a caldron? Show me these instances. For to die by hemlock is all as one with a sleeping man's continuing in a state of sleep. Nay even sweeter than sleep is this sort of death, if report say true. But if certain [of them] did endure torments, yet of these too the praise is gone to nothing. For on some disgraceful occasion they perished; some for revealing mysteries; some for aspiring to dominion; others detected in the foulest crimes; others again at random, and fruitlessly, and ignorantly, there being no reason for it, made away with themselves. But not so with us. Wherefore of their deeds nothing is said; but these flourish and daily increase.

Which Paul having in mind said, "The weakness of God is stronger than all men."

For that the Gospel is divine, even from hence is evident; namely, from what quarter could it have occurred to twelve ignorant men to attempt such great things? who sojourned in marshes, in rivers, in deserts; who never at any time perhaps had entered into a city nor into a forum: — whence did it occur, to set themselves in array against the whole world? For that they were timid and unmanly, he shows who wrote of them, not shrinking back, nor enduring to throw their failings into the shade: which indeed of itself is a very great token of the truth. What then doth he say about them? That when Christ was apprehended, after ten thousand wonders, the rest fled; and he who remained, being the leader of the rest, denied. Whence was it then that they who, when Christ was alive, endured not the attack of the Jews; now that He was dead and buried, and, as ye say, had not risen again, nor had any talk with them, nor infused courage into them,— whence did they set themselves in array against so great a world? Would they not have said among themselves, "What ever meaneth this? Himself He was not able to save, and will He protect us? Himself He defended not when alive, and will He stretch out the hand unto us now that He is dead? Himself, when alive, subdued not even one nation; and are we to convince the whole world by uttering His Name?" How, I ask, could all this be reasonable, I will not say, as something to be done, but even as something to be imagined? From whence it is plain, that had they not seen Him after He was risen, and received most ample proof of His power, they would not have ventured so great a cast.

For suppose they had possessed friends innumerable; would they not presently have got them all for enemies, disturbing ancient customs, and removing their fathers' land-marks? But as it was, they had before gotten them for enemies, all, both their own countrymen and foreigners. For although they had been recommended to veneration by everything external, would not all men have abhorred them, introducing a new polity? But now they were even void of all; and it was likely that even on that account all would hate and scorn them at once. For whom will you name? The Jews? Nay, they had against them an inexpressible hatred on account of the things which had been done unto the Master. The Greeks then? Why, first of all, these had rejected one not inferior to them; and no men know these things so well as the Greeks. For

Plato, who wished to strike out a new form of government, or rather a part of government; and that, not by changing the customs relating to the gods, but merely by substituting one line of conduct for another; being cast out of Sicily, went near to lose his life. This however did not ensue: so that he lost his liberty alone. And had not a certain Barbarian been more gentle than the tyrant of Sicily, nothing could have rescued the philosopher from slavery throughout life in a foreign land. And yet it is not all one to innovate in affairs of a kingdom, and in matters of religious worship. For the latter more than anything else causes disturbance and troubles men. For to say, " let such and such an one marry such a woman, and let the guardians [of the commonwealth] exercise their guardianship so and so," is not enough to cause any great disturbance: and especially when all this is lodged in a book, and no great anxiety on the part of the legislator to carry the proposals into practice. On the other hand, to say, " they be no gods which men worship, but demons; He who was crucified is God;" ye well know how great wrath it kindled, how severely men must have paid for it, what a flame of war it fanned.

For Protagoras, who was one of them, having dared to say, " I know of no gods," not going round the world and proclaiming it, but in a single city, was in the most imminent peril of his life. And Diagoras the Milesian, and Theodorus, who was called Atheist, although they had friends, and that influence which comes from eloquence, and were held in admiration because of their philosophy; yet nevertheless none of these profited them. And the great Socrates too, he who surpassed in philosophy all among them, for this reason drank hemlock, because in his discourses concerning the gods he was suspected of moving things a little aside. Now if the suspicion alone of innovation brought so great danger on philosophers and wise men, and on those who had attained boundless popularity; and if they were not only unable to do what they wished, but were themselves also driven from life and country; how canst thou choose but be in admiration and astonishment, when thou seest that the fisherman hath produced such an effect upon the world, and accomplished his purposes; hath overcome both Barbarians and Greeks — all of them?

But they did not, you will say, introduce strange gods as the others did. Well, and in that you are naming the very point most to be wondered at: that the innovation is twofold, both to pull down those which are, and to announce the Crucified. For from whence came it into their minds to proclaim such things? whence, to be confident about their event? Whom of those before them could they perceive to have prospered in any such attempt? Were not all men worshipping devils? Were not all used to make gods of the elements? Was not the difference [but] in the mode of impiety? But nevertheless they attacked all, and overthrew all, and overran in a short time the whole world, like a sort of winged beings; making no account of dangers, of deaths, of the difficulty of the thing, of their own fewness, of the multitude of the opponents, of the authority, the rank, the wisdom of those at war with them. For they had above all these, mightier aid, the power of Him that had been crucified and was risen again. It would not have been so wondrous, had they chosen to wage war with the world in the literal sense, as this which in fact has taken place. For according to the law of battle they might have stood over against the enemies, and occupying some adverse ground, have arrayed themselves accordingly, to meet the array of their foes, and have taken their time for attack and close conflict. But in this case it is not so. For they had no camp of their own, but were absolutely mingled with their enemies, and thus overcame them. Even in the midst of their enemies as they went about, they glided away from their hold, and became superior, and achieved a splendid victory; a victory which fulfils the prophecy that saith, "Even in the midst of thine enemies thou shalt have dominion." For this it was which was full of all astonishment, that their enemies having them in their power, and casting them into prisons and chains, not only did not vanquish them, but themselves also eventually had to stoop under them: the scourgers to the scourged, the binders in chains to those who were bound, the persecutors to the fugitives. All these things then we say unto the Greeks, yea rather more than these; for the truth has enough and greatly to spare. And if ye will follow the argument, we will teach you the whole method of fighting against them. In the mean while let us hold fast these two heads; How did the weak overcome the strong? and, From whence came it into their thoughts, being such as they were, to form such plans, unless they enjoyed Divine aid?

So far then as to what we have to say. But let us show forth by our actions all excellencies of conduct, and kindle abundantly the fire of virtue. For "ye are lights," saith he, "shining in the midst of the world." And unto each of us God hath committed a greater function than He hath to the sun: greater than heaven, and earth, and sea; and by so much greater, as spiritual things be more excellent than things sensible. When then we look unto the solar orb, and admire the beauty, and the body, and the brightness of the luminary, let us consider again that greater and better is the light which is in us, as indeed the darkness also is more dreadful unless we take heed. And in fact a deep night oppresses the whole world. This is what we have to dispel and dissolve. It is night not among heretics, nor among Greeks only, but also in the multitude on our side, in respect of doctrines and of life. For many entirely disbelieve the resurrection; many fortify themselves with their, horoscope; many adhere to superstitious observances, and to omens, and auguries, and presages. And some likewise employ amulets and charms. But to these also we will speak afterwards, when we have finished what we have to say to the Greeks.

In the mean while hold fast the things which have been said, and be ye fellow-helpers with me in the battle; by your way of life attracting them to us and changing them. For, as I am always saying, He that teaches high morality ought first to teach it in his own person, and be such as his hearers cannot do without. Let us therefore become such, and make the Greeks feel kindly towards us. And this will come to pass if we make up our minds not to do ill, but rather to suffer ill. Do we not see when little children being borne in their father's arms, give him that carries them blows on the cheek, how sweetly the father lets the boy have his fill of wrath, and when he sees that he has spent his passion, how his countenance brightens up? In like manner let us also act; and as fathers with children, so let us discourse with the Greeks. For all the Greeks are children. And this, some of their own writers have said, that "that people are children always, and no Greek is an old man." Now children cannot bear to take thought for anything useful; so also the Greeks would be for ever at play; and they lie on the ground, grovelling in posture and in affections. Moreover, children oftentimes, when we are discoursing about important things, give no heed to anything that is said, but will even be laughing all the time: such also are the Greeks. When we discourse of the Kingdom, they laugh. And as spittle dropping in abundance from an infant's mouth, which oftentimes spoils its meat and drink, such also are the words flowing from the mouth of the Greeks, vain and unclean. Even if thou art giving children their necessary food, they keep on vexing those who furnish it with evil speech, and we must bear with them all the while. Again, children, when they see a robber entering and taking away the furniture, far from resisting, even smile on him in his mischievous craft; but shouldest thou take away the little basket or the jingles or any other of their play-things, they take it to heart and fret, tear themselves, and stamp on the floor; just so do the Greeks also: when they behold the devil pilfering all their paternal wealth, and even the things which support their life, they laugh and run to him as to a friend: but should any one take away any possession, be it wealth or any childish thing whatsoever of that kind, they cry, they tear themselves. And as children expose their limbs unconsciously and blush not for shame; so the Greeks, wallowing in whoredoms and adulteries, and laying bare the laws of nature, and introducing unlawful intercourses, are not abashed.

Ye have given me vehement applause and acclamation: but with all your applause have a care lest you be among those of whom these things are said. Wherefore I beseech you all to become men: since, so long as we are children, how shall we teach them manliness? How shall we restrain them from childish folly? Let us, therefore, become men; that we may arrive at the measure of the stature which hath been marked out for us by Christ, and may obtain the good things to come: through the grace and loving-kindness of our Lord Jesus Christ, with whom unto the Father together with the Holy Spirit be glory, power, honor, now and henceforth and for evermore. Amen.

JOHN CHRYSOSTOM.
347-407.
One of the great "Fathers of the Church." He was born in Antioch, and became Bishop of Constantinople, where his rigorous ideas of conduct frequently brought him into disfavor. His Homilies have preserved the text of his discourses.

AURELIUS AUGUSTINE.
354-430.
The greatest of the "Fathers of the Church."
Augustine's writings were the principal text-book
of the clergy through the Middle Ages, and have
been the chief agent in forming the subsequent
theology of Christendom.

II

AURELIUS AUGUSTINE

354–430

A URELIUS AUGUSTINE was for a thousand years the greatest name in the history of the Christian church. He has been regarded as "the chief of the Latin Fathers," and the builder, after St. Paul, of the theology which ruled the church not only through the Middle Ages, but even to modern times; for besides the Roman Catholics, even the greatest Protestant theologians as Calvin and Edwards were his disciples. He was born at Tagaste in Numidia, a province of North Africa, A. D. 354. His early life is narrated in his "Confessions," one of the most remarkable works of autobiography ever written. His father was a pagan, though afterward converted to Christianity; but his mother was Monica, a devoted Christian whose prayers for her brilliant son, even while he was living in worldly pleasure, were answered in his conversion in 387 A. D. He became a presbyter in the church and was made Bishop of Hippo in Africa. His life was in the period while the Roman Empire was breaking up under the pressure of barbarian invasions, and his great work " The City of God " was almost a prophecy of the new Christian world destined to arise out of the dissolving empire. This sermon is taken from his "Homilies on the New Testament," a series of discourses preached to candidates for baptism. He died in 430.

ON THE LORD'S PRAYER.

" *Our Father which art in heaven, Hallowed be thy name. Thy kingdom come. Thy will be done in earth, as it is in heaven. Give us this day our daily bread. And forgive us our debts, as we forgive our debtors. And lead us not into temptation, but deliver us from evil.*"
— Matt. vi. 9–13.

THE order established for your edification requires that ye learn first what to believe, and afterwards what to ask. For so saith the Apostle, "Whosoever shall call upon the Name of the Lord, shall be saved." This testimony blessed Paul cited out of the Prophet; for by the Prophet were those times foretold, when all men should call upon God; "Whosoever shall call upon the Name of the Lord, shall be saved." And he added, "How then shall they call on Him in whom they have not believed? And how shall they believe in Him of whom they have not heard? Or how shall they hear without a preacher? Or how shall they preach except they be sent?" Therefore were preachers sent. They preached Christ. As they preached, the people heard, by hearing they believed, and by believing called upon Him. Because then it was most rightly and most truly said, "How shall they call on Him in whom they have not believed?" therefore have ye first learned what to believe: and to-day have learnt to call on Him in whom ye have believed.

The Son of God, our Lord Jesus Christ, hath taught us a Prayer; and though He be the Lord himself, as ye have heard and repeated in the Creed, the Only Son of God, yet He would not be alone. He is the Only Son, and yet would not be alone; He hath vouchsafed to have brethren. For to whom doth He say, "Say, Our Father, which art in heaven?" Whom did He wish us to call our Father, save His own Father? Did He grudge us this? Parents sometimes when they have gotten one, or two, or three children, fear to give birth to any more, lest they reduce the rest to beggary. But because the inheritance which He promised us is such as many may possess, and no one be straitened; therefore hath He called into His brotherhood the peoples of the nations; and the Only Son hath numberless brethren; who say, "Our Father, which art in heaven." So said they who have been before us; and so shall say those who will come after us. See how many brethren the Only Son hath in His grace, sharing His inheritance with those for whom He suffered death. We had a father and mother on earth, that we might be born to labors and to death: but we have found other parents, God our Father, and the Church our Mother, by whom we are born unto life eternal. Let us then consider, beloved, whose children we have begun to be; and let us live so as becomes those who have such a Father. See, how that our Creator hath condescended to be our Father!

We have heard whom we ought to call upon, and with what hope of an eternal inheritance we have begun to have a Father in heaven; let us now hear what we must ask of Him. Of such a Father what shall we ask? Do we not ask rain of Him, to-day, and yesterday, and the day before? This is no great thing to have asked of such a Father, and yet ye see with what sighings, and with what great desire we ask for rain, when death is feared,— when that is feared which none can escape. For sooner or later every man must die, and we groan, and pray, and travail in pain, and cry to God, that we may die a little later. How much more ought we to cry to Him, that we may come to that place where we shall never die!

Therefore is it said, "Hallowed be Thy Name." This we also ask of Him that His Name may be hallowed in us; for Holy is it always. And how is His Name hallowed in us, except while it makes us holy? For once we were not holy, and we are made holy by His Name; but He is always Holy, and His Name always Holy. It is for ourselves, not for God, that we pray. For we do not wish well to God, to whom no ill can ever happen. But we wish what is good for ourselves, that His Holy Name may be hallowed, that that which is always Holy, may be hallowed in us.

" Thy kingdom come." Come it surely will, whether we ask or no. Indeed, God hath an eternal kingdom. For when did He not reign? When did He begin to reign? For His kingdom hath no beginning, neither shall it have any end. But that ye may know that in this prayer also we pray for ourselves, and not for God (for we do not say, " Thy kingdom come," as though we were asking that God may reign) ; we shall be ourselves His kingdom, if believing in Him we make progress in this faith. All the faithful, redeemed by the Blood of His Only Son, will be His kingdom. And this His kingdom will come, when the resurrection of the dead shall have taken place; for then He will come himself. And when the dead are risen, He will divide them, as He himself saith, " and He shall set some on the right hand, and some on the left." To those who shall be on the right hand He will say, " Come, ye blessed of My Father, receive the kingdom." This is what we wish and pray for when we say, " Thy kingdom come; " that it may come to us. For if we shall be reprobates, that kingdom will come to others, but not to us. But if we shall be of that number, who belong to the members of His Only-begotten Son, His kingdom will come to us, and will not tarry. For are there as many ages yet remaining, as have already passed away? The Apostle John hath said,

3

"My little children, it is the last hour." But it is a long hour proportioned to this long day; and see how many years this last hour lasteth. But nevertheless, be ye as those who watch, and so sleep, and rise again, and reign. Let us watch now, let us sleep in death; at the end we shall rise again, and shall reign without end.

"Thy will be done as in heaven, so in earth." The third thing we pray for is, that His will may be done as in heaven so in earth. And in this too we wish well for ourselves. For the will of God must necessarily be done. It is the will of God that the good should reign, and the wicked be damned. Is it possible that this will should not be done? But what good do we wish for ourselves, when we say, "Thy will be done as in heaven, so in earth?" Give ear. For this petition may be understood in many ways, and many things are to be in our thoughts in this petition, when we pray God, "Thy will be done as in heaven, so in earth." As Thy Angels offend Thee not, so may we also not offend Thee. Again, how is "Thy will be done as in heaven, so in earth," understood? All the holy Patriarchs, all the Prophets, all the Apostles, all the spiritual are as it were God's heaven; and we in comparison of them are earth. "Thy will be done as in heaven, so in earth;" as in them, so in us also. Again, "Thy will be done as in heaven, so in earth;" the Church of God is heaven, His enemies are earth. So we wish well for our enemies, that they too may believe and become Christians, and so the will of God be done as in heaven, so also in earth. Again, "Thy will be done as in heaven, so in earth." Our spirit is heaven, and the flesh earth. As our spirit is renewed by believing, so may our flesh be renewed by rising again; and "the will of God be done as in heaven, so in earth." Again, our mind whereby we see truth, and delight in this truth, is heaven; as, "I delight in the law of God, after the inward man." What is the earth? "I see another law in my members, warring against the law of my mind?" When this strife shall have passed away, and a full concord be brought about of the flesh and spirit, the will of God will be done as in heaven, so also in earth. When we repeat this petition, let us think of all these things, and ask them all of the Father. Now all these things which we have mentioned, these three petitions, beloved, have respect to the life eternal. For if the Name of our God is sanctified in us, it will be for eternity. If His kingdom come, where we shall live for ever, it will be for eternity. If His will be done as in heaven, so in earth, in all the ways which I have explained, it will be for eternity.

There remain now the petitions for this life of our pilgrimage; therefore follows, " Give us this day our daily bread." Give us eternal things, give us things temporal. Thou hast promised a kingdom, deny us not the means of subsistence. Thou wilt give everlasting glory with Thyself hereafter, give us in this earth temporal support. Therefore is it *day by day,* and *to-day,* that is, in this present time. For when this life shall have passed away, shall we ask for daily bread then? For then it will not be called, *day by day,* but *to-day.* Now it is called, *day by day,* when one day passes away, and another day succeeds. Will it be called, *day by day,* when there will be one eternal day? This petition for daily bread is doubtless to be understood in two ways, both for the necessary supply of our bodily food, and for the necessities of our spiritual support. There is a necessary supply of bodily food, for the preservation of our daily life, without which we cannot live. This is food and clothing, but the whole is understood in a part. When we ask for bread, we thereby understand all things. There is a spiritual food also which the faithful know, which ye too will know when ye shall receive it at the altar of God. This also is " daily Bread," necessary only for this life. For shall we receive the Eucharist when we shall have come to Christ Himself, and begun to reign with Him for ever? So then the Eucharist is our daily bread; but let us in such wise receive it, that we be not refreshed in our bodies only, but in our souls. For the virtue which is apprehended there, is unity, that gathered together into His body, and made His members, we may be what we receive. Then will it be indeed our daily bread. Again, what I am handling before you now is " daily bread; " and the daily lessons which ye hear in church, are daily bread, and the hymns ye hear and repeat are daily bread. For all these are necessary in our state of pilgrimage. But when we shall have got to heaven, shall we hear the word, we who shall see the Word himself, and hear the Word himself, and eat and drink Him as the angels do now? Do the angels need books, and interpreters, and readers? Surely not. They read in seeing, for the Truth itself they see, and are abundantly satisfied from that fountain, from which we obtain some few drops. Therefore has it been said touching our daily bread, that this petition is necessary for us in this life.

" Forgive us our debts, as we forgive our debtors." Is this necessary except in this life? For in the other we shall have no debts. For what are debts, but sins? See, ye are on the point of being baptized, then all your sins will be blotted out, none whatever will remain. Whatever evil ye have ever done, in deed, or word, or desire, or thought, all will be blotted out. And yet if in the life which is after Baptism there were security from sin, we should not learn such a prayer as this, "Forgive us our debts." Only let us by all means do what comes next, "As we forgive our debtors." Do ye then who are about to enter in to receive a plenary and entire remission of your debts, do ye above all things see that ye have nothing in your hearts against any other, so as to come forth from Baptism secure, as it were free and discharged of all debts, and then begin to purpose to avenge yourselves on your enemies, who in time past have done you wrong. Forgive, as ye are forgiven. God can do no one wrong, and yet He forgiveth who oweth nothing. How then ought he to forgive who is himself forgiven, when He forgiveth all who oweth nothing that can be forgiven Him?

"Lead us not into temptation, but deliver us from evil." Will this again be necessary in the life to come? "Lead us not into temptation," will not be said except where there can be temptation. We read in the book of holy Job, "Is not the life of man upon earth a temptation?" What then do we pray for? Hear what. The Apostle James saith, "Let no man say when he is tempted, I am tempted of God." He spoke of those evil temptations whereby men are deceived, and brought under the yoke of the devil. This is the kind of temptation he spoke of. For there is another sort of temptation which is called a proving; of this kind of temptation it is written, "The Lord your God tempteth (proveth) you to know whether ye love Him." What means "to know?" "To make you know," for He knoweth already. With that kind of temptation whereby we are deceived and seduced, God tempteth no man. But undoubtedly in His deep and hidden judgment He abandons some. And when He hath abandoned them, the tempter finds his opportunity. For he finds in him no resistance against his power, but forthwith presents himself to him as his possessor, if God abandon him. Therefore that He may not abandon us, do we say, "Lead us not into temptation." "For every one is tempted," says the same Apostle James, "when he is drawn away of his own lust and enticed. Then lust, when it hath conceived, bringeth forth sin; and sin, when it is finished, bringeth forth death." What then has he hereby taught us? To fight against our lusts. For ye are about to put away your sins in holy Baptism; but lusts will still remain, wherewith ye must fight after that ye are regenerate. For a conflict with your own selves still remains. Let no enemy from without be feared: conquer thine own self, and the whole world is conquered. What can any tempter from without, whether the devil or the devil's minister, do against thee? Whosoever sets the hope of gain before thee to seduce thee, let him only find no covetousness in thee; and what can he who would tempt thee by gain effect? Whereas if covetousness be found in thee; thou takest fire at the sight of gain, and art taken by the bait of this corrupt food. But if he find no covetousness in thee, the trap remains spread in vain. Or should the tempter set before thee some woman of surpassing beauty; if chastity be within, iniquity from without is overcome. Therefore that he may not take thee with the bait of a strange woman's beauty, fight with thine own lust within; thou hast no sensible perception of thine enemy, but of thine own concupiscence thou hast. Thou dost not see the devil, but the object that engageth thee thou dost see. Get the mastery then over that of which thou art sensible within. Fight valiantly, for He who hath regenerated thee is thy Judge; He hath arranged the lists, He is making ready the crown. But because thou wilt without doubt be conquered, if thou have not Him to aid thee, if He abandon thee: therefore dost thou say in the prayer, "Lead us not into temptation." The Judge's wrath hath given over some to their own lusts; and the Apostle says, "God gave them over to the lusts of their hearts." How did He give them up? Not by forcing, but by forsaking them.

"Deliver us from evil," may belong to the same sentence. Therefore, that thou mayst understand it to be all one sentence, it runs thus, "Lead us not into temptation, but deliver us from evil." Therefore he added *but,* to show that all this belongs to one sentence, "Lead us not into temptation, but deliver us from evil." How is this? I will propose them singly. "Lead us not into temptation, but deliver us from evil." By delivering us from evil, He leadeth us not into temptation; by not leading us into temptation, He delivereth us from evil.

And truly it is a great temptation, dearly beloved, it is a great temptation in this life, when that in us is the subject of temptation whereby we attain pardon if, in any of our temptations, we have fallen. It is a frightful temptation when that is taken from us whereby we may be healed from the wounds of other temptations. I know that ye have not yet understood me. Give me your attention, that ye may understand. Suppose, avarice tempts a man, and he is conquered in any single tempta- tion (for sometimes even a good wrestler and fighter may get roughly handled): avarice then has got the better of a man, good wrestler though he be, and he has done some avaricious act. Or there has been a passing lust; it has not brought the man to fornication, nor reached unto adultery — for when this does take place, the man must at all events be kept back from the criminal act. But he " hath seen a woman to lust after her : " he has let his thoughts dwell on her with more pleasure than was right; he has admitted the attack; excellent combatant though he be, he has been wounded, but he has not consented to it; he has beaten back the motion of his lust, has chastised it with the bitterness of grief, he has beaten it back; and has prevailed. Still in the very fact that he had slipped, has he ground for saying, " Forgive us our debts." And so of all other temptations, it is a hard matter that in them all there should not be occasion for saying, " Forgive us our debts." What then is that frightful temptation which I have mentioned, that grievous, that tremendous temptation, which must be avoided with all our strength, with all our resolution; what is it? When we go about to avenge ourselves. Anger is kindled, and the man burns to be avenged. O frightful temptation ! Thou art losing that, whereby thou hadst to attain pardon for other faults. If thou hadst committed any sin as to other senses, and other lusts, hence mightest thou have had thy cure, in that thou mightest say, " Forgive us our debts, as we also forgive our debtors." But whoso instigateth thee to take vengeance, will lose for thee the power thou hadst to say, " As we also forgive our debtors." When that power is lost, all sins will be retained; nothing at all is remitted.

Our Lord and Master, and Saviour, knowing this dangerous tempta-tion in this life, when He taught us six or seven petitions in this Prayer, took none of them for himself to treat of, and to commend to us with greater earnestness, than this one. Have we not said, " Our Father, which art in heaven ; " and the rest which follows? Why after the conclusion of the Prayer, did He not enlarge upon it to us, either as to what He had laid down in the beginning, or concluded with at the end, or placed in the middle? For why said He not, if the Name of God be not hallowed in you, or if ye have no part in the kingdom of God, or if the will of God be not done in you, as in heaven, or if God guard you not, that ye enter not into temptation; why none of all these? but what saith He? " Verily I say unto you, that if ye forgive men their trespasses ; " in reference to that petition, " Forgive us our debts, as we also forgive our debtors." Having passed over all the other petitions which He taught us, this He taught us with an especial force. There was no need of insisting so much upon those sins in which if a man offend, he may know the means whereby he may be cured: need of it there was with regard to that sin in which, if thou sin, there is no means whereby the rest can be cured. For this thou oughtst to be ever saying, " Forgive us our debts." What debts? There is no lack of them; for we are but men; I have talked somewhat more than I ought, have said something I ought not, have laughed more than I ought, have eaten more than I ought, have listened with pleasure to what I ought not, have drunk more than I ought, have seen with pleasure what I ought not, have thought with pleasure on what I ought not; " Forgive us our debts, as we also forgive our debtors." This if thou hast lost, thou art lost thyself.

  ﾞ   Take heed, my brethren, my sons, sons of God, take heed, I beseech you, in that I am saying to you. Fight to the uttermost of your powers with your own hearts. And if ye shall see your anger making a stand against you, pray to God against it, that God may make thee conqueror of thyself, that God may make thee conqueror, I say, not of thine enemy without, but of thine own soul within. For He will give thee His present help, and will do it. He would rather that we ask this of Him, than rain. For ye see, beloved, how many petitions the Lord Christ hath taught us; and there is scarce found among them one which speaks of daily bread, that all our thoughts may be moulded after the life to come? For what can we fear that He will not give us, who hath promised and said, " Seek ye first the kingdom of God and His righteousness, and all these things shall be added unto you; for your Father knoweth that ye have need of these things before ye ask Him." " Seek ye first the kingdom of God and His righteousness, and all these things shall be added unto you." For many have been tried even with hunger, and have been found gold, and have not been forsaken by God. They would have perished with hunger, if the daily inward bread were to leave their heart. After this let us chiefly hunger. For, " Blessed are they who hunger and thirst after righteousness, for they shall be filled." But He can in mercy look upon our infirmity, and see us, as it is said, " Remember that we are dust." He who from the dust made and quickened man, for that His work of clay's sake, gave His Only Son to death. Who can explain, who can worthily so much as conceive, how much he loveth us?

III

MARTIN LUTHER

1483-1546

MARTIN LUTHER was the Apostle of the Sixteenth century — the master-mind and giant-father of the Reformation, under God. His mission was to re-open the way for God's saving grace to flow freely to men — to re-awaken mankind to the sanctity of personal conscience. The papacy interposed itself between the human soul and the Almighty, till the words of Luther,— inspired by unquestioning faith in God's declaration, " The just shall live by faith,"— fell upon it like huge sledge-hammer blows, crushing its impious assumptions into the dust. The life of this great reformer, which is an outline sketch of the Reformation, must be very briefly referred to here. Martin Luther was born the son of a miner, at Eisleben, in Saxony, November 10th, 1483. He graduated from the University at Erfurt, became doctor of philosophy, and in 1505 gave up the world to be a monk. He was made doctor of divinity in 1512. Five years later, in fulfillment of his vows as a defender of Holy Scripture, he attacked in ninety-five theses, the blasphemous sale of indulgences by Tetzel. As Pope Leo X sanctioned these practices, Europe was convulsed by a moral shock, and the Reformation began. Neither frowns nor flatteries could silence this bold minister of God. A grand pivot-scene of human history,— perhaps unequalled elsewhere by mortal,— was the firm stand of Luther before assembled monarchs and princes in the Diet at Worms, where he refused to retract in those sublime words: " Here I stand: I cannot do otherwise. God help me! Amen." In 1522 the New Testament, and in 1534 the Old Testament, were translated by him into German. He died at Eisleben, February 18th, 1546. His works are published in twenty-seven volumes, and but few have been translated into English.

THE GIFT OF GOD.

"For God so loved the world, that he gave his only begotten Son, that whosoever believeth in him should not perish, but have everlasting life. For God sent not his Son into the world to condemn the world, but that the world through him might be saved. He that believeth on him, is not condemned: but he that believeth not, is condemned already, because he hath not believed in the name of the only begotten Son of God. And this is the condemnation, that light is come into the world, and men loved darkness rather than light, because their deeds were evil. For every one that doeth evil hateth the light, neither cometh to the light, lest his deeds should be reproved. But he that doeth truth, cometh to the light, that his deeds may be made manifest, that they are wrought in God."— John iii. 16–21.

THIS Gospel is one of the most precious passages in the whole New Testament, and fully deserves, if it could be done, to be written with golden letters into our hearts. Every Christian ought to learn this consoling text by heart, and should repeat it 'once at least each day, so that we would know these words well and could readily apply them for our consolation and the strengthening of our faith. They are words which have power to gladden us when we are sad and to bring us back to life when we are dead, if we but accept them earnestly in true faith. But inasmuch as it is impossible for us to comprehend fully and to express properly the contents of this glorious text, let us pray earnestly unto God to impress these words deeply upon our hearts through His Holy Spirit, so that they may become powerful in us, and may give us much joy and consolation, Amen.

The sum and substance of this glorious, comfortable, and blessed passage is this, that God loved the world so dearly that He gave His only begotten Son to save men from eternal death and to give them everlasting life. Christ our Lord speaks to us, as it were, in these words: Heed what I tell you of a peculiar, unheard-of occurrence; yea, I will point you to a great, precious and valuable treasure, which is totally unlike any earthly gifts, by which you can now be rich and blessed for evermore. All the circumstances connected with the bestowal and reception of this precious gift are so peculiar and overwhelmingly grand that human thoughts cannot compass them, and much less can our words express their great importance.

If we consider first the Giver of this blessing, we find that the text says nothing of emperors, kings, or other dignitaries of the world, but it speaks of God himself, who is incomprehensible and omnipotent, who has created everything through His Word, who has all and preserves all and is over all, compared with whom all creation, heaven and earth, with all they contain, is but as an insignificant grain of sand. He, the Almighty, is the great Giver of all blessings, and His gifts are so glorious that the most valued treasures of men, of emperors and kings, fade away into nothingness when compared with the mercies of God. Let us, therefore, rejoice greatly and sing for gladness in view of these blessings, and let us consider as mere trifles everything else that the world can bestow. What indeed can be greater or more glorious than the Almighty Himself!

This God, who is infinite and ineffable, manifests His loving-kindness in a degree beyond all measure. What He gives He gives not as something merited, or because it is His duty to give it, but simply, as our text says, through love. He is a Giver who begrudges not his gifts, but delights in bestowing them; He gives on account of endless, divine love, as Christ says: "For God so loved the world."

There is no other virtue so glorious as love. What we dearly love we are ready to defend and protect at the risk of our life. Patience, chastity, temperance, etc., are also praiseworthy virtues, but cannot be compared with love; she is queen over them all, and comprehends them all. Surely if one is pious and righteous, he will not defraud or injure his brother, but will assist him in everything; but if we love a person, we are ever ready to devote ourselves entirely to his welfare and to assist him, according as he has need, with our counsel and our possessions. Thus, as Christ declares in our text, does God also do toward us. He gives us blessings beyond measure, not because He is patient or because we are righteous and deserve it, but through love, the greatest of all virtues. In view of this fact our hearts should awake, all our sadness should vanish, for we see before us the inexhaustible love of the divine heart, which we ought to cherish in true faith as the greatest of all gifts, knowing that God is the highest and most glorious Giver of blessings unto us, and that they all proceed from the greatest of all virtues.

The fact that anything is given from true love makes the gift itself greater and more precious. If therefore we are convinced that love prompts the bestowal of any gift, we are well pleased; but when we doubt the existence of this motive in the giver, we care but little for his gift. Thus if God had given us only one eye or one foot and we were convinced that fatherly love prompted him to do this, we would be entirely content and better satisfied than we would otherwise be if we had a hundred eyes and a hundred feet.

But the words are plain: "God so loved the world." Therefore we ought to value highly, on account of His love, all His gifts, especially those which he has ordained to our salvation and the strengthening of our faith, as Holy Baptism, the Sacrament of the Body and Blood of Christ, etc. These gifts appear not brilliant before the world, yet unto us they are heaven itself, and make us glad and cheerful because they flow from the love of our Father toward us and are instituted for our benefit. Therefore Christ in this connection not only teaches us that God will give us something, but also in what manner he will do this, namely, through divine, Fatherly love.

Thus we see how great and ineffable are the Giver and the motive which prompts Him to grant us His blessings. But the gift itself is equally glorious and inexpressible. We hear from our text that God through love does not give us a dollar, a horse, a cow, an eye, a kingdom, or even the heavens with the sun and stars, nor the whole creation, but He gives us "His only begotten Son," who is like unto Himself in everything.

This gift must surely arouse within us the deepest emotions of happiness, so that our hearts will ever be glad and leap for joy. Even as the Giver, God himself, is endless and incomprehensible in His love, so the gift itself, His Son, is eternal and unspeakable. God in this gift bestows Himself with all that He is, as St. Paul says (Rom. 8): "He that spared not His own Son, but delivered Him up for us all, how shall He not with Him also freely give us all things?" The victory over the devil, sin, death, and hell, as well as the gift of heaven, righteousness, and eternal life, is ours; yea all things are ours now, because we have the Son as our gift, in whom all else is comprehended.

If we then truly believe in this gift and accept it in real faith, all creation, be it good or evil, be it life or death, heaven or hell, must be at our service, as St. Paul in another place says: "For all things are yours; whether Paul, or Apollos, or Cephas, or the world, or life, or death, or things present, or things to come; all are yours; and ye are Christ's; and Christ is God's." (1 Cor. 3.) Indeed, if we fully consider this gift, we must confess and say that it is a boon which in value transcends all else in heaven and earth, and in comparison with which all treasures in the world are as a mite to a mountain of gold. But alas, our miserable unbelief and the terrible darkness which enshrouds us, as Christ himself shortly after this complains, prevent our hearts from realizing what a blessing we have in this gift of the Son of God; we hear these glorious words, but they rush by our outward ears, and the heart remains cold and cheerless. When we hear of a house or farm which is for sale on easy terms, we run and are as eager to make the purchase as if our existence depended upon it; but when the glorious Gospel is preached, that God so loved the world that He gave His only begotten Son for its salvation, we are shamefully and sinfully careless and lazy about hearing and accepting this blessed truth. Who is at the bottom of this wicked indifference and carelessness as to the greatest gift, so that we do not accept it nor derive from it joy and consolation? No one but the old devil himself; he blinds our hearts to such a degree that we permit the preaching of this precious Gospel to go by unheeded, while we in the meanwhile busy ourselves with temporal cares.

For this reason I remarked, at the beginning of this sermon, that we ought to repeat these words when we get out of bed in the morning and again when we retire in the evening, so that we may know them right well and praise God for His unutterable blessings. For surely all, the Giver, His love, and the Gift bestowed so undeservedly, simply through love, are most glorious and beyond our comprehension. The gift is one freely given, and will ever remain a gracious blessing which cannot be borrowed, lent, nor bought; all we have to do to obtain it is to hold out our hand and to receive willingly and gladly this treasure. Alas, that our hands and hearts are so reluctant and even unwilling to take such a glorious gift, which is so freely offered, and which is designed to be ours for evermore!

What shall those people be called who refuse to accept a kind gift and blessing? Suppose a poor, ragged beggar, nearly exhausted with hunger, meets with a great and charitable prince, who offers to give him a residence and a great yearly income, and to make him a lord, but that the beggar haughtily turns away from his benefactor without accepting his kindness, what would this foolish man be called by the world? Surely everybody would say that he is crazy and acts more like a brute than a human being. This would be the verdict of the world. Here, however, there is offered to the world no palace nor principality, no kingdom nor imperial domain, but the Son of God, and

God himself urges the world to accept and keep this gift. But alas, we men are the ones who refuse to accept this gift; we turn our backs upon God, the kind Giver. From this we can judge what a great and horrible sin unbelief is, for it is not natural that men should refuse a gift and willingly turn from it.

This proves how mad and thoughtless the world is; she does not rejoice at this gift of God, and refuses to receive it when offered. No doubt she would be quick to stretch out her hands for it if it were a dollar or a new coat; but as it is the Son of God, every one acts as if the gift were valueless.

"The world" is mentioned by name in this connection as the ungrateful one who spurns this gift which is offered to her freely. For what has the world done to merit such love and mercy of God? Nothing at all. She is the devil's bride, the greatest enemy of God and the greatest blasphemer. Yet we read here: "God so loved the world that He gave His only begotten Son."

My hearer, inscribe this truth deeply in your heart. And since you have now heard who God is, and what His gift is, which He gives alone through love, hear also what the world is. She is constituted of a multitude of people who do not believe in God and who make Him a liar; yea, they blaspheme His name and Word, and persecute it. Hence they are those who disobey father and mother, who are murderers, adulterers, treacherous persons, thieves, hypocrites, and the like, as we, alas, can see but too clearly every day of our life. The world is full of falsehood and blasphemy. Nevertheless God, through love, gives His Son to this bride of the devil, his greatest foe and persecutor.

This fact also magnifies the gift. God does not regard the sins and crimes of the world, nor her persecution of His name and Word, so as to withhold His gift on that account. It would seem as if God were too holy and His gift too precious to endure the perversion and wickedness of the world. But God does not regard the sins of the world, whether they be against the first or against the second table of the law, as too great to permit the manifestation of his love toward her; yea, on account of her sins and great misery, in which we all would have to perish if God did not grant us His help, He is merciful, and prompted by His love, He comes to our assistance.

Ought we then not to love such a merciful God in return and to trust implicitly in Him who forgives sins, and will not suffer the ungrateful world to perish for her transgressions, which are innumerable? Yea, the sins of every one of us are innumerable; who then could enumerate the sins of the whole world? Yet we read that God is ready to forgive all our transgressions; for from the love of God comes the forgiveness of sins. We ought to consider this attentively. If God gives so much, yea even himself to the world, which is His natural enemy, we are forced to conclude that His mercy and grace will also manifest itself toward us, no matter what our experiences are during this life. Therefore we ought to trust in this love, and hope for every blessing from God for Christ's sake.

Such thoughts must encourage the heart and make it glad. I and many Christians have to confess that while we were in popery we lived in great wickedness and idolatry, and were guilty of many a sin. God however did not punish such wickedness as we deserved, but manifested His love by revealing again through the Gospel His Son, whom He had given to the world. We were again permitted to hear and to understand the glorious Gospel, proclaiming that God is not wroth with the world, but that He loves us and has given His Son in our behalf. Alas, we are ungrateful and do not realize this truth as we should, else would our hearts be filled with joy, and we would be determined not only to serve God right willingly, but also to suffer without complaint everything in His service, on account of the precious treasure which we have. It is our unbelief which prevents such joy and seeks the pleasures of the world, which come from the devil and are accursed.

We have now considered four parts in our text, namely, the Giver of the gift, the gift itself, how it is given, and to whom it is given. It is impossible to express fully in words the great importance of these four considerations.

Now follows the *causa finalis,* what purpose God has in view in the bestowal of this gift. It contains no outward advantages for us; we are neither clothed by it, nor fed, nor sheltered: much less is it injurious to our bodies; it contains no poison. Thus He gives His word, Baptism and the Sacrament of the Altar, not to our injury but to our salvation. This gift of the only begotten Son is granted unto us to this end, that whosoever believeth in Him should not perish, but have everlasting life.

From this declaration we learn that this gift does not bring us money, goods, honor, or power in this world, for all such benefits would be but transitory. Yea, if we had all these things we would nevertheless still be under the dominion of the devil. But now when the Son of God is given us, through the Father's love toward us, it follows that we are freed from sin, death, and hell, if we believe in the Saviour; for He crushed the head of the serpent and despoiled it of its power; He slew sin and devoured death and extinguished the fire of hell, so that they are all vanquished for evermore and deprived of their supremacy over us. So great and glorious was this gift. Honor, praise, and glory be unto God, the merciful Giver of this blessing, for ever and for ever, Amen.

Surely we have reason enough to feel happy at this occurrence, especially since Christ Himself asserts in our text that He was given us to overpower hell and to make our timid hearts bold and full of cheerfulness. Through the firm assurance that we have a reconciled God in heaven, who loves us and who through love gave His Son for us, so that we should not perish but have everlasting life, we are made glad; for we know that death has now no authority over us, and that eternal life is ours in Christ.

This truth we cannot learn or understand too well; therefore we ought to pray every day that God may through His Holy Spirit inscribe these words deeply in our hearts, that these may be illumined and enlivened thereby. Then will we become true theologians, who know Christ aright and adhere to His doctrine, prepared to suffer for this faith all ills and adversities which, in the providence of God, may visit us. But inasmuch as we do not value these words as we should, and only hear them with our outward ears, they cannot prove their power in our hearts; we remain to-day as we were yesterday, and it is a sin and a shame that we see not with our eyes nor hear with our ears. Most certainly will the damned cry out on the day of judgment and lament, because they were so careless about the preaching and hearing of these words of consolation while yet on earth.

Let us now consider in what way this glorious gift ought to be received, in what receptacle this precious treasure should be securely laid and guarded. It is of great importance to know this. Christ himself points it out to us in the words: " That whosoever believeth in Him should not perish, but have everlasting life."

This testimony is plain and clear. It declares that faith, that is, a firm confidence in the mercy and love of God in Christ, is the receptacle into which we should receive and in which we should keep the gift of the Son of God. Love and mercy prompt God to give us such a boon, while we can receive and retain it only through faith. No work or merit of ours avails us anything in this; for even our best works are worthless in this regard. We must stretch forth our hands in faith; and as God through love is the Giver, so we must through faith in Christ be the receivers of His gift. We must believe what our text tells us, that God is kind and merciful, and that He manifests His love toward us in sending His only begotten Son into our flesh and blood, to take upon himself our sins, as John the Baptist and the prophet Isaiah declare: "This is the Lamb of God which taketh away the sins of the world." With such a gift, and assured of the love of God, we can stay our hearts against the assaults of sin and the accusations of our conscience; for we knew that he is not wroth nor terrible, but that for Christ's sake he is kind and gracious unto us. Whoever believes this is truly happy and blessed, for this gift is so great and powerful that it crushes sin, death, and every evil. As a burning fire devours a little drop of water, thus are the sins of the whole world annihilated when they come in contact with Christ; yea, if we cling to Him in faith, our sins will be removed and destroyed, even as a straw is devoured in a mighty conflagration.

Christ Himself tells us in our Gospel: "For God so loved the world, that He gave His only begotten Son, that whosoever believeth in Him should not perish, but have everlasting life." The words "whosoever believeth in Him" are of especial importance here. Christ says nothing at all of good works as means unto salvation. Faith alone can and must receive this gift. Therefore we are undisturbed by the noise of our adversaries; we cling firmly to this doctrine, for here it is said: "Whosoever believeth in Him shall not perish, but have everlasting life." If we doubt this, or change it, we accuse Christ of falsehood and set ourselves up as judges over Him.

What glorious words of consolation and eternal life! God grant that we may faithfully receive them into our hearts. Whoever has accepted them in faith will not fear the devil, nor sin, nor death, but will exclaim, in great joy and firm assurance: I am comforted, for I now have the Son of God given unto me through the Father's love toward the world. This I firmly believe, because the Word of God, the holy Gospel, thus declares it unto me. And Thy Word, O God, and Thy Son Jesus Christ cannot lie; this I know and believe. Wherein I am weak in faith, give me strength to receive and to retain this Thy great gift and love, else it will be of no advantage unto me. It behooves us therefore to become more and more acquainted with this gift and to be comforted by it; this however can only take place through faith, as Christ teaches us. The stronger our faith, the greater will be our happiness and safety, so that we can cheerfully do and suffer what God imposes upon us, and this because we know that he is merciful and full of love toward us.

Perhaps you will object and say: Yea, if I were as pious and holy as Peter, Paul, or the holy Virgin, then would I dare to believe and be comforted with this gift. They were saints, and no doubt for them this gift was intended, but I, a poor sinner, have no right to appropriate it unto myself, for I have so often and in such manifold ways offended and opposed God. Such thoughts cannot be avoided when we hear this Gospel, and then think of our condition and great transgressions. But we must watch that these thoughts do not gain such power over us that we lose sight of the Gospel; to this we must speedily return and in this find comfort. Such thoughts are really nothing but unbelief, which would keep us from this gift and its comfortable assurance of the forgiveness of our sins through faith in Christ.

Unbelief, however, can be successfully combated only with the Word of God. Christ our Saviour gives unto us this Word, so that we dare not doubt its truthfulness. He tells us that His Father in heaven, the everlasting God, so loved "the world," that He even gave for it His only begotten Son. Now it is evident that the expression "the world" does not mean Mary, Peter, Paul, etc., but that it includes the whole human race, one and all, without any exception. Or have you any doubt that you are a human being? If so, feel your chest or your nose, and you will find out whether you are different from other people. Why then will you persistently exclude yourself from the application of this expression "world," when Christ so plainly includes in it all men, and does not apply it merely to the Virgin Mary, to St. Peter, or to St. Paul? If you and I refuse to accept Christ, because we think that we have no part in him, we make him a liar, for He said that He was given for the whole world. No, we must rather come to the opposite conclusion, that we have as good a right to this gift as Peter or Paul, or any one else has, simply because we are men, and as such a part of the world. Let us therefore beware and not doubt God's words by thinking that we cannot be sure whether we belong to those, to whom and for whom He gave His Son that they might have everlasting life. With such thoughts we deny that God speaks the truth.

Let us therefore shun such doubts, and the thoughts producing them, as we would shun the very devil himself. Let us be firm in faith and

4

say: We know that God gave His gift not only to Peter and Paul, for if he had desired to bestow it only upon those perfectly worthy of it, He would have given it to the holy angels, who are pure, undefiled spirits, or to the sun and moon, which obey perfectly the law of God by continuing in their prescribed course; but we read otherwise, namely, that "God gave His Son unto the world." Therefore we all have a part in this glorious gift, just as well as David or any apostle. Who was David? Did he not commit gross sins? Who were the apostles? Were they not all sinners and unworthy of this gift?

Let no one, therefore, reason thus: I am a sinner, and am not as holy as St. Peter, consequently I dare not appropriate this gift to my consolation. Far be it from us to harbor such thoughts. Let us believe in God's Word implicitly; and because He says that He gave this gift unto the world, let us all, since we belong to the world, no matter who we are, lay hold of it in faith; for if we do not, we deny the truthfulness of God, and thereby commit a great and damnable sin.

Some perhaps might think: If God had told this unto me especially, I would believe it and be assured that it also applies to me. In this you err, my friend; God intentionally speaks in a general way, and says that He gave His Son unto the whole world, that all may be saved and none be excluded. If there are any who are not benefited by this gift, they are themselves to blame; they exclude themselves, through wicked unbelief, from the blessing of the gift of God, and will have to render an account for their faithlessness; yea, their own words will condemn them. Besides, we have the holy sacraments, instituted of Christ Himself, to be employed by us as means of grace, by which we are to obtain and to appropriate to ourselves this gift.

This is a brief and simple explanation of our beautiful and precious text to-day, which is so comprehensive that it can never be exhausted. It contains the chief doctrine of salvation, that God, through love towards the wicked world, gave His only begotten Son to be its Saviour. Let every one learn what a glorious treasure and consolation the Christians have, who God is, and what the world is, and how through faith we can obtain and enjoy this mercy, as Christ says: "Whosoever believeth in Him shall not perish, but have everlasting life." The doctrine concerning good works and their relation to faith cannot be considered in this connection, and will receive attention at some other time. Here we must consider what God gives unto us and how we ought to receive His gift.

Christ does not dwell here upon the duties which a Christian must fulfil to prove himself an obedient, beloved child of God, nor does he speak of the necessary gratitude for the love of God and the gift of eternal life. It suffices, therefore, if we in this connection restrict our consideration to the mercy of God, and to the truth that we are saved alone through this grace, which must be accepted in true faith, and with which good works on our part have nothing to do; for we are saved only through the love of God who gave His only begotten Son for us, for whose sake he now forgives us all our sins. God grant us his grace, that we may believe this truth and be happy in it in life and in death. *Prayer* We ask this for the sake of Jesus Christ, our Lord and Saviour. Amen.

IV

HUGH LATIMER

1485–1555.

ONE of the founders of English Protestantism was Hugh Latimer, bishop, reformer, and martyr. He was born at Thurcaston, in Leicestershire, about the year 1485; and was educated at Cambridge, which at that time was far in advance of Oxford in the liberality of its teachings. Latimer embraced the reformed doctrines, as taught by Luther, and by his energy in preaching them, soon attracted notice and endured persecution. For a time, King Henry VIII agreed with his views, appointed him one of his chaplains, and made him Bishop of Worcester. Later, however, Latimer's radical preaching of reform alarmed the court; he was compelled to retire to his diocese, and finally was thrown into the Tower of London. Henry VIII was the only sovereign of England who enjoyed the privilege of persecuting, even to death, *both* Protestants and Catholics. Under Edward VI, Latimer was released, and preached again, although he never resumed the work of a Bishop. But when Mary came to the throne, and restored the Roman Catholic church to power, Latimer, with many other reformers, was again thrown into prison; and on October 16, 1555, at the age of seventy years, suffered death by fire, in company with Bishop Nicholas Ridley, at Oxford. Standing at the stake, he said to his fellow-sufferers, " Be of good comfort, Brother Ridley, and play the man; we shall this day, by God's grace, light such a candle in England as shall never be put out! " As a preacher, Latimer showed high courage, deep reverence for the Scriptures, and a rugged, homely wit. An eminent English divine wrote, " If a combination of sound gospel doctrine, plain Saxon language, boldness, liveliness, directness and simplicity, can make a preacher, few, I suspect have ever equalled old Latimer."

ON CHRISTIAN LOVE.

" This is my commandment, that ye love one another, as I have loved
you."— John xv. 12.

SEEING the time is so far spent, we will take no more in hand at
this time, than this one sentence; for it will be enough for us to consider this well, and to bear it away with us. " This I command unto
you, that ye love one another." Our Saviour himself spake these words
at his last supper: it was the last sermon that he made unto his disciples
before his departure; it is a very long sermon. For our Saviour, like
as one that knows he shall die shortly, is desirous to spend that little
time that he has with his friends, in exhorting and instructing them how
they should lead their lives. Now among other things that he commanded, this was one: " This I command unto you, that ye love one another." The English expresses as though it were but one, " This is my
commandment." I examined the Greek, where it is in the plural number, and very well; for there are many things that pertain to a Christian
man, and yet all those things are contained in this one thing, that is, LOVE.
He lappeth up all things in love.

Our whole duty is contained in these words, " Love together."
Therefore St. Paul saith, " He that loveth another, fulfilleth the whole
law;" so it appeareth that all things are contained in this word Love.
This love is a precious thing; our Saviour saith, " By this shall all men
know that ye are my disciples, if ye shall love one another."

So Christ makes love his cognizance, his badge, his livery. Like
as every lord commonly gives a certain livery to his servants, whereby
they may be known that they pertain unto him; and so we say, yonder is
this lord's servants, because they wear his livery: so our Saviour, who is
the Lord above all lords, would have his servants known by their liveries
and badge, which badge is love alone. Whosoever now is endued with
love and charity, is his servant; him we may call Christ's servant; for
love is the token whereby you may know that such a servant pertaineth
to Christ; so that charity may be called the very livery of Christ. He
that hath charity is Christ's servant: he that hath not charity, is the servant of the devil. For as Christ's livery is love and charity, so the devil's
livery is hatred, malice, and discord.

But I think the devil has a great many more servants than Christ
has; for there are a great many more in his livery than in Christ's livery;

there are but very few who are endued with Christ's livery; with love and charity, gentleness and meekness of spirit; but there are a great number that bear hatred and malice in their hearts, that are proud, stout, and lofty; therefore the number of the devil's servants is greater than the number of Christ's servants.

Now St. Paul shows how needful this love is. I speak not of carnal love, which is only animal affection; but of this charitable love which is so necessary, that when a man hath it, without all other things it will suffice him. Again, if a man have all other things and lacketh that love, it will not help him, it is all vain and lost. St. Paul used it so: " Though I speak with tongues of men and angels, and yet had no love, I were even as sounding brass, or as a tinkling cymbal. And though I could prophesy and understand all secrets and all knowledge; yea, if I had all faith, so that I could move mountains out of their places, and yet had no love, I were nothing. And though I bestowed all my goods to feed the poor, and though I gave my body even that I were burned, and yet had no love, it profiteth me nothing." (1 Cor. xiii.) These are godly gifts, yet St. Paul calls them nothing when a man hath them without charity; which is a great commendation, and shows the great need of love, insomuch that all other virtues are in vain when this love is absent. And there have been some who thought that St. Paul spake against the dignity of faith; but you must understand that St. Paul speaks here not of the justifying faith, wherewith we receive everlasting life, but he understands by this word faith, the gift to do miracles, to remove hills; of such a faith he speaks. This I say to confirm this proposition. Faith only justifieth: this proposition is most true and certain. And St. Paul speaks not here of this lively justifying faith; for this right faith is not without love, for love cometh and floweth out of faith, love is a child of faith; for no man can love except he believe, so that they have two several offices, they themselves being inseparable.

St. Paul has an expression in the 13th chapter of the first of the Corinthians, which, according to the outward letter, seems much to the dispraise of this faith, and to the praise of love; these are his words, " Now abideth faith, hope, and love, even these three; but the chiefest of these is love." There are some learned men, who expound the greatness of which St. Paul speaketh here, as if meant for eternity. For when we come to God, then we believe no more, but rather see with our eyes face to face how he is; yet for all that, love remains still; so that love may be called the chiefest, because she endureth for ever. And though she is the chiefest, yet we must not attribute unto her the office which pertains unto faith only. Like as I cannot say, the mayor of Stamford must make me a pair of shoes because he is a greater man than the shoemaker is; for the mayor, though he is the greater man, yet it is not his office to make shoes; so though love be greater, yet it is not her office to save. Thus much I thought good to say against those who fight against the truth.

Now, when we would know who are in Christ's livery or not, we must learn it of St. Paul, who most evidently described charity, which is the very livery, saying, "Love is patient, she suffereth long." Now whosoever fumeth and is angry, he is out of this livery: therefore let us remember that we do not cast away the livery of Christ our master. When we are in sickness or any manner of adversities, our duty is to be patient, to suffer willingly, and to call upon him for aid, help, and comfort; for without him we are not able to abide any tribulation. Therefore we must call upon God, he has promised to help: therefore let me not think him to be false or untrue in his promises, for we cannot dishonor God more than by not believing or trusting in him. Therefore let us beware above all things of dishonoring God; and so we must be patient, trusting and most certainly believing that he will deliver us when it seems good to him, who knows the time better than we ourselves.

"Charity is gentle, friendly, and loving; she envieth not." They that envy their neighbor's profit when it goes well with him, such fellows are out of their liveries, and so out of the service of God; for to be envious is to be the servant of the devil.

"Love doth not frowardly, she is not a provoker;" as there are some men who will provoke their neighbor so far that it is very hard for them to be in charity with them; but we must wrestle with our affections; we must strive and see that we keep this livery of Christ our master; for "the devil goeth about as a roaring lion seeking to take us at a vantage," to bring us out of our liveries, and to take from us the knot of love and charity.

"Love swelleth not, is not puffed up;" but there are many swellers now-a-days, they are so high, so lofty, insomuch that they despise and contemn all others: all such persons are under the governance of the devil. God rules not them with his good Spirit; the evil spirit has occupied their hearts and possessed them.

"She doth not dishonestly; she seeketh not her own; she doth all things to the commodity of her neighbors." A charitable man will not promote himself with the damage of his neighbor. They that seek only their own advantage, forgetting their neighbors, they are not of God, they have not his livery. Further, " charity is not provoked to anger; she thinketh not evil." We ought not to think evil of our neighbor, as long as we see not open wickedness; for it is written, " You shall not judge; " we should not take upon us to condemn our neighbor. And surely the condemners of other men's works are not in the livery of Christ. Christ hateth them.

·" She rejoiceth not in iniquity; " she loveth equity and godliness. And again, she is sorry to hear of falsehood, of stealing, or such like, which wickedness is now at this time commonly used. There never was such falsehood among Christian men as there is now, at this time; truly I think, and they that have experience report it so, that among the very Infidels and Turks there is more fidelity and uprightness than among Christian men. For no man setteth anything by his promise, yea, and writings will not serve with some, they are so shameless that they dare deny their own handwriting: but, I pray you, are those false fellows in the livery of Christ? Have they his cognizance? No, no; they have the badge of the devil, with whom they shall be damned world without end, except they amend and leave their wickedness.

" She suffereth all things; she believeth all things." It is a great matter that should make us to be grieved with our neighbor; we should be patient when our neighbor doth wrong, we should admonish him of his folly, earnestly desiring him to leave his wickedness, showing the danger that follows, namely, everlasting damnation. In such wise we should study to amend our neighbor, and not to hate him or do him a foul turn again, but rather charitably study to amend him: whosoever now does so, he has the livery and cognizance of Christ, he shall be known at the last day for his servant.

" Love believeth all things: " it appears daily that they who are charitable and friendly are most deceived; because they think well of every man; they believe every man, they trust their words, and therefore are most deceived in this world, among the children of the devil. These and such like things are the tokens of the right and godly love: therefore they that have this love are soon known, for this love cannot be hid in corners, she has her operation: therefore all that have her are well enough, though they have no other gifts besides her. Again, they that lack her, though they have many other gifts besides, yet is it to no other purpose, it does them no good: for when we shall come at the great day before him, not having this livery (that is love) with us, then we are lost; he will not take us for his servants, because we have not his cognizance. But if we have this livery, if we wear his cognizance here in this world; that is, if we love our neighbor, help him in his distress, are charitable, loving, and friendly unto him, then we shall be known at the last day: but if we be uncharitable towards our neighbor, hate him, seek our own advantage with his damage, then we shall be rejected of Christ and so damned world without end.

Our Saviour saith here in this gospel, "I command you these things:" he speaketh in the plural number, and lappeth it up in one thing, which is, that we should love one another, much like St. Paul's saying in the thirteenth to the Romans, "Owe nothing to any man, but to love one another." Here St. Paul lappeth up all things together, signifying unto us, that love is the consummation of the law; for this commandment, "Thou shalt not commit adultery," is contained in this law of love: for he that loveth God will not break wedlock, because wedlock breaking is a dishonoring of God and a serving of the devil. "Thou shalt not kill:" he that loveth will not kill, he will do no harm. "Thou shalt not steal;" he that loveth his neighbor as himself, will not take away his goods. I had of late occasion to speak of picking and stealing, where I showed unto you the danger wherein they are that steal their neighbors' goods from them, but I hear nothing yet of restitution. Sirs, I tell you, except restitution is made, look for no salvation. And it is a miserable and heinous thing to consider that we are so blinded with this world, that rather than we would make restitution, we will sell unto the devil our souls which are bought with the blood of our Saviour Christ. What can be done more to the dishonoring of Christ, than to cast our souls away to the devil for the value of a little money? — the soul which he has bought with his painful passion and death! But I tell you those that will do so, and that will not make restitution when they have done wrong, or have taken away their neighbor's goods, they are not in the livery of Christ, they are not his servants; let them go as they will in this world, yet for all that they are foul and filthy enough before God; they stink before his face; and therefore they shall be cast from his presence into everlasting fire; this shall be all their good cheer that they shall have, because they have not the livery of Christ, nor his cognizance, which is love. They remember not that Christ commanded us, saying, "This I command you, that ye love one another." This is Christ's commandment. Moses, the great prophet of God, gave many laws, but he gave not the Spirit to fulfil the same laws: but Christ gave this law, and promised unto us, that when we call upon him he will give us his Holy Ghost, who shall make us able to fulfil his laws, though not so perfectly as the law requires; but yet to the contentation of God, and to the protection of our faith; for as long as we are in this world, we can do nothing as we ought to do, because our flesh leadeth us, which is ever bent against the law of God; yet our works which we do are well taken for Christ's sake, and God will reward them in heaven.

Therefore our Saviour saith, "my yoke is easy, and my burden is light," because he helpeth to bear them; else indeed we should not be able to bear them. And in another place he saith, "his commandments are not heavy;" they are heavy to our flesh, but being qualified with the Spirit of God, to the faithful which believe in Christ, to them, I say, they are not heavy; for though their doings are not perfect, yet they are well taken for Christ's sake.

You must not be offended because the Scripture commends love so highly, for he that commends the daughter, commends the mother; for love is the daughter, and faith is the mother: love floweth out of faith; where faith is, there is love, but yet we must consider their offices, faith is the hand wherewith we take hold on everlasting life.

Now let us enter into ourselves, and examine our own hearts, whether we are in the livery of God, or not: and when we find ourselves to be out of this livery, let us repent and amend our lives, so that we may come again to the favor of God, and spend our time in this world to his honor and glory, forgiving our neighbors all such things as they have done against us.

And now to make an end: mark here who gave this precept of love — Christ our Saviour himself. When and at what time? At his departing, when he should suffer death. Therefore these words ought the more to be regarded, seeing he himself spake them at his last departing from us. May God of his mercy give us grace so to walk here in this world, charitably and friendly one with another, that we may attain the joy which God hath prepared for all those that love him. Amen.

V

JOHN KNOX

1505–1572

JOHN KNOX, the Reformer of Scotland —" he who never feared the face of man," as the Earl of Morton testified at his burial — was born at Gifford, in 1505. At the age of twenty-five, having graduated at the University of St. Andrew's, he was ordained a Roman Catholic priest. Twelve years later he renounced its communion and preached the Protestant faith. Fearless, sagacious, blunt in speech, and of fiery zeal, he would not be silenced. Persecuted, his life repeatedly in danger from assassins, for two years a wretched prisoner in French galleys, later an exile with Calvin in Geneva, yet he saw with joy the establishment of the Reformed kirk in Scotland, 1560, and wrote a valuable history of the Scottish Reformation. The closing years of his life were full of ardent labors at home, till —" weary of the world," as he said — he sank to rest in Edinburgh, November 24th 1572. His religious writings are published in a volume of the " British Reformers." Only three of his sermons are preserved.

THE FIRST TEMPTATION OF CHRIST.

" Then Jesus was led by the Spirit into the desert, that he should be tempted of the devil."— Matthew iv. 1.

THE cause moving me to treat of this place of Scripture is, that such as by the inscrutable providence of God fall into divers temptations, judge not themselves by reason thereof to be less acceptable in God's presence. But, on the contrary, having the way prepared to victory by Christ Jesus, they shall not fear above measure the crafty assaults of that subtle serpent Satan — but with joy and bold courage, having such a guide as here is pointed forth, such a champion, and such weapons as

here are to be found (if with obedience we will hear, and unfeigned
faith believe), we may assure ourselves of God's present favor, and of
final victory, by the means of Him, who, for our safeguard and deliverance, entered in the battle, and triumphed over his adversary, and all his
raging fury. And that this being heard and understood, may the better
be kept in memory; this order, by God's grace, we propose to observe,
in treating the matter: *First,* What this word temptation meaneth, and
how it is used within the Scriptures. *Secondly,* Who is here tempted,
and at what time this temptation happened. *Thirdly,* How and by what
means he was tempted. *Fourthly,* Why he should suffer these temptations, and what fruits ensue to us from the same.

First. Temptation, or to tempt, in the Scriptures of God, is called to
try, to prove, or to assault the valor, the power, the will, the pleasure,
or the wisdom — whether it be of God, or of creatures. And it is taken
sometimes in good part, as when it is said that God tempted Abraham;
God tempted the people of Israel; that is, God did try and examine them,
not for his own knowledge, to whom nothing is hid, but to certify others
how obedient Abraham was to God's commandment, and how weak and
inferior the Israelites were in their journey towards the promised land.
And this temptation is always good, because it proceeds immediately
from God, to open and make manifest the secret motions of men's hearts,
the puissance and power of God's word, and the great lenity and gentleness of God towards the iniquities (yea, horrible sins and rebellions) of
those whom he hath received into his regimen and care. For who could
have believed that the bare word of God could so have moved the heart
and affections of Abraham, that to obey God's commandment he determined to kill, with his own hand, his best beloved son Isaac? who could
have trusted that, so many torments as Job suffered, he should not
speak in all his great temptations one foolish word against God? or who
could have thought that God so mercifully should have pardoned so
many, and so manifest transgressions committed by his people in the
desert, and yet that his mercy never utterly left them, but still continued with them, till at length he performed his promise made to Abraham? Who, I say, would have been persuaded of these things, unless
by trials and temptations taken of his creatures by God, they had come
by revelation made in his Holy Scriptures to our knowledge? And so
this kind of temptation is profitable, good, and necessary, as a thing
proceeding from God, who is the fountain of all goodness, to the manifestation of his own glory, and to the profit of the sufferer, however

the flesh may judge in the hour of temptation. Otherwise temptation, or to tempt, is taken in evil part; that is, he that assaults or assails intends destruction and confusion to him that is assaulted. As when Satan tempted the woman in the garden, Job by divers tribulations, and David by adultery. The scribes and Pharisees tempted Christ by divers means, questions, and subtleties. And of this matter, saith St. James, "God tempteth no man;" that is, by temptation proceeding immediately from him, he intends no man's destruction. And here you shall note, that although Satan appears sometimes to prevail against God's elect, yet he is ever frustrated of his final purpose. By temptation he led Eve and David from the obedience of God, but he could not retain them for ever under his thraldom. Power was granted to him to spoil Job of his substance and children, and to strike his body with a plague and sickness most vile and fearful, but he could not compel his mouth to blaspheme God's majesty; and, therefore, although we are laid open sometimes, as it were, to tribulation for a time, it is that when he has poured forth the venom of his malice against God's elect, it may return to his own confusion, and that the deliverance of God's children may be more to his glory, and the comfort of the afflicted: knowing that his hand is so powerful, his mercy and good-will so prompt, that he delivers his little ones from their cruel enemy, even as David did his sheep and lambs from the mouth of the lion. For a benefit received in extreme danger more moves us than the preservation from ten thousand perils, so that we fall not into them. And yet to preserve from dangers and perils so that we fall not into them, whether they are of body or spirit, is no less the work of God, than to deliver from them; but the weakness of our faith does not perceive it: this I leave at the present.

Also; to tempt means simply to prove, or try without any determinate purpose of profit or damage to ensue; as when the mind doubteth of any thing, and therein desires to be satisfied, without great love or extreme hatred of the thing that is tempted or tried. As the Queen of Sheba came to tempt Solomon in subtle questions. David tempted, that is, tried himself if he could go in harness. (1 Sam. xvii.) And Gideon said, "Let not thine anger kindle against me, if I tempt thee once again." This famous queen, not fully trusting the report and fame that was spread of Solomon, by subtle questions desired to prove his wisdom; at the first, neither extremely hating nor fervently loving the person of the king. And David, as a man not accustomed to harness, would try how he was able to go, and behave and fashion himself therein, before he would hazard battle with Goliath so armed. And Gideon, not satisfied in his conscience by the first sign that he received, desired, without contempt or hatred of God, a second time to be certified of his vocation. In this sense must the apostle be expounded when he commands us to tempt, that is, to try and examine ourselves, if we stand in the faith. Thus much for the term.

Now to the person tempted, and to the time and place of his temptation. The person tempted is the only well-beloved Son of God; the time was immediately after his baptism; and the place was the desert or wilderness. But that we derive advantage from what is related, we must consider the same more profoundly. That the Son of God was thus tempted gives instruction to us, that temptations, although they be ever so grievous and fearful, do not separate us from God's favor and mercy, but rather declare the great graces of God to appertain to us, which makes Satan to rage as a roaring lion; for against none does he so fiercely fight, as against those of whose hearts Christ has taken possession.

The time of Christ's temptation is here most diligently to be noted. And that was, as Mark and Luke witness, immediately after the voice of God the Father had commended his Son to the world, and had visibly pointed to him by the sign of the Holy Ghost; he was led or moved by the Spirit to go to a wilderness, where forty days he remained fasting among the wild beasts. This Spirit which led Christ into the wilderness was not the devil, but the holy Spirit of God the Father, by whom Christ, as touching his human and manly nature, was conducted and led; likewise by the same Spirit he was strengthened and made strong, and, finally, raised up from the dead. The Spirit of God, I say, led Christ to the place of his battle, where he endured the combat for the whole forty days and nights. As Luke saith, " He was tempted," but in the end most vehemently, after his continual fasting, and that he began to be hungry. Upon this forty days and this fasting of Christ do our papists found and build their Lent; for, say they, all the actions of Christ are our instructions; what he did we ought to follow. But he fasted forty days, therefore we ought to do the like. I answer, that if we ought to follow all Christ's actions, then ought we neither to eat or drink for the space of forty days, for so fasted Christ: we ought to go upon the waters with our feet; to cast out devils by our word; to heal and cure all sorts of maladies; to call again the dead to life; for so did

Christ. This I write only that men may see the vanity of those who, boasting themselves of wisdom, have become mad fools.

Did Christ fast thus forty days to teach us superstitious fasting? Can the papists assure me, or any other man, which were the forty days that Christ fasted? plain it is he fasted the forty days and nights that immediately followed his baptism, but which they were, or in what month was the day of his baptism, Scripture does not express; and although the day were expressed, am I or any Christian bound to counterfeit Christ's actions as the ape counterfeits the act or work of man? He himself requires no such obedience of his true followers, but saith to the apostles, " Go and preach the gospel to all nations, baptizing them in the name of the Father, the Son, and the Holy Ghost; commanding them to observe and keep all that I have commanded you." Here Christ Jesus requires the observance of his precepts and commandments, not of his actions, except in so far as he had also commanded them; and so must the apostle be understood when he saith, " Be followers of Christ, for Christ hath suffered for us, that we should follow his footsteps," which cannot be understood of every action of Christ, either in the mystery of our redemption, or in his actions and marvellous works, but only of those which he hath commanded us to observe. But where the papists are so diligent in establishing their dreams and fantasies, they lose the profit that here is to be gathered,— that is, why Christ fasted those forty days; which were a doctrine more necessary for Christians, than to corrupt the simple hearts with superstition, as though the wisdom of God, Christ Jesus, had taught us no other mystery by his fasting than the abstinence from flesh, or once on the day to eat flesh, for the space of forty days. God hath taken a just vengeance upon the pride of such men, while he thus confounds the wisdom of those that do most glory in wisdom, and strikes with blindness such as will be guides and lanterns to the feet of others, and yet refuse themselves to hear or follow the light of God's word. From such deliver thy poor flock, O Lord!

The causes of Christ's fasting these forty days I find chiefly to be two: The first, to witness to the world the dignity and excellence of his vocation, which Christ, after his baptism, was to take upon him openly; the other, to declare that he entered into battle willingly for our cause, and does, as it were, provoke his adversary to assault him: although Christ Jesus, in the eternal counsel of his Father, was appointed to be the Prince of peace, the angel (that is, the messenger) of his testament, and he alone that could fight our battles for us, yet he did not enter

in execution of it, in the sight of men, till he was commended to mankind by the voice of his heavenly Father; and as he was placed and
anointed by the Holy Ghost by a visible sign given to the eyes of men.
After which time he was led to the desert, and fasted, as before is said;
and this he did to teach us with what fear, carefulness, and reverence
the messengers of the word ought to enter on their vocation, which is
not only most excellent (for who is worthy to be God's ambassador?)
but also subject to most extreme troubles and dangers. For he that
is appointed pastor, watchman, or preacher, if he feed not with his whole
power, if he warn and admonish not when he sees the snare come, and
if, in doctrine, he divide not the word righteously, the blood and souls
of those that perish for lack of food, admonition, and doctrine, shall be
required of his hand.

But to our purpose; that Christ exceeded not the space of forty days
in his fasting, he did it to the imitation of Moses and Elias; of whom,
the one before the receiving of the law, and the other before the communication and reasoning which he had with God in Mount Horeb, in
which he was commanded to anoint Hazael king over Syria, and Jehu
king over Israel, and Elisha to be prophet, fasted the same number of
days. The events that ensued and followed this supernatural fasting
of these two servants of God, Moses and Elias, impaired and diminished
the tyranny of the kingdom of Satan. For by the law came the knowledge of sin, the damnation of such impieties, specially of idolatry, and
such as the devil had invented; and, finally, by the law came such a revelation of God's will, that no man could justly afterward excuse his sin by
ignorance, by which the devil before had blinded many. So that the law,
although it might not renew and purge the heart, for that the spirit of
Christ Jesus worketh by faith only, yet it was a bridle that did hinder
and stay the rage of external wickedness in many, and was a schoolmaster that led unto Christ. For when man can find no power in himself
to do that which is commanded, and perfectly understands, and when
he believes that the curse of God is pronounced against all those that
abide not in everything that is commanded in God's law to do them —
the man, I say, that understands and knows his own corrupt nature and
God's severe judgment, most gladly will receive the free redemption
offered by Christ Jesus, which is the only victory that overthrows Satan
and his power. And so by the giving of the law God greatly weakened,
impaired, and made frail the tyranny and kingdom of the devil. In the
days of Elias, the devil had so prevailed that kings and rulers made open

war against God, killing his prophets, destroying his ordinances, and building up idolatry, which did so prevail, that the prophet complained that of all the true fearers and worshippers of God he was left alone, and wicked Jezebel sought his life also. After this, his fasting and complaint, he was sent by God to anoint the persons aforenamed, who took such vengeance upon the wicked and obstinate idolaters, that he who escaped the sword of Hazael fell into the hands of Jehu, and those whom Jehu left, escaped not God's vengeance under Elisha.

The remembrance of this was fearful to Satan, for, at the coming of Christ Jesus, impiety was in the highest degree amongst those that pretended most knowledge of God's will; and Satan was at such rest in his kingdom, that the priests, scribes, and Pharisees had taken away the key of knowledge; that is, they had so obscured and darkened God's Holy Scriptures, by false glosses and vain traditions, that neither would they enter themselves into the kingdom of God, nor suffer and permit others to enter; but with violence restrained, and with tyranny struck back from the right way, that is, from Christ Jesus himself, such as would have entered into the possession of life everlasting by him. Satan, I say, having such dominion over the chief rulers of the visible church, and espying in Christ such graces as before he had not seen in man, and considering him to follow in fasting the footsteps of Moses and Elias, no doubt greatly feared that the quietness and rest of his most obedient servants, the priests, and their adherents, would be troubled by Christ. And, therefore, by all engines and craft, he assaults him to see what advantage he could have of him. And Christ did not repel him, as by the power of his Godhead he might have done, that he should not tempt him, but permitted him to spend all his artillery, and received the strokes and assaults of Satan's temptations in his own body, to the end he might weaken and enfeeble the strength and tyrannous power of our adversary by his long-suffering. For thus, methinks, our Master and Champion, Jesus Christ, provoked our enemy to battle: "Satan, thou gloriest of thy power and victories over mankind, that there is none able to withstand thy assaults, nor escape thy darts, but at one time or other thou givest him a wound: lo! I am a man like to my brethren, having flesh and blood, and all properties of man's nature (sin, which is thy venom, excepted); tempt, try, and assault me; I offer you here a place most convenient — the wilderness. There shall be no mortal to comfort me against thy assaults; thou shalt have time sufficient; do what thou canst, I shall not fly the place of battle.

5

If thou become victor, thou shalt still continue in possession of thy kingdom in this wretched world; but if thou canst not prevail against me, then must thy prey and unjust spoil be taken from thee; thou must grant thyself vanquished and confounded, and must be compelled to leave off from all accusation of the members of my body; for to them appertains the fruit of my battle, my victory is theirs, as I am appointed to take the punishment of their sins in my body."

O dear sisters, what comfort ought the remembrance of these signs to be to our hearts! Christ Jesus hath fought our battle; he himself hath taken us into his care and protection; however the devil may rage by temptations, be they spiritual or corporeal, he is not able to bereave us out of the hand of the almighty Son of God. To him be all glory for his mercies most abundantly poured upon us!

There remains yet to be spoken of, the time when our Lord was tempted, which began immediately after his baptism. Whereupon we have to note and mark, that although the malice of Satan never ceases, but always seeks for means to trouble the godly, yet sometimes he rages more fiercely than others, and that is commonly when God begins to manifest his love and favor to any of his children, and at the end of their battle, when they are nearest to obtain final victory. The devil, no doubt, did at all times envy the humble spirit that was in Abel, but he did not stir up the cruel heart of Cain against him till God declared his favor towards him, by accepting his sacrifice. The same we find in Jacob, Joseph, David, and most evidently in Christ Jesus. How Satan raged at the tidings of Christ's nativity! what blood he caused to be shed on purpose to have murdered Christ in his infancy! The evangelist St. Matthew witnesses that in all the coasts and borders of Bethlehem the children of two years old and of less age were murdered without mercy. A fearful spectacle and horrid example of insolent and unaccustomed tyranny! And what is the cause moving Satan thus to rage against innocents, considering that by reason of their imperfections, they could not hurt his kingdom at that instant? Oh! the crafty eye of Satan looked farther than to the present time; he heard reports by the three wise men, that they had learned, by the appearance of a star, that the King of the Jews was born; and he was not ignorant that the time prophesied of Christ's coming was then instant; for a stranger was clad with the crown and sceptre in the kingdom of Judah. The angel had declared the glad tidings to the shepherds, that a Saviour, which was Christ the Lord, was born in the city of David. All these tidings inflamed the wrath and malice of Satan, for he perfectly understood that the coming of the promised Seed was appointed to his confusion, and to the breaking down of his head and tyranny; and therefore he raged most cruelly, even at the first hearing of Christ's birth, thinking that although he could not hinder nor withstand his coming, yet he could shorten his days upon earth, lest by long life and peaceable quietness in it, the number of good men, by Christ's doctrine and virtuous life, should be multiplied; and so he strove to cut him away among the other children before he could open his mouth on his Father's message. Oh, cruel serpent! in vain dost thou spend thy venom, for the days of God's elect thou canst not shorten! And when the wheat is fallen on the ground, then doth it most multiply.

But from these things mark, dear sisters, what hath been the practice of the devil from the beginning — most cruelly to rage against God's children, when God begins to show them his mercy. And, therefore, marvel not, dearly beloved, although the like come unto you. If Satan fume or roar against you, whether it be against your bodies by persecution, or inwardly in your conscience by a spiritual battle, be not discouraged, as though you were less acceptable in God's presence, or as if Satan might at any time prevail against you. No: your temptations and storms that arise so suddenly, argue and witness that the seed which is sown, is fallen on good ground, begins to take root, and shall, by God's grace, bring forth fruit abundantly in due season and convenient time. That is it which Satan fears, and therefore thus he rages, and shall rage against you, thinking that if he can repulse you now suddenly in the beginning, that then you shall be at all times an easy prey, never able to resist his assaults. But as my hope is good, so shall my prayer be, that so you may be strengthened, that the world and Satan himself may perceive or understand that God fights your battle. For you remember, sisters, that being present with you and treating of the same place, I admonished you that Satan could not long sleep when his kingdom was threatened. And therefore I willed you, if you were in mind to continue with Christ, to prepare yourselves for the day of temptation. The person of the speaker is wretched, miserable, and nothing to be regarded, but the things that were spoken, are the infallible and eternal truth of God; without observation of which, life neither can nor shall come to mankind. God grant you continuance to the end.

This much have I briefly spoken of the temptation of Christ Jesus, who was tempted; and of the time and place of his temptation. Now remains to be spoken how he was tempted, and by what means. The most part of expositors think that all this temptation was in spirit and imagination only, the corporeal senses being nothing moved. I will contend with no man in such cases, but patiently will I suffer every man to abound in his own knowledge; and without prejudice of any man's estimations, I offer my judgment to be weighed and considered by Christian charity. It appears to me by the plain text, that Christ suffered this temptation in body and spirit. Likewise, as the hunger which Christ suffered, and the desert in which he remained, were not things offered to the imagination, but that the body did verily remain in the wilderness among beasts, and after forty days did hunger and faint for lack of food; so the external ear did hear the tempting words of Satan, which entered into the knowledge of the soul, and which, repelling the venom of such temptations, caused the tongue to speak and confute Satan, to our unspeakable comfort and consolation. It appears also that the body of Christ Jesus was carried by Satan from the wilderness unto the temple of Jerusalem, and that it was placed upon the pinnacle of the same temple, from whence it was carried to a high mountain and there tempted. If any man can show the contrary hereof by the plain Scriptures of God, with all submission and thanksgiving, I will prefer his judgment to my own; but if the matter stand only in probability and opinion of men, then it is lawful for me to believe as the Scripture here speaks. That is, that Satan spake and Christ answered, and Satan took him and carried him from one place to another. Besides the evidence of the text affirming that Satan was permitted to carry the body of Christ from place to place, and yet was not permitted to execute any further tyranny against it, is most singular comfort to such as are afflicted or troubled in body or spirit. The weak and feeble conscience of man under such temptations, commonly gathers and collects a false consequence. For man reasons thus: The body or the spirit is vexed by assaults and temptations of Satan, and he troubles or molests it, therefore God is angry with it, and takes no care of it. I answer, Tribulations or grievous vexations of body or of mind are never signs of God's displeasure against the sufferer, neither yet does it follow that God has cast away the care of his creatures, because he permits them to be molested and vexed for a time. For if any sort of tribulation were the infallible sign of God's displeasure, then should we condemn the best beloved children of God. But of this we may speak hereafter. Now to the temptation.

Verse 2d. "And when he had fasted forty days and forty nights, he was afterwards hungry." Verse 3d. "Then came to him the tempter, and said, If you be the Son of God, command that these stones be made bread," etc. Why Christ fasted forty days and would not exceed the same, without sense and feeling of hunger, is before touched upon, that is, he would provoke the devil to battle by the wilderness and long abstinence, but he would not usurp or arrogate any more to himself in that case than God had wrought with others, his servants and messengers before. But Christ Jesus (as St. Augustine more amply declares), without feeling of hunger, might have endured the whole year, or to time without end, as well as he did endure the space of forty days. For the nature of mankind was sustained those forty days by the invisible power of God, which is at all times of equal power. But Christ, willing to offer further occasion to Satan to proceed in tempting of him, permitted the human nature to crave earnestly that which it lacked, that is to say, refreshing of meat; which Satan perceiving took occasion, as before, to tempt and assault. Some judge that Satan tempted Christ to gluttony, but this appears little to agree with the purpose of the Holy Ghost; who shows us this history to let us understand that Satan never ceases to oppugn the children of God, but continually, by one mean or other, drives or provokes them to some wicked opinions of their God; and to have them desire stones to be converted into bread, or to desire hunger to be satisfied, has never been sin, nor yet a wicked opinion of God. And therefore I doubt not but the temptation was more spiritual, more subtle, and more dangerous. Satan had respect to the voice of God, which had pronounced Christ to be his well-beloved Son, etc. Against this voice he fights, as his nature is ever to do against the assured and immutable word of God: for such is his malice against God, and against his chosen children, that where and to whom God pronounces love and mercy, to these he threatens displeasure and damnation; and where God threatens death, there is he bold to pronounce life; and for this cause is Satan called a liar from the beginning. And so the purpose of Satan was to drive Christ into desperation, that he should not believe the former voice of God his Father; which appears to be the meaning of this temptation: "Thou hast heard," would Satan say, "a voice proclaimed in the air, that thou wast the beloved Son of God, in whom his soul was well pleased; but mayst thou not be judged more than mad, and weaker than the brainless fool if thou believest any such promise? Where are the signs of his love? Art thou not cast out from comfort of all creatures? Thou art in worse case than the brute beasts, for every day they hunt for their prey, and the earth produces grass and herbs for their sustenance, so that none of them are pined and consumed away by hunger; but thou hast fasted forty days and nights, ever waiting for some relief and comfort from above, but thy best provision is hard stones! If thou dost glory in thy God, and dost verily believe the promise that is made, command that these stones be bread. But evident it is, that so thou canst not do; for if thou couldst, or if thy God would have showed thee any such pleasure, thou mightest long ago have removed thy hunger, and needest not have endured this languishing for lack of food. But seeing thou hast long continued thus, and no provision is made for thee, it is vanity longer to believe any such promise, and therefore despair of any help from God's hand, and provide for thyself by some other means!"

Many words have I used here, dearly beloved, but I cannot express the thousandth part of the malicious despite which lurked in this one temptation of Satan. It was a mocking of Christ and of his obedience. It was a plain denial of God's promise. It was the triumphing voice of him that appeared to have gotten victory. Oh how bitter his temptation was, no creature can understand, but such as feel the grief of such darts as Satan casts at the tender conscience of those that gladly would rest and repose in God, and in the promises of his mercy. But here is to be noted the ground and foundation. The conclusion of Satan is this: Thou art none of God's elect, much less his well-beloved Son. His reason is this: Thou art in trouble and findest no relief. There the foundation of the temptation was Christ's poverty, and the lack of food without hope of remedy to be sent from God. And it is the same temptation which the devil objected to him by the princes of the priests in his grievous torments upon the cross; for thus they cried, "If he be the Son of God, let him come down from the cross, and we will believe in him; he trusted in God, let him deliver him, if he have pleasure in him." As though they would say, God is the deliverer of his servants from troubles; God never permits those that fear him to come to confusion; this man we see in extreme trouble; if he be the Son of God, or even a true worshipper of his name, he will deliver him from this calamity. If he deliver him not, but suffer him to perish in these anguishes, then it is an assured sign that God has rejected him as a hypocrite, that shall have no portion of his glory. Thus, I say, Satan takes occasion to tempt, and moves also others to judge and condemn God's elect and chosen children, by reason that troubles are multiplied upon them.

But with what weapons we ought to fight against such enemies and assaults, we shall learn in the answer of Christ Jesus, which follows: But he, answering, said, " It is written, Man lives not by bread only, but by every word which proceeds out of the mouth of God." This answer of Christ proves the sentence which we have brought of the aforesaid temptation, to be the very meaning of the Holy Ghost; for unless the purpose of Satan had been to have removed Christ from all hope of God's merciful providence towards him in that his necessity, Christ had not answered directly to his words, saying, " Command that these stones be made bread." But Christ Jesus, perceiving his art and malicious subtilty, answered directly to his meaning, his words nothing regarded; by which Satan was so confounded, that he was ashamed to reply any further.

But that you may the better understand the meaning of Christ's answer, we will express and repeat it over in more words. " Thou laborest, Satan," would Christ say, " to bring into my heart a doubt and suspicion of my Father's promise, which was openly proclaimed in my baptism, by reason of my hunger, and that I lack all carnal provision. Thou art bold to affirm that God takes no care for me, but thou art a deceitful and false corrupt sophister, and thy argument too is vain, and full of blasphemies; for thou bindest God's love, mercy, and providence, to the having or wanting of bodily provision, which no part of God's Scriptures teach us, but rather the express contrary. As it is written, ' Man liveth not by bread alone, but by every word that proceedeth from the mouth of God.' That is, the very life and felicity of man consists not in the abundance of bodily things, or, the possession and having of them makes no man blessed or happy; neither shall the lack of them be the cause of his final misery; but the very life of man consists in God, and in his promises pronounced by his own mouth, unto which whoso cleaves unfeignedly, shall live the life everlasting. And although all creatures in earth forsake him, yet shall not his bodily life perish till the time appointed by God approach. For God has means to feed, preserve, and maintain, unknown to man's reason, and contrary to the common course of nature. He fed his people Israel in the desert forty years without the provision of man. He preserved Jonah in the whale's belly; and maintained and kept the bodies of the three children in the furnace of fire. Reason and the natural man could have seen nothing in these cases but destruction and death, and could have judged nothing but that God had cast away the care of these his creatures, and yet his providence was most vigilant towards them in the extremity of their dangers, from which he did so deliver them, and in the midst of them did so assist them, that his glory, which is his mercy and goodness, did more appear and shine after their troubles, than it could have done if they had fallen in them. And therefore I measure not the truth and favor of God, by having or by lacking of bodily necessities, but by the promise which he has made to me. As he himself is immutable, so is his word and promise constant, which I believe, and to which I will adhere, and so cleave, whatever can come to the body outwardly."

In this answer of Christ we may perceive what weapons are to be used against our adversary the devil, and how we may confute his arguments, which craftily, and of malice, he makes against God's elect. Christ might have repulsed Satan with a word, or by commanding him to silence, as he to whom all power was given in heaven and earth; but it pleased his mercy to teach us how to use the sword of the Holy Ghost, which is the word of God, in battle against our spiritual enemy. The Scripture that Christ brings is written in the eighth chapter of Deuteronomy. It was spoken by Moses a little before his death, to establish the people in God's merciful providence. For in the same chapter, and in certain others that go before, he reckons the great travail and divers dangers with the extreme necessities that they had sustained in the desert, the space of forty years, and yet, notwithstanding how constant God had been in keeping and performing his promise, for throughout all perils he had conducted them to the sight and borders of the promised land. And so this Scripture more directly answers to the temptation of Satan; for thus does Satan reason, as before is said, " Thou art in poverty and hast no provision to sustain thy life. Therefore God takes no regard nor care of thee, as he doth over his chosen children." Christ Jesus answered: " Thy argument is false and vain; for poverty or necessity precludes not the providence or care of God; which is easy to be proved by the people of God, Israel, who, in the desert, oftentimes lacked things necessary to the sustenance of life, and for lack of the same they grudged and murmured; yet the Lord never cast away the providence and care of them, but according to the word that he had once pronounced, to wit, that they were his peculiar people; and according to the promise made to Abraham, and to them before their departure from Egypt, he still remained their conductor and guide, till he placed them in peaceable possession of the land of Canaan, their great infirmities and manifold transgressions notwithstanding."

Thus are we taught, I say, by Christ Jesus, to repulse Satan and his assaults by the word of God, and to apply the examples of his mercies, which he has shown to others before us, to our own souls in the hour of temptation, and in the time of our trouble. For what God doth to one at any time, the same appertains to all that depend upon God and his promises. And, therefore, however we are assaulted by Satan, our adversary, within the word of God is armour and weapons sufficient. The chief craft of Satan is to trouble those that begin to decline from his obedience, and to declare themselves enemies to iniquity, with divers assaults, the design whereof is always the same, that is, to put variance betwixt them and God, into their conscience, that they should not repose and rest themselves in his assured promises. And to persuade this, he uses and invents divers arguments. Sometimes he calls the sins of their youth, and which they have committed in the time of blindness, to their remembrance; very often he objects their unthankfulness towards God and present imperfections. By sickness, poverty, tribulations in their household, or by persecution, he can allege that God is angry, and regards them not. Or, by the spiritual cross, which few feel and fewer understand the utility and profit of, he would drive God's children to desperation, and by infinite means more, he goeth about seeking, like a roaring lion, to undermine and destroy our faith. But it is impossible for him to prevail against us, unless we obstinately refuse to use the defense and weapons that God has offered. Yea, I say, that God's elect cannot refuse it, but seek for their Defender when the battle is most strong; for the sobs, groans, and lamentations of such as fight, yea, the fear they have lest they be vanquished, the calling and prayer for continuance, are the undoubted and right seeking of Christ our champion. We refuse not the weapon, although sometimes, by infirmity, we cannot use it as we would. It suffices that your hearts unfeignedly sob for greater strength, for continuance, and for final deliverance by Christ Jesus; that which is wanting in us, his sufficiency doth supply; for it is he that fighteth and overcometh for us. But for bringing of the examples of the Scriptures, if God permit, in the end we shall speak more largely when it shall be treated why Christ permitted himself thus to be tempted. Sundry impediments now call me from writing in this matter, but, by God's grace, at convenient leisure I purpose to finish, and to send it to you. I grant the matter that proceeds from me is not worthy of your pain and labor to read it; yet, seeing it is a testimony of my good mind towards you, I doubt not but you will accept it in good part. God, the Father of our Lord Jesus Christ, grant unto you to find favor and mercy of the Judge, whose eyes and knowledge pierce through the secret cogitations of the heart, in the day of temptation, which shall come upon all flesh, according to that mercy which you (illuminated and directed by his Holy Spirit) have showed to the afflicted. Now the God of all comfort and consolation confirm and strengthen you in his power unto the end. Amen.

VI

JOHN CALVIN

1509–1564

JOHN CALVIN, a chief reformer and theologian — well termed by Dr. Mason " the Paul of the Reformation "— was born at Noyon in Picardy, France, July 10th 1509, and died in Geneva, May 27th 1564. He graduated from the University of Paris, studied law and Greek at Orleans, and became an ardent student of the Scriptures. Converted to the reformed doctrines, he gave up the Roman Catholic chaplaincy conferred on him in his childhood, and eloquently preached the freeness of Gospel salvation. Persecuted in one city, he fled to another, everywhere bearing testimony to the power of God's grace. In his twenty-fifth year, he issued his " Institutes of the Christian Religion," a masterly statement and vindication of evangelical doctrines as freed from the traditions and perversions of the papal theologians. The best of its principles still remain as the heritage of the saints, although some of its severer doctrines are now held by few theologians. In 1535 he began his ministerial labors and ecclesiastical rule in Geneva, which continued nearly thirty years, excepting a three years' banishment from 1538. By his firm control Geneva became the stronghold of French Protestantism, a city of refuge from persecution and death for all who longed to worship God with a pure conscience. One of the profoundest theologians, and a most able expositor of the Scriptures, Calvin was also an extremely conscientious, earnest, and abstemious man. His works, in fifty-one volumes, have been published by the Calvin Translation Society, Edinburgh. Only four of his Sermons are extant. They have a closeness of thought and homeliness of illustration, above all abounding in inspiring exhortations for each to stand firm as a witness for Gospel truth, at a time when monstrous cruelties were heaped upon Huguenots and Protestants.

ON ENDURING PERSECUTION FOR CHRIST.

" Let us go forth out of the tents after Christ, bearing his reproach."—
Hebrews xiii. 13.

ALL the exhortations which can be given us to suffer patiently for
the name of Jesus Christ, and in defence of the gospel, will have no effect,
if we do not feel assured of the cause for which we fight. For when
we are called to part with life, it is absolutely necessary to know on what
grounds. The firmness necessary we cannot possess, unless it be founded
on certainty of faith.

It is true that persons may be found who will foolishly expose
themselves to death in maintaining some absurd opinions and reveries
conceived by their own brain, but such impetuosity is more to be regarded
as frenzy than as Christian zeal; and, in fact, there is neither firmness nor
sound sense in those who thus, at a kind of hap-hazard, cast themselves
away. But however this may be, it is in a good cause only that God can
acknowledge us as his martyrs. Death is common to all, and the children of God are condemned to ignominy and tortures just as criminals
are; but God makes the distinction between them, inasmuch as he cannot
deny his truth. On our part, then, it is requisite that we have sure and
infallible evidence of the doctrine which we maintain; and hence, as I
have said, we cannot be rationally impressed by any exhortations which
we receive to suffer persecution for the gospel, if no true certainty of
faith has been imprinted in our hearts. For to hazard our life upon
a peradventure is not natural, and though we were to do it, it would
only be rashness, not Christian courage. In a word, nothing that we
do will be approved of God if we are not thoroughly persuaded that it
is for him and his cause we suffer persecution, and the world is our
enemy.

Now, when I speak of such persuasion, I mean not merely that we
must know how to distinguish between true religion and the abuses or
follies of men, but also that we must be thoroughly persuaded of the
heavenly life, and the crown which is promised us above, after we shall
have fought here below. Let us understand, then, that both of these
requisites are necessary, and cannot be separated from each other. The
points, accordingly, with which we must commence, are these:— We
must know well what our Christianity is, what the faith which we have
to hold and follow — what the rule which God has given us; and we

must be so well furnished with such instructions as to be able boldly to condemn all the falsehoods, errors, and superstitions, which Satan has introduced to corrupt the pure simplicity of the doctrine of God. Hence, we ought not to be surprised that, in the present day, we see so few persons disposed to suffer for the Gospel, and that the greater part of those who call themselves Christians know not what it is. For all are as it were lukewarm; and instead of making it their business to hear or read, count it enough to have had some slight taste of Christian faith. This is the reason why there is so little decision, and why those who are assailed immediately fall away. This fact should stimulate us to inquire more diligently into divine truth, in order to be well assured with regard to it.

Still, however, to be well informed and grounded is not the whole that is necessary. For we see some who seem to be thoroughly imbued with sound doctrine, and who, notwithstanding, have no more zeal or affection than if they had never known any more of God than some fleeting fancy. Why is this? Just because they have never comprehended the majesty of the Holy Scriptures. And, in fact, did we, such as we are, consider well that it is God who speaks to us, it is certain that we would listen more attentively, and with greater reverence. If we would think that in reading Scripture we are in the school of angels, we would be far more careful and desirous to profit by the doctrine which is propounded to us.

We now see THE TRUE METHOD OF PREPARING TO SUFFER FOR THE GOSPEL. *First,* We must have profited so far in the school of God as to be decided in regard to true religion and the doctrine which we are to hold; and we must despise all the wiles and impostures of Satan, and all human inventions, as things not only frivolous but also carnal, inasmuch as they corrupt Christian purity; therein differing, like true martyrs of Christ, from the fantastic persons who suffer for mere absurdities. *Second,* Feeling assured of the good cause, we must be inflamed, accordingly, to follow God whithersoever he may call us: his word must have such authority with us as it deserves, and, having withdrawn from this world, we must feel as it were enraptured in seeking the heavenly life.

But it is more than strange, that though the light of God is shining more brightly than it ever did before, there is a lamentable want of zeal! If the thought does not fill us with shame, so much the worse. For we must shortly come before the great Judge, where the iniquity which we endeavor to hide will be brought forward with such upbraidings, that we shall be utterly confounded. For, if we are obliged to bear testimony to God, according to the measure of the knowledge which he has given us, to what is it owing, I would ask, that we are so cold and timorous in entering into battle, seeing that God has so fully manifested himself at this time, that he may be said to have opened to us and displayed before us the great treasures of his secrets? May it not be said that we do not think we have to do with God? For had we any regard to his majesty we would not dare to turn the doctrine which proceeds from his mouth into some kind of philosophic speculation. In short, it is impossible to deny that it is to our great shame, not to say fearful condemnation, that we have so well known the truth of God, and have so little courage to maintain it!

Above all, when we look to the Martyrs of past times, well may we detest our own cowardice! The greater part of those were not persons much versed in Holy Scripture, so as to be able to dispute on all subjects. They knew that there was one God, whom they behoved to worship and serve — that they had been redeemed by the blood of Jesus Christ, in order that they might place their confidence of salvation in him and in his grace — and that, all the inventions of men being mere dross and rubbish, they ought to condemn all idolatries and superstitions. In one word, their theology was in substance this,— There is one God who created all the world, and declared his will to us by Moses and the Prophets, and finally by Jesus Christ and his Apostles; and we have one sole Redeemer, who purchased us by his blood, and by whose grace we hope to be saved: All the idols of the world are cursed, and deserve execration.

With a system embracing no other points than these, they went boldly to the flames, or to any other kind of death. They did not go in twos or threes, but in such bands, that the number of those who fell by the hands of tyrants is almost infinite! We, on our part, are such learned clerks, that none can be more so (so at least we think), and, in fact, so far as regards the knowledge of Scripture, God has so spread it out before us, that no former age was ever so highly favored. Still, after all, there is scarcely a particle of zeal. When men manifest such indifference, it looks as if they were bent on provoking the vengeance of God.

What then should be done in order to inspire our breasts with true courage? We have, in the first place, to consider how precious the

Confession of our Faith is in the sight of God. We little know how much God prizes it, if our life, which is nothing, is valued by us more highly. When it is so, we manifest a marvellous degree of stupidity. We cannot save our life at the expense of our confession, without acknowledging that we hold it in higher estimation than the honor of God and the salvation of our souls.

A heathen could say, that " It was a miserable thing to save life by giving up the only things which made life desirable!" And yet he and others like him never knew for what end men are placed in the world, and why they live in it. It is true they knew enough to say that men ought to follow virtue, to conduct themselves honestly and without reproach; but all their virtues were mere paint and smoke. We know far better what the chief aim of life should be, namely, to glorify God, in order that he may be our glory. When this is not done, woe to us! And we cannot continue to live for a single moment upon the earth without heaping additional curses on our heads. Still we are not ashamed to purchase some few days to languish here below, renouncing the eternal kingdom by separating ourselves from him by whose energy we are sustained in life.

Were we to ask the most ignorant, not to say the most brutish persons in the world, Why they live? they would not venture to answer simply, that it is to eat, and drink, and sleep; for all know that they have been created for a higher and holier end. And what end can we find if it be not to honor God, and allow ourselves to be governed by him, like children by a good parent; so that after we have finished the journey of this corruptible life, we may be received into his eternal inheritance? Such is the principal, indeed the sole end. When we do not take it into account, and are intent on a brutish life, which is worse than a thousand deaths, what can we allege for our excuse? To live and not know why, is unnatural. To reject the causes for which we live, under the influence of a foolish longing for a respite of some few days, during which we are to live in the world, while separated from God — I know not how to name such infatuation and madness!

But as persecution is always harsh and bitter, let us consider, How AND BY WHAT MEANS CHRISTIANS MAY BE ABLE TO FORTIFY THEMSELVES WITH PATIENCE, SO AS UNFLINCHINGLY TO EXPOSE THEIR LIFE FOR THE TRUTH OF GOD. The text which we have read out, when it is properly understood, is sufficient to induce us to do so. The Apostle says, " Let us go forth from the city after the Lord Jesus, bearing his reproach."

In the first place, he reminds us, although the swords should not be drawn over us nor the fires kindled to burn us, that we cannot be truly united to the Son of God while we are rooted in this world. Wherefore, a Christian even in repose, must always have one foot lifted to march to battle, and not only so, but he must have his affections withdrawn from the world, although his body is dwelling in it. Grant that this at first sight seems to us hard, still we must be satisfied with the words of St. Paul (1 Thess. iii. 3), "We are called and appointed to suffer." As if he had said, Such is our condition as Christians; this is the road by which we must go, if we would follow Christ.

Meanwhile, to solace our infirmity and mitigate the vexation and sorrow which persecution might cause us, a good reward is held forth: In suffering for the cause of God, we are walking step by step after the Son of God, and have him for our guide. Were it simply said, that to be Christians we must pass through all the insults of the world boldly, to meet death at all times and in whatever way God may be pleased to appoint, we might apparently have some pretext for replying, It is a strange road to go at peradventure. But when we are commanded to follow the Lord Jesus, his guidance is too good and honorable to be refused. Now, in order that we may be more deeply moved, not only is it said that Jesus Christ walks before us as our Captain, but that we are made comfortable to his image; as St. Paul speaks in the eighth chapter to the Romans (Rom. viii. 29), "God hath ordained all those whom he hath adopted for his children, to be made conformable to him who is the pattern and head of all."

Are we so delicate as to be unwilling to endure anything? Then we must renounce the grace of God by which he has called us to the hope of salvation. For there are two things which cannot be separated — to be members of Christ, and to be tried by many afflictions. We certainly ought to prize such a conformity to the Son of God much more than we do. It is true, that in the world's judgment there is disgrace in suffering for the gospel. But since we know that unbelievers are blind, ought we not to have better eyes than they? It is ignominy to suffer from those who occupy the seat of justice, but St. Paul shows us by his example that we have to glory in scourings for Jesus Christ, as marks by which God recognises us and avows us for his own. And we know what St. Luke narrates of Peter and John (Acts v. 41), namely, that they rejoiced to have been " counted worthy to suffer infamy and reproach for the name of the Lord Jesus."

Ignominy and dignity are two opposites: so says the world which, being infatuated, judges against all reason, and in this way converts the glory of God into dishonor. But, on our part, let us not refuse to be vilified as concerns the world, in order to be honored before God and his angels. We see what pains the ambitious take to receive the commands of a king, and what a boast they make of it. The Son of God presents his commands to us, and every one stands back! Tell me, pray, whether in so doing are we worthy of having anything in common with him? There is nothing here to attract our sensual nature, but such notwithstanding are the true escutcheons of nobility in the heavens. Imprisonment, exile, evil report, imply in men's imagination whatever is to be vituperated; but what hinders us from viewing things as God judges and declares them, save our unbelief? Wherefore, let the Name of the Son of God have all the weight with us which it deserves, that we may learn to count it honor when he stamps his marks upon us: If we act otherwise our ingratitude is insupportable!

Were God to deal with us according to our deserts, would he not have just cause to chastise us daily in a thousand ways? Nay more, a hundred thousand deaths would not suffice for a small portion of our misdeeds! Now, if in his infinite goodness he puts all our faults under his foot and abolishes them, and instead of punishing us according to our demerit, devises an admirable means to convert our afflictions into honor and a special privilege, inasmuch as through them we are taken into partnership with his Son, must it not be said, when we disdain such a happy state, that we have indeed made little progress in Christian doctrine?

Accordingly St. Peter, after exhorting us (1 Peter iv. 15) to walk so purely in the fear of God, as "not to suffer as thieves, adulterers, and murderers," immediately adds, "If we must suffer as Christians, let us glorify God for the blessing which he thus bestows upon us." It is not without cause he speaks thus. For who are we, I pray, to be witnesses of the truth of God, and advocates to maintain his cause? Here we are poor worms of the earth, creatures full of vanity, full of lies, and yet God employs us to defend his truth — an honor which pertains not even to the angels of heaven! May not this consideration alone well inflame us to offer ourselves to God to be employed in any way in such honorable service?

Many persons, however, cannot refrain from pleading against God, or, at least, from complaining against him for not better supporting their

6

weakness. It is marvellously strange, they say, how God, after having chosen us for his children, allows us to be so trampled upon and tormented by the ungodly. I answer: Even were it not apparent why he does so, he might well exercise his authority over us, and fix our lot at his pleasure. But when we see that Jesus Christ is our pattern, ought we not, without inquiring farther, to esteem it great happiness that we are made like to him? God, however, makes it very apparent what the reasons are for which he is pleased that we should be persecuted. Had we nothing more than the consideration suggested by St. Peter (1 Peter i. 7), we were disdainful indeed not to acquiesce in it. He says, " Since gold and silver, which are only corruptible metals, are purified and tested by fire, it is but reasonable that our faith, which surpasses all the riches of the world, should be tried."

It were easy indeed for God to crown us at once without requiring us to sustain any combats; but as it is his pleasure that until the end of the world Christ shall reign in the midst of his enemies (Psalm cx.), so it is also his pleasure that we, being placed in the midst of them, shall suffer their oppression and violence till he deliver us. I know, indeed, that the flesh kicks when it is to be brought to this point, but still the will of God must have the mastery. If we feel some repugnance in ourselves, it need not surprise us; for it is only too natural for us to shun the cross. Still let us not fail to surmount it, knowing that God accepts our obedience, provided we bring all our feelings and wishes into captivity, and make them subject to him.

When the Prophets and Apostles went to death, it was not without feeling some inclination to recoil. " They will lead thee whither thou wouldst not," said our Lord Jesus Christ to Peter. (John xxi. 18.) When such fears of death arise within us, let us gain the mastery over them, or rather let God gain it; and meanwhile, let us feel assured that we offer him a pleasing sacrifice when we resist and do violence to our inclinations for the purpose of placing ourselves entirely under his command: This is the principal war in which God would have his people to be engaged. He would have them strive to suppress every rebellious thought and feeling which would turn them aside from the path to which he points. And the consolations are so ample, that it may well be said, we are more than cowards if we give way!

In ancient times vast numbers of people, to obtain a simple crown of leaves, refused no toil, no pain, no trouble; nay, it even cost them nothing to die, and yet every one of them fought for a peradventure, not knowing whether he was to gain or lose the prize. God holds forth to us the immortal crown by which we may become partakers of his glory: He does not mean us to fight at hap-hazard, but all of us have a promise of the prize for which we strive. Have we any cause then to decline the struggle? Do we think it has been said in vain, "If we die with Jesus Christ we shall also live with him?" (2 Tim. ii. 11.) Our triumph is prepared, and yet we do all we can to shun the combat.

But it is said that all we teach on this subject is repugnant to human judgment. I confess it. And hence when our Saviour declares, "Blessed are they who are persecuted for righteousness' sake (Matt. v. 10), he gives utterance to a sentiment which is not easily received in the world. On the contrary, he wishes to account that as happiness which in the judgment of sense is misery. We seem to ourselves miserable when God leaves us to be trampled upon by the tryanny and cruelty of our enemies; but the error is that we look not to the promises of God, which assure us that all will turn to our good. We are cast down when we see the wicked stronger than we, and planting their foot on our throat; but such confusion should rather, as St. Paul says, cause us to lift lift up our heads. Seeing we are too much disposed to amuse ourselves with present objects, God, in permitting the good to be maltreated, and the wicked to have sway, shows by evident tokens that a day is coming on which all that is now in confusion will be reduced to order. If the period seems distant, let us run to the remedy, and not flatter ourselves in our sin; for it is certain that we have no faith if we cannot carry our views forward to the coming of Jesus Christ.

To leave no means which may be fitted to stimulate us unemployed, God sets before us PROMISES on the one hand, and THREATENINGS on the other. Do we feel that the promises have not sufficient influence, let us strengthen them by adding the threatenings. It is true we must be perverse in the extreme not to put more faith in the promises of God, when the Lord Jesus says that he will own us as his before his Father, provided we confess him before men. (Matt. x. 32; Luke xii. 8.) What should prevent us from making the confession which he requires? Let men do their utmost, they cannot do worse than murder us! and will not the heavenly life compensate for this? I do not here collect all the passages in Scripture which bear on this subject: they are so often reiterated that we ought to be thoroughly satisfied with them. When the struggle comes, if three or four passages do not suffice, a hundred surely ought to make us proof against all contrary temptations!

But if God cannot win us to himself by gentle means, must we not be mere blocks if his threatenings also fail? Jesus Christ summons all those who from fear of temporal death shall have denied the truth, to appear at the bar of God his Father, and says, that then both body and soul will be consigned to perdition. (Matt. x. 28; Luke xii. 5.) And in another passage he says that he will disclaim all those who shall have denied him before men. (Matt. x. 33; Luke xii. 10.) These words, if we are not altogether impervious to feeling, might well make our hair stand on end! Be this as it may, this much is certain; if these things do not move us as they ought, nothing remains for us but a fearful judgment. (Heb. x. 27.) All the words of Christ having proved unavailing, we stand convicted of gross infidelity.

It is in vain for us to allege that pity should be shown us, inasmuch as our nature is so frail; for it is said, on the contrary, that Moses having looked to God by faith was fortified so as not to yield under any temptation. Wherefore, when we are thus soft and easy to bend, it is a manifest sign, I do not say that we have no zeal, no firmness, but that we know nothing either of God or his kingdom. When we are reminded that we ought to be united to our Head, it seems to us a fine pretext for exemption to say, that we are men! But what were those who have trodden the path before us? Indeed, had we nothing more than pure doctrine, all the excuses we could make would be frivolous; but having so many examples which ought to supply us with the strongest proof, the more deserving are we of condemnation.

There are two points to be considered. The first is, that the whole body of the Church in general has always been, and to the end will be, liable to be afflicted by the wicked, as is said in the Psalms (Psalms cxxix. 1), "From my youth up they have tormented me, and dragged the plough over me from one end to the other." The Holy Spirit there brings in the ancient Church, in order that we, after being much acquainted with her afflictions, may not regard it as either new or vexatious, when the like is done to ourselves in the present day. St. Paul, also, in quoting from another Psalm (Rom. viii. 36; Psalm xliv. 22), a passage which says, "We have been led like sheep to the slaughter;" shows that that has not been for one age only, but is the ordinary condition of the Church, and shall be.

Therefore, on seeing how the Church of God is trampled upon in the present day by proud worldlings, how one barks and another bites, how they torture, how they plot against her, how she is assailed incessantly by mad dogs and savage beasts, let it remind us that the same thing was done in all the olden time. It is true God sometimes gives her a truce and time of refreshment, and hence in the Psalm above quoted, it is said, " He cutteth the cords of the wicked;" and in another passage (Psalm cxxv. 3), " He breaks their staff, lest the good should fall away, by being too hardly pressed." But still it has pleased him that his Church should always have to battle so long as she is in this world, her repose being treasured up on high in the heavens. (Heb. iii. 9.)

Meanwhile, the issue of her afflictions has always been fortunate. At all events, God has caused that though she has been pressed by many calamities, she has never been completely crushed; as it is said (Psalm vii. 15), " The wicked with all their efforts have not succeeded in that at which they aimed." St. Paul glories in the fact, and shows that this is the course which God in mercy always takes. He says (1 Cor. iv. 12), " We endure tribulations, but we are not in agony; we are impoverished, but not left destitute; we are persecuted, but not forsaken; cast down, but we perish not; bearing everywhere in our body the mortification of the Lord Jesus, in order that his life may be manifested in our mortal bodies." Such being, as we see, the issue which God has at all times given to the persecutions of his Church, we ought to take courage, knowing that our forefathers, who were frail men like ourselves, always had the victory over their enemies, by remaining firm in endurance.

I only touch on this article briefly to come to the *second*, which is more to our purpose, viz., that WE OUGHT TO TAKE ADVANTAGE OF THE PARTICULAR EXAMPLES OF THE MARTYRS WHO HAVE GONE BEFORE US. These are not confined to two or three, but are, as the Apostle says (Heb. xii. 1), " a great and dense cloud." By this expression he intimates that the number is so great that it ought as it were completely to engross our sight. Not to be tedious, I will only mention the Jews, who were persecuted for the true Religion, as well under the tyranny of King Antiochus as a little after his death. We cannot allege that the number of sufferers was small, for it formed as it were a large army of martyrs. We cannot say that it consisted of prophets whom God had set apart from common people; for women and young children formed part of the band. We cannot say that they got off at a cheap rate, for they were tortured as cruelly as it was possible to be. Accordingly, we hear what the Apostle says (Heb. xi. 35), " Some were stretched out like drums, not caring to be delivered, that they might obtain a better resurrection; others were proved by mockery and blows, or bonds and prisons; others were stoned or sawn asunder; others travelled up and down, wandering among mountains and caves."

Let us now compare their case with ours. If they so endured for the truth which was at that time so obscure, what ought we to do in the clear light which is now shining? God speaks to us with open mouth; the great gate of the kingdom of heaven has been opened, and Jesus Christ calls us to himself, after having come down to us that we might have him as it were present to our eyes. What a reproach would it be to us to have less zeal in suffering for the Gospel, than those had who only hailed the promises afar off — who had only a little wicket opened whereby to come to the kingdom of God, and who had only some memorial and type of Jesus Christ? These things cannot be expressed in word as they deserve, and therefore I leave each to ponder them for himself.

The doctrine now laid down, as it is general, ought to be carried into practice by all Christians, each applying it to his own use according as may be necessary. This I say, in order that those who do not see themselves in apparent danger may not think it superfluous as regards them. They are not at this hour in the hands of tyrants, but how do they know what God means to do with them hereafter? We ought therefore to be so forearmed, that if some persecution which we did not expect arrives, we may not be taken unawares. But I much fear that there are many deaf ears in regard to this subject. So far are those who are sheltered and at their ease from preparing to suffer death when need shall be, that they do not even trouble themselves about serving God in their lives. It nevertheless continues true that this preparation for persecution ought to be our ordinary study, and especially in the times in which we live.

Those, again, whom God calls to suffer for the testimony of his Name, ought to show by deeds that they have been thoroughly trained to patient endurance. Then ought they to recall to mind all the exhortations which were given them in times past, and bestir themselves just as the soldier rushes to arms when the trumpet sounds. But how different is the result! The only question is how to find out subterfuges for escaping. I say this in regard to the greater part; for persecution is a true touchstone by which God ascertains who are his. And few are so faithful as to be prepared to meet death boldly.

It is a kind of monstrous thing, that persons who make a boast of having heard a little of the gospel, can venture to open their lips to give utterance to such quibbling. Some will say, What do we gain by confessing our faith to obstinate people who have deliberately resolved to fight against God? Is not this to cast pearls before swine? As if Jesus Christ had not distinctly declared (Matt. viii. 38), that he wishes to be confessed among the perverse and malignant. If they are not instructed thereby, they will at all events remain confounded; and hence confession is an odor of a sweet smell before God, even though it be deadly to the reprobate. There are some who say, What will our death profit? Will it not rather prove an offence? As if God had left them the choice of dying when they should see it good and find the occasion opportune. On the contrary, we approve our obedience by leaving in his hand the profit which is to accrue from our death.

In the *first* place, then, the Christian man, wherever he may be, must resolve, notwithstanding of dangers or threatenings, to walk in simplicity as God has commanded. Let him guard as much as he can against the ravening of the wolves, but let it not be with carnal craftiness. Above all, let him place his life in the hands of God. Has he done so? Then if he happens to fall into the hands of the enemy, let him think that God, having so arranged, is pleased to have him for one of the witnesses of his Son, and therefore that he has no means of drawing back without breaking faith with him to whom we have promised all duty in life and in death — him whose we are and to whom we belong, even though we should have made no promise.

In saying this I do not lay all under the necessity of making a full and entire Confession of everything which they believe, even should they be required to do so. I am aware also of the measure observed by St. Paul, although no man was ever more determined boldly to maintain the cause of the gospel as he ought. And hence it is not without cause our Lord promises to give us, on such an occasion, " a mouth and wisdom " (Luke xxi. 15); as if he had said, that the office of the Holy Spirit is not only to strengthen us to be bold and valiant, but also to give us prudence and discretion, to guide us in the course which it will be expedient to take.

The substance of the whole is, that those who are in such distress are to ask and obtain such prudence from above, not following their own carnal wisdom, in searching out for a kind of loop-holes by which to escape. There are some who tell us that our Lord himself gave no answer to those who interrogated him. But I rejoin, *First,* That this does not abolish the rule which he has given us to make Confession of our Faith when so required. (1 Peter iii. 15.) *Secondly,* That he never used any disguise to save his life: and, *Thirdly,* That he never gave an answer so ambiguous, as not to embody a sufficient testimony to all that he had to say; and that, moreover, he had already satisfied those who came to interrogate him anew, with the view not of obtaining information, but merely of laying traps to ensnare him.

Let it be held, then, as a fixed point among all Christians, that they ought not to hold their life more precious than the testimony to the truth, inasmuch as God wishes to be glorified thereby. Is it in vain that he gives the name of WITNESSES (for this is the meaning of the word *Martyr*) to all who have to answer before the enemies of the faith? Is it not because he wishes to employ them for such a purpose? Here every one is not to look for his fellow, for God does not honor all alike with the call. And as we are inclined so to look, we must be the more on our guard against it. Peter having heard from the lips of our Lord Jesus (John xxi. 18), that he should be led in his old age where he would not, asked, What was to become of his companion John? There is not one amongst us who would not readily have put the same question; for the thought which instantly rises in our minds, is Why do I suffer rather than others? On the contrary, Jesus Christ exhorts all of us in common, and each of us in particular, to hold ourselves "ready" in order that according as he shall call this one or that one, we may march forth in our turn.

I explained above how little prepared we shall be to suffer martyrdom, if we be not armed with the divine PROMISES. It now remains to show somewhat more fully what the purport and aim of these promises are — not to specify them all in detail, but to show the principal things which God wishes us to hope from him, to console us in our afflictions. Now these things, taken summarily, are three. The *first* is, *that inasmuch as our life and death are in his hand, he will so preserve us by his might that not a hair will be plucked out of our heads without his leave.* Believers, therefore, ought to feel assured into whatever hands they may fall, that God is not divested of the guardianship which he exercises over their persons. Were such a persuasion well imprinted on our hearts, we should be delivered from the greater part of the doubts and perplexities which torment us and obstruct us in our duty.

We see tyrants let loose: thereupon it seems to us that God no longer possesses any means of saving us, and we are tempted to provide for our own affairs as if nothing more were to be expected from him. On the contrary, his Providence, as he unfolds it, ought to be regarded by us as an impregnable fortress. Let us labor, then, to learn the full import of the expression, that our bodies are in the hands of him who created them. For this reason he has sometimes delivered his people in a miraculous manner, and beyond all human expectation, as Shedrach, Meshach, and Abednego, from the fiery furnace, Daniel from the den of lions, Peter from Herod's prison, where he was locked in, chained, and guarded so closely. By these examples he meant to testify that he holds our enemies in check, although it may not seem so, and has power to withdraw us from the midst of death when he pleases: Not that he always does it; but in reserving authority to himself to dispose of us for life and for death, he would have us to feel fully assured that he has us under his charge; so that whatever tyrants attempt, and with whatever fury they may rush against us, it belongs to him alone to order our life.

If he permits tyrants to slay us, it is not because our life is not dear to him, and in greater honor an hundred times than it deserves. Such being the case, having declared by the mouth of David (Psalm cxvi, 13), that the death of the saints is precious in his sight, he says also by the mouth of Isaiah (xxvi, 21), that the earth will discover the blood which seems to be concealed. Let the enemies of the gospel, then, be as prodigal as they will of the blood of Martyrs, they shall have to render a fearful account of it even to its last drop! In the present day, they indulge in proud derision while consigning believers to the flames; and after having bathed in their blood, they are intoxicated by it to such a degree as to count all the murders which they commit mere festive sport. But if we have patience to wait, God will show in the end that it is not in vain he has taxed our life at so high a value. Meanwhile, let it not offend us that it seems to confirm the gospel, which in worth surpasses heaven and earth!

To be better assured that God does not leave us as it were forsaken in the hands of tyrants, let us remember the declarations of Jesus Christ, when he says (Acts ix. 4) that he himself is persecuted in his members. God had indeed said before, by Zechariah (Zech. ii, 8), " He who touches you touches the apple of mine eye:" But here it is said much more expressly, that if we suffer for the gospel, it is as much as if the Son of God were suffering in person. Let us know, therefore, that Jesus Christ must forget himself before he can cease to think of us when we are in prison, or in danger of death for his cause; and let us know that God will take to heart all the outrages which tyrants commit upon us, just as if they were committed on his own Son.

Let us now come to the *second* point which God declares to us in his promise for our consolation. It is, that he *will so sustain us by the energy of his Spirit that our enemies, do what they may, even with Satan at their head, will gain no advantage over us.* And we see how he displays his gifts in such an emergency; for the invincible constancy which appears in the martyrs abundantly and beautifully demonstrates that God works in them mightily. In persecution there are two things grievous to the flesh, the Vituperation and insult of men, and the Tortures which the body suffers. Now, God promises to hold out his hand to us so effectually, that we shall overcome both by patience. What he thus tells us he confirms by fact. Let us take this buckler, then, to ward off all fears by which we are assailed, and let us not confine the working of the Holy Spirit within such narrow limits as to suppose that he will not easily surmount all the cruelties of men.

Of this we have had, among other examples, one which is particularly memorable. A young man who once lived with us here, having been apprehended in the town of Tournay, was condemned to have his head cut off if he recanted, and to be burned alive if he continued steadfast to his purpose! When he was asked, What he meant to do? he replied simply, "He who will give me grace to die patiently for his Name, will surely give me grace to bear the fire!" We ought to take this expression not as that of a mortal man, but as that of the Holy Spirit, to assure us that God is not less powerful to strengthen us, and render us victorious over tortures, than to make us submit willingly to a milder death. Moreover, we oftentimes see what firmness he gives to unhappy malefactors who suffer for their crimes. I speak not of the hardened, but of those who derive consolation from the grace of Jesus Christ, and by this means, with a peaceful heart, undergo the most grievous punishment which can be inflicted. One beautiful instance is seen in the thief who was converted at the death of our Lord. Will God, who thus powerfully assists poor criminals when enduring the punishment of their misdeeds, be so wanting to his own people, while fighting for his cause, as not to give them invincible courage?

The *third* point for consideration in the promises which God gives his Martyrs is, *The fruit which they ought to hope for from their sufferings, and in the end, if need be, from their death.* Now, this fruit is, that after having glorified his Name — after having edified the Church by their constancy — they will be gathered together with the Lord Jesus into his immortal glory.   But as we have above spoken of this at some length, it is enough here to recall it to remembrance.   Let believers, then, learn to lift up their heads towards the crown of glory and immortality to which God invites them, thus they may not feel reluctant to quit the present life for such a recompense; and, to feel well assured of this inestimable blessing, let them have always before their eyes the conformity which they thus have to our Lord Jesus Christ; beholding death in the midst of life, just as he, by the reproach of the cross, attained to THE GLORIOUS RESURRECTION, wherein consists all our felicity, joy, and triumph!

VII

JEREMY TAYLOR

1613–1667

JEREMY TAYLOR, D. D., whom Emerson calls "the Shakespeare of divines," was one of the most gifted, learned, and devout churchmen and theologians of England. At times, scholastic conceits detract from the force and clearness of his thoughts; but his comprehensive glance, incisiveness of argument, wealth of fancy, and strong practical piety, would atone for greater derelictions. He was born in Cambridge, the son of a barber, August 15th, 1613. Entering Caius College as a sizar or servitor, he graduated with honors, and at twenty-three became chaplain in ordinary to Charles I. After the defeat of the royalists, he withdrew into Wales in 1645, and taught school for a livelihood. Here he became chaplain to the Earl of Carberry, to whom he dedicated his "Course of Sermons for all the Sundays in the year," published in 1651. His celebrated "Holy Living," "Holy Dying," and "Life of Christ," appeared about the same time. In 1660 Charles II appointed him Bishop of Down and Connor, in Ireland. He died August 13th, 1667. From the second and revised edition of his Sermons, the following is selected. It is the second of a series of three, the first of which treats of the universality of the Judgment, and the third of the sentence of condemnation or justification awaiting each mortal. His frequent Greek and Latin quotations are omitted.

CHRIST'S ADVENT TO JUDGMENT.

"For we must all appear before the judgment-seat of Christ, that every one may receive the things done in his body, according to that he hath done, whether it be good or bad."— 2 Cor. v. 10.

1. If we consider the person of the Judge, we first perceive that he is interested in the injury of the crimes he is to sentence: " They shall look on him whom they have pierced." It was for thy sins that the Judge did suffer such unspeakable pains as were enough to reconcile all the world to God; the sum and spirit of which pains could not be better understood than by the consequence of his own words, " My God, my God, why hast thou forsaken me?" meaning, that he felt such horrible, pure, unmingled sorrows, that, although his human nature was personally united to the Godhead, yet at that instant he felt no comfortable emanations by sensible perception from the Divinity, but he was so drenched in sorrow that the Godhead seemed to have forsaken him. Beyond this, nothing can be added: but then, that thou hast for thy own particular made all this in vain and ineffective, that Christ thy Lord and Judge should be tormented for nothing, that thou wouldst not accept felicity and pardon when he purchased them at so dear a price, must needs be an infinite condemnation to such persons. How shalt thou look upon him that fainted and died for love of thee, and thou didst scorn his miraculous mercies? How shall we dare to behold that holy face that brought salvation to us, and we turned away and fell in love with death, and kissed deformity and sins? and yet in the beholding that face consists much of the glories of eternity. All the pains and passions, the sorrows and the groans, the humility and poverty, the labors and the watchings, the prayers and the sermons, the miracles and the prophecies, the whip and the nails, the death and the burial, the shame and the smart, the cross and the grave of Jesus, shall be laid upon thy score, if thou hast refused the mercies and design of all their holy ends and purposes. And if we remember what a calamity that was which broke the Jewish nation in pieces, when Christ came to judge them for their murdering him who was their King and the Prince of life, and consider that this was but a dark image of the terrors of the day of judgment, we may then apprehend that there is some strange unspeakable evil that attends them that are guilty of this death, and of so much evil to their Lord. Now it is certain if thou wilt not be saved by his death, you are guilty of his death; if thou wilt not suffer him to have thee, thou art guilty of destroying him; and then let it be considered what is to be expected from that Judge before whom you stand as his murderer and betrayer. But this is but half of this consideration.

2. Christ may be crucified again, and upon a new account put to an open shame. For after that Christ had done all this by the direct ac-

tions of his priestly office, of sacrificing himself for us, he hath also done very many things for us which are also the fruits of his first love and prosecutions of our redemption. I will not instance in the strange arts of mercy that our Lord uses to bring us to live holy lives; but I consider, that things are so ordered, and so great a value set upon our souls since they are the images of God, and redeemed by the blood of the Holy Lamb, that the salvation of our souls is reckoned as a part of Christ's reward, a part of the glorification of his humanity. Every sinner that repents causes joy to Christ, and the joy is so great that it runs over and wets the fair brows and beauteous locks of cherubim and seraphim, and all the angels have a part of that banquet; then it is that our blessed Lord feels the fruits of his holy death, the acceptation of his holy sacrifice, the graciousness of his person, the return of his prayers. For all that Christ did or suffered, and all that he now does as a priest in heaven, is to glorify his Father by bringing souls to God. For this it was that he was born and died, that he descended from heaven to earth, from life to death, from the cross to the grave; this was the purpose of his resurrection and ascension, of the end and design of all the miracles and graces of God manifested to all the world by him; and now what man is so vile, such a malicious fool, that will refuse to bring joy to his Lord by doing himself the greatest good in the world? They who refuse to do this, are said to crucify the Lord of Life again, and put him to an open shame — that is, they, as much as in them lies, bring Christ from his glorious joys to the labors of his life and the shame of his death; they advance his enemies, and refuse to advance the kingdom of their Lord; they put themselves in that state in which they were when Christ came to die for them; and now that he is in a state that he may rejoice over them (for he hath done all his share towards it), every wicked man takes his head from the blessing, and rather chooses that the devil should rejoice in his destruction, than that his Lord should triumph in his felicity. And now upon the supposition of these premises, we may imagine that it will be an infinite amazement to meet that Lord to be our Judge whose person we have murdered, whose honor we have disparaged, whose purposes we have destroyed, whose joys we have lessened, whose passion we have made ineffectual, and whose love we have trampled under our profane and impious feet.

3. But there is yet a third part of this consideration. As it will be inquired at the day of judgment concerning the dishonors to the person of Christ, so also concerning the profession and institution of Christ, and

concerning his poor members; for by these also we make sad reflections upon our Lord. Every man that lives wickedly disgraces the religion and institution of Jesus, he discourages strangers from entering into it, he weakens the hands of them that are in already, and makes that the adversaries speak reproachfully of the name of Christ; but although it is certain our Lord and Judge will deeply resent all these things, yet there is one thing which he takes more tenderly, and that is, the uncharitableness of men towards his poor. It shall then be upbraided to them by the Judge, that himself was hungry and they refused to give meat to him that gave them his body and heart-blood to feed them and quench their thirst; that they denied a robe to cover his nakedness, and yet he would have clothed their souls with the robe of his righteousness, lest their souls should be found naked on the day of the Lord's visitation; and all this unkindness is nothing but that evil men were uncharitable to their brethren, they would not feed the hungry, nor give drink to the thirsty, nor clothe the naked, nor relieve their brothers' needs, nor forgive their follies, nor cover their shame, nor turn their eyes from delighting in their affronts and evil accidents; this is it which our Lord will take so tenderly, that his brethren for whom he died, who sucked the paps of his mother, that fed on his body and are nourished with his blood, whom he hath lodged in his heart and entertains in his bosom, the partners of his spirit and co-heirs of his inheritance, that these should be denied relief and suffered to go away ashamed, and unpitied; this our Blessed Lord will take so ill, that all those who are guilty of this unkindness, have no reason to expect the favor of the Court.

4. To this if we add the almightiness of the Judge, his infinite wisdom and knowledge of all causes, and all persons, and all circumstances, that he is infinitely just, inflexibly angry, and impartial in his sentence, there can be nothing added either to the greatness or the requisites of a terrible and an Almighty Judge. For who can resist him who is almighty? Who can evade his scrutiny that knows all things? Who can hope for pity of him that is inflexible? Who can think to be exempted when the Judge is righteous and impartial? But in all these annexes of the Great Judge, that which I shall now remark, is that indeed which hath terror in it, and that is, the severity of our Lord. For then is the day of vengeance and recompenses, and no mercy at all shall be showed, but to them that are the sons of mercy; for the other, their portion is such as can be expected from these premises.

1. If we remember the instances of God's severity in this life, in

the days of mercy and repentance, in those days when judgment waits upon mercy, and receives laws by the rules and measures of pardon, and that for all the rare streams of loving-kindness issuing out of paradise and refreshing all our fields with a moisture more fruitful than the floods of Nilus, still there are mingled some storms and violences, some fearful instances of the divine justice, we may more readily expect it will be worse, infinitely worse, at that day, when Judgment shall ride in triumph, and Mercy shall be the accuser of the wicked. But so we read, and are commanded to remember, because they are written for our example, that God destroyed at once five cities of the plain, and all the country, and Sodom and her sisters are set forth for an example, suffering the vengeance of eternal fire. Fearful it was when God destroyed at once twenty-three thousand for fornication, and an exterminating angel in one night killed one hundred and eight-five thousand of the Assyrians, and the first-born of all the families of Egypt, and for the sin of David in numbering the people, three-score and ten thousand of the people died, and God sent ten tribes into captivity and eternal oblivion and indistinction from a common people for their idolatry. Did not God strike Korah and his company with fire from heaven? and the earth opened and swallowed up the congregation of Abiram? And is not evil come upon all the world for one sin of Adam? Did not the anger of God break the nation of the Jews all in pieces with judgments so great, that no nation ever suffered the like, because none ever sinned so? And at once it was done, that God in anger destroyed all the world, and eight persons only escaped the angry baptism of water, and yet this world is the time of mercy; God hath opened here his magazines, and sent his Holy Son as the great channel and fountain of it, too: here he delights in mercy, and in judgment loves to remember it, and it triumphs over all his works, and God contrives instruments and accidents, chances and designs, occasions and opportunities for mercy. If, therefore, now the anger of God makes such terrible eruptions upon the wicked people that delight in sin, how great may we suppose that anger to be, how severe that judgment, how terrible that vengeance, how intolerable those inflictions which God reserves for the full effusion of indignation on the great day of vengeance!

2. We may also guess at it by this: if God upon all single instances, and in the midst of our sins, before they are come to the full, and sometimes in the beginning of an evil habit, be so fierce in his anger, what can we imagine it to be in that day when the wicked are to drink the

dregs of that horrid potion, and count over all the particulars of their whole treasure of wrath? "This is the day of wrath, and God shall reveal, or bring forth, his righteous judgments." The expression is taken from Deut. xxxii. 34: "Is not this laid up in store with me, and sealed up among my treasures? I will restore it in the day of vengeance, for the Lord shall judge his people, and repent himself for his servants." For so did the Lybian lion that was brought up under discipline, and taught to endure blows, and eat the meat of order and regular provision, and to suffer gentle usages and the familiarities of societies; but once he brake out into his own wildness, and killed two Roman boys; but those that forage in the Lybian mountains tread down and devour all that they meet or master; and when they have fasted two days, lay up an anger great as is their appetite, and bring certain death to all that can be overcome. God is pleased to compare himself to a lion; and though in this life he hath confined himself with promises and gracious emanations of an infinite goodness, and limits himself by conditions and covenants, and suffers himself to be overcome by prayers, and himself hath invented ways of atonement and expiation; yet when he is provoked by our unhandsome and unworthy actions, he makes sudden breaches, and tears some of us in pieces, and of others he breaks their bones or affrights their hopes and secular gayeties, and fills their house with mourning and cypress, and groans and death. But when this Lion of the tribe of Judah shall appear upon his own mountain, the mountain of the Lord, in his natural dress of majesty, and that Justice shall have her chain and golden fetters taken off, then Justice shall strike, and Mercy shall not hold her hands; she shall strike sore strokes, and Pity shall not break the blow; and God shall account with us by minutes, and for words, and for thoughts, and then he shall be severe to mark what is done amiss; and that Justice may reign entirely, God shall open the wicked man's treasure, and tell the sums, and weigh grains and scruples. Said Philo upon the place of Deuteronomy before quoted: As there are treasures of good things, and God has crowns and sceptres in store for his saints and servants, and coronets for martyrs, and rosaries for virgins, and phials full of prayers, and bottles full of tears, and a register of sighs and penitential groans, so God hath a treasure of wrath and fury, of scourges and scorpions, and then shall be produced the shame of lust, and the malice of envy, and the groans of the oppressed, and the persecutions of the saints, and the cares of covetousness, and the troubles of ambition, and the insolencies of traitors, and the violences

7

of rebels, and the rage of anger, and the uneasiness of impatience, and the restlessness of unlawful desires; and by this time the monsters and diseases will be numerous and intolerable, when God's heavy hand shall press the *sanies* and the intolerableness, the obliquity and the unreasonableness, the amazement and the disorder, the smart and the sorrow, the guilt and the punishment, out from all our sins, and pour them into one chalice, and mingle them with an infinite wrath, and make the wicked drink off all the vengeance, and force it down their unwilling throats with the violence of devils and accursed spirits.

3. We may guess at the severity of the Judge by the lesser strokes of that judgment which he is pleased to send upon sinners in this world, to make them afraid of the horrible pains of doomsday — I mean the torments of an unquiet conscience, the amazement and confusions of some sins and some persons. For I have sometimes seen persons surprised in a base action, and taken in the circumstances of crafty theft and secret injustices, before their excuse was ready. They have changed their color, their speech hath faltered, their tongue stammered, their eyes did wander and fix nowhere, till shame made them sink into their hollow eye-pits to retreat from the images and circumstances of discovery; their wits are lost, their reason useless, the whole order of their soul is discomposed, and they neither see, nor feel, nor think, as they used to do, but they are broken into disorder by a stroke of damnation and a lesser stripe of hell; but then if you come to observe a guilty and a base murderer, a condemned traitor, and see him harassed first by an evil conscience, and then pulled in pieces by the hangman's hooks, or broken upon sorrows and the wheel, we may then guess (as well as we can in this life) what the pains of that day shall be to accursed souls. But those we shall consider afterwards in their proper scene; now only we are to estimate the severity of our Judge by the intolerableness of an evil conscience; if guilt will make a man despair — and despair will make a man mad, confounded, and dissolved in all the regions of his senses and more noble faculties, that he shall neither feel, nor hear, nor see, anything but spectres and illusions, devils and frightful dreams, and hear noises, and shriek fearfully, and look pale and distracted, like a hopeless man from the horrors and confusions of a lost battle, upon which all his hopes did stand — then the wicked must at the day of judgment expect strange things and fearful, and such which now no language can express, and then no patience can endure. Then only it can truly be said that he is inflexible and inexorable. No prayers then can move him, no groans

can cause him to pity thee; therefore pity thyself in time, that when the Judge comes thou mayest be one of the sons of everlasting mercy, to whom pity belongs as part of thine inheritance, for all else shall without any remorse (except his own) be condemned by the horrible sentence!

4. That all may think themselves concerned in this consideration, let us remember that even the righteous and most innocent shall pass through a severe trial. Many of the ancients explicated this severity by the fire of conflagration, which say they shall purify those souls at the day of judgment, which in this life have built upon the foundation (hay and stubble) works of folly and false opinions, and states of imperfection. So St. Augustine's doctrine was: " The great fire at doomsday shall throw some into the portion of the left hand, and others shall be purified and represented on the right." And the same is affirmed by Origen and Lactantius; and St. Hilary thus expostulates: " Since we are to give account for every idle word, shall we long for the day of judgment, wherein we must, every one of us, pass that unwearied fire in which those grievous punishments for expiating the soul from sins must be endured; for to such as have been baptized with the Holy Ghost it remaineth that they be consummated with the fire of judgment." And St. Ambrose adds: " That if any be as Peter or as John, they are baptized with this fire, and he that is purged here had need to be purged there again. Let him also purify us, that every one of us being burned with that flaming sword, not burned up or consumed, we may enter into Paradise, and give thanks unto the Lord who hath brought us into a place of refreshment." This opinion of theirs is, in the main of it, very uncertain; relying upon the sense of some obscure place of Scripture, is only apt to represent the great severity of the Judge at that day, and it hath in it this only certainty, that even the most innocent person hath great need of mercy, and he that hath the greatest cause of confidence, although he runs to no rocks to hide him, yet he runs to the protection of the cross, and hides himself under the shadow of the divine mercies: and he that shall receive the absolution of the blessed sentence, shall also suffer the terrors of the day, and the fearful circumstances of Christ's coming. The effect of this consideration is this: That if the righteous scarcely be saved, where shall the wicked and the sinner appear? And if St. Paul, whose conscience accused him not, yet durst not be too confident, because he was not hereby justified, but might be found faulty by the severer judgment of his Lord, how shall we appear, with all our crimes and evil habits round about us? If

there be need of much mercy to the servants and friends of the Judge, then his enemies shall not be able to stand upright in judgment.

5. But the matter is still of more concernment. The Pharisees believed that they were innocent if they abstained from criminal actions, such as were punishable by the Judge; and many Christians think all is well with them if they abstain from such sins as have a name in the tables of their laws; but because some sins are secret and not discernible by man, others are public, but not punished, because they are frequent and perpetual, and without external mischiefs in some instances, and only provocations against God, men think that in their concernment they have no place; and such are jeering, and many instances of wantonness, and revelling, doing petty spites, and doggedness, and churlishness, lying and pride; and beyond this, some are very like virtues; as too much gentleness and slackness in government, or too great severity and rigor of animadversions, bitterness in reproof of sinners, uncivil circumstances, imprudent handlings of some criminals, and zeal. Nay, there are some vile things, which, through the evil discoursings and worse manners of men, are passed into an artificial and false reputation, and men are accounted wits for talking atheistically, and valiant for being murderers, and wise for deceiving and circumventing our brothers; and many irregularities more, for all which we are safe enough here. But when the day of judgment comes, these shall be called to a severe account, for the Judge is omniscient and knows all things, and his tribunal takes cognizance of all causes, and hath a coercitive for all. "All things are naked and open to his eyes," saith St. Paul, therefore nothing shall escape for being secret. And all prejudices being laid aside, it shall be considered concerning our evil rules and false principles: "When I shall receive the people, I shall judge according unto right," (so we read); "When we shall receive time, I will judge justices and judgments," so the vulgar Latin reads it — that is, in the day of the Lord, when time is put into his hand and time shall be no more, he shall judge concerning those judgments which men here make of things below; and the fighting man shall perceive the noises of drunkards, and fools that cried him up for daring to kill his brother, to have been evil principles; and then it will be declared, by strange effects, that wealth is not the greatest fortune, and ambition was not but an ill counsellor, and to lie for a good cause was no piety, and to do evil for the glory of God was but an ill worshipping him, and that good-nature was not well employed when it spent itself in vicious company and evil compliances, and that piety was not softness and want of courage, and that

poverty ought not to have been contemptible, and that cause that is unsuccessful is not therefore evil, and what is folly here shall be wisdom there. Then shall men curse their evil guides and their accursed superinduced necessities and the evil guises of the world, and then when silence shall be found innocence, and eloquence in many instances condemned as criminal, when the poor shall reign and generals and tyrants shall lie low in horrible regions, when he that lost all shall find a treasure, and he that spoiled him shall be found naked and spoiled by the destroyer,— then we shall find it true that we ought here to have done what our Judge, our Blessed Lord, shall do there, that is, take our measures of good and evil by the severities of the word of God, by the sermons of Christ, and the four Gospels, and by the Epistles of St. Paul, by justice and charity, by the laws of God and the laws of wise princes and republics, by the rules of nature and the just proportions of reason, by the examples of good men and the proverbs of wise men, by severity and the rules of discipline; for then it shall be that truth shall ride in triumph, and the holiness of Christ's sermons shall be manifest to all the world, that the word of God shall be advanced over all the discources of men, and Wisdom shall be justified by all her children. Then shall be heard those words of an evil and tardy repentance and the just rewards of folly: "We fools thought their life madness; but behold they are justified before the throne of God, and we are miserable for ever." Here men think it strange if others will not run into the same excess of riot; but there they will wonder how themselves should be so mad and infinitely unsafe by being strangely and inexcusably unreasonable. The sum is this: The Judge shall appear clothed with wisdom, and power, and justice, and knowledge, and an impartial Spirit, making no separations by the proportions of this world, but by the measures of God, not giving sentence by the principles of our folly and evil customs, but by the severity of his own laws and measures of the Spirit. "God does not judge as man judges."

6. Now that the Judge is come thus arrayed, thus prepared, so instructed, let us next consider the circumstances of our appearing and his sentence; and first I consider that men at the day of judgment that belong not to the portion of life, shall have three sorts of accusers: 1. Christ himself, who is their judge; 2. Their own conscience, whom they have injured and blotted with characters of death and foul dishonor; 3. The devil, their enemy, whom they served.

1. Christ shall be their accuser, not only upon the stock of those direct injuries (which I before reckoned) of crucifying the Lord of life,

once and again, etc., but upon the titles of contempt and unworthiness, of unkindness and ingratitude; and the accusation will be nothing else but a plain representation of those artifices and assistances, those bonds and invitations, those constrainings and importunities, which our dear Lord used to us to make it almost impossible to lie in sin, and necessary to be saved. For it will, it must needs be, a fearful exprobration of our unworthiness, when the Judge himself shall bear witness against us that the wisdom of God himself was strangely employed in bringing us safely to felicity. I shall draw a short scheme, which, although it must needs be infinitely short of what God hath done for us, yet it will be enough to shame us. God did not only give his Son for an example, and the Son gave himself for a price for us, but both gave the Holy Spirit to assist us in mighty graces, for the verifications of faith, and the entertainments of hope, and the increase and perseverance of charity. God gave to us a new nature, he put another principle into us, a third part of a perfective constitution; we have the Spirit put into us, to be a part of us, as properly to produce actions of a holy life, as the soul of man in the body does produce the natural. God hath exalted human nature, and made it in the person of Jesus Christ, to sit above the highest seat of angels, and the angels are made ministering spirits, ever since their Lord became our brother. Christ hath by a miraculous sacrament given us his body to eat and his blood to drink, he made ways that we may become all one with him. He hath given us an easy religion, and hath established our future felicity upon natural and pleasant conditions, and we are to be happy hereafter if we suffer God to make us happy here; and things are so ordered that a man must take more pains to perish than to be happy. God hath found out rare ways to make our prayers acceptable, our weak petitions, the desires of our imperfect souls, to prevail mightily with God, and to lay a holy violence and an undeniable necessity upon himself; and God will deny us nothing but when we ask of him to do us ill offices, to give us poisons and dangers, and evil nourishment, and temptations; and he that hath given such mighty power to the prayers of his servants, yet will not be moved by those potent and mighty prayers to do any good man an evil turn, or to grant him one mischief — in that only God can deny us. But in all things else God hath made all the excellent things in heaven and earth to join towards the holy and fortunate effects; for he that appointed an angel to present the prayers of saints, and Christ makes intercession for us, and the Holy Spirit makes intercession for us with groans unutterable, and all the holy men in the world pray for all and for every one, and God hath instructed us with scriptures, and precedents, and collateral and direct assistances to pray, and he encouraged us with divers excellent promises, and parables, and examples, and teaches us what to pray, and how, and gives one promise to public prayer, and another to private prayer, and to both the blessing of being heard.

Add to this account that God did heap blessings upon us without order, infinitely, perpetually, and in all instances, when we needed and when we needed not. He heard us when we prayed, giving us all, and giving us more, than we desired. He desired that we should ask, and yet he hath also prevented our desires. He watched for us, and at his own charge sent a whole order of men whose employment is to minister to our souls; and if all this had not been enough, he had given us more also. He promised heaven to our obedience, a province for a dish of water, a kingdom for a prayer, satisfaction for desiring it, grace for receiving, and more grace for accepting and using the first. He invited us with gracious words and perfect entertainments; he threatened horrible things to us if we would not be happy; he hath made strange necessities for us, making our very repentance to be a conjugation of holy actions, and holy times, and a long succession; he hath taken away all excuses from us; he hath called us off from temptation; he bears our charges; he is always beforehand with us in every act of favor, and perpetually slow in striking, and his arrows are unfeathered; and he is so long, first, in drawing his sword, and another long while in whetting it, and yet longer in lifting his hand to strike, that before the blow comes the man hath repented long, unless he be a fool and impudent; and then God is so glad of an excuse to lay his anger aside, that certainly, if after all this, we refuse life and glory, there is no more to be said; this plain story will condemn us: but the story is very much longer; and, as our conscience will represent all our sins to us, so the Judge will represent all his Father's kindnesses, as Nathan did to David, when he was to make the justice of the divine sentence appear against him. Then it shall be remembered that the joys of every day's piety would have been a greater pleasure very night than the remembrance of every night's sin could have been in the morning; that every night the trouble and labor of the day's virtue would have been as much passed and turned to as very a nothing as the pleasure of that day's sin, but that they would be infinitely distinguished by the remanent effects. So Musonius expressed the sense of this inducement; and that this argument would have grown so great by that time we come to die that the certain pleasures, and rare confidences, and holy hopes of a death-bed would be a strange felicity to the man when he remembers he did obey, if they were compared to the fearful expectations of a dying sinner, who feels by a formidable and affrighting remembrance that of his sins nothing remains but the gains of a miserable eternity. The offering ourselves to God every morning, and the thanksgiving to God every night, hope and fear, shame and desire, the honor of leaving a fair name behind us, and the shame of dying like a fool,—everything indeed in the world is made to be an argument and an inducement to us to invite us to come to God and be saved; and therefore when this, and infinitely more shall by the Judge be exhibited in sad remembrances, there needs no other sentence; we shall condemn ourselves with a hasty shame, and a fearful confusion, to see how good God hath been to us, and how base we have been to ourselves. Thus Moses is said to accuse the Jews; and thus also he that does accuse, is said to condemn, as Verres was by Cicero, and Claudia by Domitius her accuser, and the world of impenitent persons by the men of Nineveh, and all by Christ, their Judge. I represent the horror of this circumstance to consist in this, besides the reasonableness of the judgment, and the certainty of the condemnation, it cannot but be an argument of an intolerable despair to perishing souls, when he that was our Advocate all our life, shall, in the day of that appearing, be our Accuser and our Judge, a party against us, an injured person in the day of his power and of his wrath, doing execution upon all his own foolish and malicious enemies.

2. Our conscience shall be our accuser. But this signifies but these two things: First. That we shall be condemned for the evils that we have done and shall then remember, God by his power wiping away the dust from the tables of our memory, and taking off the consideration and the voluntary neglect and rude shufflings of our cases of conscience. For then we shall see things as they are, the evil circumstances and the crooked intentions, the adherent unhandsomeness and the direct crimes; for all things are laid up safely, and though we draw a curtain of cobweb over them, and few fig-leaves before our shame, yet God shall draw away the curtain, and forgetfulness shall be no more, because, with a taper in the hand of God, all the corners of our nastiness shall be discovered. And, secondly, it signifies this also, that not only the justice of God shall be confessed by us in our own shame and condemnation, but the evil of the sentence shall be received into us, to melt our bowels and to break our heart in pieces within us, because we are the authors of our own death, and our own inhuman hands have torn our souls in pieces. Thus

far the horrors are great, and when evil men consider it, it is certain they must be afraid to die. Even they that have lived well, have some sad considerations, and the tremblings of humility, and suspicion of themselves. I remember St. Cyprian tells of a good man who in his agony of death saw a phantasm of a noble and angelical shape, who, frowning and angry, said to him: "Ye cannot endure sickness, ye are troubled at the evils of the world, and yet you are loth to die and to be quit of them; what shall I do to you?" Although this is apt to represent every man's condition more or less, yet, concerning persons of wicked lives, it hath in it too many sad degrees of truth; they are impatient of sorrow, and justly fearful of death, because they know not how to comfort themselves in the evil accidents of their lives; and their conscience is too polluted to take death for sanctuary, and to hope to have amends made to their condition by the sentence of the day of judgment. Evil and sad is their condition who cannot be contented here nor blessed hereafter, whose life is their misery and their conscience is their enemy, whose grave is their prison and death their undoing, and the sentence of doomsday the beginning of an intolerable condition!

3. The third sort of accusers are the devils, and they will do it with malicious and evil purposes. The prince of the devils hath Diabolus for one of his chiefest appellatives. The accuser of the brethren he is by his professed malice and employment; and therefore God, who delights that his mercy should triumph and his goodness prevail over all the malice of men and devils, hath appointed one whose office is to reprove the accuser and to resist the enemy, and to be a defender of their cause who belong to God. The Holy Spirit is a defender; the evil spirit is the accuser; and they that in this life belong to one or the other, shall in the same proportion be treated at the day of judgment. The devil shall accuse the brethren, that is, the saints and servants of God, and shall tell concerning their follies and infirmities, the sins of their youth and weakness of their age, the imperfect grace and the long schedule of omissions of duty, their scruples and their fears, their diffidences and pusillanimity, and all those things which themselves by strict examination find themselves guilty of and have confessed, all their shame and the matter of their sorrows, their evil intentions and their little plots, their carnal confidences and too fond adherences to the things of this world, their indulgence and easiness of government, their wilder joys and freer meals, their loss of time and their too forward and apt compliances, their trifling arrests and little peevishnesses, the mixtures of the world with the things of the Spirit,

and all the incidences of humanity he will bring forth and aggravate them by circumstance of ingratitude, and the breach of promise, and the evacuating all their holy purposes, and breaking their resolutions, and rifling their vows, and all these things, being drawn into an entire representment, and the bills clogged by numbers, will make the best man in the world seem foul and unhandsome, and stained with the characters of death and evil dishonor. But for these there is appointed a defender. The Holy Spirit that maketh intercession for us shall then also interpose, and against all these things shall oppose the passion of our Blessed Lord, and upon all their defects shall cast the *robe of his righteousness;* and the sins of their youth shall not prevail so much as the repentance of their age, and their omissions be excused by probable intervening causes, and their little escapes shall appear single and in disunion, because they were always kept asunder by penitential prayers and sighings, and their seldom returns of sin by their daily watchfulness, and their often infirmities by the sincerity of their souls, and their scruples by their zeal, and their passions by their love, and all by the mercies of God and the sacrifice which their Judge offered and the Holy Spirit made effective by daily graces and assistances. These, therefore, infallibly go to the portion of the right hand, because the Lord our God shall answer for them. But as for the wicked, it is not so with them; for although the plain story of their life be to them a sad condemnation, yet what will be answered when it shall be told concerning them, that they despised God's mercies, and feared not his angry judgments; that they regarded not his word, and loved not his excellencies; that they were not persuaded by the promises, nor affrighted by his threatenings; that they neither would accept his government nor his blessings; that all the sad stories that ever happened in both the worlds (in all which himself did escape till the day of his death, and was not concerned in them save only that he was called upon by every one of them, which he ever heard or saw or was told of, to repentance), that all these were sent to him in vain? But cannot the accuser truly say to the Judge concerning such persons, " They were thine by creation, but mine by their own choice; thou didst redeem them indeed, but they sold themselves to me for a trifle, or for an unsatisfying interest; thou diedst for them, but they obeyed my commandments; I gave them nothing, I promised them nothing but the filthy pleasures of a night, or the joys of madness, or the delights of a disease; I never hanged upon the cross three long hours for them, nor endured the labors of a poor life thirty-three years together for their interest; only when

they were thine by the merit of thy death, they quickly became mine by
the demerit of their ingratitude; and when thou hadst clothed their soul
with thy robe, and adorned them by thy graces, we stripped them naked
as their shame, and only put on a robe of darkness, and they thought
themselves secure and went dancing to their grave like a drunkard to a
fight, or a fly unto a candle; and therefore they that did partake with
us in our faults must divide with us in our portion and fearful interest."
This is a sad story because it ends in death, and there is nothing to abate
or lessen the calamity. It concerns us therefore to consider in time that
he that tempts us will accuse us, and what he calls pleasant now he shall
then say was nothing, and all the gains that now invite earthly souls and
mean persons to vanity, was nothing but the seeds of folly, and the
harvest is pain and sorrow and shame eternal. But then, since this horror
proceeds upon the account of so many accusers, God hath put it into our
power by a timely accusation of ourselves in the tribunal of the court
Christian, to prevent all the arts of aggravation which at doomsday shall
load foolish and undiscerning souls. He that accuses himself of his
crimes here, means to forsake them, and looks upon them on all sides,
and spies out his deformity, and is taught to hate them, he is instructed
and prayed for, he prevents the anger of God and defeats the devil's
malice, and, by making shame the instrument of repentance, he takes
away the sting, and makes that to be his medicine which otherwise would
be his death: and, concerning this exercise, I shall only add what the
patriarch of Alexandria told an old religious person in his hermitage.
Having asked him what he found in that desert, he was answered, " Only
this, to judge and condemn myself perpetually; that is the employment of
my solitude." The patriarch answered, " There is no other way." By
accusing ourselves we shall make the devil's malice useless, and our own
consciences dear, and be reconciled to the Judge by the severities of an
early repentance, and then we need to fear no accusers.

VIII

RICHARD BAXTER

1615–1691

RICHARD BAXTER was among the greatest of the divines of the seventeenth century. He belonged to the large and eminent class known as "Nonconformists," because they refused to submit to the bigoted rule of the Church of England. He is said to have "preached more sermons, engaged in more controversies, and written more books" than any other man of his party and age. Dr. Isaac Barrow said of him that "his practical writings were never mended, and his controversial seldom confuted." The number of books written by him was more than 160; through a stirring and active life, although in a physical condition always delicate and often feeble. He was born in 1615, at Rowton, in Shropshire, England; was parish clergyman at Kidderminster from 1640 most of the time until 1662, when the Act of Uniformity, to which he could not conscientiously submit, compelled him to leave his church. He was never a radical, but in politics was equally opposed to the autocratic rule of Charles I and later of Oliver Cromwell; and in theology he endeavored to reconcile the views of Calvin with those of Arminius, Calvin's great antagonist. He suffered persecution for his opinions, was more than once driven away from his parish at Kidderminster, was sent to prison by the infamous Judge Jeffreys in 1685, and was kept in jail for eighteen months. But his last years were peaceful, prosperous and honored. He died in London, in 1691. Among his many writings, the most widely circulated were "The Saints' Everlasting Rest" and "A call to the Unconverted," books which have been translated into many languages and read even in our own time.

RICHARD BAXTER.
1615-1691.
One of the greatest "Nonconformists." Baxter
opposed both Cromwell and the Cavaliers, and
consequently suffered many persecutions. He
wrote more than 160 volumes of sermons and controversial letters.

JEREMY TAYLOR.
1613-1667.
The famous author of "Holy Living" and "Holy
Dying" was one of the most pious scholars of
English history. He was the son of a barber,
became chaplain to King Charles I, and rose high
in the favor of Charles II.

MAKING LIGHT OF CHRIST AND SALVATION.

"But they made light of it."— Matt. xxii. 5.

SEEING this is the great condemning sin, before we inquire after it into the hearts of our hearers, it beseems us to begin at home, and see that we, who are preachers of the Gospel, be not guilty of it ourselves. The Lord forbid that they that have undertaken the sacred office of revealing the excellences of Christ to the world, should make light of Him themselves, and slight that salvation which they do daily preach. The Lord knows we are all of us so low in our estimation of Christ, and do this great work so negligently, that we have cause to be ashamed of our best sermons; but should this sin prevail in us, we were the most miserable of all men. Brethren, I love not censoriousness; yet dare not befriend so vile a sin in myself or others, under pretense of avoiding it; especially when there is so great necessity that it should be healed first in them that make it their work to heal it in others. Oh that there were no cause to complain that Christ and salvation are made light of by the preachers of it! But, do not the negligent studies of some speak it out? Doth not their dead and drowsy preaching declare it? Do not they make light of the doctrine they preach, that do it as if they were half asleep, and feel not what they speak themselves? Doth not the carelessness of some men's private endeavors discover it? What do they for souls? How slightly do they reprove sin! How little do they when they are out of the pulpit for the saving of men's souls! Doth not the continued neglect of those things wherein the interest of Christ consisteth discover it? 1. The Church's purity and reformation. 2. Its unity. Do not the covetous and worldly lives of too many discover it, losing advantages for men's souls for a little gain to themselves? And most of this is because men are preachers before they are Christians, and tell men of that which they never felt themselves. Of all men on earth there are few that are in so sad a condition as such ministers: and if, indeed, they do believe that Scripture which they preach, methinks it should be terrible to them in their studying and preaching it.

Beloved hearers; the office that God hath called us to, is by declaring the glory of His grace, to help under Christ to the saving of men's souls. I hope you think not that I come hither to-day on any other errand. The Lord knows I had not set a foot out of doors but in hope to succeed in this work for your souls. I have considered, and often considered, what is the matter that so many thousands should perish when God hath done so much for their salvation; and I find this that is mentioned in my text is the cause. It is one of the wonders of the world, that when God hath so loved the world as to send His Son, and Christ hath made a satisfaction by His death sufficient for them all, and offereth the benefits of it so freely to them, even without money or price, that yet the most of the world should perish; yea, the most of those that are thus called by His word! Why, here is the reason, when Christ hath done all this, men make light of it. God hath showed that He is not unwilling; and Christ hath showed that He is not unwilling that men should be restored to God's favor and be saved; but men are actually unwilling themselves. God takes not pleasure in the death of sinners, but rather that they return and live. But men take such pleasure in sin that they will die before they will return. The Lord Jesus was content to be their Physician, and hath provided them a sufficient plaster of His own blood: but if men make light of it, and will not apply it, what wonder if they perish after all? This Scripture giveth us the reason of their perdition. This, sad experience tells us, the most of the world is guilty of. It is a most lamentable thing to see how most men do spend their care, their time, their pains, for known vanities, while God and glory are cast aside; that He who is all should seem to them as nothing, and that which is nothing should seem to them as good as all; that God should set mankind in such a race where heaven or hell is their certain end, and that they should sit down, and loiter, or run after the childish toys of the world, and so much forget the prize that they should run for. Were it but possible for one of us to see the whole of this business as the all-seeing God doth; to see at one view both heaven and hell, which men are so near; and see what most men in the world are minding, and what they are doing every day, it would be the saddest sight that could be imagined. Oh how should we marvel at their madness, and lament their self-delusion! Oh poor distracted world! what is it you run after? and what is it that you neglect? If God had never told them what they were sent into the world to do, or whither they were going, or what was before them in another world, then they had been excusable; but He hath told them over and over, till they were weary of it. Had He left it doubtful, there had been some excuse; but it is His sealed word, and they profess to believe it, and would take it ill of us if we should question whether they do believe it or not.

Beloved, I come not to accuse any of you particularly of this crime;

but seeing it is the commonest cause of men's destruction, I suppose you will judge it the fittest matter for our inquiry, and deserving our greatest care for the cure. To which end I shall, 1. Endeavor the conviction of the guilty. 2. Shall give them such considerations as may tend to humble and reform them. 3. I shall conclude with such direction as may help them that are willing to escape the destroying power of this sin. And for the first, consider:

I. It is the case of most sinners to think themselves freest from those sins that they are most enslaved to; and one reason why we can not reform them, is because we can not convince them of their guilt. It is the nature of sin so far to blind and befool the sinner, that he knoweth not what he doth, but thinketh he is free from it when it reigneth in him, or when he is committing it: it bringeth men to be so much unacquainted with themselves that they know not what they think, or what they mean and intend, nor what they love or hate, much less what they are habituated and disposed to. They are alive to sin, and dead to all the reason, consideration, and resolution that should recover them, as if it were only by their sinning that we must know they are alive. May I hope that you that hear me to-day are but willing to know the truth of your case, and then I shall be encouraged to proceed to an inquiry. God will judge impartially; why should not we do so? Let me, therefore, by these following questions, try whether none of you are slighters of Christ and your own salvation. And follow me, I beseech you, by putting them close to your own hearts, and faithfully answering them.

1. Things that men highly value will be remembered; they will be matter of their freest and sweetest thoughts. This is a known case.

Do not those then make light of Christ and salvation that think of them so seldom and coldly in comparison of other things? Follow thy own heart, man, and observe what it daily runneth after; and then judge whether it make not light of Christ.

We can not persuade men to one hour's sober consideration what they should do for an interest in Christ, or in thankfulness for His love, and yet they will not believe that they make light of him.

2. Things that we highly value will be matter of our discourse; the judgment and heart will command the tongue. Freely and delightfully will our speech run after them. This also is a known case.

Do not those men make light of Christ and salvation that shun the mention of His name, unless it be in a vain or sinful use? Those that love not the company where Christ and Salvation is much talked of, but think it troublesome, precise discourse: that had rather hear some merry jests, or idle tales, or talk of their riches or business in the world. When you may follow them from morning to night, and scarce have a savory word of Christ; but perhaps some slight and weary mention of Him sometimes; judge whether these make not light of Christ and salvation. How seriously do they talk of the world and speak of vanity! but how heartlessly do they make mention of Christ and salvation!

3. The things that we highly value we would secure the possession of, and therefore would take any convenient course to have all doubts and fears about them well resolved. Do not those men then make light of Christ and salvation that have lived twenty or thirty years in uncertainty whether they have any part in these or not, and yet never seek out for the right resolution of their doubts? Are all that hear me this day certain they shall be saved? Oh that they were! Oh, had you not made light of salvation, you could not so easily bear such doubting of it; you could not rest till you had made it sure, or done your best to make it sure. Have you nobody to inquire of, that might help you in such a work? Why, you have ministers that are purposely appointed to that office. Have you gone to them, and told them the doubtfulness of your case, and asked their help in the judging of your condition? Alas, ministers may sit in their studies from one year to another, before ten persons among a thousand will come to them on such an errand! Do not these make light of Christ and salvation? When the Gospel pierceth the heart indeed, they cry out, "Men and brethren, what shall we do to be saved?" Trembling and astonished, Paul cries out, "Lord, what wilt Thou have me to do?" And so did the convinced Jews to Peter. But when hear we such questions?

4. The things that we value do deeply affect us, and some motions will be in the heart according to our estimation of them. O sirs, if men made not light of these things, what working would there be in the hearts of all our hearers! What strange affections would it raise in them to hear of the matters of the world to come! How would their hearts melt before the power of the Gospel! What sorrow would be wrought in the discovery of their sins! What astonishment at the consideration of their misery! What unspeakable joy at the glad tidings of salvation by the blood of Christ! What resolution would be raised in them upon the discovery of their duty! Oh what hearers should we have, if it were not for this sin! Whereas now we are likelier to weary them, or preach them asleep with matters of this unspeakable moment. We talk to them

of Christ and salvation till we make their heads ache: little would one think by their careless carriage that they heard and regarded what we said, or thought we spoke at all to them.

5. Our estimation of things will be seen in the diligence of our endeavors. That which we most highly value, we shall think no pains too great to obtain. Do not those men then make light of Christ and salvation that think all too much that they do for them; that murmur at His service, and think it too grievous for them to endure? that ask of His service as Judas of the ointment, What need this waste? Can not men be saved without so much ado? This is more ado than needs. For the world they will labor all the day and all their lives; but for Christ and salvation they are afraid of doing too much. Let us preach to them as long as we will, we can not bring them to relish or resolve upon a life of holiness. Follow them to their houses, and you shall not hear them read a chapter, nor call upon God with their families once a day: nor will they allow Him that one day in seven which He hath separated to His service. But pleasure, or worldly business, or idleness, must have a part. And many of them are so far hardened as to reproach them that will not be as mad as themselves. And is not Christ worth the seeking? Is not everlasting salvation worth more than all this? Doth not that soul make light of all these that thinks His ease more worthy than they? Let but common sense judge.

6. That which we most highly value, we think we can not buy too dear: Christ and salvation are freely given, and yet the most of men go without them because they can not enjoy the world and them together. They are called but to part with that which would hinder them from Christ, and they will not do it. They are called but to give God His own, and to resign all to His will, and let go the profits and pleasures of this world, when they must let go either Christ or them, and they will not. They think this too dear a bargain, and say they can not spare these things: they must hold their credit with men; they must look to their estates: how shall they live else? They must have their pleasure, whatsoever becomes of Christ and salvation: as if they could live without Christ better than without these: as if they were afraid of being losers by Christ, or could make a saving match by losing their souls to gain the world. Christ hath told us over and over that if we will not forsake all for Him we can not be His disciples. Far are these men from forsaking all, and yet will needs think that they are His disciples indeed.

7. That which men highly esteem, they would help their friends

8

to as well as themselves. Do not those men make light of Christ and salvation that can take so much care to leave their children portions in the world, and do so little to help them to heaven? that provide outward necessaries so carefully for their families, but do so little to the saving of their souls? Their neglected children and friends will witness that either Christ, or their children's souls, or both, were made light of.

8. That which men highly esteem, they will so diligently seek after that you may see it in the success, if it be a matter within their reach. You may see how many make light of Christ, by the little knowledge they have of Him, and the little communion with Him, and communication from Him; and the little, yea, none of His special grace in them. Alas! how many ministers can speak it to the sorrow of their hearts, that many of their people know almost nothing of Christ, though they hear of Him daily! Nor know they what they must do to be saved: if we ask them an account of these things, they answer as if they understood not what we say to them, and tell us they are no scholars, and therefore think they are excusable for their ignorance. Or if these men had not made light of Christ and their salvation, but had bestowed but half as much pains to know and enjoy Him as they have done to understand the matters of their trades and callings in the world, they would not have been so ignorant as they are: they make light of these things, and therefore will not be at the pains to study or learn them. When men that can learn the hardest trade in a few years have not learned a catechism, nor how to understand their creed, under twenty or thirty years' preaching, nor can abide to be questioned about such things, doth not this show that they have slighted them in their hearts? How will these despisers of Christ and salvation be able one day to look Him in the face, and to give an account of these neglects?

Thus much I have spoken in order to your conviction. Do not some of your consciences by this time smite you, and say, I am the man that have made light of my salvation? If they do not, it is because you make light of it still, for all that is said to you. But because, if it be the will of the Lord, I would fain have this damning distemper cured, and am loath to leave you in such a desperate condition, if I knew how to remedy it, I will give you some considerations, which may move you, if you be men of reason and understanding, to look better about you; and I beseech you to weigh them, and make use of them as we go, and lay open your hearts to the work of grace, and sadly bethink you what a case you are in, if you prove such as make light of Christ.

Consider, 1. Thou makest light of Him that made not light of thee who didst deserve it. Thou wast worthy of nothing but contempt. As a man, what art thou but a worm to God? As a sinner, thou art far viler than a toad: yet Christ was so far from making light of thee and thy happiness, that He came down into the flesh, and lived a life of suffering, and offered himself a sacrifice to the justice which thou hadst provoked, that thy miserable soul might have a remedy. It is no less than miracles of love and mercy that He hath showed to us; and yet shall we slight them after all?

Angels admire them, whom they less concern, and shall redeemed sinners make light of them? What barbarous, yea, devilish, yea, worse than devilish ingratitude is this! The devils never had a saviour offered them; but thou hast, and dost thou yet make light of Him?

2. Consider, the work of man's salvation by Jesus Christ is the masterpiece of all the works of God, wherein He would have His love and mercy to be magnified. As the creation declareth His goodness and power, so doth redemption His goodness and mercy; He hath contrived the very frame of His worship so that it shall much consist in the magnifying of this work; and, after all this, will you make light of it? "His name is Wonderful." "He did the work that none could do." "Greater love could none show than His." How great was the evil and misery that He delivered us from! the good procured for us! All are wonders, from His birth to His ascension; from our new birth to our glorification, all are wonders of matchless mercy — and yet do you make light of them?

3. You make light of matters of greatest excellency and moment in the world: you know not what it is that you slight: had you well known, you would not have done it. As Christ said to the woman of Samaria, "Hadst thou known who it is that speakest to thee, thou wouldst have asked of Him the waters of life;" had they known they would not have crucified the Lord of glory. So had you known what Christ is, you would not have made light of Him; had you been one day in heaven, and but seen what they possess, and seen also what miserable souls must endure that are shut out, you would never sure have made so light of Christ again.

O sirs, it is no trifles or jesting matters that the Gospel speaks of. I must needs profess to you that when I have the most serious thoughts of these things myself, I am ready to marvel that such amazing matters do not overwhelm the souls of men; that the greatness of the subject doth

not so much overmatch our understandings and affections as even to
drive men beside themselves, but that God hath always somewhat allayed
it by the distance; much more that men should be so blockish as to make
light of them. O Lord, that men did but know what everlasting glory
and everlasting torments are: would they then hear us as they do? would
they read and think of these things as they do? I profess I have been
ready to wonder, when I have heard such weighty things delivered, how
people can forbear crying out in the congregation; much more how they
can rest till they have gone to their ministers, and learned what they
should do to be saved, that this great business might be put out of doubt.
Oh that heaven and hell should work no more on men! Oh that ever-
lastingness should work no more! Oh how can you forbear when you
are alone to think with yourselves what it is to be everlastingly in joy or
in torment! I wonder that such thoughts do not break your sleep, and
that they come not in your mind when you are about your labor! I
wonder how you can almost do any thing else! how you can have any
quietness in your minds! how you can eat, or drink, or rest, till you have
got some ground of everlasting consolations! Is that a man or a corpse
that is not affected with matters of this moment? that can be readier to
sleep than to tremble when he heareth how he must stand at the bar of
God? Is that a man or a clod of clay that can rise or lie down without
being deeply affected with his everlasting estate? that can follow his
worldly business and make nothing of the great business of salvation or
damnation; and that when they know it is hard at hand! Truly, sirs,
when I think of the weight of the matter, I wonder at the very best of
God's saints upon earth that they are no better, and do no more in so
weighty a case. I wonder at those whom the world accounteth more
holy than needs, and scorns for making too much ado, that they can put
off Christ and their souls with so little; that they pour not out their souls
in every supplication; that they are not more taken up with God; that
their thoughts be not more serious in preparation for their account. I
wonder that they be not a hundred times more strict in their lives, and
more laborious and unwearied in striving for the crown, than they are.
And for myself, as I am ashamed of my dull and careless heart, and of
my slow and unprofitable course of life, so the Lord knows I am ashamed
of every sermon that I preach: when I think what I have been speaking
of, and who sent me, and that men's salvation or damnation is so much
concerned in it, I am ready to tremble lest God should judge me as a
slighter of His truth and the souls of men, and lest in the best sermon I

should be guilty of their blood.   Methinks we should not speak a word to men in matters of such consequence without tears, or the greatest earnestness that possibly we can: were not we too much guilty of the sin which we reprove, it would be so.   Whether we are alone, or in company, methinks our end, and such an end, should still be in our mind, and as before our eyes; and we should sooner forget any thing, and set light by any thing, or by all things, than by this.

Consider, 4. Who is it that sends this weighty message to you?   Is it not God Himself?   Shall the God of heaven speak, and men make light of it?   You would not slight the voice of an angel or a prince.

5. Whose salvation is it that you make light of?   Is it not your own? Are you no more near or dear to yourselves than to make light of your own happiness or misery?   Why, sirs, do you not care whether you be saved or damned?   Is self-love lost? are you turned your own enemies? As he that slighteth his meat doth slight his life; so if you slight Christ, whatsoever you may think, you will find it was your own salvation that you slighted.   Hear what He saith, "All they that hate Me love death."

6. Your sin is greater, in that you profess to believe the Gospel which you make so light of.   For a professed infidel to do it, that believes not that ever Christ died, or rose again, or doth not believe that there is a heaven or hell, this were no such marvel — but for you, that make it your creed, and your very religion, and call yourselves Christians, and have been baptized into this faith, and seem to stand to it, this is the wonder, and hath no excuse.   What! believe that you shall live in endless joy or torment, and yet make no more of it to escape torment, and obtain that joy!   What! believe that God will shortly judge you, and yet make no more preparation for it!   Either say plainly, I am no Christian, I do not believe these wonderful things, I will believe nothing but what I see, or else let your hearts be affected with your belief, and live as you say you do believe.   What do you think when you repeat the creed, and mention Christ's judgment and everlasting life?

7. What are these things you set so much by as to prefer them before Christ, and the saving of your souls?   Have you found a better friend, a greater and a surer happiness than this?   Good Lord! what dung is it that men make so much of, while they set so light by everlasting glory?   What toys are they that they are daily taken up with, while matters of life and death are neglected?   Why, sirs, if you had every one a kingdom in your hopes, what were it in comparison of the everlasting

kingdom? I can not but look upon all the glory and dignity of this world, lands and lordships, crowns and kingdoms, even as on some brain-sick, beggarly fellow, that borroweth fine clothes, and plays the part of a king or a lord for an hour on a stage, and then comes down, and the sport is ended, and they are beggars again. Were it not for God's interest in the authority of magistrates, or for the service they might do Him, I should judge no better of them. For, as to their own glory, it is but a smoke: what matter is it whether you live poor or rich, unless it were a greater matter to die rich than it is. You know well enough that death levels all. What matter is it at judgment, whether you be to answer for the life of a rich man or a poor man? Is Dives, then, any better than Lazarus? O that men knew what a poor, deceiving shadow they grasp at while they let go the everlasting substance! The strongest, and richest, and most voluptuous sinners, do they lay in fuel for their sorrows, while they think they are gathering together a treasure. Alas! they are asleep, and dream that they are happy; but when they awake, what a change will they find! Their crown is made of thorns: their pleasure hath such a sting as will stick in the heart through all eternity, except unfeigned repentance do prevent it. O how sadly will these wretches be convinced ere long, what a foolish bargain they made in selling Christ and their salvation for these trifles! Let your farms and merchandize then, save you, if they can, and do that for you that Christ would have done. Cry then to Baal, to save thee! Oh, what thoughts have drunkards, and adulterers, etc., of Christ, that will not part with the basest lust for Him? "For a piece of bread," saith Solomon, "such men do transgress."

8. To set so light by Christ and salvation is a certain mark that thou hast no part in them, and if thou so continue, that Christ will set as light by thee: "Those that honor Him He will honor, and those that despise Him shall be lightly esteemed." Thou wilt feel one day that thou canst not live without Him; thou wilt confess then thy need of Him; and then thou mayest go look for a saviour where thou wilt; for He will be no Saviour for thee hereafter, that wouldst not value Him, and submit to Him here. Then who will prove the loser by thy contempt? O what a thing will it be for a poor miserable soul to cry to Christ for help in the day of extremity, and to hear so sad an answer as this! Thou didst set lightly by Me and My law in the day of thy prosperity, and I will now set as light by thee in the day of thy adversity. Read Prov. i. 24, to the end. Thou that, as Esau, didst sell thy birthright for a mess of pottage,

shalt then find no place for repentance, though thou seek it with tears. Do you think that Christ shed His blood to save them that continue to make light of it? and to save them that value a cup of drink or a lust before His salvation? I tell you, sirs, though you set so light by Christ and salvation, God doth not so: He will not give them on such terms as these: He valueth the blood of His Son, and the everlasting glory, and He will make you value them if ever you have them. Nay, this will be thy condemnation, and leaveth no remedy. All the world 'can not save him that sets lightly by Christ. None of them shall taste of His Supper. Nor can you blame Him to deny you what you make light of yourselves. Can you find fault if you miss of the salvation which you slighted?

9. The time is near when Christ and salvation will not be made light of as now they are. When God hath shaken those careless souls out of their bodies, and you must answer for all your sins in your own name, oh then what would you give for a saviour! When a thousand bills shall be brought in against you, and none to relieve you, then you will consider, Oh! Christ would now have stood between me and the wrath of God: had I not despised Him, He would have answered all. When you see the world hath left you, and your companions in sin have deceived themselves and you, and all your merry days are gone, then what would you give for that Christ and salvation that now you account not worth your labor! Do you think that when you see the judgment set, and you are doomed to everlasting perdition for your wickedness, that you should then make as light of Christ as now? Why will you not judge now as you know you shall judge then? Will He then be worth ten thousand worlds? and is He not now worth your highest estimation and dearest affection?

10. God will not only deny these that salvation thou madest light of, but He will take from thee all that which thou didst value before it: he that most highly esteems Christ shall have Him, and the creatures, so far as they are good here, and Him without the creature hereafter, because the creature is not useful; and he that sets more by the creature than by Christ, shall have some of the creature without Christ here, and neither Christ nor it hereafter.

So much of these considerations, which may show the true face of this heinous sin.

What think you now, friends, of this business? Do you not see by this time what a case that soul is in that maketh light of Christ and salvation? What need then is there that you should take heed lest this should prove your own case! The Lord knows it is too common a case.

Whoever is found guilty at the last of this sin, it were better for that man he had never been born. It were better for him he had been a Turk or Indian, that never had heard the name of a Saviour, and that never had salvation offered to him: for such men " have no cloak for their sin." Besides all the rest of their sins, they have this killing sin to answer for, which will undo them. And this will aggravate their misery, that Christ whom they set light by must be their Judge, and for this sin will He judge them. Oh that such would now consider how they will answer that question that Christ put to their predecessors: " How will ye escape the damnation of hell?" or, " How shall we escape if we neglect so great salvation?" Can you escape without a Christ? or will a despised Christ save you then? If he be accursed that sets light by father or mother, what then is he that sets light by Christ? It was the heinous sin of the Jews, that among them were found such as set light by father and mother. But among us, men slight the Father of spirits! In the name of God, brethren, I beseech you to consider how you will then bear this anger which you now make light of! You that can not make light of a little sickness or want, or of natural death, no, not of a tooth-ache, but groan as if you were undone; how will you then make light of the fury of the Lord, which will burn against the contemners of His grace! Doth it not behoove you beforehand to think of these things?

Hitherto I have been convincing you of the evil of the sin, and the danger that followeth: I come now to know your resolution for the time to come. What say you? Do you mean to set as light by Christ and salvation as hitherto you have done; and to be the same men after all this? I hope not. Oh let not your ministers that would fain save you, be brought in as witnesses against you to condemn you; at least, I beseech you put not this upon me. Why, sirs, if the Lord shall say to us at judgment, Did you never tell these men what Christ did for their souls, and what need they had of Him, and how nearly it did concern them to look to their salvation, that they made light of it? We must needs say the truth: Yea, Lord, we told them of it as plainly as we could; we would have gone on our knees to them if we had thought it would have prevailed; we did entreat them as earnestly as we could to consider these things; they heard of these things every day; but, alas, we could never get them to their hearts: they gave us the hearing, but they made light of all that we could say to them. Oh! sad will it prove on your side, if you force us to such an answer as this.

Dearly beloved in the Lord, I have now done that work which I came upon; what effect it hath, or will have, upon your hearts, I know not, nor is it any further in my power to accomplish that which my soul desireth for you.   Were it the Lord's will that I might have my wish herein, the words that you have this day heard should so stick by you that the secure should be awakened by them, and none of you should perish by the slighting of your salvation.   I can not now follow you to your several habitations to apply this word to your particular necessities; but O that I could make every man's conscience a preacher to himself that it might do it, which is ever with you!   That the next time you go prayerless to bed, or about your business, conscience might cry out, dost thou set no more by Christ and thy salvation?   That the next time you are tempted to think hardly of a holy and diligent life (I will not say to deride it as more ado than needs), conscience might cry out to thee, Dost thou set so light by Christ and thy salvation?   That the next time you are ready to rush upon known sin, and to please your fleshly desires against the command of God, conscience might cry out, Is Christ and salvation no more worth than to cast them away, or venture them for lusts?   That when you are following the world with your most eager desires, forgetting the world to come, and the change that is a little before you, conscience might cry out to you, Is Christ and salvation no more worth than so?   That when you are next spending the Lord's day in idleness or vain sports, conscience might tell you what you are doing.   In a word, that in all your neglects of duty, your sticking at the supposed labor or cost of a godly life, yea, in all your cold and lazy prayers and performances, conscience might tell you how unsuitable such endeavors are to the reward; and that Christ and salvation should not be so slighted.   I will say no more but this at this time, It is a thousand pities that when God hath provided a Saviour for the world, and when Christ had suffered so much for their sins, and made so full a satisfaction to justice, and purchased so glorious a kingdom for his saints, and all this is offered so freely to sinners, to lost, unworthy sinners, even for nothing, that yet so many millions should everlastingly perish because they make light of their Saviour and salvation, and prefer the vain world and their lusts before them.   I have delivered my message, the Lord open your hearts to receive it. I have persuaded you with the word of truth and soberness; the Lord persuade you more effectually, or else all this is lost.   Amen.

IX

JOHN BUNYAN

1628–1688

EVERYONE knows that " The Pilgrim's Progress " by John Bunyan has passed through more editions, been translated into more
languages, and been read by more people than any other book written
by one man; but comparatively few people know that the author of this
book was also the most popular preacher of his generation in England.
John Bunyan came of lowly origin. He was born in the village of
Elstow, near Bedford in 1628. He followed his father's trade as a
" tinker," or mender of metal pots and pans; received very little
education; and according to his own account lived a wild life in his
youth, being especially notorious for his profanity. He was a soldier
on the side of the Commonwealth in the Civil War, between 1644
and 1646. Recently the muster-roll of his company has been discovered, bearing his name. His marriage in 1648 was the turning-
point of his life, for it led to his conversion to Christ in 1653,— a conversion powerfully marked, of which he afteward told the story in his
" Grace Abounding." He united with a Baptist society, and uneducated as he was, soon began to preach. His fervent spirit, wide
eloquence, and quaintness of speech made him famous throughout
the midland counties of England. On the accession of Charles II all
religious services except those of the church of England were forbidden; but Bunyan persisted in preaching, and for that reason was
sent to prison at Bedford. Here he remained twelve years, from
1660 to 1672, though not all the time in close confinement; for he
was permitted occasionally to go upon the street, leading his blind
little girl, and selling the " tagged laces," which he had woven as a
support for himself and his family. While in Bedford jail he wrote
his immortal allegory, " The Pilgrim's Progress." Released at last,

he again entered upon his work of preaching, and won increased popularity throughout the kingdom. He died at Snowhill, near London, August 31, 1688. Next to his " Pilgrim's Progress," the most widely read of his many writings is " The Holy War," also an allegory. This sermon is a good example of his preaching. Owing to its length some minor parts have been omitted, but its plan and spirit are preserved.

THE HEAVENLY FOOTMAN.

"So run that ye may obtain."— 1 Cor. ix. 24.

HEAVEN and happiness is that which every one desireth, insomuch that wicked Balaam could say, " Let me die the death of the righteous, and let my last end be like his." Yet, for all this, there are but very few that do obtain that ever-to-be-desired glory, insomuch that many eminent professors drop short of a welcome from God into this pleasant place. The apostle, therefore, because he did desire the salvation of the souls of the Corinthians, to whom he writes this epistle, layeth them down in these words such counsel which, if taken, would be for their help and advantage.

First. Not to be wicked, and sit still, and wish for heaven; but to run for it.

Secondly. Not to content themselves with every kind of running, but, saith he, " So run that ye may obtain." As if he should say, some, because they would not lose their souls, they begin to run betimes, they run apace, they run with patience, they run the right way. Do you so run. Some run from both father and mother, friends and companions, and thus, they may have the crown. Do you so run. Some run through temptations, afflictions, good report, evil report, that they may win the pearl. Do you so run. " So run that ye may obtain."

These words they are taken from men's running for a wager: a very apt similitude to set before the eyes of the saints of the Lord. " Know you not that they which run in a race run all, but one obtains the prize? So run that ye may obtain." That is, do not only run, but be sure you win as well as run. " So run that ye may obtain."

I shall not need to make any great ado in opening the words at this time, but shall rather lay down one doctrine that I do find in them; and in prosecuting that, I shall show you, in some measure, the scope of the words.

The doctrine is this: They that will have heaven, must run for it; I say, they that will have heaven, they must run for it. I beseech you to heed it well. "Know ye not, that they which run in a race run all, but one obtaineth the prize? So run ye." The prize is heaven, and if you will have it, you must run for it. You have another scripture for this in the 12th of the Hebrews, the 1st, 2d, and 3d verses: "Wherefore seeing also," saith the apostle, "that we are compassed about with so great a cloud of witnesses, let us lay aside every weight, and the sin which doth so easily beset us, and let us run with patience the race that is set before us." And let us run, saith he.

Again, saith Paul, "I so run, not as uncertainly: so fight I," etc.

But before I go any farther:

1. Fleeing. Observe, That this running is not an ordinary, or any sort of running, but it is to be understood of the swiftest sort of running; and therefore, in the 6th of the Hebrews, it is called a fleeing: "That we might have strong consolation, who have fled for refuge, to lay hold on the hope set before us." Mark, who have fled. It is taken from that 20th of Joshua, concerning the man that was to flee to the city of refuge, when the avenger of blood was hard at his heels, to take vengeance on him for the offence he had committed; therefore it is a running or fleeing for one's life: A running with all might and main, as we use to say. So run.

2. Pressing. Secondly, This running in another place is called a pressing. "I press toward the mark;" which signifieth, that they that will have heaven, they must not stick at any difficulties they meet with; but press, crowd, and thrust through all that may stand between heaven and their souls. So run.

3. Continuing. Thirdly, This running is called in another place, a continuing in the way of life. "If you continue in the faith grounded, and settled, and be not moved away from the hope of the gospel of Christ." Not to run a little now and then, by fits and starts, or half-way, or almost thither, but to run for my life, to run through all difficulties, and to continue therein to the end of the race, which must be to the end of my life. "So run that ye may obtain." And the reasons for this point are these:

1. Because all or every one that runneth doth not obtain the prize; there may be many that do run, yea, and run far too, who yet miss of the

crown that standeth at the end of the race. You know that all that run in a race do not obtain the victory; they all run, but one wins. And so it is here; it is not every one that runneth, nor every one that seeketh, nor every one that striveth for the mastery, that hath it. "Though a man do strive for the mastery," saith Paul, " yet he is not crowned, unless he strive lawfully;" that is, unless he so run, and so strive, as to have God's approbation. What, do ye think that every heavy-heeled professor will have heaven? What, every lazy one? every wanton and foolish professor, that will be stopped by anything, kept back by anything, that scarce runneth so fast heavenward as a snail creepeth on the ground? Nay, there are some professors that do not go on so fast in the way of God as a snail doth go on the wall; and yet these think, that heaven and happiness is for them. But stay, there are many more that run than there be that obtain; therefore he that will have heaven must run for it.

2. Because you know, that though a man do run, yet if he do not overcome, or win, as well as run, what will they be the better for their running? They will get nothing. You know the man that runneth, he doth do it that he may win the prize; but if he doth not obtain it, he doth lose his labor, spend his pains and time, and that to no purpose; I say, he getteth nothing. And ah! how many such runners will there be found in the day of judgment? Even multitudes, multitudes that have run, yea, run so far as to come to heaven-gates, and not able to get any farther, but there stand knocking, when it is too late, crying, Lord, Lord, when they have nothing but rebukes for their pains. Depart from me, you come not here, you come too late, you run too lazily; the door is shut. " When once the master of the house is risen up," saith Christ, " and hath shut to the door, and ye begin to stand without, and to knock, saying, Lord, Lord, open to us, I will say, I know you not, Depart," etc. O sad will the state of those be that run and miss; therefore, if you will have heaven, you must run for it; and " so run that ye may obtain."

3. Because the way is long (I speak metaphorically), and there is many a dirty step, many a high hill, much work to do, a wicked heart, world, and devil to overcome; I say, there are many steps to be taken by those that intend to be saved, by running or walking in the steps of that faith of our father Abraham. Out of Egypt thou must go through the Red Sea; thou must run a long and tedious journey, through the vast howling wilderness, before thou come to the land of promise.

4. They that will go to heaven they must run for it; because, as the way is long, so the time in which they are to get to the end of it is very

uncertain; the time present is the only time; thou hast no more time allotted thee than that thou now enjoyest: "Boast not thyself of to-morrow, for thou knowest not what a day may bring forth." Do not say, I have time enough to get to heaven seven years hence: for I tell thee, the bell may toll for thee before seven days more be ended; and when death comes, away thou must go, whether thou art provided or not; and therefore look to it; make no delays; it is not good dallying with things of so great concernment as the salvation or damnation of thy soul. You know he that hath a great way to go in a little time, and less by half than he thinks of, he had need to run for it.

5. They that will have heaven, they must run for it; because the devil, the law, sin, death, and hell follow them. There is never a poor soul that is going to heaven, but the devil, the law, sin, death, and hell, make after that soul. "The devil, your adversary, as a roaring lion, goeth about, seeking whom he may devour." And I will assure you, the devil is nimble, he can run apace, he is light of foot, he hath overtaken many, he hath turned up their heels, and hath given them an everlasting fall. Also the law, that can shoot a great way, have a care thou keep out of the reach of those great guns, the ten commandments. Hell also hath a wide mouth; it can stretch itself farther than you are aware of. And as the angel said to Lot, "Take heed, look not behind thee, neither tarry thou in all the plain" (that is, anywhere between this and heaven), "lest thou be consumed;" so say I to thee, Take heed, tarry not, lest either the devil, hell, or the fearful curses of the law of God, do overtake thee, and throw thee down in the midst of thy sins, so as never to rise and recover again. If this were well considered, then thou, as well as I, wouldst say, They that will have heaven must run for it.

6. They that will go to heaven must run for it; because perchance the gates of heaven may be shut shortly. Sometimes sinners have not heaven-gates open to them so long as they suppose; and if they be once shut against a man, they are so heavy, that all the men in the world, nor all the angels in heaven, are not able to open them. "I shut, and no man can open," saith Christ. And how if thou shouldst come but one quarter of an hour too late? I tell thee, it will cost thee an eternity to bewail thy misery in. Francis Spira can tell thee what it is to stay till the gate of mercy be quite shut; or to run so lazily, that they be shut before thou get within them. What, to be shut out! what, out of heaven! Sinner, rather than lose it, run for it; yea, and "so run that thou mayst obtain."

7. *Lastly,* Because if thou lose, thou losest all, thou losest soul, God, Christ, heaven, ease, peace, etc. Besides, thou layest thyself open to all the shame, contempt, and reproach, that either God, Christ, saints, the world, sin, the devil, and all, can lay upon thee. As Christ saith of the foolish builder, so will I say of thee, if thou be such a one who runs and. misses; I say, even all that go by will begin to mock at thee, saying, This man began to run well, but was not able to finish. But more of this anon.

Quest. But how should a poor soul do to run? For this very thing is that which afflicteth me sore (as you say), to think that I may run, and yet fall short. Methinks to fall short at last, O, it fears me greatly! Pray tell me, therefore, how I should run.

Ans. That thou mayst indeed be satisfied in this particular consider these following things.

The first direction. If thou wouldst so run as to obtain the kingdom of heaven, then be sure that thou get into the way that leadeth thither: For it is a vain thing to think that ever thou shalt have the prize, though thou runnest never so fast, unless thou art in the way that leads to it. Set the case, that there should be a man in London that was to run to York for a wager; now, though he run never so swiftly, yet if he run full south, he might run himself quickly out of breath, and be never the nearer the prize, but rather the farther off. Just so is it here; it is not simply the runner, nor yet the hasty runner, that winneth the crown, unless he be in the way that leadeth thereto. I have observed, that little time which I have been a professor, that there is a great running to and fro, some this way, and some that way, yet it is to be feared most of them are out of the way, and then, though they run as swift as the eagle can fly, they are benefited nothing at all.

Here is one runs a-quaking, another a-ranting; one again runs after the baptism, and another after the Independency: Here is one for Free-will, and another for Presbytery; and yet possibly most of all these sects run quite the wrong way, and yet every one is for his life, his soul, either for heaven or hell.

If thou now say, Which is the way? I tell thee it is Christ, the Son of Mary, the Son of God. Jesus saith, " I am the way, the truth, and the life; no man cometh to the Father but by me." So then thy business is (if thou wouldst have salvation), to see if Christ be thine, with all his benefits; whether he hath covered thee with his righteousness, whether he hath showed thee that thy sins are washed away with his heart-blood, whether thou are planted into him, and whether you have faith in him, so as to make a life out of him, and to conform thee to him; that is, such faith as to conclude that thou art righteous, because Christ is thy righteousness, and so constrained to walk with him as the joy of thy heart, because he saveth thy soul. And for the Lord's sake take heed, and do not deceive thyself, and think thou art in the way upon too slight grounds; for if thou miss of the way, thou wilt miss of the prize, and if thou miss of that I am sure thou wilt lose thy soul, even that soul which is worth more than the whole world.

Mistrust thy own strength, and throw it away; down on thy knees in prayer to the Lord for the spirit of truth; search his word for direction; flee seducers' company; keep company with the soundest Christians, that have most experience of Christ; and be sure thou have a care of Quakers, Ranters, Free-willers: Also do not have too much company with some Anabaptists, though I go under that name myself. I tell thee this is such a serious matter, and I fear thou wilt so little regard it, that the thought of the worth of the thing, and of thy too light regarding of it, doth even make my heart ache whilst I am writing to thee. The Lord teach thee the way by his Spirit, and then I am sure thou wilt know it. So run.

The second direction. As thou shouldst get into the way, so thou shouldst also be much in studying and musing on the way. You know men that would be expert in anything, they are usually much in studying of that thing, and so likewise is it with those that quickly grow expert in any way. This therefore thou shouldst do; let thy study be much exercised about Christ, which is the way, what he is, what he hath done, and why he is what he is, and why he hath done what is done; as, why "he took upon him the form of a servant," (Phil. ii.); why he was "made in the likeness of man;" why he cried; why he died; why he "bare the sin of the world;" why he was made sin, and why he was made righteousness; why he is in heaven in the nature of man, and what he doth there. Be much in musing and considering of these things; be thinking also enough of those places which thou must not come near, but leave some on this hand, and some on that hand; as it is with those that travel into other countries; they must leave such a gate on this hand, and such a bush on that hand, and go by such a place, where standeth such a thing. Thus therefore you must do: "Avoid such things, which are expressly forbidden in the word of God." Withdraw thy foot far from her, "and come not nigh the door of her house, for her steps take hold of hell, going down to the chambers of death." And so of everything that is not in the way, have a care of it, that thou go not by it; come not near it, have nothing to do with it. So run.

The third direction. Not only thus, but in the next place, Thou must strip thyself of those things that may hang upon thee, to the hindering of thee in the way to the kingdom of heaven, as covetousness, pride, lust, or whatever else thy heart may be inclining unto, which may hinder thee in this heavenly race. Men that run for a wager, if they intend to win as well as run, they do not use to encumber themselves, or carry those things about them that may be an hindrance to them in their running. " Every man that striveth for the mastery is temperate in all things:" That is, he layeth aside everything that would be anywise a disadvantage to him; as saith the apostle, " Let us lay aside every weight, and the sin that doth so easily beset us, and let us run with patience the race that is set before us." It is but a vain thing to talk of going to heaven, if thou let thy heart be encumbered with those things that would hinder. Would you not say that such a man would be in danger of losing, though he run, if he fill his pockets with stones, hang heavy garments on his shoulders, and get lumpish shoes on his feet? So it is here; thou talkest of going to heaven, and yet fillest thy pocket with stones, i. e., fillest thy heart with this world, lettest that hang on thy shoulders, with its profits and pleasures: Alas, alas, thou art widely mistaken: if thou intendest to win, thou must strip, thou must lay aside every weight, thou must be temperate in all things. Thou must so run.

The fourth direction. Beware of by-paths; take heed thou dost not turn into those lanes which lead out of the way. There are crooked paths, paths in which men go astray, paths that lead to death and damnation, but take heed of all those. Some of them are dangerous because of practice, some because of opinion, but mind them not; mind the path before thee, look right before thee, turn neither to the right hand nor to the left, but let thine eyes look right on, even right before thee; " Ponder the path of thy feet, and let all thy ways be established." Turn not to the right hand nor to the left: " Remove thy foot far from evil." This counsel being not so seriously taken as given, is the reason of that starting from opinion to opinion, reeling this way and that way, out of this lane into that lane, and so missing the way to the kingdom. Though the way to heaven be but one, yet there are many crooked lanes and by-paths shoot down upon it, as I may say. And again, notwithstanding the kingdom of heaven be the biggest city, yet usually those by-paths are most

9

beaten, most travellers go those ways; and therefore the way to heaven is hard to be found, and as hard to be kept in, by reason of these. Yet, nevertheless, it is in this case as it was with the harlot of Jericho; she had one scarlet thread tied in her window, by which her house was known: So it is here, the scarlet streams of Christ's blood run throughout the way to the kingdom of heaven; therefore mind that, see if thou do find the besprinkling of the blood of Christ in the way, and if thou do, be of good cheer, thou art in the right way; but have a care thou beguile not thyself with a fancy; for then thou mayst light into any lane or way; but that thou mayst not be mistaken, consider, though it seem never so pleasant, yet if thou do not find that in the very middle of the road there is written with the heart-blood of Christ, that he came into the world to save sinners, and that we are justified, though we are ungodly, shun that way; for this it is which the apostle meaneth when he saith, " We have boldness to enter into the holiest by the blood of Jesus, by a new and living way which he hath consecrated for us, through the vail, that is to say, his flesh." How easy a matter it is in this our day, for the devil to be too cunning for poor souls, by calling his by-paths the way to the kingdom! If such an opinion or fancy be but cried up by one or more, this inscription being set upon it by the devil, [This is the way of God] how speedily, greedily, and by heaps, do poor simple souls throw away themselves upon it; especially if it be daubed over with a few external acts of morality, if so good! But this is because men do not know painted by-paths from the plain way to the kingdom of heaven. They have not yet learned the true Christ, and what his righteousness is, neither have they a sense of their own insufficiency; but are bold, proud, presumptuous, self-conceited. And therefore,

The fifth direction. Do not thou be too much in looking too high in thy journey heavenwards. You know men that run a race do not use to stare and gaze this way and that, neither do they use to cast up their eyes too high, lest haply, through their too much gazing with their eyes after other things, they in the mean time stumble, and catch a fall. The very same case is this; if thou gaze and stare after every opinion and way that comes into the world, also if thou be prying overmuch into God's secret decrees, or let thy heart too much entertain questions about some nice foolish curiosities, thou mayst stumble and fall, as many hundreds in England have done, both in ranting and quakery, to their own eternal overthrow, without the marvellous operation of God's grace be suddenly stretched forth to bring them back again. Take heed, therefore; follow not that proud, lofty spirit, that, devil-like, cannot be content with his own station. David was of an excellent spirit, where he saith, " Lord, my heart is not haughty, nor mine eyes lofty, neither do I exercise myself in great matters, or things too high for me. Surely I have behaved and quieted myself as a child that is weaned of his mother : My soul is even as a weaned child." Do thou so run.

The sixth direction. Take heed that you have not an ear open to every one that calleth after you as you are in your journey. Men that run, you know, if any do call after them, saying, I would speak with you, or go not too fast, and you shall have my company with you, if they run for some great matter, they use to say, Alas, I cannot stay, I am in haste, pray talk not to me now ; neither can I stay for you, I am running for a wager : If I win I am made, if I lose I am undone, and therefore hinder me not. Thus wise are men when they run for corruptible things, and thus shouldst thou do, and thou hast more cause to do so than they, forasmuch as they run for things that last not, but thou for an incorruptible glory. I give thee notice of this betimes, knowing that thou shalt have enough call after thee, even the devil, sin, this world, vain company, pleasures, profits, esteem among men, ease, pomp, pride together with an innumerable company of such companions ; one crying, Stay for me ; the other saying, Do not leave me behind ; a third saying, And take me along with you. What, will you go, saith the devil, without your sins, pleasures, and profits? Are you so hasty? Can you not stay and take these along with you? Will you leave your friends and companions behind you? Can you not do as your neighbors do, carry the world, sin, lust, pleasure, profit, esteem among men, along with you? Have a care thou do not let thine ear now be open to the tempting, enticing, alluring, and soul-entangling flatteries of such sink-souls as these are. " My son," saith Solomon, " If sinners entice thee, consent thou not."

You know what it cost the young man which Solomon speaks of in the 7th of the Proverbs, that was enticed by a harlot: " With much fair speech she won him, and caused him to yield, with the flattering of her lips she forced him, till he went after her as an ox to the slaughter, or as a fool to the correction of the stocks ;" even so far, " till the dart struck through his liver, and knew not that it was for his life. Hearken unto me now therefore," saith he, " O ye children, and attend to the words of my mouth, let not thine heart decline to her ways, go not astray in her paths, for she hast cast down many wounded, yea, many strong men have been slain (that is, kept out of heaven) ; by her house is the way to hell, going down to the chambers of death." Soul, take this counsel, and say, Satan, sin, lust, pleasure, profit, pride, friends, companions, and everything else, let me alone, stand off, come not nigh me, for I am running for heaven, for my soul, for God, for Christ, from hell and everlasting damnation; if I win, I win all; and if I lose, I lose all; let me alone, for I will not hear. So run.

The seventh direction. In the next place, be not daunted though thou meetest with never so many discouragements in thy journey thither. That man that is resolved for heaven, if Satan cannot win him by flatteries, he will endeavor to weaken him by discouragements; saying, Thou art a sinner, thou hast broken God's law, thou art not elected, thou comest too late, the day of grace is passed, God doth not care for thee, thy heart is naught, thou art lazy, with a hundred other discouraging suggestions. And thus it was with David, where he saith, " I had fainted, unless I had believed to see the loving-kindness of the Lord in the land of the living." As if he should say, the devil did so rage, and my heart was so base, that had I judged according to my own sense and feeling, I had been absolutely distracted; but I trusted to Christ in the promise, and looked that God would be as good as his promise, in having mercy upon me, an unworthy sinner; and this is that which encouraged me, and kept me from fainting. And thus must thou do when Satan, or the law, or thy own conscience, do go about to dishearten thee, either by the greatness of thy sins, the wickedness of thy heart, the tediousness of the way, the loss of outward enjoyments, the hatred that thou wilt procure from the world or the like; then thou must encourage thyself with the freeness of the promises, the tender-heartedness of Christ, the merits of his blood, the freeness of his invitations to come in, the greatness of the sin of others that have been pardoned, and that the same God, through the same Christ, holdeth forth the same grace as free as ever. If these be not thy meditations, thou wilt draw very heavily in the way of heaven, if thou do not give up all for lost, and so knock off from following any farther; therefore, I say, take heart in thy journey, and say to them that seek thy destruction, " Rejoice not against me, O my enemy, for when I fall I shall arise, when I sit in darkness the Lord shall be a light unto me." So run.

The eighth direction. Take heed of being offended at the cross that thou must go by before thou come to heaven. You must understand (as I have already touched) that there is no man that goeth to heaven but he must go by the cross. The cross is the standing way-mark by which all they that go to glory must pass.

"We must through much tribulation enter into the kingdom of heaven." "Yea, and all that will live godly in Christ Jesus shall suffer persecution." If thou art in thy way to the kingdom, my life for thine thou wilt come at the cross shortly (the Lord grant thou dost not shrink at it, so as to turn thee back again). "If any man will come after me," saith Christ, "let him deny himself, and take up his cross daily, and follow me." The cross it stands, and hath stood, from the beginning, as a way-mark to the kingdom of heaven. You know, if one ask you the way to such and such a place, you, for the better direction, do not only say, This is the way, but then also say, You must go by such a gate, by such a stile, such a bush, tree, bridge, or such like: Why, so it is here; art thou inquiring the way to heaven? Why, I tell thee, Christ is the way; into him thou must get, into his righteousness, to be justified; and if thou art in him, thou wilt presently see the cross, thou must go close by it, thou must touch it, nay, thou must take it up, or else thou wilt quickly go out of the way that leads to heaven, and turn up some of those crooked lanes that lead down to the chambers of death.

It is the cross which keepeth those that are kept from heaven. I am persuaded, were it not for the cross, where we have one professor we should have twenty; but this cross, that is it which spoileth all.

Some men, as I said before, when they come at the cross they can go no farther, but back again to their sins they must go. Others they stumble at it, and break their necks; others again, when they see the cross is approaching, they turn aside to the left hand, or to the right hand, and so think to get to heaven another way; but they will be deceived. "For all that will live godly in Christ Jesus shall," mark, "shall be sure to suffer persecution." There are but few when they come at the cross, cry, Welcome cross! as some of the martyrs did to the stake they were burned at: Therefore, if you meet with the cross in thy journey, in what manner soever it be, be not daunted, and say, Alas, what shall I do now! But rather take courage, knowing, that by the cross is the way to the kingdom. Can a man believe in Christ, and not be hated by the devil? Can he make a profession of this Christ, and that sweetly and convincingly, and the children of Satan hold their tongue? Can darkness agree with light? or the devil endure that Christ Jesus should be honored both by faith and a heavenly conversation, and let that soul alone at quiet? Did you never read that "the dragon persecuted the woman?" And that Christ saith, "In the world you shall have tribulations?"

The ninth direction. Beg of God that he would do these two things for thee: First, Enlighten thine understanding: And, secondly, Inflame thy will. If these two be but effectually done, there is no fear but thou wilt go safe to heaven.

One of the great reasons why men and women do so little regard the other world, it is because they see so little of it: And the reason why they see so little of it is, because they have their understanding darkened: And therefore, saith Paul, "Do not you believers walk as do other Gentiles, even in the vanity of their minds, having their understanding darkened, being alienated from the life of God through the ignorance (or foolishness) that is in them, because of the blindness of their heart." Walk not as those, run not with them: alas, poor souls, they have their understandings darkened, their hearts blinded, and that is the reason they have such undervaluing thoughts of the Lord Jesus Christ, and the salvation of their souls. For when men do come to see the things of another world, what a God, what a Christ, what a heaven, and what an eternal glory there is to be enjoyed; also when they see that it is possible for them to have a share in it, I tell you it will make them run through thick and thin to enjoy it. Moses, having a sight of this, because his understanding was enlightened, "He feared not the wrath of the king, but chose rather to suffer afflictions with the people of God, than to enjoy the pleasures of sin for a season. He refused to be called the son of the king's daughter;" accounting it wonderful riches to be accounted worthy of so much as to suffer for Christ, with the poor despised saints; and that was because he saw him who was invisible, and had respect unto the recompense of reward. And this is that which the apostle usually prayeth for in his epistles for the saints, namely, "That they might know what is the hope of God's calling, and the riches of the glory of his inheritance in the saints; and that they might be able to comprehend with all saints, what is the breadth, and length, and depth, and height, and know the love of Christ, which passeth knowledge." Pray therefore that God would enlighten thy understanding; that will be a very great help unto thee. It will make thee endure many a hard brunt for Christ; as Paul saith, "After you were illuminated, ye endured a great sight of afflictions.—— You took joyfully the spoiling of your goods, knowing in yourselves that ye have in heaven a better and an enduring substance." If there be never such a rare jewel lie just in a man's way, yet if he sees it not, he will rather trample upon it than stoop for it, and it is because he sees it not. Why, so it is here, though heaven be worth never so much, and thou hast never so much need of it, yet if thou see it not, that is, have not thy understanding opened or enlightened to see, thou wilt not regard at all: therefore cry to the Lord for enlightening grace, and say, " Lord, open my blind eyes; Lord, take the veil off my dark heart," show me the things of the other world, and let me see the sweetness, glory, and excellency of them for Christ's sake. This is the first.

The tenth direction. Cry to God that he would inflame thy will also with the things of the other world. For when a man's will is fully set to do such or such a thing, then it must be a very hard matter that shall hinder that man from bringing about his end. When Paul's will was set resolvedly to go up to Jerusalem (though it was signified to him before, what he should there suffer), he was not daunted at all; nay, saith he, " I am ready (or willing) not only to be bound, but also to die at Jerusalem for the name of the Lord Jesus." His will was inflamed with love to Christ; and therefore all the persuasions that could be used wrought nothing at all.

Your self-willed people nobody knows what to do with them: we use to say, He will have his own will, do all what you can. Indeed to have such a will for heaven, is an admirable advantage to a man that undertaketh a race thither; a man that is resolved, and hath his will fixed, saith he, I will do my best to advantage myself; I will do my worst to hinder my enemies; I will not give out as long as I can stand; I will have it or I will lose my life; " though he slay me yet will I trust in him. I will not let thee go except thou bless me." I will, I will, I will, O this blessed inflamed will for heaven! What is it like? If a man be willing, then any argument shall be a matter of encouragement; but if unwilling, then any argument shall give discouragement; this is seen both in saints and sinners; in them that are the children of God, and also those that are the children of the devil. As,

1. The saints of old, they being willing and resolved for heaven, what could stop them? Could fire and faggot, sword or halter, stinking dungeons, whips, bears, bulls, lions, cruel rackings, stoning, starving, nakedness, etc., " and in all these things they were more than conquerors, through him that loved them;" who had also made them " willing in the day of his power."

2. See again, on the other side, the children of the devil, because they are not willing, how many shifts and starting-holes they will have.

I have married a wife, I have a farm, I shall offend my landlord, I shall offend my master, I shall lose my trading, I shall lose my pride, my pleasures, I shall be mocked and scoffed, therefore I dare not come. I, saith another, will stay till I am older, till my children are out, till I am got a little aforehand in the world, till I have done this and that, and the other business: but alas, the thing is, they are not willing; for, were they but soundly willing, these, and a thousand such as these, would hold them no ·faster than the cords held Samson, when he broke them like burnt flax. I tell you the will is all: that is one of the chief things which turns the wheel either backwards or forwards; and God knoweth that full well, and so likewise doth the devil; and therefore they both endeavor very much to strengthen the will of their servants; God, he is for making of his a willing people to serve him; and the devil, he doth what he can to possess the will and affection of those that are his with love to sin; and therefore when Christ comes close to the matter, indeed, saith he, " You will not come to me. How often would I have gathered you as a hen doth her chickens, but you would not." The devil had possessed their wills, and so long he was sure enough of them. O therefore cry hard to God to inflame thy will for heaven and Christ: thy will, I say, if that be rightly set for heaven, thou wilt not be beat off with discouragements; and this was the reason that when Jacob wrestled with the angel, though he lost a limb, as it were, and the hollow of his thigh was put out of joint as he wrestled with him, yet, saith he, " I will not," mark, " I will not let thee go except thou bless me." Get thy will tipt with the heavenly grace, and resolution against all discouragements, and then thou goest full speed for heaven; but if thou falter in thy will, and be not found there, thou wilt run hobbling and halting all the way thou runnest, and also to be sure thou wilt fall short at last. The Lord give thee a will and courage.

Thus have I done with directing thee how to run to the kingdom; be sure thou keep in memory what I have said unto thee, lest thou lose thy way. But because I would have thee think of them, take all in short in this little bit of paper.

1. Get into the way. 2. Then study on it. 3. Then strip, and lay aside everything that would hinder. 4. Beware of by-paths. 5. Do not gaze and stare too much about thee, but be sure to ponder the path of thy feet. 6. Do not stop for any that call after thee, whether it be the world, the flesh, or the devil: for all these will hinder thy journey, if possible. 7. Be not daunted with any discouragements thou meetest with as

thou goest. 8. Take heed of stumbling at the cross. 9. Cry hard to God for an enlightened heart, and a willing mind, and God give thee a prosperous journey.

Provocation. Now that you may be provoked to run with the foremost, take notice of this. When Lot and his wife were running from cursed Sodom to the mountains, to save their lives, it is said, that his wife looked back from behind him, and she became a pillar of salt; and yet you see that neither her practice, nor the judgment of God that fell upon her for the same, would cause Lot to look behind him. I have sometimes wondered at Lot in this particular; his wife looked behind her, and died immediately, but let what would become of her, Lot would not so much as look behind him to see her. We do not read that he did so much as once look where she was, or what was become of her; his heart was indeed upon his journey, and well it might: there was the mountain before him, and the fire and brimstone behind him; his life lay at stake, and he had lost it if he had but looked behind him. Do thou so run: and in thy race remember Lot's wife, and remember her doom; and remember for what that doom did overtake her; and remember that God made her an example for all lazy runners, to the end of the world; and take heed thou fall not after the same example. But,

If this will not provoke thee, consider thus, 1. Thy soul is thy own soul, that is either to be saved or lost; thou shalt not lose my soul by thy laziness. It is thy own soul, thy own ease, thy own peace, thy own advantage or disadvantage. If it were my own that thou art desired to be good unto, methinks reason should move thee somewhat to pity it. But alas, it is thy own, thy own soul. "What shall it profit a man if he shall gain the whole world, and lose his own soul?" God's people wish well to the souls of others, and wilt not thou wish well to thy own? And if this will not provoke thee, then think.

Again, 2. If thou lose thy soul, it is thou also that must bear the blame. It made Cain stark mad to consider that he had not looked to his brother Abel's soul. How much more will it perplex thee to think, that thou hadst not a care of thy own? And if this will not provoke thee to bestir thyself, think again.

3. That, if thou wilt not run, the people of God are resolved to deal with thee even as Lot dealt with his wife, that is, leave thee behind them. It may be thou hast a father, mother, brother, etc., going post-haste to heaven, wouldst thou be willing to be left behind them? Surely no.

Again, 4. Will it not be a dishonor to thee to see the very boys and girls in the country to have more with than thyself? It may be the servants of some men, as the housekeeper, ploughman, scullion, etc., are more looking after heaven than their masters. I am apt to think, sometimes, that more servants than masters, that more tenants than landlords, will inherit the kingdom of heaven. But is not this a shame for them that are such? I am persuaded you scorn, that your servants should say that they are wiser than you in the things of this world; and yet I am bold to say, that many of them are wiser than you in the things of the world to come, which are of greater concernment.

Expostulation. Well, then, sinner, what sayest thou? Where is thy heart? Wilt thou run? Art thou resolved to strip? Or art thou not? Think quickly, man, it is not dallying in this matter. Confer not with flesh and blood; look up to heaven, and see how thou likest it; also to hell (of which thou mayest understand something in my book, called, A few sighs from hell; or, The groans of a damned soul, which I wish thee to read seriously over), and accordingly devote thyself. If thou dost not know the way, inquire at the word of God; if thou wantest company, cry for God's Spirit; if thou wantest encouragement, entertain the promises. But be sure thou begin betimes; get into the way, run apace, and hold out to the end; and the Lord give thee a prosperous journey. FAREWELL.

JOHN BUNYAN.
1628-1688.
"Pilgrim's Progress" has immortalized for posterity this most popular preacher of his time. Twelve years of his life were spent in jail, for preaching contrary to an order of the King, and there his most famous book was written.

JEAN BAPTISTE MASSILLON.
1663-1742.
This most famous preacher of France remained
through his long life a devout Roman Catholic.
His sermons are distinguished by their keen
penetration and their great emotional appeal.

X

JEAN BAPTISTE MASSILLON

1663–1742

AMONG French preachers, there can be no question that the highest place belongs to Jean Baptiste Massillon, who has been called " The Whitefield of France." He was born at Hyères, June 24, 1663; and lived and died in the Roman Catholic communion. While teaching theology at Meaux, he was called to Paris, and became the head of a seminary or training school for priests. In 1717 he was made Bishop of Clermont; and in 1742 he died. Although an able professor of theology and a faithful bishop, he found his fame as the most eloquent preacher of his generation. A historian of the pulpit, (Dr. H. C. Fish) has written of Massillon that " the peculiarities of his sermonizing are great clearness of thought, perfect sobriety of judgment, tender emotions, melting pathos, novelty of illustration, copiousness of language, and unerring taste and skill." Louis XIV, " le Grand Monarque," once said to him, " Father, I have heard many great orators in this chapel, and have been highly pleased with them, but whenever I hear you, I go away displeased with myself, for I see my own character." The sermon here given is one of his most celebrated, but great allowance must be made for the translation from the French into the English language.

THE SMALL NUMBER OF THE SAVED.

" And many lepers were in Israel in the time of Eliseus the prophet; and none of them was cleansed, saving Naaman the Syrian."—Luke, iv. 27.

EVERY day, my brethren, you continue to ask of us, whether the road to heaven is really so difficult, and the number of the saved really so small as we represent? To a question so often proposed, and still oftener resolved, our Saviour answers you here, that there were many widows in Israel afflicted with famine; but the widow of Sarepta was alone found worthy the succor of the prophet Elias; that the number of lepers was great in Israel in the time of the prophet Eliseus; and that Naaman was only cured by the man of God.

Were I here, my brethren, for the purpose of alarming, rather than instructing you, I had need only to recapitulate what in the holy writings we find dreadful with regard to this great truth; and, running over the history of the just, from age to age, show you that, in all times, the number of the saved has been very small. The family of Noah alone saved from the general flood; Abraham chosen from among men to be the sole depositary of the covenant with God; Joshua and Caleb the only two of six hundred thousand Hebrews who saw the Land of Promise; Job the only upright man in the land of Uz — Lot, in Sodom. To representations so alarming, would have succeeded the sayings of the prophets. In Isaiah you would see the elect as rare as the grapes which are found after the vintage, and have escaped the search of the gatherer; as rare as the blades which remain by chance in the field, and have escaped the scythe of the mower. The Evangelist would still have added new traits to the terrors of these images. I might have spoken to you of two roads — of which one is narrow, rugged, and the path of a very small number; the other broad, open, and strewed with flowers, and almost the general path of men: that everywhere, in the holy writings, the multitude is always spoken of as forming the party of the reprobate; while the saved, compared with the rest of mankind, form only a small flock, scarcely perceptible to the sight. I would have left you in fears with regard to your salvation; always cruel to those who have not renounced faith and every hope of being among the saved. But what would it serve to limit the fruits of this instruction to the single point of setting forth how few persons will be saved? Alas! I would make the danger known, without instructing you how to avoid it; I would allow you, with the prophet, the sword of the wrath of God suspended over your heads, without assisting you to escape the threatened blow; I would alarm but not instruct the sinner.

My intention is, therefore, to-day, to search for the cause of this small number, in our morals and manner of life. As every one flatters himself he will not be excluded, it is of importance to examine if his confidence be well founded. I wish not, in marking to you the causes which render salvation so rare, to make you generally conclude that few will be saved, but to bring you to ask yourselves if, living as you live, *you* can hope to be saved. Who am I? What am I doing for heaven? And what can be my hopes in eternity? I propose no other order in a matter of such importance. What are the causes which render salvation so rare? I mean to point out three principal causes, which is the only arrangement of this discourse. Art, and far-sought reasonings, would here be ill-timed. O attend, therefore, be ye whom ye may! No subject can be more worthy your attention, since it goes to inform you what may be the hopes of your eternal destiny.

Part I.— Few are saved, because in that number we can only comprehend two descriptions of persons:— either those who have been so happy as to preserve their innocence pure and undefiled, or those who, after having lost, have regained it by penitence. This is the first cause. There are only these two ways of salvation: heaven is only open to the innocent or to the penitent. Now, of which party are you? Are you innocent? Are you penitent?

Nothing unclean shall enter the kingdom of God. We must consequently carry there either an innocence unsullied, or an innocence regained. Now to die innocent, is a grace to which few souls can aspire: and to live penitent, is a mercy which the relaxed state of our morals renders equally rare. Who, indeed, will pretend to salvation by the claim of innocence? Where are the pure souls in whom sin has never dwelt, and who have preserved to the end the sacred treasure of grace confided to them by baptism, and which our Saviour will re-demand at the awful day of punishment?

In those happy days when the whole Church was still but an assembly of saints, it was very uncommon to find an instance of a believer, who, after having received the gifts of the Holy Spirit, and acknowledged Jesus Christ in the sacrament which regenerates us, fell back to his former irregularities of life. Ananias and Sapphira, were the only prevaricators in the Church of Jerusalem; that of Corinth had only one incestuous sinner. Church-penitence was then a remedy almost unknown; and scarcely was there found among these true Israelites one single leper whom they were obliged to drive from the holy altar, and separate from communion with his brethren. But, since that time the number of the upright diminishes, in proportion as that of believers increases. It would appear that the world, pretending now to have become almost generally Christian, has brought with it into the Church its corruptions and its maxims.

Alas! we all go astray, almost from the breast of our mothers! The first use which we make of our heart is a crime; our first desires are passions; and our reason only expands and increases on the wrecks of our innocence. The earth, says a prophet, is infected by the corruption of those who inhabit it: all have violated the laws, changed the ordinances, and broken the alliance which should have endured for ever: all commit sin, and scarcely is there one to be found who does the work of the Lord. Injustice, calumny, lying, treachery, adultery, and the blackest crimes have deluged the earth. The brother lays snares for his brother; the father is divided from his children; the husband from his wife: there is no tie which a vile interest does not sever. Good faith and probity are no longer virtues except among the simple people. Animosities are endless; reconciliations are feints, and never is a former enemy regarded as a brother: they tear, they devour each other. Assemblies are no longer but for the purpose of public and general censure. The purest virtue is no longer a protection from the malignity of tongues. Gaming is become either a trade, a fraud, or a fury. Repasts — those innocent ties of society — degenerate into excesses of which we dare not speak. Our age witnesses horrors with which our forefathers were unacquainted.

Behold, then, already one path of salvation shut to the generality of men. All have erred. Be ye whom ye may listen to me now, the time has been when sin reigned over you. Age may perhaps have calmed your passions, but what was your youth? Long and habitual infirmities may perhaps have disgusted you with the world; but what use did you formerly make of the vigor of health? A sudden inspiration of grace may have turned your heart, but do you not most fervently entreat that every moment prior to that inspiration may be effaced from the remembrance of the Lord.

But with what am I taking up time? We are all sinners, O my God! and Thou knowest our hearts! What we know of our errors, is, perhaps, in Thy sight, the most pardonable; and we all allow, that by innocence we have no claim to salvation. There remains, therefore, only one resource, which is penitence. After our shipwreck, say the saints, it is the timely plank which alone can conduct us into port; there is no other means of salvation for us. Be ye whom ye may, prince or subject, high or low, penitence alone can save you. Now permit me to ask:

Where are the penitent? You will find more, says a holy father, who have never fallen, than who, after their fall, have raised themselves by true repentance. This is a terrible saying; but do not let us carry things too far: the truth is sufficiently dreadful without adding new terrors to it by vain declamation.

Let us only examine as to whether the majority of us have a right, through penitence, to salvation. What is a penitent? According to Tertullian, a penitent is a believer who feels every moment his former unhappiness in forsaking and losing his God. One who has his guilt incessantly before his eyes; who finds everywhere the traces and remembrance of it.

A penitent is a man intrusted by God with judgment against himself; one who refuses himself the most innocent pleasures because he had formerly indulged in those the most criminal; one who puts up with the most necessary gratification with pain; one who regards his body as an enemy whom it is necessary to conquer — as an unclean vessel which must be purified — as an unfaithful debtor of whom it is proper to exact to the last farthing. A penitent regards himself as a criminal condemned to death, because he is no longer worthy of life. In the loss of riches or health, he sees only a withdrawal of favors that he had formerly abused: in the humiliations which happen to him, only the pains of his guilt: in the agonies with which he is racked, only the commencement of those punishments he has justly merited. Such is a penitent.

But I again ask you — Where, among us, are penitents of this description? Now look around you. I do not tell you to judge your brethren, but to examine what are the manners and morals of those who surround you. Nor do I speak of those open and avowed sinners who have thrown off even the appearance of virtue. I speak only of those who, like yourselves, live as most live, and whose actions present nothing to the public view particularly shameful or depraved. They are sinners and they admit it: you are not innocent, and you confess it. Now are they penitent? or are you? Age, avocation, more serious employments, may perhaps have checked the sallies of youth. Even the bitterness which the Almighty has made attendant on our passions, the deceits, the treacheries of the world, an injured fortune, with ruined constitution, may have cooled the ardor, and confined the irregular desires of your hearts. Crimes may have disgusted you even with sin itself — for passions gradually extinguish themselves. Time, and the

natural inconstancy of the heart will bring these about; yet, nevertheless, though detached from sin by incapability, you are no nearer
your God. According to the world you are become more prudent, more
regular, to a greater extent what it calls men of probity, more exact
in fulfilling your public or private duties. But you are not penitent.
You have ceased from your disorders, but you have not expiated them.
You are not converted: this great stroke, this grand operation on the
heart, which regenerates man, has not yet been felt by you. Nevertheless, this situation, so truly dangerous, does not alarm you. Sins
which have never been washed away by sincere repentance, and consequently never obliterated from the book of life, appear in your eyes
as no longer existing; and you will tranquilly leave this world in a
state of impenitence, so much the more dangerous as you will die without
being sensible of your danger.

What I say here, is not merely a rash expression, or an emotion
of zeal; nothing is more real, or more exactly true: it is the situation
of almost all men, even the wisest and most esteemed of the world.
The morality of the younger stages of life is always lax, if not licen-
tious. Age, disgust, and establishment for life, fix the heart, and
withdraw it from debauchery: but where are those who are converted?
Where are those who expiate their crimes by tears of sorrow and true
repentance? Where are those who, having begun as sinners, end as
penitents? Show me, in your manner of living, the smallest trace of
penitence! Are your graspings at wealth and power, your anxieties
to attain the favor of the great (and by these means an increase of employments and influence) — are these proofs of it? Would you wish to
reckon even your crimes as virtues?— that the sufferings of your ambition, pride, and avarice, should discharge you from an obligation which
they themselves have imposed? You are penitent to the world, but
are you so to Jesus Christ? The infirmities with which God afflicts you,
the enemies He raised up against you, the disgraces and losses with
which He tries you — do you receive them all as you ought, with humble
submission to His will? or, rather, far from finding in them occasions
of penitence, do you not turn them into the objects of new crimes? It
is the duty of an innocent soul to receive with submission the chastisements of the Almighty; to discharge, with courage, the painful duties
of the station allotted to him, and to be faithful to the laws of the Gospel — but do sinners owe nothing beyond this? And yet they pretend
to salvation! Upon what claim? To say that you are innocent before

God, your own consciences will witness against you. To endeavor to persuade yourselves that you are penitent, you dare not; and you would condemn yourselves by your own mouths. Upon *what,* then, dost thou depend, O man! who thus livest so tranquil?

And what renders it still more dreadful is that, acting in this manner you only follow the current; your morals are the morals of well-nigh all men. You may, perhaps, be acquainted with some still more guilty (for I suppose you too have still remaining some sentiments of religion, and regard for your salvation), but do you know any real penitents? I am afraid we must search the deserts and solitudes for them. You possibly may mention, among persons of rank and worldly custom, a small number whose morals and mode of life, more austere and guarded than the generality, attract the attention, and very likely the censure of the public. But all the rest walk in the uniform path. I see clearly that every one comforts himself by the example of his neighbor: that, in that point, children succeed to the false security of their fathers; that none live innocent, that none die penitent: I see it, and I cry, O God! if Thou hast not deceived us; if all Thou hast told us with regard to the road to eternal life shall be strictly fulfilled, if the number of those who must perish shall not influence Thee to abate from the severity of Thy laws — what will become of that immense multitude of creatures which every hour disappears from the face of the earth? Where are our friends, our relations who have gone before us? and what is their lot in the eternal regions of the dead? What shall we ourselves become?

When formerly a prophet complained to the Lord that all Israel had forsaken His protection, He replied that seven thousand still remained who had not bowed the knee to Baal. Behold the number of pure and faithful souls which a whole kingdom then contained! But couldst Thou still, O my God! comfort the anguish of Thy servants to-day by the same assurance! I know that Thine eye discerns still some upright among us; that the priesthood has still its Phineases; the magistracy its Samuels; the sword its Joshuas; the court its Daniels, its Esthers, and its Davids: for the world only exists for Thy chosen, and all would perish were the number accomplished. But those happy remnants of the children of Israel who shall inherit salvation — what are they, compared to the grains of sand in the sea; I mean, to that number of sinners who fight for their own destruction? Come you after this, my brethren, to inquire if it be true that few shall be saved?

10

Thou hast said it, O, my God! and hence it is a truth which shall endure forever.

But, even admitting that the Almighty had not spoken thus, I would wish, in the second place, to review, for an instant, what passes among men:— the laws by which they are governed; the maxims by which the multitude is regulated: this is the second cause of the paucity of the saved; and, properly speaking, is only a development of the first — the force of habit and customs.

Part II.— Few people are saved, because the maxims most universally received in all countries, and upon which depend, in general, the morals of the multitude, are incompatible with salvation. The rules laid down, approved, and authorized by the world with regard to the application of wealth, the love of glory, Christian moderation, and the duties of offices and conditions, are directly opposed to those of the evangelists, and consequently can lead only to death. I shall not, at present, enter into a detail too extended for a discourse, and too little serious, perhaps, for Christians.

I need not tell you that this is an established custom in the world, to allow the liberty of proportioning expenses to rank and wealth; and, provided, it is a patrimony we inherit from our ancestors, we may distinguish ourselves by the use of it, without restraint to our luxury, or without regard, in our profusion, to anything but our pride and caprice.

But Christian moderation has its rules. We are not the absolute masters of our riches; nor are we entitled to abuse what the Almighty has bestowed upon us for better purposes. Above all, while thousands of unfortunate wretches languish in poverty, whatever we make use of beyond the wants and necessary expenses of our station, is an inhumanity and a theft from the poor. "These are refinements of devotion," they say. "And, in matters of expense and profusion, nothing is excessive or blamable, according to the world, but what may tend to derange the fortune." I need not tell you that it is an approved custom to decide our lots, and to regulate our choice of professions or situations in life, by the order of our birth, or the interests of fortune. But, O my God! does the ministry of Thy Gospel derive its source from the worldly considerations of a carnal birth? "We can not fix everything," says the world, "and it would be melancholy to see persons of rank and birth in avocations unworthy of their dignity. If born to a name distinguished in the world, you must get forward by dint of intrigue, meanness, and expense: make fortune your idol: that ambition, however much condemned by the laws of the Gospel, is only a sentiment worthy your name and birth: you are of a sex and rank which introduce you to the gayeties of the world: you can not but do as others do: you must frequent all the public places, where those of your age and rank assemble: enter into the same pleasures: pass your days in the same frivolities, and expose yourself to the same dangers: these are the received maxims, and you are not made to reform them." *Such is the doctrine of the world!*

Now, permit me to ask you here, who confirms you in these ways? By what rule are they justified to your mind? Who authorizes you in this dissipation, which is neither agreeable to the title you have received by baptism, nor perhaps to those you hold from your ancestors? Who authorizes those public pleasures, which you only think innocent because your soul, already too familiarized with sin, feels no longer the dangerous impressions or tendency of them? Who authorizes you to lead an effeminate and sensual life, without virtue, sufferance, or any religious exercise?— to live like a stranger in the midst of your own family, disdaining to inform yourself with regard to the morals of those dependent upon you?— through an affected state, to be ignorant whether they believe in the same God; whether they fulfill the duties of the religion you profess? Who authorizes you in maxims so little Christian? Is it the Gospel of Jesus Christ? Is it the doctrine of the Apostles and saints? For surely some rule is necessary to assure us that we are in safety. What is yours? *" Custom:"* *that* is the only reply you can make! " We see none around us but what conduct themselves in the same way, and by the same rule. Entering into the world, we find the manners already established: our fathers lived thus, and from them we copy our customs: the wisest conform to them: an individual can not be wiser than the whole world, and must not pretend to make himself singular, by acting contrary to the general voice." Such, my brethren, are your only comforters against all the terrors of religion! None act up to the law. The public example is the only guarantee of our morals. We never reflect that, as the Holy Spirit says, the laws of the people are vain: that our Saviour has left us rules, in which neither times, ages, nor customs, can ever authorize the smallest change: that the heavens and the earth shall pass away, that customs and manners shall change, but that the Divine laws will everlastingly be the same.

We content ourselves with looking around us. We do not reflect that what, at present, we call *custom,* would, in former times, before the morals of Christians became degenerated, have been regarded as monstrous singularities; and, if corruption has gained since that period, these vices, though they have lost their singularity, have not lost their guilt. We do not reflect that we shall be judged by the Gospel, and not by custom; by the examples of the holy, and not by men's opinions;— that the habits, which are only established among believers by the relaxation of faith, are abuses we are to lament, not examples we are to follow;— that, in changing the manners, they have not changed our duties;— that the common and general example which authorizes them, only proves that virtue is rare, but not that profligacy is permitted;— in a word, that piety and a real Christian life are too repulsive to our depraved nature to be practiced by the majority of men.

Come now, and say that you only do as others do. It is exactly by that you condemn yourselves. What! the most terrible certainty of your condemnation shall become the only motive for your confidence! Which, according to the Scriptures, is the road that conducts to death? Is it not that which the majority pursue? Which is the party of the reprobate? Is it not the multitude? You do nothing but what others do! But thus, in the time of Noah, perished all who were buried under the waters of the deluge: all who, in the time of Nebuchadnezzar, prostrated themselves before the golden calf: all who, in the time of Elijah, bowed the knee to Baal; all who, in the time of Eleazer, abandoned the law of their fathers. You only do what others do! But that is precisely what the Scriptures forbid. "Do not," say they, "conform yourselves to this corrupted age." Now, the corrupted age means not the small number of the just, whom you endeavor not to imitate; it means the multitude whom you follow. You only do what others do! You will consequently experience the same lot. " Misery to thee " (cried formerly St. Augustine), " fatal torrent of human customs! Wilt thou never suspend thy course! Wilt thou, to the end, draw the children of Adam into thine immense and terrible abyss! "

In place of saying to ourselves, " What are my hopes? " In the Church of Christ there are two roads; one broad and open, by which almost the whole world passes, and which leads to death; the other narrow, where few indeed enter, and which conducts to life eternal; in which of these am I? Are my morals those which are common to persons of my rank, age, and situation in life? Am I with the great number? Then I am not in the right path. I am losing myself. The great number in every station is not the party saved," not far from reasoning in *this* manner, we say to ourselves, " I am not in a worse state than others! Those of my rank and age live as I do! Why should I not live like them?" *Why,* my dear hearers? For that very reason! The general mode of living can not be that of a Christian life. In all ages, the holy have been remarkable and singular men. Their manners were always different from those of the world; and they have only been saints because their lives had no similarity to those of the rest of mankind. In the time of Esdras, in spite of the defense against it, the custom prevailed of intermarrying with strange women: this abuse became general: the priests and the people no longer made any scruple of it. But what did this holy restorer of the law? Did he follow the example of his brethren? Did he believe that guilt, in becoming general, became more legitimate? No: he recalled the people to a sense of the abuse. He took the book of the law in his hand, and explained it to the affrighted people — corrected the custom by the truth.

Follow, from age to age, the history of the just; and see if Lot conformed himself to the habits of Sodom, or if nothing distinguished him from the other inhabitants; if Abraham lived like the rest of his age; if Job resembled the other princes of his nation; if Esther conducted herself, in the court of Ahasuerus like the other women of that prince; if many widows in Israel resembled Judith; if, among the children of the captivity, it is not said of Tobias alone that he copied not the conduct of his brethren, and that he even fled from the danger of their commerce and society. See, if in those happy ages, when Christians were all saints, they did not shine like stars in the midst of the corrupted nations; and if they served not as a spectacle to angels and men, by the singularity of their lives and manners. If the pagans did not reproach them for their retirement, and shunning of all public theatres, places, and pleasures. If they did not complain that the Christians affected to distinguish themselves in everything from their fellow-citizens; to form a separate people in the midst of the people; to have their particular laws and customs; and if a man from their side embraced the party of the Christians, they did not consider him as forever lost to their pleasures, assemblies and customs. In a word, see, if in all ages the saints whose lives and actions have been transmitted down to us, have resembled the rest of mankind.

You will perhaps tell us that all these are singularities and exceptions, rather than rules which the world is obliged to follow. They are exceptions, it is true: but the reason is, that the general rule is to reject salvation; that a religious and pious soul in the midst of the world is always a singularity approaching to a miracle. The whole world, you say, is not obliged to follow these examples. But is not piety alike the duty of all? To be saved, must we not be holy? Must heaven, with difficulty and sufferance, be gained by some, and by others with ease? Have you any other Gospel to follow? Any other duties to fulfill? Any other promises to hope for, than those of the Holy Bible? Ah! since there was another way more easy to arrive at salvation, wherefore — ye pious Christians, who at this moment enjoy the kingdom gained with toil, and at the expense of your blood — did ye leave us examples so dangerous and vain? Wherefore have ye opened for us a road, rugged, disagreeable, and calculated to repress our ardor, seeing there was another you could have pointed out more easy, and more likely to attract us, by facilitating our progress? Great God! how little does mankind consult reason in the point of eternal salvation!

Will you console yourselves, after this, with the *multitude,* as if the greatness of the *number* could render the guilt unpunished, and the Almighty durst not condemn all those who live like you? What are all creatures in the sight of God? Did the multitude of the guilty prevent Him from destroying all flesh at the deluge? from making fire from heaven descend upon the five iniquitous cities? from burying, in the waters of the Red Sea, Pharoah and all his army? from striking with death all who murmured in the desert? Ah! the kings of the earth may reckon upon the number of the guilty, because the punishment becomes impossible, or at least difficult, when the fault is become general. But God, who, as Job says, wipes the impious from the face of the earth, as one wipes the dust from off a garment — God, in whose sight all people and nations are as if they were not — numbers not the guilty. He has regard only to the crimes; and all that the weak and miserable sinner can expect from his unhappy accomplices, is to have them as companions in his misery.

So few are saved, because the maxims most universally adopted are maxims of sin. So few are saved, because the maxims and duties most universally unknown, or rejected, are those most indispensable to salvation. This is the last reflection, which is indeed nothing more than the proof and the development of the former ones.

What are the engagements of the holy vocation to which we have all been called? The solemn promises of baptism. What have we promised at baptism? To renounce the world, the devil, and the flesh. These are our vows. This is the situation of the Christian. These are the essential conditions of our covenant with God, by which eternal life has been promised to us. These truths appear familiar, and destined for the common people; but it is a mistake. Nothing can be more sublime; and, alas! nothing is more generally unknown! It is in the courts of kings, and to the princes of the earth, that without ceasing we ought to announce them. Alas! they are well instructed in all the affairs of the world, while the first principles of Christian morality are frequently more unknown to them than to humble and simple hearts!

At your baptism, then, you have renounced *the world*. It is a promise you have made to God, before the holy altar; the Church has been the guaranty and depository of it; and you have only been admitted into the number of believers, and marked with the indefeasible seal of salvation, upon the faith that you have sworn to the Lord, to love neither the world, nor what the world loves. Had you then answered, what you now repeat every day, that you find not the world so black and pernicious as we say; that, after all, it may innocently be loved; and that we only decry it so much because we do not know it; and since you are to live in the world you wish to live like those who are in it — had you answered thus, the Church would not have received you into its bosom; would not have connected you with the hope of Christians, nor joined you in communion with those who have overcome the world. She would have advised you to go and live with those unbelievers who know not our Saviour. For this reason it was, that in former ages, those of the Catechumen, who could not prevail upon themselves to renounce the world and its pleasures, put off their baptism till death; and durst not approach the holy altar, to contract, by the sacrament, which regenerates us, engagements of which they knew the importance and sanctity; and to fulfill which they felt themselves still unqualified.

You are therefore required, by the most sacred of all vows, to hate the world; that is to say, not to conform yourselves to it. If you love it, if you follow its pleasures and customs, you are not only, as St. John says, the enemy of God, but you likewise renounce the faith given in baptism; you abjure the gospel of Jesus Christ; you are an apostate from religion, and trample under foot the most sacred and irrevocable vows that man can make.

Now, what is this world which you ought to hate? I have only to answer that it is the one you love. You will never mistake it by this mark. This world is a society of sinners, whose desires, fears, hopes, cares, projects, joys, and chagrins, no longer turn but upon the successes or misfortunes of this life. This world is an assemblage of people who look upon the earth as their country; the time to come as an exilement; the promises of faith as a dream; and death as the greatest of all misfortunes. This world is a temporal kingdom, where our Saviour is unknown; where those acquainted with His name, glorify Him as their Lord, hate His maxims, despise His followers, and neglect or insult Him in His sacraments and worship. In a word, to give a proper idea at once of this world, it is the vast multitude. Behold the world which you ought to shun, hate, and war against by your example.

Now, is this your situation in regard to the world? Are its pleasures a fatigue to you? Do its accesses afflict you? Do you regret the length of your pilgrimage here? Or on the contrary, are not its laws your laws; its maxims your maxims? What it condemns, do you not condemn? What it approves do you not approve? And should it happen, that you alone were left upon the earth, may we not say that the corrupt world would be revived in you; and that you would leave an exact model of it to your posterity? When I say you, I mean, and I address myself to almost all men.

Where are those who sincerely renounce the pleasures, habits, maxims, and hopes of this world? We find many who complain of it, and accuse it of injustice, ingratitude, and caprice; who speak warmly of its abuses and errors. But in decrying, they continue to love and follow it; they can not bring themselves to do without it. In complaining of its injustice, they are only piqued at it, they are not undeceived. They feel its hard treatment, but they are unacquainted with its dangers. They censure, but where are those who hate it? And now my brethren, you may judge if many can have a claim to salvation.

In the second place, you have renounced *the flesh* at your baptism; that is to say, you are engaged not to live according to the sensual appetites; to regard even indolence and effeminacy as crimes; not to flatter the corrupt desires of the flesh; but to chastise, crush, and crucify it. This is not an acquired perfection; it is a vow: It is the first of all duties; the character of a true Christian and inseparable from faith. In a word, you have anathematized Satan and all his works. And what are his works? That which composes almost the thread and end of your life; pomp, pleasure, luxury, and dissipation; lying, of which he is the father; pride, of which he is the model; jealousy and contrition, of which he is the artisan.

But I ask you, where are those who have not withdrawn the anathema they had pronounced against Satan? Now, consequently (to mention it as we go along), behold many of the questions answered! You continually demand of us, if theaters, and other public places of amusement, be innocent recreations for Christians? In return, I have only one question to ask you: Are they the works of Satan or of Jesus Christ? for there can be no medium in religion. I do not mean to say that there are not many recreations and amusements which may be termed indifferent. But the most indifferent pleasures which religion allows, and which the weakness of our nature renders even necessary, belong, in one sense, to Jesus Christ, by the facility with which they ought to enable us to apply ourselves to more holy and more serious duties. Everything we do, everything we rejoice or weep at, ought to be of such a nature as to have a connection with Jesus Christ, and to be done for his glory.

Now, upon this principle,— the most incontestable, and most universally allowed in Christian morality — you have only to decide whether you can connect the glory of Jesus Christ with the pleasures of a theater. Can our Saviour have any part in such a species of recreation? And before you enter them, can you, with confidence, declare to Him that, in so doing, you only propose His glory, and to enjoy the satisfaction of pleasing Him! *What!* the theaters, such as they are at present, still more criminal by the public licentiousness of those unfortunate creatures who appear on them than by the impure and passionate scenes they represent — the theaters works of *Jesus Christ!* Jesus Christ would animate a mouth, from whence are to proceed lascivious words, adapted to corrupt the heart! But these blasphemies strike me with horror. Jesus Christ would preside in assemblies of sin, where everything we hear weakens His doctrines! where the poison enters into the soul through all the senses! where every art is employed to inspire, awaken, and justify the passions He condemns! Now, says Tertullian, if they are not the works of Jesus Christ they must be the works of Satan. Every Christian, therefore, ought to abstain from them. When he partakes of them, he violates the vows of baptism. However innocent he may flatter himself to be, in bringing from these places an untainted heart, it is sullied by being there; since by his presence alone he has participated in the works of Satan, which he had renounced at baptism, and violated the most sacred promises he had made to Jesus Christ and to His Church.

These, my brethren, as I have already told you, are not merely advices and pious arts; they are the most essential of our obligations. But, alas! who fulfills them? Who even knows them? Ah! my brethren, did you know how far the title you bear, of Christian, engages you; could you comprehend the sanctity of your state; the hatred of the world, of yourself, and of everything which is not of God, that it enjoins that Gospel life, that constant watching, that guard over the passions, in a word, that conformity with Jesus Christ crucified, which it exacts of you — could you comprehend it, could you remember that as you ought to love God with all your heart, and all your strength, a single desire that has not connection with Him defiles you — you would appear a monster in your own sight. How! you would exclaim. Duties so holy, and morals so profane! A vigilance so continual, and a life so careless and dissipated! A love of God so pure, so complete, so universal, and a heart the continual prey of a thousand impulses, either foreign or criminal! If thus it is, who, O my God! will be entitled to salvation? Few indeed, I fear, my dear hearers! At least it will not be *you* (unless a change takes place) nor those who resemble you; it will not be the multitude!

Who *shall* be saved? Those who work out their salvation with fear and trembling; who live in the world without indulging in its vices. Who shall be saved? That Christian woman, who, shut up in the circle of her domestic duties, rears up her children in faith and in piety; divides her heart only between her Saviour and her husband; is adorned with delicacy and modesty; sits not down in the assemblies of vanity; makes not a law of the ridiculous customs of the world, but regulates those customs by the law of God; and makes virtue appear more amiable by her rank and her example. Who shall be saved? That believer, who, in the relaxation of modern times, imitates the manners of the first Christians — whose hands are clean, and his heart pure — who is watchful — who hath not lift up his soul to vanity — but who, in the midst of the dangers of the great world, continually applies himself to purify it; just — who swears not deceitfully against his neighbor, nor is indebted to fraudulent ways for the innocent aggrandizement of his fortune; generous, who with benefits repays the enemy who sought his ruin; sincere — who sacrifices not the truth to a vile interest, and knows not the part of rendering himself agreeable, by betraying his conscience; charitable — who makes his house and interest the refuge of his fellow-creatures, and himself the consolation of the afflicted; regards his wealth as the property of the poor; humble in affliction — a Christian under injuries, and penitent even in prosperity. *Who* will merit salvation? You, my dear hearer, if you will follow these examples; for such are the souls to be saved. Now these assuredly do not form the greatest number. While you continue, therefore, to live like the multitude, it is a striking proof that you disregard your salvation.

These, my brethren, are truths which should make us tremble! nor are they those vague ones which are told to all men, and which none apply to themselves. Perhaps there is not in this assembly an individual who may not say of himself, " I live like the great number; like those of my rank, age, and situation; I am lost, should I die in this path." Now, can anything be more capable of alarming a soul, in whom some remains of care for his salvation still exist? It is the multitude, nevertheless, who tremble not. There is only a small number of the just who work out severally their salvation, with fear and trembling. All the rest are tranquil. After having lived with the multitude, they flatter themselves they shall be particularized at death. Every one augurs favorably for himself, and vainly imagines that he shall be an exception.

On this account it is, my brethren, that I confine myself to you who are now here assembled. I include not the rest of men; but consider you as alone existing on the earth. The idea which fills and terrifies me, is this — I figure to myself the present as your last hour, and the end of the world! the heavens opening above your heads — the Saviour, in all His glory, about to appear in the midst of His temple — you only assembled here as trembling criminals, to wait His coming, and hear the sentence, either of life eternal, or everlasting death! for it is vain to flatter yourselves that you shall die more innocent than you are at this hour. All those desires of change with which you are amused, will continue to amuse you till death arrives. The experience of all ages proves it. The only difference you have to expect, will most likely be only a larger balance against you than what you would have to answer for now; and from what would be your destiny, were you to be judged in this moment, you may almost decide upon what it will be at death. Now, I ask you — and, connecting my own lot with yours, I ask it with dread — were Jesus Christ to appear in this temple, in the midst of this assembly, to judge us, to make the awful separation between the sheep and the goats, do you believe that the most of us would be placed at His right hand? Do you believe that the number would at least be equal? Do you believe that there would even be found *ten* upright and faithful servants of the Lord, when formerly *five cities* could not furnish that number? I ask you! You know not! I know it not! Thou alone, O my God! knowest who belong to Thee.

But if we know not who belong to Him, at least we know that *sinners* do not. Now, who are the just and faithful assembled here at present? Titles and dignities avail nothing; you are stripped of all these in the presence of your Saviour! Who are they? Many sinners who wish not to be converted; many more who wish, but always put it off; many others who are only converted in appearance, and again fall back to their former course; in a word, a great number, who flatter themselves they have no occasion for conversion. This is the party of the reprobate! Ah! my brethren, cut off from this assembly these four classes of sinners, for they will be cut off at the great day! And now stand forth ye righteous:— where are ye? O God, where are Thine elect! What remains as Thy portion!

My brethren, our ruin is almost certain! Yet we think not of it! If in this terrible separation, which will one day take place; there should be but *one* sinner in the assembly on the side of the reprobate, and a voice from heaven should assure us of it, without particularizing him, who of us would not tremble, lest *he* should be the unfortunate and devoted wretch? Who of us would not immediately apply to his conscience, to examine if its crimes merited not this punishment? Who of us, seized with dread, would not demand of our Saviour, as did the Apostles, crying out, "Lord, is it I?" And should a small respite be allowed to our prayers, who of us would not use every effort, by tears, supplication, and sincere repentance, to avert the misfortune?

Are we in our senses, my dear hearers? Perhaps among all who listen to me now, ten righteous ones would not be found. It may be fewer still. What do I perceive, O my God! I dare not, with a fixed eye, regard the depths of Thy judgments and justice! Not more than *one,* perhaps, would be found among us all! And this danger affects you not, my dear hearer! You persuade yourself that in this great number who shall perish, you will be the happy individual! You, who have less reason, perhaps, than any other to believe it! You, upon whom alone the sentence of death should fall, were only one of all who hear me to suffer! Great God! how little are the terrors of Thy law known to the world? In all ages, the just have shuddered with dread, in reflecting on the severity and extent of Thy judgments, touching the destinies of men! Alas! what are they laying up in store for the sons of men!

But what are we to conclude from these awful truths? That all must despair of salvation? God forbid! The impious alone, to quiet his own feelings in his debaucheries, endeavors to persuade himself that all men shall perish as well as he. This idea ought not to be the fruit of the present discourse. It is intended to undeceive you with regard to the general error, that any one may do whatever is done by others. To convince you that, in order to merit salvation, you must distinguish yourself from the rest; that in the midst of the world you are to live for God's glory, and not follow after the multitude.

When the Jews were led in captivity from Judea to Babylon, a little before they quitted their own country, the prophet Jeremiah, whom the Lord had forbidden to leave Jerusalem, spoke thus to them: "Children of Israel, when you shall arrive at Babylon, you will behold the inhabitants of that country, who carry upon their shoulders gods of silver and gold. All the people will prostrate themselves, and adore them. But you, far from allowing yourselves, by these examples, to be led to impiety, say to yourselves in secret, It is Thou, O Lord! whom we ought to adore."

Let me now finish, by addressing to you the same words.

At your departure from this temple, you go to enter into another Babylon. You go to see the idols of gold and silver, before which all men prostrate themselves. You go to regain the vain objects of human passions, wealth, glory, and pleasure, which are the gods of this world and which almost all men adore. You will see those abuses which all the world permits, those errors which custom authorizes, and those debaucheries, which an infamous fashion has almost constituted as laws. Then, my dear hearer, if you wish to be of the small number of true Israelites, say, in the secrecy of your heart, "It is Thou alone, O my

God! whom we ought to adore. I wish not to have connection with a people which know Thee not; I will have no other law than Thy holy law; the gods which this foolish multitude adores, are not gods: they are the work of the hands of men; they will perish with them: Thou alone, O my God! are immortal; and Thou alone deservest to be adored. The customs of Babylon have no connection with the holy laws of Jerusalem. I will continue to worship Thee with that small number of the children of Abraham which still, in the midst of an infidel nation, composes Thy people; with them I will turn all my desires toward the holy Zion. The singularity of my manners will be regarded as a weakness; but blessed weakness, O my God! which will give me strength to resist the torrent of customs, and the seduction of example. Thou wilt be my God in the midst of Babylon, as Thou wilt one day be in Jerusalem above!"

"Ah! the time of the captivity will at last expire. Thou wilt call to Thy remembrance Abraham and David. Thou wilt deliver Thy people. Thou wilt transport us to the holy city. Then wilt Thou alone reign over Israel, and over the nations which at present know Thee not. All being destroyed, all the empires of the earth, all the monuments of human pride annihilated, and Thou alone remaining eternal, we then shall know that Thou art the Lord of hosts, and the only God to be adored.

Behold the fruit which you ought to reap from this discourse! Live apart. Think, without ceasing, that the great number work their own destruction. Regard as nothing all customs of the earth, unless authorized by the law of God, and remember, that holy men in all ages have been looked upon as a peculiar people.

It is thus that, after distinguishing yourselves from the sinful on earth, you will be gloriously distinguished from them in eternity!

Now, to God the Father, etc.

XI

JONATHAN EDWARDS

1703–1758

"I CONSIDER Jonathan Edwards the greatest of the sons of men. He ranks with the brightest luminaries of the Christian Church, not excluding any country or any age since the apostolic:" such is the tribute paid by the eminent Robert Hall to one of America's ablest divines and metaphysicians. Jonathan Edwards was born October 5th, 1703, at Windsor, Connecticut, where his father ministered for sixty years. As a child, he was a scholar and logician.. He graduated from Yale College at seventeen, was licensed to preach two years later, and in 1727 was installed in the Congregational Church, Northampton. His pastorate of twenty-four years, at first blessed by a thrilling revival of religion, ended in his expulsion by his congregation. His offences were too faithful rebukes of the sins of his people, and the exclusion of unconverted people from the Lord's Supper. Six years of his life were now given to miserably paid missionary labors among the Indians at Stockbridge, Massachusetts. These years gave him the opportunity of writing his "Freedom of the Will," perhaps the greatest work on its theme ever published. He was at last recognized in being chosen to the presidency of Princeton College, but died a few months after of small-pox, March 22d, 1758. His last words were: "Trust in God, and ye need not fear." His most powerful Sermons appeal to the conscience by the terrors of condemnation awaiting the unregenerate.

WRATH UPON THE WICKED TO THE UTTERMOST.

"To fill up their sins alway; for the wrath is come upon them to the uttermost."— 1 Thess. ii. 16.

IN verse 14 the apostle commends the Christian Thessalonians, that they became the followers of the churches of God in Judea, both in faith and in sufferings; in *faith,* in that they received the word, not as the word of man, but as it is in truth the word of God: in *sufferings,* in that they had suffered like things of their own countrymen, as *they* had of the Jews. Upon which the apostle sets forth the persecuting, cruel, and perverse wickedness of that people, " who both killed the Lord Jesus and their own prophets, and have," says he, " persecuted us; and they please not God, and are contrary to all men, forbidding us to speak to the Gentiles, that they might be saved." Then come in the words of the text: " To fill up their sins always; for the wrath is come upon them to the uttermost."

In these words we may observe two things:

1. To what effect was the heinous wickedness and obstinacy of the Jews, viz. *to fill up their sins.* God hath set bounds to every man's wickedness; he suffers men to live, and to go on in sin, till they have filled up their measure, and then cuts them off. To this effect was the wickedness and obstinacy of the Jews: they were exceedingly wicked, and thereby filled up the measure of their sins a great pace. And the reason why they were permitted to be so obstinate under the preaching and miracles of Christ, and of the apostles, and under all the means used with them, was that they might fill up the measure of their sins. This is agreeable to what Christ said, Matt. xxiii. 31, 32. " Wherefore ye be witnesses unto yourselves, that ye are the children of them which killed the prophets. Fill ye up then the measure of your fathers."

2. The punishment of their wickedness: " The wrath is come upon them to the uttermost." There is a connection between the measure of men's sin, and the measure of punishment. When they have filled up the measure of their sin, then is filled up the measure of God's wrath.

The degree of their punishment, is the *uttermost degree.* This may respect both a national and personal punishment. If we take it as a *national* punishment, a little after the time when the epistle was written, wrath came upon the nation of the Jews to the uttermost, in their terrible destruction by the Romans; when, as Christ said, " was great tribulation, such as never was since the beginning of the world to that time," Matt. xxiv. 21. That nation had before suffered many of the fruits of divine wrath for their sins; but this was beyond all, this was their highest degree of punishment as a nation. If we take it as a *personal* punishment, then it respects their punishment in hell. God often punishes men very dreadfully in this world; but in hell " wrath comes on them to the *uttermost.*"

By this expression is also denoted the *certainty* of this punishment. For though the punishment was then future, yet it is spoken of as present: "The wrath *is* come upon them to the uttermost." It was as certain as if it had already taken place. God, who knows all things, speaks of things that are not as though they were; for things present and things future are equally certain with him. It also denotes the *near approach* of it. The wrath is *come;* i. e. it is just at hand; it is at the door; as it proved with respect to that nation; their terrible destruction by the Romans was soon after the apostle wrote this epistle.

DOCTRINE. When those that continue in sin shall have filled up the measure of their sin, then wrath will come upon them to the uttermost.

I. There is a *certain measure* that God hath set to the sin of every wicked man. God says concerning the sin of man, as he says to the raging waves of the sea, Hitherto shalt thou come, and no farther. The measure of some is much greater than of others. Some reprobates commit but a little sin in comparison with others, and so are to endure proportionably a smaller punishment. There are many vessels of wrath; but some are smaller, and others greater vessels; some will contain comparatively but little wrath, others a greater measure of it. Sometimes, when we see men go to dreadful lengths, and become very heinously wicked, we are ready to wonder that God lets them alone. He sees them go on in such audacious wickedness, and keeps silence, nor does anything to interrupt them, but they go smoothly on, and meet with no hurt. But sometimes the reason why God lets them alone is, because they have not filled up the measure of their sins. When they live in dreadful wickedness, they are but filling up the measure which God hath *limited* for them. This is sometimes the reason why God suffers very wicked men to live so long; because their iniquity is not full: Gen. xv. 16. "The iniquity of the Amorites is not yet full." For this reason also God sometimes suffers them to live in prosperity. Their prosperity is a snare to them, and an occasion of their sinning a great deal more. Wherefore God suffers them to have such a snare, because he suffers them to fill up a larger measure. So, for this cause, he sometimes suffers them to live under great light, and great means and advantages, at the same time to neglect and misimprove all. Every one shall live till he hath filled up his measure.

II. While men continue in sin, they are filling the measure set them. This is the work in which they spend their whole lives; they begin in their childhood; and, if they live to grow old in sin, they still go on with this work. It is the work with which every day is filled up. They may alter their business in other respects; they may sometimes be about one thing, and sometimes about another; but they never change from this work of filling up the measure of their sins. Whatever they put their hands to, they are still employed in this work. This is the first thing that they set themselves about when they awake in the morning, and the last thing they do at night. They are all the while treasuring up wrath against the day of wrath, and the revelation of the righteous judgment of God. It is a gross mistake of some natural men, who think that when they read and pray, they do not add to their sins; but, on the contrary, think they diminish their guilt by these exercises. They think, that instead of adding to their sins, they do something to satisfy for their past offences; but instead of that, they do but add to the measure by their best prayers, and by those services with which they themselves are most pleased.

III. When once the measure of their sins is filled up, then wrath will come upon them to the uttermost. God will then wait no longer upon them. Wicked men think that God is altogether such an one as themselves, because, when they commit such wickedness, he keeps silence. "Because judgment against an evil work is not executed speedily, therefore the heart of the children of men is fully set in them to do evil." But when once they shall have filled up the measure of their sins, judgment will be executed; God will not bear with them any longer. Now is the day of grace, and the day of patience, which they spend in filling up their sins; but when their sins shall be full, then will come the day of wrath, the day of the fierce anger of God.— God often executes his wrath on ungodly men in a less degree, in this world. He sometimes brings afflictions upon them, and that in wrath. Sometimes he expresses his wrath in very sore judgments; sometimes he appears in a terrible manner, not only outwardly, but also in the inward expressions of it on their consciences. Some, before they died, have had the wrath of God inflicted on their souls in degrees that have been intolerable. But these things are only forerunners of their punishment, only slight foretastes of wrath. God never stirs up all his wrath against wicked men while in this world; but when once wicked men shall have filled up the measure of their sins, then wrath will come upon them to the uttermost; and that in the following respects:

1. Wrath will come upon them without any *restraint* or moderation

in the degree of it. God doth always lay, as it were, a restraint upon himself; he doth not stir up his wrath; he stays his rough wind in the day of his east wind; he lets not his arm light down on wicked men with its full weight. But when sinners shall have filled up the measure of their sins, there will be no caution, no restraint. His rough wind will not be stayed nor moderated. The wrath of God will be poured out like fire. He will come forth, not only in anger, but in the fierceness of his anger; he will execute wrath with power, so as to show what his wrath is, and make his power known. There will be nothing to alleviate his wrath; his heavy wrath will lie on them, without anything to lighten the burthen, or to keep off, in any measure, the full weight of it from pressing the soul. His eye will not spare, neither will he regard the sinner's cries and lamentations, however loud and bitter. Then shall wicked men know that God is the Lord; they shall know how great that majesty is which they have despised, and how dreadful that threatened wrath is which they have so little regarded. Then shall come on wicked men that punishment which they deserve. God will exact of them the uttermost farthing. Their iniquities are marked before him; they are all written in his book; and in the future world he will reckon with them, and they must pay all the debt. Their sins are laid up in store with God; they are sealed up among his treasures; and them he will recompense, even recompense into their bosoms. The consummate degree of punishment will not be executed till the day of judgment; but the wicked are sealed over to this consummate punishment immediately after death; they are cast into hell, and there bound in chains of darkness to the judgment of the great day; and they know that the highest degree of punishment is coming upon them. Final wrath will be executed without any mixture; all mercy, all enjoyments will be taken away. God sometimes expresses his wrath in this world; but here good things and evil are mixed together; in the future there will be only evil things.

2. Wrath will then be executed without any *merciful* circumstances. The judgments which God executes on ungodly men in this world, are attended with many merciful circumstances. There is much patience and long-suffering, together with judgments; judgments are joined with continuance of opportunity to seek mercy. But in hell there will be no more exercises of divine patience. The judgments which God exercises on ungodly men in this world are warnings to them to avoid greater punishments; but the wrath which will come upon them, when they shall have filled up the measure of their sin, will not be of the nature of

warnings. Indeed they will be effectually awakened, and made thoroughly sensible, by what they shall suffer; yet their being awakened and made sensible will do them no good. Many a wicked man hath suffered very awful things from God in this world, which have been a means of saving good; but that wrath which sinners shall suffer after death will be no way for their good. God will have no merciful design in it; neither will it be possible that they should get any good by that or by anything else.

3. Wrath will so be executed as to perfect the work to which wrath tends, viz., *utterly to undo* the subject of it. Wrath is often so executed in this life as greatly to distress persons, and bring them into great calamity; yet not so as to complete the ruin of those who suffer it; but in another world it will be so executed as to finish their destruction, and render them utterly and perfectly undone; it will take away all comfort, all hope, and all support. The soul will be, as it were, utterly crushed; the wrath will be wholly intolerable. It must sink, and will utterly sink, and will have no more strength to keep itself from sinking than a worm would have to keep itself from being crushed under the weight of a mountain. The wrath will be so great, so mighty and powerful, as wholly to abolish all manner of welfare: Matt. xxi. 44, "But on whomsoever it shall fall, it will grind him to powder."

4. When persons shall have filled up the measure of their sin, that wrath will come upon them which is *eternal*. Though men may suffer very terrible and awful judgments in this world, yet those judgments have an end. They may be long continued, yet they commonly admit of relief. Temporal distresses and sorrows have intermissions and respite, and commonly by degrees abate and wear off; but the wrath that shall be executed, when the measure of sin shall have been filled up, will have no end. Thus it will be to the uttermost as to its duration; it will be of so long continuance that it will be impossible it should be longer. Nothing can be longer than eternity.

5. When persons shall have filled up the measure of their sin, then wrath will come upon them to the uttermost of what is *threatened*. Sin is an infinite evil; and the punishment which God hath threatened against it is very dreadful. The threatenings of God against the workers of iniquity are very awful; but these threatenings are never fully accomplished in this world. However dreadful things some men may suffer in this life, yet God never fully executes his threatenings for so much as one sin, till they have filled up the whole measure. The threatenings of

the law are never answered by anything that any man suffers here. The most awful judgment in this life doth not answer God's threatenings, either in degree, or in circumstances, or in duration. If the greatest sufferings that ever are endured in this life should be eternal, it would not answer the threatening. Indeed temporal judgments *belong* to the threatenings of the law; but these are not *answered* by them; they are but foretastes of the punishment. "The wages of sin is death." No expressions of wrath that are suffered before men have filled up the measure of their sin, are its full wages. But *then* God will reckon with them, and will recompense into their bosoms the full deserved sum.

The use I would make of this doctrine is, of warning to natural men to rest no longer in sin, and to make haste to flee from it. The things which have been said, under this doctrine, may well be awakening, awful considerations to you. It is awful to consider whose wrath it is that abides upon you, and of what wrath you are in danger. It is impossible to express the misery of a natural condition. It is like being in Sodom, with a dreadful storm of fire and brimstone hanging over it, just ready to break forth, and to be poured down upon it. The clouds of divine vengeance are full and just ready to burst. Here let those who yet continue in sin, in this town, consider particularly:

1. Under what *great means* and advantages you continue in sin. God is now favoring us with very great and extraordinary means and advantages, in that we have such extraordinary tokens of the presence of God among us; his spirit is so remarkably poured out, and multitudes of all ages and all sorts are converted and brought home to Christ. God appears among us in the most extraordinary manner, perhaps, that ever he did in New England. The children of Israel saw many mighty works of God when he brought them out of Egypt; but we, at this day, see works more mighty, and of a more glorious nature.

We, who live under such light, have had loud calls; but now, above all. Now is a day of salvation. The fountain hath been set open among us in an extraordinary manner, and hath stood open for a considerable time: Yet you continue in sin, and the calls that you have hitherto had, have not brought you to be washed in it. What extraordinary advantages have you lately enjoyed, to stir you up! How hath everything in the town, of late, been of that tendency! Those things which used to be the greatest hindrances have been removed. You have not the ill examples of immoral persons to be a temptation to you.

There is not now that vain worldly talk and evil company to divert you, and to be a hindrance to you, which there used to be. Now you have multitudes of good examples set before you; there are many now all around you who, instead of diverting and hindering you, are earnestly desirous of your salvation, and willing to do all that they can to move you to flee to Christ: they have a thirsting desire for it. The chief talk in the town has of late been about the things of religion, and has been such as hath tended to promote, and not to hinder, your souls' good. Everything all around you hath tended to stir you up; and will you yet continue in sin!

Some of you have continued in sin till you are far advanced in life. You were warned when you were children; and some of you had awakenings then; however, the time went away. You became men and women; and then you were stirred up again, you had the strivings of God's Spirit; and some of you have fixed the times when you would make thorough work of seeking salvation. Some of you perhaps determined to do it when you should be married and settled in the world; others when you should have finished such a business, and when your circumstances should be so and so altered. Now these times have come and are past, yet you continue in sin.

Many of you have had remarkable warnings of Providence. Some of you have been warned by the deaths of near *relations;* you have stood by and seen others die and go into eternity; yet this hath not been effectual. Some of you have been near death *yourselves,* have been brought nigh the grave in sore sickness, and were full of your promises how you would behave yourselves, if it should please God to spare your lives. Some of you have very narrowly escaped death by dangerous accidents; but God was pleased to spare you, to give you a further space to repent; yet you continue in sin.

Some of you have seen times of remarkable outpourings of the Spirit of God in this town in times past; but it had no good effect on you. *You* had the strivings of the Spirit of God, as well as others. God did not pass so by your door, but that he came and knocked; yet you stood it out. Now God hath come again in a more remarkable manner than ever before, and hath been pouring out his Spirit for some months in its most gracious influence: yet you remain in sin until now. In the beginning of this awakening you were warned to flee from wrath, and to forsake your sins. You were told what a wide door there was open, what an accepted time it was, and were urged to press into the kingdom of God. And many did press in; they forsook their sins, and believed in Christ; *but you, when you had seen it, repented not that you might believe him.*

Then you were warned again, and still others have been pressing and thronging into the kingdom of God. Many have fled for refuge and have laid hold on Christ: yet you continue in sin and unbelief. You have seen multitudes of all sorts, of all ages, young and old, flocking to Christ, and many of about your age and your circumstances; but you still are in the same miserable condition in which you used to be. You have seen persons daily flocking to Christ, as doves to their windows. God hath not only poured out his Spirit on this town, but also on other towns around us, and they are flocking in there as well as here. This blessing spreads farther and farther; many, far and near, seem to be setting their faces Zion-ward: yet you who live here, where this work first began, continue behind still; you have no lot nor portion in this matter.

2. How *dreadful* the wrath of God is, when it is executed to the uttermost. To make you in some measure sensible of that, I desire you to consider whose wrath it is. The wrath of a king is the roaring of a lion; but this is the wrath of Jehovah, the Lord God Omnipotent. Let us consider, what can we rationally think of it? How dreadful must be the wrath of such a Being, when it comes upon a person to the uttermost, without any pity, or moderation, or merciful circumstances! What must be the uttermost of his wrath, who made heaven and earth by the word of his power; who spake, and it was done, who commanded, and it stood fast! What must his wrath be, who commandeth the sun, and it rises not, and sealeth up the stars! What must his wrath be, who shaketh the earth out of its place, and causeth the pillars of heaven to tremble! What must his wrath be, who rebuketh the sea and maketh it dry, who removeth the mountains out of their places, and overturneth them in his anger? What must his wrath be, whose majesty is so awful that no man could live in the sight of it? What must the wrath of such a Being be, when it comes to the uttermost, when he makes his majesty appear and shine bright in the misery of wicked men? And what is a worm of the dust before the fury and under the weight of this wrath, which the stoutest devils cannot bear, but utterly sink and are crushed under it? Consider how dreadful the wrath of God is sometimes in this world, only in a little taste or view of it. Sometimes when God only enlightens conscience to have some sense of his wrath, it causes the stout-hearted to cry out; nature is ready to sink under it, when in-

deed it is but a little glimpse of divine wrath that is seen. This hath been observed in many cases. But if a slight taste and apprehension of wrath be so dreadful and intolerable, what must it be when it comes upon persons to the uttermost? When a few drops or a little sprinkling of wrath is so distressing and overbearing to the soul, how must it be when God opens the flood-gates, and lets the mighty deluge of his wrath come pouring down upon men's guilty heads, and brings in all his waves and billows upon their souls? How little of God's wrath will sink them! Psalm ii, 12, "When his wrath is kindled but a little, blessed are all they that put their trust in him."

3. Consider, you know not what wrath God may be about to execute upon wicked men in *this world*. Wrath may, in some sense, be coming upon them in the present life, to the uttermost, for aught we know. When it is said of the Jews, "the wrath is come upon them to the uttermost," respect is had, not only to the execution of divine wrath on that people in hell, but that terrible destruction of Judea and Jerusalem, which was then near approaching, by the Romans. We know not but the wrath is now coming, in some peculiarily awful manner, on the wicked world. God seems, by the things which he is doing among us, to be coming forth for some great thing. The work which hath been lately wrought among us is no ordinary thing. He doth not work in his usual way, but in a way very extraordinary; and it is probable that it is a forerunner of some very great revolution. We must not pretend to say what is in the womb of Providence, or what is in the book of God's secret decrees; yet we may and ought to discern the signs of these times.

Though God be now about to do glorious things for his church and people, yet it is probable that they will be accompanied with dreadful things to his enemies. It is the manner of God, when he brings about any glorious revolution for his people, at the same time to execute very awful judgments on his enemies: Deut. xxxii. 43. "Rejoice, O ye nations, with his people; for he will avenge the blood of his servants, and will render vengeance to his adversaries, and will be merciful unto his land and to his people." Isa. iii. 10, 11. "Say ye to the righteous, it shall be well with him: for they shall eat the fruit of their doings. Woe unto the wicked, it shall be ill with him: for the reward of his hands shall be given him." Isa. lxv. 13, 14. "Therefore, thus saith the Lord God, Behold, my servants shall eat, but ye shall be hungry: behold, my servants shall drink, but ye shall be thirsty; behold, my servants shall rejoice, but ye shall be ashamed: behold, my servants shall sing for joy of heart, but ye shall cry for sorrow of heart, and shall howl for vexation of spirit." We find in Scripture that where glorious times are prophesied to God's people, there are at the same time awful judgments foretold to his enemies. What God is now about to do, we know not: but this we may know, that there will be no safety to any but those who are in the ark.— Therefore it behoves all to haste and flee for their lives, to get into a safe condition, to get into Christ; then they need not fear, though the earth be removed, and the mountains carried into the midst of the sea; though the waters thereof roar and be troubled; though the mountains shake with the swelling thereof: for God will be their refuge and strength; they need not be afraid of evil tidings; their hearts may be fixed, trusting in the Lord.

XII

· JOHN WESLEY

1703-1791

FOR four generations, the Wesley family gave ministers of Puritan principles to the Church of England. The last and greatest of these was John Wesley, who was born at Epworth, Lincolnshire, June 17th, 1703, and died in London, March 2d, 1791. He graduated with distinction from Christ Church, Oxford, and was ordained priest in 1728. Of the origin of Methodism he relates: " In 1729 two young men in England, reading the Bible, saw they could not be saved without holiness; followed after it, and incited others so to do. In 1737 they saw, likewise, that men are justified before they are sanctified; but still holiness was their object. God then thrust them out to raise a holy people." Yet he dates his own conversion to May 24th, 1738, soon after his return from a missionary visit with the Moravians to Georgia. The remainder of his life is a wonderful record of Christian evangelization, patient industry, and herculean labors. Since the Apostle Paul, he was the chief missionary of the Gospel to the poor, meeting them in the churchyards, at their workshops, and in their homes. During these fifty-three years he travelled 225,000 miles, and preached more than 40,000 sermons — never missing a single appointment. Many million members in the various Methodist denominations are the living fruits of his labors, but even greater than this was the evangelical inpulse given to the church of England, and to all the various churches of the English-speaking world. The highest historical authorities concur in the statement that the labors of John Wesley saved England from the horrors of the French Revolution. His writings are voluminous and of varying value, extending to thirty-two volumes. Clearness of thought, directness of address, and calmness of appeal, characterize his sermons.

GOD'S LOVE TO FALLEN MAN.

"Not as the Transgression, so is the Free Gift."— Romans v. 15.

How exceedingly common, and how bitter is the outcry against our first parent, for the mischief which he not only brought upon himself, but entailed upon his latest posterity! It was by his wilful rebellion against God, "that sin entered into the world." "By one man's disobedience," as the Apostle observes, *the many,* as many as were then in the loins of their forefathers, *were made,* or constituted *sinners:* not only deprived of the favor of God, but also of his image; of all virtue, righteousness, and true holiness, and sunk partly into the image of the devil, in pride, malice, and all other diabolical tempers; partly into the image of the brute, being fallen under the dominion of brutal passions and grovelling appetites. Hence also Death entered into the world, with all his forerunners and attendants; pain, sickness, and a whole train of uneasy as well as unholy passions and tempers.

"For all this we may thank Adam," has been echoed down from generation to generation. The self-same charge has been repeated in every age and every nation where the oracles of God are known, in which alone this grand and important event has been discovered to the children of men. Has not *your* heart, and probably *your* lips too, joined in the general charge? How few are there of those who believe the scriptural relation of the Fall of Man, that have not entertained the same thought concerning our first parent? Severely condemning him, that, through wilful disobedience to the sole command of his Creator,

"Brought death into the world and all our woe."

Nay, it were well if the charge rested here: but it is certain it does not. It cannot be denied that it frequently glances from Adam to his Creator. Have not thousands, even of those that are called Christians, taken the liberty to call his mercy, if not his justice also, into question, on this very account? Some indeed have done this a little more modestly, in an oblique and indirect manner: but others have thrown aside the mask, and asked, "Did not God foresee that Adam would abuse his liberty? And did he not know the baneful consequences which this must naturally have on all his posterity? And why then did he permit that disobedience? Was it not easy for the Almighty to have prevented it?" He certainly did foresee the whole. This cannot be denied. "For

known unto God are all his works from the beginning of the world."
(Rather from all eternity, as the words ἀπ' αιωνος properly signify.)
And it was undoubtedly in his power to prevent it; for he hath all power
both in heaven and earth. But it was known to him at the same time,
that it was best upon the whole not to prevent it. He knew, that, " not
as the transgression, so is the free gift:" that the evil resulting from the
former was not as the good resulting from the latter, not worthy to be
compared with it. He saw that to permit the fall of the first man was
far best for mankind in general: that abundantly more good than evil
would accrue to the posterity of Adam by his fall: that if " sin abounded "
thereby over all the earth, yet grace " would much more abound:" yea,
and that to every individual of the human race, unless it was his own
choice.

It is exceedingly strange that hardly anything has been written,
or at least published, on this subject: nay, that it has been so little
weighed or understood by the generality of Christians: especially considering that it is not a matter of mere curiosity, but a truth of the
deepest importance; it being impossible, on any other principle,

> " To assert a gracious Providence,
>   And justify the ways of God with men:"

and considering withal, how plain this important truth is, to all sensible
and candid inquirers. May the Lover of Men open the eyes of our
understanding, to perceive clearly that by the fall of Adam mankind in
general have gained a capacity,

First, of being more holy and happy on earth, and,

Secondly, of being more happy in heaven than otherwise they could
have been.

And, first, mankind in general have gained by the fall of Adam,
a capacity of attaining more holiness and happiness on earth than it
would have been possible for them to attain if Adam had not fallen. For
if Adam had not fallen, Christ had not died. Nothing can be more clear
than this: nothing more undeniable: the more thoroughly we consider
the point, the more deeply shall we be convinced of it. Unless all the
partakers of human nature had received that deadly wound in Adam,
it would not have been needful for the Son of God to take our nature
upon him. Do you not see that this was the very ground of his coming
into the world? " By one man sin entered into the world, and death
by sin. And thus death passed upon all " through him, " in whom all

men sinned." (Rom. v. 12.) Was it not to remedy this very thing, that "the Word was made flesh?" that "as in Adam all died, so in Christ all might be made alive?" Unless, then, *many* had been made sinners by the disobedience of one, by the obedience of one, *many* would not have been *made righteous*. (Ver. 18.) So there would have been no room for that amazing display of the Son of God's love to mankind. There would have been no occasion for his "being obedient unto death, even the death of the cross." It could not then have been said, to the astonishment of all the hosts of heaven, "God so loved the world," yea, the ungodly world, which had no thought or desire of returning to him, "that he gave his Son" out of his bosom, his only begotten Son, "to the end that whosoever believeth on him should not perish, but have everlasting life." Neither could we then have said, "God was in Christ reconciling the world to himself:" or that he "made him to be sin," that is, a *sin-offering* "for us, who knew no sin, that we might be made the righteousness of God through him." There would have been no such occasion for such "an Advocate with the Father," as "Jesus Christ the Righteous:" neither for his appearing "at the right hand of God, to make intercession for us."

What is the necessary consequence of this? It is this: there could then have been no such thing as faith in God, *thus loving the world,* giving his only Son for us men, and for our salvation. There could have been no such thing as faith in the Son of God, "as loving us and giving himself for us." There could have been no faith in the Spirit of God, as renewing the image of God in our hearts, as raising us from the death of sin unto the life of righteousness. Indeed, the whole privilege of justification by faith could have no existence; there could have been no redemption in the blood of Christ: neither could Christ have been "made of God unto us," either "wisdom, righteousness, sanctification, or redemption."

And the same grand blank which was in our faith, must likewise have been in our love. We might have loved the Author of our being, the Father of angels and men, as our Creator and Preserver: we might have said, "O Lord our Governor, how excellent is thy name in all the earth!" But we could not have loved him under the nearest and dearest relation, "as delivering up his Son for us all." We might have loved the Son of God, as being the "brightness of his Father's glory, the express image of his person": (although this ground seems to belong rather to the inhabitants of heaven than earth.) But we could not have loved him as "bearing our sins in his own body on the tree," and "by that one oblation of himself once offered, making a full oblation, sacrifice, and satisfaction, for the sins of the whole world." We could not have been "made comformable to his death," nor "have known the power of his resurrection." We could not have loved the Holy Ghost as revealing to us the Father and the Son, as opening the eyes of our understanding, bringing us out of darkness into his marvellous light, renewing the image of God in our soul, and sealing us unto the day of redemption. So that, in truth, what is now "in the sight of God, even the Father," not of fallible men, "pure religion and undefiled," would then have had no being: inasmuch as it wholly depends on those grand principles, "By grace ye are saved through faith:" and "Jesus Christ is of God made unto us wisdom, and righteousness, and sanctification, and redemption."

We see then what unspeakable advantage we derive from the fall of our first parent, with regard to faith: faith both in God the Father, who spared not his own Son, his only Son, but "wounded him for our transgressions," and "bruised him for our iniquities:" and in God the Son, who poured out his soul for us transgressors, and washed us in his own blood. We see what advantage we derive therefrom with regard to the love of God, both of God the Father, and God the Son. The chief ground of this love, as long as we remain in the body, is plainly declared by the Apostle, "We love him, because he first loved us." But the greatest instance of his love had never been given, if Adam had not fallen.

And as our faith, both in God the Father and the Son, receives an unspeakable increase, if not its very being, from this grand event, as does also our love both of the Father and the Son: so does the love of our neighbor also, our benevolence to all mankind: which cannot but increase in the same proportion with our faith and love of God. For who does not apprehend the force of that inference drawn by the loving Apostle, "Beloved, if God so loved us, we ought also to love one another." If God *so* loved us — observe, the stress of the argument lies on this very point: *so loved us!* as to deliver up his only Son to die a cursed death for our salvation. "Beloved, what manner of love is this," wherewith God hath loved us? So as to give his *only Son!* In glory equal with the Father: in majesty co-eternal! What manner of love is this wherewith the only begotten Son of God hath loved us, as to *empty himself,* as far as possible, of his eternal Godhead; as to divest himself of that glory, which he had with the Father before the world began; as to "take upon him the form of a servant, being found in fashion as a man!" And then to humble himself still further, "being obedient unto death, even the death of the cross!" If God *so* loved us, how ought we to love one another? But this motive to brotherly love had been totally wanting, if Adam had not fallen. Consequently we could not then have loved one another in so high a degree as we may now. Nor could there have been that height and depth in the command of our Blessed Lord, "As I have loved you, so love one another."

Such gainers may we be by Adam's fall, with regard both to the love of God and of our neighbor. But there is another grand point, which, though little adverted to, deserves our deepest consideration. By that one act of our first parent, not only "sin entered into the world," but pain also, and was alike entailed on his whole posterity. And herein appeared, not only the justice, but the unspeakable goodness of God. For how much good does he continually bring out of this evil! How much holiness and happiness out of pain!

How innumerable are the benefits which God conveys to the children of men through the channel of sufferings! So that it might well be said, "What are termed afflictions in the language of men, are in the language of God styled blessings." Indeed had there been no suffering in the world, a considerable part of religion, yea, and in some respects, the most excellent part, could have had no place therein: since the very existence of it depends on our suffering: so that had there been no pain, it could have had no being. Upon this foundation, even our suffering, it is evident all our passive graces are built; yea, the noblest of all Christian graces, *love enduring all things.* Here is the ground for resignation to God, enabling us to say from the heart, in every trying hour, "It is the Lord: let him do what seemeth him good." "Shall we receive good at the hand of the Lord, and shall we not receive evil?" And what a glorious spectacle is this? Did it not constrain even a heathen to cry out, *"Ecce spectaculum Deo dignum!* See a sight worthy of God: a good man struggling with adversity, and superior to it." Here is the ground for confidence in God, both with regard to what we feel, and with regard to what we should fear, were it not that our soul is calmly stayed on him. What room could there be for trust in God, if there was no such thing as pain or danger? Who might not say then, "The cup which my Father hath given me, shall I not drink it?" It is by sufferings that our faith is tried, and, therefore, made more acceptable to God. It is in the day of trouble that we have occasion to say, "Though he slay me, yet will I trust in him." And this is well pleasing to God, that we should own him in the face of danger; in defiance of sorrow, sickness, pain, or death.

Again: Had there been neither natural nor moral evil in the world, what must have become of patience, meekness, gentleness, long-suffering? It is manifest they could have had no being: seeing all these have evil for their object. If, therefore, evil had never entered into the world, neither could these have had any place in it. For who could have *returned good for evil,* had there been no evil-doer in the universe? How had it been possible, on that supposition, to *overcome evil with good?* Will you say, "But all these graces might have been divinely infused into the hearts of men." Undoubtedly they might: but if they had, there would have been no use or exercise for them. Whereas in the present state of things we can never long want occasion to exercise them. And the more they are exercised, the more all our graces are strengthened and increased. And in the same proportion as our resignation, our confidence in God, our patience and fortitude, our meekness, gentleness, and long-suffering, together with our faith and love of God and man increase, must our happiness increase, even in the present world.

Yet again: As God's permission of Adam's fall gave all his posterity a thousand opportunities of *suffering,* and thereby of exercising all those passive graces which increase both their holiness and happiness: so it gives them opportunities of *doing good* in numberless instances, of exercising themselves in various good works, which otherwise could have had no being. And what exertions of benevolence, of compassion, of godlike mercy, had then been totally prevented! Who could then have said to the lover of men,

> "Thy mind throughout my life be shown,
> While listening to the wretches' cry,
> The widow's or the orphan's groan;
> On mercy's wings I swiftly fly.
> The poor and needy to relieve;
> Myself, my all, for them to give?"

It is the just observation of a benevolent man,

> ———"All worldly joys are less,
> Than that one joy of doing kindnesses."

Surely *in keeping* this commandment, if no other, there is great reward. "As we have time, let us do good unto all men;" good of every kind and in every degree. Accordingly the more good we do (other circumstances being equal), the happier we shall be. The more we deal our bread to the hungry, and cover the naked with garments; the more we relieve the stranger, and visit them that are sick or in prison: the more kind offices we do to those that groan under the various evils of human life: the more comfort we receive even in the present world; the greater the recompense we have in our own bosom.

To sum up what has been said under this head: As the more holy we are upon earth, the more happy we must be (seeing there is an inseparable connection between holiness and happiness); as the more good we do to others, the more of present reward rebounds into our own bosom: even as our sufferings for God lead us to *rejoice* in him "with joy unspeakable and full of glory:" therefore, the fall of Adam, First, by giving us an opportunity of being far more holy; Secondly, by giving us the occasions of doing innumerable good works, which otherwise could not have been done; and, Thirdly, by putting it into our power to suffer for God, whereby "the Spirit of glory and of God rests upon us:" may be of such advantage to the children of men, even in the present life, as they will not thoroughly comprehend till they attain life everlasting.

It is then we shall be enabled fully to comprehend, not only the advantages which accrue at the present time to the sons of men by the fall of their first Parent, but the infinitely greater advantages which they may reap from it in eternity. In order to form some conception of this, we may remember the observation of the Apostle, "As one star differeth from another star in glory, so also is the resurrection of the dead." The most glorious stars will undoubtedly be those who are the most holy; who bear most of that image of God wherein they were created. The next in glory to these will be those who have been most abundant in good works: and next to them, those that have suffered most, according to the will of God. But what advantages in every one of these respects, will the children of God receive in heaven, by God's permitting the introduction of pain upon earth, in consequence of sin? By occasion of this they attained many holy tempers, which otherwise could have had no being: resignation to God, confidence in him in times of trouble and danger, patience, meekness, gentleness, long-suffering, and the whole train of passive virtues. And on account of this superior holiness they will then enjoy superior happiness. Again: every one will then "receive his own reward, according to his own labor." Every individual will be "rewarded according to his work." But the fall gave rise to innumerable good works, which could otherwise never have existed,

12

such as ministering to the necessities of the saints, yea, relieving the distressed in every kind.   And hereby innumerable stars will be added to
their eternal crown.   Yet again: there will be an abundant reward in
heaven, for *suffering,* as well as for *doing,* the will of God: "these light
afflictions, which are but for a moment, work out for us a far more exceeding and eternal weight of glory."   Therefore that event, which occasioned the entrance of suffering into the world, has thereby occasioned,
to all the children of God, an increase of glory to all eternity.   For although the sufferings themselves will be at an end: although

> "The pain of life shall then be o'er,
>   The anguish and distracting care;
>   The sighing grief shall weep no more;
>   And sin shall never enter there:"—

yet the joys occasioned thereby shall never end, but flow at God's right
hand for evermore.

There is one advantage more than we reap from Adam's fall, which
is not unworthy our attention.   Unless in Adam all had died, being in
the loins of their first Parent, every descendant of Adam, every child
of man, must have personally answered for himself to God: it seems to
be a necessary consequence of this, that if he had once fallen, once violated any command of God, there would have been no possibility of his
rising again; there was no help, but he must have perished without
remedy.   For that Covenant knew not to show mercy: the word was,
"The soul that sinneth, it shall die."   Now who would not rather be
on the footing he is now; under a covenant of mercy?   Who would
wish to hazard a whole eternity upon one stake?   Is it not infinitely
more desirable, to be in a state wherein, though encompassed with infirmities, yet we do not run such a desperate risk, but if we fall, we may
rise again?   Wherein we may say,

> "My trespass is grown up to heaven!
>   But, far above the skies,
> In Christ abundantly forgiven,
>   I see thy mercies rise!"

In Christ!   Let me entreat every serious person, once more to fix
his attention here.   All that has been said, all that can be said, on these
subjects, centres in this point.   The fall of Adam produced the death of
Christ!   Hear, O heavens, and give ear, O earth!   Yea,

"Let earth and heaven agree,
  Angels and men be joined,
To celebrate with me
  The Saviour of mankind;
To adore the all-atoning Lamb,
And bless the sound of JESUS' Name!

If God had prevented the fall of man, *The Word* had never been *made flesh:* nor had we ever " seen his glory, the glory as of the only begotten of the Father." Those mysteries had never been displayed, " which the very angels desire to look into." Methinks this consideration swallows up all the rest, and should never be out of our thoughts. Unless " by one man, judgment had come upon all men to condemnation," neither angels nor men could ever have known " the unsearchable riches of Christ."

See then, upon the whole, how little reason we have to repine at the fall of our first Parent, since herefrom we may derive such unspeakable advantages, both in time and eternity. See how small pretence there is for questioning the mercy of God in permitting that event to take place! Since therein, mercy, by infinite degrees, rejoices over judgment! Where, then, is the man that presumes to blame God, for not preventing Adam's sin? Should we not rather bless him from the ground of the heart, for therein laying the grand scheme of man's redemption, and making way for that glorious manifestation of his wisdom, holiness, justice, and mercy? If indeed God had decreed before the foundation of the world, that millions of men should dwell in everlasting burnings, because Adam sinned, hundreds or thousands of years before they had a being; I know not who could thank him for this, unless the devil and his angels: seeing, on this supposition, all those millions of unhappy spirits would be plunged into hell by Adam's sin, without any possible advantage from it. But, blessed be God, this is not the case. Such a decree never existed. On the contrary, every one born of a woman, may be an unspeakable gainer thereby: and none ever was or can be a loser, but by his own choice.

We see here a full answer to that plausible account " of the origin of evil," published to the world some years since, and supposed to be unanswerable: that it " necessarily resulted from the nature of matter, which God was not able to alter." It is very kind in this sweet-tongued orator to make an excuse for God! But there is really no occasion for it: God hath answered for himself. He made man in his own image, a spirit endued with understanding and liberty. Man abusing that liberty, produced evil; brought sin and pain into the world. This God permitted, in order to a fuller manifestation of his wisdom, justice, and mercy, by bestowing on all who would receive it an infinitely greater happiness than they could possibly have attained, if Adam had not fallen.

"O the depth of the riches both of the wisdom and knowledge of God!" Although a thousand particulars of "his judgments, and of his ways are unsearchable" to us, and *past* our *finding out,* yet we may discern the general scheme, running through time into eternity. "According to the council of his own will," the plan he had laid before the foundation of the world, he created the parent of all mankind in his own image. And he permitted *all men* to be *made sinners by the disobedience of* this *one* man, that, *by the obedience of one,* all who receive *the free gift,* may be infinitely holier and happier to all eternity!

XIII

GEORGE WHITEFIELD

1714–1770

I N the spiritual deadness of the eighteenth century, a most impassioned pioneer of the gospel consecrated his life to declaring its
glad tidings of salvation throughout England and her American
colonies. George Whitefield was born December 27th, 1714, the
son of a Gloucester innkeeper. He entered Pembroke College, Oxford, as a servitor, and allied himself with the little band of worshippers called "Methodists." In his twenty-second year, he was
ordained a deacon. Excluded from the churches of Bristol, he un-
dauntedly began preaching in the open air three years later. Whitefield and Wesley separated in 1741, because of doctrinal differences,
and the former henceforth ministered as a Calvinistic Methodist. Of
his vast labors, he briefly records that " from the time of his ordination, to a period embracing 34 years, he preached upwards of 18,000
sermons, crossed the Atlantic seven times, and travelled thousands of
miles both in England and America." He died at Newburyport,
Massachusetts, September 30th, 1770. Several volumes of his discourses, imperfectly reported, are of little value. This thrilling sermon
was preached in the High-Church Yard of Glasgow on Sunday
morning, September 13th 1741, and is evidently a verbatim transcript.
It, with two others, is printed in the " Revivals of the Eighteenth
Century," published by the Free Church of Scotland.

THE METHOD OF GRACE.

*" They have healed also the hurt of the daughter of my people
slightly, saying, peace, 'peace; when there is no peace."*— Jeremiah vi. 14.

As God can send a nation or people no greater blessing than to give
them faithful, sincere, and upright ministers, so the greatest curse that

God can possibly send upon a people in this world, is to give them over to blind, unregenerate, carnal, lukewarm, and unskilful guides. And yet, in all ages, we find that there have been many wolves in sheep's clothing, many that daubed with untempered mortar, that prophesied smoother things than God did allow. As it was formerly, so it is now; there are many that corrupt the Word of God and deal deceitfully with it. It was so in a special manner in the prophet Jeremiah's time; and he, faithful to his Lord, faithful to that God who employed him, did not fail from time to time to open his mouth against them, and to bear a noble testimony to the honor of that God in whose name he from time to time spake. If you will read his prophecy, you will find that none spake more against such ministers than Jeremiah, and here especially in the chapter out of which the text is taken, he speaks very severely against them — he charges them with several crimes; particularly, he charges them with covetousness: "For," says he in the 13th verse, "from the least of them even to the greatest of them, every one is given to covetousness; and from the prophet even unto the priest, every one dealeth falsely." And then, in the words of the text, in a more special manner, he exemplifies how they had dealt falsely, how they had behaved treacherously to poor souls: says he, "They have healed also the hurt of the daughter of my people slightly, saying, Peace, peace, when there is no peace." The prophet, in the name of God, had been denouncing war against the people, he had been telling them that their house should be left desolate, and that the Lord would certainly visit the land with war. "Therefore," says he, in the 11th verse, "I am full of the fury of the Lord; I am weary with holding in; I will pour it out upon the children abroad, and upon the assembly of young men together; for even the husband with the wife shall be taken, the aged with him that is full of days. And their houses shall be turned unto others, with their fields and wives together; for I will stretch out my hand upon the inhabitants of the land, saith the Lord." The prophet gives a thundering message, that they might be terrified and have some convictions and inclinations to repent; but it seems that the false prophets, the false priests, went about stifling people's convictions, and when they were hurt or a little terrified, they were for daubing over the wound, telling them that Jeremiah was but an enthusiastic preacher, that there could be no such thing as war among them, and saying to people, Peace, peace, be still, when the prophet told them there was no peace. The words, then, refer primarily unto outward things, but I verily believe have also a further reference to the soul, and are to be referred to those false teachers, who, when people were under conviction of sin, when people were beginning to look towards heaven, were for stifling their convictions and telling them they were good enough before. And, indeed, people generally love to have it so; our hearts are exceedingly deceitful, and desperately wicked; none but the eternal God knows how treacherous they are. How many of us cry, Peace, peace, to our souls, when there is no peace! How many are there who are now settled upon their lees, that now think they are Christians, that now flatter themselves that they have an interest in Jesus Christ; whereas if we come to examine their experiences, we shall find that their peace is but a peace of the devil's making — it is not a peace of God's giving — it is not a peace that passeth human understanding. It is matter, therefore, of great importance, my dear hearers, to know whether we may speak peace to our hearts. We are all desirous of peace; peace is an unspeakable blessing; how can we live without peace? And, therefore, people from time to time must be taught how far they must go, and what must be wrought in them, before they can speak peace to their hearts. This is what I design at present, that I may deliver my soul, that I may be free from the blood of all those to whom I preach — that I may not fail to declare the whole counsel of God. I shall, from the words of the text, endeavor to show you what you must undergo, and what must be wrought in you before you can speak peace to your hearts.

But before I come directly to this, give me leave to premise a caution or two. And the first is, that I take it for granted you believe religion to be an inward thing; you believe it to be a work in the heart, a work wrought in the soul by the power of the Spirit of God. If you do not believe this, you do not believe your Bibles. If you do not believe this, though you have got your Bibles in your hand, you hate the Lord Jesus Christ in your heart; for religion is everywhere represented in Scripture as the work of God in the heart. "The kingdom of God is within us," says our Lord; and, "He is not a Christian who is one outwardly; but he is a Christian who is one inwardly." If any of you place religion in outward things, I shall not perhaps please you this morning; you will understand me no more when I speak of the work of God upon a poor sinner's heart than if I were talking in an unknown tongue. I would further premise a caution, that I would by no means confine God to one way of acting. I would by no means say, that all persons, before they come to have a settled peace in their hearts, are obliged to undergo the same degrees of conviction. No; God has various ways of bringing his children home; his sacred Spirit bloweth when, and where, and how it listeth. But, however, I will venture to affirm this: that before ever you can speak peace to your heart, whether by shorter or longer continuance of your convictions, whether in a more pungent or in a more gentle way, you must undergo what I shall hereafter lay down in the following discourse.

First, then, before you can speak peace to your hearts, you must be made to see, made to feel, made to weep over, made to bewail, your actual transgressions against the law of God. According to the covenant of words, "The soul that sinneth it shall die;" cursed is that man, be he what he may, be he who he may, that continueth not in all things that are written in the book of the law to do them. We are not only to do some things, but we are to do all things, and we are to continue so to do; so that the least deviation from the moral law, according to the covenant of works, whether in thought, word, or deed, deserves eternal death at the hand of God. And if one evil thought, if one evil word, if one evil action, deserves eternal damnation, how many hells, my friends, do every one of us deserve, whose whole lives have been one continued rebellion against God! Before ever, therefore, you can speak peace to your hearts, you must be brought to see, brought to believe, what a dreadful thing it is to depart from the living God. And now, my dear friends, examine your hearts, for I hope you came hither with a design to have your souls made better. Give me leave to ask you, in the presence of God, whether you know the time, and if you do not know exactly the time, do you know there was a time, when God wrote bitter things against you, when the arrows of the Almighty were within you? Was ever the remembrance of your sins grievous to you? Was the burden of your sins intolerable to your thoughts? Did you ever see that God's wrath might justly fall upon you, on account of your actual transgressions against God? Were you ever in all your life sorry for your sins? Could you ever say, My sins are gone over my head as a burden too heavy for me to bear? Did you ever experience any such thing as this? Did ever any such thing as this pass between God and your soul? If not, for Jesus Christ's sake, do not call yourselves Christians; you may speak peace to your hearts, but there is no peace. May the Lord awaken you, may the Lord convert you, may the Lord give you peace, if it be his will, before you go home!

But further: you may be convinced of your actual sins, so as to be made to tremble, and yet you may be strangers to Jesus Christ, you may have no true work of grace upon your hearts. Before ever, therefore, you can speak peace to your hearts, conviction must go deeper; you must not only be convinced of your actual transgressions against the law of God, but likewise of the foundation of all your transgressions. And what is that? I mean original sin, that original corruption each of us brings into the world with us, which renders us liable to God's wrath and damnation. There are many poor souls that think themselves fine reasoners, yet they pretend to say there is no such thing as original sin; they will charge God with injustice in imputing Adam's sin to us; although we have got the mark of the beast and of the devil upon us, yet they tell us we are not born in sin. Let them look abroad into the world and see the disorders in it, and think, if they can, if this is the paradise in which God did put man. No! everything in the world is out of order. I have often thought, when I was abroad, that if there were no other argument to prove original sin, the rising of wolves and tigers against man, nay, the barking of a dog against us, is a proof of original sin. Tigers and lions durst not rise against us, if it were not for Adam's first sin: for when the creatures rise up against us, it is as much as to say, You have sinned against God, and we take up our Master's quarrel. If we look inwardly, we shall see enough of lusts and man's temper contrary to the temper of God. There is pride, malice, and revenge, in all our hearts; and this temper cannot come from God; it comes from our first parent, Adam, who, after he fell from God, fell out of God into the devil. However, therefore, some people may deny this, yet when conviction comes, all carnal reasonings are battered down immediately, and the poor soul begins to feel and see the fountain from which all the polluted streams do flow. When the sinner is first awakened, he begins to wonder — How came I to be so wicked? The Spirit of God then strikes in, and shows that he has no good thing in him by nature; then he sees that he is altogether gone out of the way, that he is altogether become abominable, and the poor creature is made to lie down at the foot of the throne of God, and to acknowledge that God would be just to damn him, just to cut him off, though he never had committed one actual sin in his life. Did you ever feel and experience this, any of you — to justify God in your damnation — to own that you are by nature children of wrath, and that God may justly cut you off, though you never actually had offended him in all your life? If you were ever truly convicted, if your hearts were ever truly cut, if self were truly taken out of you, you would be made to see and feel this. And if you have never felt the weight of original sin, do not call yourselves Christians. I am verily persuaded original sin is the greatest burden of a true convert; this ever grieves the regenerate soul, the sanctified soul. The indwelling of sin in the heart is the burden of a converted person; it is the burden of a true Christian. He continually cries out, "O! who will deliver me from this body of death, this indwelling corruption in my heart?" This is that which disturbs a poor soul most. And, therefore, if you never felt this inward corruption, if you never saw that God might justly curse you for it, indeed, my dear friends, you may speak peace to your hearts, but I fear, nay, I know, there is no true peace.

Further: before you can speak peace to your hearts, you must not only be troubled for the sins of your life, the sins of your nature, but likewise for the sins of your best duties and performances. When a poor soul is somewhat awakened by the terrors of the Lord, then the poor creature, being born under the covenant of works, flies directly to a covenant of works again. And as Adam and Eve hid themselves among the trees of the garden, and sewed fig leaves together to cover their nakedness, so the poor sinner, when awakened, flies to his duties and to his performances, to hide himself from God, and goes to patch up a righteousness of his own. Says he, I will be mighty good now — I will reform — I will do all I can; and then certainly Jesus Christ will have mercy on me. But before you can speak peace to your heart, you must be brought to see that God may damn you for the best prayer you ever put up; you must be brought to see that all your duties — all your righteousness — as the prophet elegantly expresses it — put them all together, are so far from recommending you to God, are so far from being any motive and inducement to God to have mercy on your poor soul, that he will see them to be filthy rags, a menstruous cloth — that God hates them, and cannot away with them, if you bring them to him in order to recommend you to his favor. My dear friends, what is there in our performances to recommend us unto God? Our persons are in an unjustified state by nature, we deserve to be damned ten thousand times over; and what must our performances be? We can do no good thing by nature: "They that are in the flesh cannot please God." You may do things materially good, but you cannot do a thing formally and rightly good; because nature cannot act above itself. It is impossible that a man who is unconverted can act for the glory of God; he cannot do anything in, faith and " whatsoever is not of faith is sin." After we are renewed, yet we are renewed but in part, indwelling sin continues in us, there is a mixture of corruption in every one of our duties; so that after we are converted, were Jesus Christ only to accept us according to our works, our works would damn us, for we cannot put up a prayer but it is far from that perfection which the moral law requireth. I do not know what you may think, but I can say that I cannot pray but I sin — I cannot preach to you or any others but I sin — I can do nothing without sin; and, as one expresseth it, my repentance wants to be repented of, and my tears to be washed in the precious blood of my dear Redeemer. Our best duties are as so many splendid sins. Before you can speak peace to your heart, you must not only be sick of your original and actual sin, but you must be made sick of your righteousness, of all your duties and performances. There must be a deep conviction before you can be brought out of your self-righteousness; it is the last idol taken out of our heart. The pride of our heart will not let us submit to the righteousness of Jesus Christ. But if you never felt that you had no righteousness of your own, if you never felt the deficiency of your own righteousness, you cannot come to Jesus Christ. There are a great many now who may say, Well, we believe all this; but there is a great difference betwixt talking and feeling. Did you ever feel the want of a dear Redeemer? Did you ever feel the want of Jesus Christ, upon the account of the deficiency of your own righteousness? And can you now say from your heart, Lord, thou mayst justly damn me for the best duties that ever I did perform? If you are not thus brought out of self, you may speak peace to yourselves, but yet there is no peace.

But then, before you can speak peace to your souls, there is one particular sin you must be greatly troubled for, and yet I fear there are few of you think what it is; it is the reigning, the damning sin of the Christian world, and yet the Christian world seldom or never think of it. And pray what is that? It is what most of you think you are not guilty of — and that is, the sin of unbelief. Before you can speak peace to your heart, you must be troubled for the unbelief of your heart. But, can it be supposed that any of you are unbelievers here in this churchyard, that are born in Scotland, in a reformed country, that go to church every Sabbath? Can any of you that receive the sacrament once a year — O that it were administered oftener! — can it be supposed that you who had tokens for the sacrament, that you who keep up family prayer, that any of you do not believe in the Lord

Jesus Christ? I appeal to your own hearts, if you would not think me uncharitable, if I doubted whether any of you believed in Christ; and yet, I fear upon examination, we should find that most of you have not so much faith in the Lord Jesus Christ as the devil himself. I am persuaded the devil believes more of the Bible than most of us do. He believes the divinity of Jesus Christ; that is more than many who call themselves Christians do; nay, he believes and trembles, and that is more than thousands amongst us do. My friends, we mistake a historical faith for a true faith, wrought in the heart by the Spirit of God. You fancy you believe, because you believe there is such a book as we call the Bible — because you go to church; all this you may do, and have no true faith in Christ. Merely to believe there was such a person as Christ, merely to believe there is a book called the Bible, will do you no good, more than to believe there was such a man as Cæsar or Alexander the Great. The Bible is a sacred depository. What thanks have we to give to God for these lively oracles! But yet we may have these, and not believe in the Lord Jesus Christ. My dear friends, there must be a principle wrought in the heart by the Spirit of the living God. Did I ask you how long it is since you believed in Jesus Christ, I suppose most of you would tell me, you believed in Jesus Christ as long as ever you remember — you never did misbelieve. Then, you could not give me a better proof that you never yet believed in Jesus Christ, unless you were sanctified early, as from the womb; for, they that otherwise believe in Christ know there was a time when they did not believe in Jesus Christ. You say you love God with all your heart, soul, and strength. If I were to ask you how long it is since you loved God, you would say, As long as you can remember; you never hated God, you know no time when there was enmity in your heart against God. Then, unless you were sanctified very early, you never loved God in your life. My dear friends, I am more particular in this, because it is a most deceitful delusion, whereby so many people are carried away, that they believe already. Therefore, it is remarked of Mr. Marshall, giving account of his experiences, that he had been working for life, and he had ranged all his sins under the ten commandments, and then coming to a minister, asked him the reason why he could not get peace. The minister looked to his catalogue, Away, says he, I do not find one word of the sin of unbelief in all your catalogue. It is the peculiar work of the Spirit of God to convince us of our unbelief — that we have got no faith. Says Jesus Christ, " I will send the Comforter; and when he is come, he will reprove the world " of the sin of unbelief;

" of sin," says Christ, " because they believe not on me."   Now, my dear
friends, did God ever show you that you had no faith?   Were you ever
made to bewail a hard heart of unbelief?   Was it ever the language of
your heart, Lord, give me faith; Lord, enable me to lay hold on thee;
Lord, enable me to call thee *my* Lord and *my* God?   Did Jesus Christ
ever convince you in this manner?   Did he ever convince you of your
inability to close with Christ, and make you to cry out to God to give you
faith?   If not, do not speak peace to your heart.   May the Lord awaken
you, and give you true, solid peace before you go hence and be no more!

Once more, then: before you can speak peace to your heart, you
must not only be convinced of your actual and original sin, the sins of
your own righteousness, the sin of unbelief, but you must be enabled to
lay hold upon the perfect righteousness, the all-sufficient righteousness,
of the Lord Jesus Christ; you must lay hold by faith on the righteousness
of Jesus Christ, and then you shall have peace.   " Come," says Jesus,
" unto me, all ye that are weary and heavy laden, and I will give you
rest."   This speaks encouragement to all that are weary and heavy
laden; but the promise of rest is made to them only upon their coming
and believing, and taking him to be their God and their all.   Before we
can ever have peace with God, we must be justified by faith through our
Lord Jesus Christ, we must be enabled to apply Christ to our hearts, we
must have Christ brought home to our souls, so as his righteousness may
be made our righteousness, so as his merits may be imputed to our souls.
My dear friends, were you ever married to Jesus Christ?   Did Jesus
Christ ever give himself to you?   Did you ever close with Christ by a
lively faith, so as to feel Christ in your hearts, so as to hear him speaking
peace to your souls?   Did peace ever flow in upon your hearts like a
river?   Did you ever feel that peace that Christ spoke to his disciples?   I
pray God he may come and speak peace to you.   These things you must
experience.   I am now talking of the invisible realities of another world,
of inward religion, of the work of God upon a poor sinner's heart.   I
am now talking of a matter of great importance, my dear hearers; you
are all concerned in it, your souls are concerned in it, your eternal salvation is concerned in it.   You may be all at peace, but perhaps the devil
has lulled you asleep into a carnal lethargy and security, and will endeavor
to keep you there, till he get you to hell, and there you will be awakened;
but it will be dreadful to be awakened and find yourselves so fearfully
mistaken, when the great gulf is fixed, when you will be calling to all
eternity for a drop of water to cool your tongue, and shall not obtain it.

Give me leave, then, to address myself to several sorts of persons; and O may God, of his infinite mercy, bless the application! There are some of you perhaps can say, Through grace we can go along with you. Blessed be God, we have been convinced of our actual sins, we have been convinced of original sin, we have been convinced of self-righteousness, we have felt the bitterness of unbelief, and through grace we have closed with Jesus Christ; we can speak peace to our hearts, because God hath spoken peace to us. Can you say so? Then I will salute you, as the angels did the women the first day of the week, All hail! fear not ye, my dear brethren, you are happy souls; you may lie down and be at peace indeed, for God hath given you peace; you may be content under all the dispensations of providence, for nothing can happen to you now, but what shall be the effect of God's love to your soul; you need not fear what fightings may be without, seeing there is peace within. Have you closed with Christ? Is God your friend? Is Christ your friend? Then look up with comfort; all is yours, and you are Christ's, and Christ is God's. Everything shall work together for your good; the very hairs of your head are numbered; he that toucheth you, toucheth the apple of God's eye. But then, my dear friends, beware of resting on your first conversion. You that are young believers in Christ, you should be looking out for fresh discoveries of the Lord Jesus Christ every moment; you must not build upon your past experiences, you must not build upon a work within you, but always come out of yourselves to the righteousness of Jesus Christ without you; you must be always coming as poor sinners to draw water out of the wells of salvation; you must be forgetting the things that are behind, and be continually pressing forward to the things that are before. My dear friends, you must keep up a tender, close walk with the Lord Jesus Christ. There are many of us who lose our peace by our untender walk; something or other gets in betwixt Christ and us, and we fall into darkness; something or other steals our hearts from God, and this grieves the Holy Ghost, and the Holy Ghost leaves us to ourselves. Let me, therefore, exhort you that have got peace with God, to take care that you do not lose this peace. It is true, if you are once in Christ, you cannot finally fall from God: "There is no condemnation to them that are in Christ Jesus;" but if you cannot fall finally, you may fall foully, and may go with broken bones all your days. Take care of backslidings; for Jesus Christ's sake, do not grieve the Holy Ghost — you may never recover your comfort while you live. O take care of going a gadding and wandering from God, after you have closed with Jesus Christ. My dear friends, I have paid dear for backsliding. Our hearts are so cursedly wicked, that if you take not care, if you do not keep up a constant watch, your wicked hearts will deceive you, and draw you aside. It will be sad to be under the scourge of a correcting Father; witness the visitations of Job, David, and other saints in Scripture. Let me, therefore, exhort you that have got peace to keep a close walk with Christ. I am grieved with the loose walk of those that are Christians, that have had discoveries of Jesus Christ; there is so little difference betwixt them and other people, that I scarce know which is the true Christian. Christians are afraid to speak for God — they run down with the stream; if they come into worldly company, they will talk of the world as if they were in their element; this you would not do when you had the first discoveries of Christ's love; you could talk then of Christ's love for ever, when the candle of the Lord shined upon your soul. That time has been when you had something to say for your dear Lord; but now you can go into company and hear others speaking about the world bold enough, and you are afraid of being laughed at if you speak for Jesus Christ. A great many people have grown conformists now in the worst sense of the word; they will cry out against the ceremonies of the church, as they may justly do; but then you are mighty fond of ceremonies in your behavior; you will conform to the world, which is a great deal worse. Many will stay till the devil bring up new fashions. Take care, then, not to be conformed to the world. What have Christians to do with the world? Christians should be singularly good, bold for their Lord, that all who are with you may take notice that you have been with Jesus. I would exhort you to come to a settlement in Jesus Christ, so as to have a continual abiding of God in your heart. We go a-building on our faith of adherence, and lose our comfort; but we should be growing up to a faith of assurance, to know that we are God's, and so walk in the comfort of the Holy Ghost and be edified. Jesus Christ is now much wounded in the house of his friends. Excuse me in being particular; for, my friends, it grieves me more that Jesus Christ should be wounded by his friends than by his enemies. We cannot expect anything else from Deists; but for such as have felt his power to fall away, for them not to walk agreeably to the vocation wherewith they are called — by these means we bring our Lord's religion into contempt, to be a by-word among the heathen. For Christ's sake, if you know Christ keep close by him; if God have spoken peace, O keep that peace by looking up to Jesus Christ every moment. Such as have got peace with God, if you are under trials, fear not, all things shall work for your good; if you are under temptations, fear not. If he has spoken peace to your hearts, all these things shall be for your good.

But what shall I say to you that have got no peace with God?—and these are, perhaps, the most of this congregation; it makes me weep to think of it. Most of you, if you examine your hearts, must confess that God never yet spoke peace to you; you are children of the devil, if Christ is not in you, if God has not spoken peace to your heart. Poor soul! what a cursed condition are you in! I would not be in your case for ten thousand, thousand worlds. Why? You are just hanging over hell. What peace can you have when God is your enemy, when the wrath of God is abiding upon your poor soul? Awake, then, you that are sleeping in a false peace; awake, ye carnal professors, ye hypocrites that go to church, receive the sacrament, read your Bibles, and never felt the power of God upon your hearts; you that are formal professors, you that are baptized heathens; awake, awake, and do not rest on a false bottom. Blame me not for addressing myself to you; indeed, it is out of love to your souls. I see you are lingering in your Sodom, and wanting to stay there; but I come to you as the angel did to Lot, to take you by the hand. Come away, my dear brethren—fly, fly, fly for your lives to Jesus Christ, fly to a bleeding God, fly to a throne of grace; and beg of God to break your hearts, beg of God to convince you of your actual sins, beg of God to convince you of your original sin, beg of God to convince you of your self-righteousness — beg of God to give you faith, and to enable you to close with Jesus Christ. O you that are secure, I must be a son of thunder to you, and O that God may awaken you, though it be with thunder: it is out of love, indeed, that I speak to you. I know by sad experience what it is to be lulled asleep with a false peace; long was I lulled asleep, long did I think myself a Christian, when I knew nothing of the Lord Jesus Christ. I went perhaps farther than many of you do; I used to fast twice a week, I used to pray sometimes nine times a day, I used to receive the sacrament constantly every Lord's-day; and yet I knew nothing of Jesus Christ in my heart, I knew not that I must be a new creature — I knew nothing of inward religion in my soul. And perhaps, many of you may be deceived as I, poor creature, was; and, therefore, it is out of love to you indeed, that I speak to you. O if you do not take care, a form of religion will destroy your soul; you will rest in it, and will not come to Jesus Christ at all; whereas, these things are only the means, and not the end of religion; Christ is the end of the law for righteousness to all that believe. O, then, awake, you that are settled on your lees; awake you Church professors; awake you that have got a name to live, that are rich and think you want nothing, not considering that you are poor, and blind, and naked; I counsel you to come and buy of Jesus Christ gold, white raiment, and eye-salve. But I hope there are some that are a little wounded; I hope God does not intend to let me preach in vain; I hope God will reach some of your precious souls, and awaken some of you out of your carnal security; I hope there are some who are willing to come to Christ, and beginning to think that they have been building upon a false foundation. Perhaps the devil may strike in, and bid you despair of mercy; but fear not, what I have been speaking to you is only out of love to you — is only to awaken you, and let you see your danger. If any of you are willing to be reconciled to God, God the Father, Son, and Holy Ghost, is willing to be reconciled to you. O then, though you have no peace as yet, come away to Jesus Christ; he is our peace, he is our peace-maker — he has made peace betwixt God and offending man. Would you have peace with God? Away, then, to God through Jesus Christ, who has purchased peace; the Lord Jesus has shed his heart's blood for this. He died for this; he rose again for this; he ascended into the highest heaven, and is now interceding at the right hand of God. Perhaps you think there will be no peace for you. Why so? Because you are sinners? because you have crucified Christ — you have put him to open shame — you have trampled under foot the blood of the Son of God? What of all this? Yet there is peace for you. Pray, what did Jesus Christ say to his disciples, when he came to them the first day of the week? The first word he said was, " Peace be unto you; " he showed them his hands and his side, and said, " Peace be unto you." It is as much as if he had said, Fear not, my disciples; see my hands and my feet how they have been pierced for your sake; therefore, fear not. How did Christ speak to his disciples? " Go tell my brethren, and tell broken-hearted Peter in particular, that Christ is risen, that he is ascended unto his Father and your Father, to his God and your God." And after Christ rose from the dead, he came preaching peace, with an olive branch of peace, like Noah's dove: " My peace I leave with you." Who were they? They were enemies of Christ as well as we, they were deniers of Christ once as well as we. Perhaps some of you have backslidden and lost your peace, and you think you deserve no peace; and no more you do. But, then, God will heal your backslidings, he will love you freely. As for you that are wounded, if you are made willing to come to Christ, come away. Perhaps some of you want to dress yourselves in

13

your duties, that are but rotten rags. No, you had better come naked as you are, for you must throw aside your rags, and come in your blood. Some of you may say, We would come, but we have got a hard heart. But you will never get it made soft till ye come to Christ; he will take away the heart of stone, and give you an heart of flesh; he will speak peace to your souls; though ye have betrayed him, yet he will be your peace. Shall I prevail upon any of you this morning to come to Jesus Christ? There is a great multitude of souls here; how shortly must you all die, and go to judgment! Even before night, or to-morrow's night, some of you may be laid out for this kirk-yard. And how will you do if you be not at peace with God — if the Lord Jesus Christ has not spoken peace to your heart? If God speak not peace to you here, you will be damned for ever. I must not flatter you, my dear friends, I will deal sincerely with your souls. Some of you may think I carry things too far. But, indeed, when you come to judgment, you will find what I say is true, either to your eternal damnation or comfort. May God influence your hearts to come to him! I am not willing to go away without persuading you. I cannot be persuaded but God may make use of me as a means of persuading some of you to come to the Lord Jesus Christ. O did you but feel the peace which they have that love the Lord Jesus Christ! "Great peace have they," says the psalmist, "that love thy law; nothing shall offend them." But there is no peace to the wicked. I know what it is to live a life of sin; I was obliged to sin in order to stifle conviction. And I am sure this is the way many of you take; if you get into company you drive off conviction. But you had better go to the bottom at once; it must be done — your wound must be searched, or you must be damned. If it were a matter of indifference, I would not speak one word about it. But you will be damned without Christ. He is the way, he is the truth, and the life. I cannot think you should go to hell without Christ. How can you dwell with everlasting burnings? How can you abide the thought of living with the devil for ever? Is it not better to have some soul-trouble here, than to be sent to hell by Jesus Christ hereafter? What is hell, but to be absent from Christ? If there were no other hell, that would be hell enough. It will be hell to be tormented with the devil for ever. Get acquainted with God, then, and be at peace. I beseech you, as a poor worthless ambassador of Jesus Christ, that you would be reconciled to God. My business this morning, the first day of the week, is to tell you that Christ is willing to be reconciled to you. Will any of you be reconciled to Jesus Christ? Then he will forgive you all your sins, he will blot out all your transgressions. But if you will go on and rebel against Christ, and stab him daily — if you will go on and abuse Jesus Christ, the wrath of God you must expect will fall upon you. God will not be mocked; that which a man soweth, that shall he also reap. And if you will not be at peace with God, God will not be at peace with you. Who can stand before God when he is angry? It is a dreadful thing to fall into the hands of an angry God. When the people came to apprehend Christ, they fell to the ground when Jesus said, " I am he." And if they could not bear the sight of Christ when clothed with the rags of mortality, how will they bear the sight of him when he is on his Father's throne? Methinks I see the poor wretches dragged out of their graves by the devil; methinks I see them trembling, crying out to the hills and rocks to cover them. But the devil will say, Come, I will take you away; and then they shall stand trembling before the judgment-seat of Christ. They shall appear before him to see him once, and hear him pronounce that irrevocable sentence, " Depart from me, ye cursed." Methinks I hear the poor creatures saying, Lord, if we must be damned, let some angel pronounce the sentence. No, the God of love, Jesus Christ, will pronounce it. Will ye not believe this? Do not think I am talking at random, but agreeably to the Scriptures of truth. If you do not, then show yourselves men, and this morning go away with full resolution, in the strength of God, to cleave to Christ. And may you have no rest in your souls till you rest in Jesus Christ! I could still go on, for it is sweet to talk of Christ. Do you not long for the time when you shall have new bodies — when they shall be immortal, and made like Christ's glorious body? and then they will talk of Jesus Christ for evermore. But it is time, perhaps, for you to go and prepare for your respective worship, and I would not hinder any of you. My design is, to bring poor sinners to Jesus Christ. O that God may bring some of you to himself! May the Lord Jesus now dismiss you with his blessing, and may the dear Redeemer convince you that are unawakened, and turn the wicked from the evil of their way! And may the love of God, that passeth all understanding, fill your hearts! Grant this, O Father, for Christ's sake; to whom, with thee and the blessed Spirit, be all honor and glory, now and for evermore. Amen.

XIV

ROWLAND HILL

1744–1833

QUAINT Rowland Hill! honest, untiring in gospel zeal, yet abounding in an eccentric humor that either offended or conquered the hearts of all who heard him; in figure so noble and commanding, that, even when almost fourscore and ten, his congregation were used to say, " It does us good if we can only see him! " This founder of the noted Surrey Chapel, London, was the son of Sir R. Hill, and was born at Hawkstone, Shropshire, August 23d, 1744. He graduated at St. John's College, Cambridge, and was ordained deacon in the Church of England. Yet he soon became a devoted and able disciple of Whitefield. For fifty winters he ministered to his great London congregation, and gave his summers to itinerant preaching, closing his labors only with his life, April 11th, 1833. His " Village Dialogues," a defence of Christian doctrine in a series of attractive conversations, were widely popular. He lived a whole-souled evangelist. Sheridan said of him: " His ideas come red-hot from the heart." The following Sermon, reported as delivered, was preached in Surrey Chapel on his last New Year's Day on earth. It attests his devoutness and earnestness of spirit, despite the infirmities of his eighty-ninth year.

THE IMPROVEMENT OF TIME.

" This month shall be unto you the beginning of months; it shall be the first month of the year to you."— Exodus xii. 2.

BRETHREN, time passes very quickly. We are now beginning a new year — which of us will be alive when the year is concluded? Many of

196

my friends have been swept away by the scythe of time into eternity since this time twelve months; and there is one standing among you now who does not expect to see this year out. The days of my pilgrimage must be nearly ended. Dear brethren, do let me offer a few hints another time for your eternal good. I dread the thought of having the sun set, in my poor little way, in a manner that is inconsistent with former mercies. Oh, it is beautiful to see the setting sun on a summer's day — though the rays are faint, yet they are still bright and clear. So while the rays of my poor abilities begin to get very feeble, God can still give a light to them — I pray that he may be a light and life to your souls.

Now, what have we here in the text? Why, that which may instruct us all. The words, perhaps, may not strike you as being very appropriate, but they will be a good starting-post for me, perhaps, and instruct me to speak profitably upon more things than one.

There is no good done to the souls of men, but as divine knowledge is communicated to our hearts through Him who is the fountain of all knowledge and all wisdom whatsoever. What is a man without an understanding? And what is that understanding, unless the Lord give light to the understanding? How beautiful is that prayer which you sometimes offer, that " the eyes of your understanding being enlightened, that ye may know what is the hope of his calling, and what the riches of the glory of his inheritance in the saints, and what is the exceeding great-ness of his power to us-ward who believe, according to the working of his mighty power."

But we must not only have a door-way into the mind, by the medium of the understanding — but when we get into the mind, the great matter is, to bring God to you. Lord, grant that we may never come to the house of God without humbly waiting on God, in order that we may re-ceive the food of his house. How miserably off is that man who calls at a house where is plenty of food, and where he is permitted to take what he pleases, and still prefers joining with them who are under the penalty of starvation! Oh, that the Lord would give me food for you; and oh, that the Lord would give you appetites to eat it!

The Lord was determined to take a people to himself, according to his own wisdom, and to bring them to the promised land, where he was to instruct them in things that were figurative for the day, having " a shadow of good things to come," (we have the happiness to enjoy these things more plainly) by different types, and ceremonies, and sacrifices. Now the day at length approaches when Israel is to be delivered, by the outstretched arm of Omnipotence itself, from the bonds of their Egyptian taskmasters and tyrants. The day approaches and the work must be done, because God determined it should be done. What a mercy it is that God's determinations must be accomplished! Let me know his will, let me ask to have that will engraven upon my heart; and, as sure as God is omnipotent, so shall I have that glorious will of his accomplished upon me for my everlasting good. I wish I could lift up my heart more abundantly to Him who is the author of omnipotent power, when I make use of that but one expression in the Lord's Prayer, " Thy will be done." And, blessed be his name, what a glorious promise is that, " I will give them a heart to know me, that I am the Lord:" I have given them minds, and I will feed and direct those minds for their good; and their minds shall be directed according to my holy mind and will. So that there shall be a happy communication between unworthy sinners that seek him, and God that gives them to understand.

Well, he gave the children of Israel divers ordinances; and the first grand institution God points out before us this morning, namely, that of the passover, the account of which we have in this chapter. We are certain that the Gospel was meant in all that institution, when we are told that " Christ our passover is sacrificed for us." Not one drop of blood was ever shed from any of the animals that were sacrificed in ancient times, but all pointed beautifully to the dear Lamb of God who came into the world, and took away sin by the sacrifice of himself. All of them went to pre-figure the glorious days when the fullness of the time shall come, when all these typical representations shall be really and gloriously exemplified. I met with a person the other day who thought there could be no use in common people reading the account of the Levitical institutions; I trust you are all convinced that those institutions were the Gospel of the Old Testament dispensation, and were all typical of the Lamb of God, who was to come in the fullness of time — oh, it is a fine expression, — to " put away sin by the sacrifice of himself." Oh, thanks be to God for the redemption! My debts are all discharged! I love to represent Christ to you in the way of a substituted surety; he paid the debts for me. I remember once myself being a considerable sufferer by being a surety for a debtor. In such case they come on you the same as if you had contracted the debt, though you did not contract a farthing of it. So the Lord comes on us to demand payment of the law; then the Lord Jesus, our beloved surety, comes in: " I have paid thy debts — I have suffered thy penalty — I died;" what a fine reason that is! " the just for the unjust, that I might bring you to God." Oh, the latter part of the business is charming; we are to be brought to God through Jesus Christ, being renewed in the spirit of our minds.

Wherever redemption through Christ is not preached fully, and freely, and distinctively, to the hearts of men, we never find a blessing upon the preached word. How dare I come, with all my imperfections about me, to a God of infinite holiness and purity? But now, all my sins are buried in the grave of Christ. Yes, and I may look upon the glorious voice which revivified the body of Christ, when he was raised from the dead by the power of the Father (as well as by his own power too, for he had "power to lay down his life," and he had "power to take it again,") as a proof of my resurrection to everlasting life. "He that believeth on me, though he were dead, yet shall he live; and whosoever liveth, and believeth in me, shall never die." And as a sweet pledge of the certainty of my resurrection, what did he do for his people? He blessed them with a spiritual resurrection: "And you hath he quickened who were dead in trespasses and in sins." The vivifying grace of Christ in the soul in an earnest of that second, glorious resurrection in Christ, when body and soul shall be reunited, when we shall see our Redeemer as he is, know as we are known and "be for ever with the Lord."

Now, what was ordered to be done by the Israelites in this chapter? Why here we are told of the lamb that was to be slain, the paschal lamb in the time of the passover. It was the first of all the ordinances that God ordained in the Jewish church, it was to be with them the beginning of the year. My dear brethren, we never begin to live till we live to God. I remember once seeing an old man, I suppose he must have been seventy or eighty years of age; and I asked him how old he was. He looked at me — he was brought to me as a monument of mercy,— he looked at me for a time, and faltered in his voice, the tears trickling down his cheeks; says he, "I am two years old." "Two years old?" "Ah, sir," says he, "till a little time ago I lived the life of a dead man; and I never knew what life was till I met with the life which is 'hid with Christ in God.'" Oh, it is a glorious truth; we have a life in God. And we may further add, "When Christ" (that is a fine idea — God engrave it on my heart!) "When Christ, who is our life (that he is) shall appear, then shall we also "— Oh what miracles of mercy shall we be! —" then shall we also appear with him in glory."

There is a number of fine mysteries connected with this lamb's being offered. It was to be the night of their deliverance: then began their day of happiness and deliverance: and there were ceremonies appointed which are very significant to us in this present day. They were to eat the paschal lamb with their staff in their hand, with their shoes on their feet, and with their loins girded. God give us the staff of promise, with which we may fight our enemies. Nothing in the world repels the enemy's temptations so well as when we can fasten on a good promise, and set it against the devil's malice against our precious souls.

They were to have their shoes on their feet, so that they might be ready to march immediately. God be praised, Christians are not to have one single idle hour. Be always ready, morning, noon, and night; that, if you are awakened out of your sleep by the coming of the Lord, you may be ready to say, "Here I am, Lord, prepared to meet you." May sloth be gone, and may we be filled with that activity and sacred zeal which shall bring us safe through all our labors.

They were also to have their "loins girded." We are told of the girdle of truth — of the loins being "girt about with truth." I have seen poor men when at hard labor with a girdle about their loins by way of strengthening them. "Gird up the loins of your mind," says the apostle; "be sober, and hope to the end." Be always ready for the work whenever you may be called to it. Oh, this is a good word for any part of our sermon — as it is good for the beginning of our life, so it will be while we continue and go on with our days. "Therefore, my beloved brethren, be steadfast, unmovable, always abounding in the work of the Lord"— can any one of you get beyond the lovely practice of that one thing?—"forasmuch as ye know that your labor is not in vain in the Lord." Hence it is that we are beautifully instructed to understand religion to be a persevering work: "So run that ye may obtain." What a mercy it is when we are kept watching and praying that we enter not into temptation!

I thank God the Bible is a very practical book. Though I know there are a great number of things beyond my own power of obtaining them, yet the promises are brought sweetly to my mind when I go to Him for strength who alone gives it me to perform duties. Oh, those beautiful expressions of the Apostle Paul! — I fear not the language of the commandment when the language of the promise is so rich and free.—"Work out your own salvation." Who can do it for you? I pray God he may help you; but if you don't help yourselves it will be in vain. I don't doubt this will sound a little comical in the ears of some. God helps them who help themselves: God gives strength to work, and man works by the strength which God gives him. "Work out your own salvation with fear and trembling;" and then directly I have the promise, and a glorious promise it is. If ten thousand angels had put all their strength together, they could not have given me a promise of equal value. "Work out your own salvation with fear and trembling. For it is God which worketh in you"—he that gives strength to all his bright seraphs above will give you strength—"to will and to do of his good pleasure." He gives a will by the breath of omnipotence, and then we see the activity of real Christians when the activity of God is in them, when the Spirit of the Lord is said to work in them mightily, when they are "strengthened with all might by his Spirit in the inner man." Dear brethren, I wish to have stronger faith in these strong promises of God. Indeed they are large promises, such as nobody could ever have dared to expect if he had not enabled believers to perform the same by the power of his mighty Spirit. I want no other evidence of the truth of these things, my dear brethren, than the life and conversation of you that truly believe in the Lord Jesus, you who, by your walk and behavior, are lights to the world. See what grace does when it reigns in the heart, and how you become more than conquerors over all your corruptions.

There was not only to be the staff of profession in their hand, and their feet shod with the preparation of the gospel of peace; but they were to be ready to march immediately the Lord sent them out to work. Here it is to be further observed, that directly the commandment was given, they were said to obey it; they had no time to hesitate, and there was no time to lose: their loins were girt, their staff was in their hands, and they were ready to go.

They were to suffer no leaven to be in their houses at the time they celebrated the passover. You know what leaven means; the leaven of malice and wickedness, the swelling pride of the human heart, and the abominable evils that are produced thereby. No unclean thing was to be eaten by them: not that any outward uncleanness will make us inwardly unclean: thanks be to God that he has ordered it that that which was the duty of the Jews is no longer our duty. But at the same time I thank my God for that charming command—there is no command but, if we obey it, will be charming,—"Come out from among them, and be ye separate, saith the Lord, and touch not the unclean thing." No unclean thing was to be touched or eaten by the Jews of old. We should so hate sin that we will not touch it. Who in the world would like to touch a filthy carcass if he could keep away from it?

These are some of the particulars connected with the manner in which the Jews were commanded to eat the passover. There are other things respecting it, on which we may observe. It was to be a lamb of the first year. Christ died in the beginning of the prime of his life. Christ suffered himself to be bound by the law's curse; he received the curse "the just for the unjust, that he might bring us to God." What a day was that when all the sins of God's people were laid upon the Lord Jesus Christ! Sometimes we sing,

> "The Lord, in the day
> Of his anger, did lay
> Our sins on the Lamb, and he bore them away."

He bore them away into the land of eternal forgetfulness. "Thy sins and thy iniquities," said the God of love, "will I remember no more." Now and then you and I have a person who has offended us; and we find that if they repent we can forgive them through the grace of God, when all that is angry and bad is subdued by the contrary spirit: but we cannot say — I cannot, at least, and I dare say you cannot, that we entirely forget it; to say that we remember no more, is more than we can do. Now, God's promise is even to forget our sins; he will bury them in the grave of Christ, and they are never to appear any more against us.

It should be, moreover, further observed, that this lamb that was to be slain, when slaughtered was not to be divided. God give me an undivided good. There are some people talk about the atonement of Christ, and don't like to talk about the influence of the Holy Spirit to sanctify and purify the heart. If I preach one sermon on justification, I would at least preach another on sanctification. If I tell people how God has freely forgiven them, so I will tell them of his grace working righteousness in the heart; it has wrought out not only righteousness for me, but it works righteousness in me, and makes me righteous. Don't let us forget that fine doctrine. He is just as willing to give his grace for the purifying our hearts, as he was free to give us of his blood for the justification of our persons. If ever we preach the gospel in a sort of partial manner, without giving equal weight to both parts of divine truth, we do injury to the souls of men. There is not an hour in my life in which I need not view "the Lamb of God which taketh away the sins of the world." I cannot spend a single day upon the earth, but I am compelled to cry out,

> "Open, O Lord, for this day's sins,
> The fountain of thy blood."

But still I want his Holy Spirit, that I may sin less, love him more, obey and serve him better, and live more to his glory and praise. Don't be partial in your believing: remember that all the doctrines are equally valuable. Not a bone of this sacrifice was ever to be broken; it was to be eaten whole. So may you and I fix on the Lamb of God as one complete and whole salvation without dividing part from part. I remember a very pretty remark a child made, when asked a rather improper question: "Which do you love best, your father or your mother?" The poor little child did not know what to answer: for a while, he did not know what to answer: he looked first at one, and then at the other: and at last the poor little creature cried out, "I love them both best." So I would have you love justification by the blood of Christ, to feel his holy righteousness which he has given you, equally with his sanctification whereby you are able to live to God. If I have been convinced by the power of the Holy Ghost, sin will be my plague and grief all the days of my life. If God himself were to tell me to be happy without being holy, I could not be so: it would be impossible to be content with pardon without purification, and being among the blessed number of those who are "pure in heart." I never wish you to have the consolations of religion without having the sanctifying influences of it, and without finding that your happiness is increased as your holiness is increased. You need not be afraid, according to the cant of some bad professors, of being legal; for the more holy you are, the more you will feel yourselves indebted to Him who has made you holy; and the more you will acknowledge your obligations to that God who has carried on his work of grace with power in your souls, and who has promised never to leave you till he brings you to his everlasting glory.

Then we find how the lamb was to be eaten. It was to be eaten by families, and to be "roast with fire." Oh, my God, what did our Redeemer feel, when, if I may so express myself, resting under his Father's wrath, he cried out in the agonies of his soul, "Father, if it be possible, let this cup pass from me!" and when "his sweat was as it were great drops of blood falling down to the ground." I do like that prayer; "By thine agony and bloody sweat, Good Lord deliver us." O that I may learn to be crucified with Christ! O that I may learn to have all my sins mortified through his mortification, and live to his glory and his praise.

This great work was to be done for and in the children of Israel, and it was done for them; and it will be wrought in all them that believe in the Lord Jesus. Pray, my dear brethren, what is life? It is a wonderful emanation from God himself. Why is it I have not the life of a beast? I don't know but what human life is of the same nature, in regard to the mere point of life, as is the life of any other animal: but there is a glorious difference in this respect; it is a life which is filled with mind, and in that life I can climb to God himself. And when the Lord is pleased to vivify my dead soul, to reanimate me from the grave of sin, to make me " a new creature in Christ Jesus," to give me a new nature; when all these pretty texts are brought home to the heart, and I know their meaning by feeling their power, then I know that my life is worth a thousand worlds. It is " hid with Christ in God." Christ is my life in time, and he will permit me to be with him in the mansions of eternity. Oh what a mercy it is to feel that we have a present life, a spiritual life, in order that we may rise to live with God for ever. " And you hath he quickened who were dead in trespasses and sins." " I live," saith the apostle, "yet not I, but Christ liveth in me: and the life which I now live in the flesh I live by faith in the Son of God." Dear brethren, is it not a happiness to have all these powers communicated to us, through the gospel of our Redeemer, whereby we may live to his praise, and be for ever with the Lord?

But there is one thing which must not be forgotten. This Lamb that was to be slain was to have its blood sprinkled on the door-posts of the house, and on the lintel; but not upon the threshold. We are not to trample on the blood of Christ; but we are to look at it as a security from that death and condemnation which we as sinners deserve before God. When the destroying angel came to a house, and saw the blood sprinkled there, not an Israelite's child was to be smitten; while the children of the Egyptians were sure to lose their offspring as an instance of the vengeance of God.

Now, my dear brethren, do pray the Lord to make this part of the sermon profitable. Do remember that, precious as the blood of the Lamb is, it never will secure you, unless it be sprinkled on the door-posts of your heart; it never will avail unless applied. That is the grand work of faith: faith not only believes that Christ died for sinners, but faith goes more particularly to the application of it to the mind. I may hear of a rich man who has paid the debts of many people; but unless he has paid mine, his generosity to others is of no value to me. I want to know that all my debts are pardoned, and to have the certainty of it by the sanctifying influence of the Holy Spirit possessing my soul.

May the Lord bless these imperfect hints, for his Name's sake. Amen.

XV

TIMOTHY DWIGHT

1752–1817

TIMOTHY DWIGHT, S. T. D., LL.D., a learned theologian and a great educator, was born in Northampton, Massachusetts, May 14th, 1752. Much of his worth and labors in life were owing to his mother's training — a daughter of the great Jonathan Edwards. At the age of seventeen he graduated with honors from Yale College, acted as a tutor therein for six years, was licensed to preach in 1777, and served the year following as a chaplain in the American army. Pastoral and academic duties, mainly at Greenfield, intervened till his appointment as president of Yale College and professor of theology, in 1795. These duties he discharged with conspicuous ability till his death, January 11th, 1817. To each course of students he preached a series of Sermons, forming a systematic survey of theology. These were first published in 1846 in five volumes, entitled: " Theology Explained and Defended in a Series of Sermons." It has been said that these sermons, given at a time when a wave of infidelity after the French Revolution was sweeping over the land maintained the faith and held the students of Yale loyal to Christianity.

THE SOVEREIGNTY OF GOD.

" O Lord, I know that the way of man is not in himself: it is not in man that walketh to direct his steps."— Jeremiah x. 23.

IN this passage of Scripture, the prophet, after uttering a variety of sublime declarations concerning the perfections and providence of God, and the follies and sins of men, exhibits the progress of life as a Way. In this Way, all men are considered as travelling. We commence the journey at our birth; pass on through the several stages of childhood, youth, manhood, and old age, and finish it when we enter eternity. The accommodations, and the fare, are greatly varied among the various travellers. Some find their entertainment plentiful, and agreeable: and some, even luxurious and splendid. Others are slenderly provided with food, raiment, and lodging; are almost mere sufferers; and literally, *have not where to lay their heads.*

In the mean time, sorrow and disease, dangers and accidents, like a band of marauders, lie in wait for the travellers; and harass, and destroy, a great proportion of their number. Of the vast multitude, who continually walk in the path of life, almost all disappear long before they reach the goal at which it terminates. A very few arrive at the end. Of these, every one, dragging heavily his weary feet over the last division of the road, teaches us, that this part of his progress is only *labor and sorrow.*

A remarkable fact, universally attendant on our journey, is recited in the text. "O Lord," says the deeply humbled prophet, "I know that the way of man is not in himself; it is not in man that walketh to direct his steps." The enterprise is not contrived by ourselves. We are placed in it, and necessitated to accomplish it, by a superior and irresistible hand. It cannot but seem strange, that in such a journey we should originally be prevented from the ability to direct ourselves; and that, while we are compelled to the undertaking, we should be furnished for it in a manner so imperfect. Yet such is unquestionably the fact. Nor is the explanation so difficult, or so unsatisfactory, as we are prone to believe. God originally intended, that all his creatures should be dependent on him for aid, guidance, and protection. Nor can it be rationally supposed, that such a dependence on his perfections and providence is either unreasonable or undesirable. *The Sovereignty of God* which is so clearly and strongly visible in this interesting subject, has ever been questioned, and very often denied, by mankind. To establish this doctrine in the minds of my audience, is the peculiar design of the present discourse. In a sermon, lately delivered in this place on *the decrees of God,* I explained what I intend by the divine Sovereignty. It was then observed, that "the conduct of God is sovereign, in this sense; that he does according to his will, independently and irresistibly, without giving an account of any of his matters any farther than he pleases; but that he wills nothing without the best reason, whether that reason be disclosed to his creatures, or not; that real glory to himself, and real good to his creation, not otherwise attainable, are universally the object to which his pleasure is directed, whether it respects the existence and motions of an insect, or the salvation of a man." It was remarked, also, at that time, that, in the ordinary sense of the word, *God never acts arbitrarily; and that to say, he wills a thing because he wills it, is to speak without meaning.* All his pleasure, all his determinations, are perfectly wise and good; founded on the best of all reasons, and directed to the best of all purposes. Were he to act in any other manner, his providence would be less wise, and less desirable.

It will not be questioned, that this doctrine is deeply interesting to man. On this life is suspended that which is to come. Consequences, eternal and incomprehensible, will flow from those doctrines, which we adopt in the present world. All our conduct will then be examined; and will either be approved, or condemned. If we have chosen the strait and narrow way prescribed to us, the termination will be happy. If we have preferred *the broad and crooked road,* it will be deplorable.

Few of this audience will probably deny the truth of a direct Scriptural declaration. With as little, reason can it be denied, that most of them apparently live in the very manner, in which they would live, if the doctrine were false: or that they rely, chiefly at least, on their own sagacity, contrivance, and efforts, for success in this life, and that which is to come. As little can it be questioned, that such self-confidence is a guide eminently dangerous and deceitful. Safe as we may feel under its direction, our safety is imaginary. The folly of *others* in trusting to themselves *we* discern irresistibly. The same folly *they* perceive, with equal evidence, in *us.* Our true wisdom lies in willingly feeling, and cheerfully acknowledging, our dependence on God; and in committing ourselves with humble reliance to his care and direction.

With these observations, I will now proceed to illustrate the truth of the doctrine. The mode which I shall pursue will, probably, be thought singular. I hope it will be useful. Metaphysical arguments, which are customarily employed for the purpose of establishing this and several other doctrines of theology, are, if I mistake not, less satisfactory to the minds of men at large, than the authors of them appear to believe. Facts, wherever they can be fairly adduced for this end, are attended with a superior power of conviction; and commonly leave little doubt behind them. On these, therefore, I shall at the present time rely for the accomplishment of my design. In the

1st place, *The doctrine of the text is evident, from the great fact, that the birth and education of all men depend not on themselves.*

The succeeding events of life are derived, in a great measure at least, from our birth. By this event, it is in a prime degree determined whether men shall be princes or peasants, opulent or poor, learned or ignorant, honorable or despised; whether they shall be civilized or savage, freemen or slaves, Christians or Heathen, Mohammedans or Jews.

A child is born of Indian parents in the western wilderness. By his birth he is, of course, a savage. His friends, his mode of life, his habits, his knowledge, his opinions, his conduct, all grow out of this single event. His first thoughts, his first instructions, and all the first objects with which he is conversant, the persons whom he loves, the life to which he addicts himself, and the character which he assumes, are all savage. He is an Indian from the cradle: he is an Indian to the grave. To say, that he could not be otherwise, we are not warranted; but that he is not, is certain.

Another child is born of a Bedouin Arab. From this moment he begins to be an Arabian. *His hand is against every man; and every man's hand is against him.* Before he can walk, or speak, he is carried through pathless wastes in search of food; and roams in the arms of his mother, and on the back of a camel, from spring to spring, and from pasture to pasture. Even then he begins his conflict with hunger and thirst; is scorched by a vertical sun; shrivelled by the burning sand beneath; and poisoned by the breath of the Simoom. Hardened thus through his infancy and childhood, both in body and mind, he becomes, under the exhortations and example of his father, a robber from his youth; attacks every stranger whom he is able to overcome; and plunders every valuable thing on which he can lay his hand.

A third receives his birth in the palace of a British nobleman; and is welcomed to the world as the heir apparent of an ancient, honorable, and splendid family. As soon as he opens his eyes on the light, he is surrounded by all the enjoyments which opulence can furnish, ingenuity contrive, or fondness bestow. He is dandled on the knee of indulgence; encircled by attendants, who watch and prevent alike his necessities and wishes; cradled on down; and charmed to sleep by the voice of tenderness and care. From the dangers and evils of life he is guarded with anxious solicitude. To its pleasures he is conducted by the ever-ready hand of maternal affection. His person is shaped and improved by a succession of masters; his mind is opened, invigorated, and refined, by the assiduous superintendence of learning and wisdom. While a child, he is served by a host of menials, and flattered by successive trains of visitors. When a youth, he is regarded by a band of tenants with reverence and awe. His equals in age bow to his rank; and multitudes, of superior years, acknowledge his distinction by continual testimonies of marked respect. When a man, he engages the regard of his sovereign; commands the esteem of the senate; and earns the love and applause of his country.

A fourth child, in the same kingdom, is begotten by a beggar and born under a hedge. From his birth, he is trained to suffering and hardihood. He is nursed, if he can be said to be nursed at all, on a coarse, scanty, and precarious pittance; holds life only as a tenant at will; combats from the first dawnings of intellect with insolence, cold, and nakedness; is originally taught to beg and to steal; is driven from the doors of men by the porter or the house-dog; and is regarded as an alien from the family of Adam. Like his kindred worms, he creeps through life in the dust; dies under the hedge, where he is born; and is then, perhaps, cast into a ditch, and covered with earth, by some stranger, who remembers, that, although a beggar, he still was a man.

A child enters the world in China; and unites, as a thing of course, with his sottish countrymen in the stupid worship of the idol Fo. Another prostrates himself before the Lama, in consequence of having received his being in Thibet, and of seeing the Lama worshipped by all around him.

A third, who begins his existence in Turkey, is carried early to the mosque; taught to lisp with profound reverence the name of Mohammed; habituated to repeat the prayers and sentences of the Koran as the means of eternal life; and induced, in a manner irresistibly, to complete his title to Paradise by a pilgrimage to Mecca.

The Hindoo infant grows into a religious veneration for the cow; and perhaps never doubts, that, if he adds to this a solemn devotion to Juggernaut, the Gooroos, and the Dewtahs, and performs carefully his ablutions in the Ganges, he shall wash away all his sins, and obtain, by the favor of Brahma, a seat among the blessed.

In our own favored country, one child is born of parents devoted solely to this world. From his earliest moments of understanding, he hears and sees nothing commended, but hunting, horse-racing, visiting, dancing, dressing, riding, parties, gaming, acquiring money with eagerness and skill, and spending it in gayety, pleasure, and luxury. These things, he is taught by conversation and example, constitute all the good of man. His taste is formed, his habits are riveted, and the whole character of his soul is turned to them, before he is fairly sensible that there is any other good. The question, whether virtue and piety are either duties or blessings, he probably never asks. In the dawn of life he sees them

14

neglected and despised by those whom he most reverences; and learns only to neglect and despise them also. Of Jehovah he thinks as little, and for the same reason, as a Chinese or a Hindoo. *They* pay their devotions to Fo and to Juggernaut: *he,* his to money and pleasure. Thus he lives, and dies, a mere animal; a stranger to intelligence and morality, to his duty and his God.

Another child comes into existence in the mansion of Knowledge and Virtue. From his infancy, his mind is fashioned to wisdom and piety. In his infancy he is taught and allured to remember his Creator; and to unite, first in form, and then in affection, in the household devotions of the morning and evening. God he knows almost as soon as he can know anything. The presence of that glorious being he is taught to realize almost from the cradle; and from the dawn of intelligence, to understand the perfections and government of his Creator. His own accountableness as soon as he can comprehend it, he begins to feel habitually, and always. The way of life through the Redeemer is early, and regularly explained to him by the voice of parental love; and enforced and endeared in the house of God. As soon as possible, he is enabled to read and persuaded to " search, the Scriptures." Of the approach, the danger, and the mischiefs of temptations, he is tenderly warned. At the commencement of sin, he is kindly checked in his dangerous career. To God he was solemnly given in baptism. To God he was daily commended in fervent prayer. Under this happy cultivation he grows up, " like an olive tree in the courts of the Lord; " and, green, beautiful, and flourishing, he blossoms; bears fruit; and is prepared to be transplanted by the Divine hand to a kinder soil in the regions above.

How many, and how great, are the differences in these several children! How plainly do they all, in ordinary circumstances, arise out of their birth! From their birth is derived, of course, the education which I have ascribed to them; and from this education spring in a great measure both their character and their destiny. The place, the persons, the circumstances, are here evidently the great things which, in the ordinary course of Providence, appear chiefly to determine what the respective men shall be; and what shall be those allotments which regularly follow their respective characters. As, then, they are not at all concerned in contriving or accomplishing either their birth or their education; it is certain that, in these most important particulars, the way of man is not in himself. God only can determine what child shall spring from parents, wise or foolish, virtuous or sinful, rich or poor, honorable or infamous, civilized or savage, Christian or Heathen.

I wish it to be distinctly understood, and carefully remembered, that " in the moral conduct of all these individuals no physical necessity operates." Every one of them is absolutely a free agent; as free as any created agent can be. Whatever he does is the result of choice, absolutely unconstrained.

Let me add, that not one of them is placed in a situation in which, if he learns and performs his duty to the utmost of his power, he will fail of being finally accepted.

2dly. *The doctrine is strikingly evident from this great fact also; that the course of life, which men usually pursue, is very different from that, which they have intended.*

Human life is ordinarily little else than a collection of disappointments. Rarely is the life of man such as he designs it shall be. Often do we fail in pursuing, at all, the business originally in our view. The intentional farmer becomes a mechanic, a seaman, a merchant, a lawyer, a physician, or a divine. The very place of settlement, and of residence through life, is often different, and distant, from that which was originally contemplated. Still more different is the success which follows our efforts.

All men intend to be rich and honorable; to enjoy ease; and to pursue pleasure. But how small is the number of those who compass these objects! In this country, the great body of mankind are, indeed, possessed of competence; a safer and happier lot than that to which they aspire; yet few, very few are rich. Here also, the great body of mankind possess a character, generally reputable; but very limited is the number of those who arrive at the honor which they so ardently desire, and of which they feel assured. Almost all stop at the moderate level, where human efforts appear to have their boundary established in the determination of God. Nay, far below this level, creep multitudes of such as began life with full confidence in the attainment of distinction and splendor.

The Lawyer, emulating the eloquence, business, and fame, of Murray or Dunning, and secretly resolved not to slacken his efforts, until all his rivals in the race of glory are out-stripped, is often astonished, as well as broken-hearted, to find business and fame pass by his door, and stop at the more favored mansion of some competitor, in his view less able, and less discerning, than himself.

The physician, devoted to medical science, and possessed of distinguished powers of discerning and removing diseases, is obliged to walk; while a more fortunate empiric, ignorant and worthless, rolls through the streets in his coach.

The Legislator beholds with anguish and amazement, the suffrages of his countrymen given eagerly to a rival candidate, devoid of knowledge and integrity; but skilled in flattering the base passions of men, and deterred by no hesitations of conscience, and no fears of infamy, from saying and doing anything which may secure his election.

The Merchant often beholds with a despairing eye his own ships sunk in the ocean; his debtors fail; his goods unsold; his business cramped; and himself, his family, and his hopes, ruined: while a less skilful but more successful neighbor sees wealth blown to him by every wind, and floated on every wave.

The crops of the Farmer are stinted; his cattle die; his markets are bad; and the purchaser of his commodities proves to be a cheat who deceives his confidence, and runs away with his property.

Thus the darling schemes and fondest hopes of man are daily frustrated by time. While sagacity contrives, patience matures, and labor industriously executes; disappointment laughs at the curious fabric, formed by so many efforts, and gay with so many brilliant colors; and while the artists imagine the work arrived at the moment of completion, brushes away the beautiful web, and leaves nothing behind.

The designs of men, however, are in many respects not unfrequently successful. The Lawyer and Physician acquire business and fame; the Statesman, votes; and the Farmer, wealth. But their real success, even in this case, is often substantially the same with that already recited. In all plans and all labors, the supreme object is *to become happy*. Yet, when men have actually acquired riches and honor, or secured to themselves popular favor, they still find the happiness, which they expected, eluding their grasp. Neither wealth, fame, office, nor sensual pleasure can yield such good as *we* need. As these coveted objects are accumulated; the wishes of man always grow faster than his gratifications. Hence, whatever he acquires he is usually as little satisfied and often less than before.

A principal design of the mind in laboring for these things is *to become superior to others*. But almost all rich men are obliged to see, and usually with no small anguish, others richer than themselves; honorable men, others more honorable; voluptuous men, others who enjoy more pleasure. The great end of the strife is therefore unobtained; and the happiness expected never found. Even the successful competitor in the race utterly misses his aim. The real enjoyment existed, although it was unperceived by him, in the mere strife for superiority. When he has outstripped all his rivals, the contest is at an end: and his spirits, which were invigorated only by contending, languish for want of a competitor.

Besides, the happiness in view was only the indulgence of pride, or mere animal pleasure. Neither of these can satisfy or endure. A rational mind may be, and often is, so narrow and grovelling, as not to aim at any higher good, to understand its nature, or to believe its existence. Still, in its original constitution, it was formed with a capacity for intellectual and moral good, and was destined to find in this good its only satisfaction. Hence, no inferior good will fill its capacity or its desires. Nor can this bent of its nature ever be altered. Whatever other enjoyment, therefore, it may attain; it will, without this, still crave and still be unhappy.

No view of the ever-varying character and success of mankind in their expectations of happiness, and their efforts to obtain it, can illustrate this doctrine more satisfactorily than that of the progress and end of a class of students in this seminary. At their first appearance here they are all exactly on the same level. Their character, their hopes and their destination are the same. They are enrolled on one list; and enter upon a collegiate life with the same promise of success. At this moment they are plants, appearing just above the ground; all equally fair and flourishing. Within a short time, however, some begin to rise above others; indicating by a more rapid growth a structure of superior vigor, and promising both more early and more abundant fruit.

Some are studious, steadfast, patient of toil, resolved on distinction, in love with science, and determined with unbroken ambition never to be left behind by their companions. Of these a part are amiable, uniform in their morals, excellent in their dispositions, and honorable by their piety. Another part, although less amiable, are still decent, pleasant in their temper, uncensurable in their conduct, and reputable in their character.

Others are thoughtless, volatile, fluttering from object to object, particularly from one scene of pleasure to another, alighting only for a mo-

ment, never settling, regardless of everything except the present gratification, and most regardless of their time, their talents, their duty, and
their souls.

Others still are openly vicious, idle, disorderly; gamblers, profane,
apparently infidels; enemies to themselves, undutiful to their parents, cor-
rupters of their companions, and disturbers of the collegiate peace.

When the class, which these individuals originally constituted, leaves
this seat of science; a number of them will always be missing. Some of
these have been sent away by the mandate of law; some have voluntarily
deserted their education; and some not very unfrequently have gone to
the grave. Of those who remain, the character and the prospects have
usually become widely different. The original level is broken, and broken
for ever.

How different from all this were their parents' expectations and
their own!

Still, when they enter the world, they all intend to be rich, honorable,
and happy. Could they look into futurity, and discern the events which
it will shortly unfold; how changed would be their apprehensions!

One, almost at his entrance into life, knowing but inexperienced, discerning but not wise, urged by strong passions, and secure in self-confidence, pushes boldly forward to affluence and distinction; but, marked as
the prey of cunning and the victim of temptation, is seduced from prudence and worth to folly, vice, and ruin. His property is lost by bold
speculation, his character by licentiousness, and the man himself by the
disappointment of his hopes and the breaking of his heart.

Another, timid, humble, reluctant to begin, and easily discouraged
from pursuing, insensible to the charms of distinction, and a stranger to
the inspiration of hope, without friends to sustain and without prospects
to animate, begins to flag, when he commences his connection with the
world, creeps through life because he dares not attempt to climb, and
lives and dies, scarcely known beyond the limits of his native village.

A third yields himself up a prey to sloth, and shrinks into insig-
nificance for want of exertion.

A fourth, possessed of moderate wishes, and preferring safety to
grandeur, steers of design between poverty and riches, obscurity and
distinction, walks through life without envying those who ride, and finds,
perhaps, in quiet and safety, in an even course of enjoyment, and in
the pleasure of being beloved rather than admired, the happiness which

his more restless companions seek from opulence, power, and splendor in vain.

A fifth, cheerful, fraught with hope, and assured by the gayety and bustle, which he sees around him, that the world is filled with good, moves onward to acquire it, without a suspicion of disappointment or danger. At once he is astonished to find, that men, who look pleasantly on him, are not his friends; that a smile of approbation is no evidence of good-will; and that professions and promises convey to him no assurance of aid or comfort. To be dependent, he soon learns, is to be friendless, and to need assistance, a sufficient reason for having it refused. The business, which he expected to court his acceptance, flies from him; the countenance, on which he reposed, is withdrawn, and the hopes, which he gayly cherished, begin early to wither. Alone, forgotten, unprepared for struggles, and never mistrusting that struggles would be necessary, he is overset by the suddenness and violence of the shock, and either falls into listlessness and stupor, or dies of a broken heart.

A sixth, from imbecility of constitution or the malignant power of accident, sickens and expires, when he has scarcely begun to live.

A seventh, with vigorous industry, effort, and perseverance, goes steadily forward to wealth and distinction. Yet even *he* finds the void of his mind unsupplied by real good. He is rich and great, but not happy. That enchanting object, happiness, wrought into such elegance of form and adorned with such brilliant colors, has ever fascinated his mind. Lost in wonder and delight, and gazing with an eager and bewildered eye, he never considered, that in this world the rainbow with all its splendor was only painted on a cloud; and, while he roves from field to field, and climbs from one height to another in pursuit of the fairy vision, is astonished to behold it still retreat before him, and finally vanish for ever.

Were I to ask the youths who are before me, what are their designs and expectations concerning their future life, and write down their several answers; what a vast difference would ultimately be found between those answers, and the events which would actually befall them! To how great a part of that difference would facts, over which they could have no control, give birth! How many of them will in all probability be less prosperous, rich, and honorable than they now intend: how many, devoted to employments, of which at present they do not even dream; in circumstances, of which they never entertained even a thought; behind those whom they expected to outrun, poor, sick, in sorrow or in the grave.

3dly. *The doctrine is further evident from the fact, that Life does not depend upon man.*

All intend to live, and feel secure of many years: but how often does death frustrate this intention, and dissolve the charm of this security! How many leave the world at an immature age! How many, in the midst of bold projects, sanguine desires, and strenuous exertions! How many asterisks appear with a melancholy aspect even in the younger classes of the triennial catalogue: marking solemnly, to a considerate mind, the termination of parental hopes, and the vanity of youthful designs! Where now are multitudes of those who a little while since lived, and studied and worshipped, here, with fond views of future eminence and prosperity, and with as fair a promise as can be found, of future success, usefulness, and honor?

As we are unable to assure ourselves even of a single day, much more of a long life, it is plain, that our eternal state lies beyond our control. As death finds us, so the judgment will certainly find us. He therefore, who *kills,* as well as *makes alive,* at his pleasure, must of course hold in his hands, only, all our allotments which lie beyond the grave.

I have not called up this doctrine at the present time, for the purpose of entering into any of those metaphysical disquisitions, which restless curiosity, rather than sound wisdom, has commonly founded on it; but on the one hand to give it its proper place in this system of discourses, and on the other to derive from it several practical observations, which, there is reason to hope, may, by the blessing of God, be useful to those who hear me, especially to those who are students in this seminary.

REMARKS.

1st. *You see here, my young friends, the most solid reasons for gratitude to your Creator.*

God, only, directed that you should be born in this land, and in the midst of peace, plenty, civilization, freedom, learning, and religion; and that your existence should not commence in a Tartarian forest or an African waste. God, alone, ordered that you should be born of parents who knew and worshipped Him, the glorious and eternal Jehovah; and not of parents who bowed before the Lama or the ox, an image of brass or the stock of a tree. In the book of his counsels, your names, so far as we are able to judge, were written in the fair lines of mercy.

It is of his overflowing goodness, that you are now here; surrounded with privileges, and beset with blessings, educated to knowledge, usefulness, and piety, and prepared to begin an endless course of happiness and glory. All these delightful things have been poured into your lap, and have come, unbidden, to solicit your acceptance. If these blessings awaken not gratitude, it cannot be awakened by blessings in the present world. If they are not thankfully felt by *you,* it is because you know not how to be thankful. Think what you are, and where you are; and what and where you just as easily might have been. Remember, that, instead of cherishing tender affections, imbibing refined sentiments, exploring the field of science, and assuming the name and character of the sons of God, you might as easily have been dozing in the smoke of a wigwam, brandishing a tomahawk, or dancing round an embowelled captive; or that you might yourselves have been embowelled by the hand of superstition, and burnt on the altars of Moloch. If you remember these things, you cannot but call to mind, also, *who made you to differ* from the miserable beings who have thus lived and died.

2dly. *This doctrine forcibly demands of you moderate desires and expectations.*

There are two modes, in which men seek happiness in the enjoyments of the present world. "Most persons freely indulge their wishes, and intend to find objects sufficient in number and value, to satisfy them." A few "aim at satisfaction by proportioning their desires to the number and measure of their probable gratifications." By the doctrine of the text, the latter method is stamped with the name of wisdom, and on the former is inscribed the name of folly. Desires indulged grow faster and farther than gratifications extend. Ungratified desire is misery. Expectations eagerly indulged and terminated by disappointment, are often exquisite misery. But how frequently are expectations raised, only to be disappointed, and desires let loose, only to terminate in distress! The child pines for a toy: the moment he possesses it, he throws it by, and cries for another. When they are piled up in heaps around him, he looks at them without pleasure, and leaves them without regret. He knew not, that all the good, which they could yield, lay in expectation; nor that his wishes for more would increase faster than toys could be multiplied, and is unhappy at last for the same reason as at first: his wishes are ungratified. Still indulging them, and still believing that the gratification of them will furnish the enjoyment for which he pines, he goes on, only to be unhappy.

Men are merely taller children. Honor, wealth, and splendor are the toys for which grown children pine; but which, however accumulated, leave them still disappointed and unhappy. God never designed that intelligent beings should be satisfied with these enjoyments. By his wisdom and goodness they were formed to derive their happiness from Virtue.

Moderated desires constitute a character fitted to acquire all the good which this world can yield. He, who is prepared, *in whatever situation he is, therewith to be content,* has learned effectually the science of being happy, and possesses the alchymic stone, which will change every metal into gold. Such a man will smile upon a stool, while Alexander at his side sits weeping on the throne of the world.

The doctrine of the text teaches you irresistibly, that since you cannot command gratifications, you should command your desires; and that, as the events of life do not accord with your wishes, your wishes should accord with *them.* Multiplied enjoyments fall to but few men, and are no more rationally expected than the highest prize in a lottery. But a well regulated mind, a dignified independence of the world, and a wise preparation to possess one's soul in patience, whatever circumstances may exist, is in the power of every man, and is greater wealth than that of both Indies, and greater honor than Cæsar ever acquired.

3dly. *As your course and your success through life are not under your control, you are strongly urged to commit yourselves to God, who can control both.*

That you cannot direct your course through the world, that your best concerted plans will often fail, that your sanguine expectations will be disappointed, and that your fondest worldly wishes will terminate in mortification, cannot admit of a momentary doubt. That God can direct you, that he actually controls all your concerns, and that, if you commit yourselves to his care, he will direct you kindly and safely, can be doubted only of choice. Why, then, do you hesitate to yield yourselves and your interests to the guidance of your Maker? There are two reasons, which appear especially to govern mankind in this important concern: they do not and will not realize the agency of God in their affairs; and they do not choose to have them directed as they imagine he will direct them. The former is the result of stupidity; the latter, of impiety. Both are foolish in the extreme, and not less sinful than foolish.

The infinitely wise, great, and glorious Benefactor of the universe has offered to take men by the hand, lead them through the journey of life, and conduct them to his own house in the heavens. The proof of his sincerity in making this offer has been already produced. He has given his own Son to live, and die, and rise, and reign, and intercede for our race. "Herein is love," if there ever was love; "not that we have loved him, but that he has loved us." That he, who has done this, should not be sincere, is impossible. St. Paul, therefore, triumphantly asks what none can answer: "He, that spared not his own Son, but delivered him up for us all, how shall he not with him also freely give us all things?" Trust, then, his word with undoubting confidence; take his hand with humble gratitude, and with all the heart obey his voice, which you will everywhere hear, saying, "this is the way, walk ye therein." In sickness and in health, by night and by day, at home and in crowds, he will watch over you with tenderness inexpressible. He will "make you lie down in green pastures, lead you beside the still waters, and guide you in paths of righteousness, for his Name's sake. He will prepare a table before you in the presence of your enemies, and cause your cup to run over with blessings. When you pass through the waters of affliction, he will be with you, and through the rivers, they shall not overflow you. When you walk through the fire, you shall not be burned; neither shall the flame kindle on you." From their native heavens, he will commission those charming twin-sisters, Goodness and Mercy, to descend and "follow you all your days."

But if you wish God to be your guide and your friend, you must conform to his pleasure. Certainly you cannot wonder, that the infinitely Wise should prefer his own wisdom to yours, and that he should choose for his children their allotments, rather than leave them to choose for themselves. That part of his pleasure, which you are to obey, is all summed up in the single word, Duty, and is perfectly disclosed in the Scriptures. The whole scheme is so formed as to be plain, easy, profitable, and delightful; profitable in hand, delightful in the possession. Every part and precept of the whole, is calculated for this end, and will make you only wise, good, and happy.

Life has been often styled an ocean, and our progress through it a voyage. The ocean is tempestuous and billowy, overspread by a cloudy sky, and fraught beneath with shelves and quicksands. The voyage is eventful beyond comprehension, and at the same time full of uncertainty, and replete with danger. Every adventurer needs to be well prepared for whatever may befall him, and well secured against the manifold hazards of losing his course, sinking in the abyss, or of being wrecked against the shore.

These evils have existed at all times. The present, and that part of the past which is known to you by experience, has seen them multiplied beyond example. It has seen the ancient and acknowledged standards of thinking violently thrown down. Religion, morals, government, and the estimate formed by man of crimes and virtues, and of all the means of usefulness and enjoyment, have been questioned, attacked, and in various places, and with respect to millions of the human race, finally overthrown. A licentiousness of opinion and conduct, daring, outrageous, and rending asunder every bond, formed by God or man, has taken place of former good sense and sound morals, and has long threatened the destruction of human good. Industry, cunning, and fraud have toiled with unrivalled exertions, to convert man into a savage, and the world into a desert. A wretched and hypocritical philanthropy, also, not less mischievous, has stalked forth as the companion of these ravagers: a philanthropy born in a dream, bred in a novel, and living only in professions. This guardian genius of human interests, this friend of human rights, this redresser of human wrongs, is yet without a heart to feel, and without a hand to bless. But she is well furnished with lungs, with eyes, and a tongue. She can talk, and sigh, and weep at pleasure, but can neither pity nor give. The objects of her attachment are either knaves and villains at home, or unknown sufferers beyond her reach abroad. To the former, she ministers the sword and the dagger, that they may fight their way into place, and power, and profit. At the latter, she only looks through a telescope of fancy, as an astronomer searches for stars invisible to the eye. To every real object of charity within her reach, she complacently says, " Be thou warmed, and be thou filled; depart in peace."

By the daring spirit, the vigorous efforts, and the ingenious cunning, so industriously exerted on the one hand, and the smooth and gentle benevolence, so softly professed on the other, multitudes have been, and you easily may be, destroyed. The mischief has indeed been met, resisted, and overcome; but it has the heads and the lives of the Hydra, and its *wounds,* which at times have seemed *deadly,* are much more readily *healed,* than any good man could wish, than any sober man could expect. Hope not to escape the assaults of this enemy: To feel that you are in danger, will ever be a preparation for your safety. But it will be only such a preparation; your deliverance must ultimately and only flow from your Maker. Resolve, then, to commit yourselves to him with a cordial reliance on his wisdom, power, and protection. Consider how much you have at stake, that you are bound to eternity, that your existence will be immortal, and that you will either rise to endless glory or be lost in absolute perdition. Heaven is your proper home. The path, which I have recommended to you, will conduct you safely and certainly to that happy world. Fill up life, therefore, with obedience to God, with faith in the Lord Jesus Christ, and repentance unto life, the obedience to the two great commands of the Gospel, with supreme love to God and universal good-will to men, the obedience to the two great commands of the law. On all your sincere endeavors to honor him, and befriend your fellow-men, he will smile; every virtuous attempt he will bless: every act of obedience he will reward. Life in this manner will be pleasant amid all its sorrows; and beams of hope will continually shine through the gloom, by which it is so often overcast. Virtue, the seed that cannot die, planted from heaven, and cultivated by the divine hand, will grow up in your hearts with increasing vigor, and blossom in your lives with supernal beauty. Your *path* will be that of *the just,* and will gloriously resemble the dawning light, "which shines brighter and brighter, to the perfect day." Peace will take you by the hand, and offer herself as the constant and delightful companion of your progress. Hope will walk before you, and with an unerring finger point out your course; and Joy, at the end of the journey, will open her arms to receive you. You will "wait on the Lord, and renew your strength; will mount up with wings, as eagles; will run, and not be weary; will walk, and not faint."

XVI

ROBERT HALL

1764–1831

ROBERT HALL, one of the great lights of the Baptist church, in England, was born at Arnesby, Leicestershire, May 2d, 1764, and died February 21st, 1831. He studied at King's College, Aberdeen, and at nineteen became an assistant Baptist minister in Broadmead Chapel, near Bristol. Subsequently he labored in Cambridge and Leicester, returning to Bristol in 1835. His treasures of learning and gifts of glowing eloquence were unsurpassed. Artless, earnest, sincere, and wholly absorbed in his discourse, his hearers would grow so entranced by his sublime appeals, that often many would start to their feet and remain standing till he ceased speaking. Dugald Stewart called him a writer of English in its perfection, "combining the beauties of Johnson, Addison, and Burke, without their imperfections." He suffered acutely from spine disease, and had several attacks of mental derangement, but was till death a faithful pastor and student.

MARKS OF LOVE TO GOD.

" But I know you, that ye have not the love of God in you."— John v. 42.

THE persons whom our Lord addressed in these words made a high profession of religion, valued themselves upon their peculiar opportunities of knowing the true God and his will, and proclaimed themselves as the Israel and the temple of the Lord, while they despised the surrounding pagans as those who were strangers to the divine law. Yet the self complacent Pharisees of our Saviour's age were as far from the love of God, he assures them in the text, as any of those who had never heard of his name. In this respect, *many of " the first were*

ROBERT HALL.
1764-1831.
A great English Baptist, noted for his learning
and his eloquence, in spite of great bodily infirmities. He is rated among the most perfect writers
of literary English.

TIMOTHY DWIGHT.
1752-1817.
A grandson of Jonathan Edwards, served as
chaplain in the American army during the Revolution and later as professor at Yale; exerted a
great influence in behalf of orthodox Christianity.

last, and the last first." The rejection of the gospel evinces a hardness of heart which is *decisive* against the character; and, in the case of the Pharisees, it gave ample evidence that they possessed no love of God. Had they really known *God,* as our Lord argues, they would have known *himself* to be sent by God: whereas, in proving the bitter enemies of Christ, they proved that they were in a state of enmity against God. By parity of reason, *we,* my brethren, who know God and his word in the way of Christian profession, ought *not* to take it for granted that we possess the love of God, and are in the way of eternal life: the same self-delusion may overtake *us* also; and similar admonitions may be no less necessary to many present, than to the Pharisees of old. Suffer then, my brethren, the word of exhortation, while I invite each individual seriously to consider this subject, with a view to the discovery of his real character.

In proceeding to lay down certain *marks* of grace, let it be premised, that either these marks partake of the *nature* of true religion, or they do *not.* If they *do,* they must be *identified* with it, and here the mark is the *thing:* if they do *not* partake of its nature, some of them may exist as indications where genuine religion is not. It is necessary, then, that we combine a *variety* of particular *signs* of grace: any *one* taken by itself, may, or may *not,* exist, *without* true religion; but where *many* are combined, no just doubt can remain.

Whether you have the love of God in your soul, presents a most critical subject of inquiry; since the love of God will be acknowledged by all to be the great, the essential, principle of true religion. The simple question, then, to which I would call your attention, is this: " Am I, or am I not, a sincere lover of the Author of my being? "

In endeavoring to assist you in the decision of this momentous question, as it respects yourselves,

I. I shall entreat your attention while I suggest a variety of *marks* which indicate love to God; and

II. Supposing the conviction produced by the statement to be, that you have *not* the love of God, I shall point out the proper improvement of such a conviction.

I. In suggesting various marks by which you may ascertain whether you love God, or not, I would mention,

1. The *general* bent and turn of your *thoughts,* when not under the immediate control of circumstances; for these, you are aware, give a new and peculiar bias to our thoughts, and stamp them with an impress

of their own. There is an infinite variety of thoughts continually passing through the mind of every individual: of these, some are thrown up by occasions; but others, and often the greater part, follow the habitual train of our associations. It is not to thoughts of the former kind that I refer; it is to those of the latter class,— those *voluntary* thoughts which spring up of *themselves* in the mind of every person: it is these, not the former, that afford clear indication of the *general temper and disposition.* The question I would propose to you is, What is the bent of your thoughts, when, disengaged from the influence of any particular occurrence, you are left *to yourselves,* in the intervals of retirement and tranquillity, in the silence of the midnight watches, and, in short, whenever your mind is left free to its own spontaneous musings? Are the thoughts most familiar to your mind, at such times, thoughts of God and the things of God;— or, are they thoughts that turn upon the present world and its transient concerns? Are they confined, for the most part, within the narrow circle of time and sense; or, do they make frequent and large excursions into the spiritual and eternal world? The answer to *this* question will go far to decide whether you have, or have *not,* the love of God. It is impossible that such an object as the Divine Being should be absent long from your thoughts; impossible that *his* remembrance should long remain merged in the stream of other imaginations; unless you are supposed chargeable with a *decided indifference* to divine things! Unless you are destitute of love to God, you can never be so utterly uncongenial in sentiment and feeling with the Psalmist, when he says, " My mouth shall praise thee with joyful lips, while I meditate upon thee in the night watches: " " How precious are thy thoughts unto me, O God! " When that man of God gazed upon the starry heavens, his mind was not merely wrought into astonishment at the physical energy there displayed; he was still more deeply lost in grateful admiration of the mercy of Providence as manifested to *man:*— a sinful child of dust, and yet visited by God in the midst of so magnificent a universe! But when day passes after day, and night after night, without any serious thoughts of God, it is plain that He is not the *home* of your mind, not your *portion, centre,* and *resting-place:* and, if this is the case, it is equally plain that you are not in a state of acceptance with Him; since nothing can be more certain than that, *as* our thoughts are, *such* must be our *character.* I do not ask what are your thoughts at particular *times,* or under the influence of some particular *event:* there may be little difference, on some oc-

casions, between those who remember, and those who neglect, God
habitually. The charge against the ungodly is, that " God is not in *all*
their thoughts." If there are any here who feel this charge as bearing
against *themselves,* let them take that solemn warning given by God
himself at the close of the fiftieth Psalm " Oh, consider this, ye that
forget God, lest I tear you in pieces, and there be none to deliver you!"

2. Let me request you to consider seriously how you stand disposed
to the *exercises of religion.* If God is the object of your love, you will
gladly avail yourselves of the most favorable opportunities of cultivating
a closer friendship with the Father of your spirits: on the contrary, he
who feels no regard for these opportunities, proves that he has no love
to God, and will never be able to establish the conviction that God is
his friend. Wherever there exists a sincere friendship, opportunities of
cultivating it are gladly embraced, and the opposite privations are re-
gretted. Where an *habitual neglect* of sacred exercises prevails, it must
be interpreted as if it said, like those whom the prophet describes, " Cause
the Holy One of Israel to cease from amongst us. Depart from us, for
we desire not the knowledge of thy ways!" If your closets seldom
witness your private devotions, if your moments in retirement are languid and uninteresting,— your religion can have no hold on your heart;
and the reason why your religion has no hold on your heart, is because
you have no love of God. There are some whose religion sits easy and
delightful upon them; its acts and functions are free and lively: there
are others who seem to bear their religion as a burthen, to drag their
duties as a *chain* — as *no vital part of themselves,* but rather a cumbrous
appendage: this is a decisive and melancholy symptom of a heart
alienated from God. There is no genuine religion, no real contact of
the heart with the best of beings, unless it makes us continually resort
to Him as our *chief joy.* The Psalmist is always expressing his fervent
desires after God: after the light of the divine countenance, and the
sense of the divine favor: but do you suppose such desires *peculiar*
to the state of believers under the *Old* Testament? *No,* my brethren;
there exist more abundant reasons than ever, since the gospel of Christ
has been displayed in all the glorious fullness of its blesssings, why
our souls should be inflamed with such feelings as those which inspired
the Psalmist, when he exclaimed, " As the hart panteth for the water-
brooks, so longeth my soul after thee, O God!"

3. If you would ascertain whether you love God, consider how
you stand affected toward the *word* of God. We can entertain no just

15

thoughts of God, but such as we derive from his own word: we can
acquire no true knowledge of God, nor cherish any suitable affections
towards him, unless they are such as his own revelation authorizes.
Otherwise we must suppose that revelation insufficient for its specific
purposes, and set the *means* against the *end*. All, therefore, who sincerely love God, are *students* of his word; they here, also, accord in
soul with the Psalmist, and, like him, can say, "O how I love thy word!
in it is my meditation all the day:" they eat it as food for their souls,
and find it *sweeter than honey*. They go to it as to an inexhaustible
fountain, and drink from it streams of sacred light and joy. A neglected Bible is too unambiguous a sign of an unsanctified heart; since
that blessed book cannot fail to attract every one that loves its Divine
Author. How is it possible to delight in God, and yet neglect *that*
word which alone reveals him in his true and glorious character,—
alone discovers the way by which he comes into unison with us, and
condescends to pardon us, to love us, and to guide us through all this
mysterious state of being? It is observable, that the *only* persons who
are inattentive to their own sacred books are to be found among *Christians*. *Mahomedans* commit large portions of the Koran to memory; the
Jews regard the Old Testament with reverence; the *Hindoo Bramins*
are enthusiastically attached to their Shaster; while *Christians* alone
neglect their Bible. And the reason is, that the *Scriptures* are so much
more spiritual than the religious books received by others: they afford
so little scope for mere amusement or self-complacency;— they place
the reader *alone with God,*— they withdraw him from the things that
are seen and temporal, and fix him among the things that are unseen
and eternal,— they disclose to his view at once the secret evils of his
own condition, and the awful purity of that Being with whom he has
to do. No wonder the ungodly man hates their light, neither comes
to their light, but retires from it farther and farther into the shades
of guilty ignorance. How melancholy the infatuation of such a character!

4. Estimate your character in respect to your love of God, by
reflecting, with what sentiments you regard the *people* of God. God
has a people peculiarly his own: they are *not* of that world to which they
outwardly belong,— not conformed to it in the spirit of their mind;
they stand apart, many of them at least, in conspicuous conformity to
Jesus Christ, and earnest expectation of the glory which He has promised. How, then, do you regard these decided followers of God? Do

you shun their society with aversion and secret shame; or do you enjoy their communion as one of the most delightful among your Christian privileges? Are you content merely to be the companion of those who " have a *name* to live, but are dead: " or can you say with the Psalmist, " My delight is in the excellent of the earth? " or, with the beloved disciple, " We know that we have passed from death unto life, because we love the brethren? " for, as he adds, " He that loveth him that begot, loveth him that is begotten:" if you do not love the *image* which you have *seen,* how can you love the *unseen* original? If the features of holiness and grace in the *creature* are not attractive to your view, how can your affections rise to the perfect *essence?* How can you ascend to the very *Sun* itself, when you cannot enjoy even the faint *reflection* of its glory? He who knew the heart, could alone say to those around him, " I *know you,* that ye have not the love of God in you: " but though none can address you now in the same tone of divine authority, yet you may hear it uttered by a voice within —the voice of your own conscience: you may know, without any perturbations of hope or fear, by the spiritual insensibility and inaction of your soul,— by *this* you may know, with equal certainty as by a voice from heaven, that *you have not the love of God in you!*

5. Consider the disposition you entertain toward the person and office of the *Son of God.* " If ye had loved the Father, ye would have loved me also," was the constant argument of Jesus Christ to those Pharisees whom he addresses in the text. For Jesus Christ is the express *image* of God: the effulgence of the divine character is attempered in *him,* to suit the views of sinful humanity. In the life of Jesus Christ, we see how the Divine Being conducts himself in human form and in our own circumstances: we behold how he bears all the sorrows, and passes through all the temptations, of flesh and blood. Such, indeed, is the identity, so perfect the *oneness* of character, between the *man Christ Jesus* and the *Divine Being,*— that our Saviour expressly assures us, " He that hath seen *me,* hath seen the *Father; I* and my Father are *one."* The purpose for which God was manifested in the flesh was, not to reveal high speculations concerning the nature of the Deity: it was to *bear* our sorrows, and to *die* for our sins. But can *you* contemplate Him, thus stooping to your condition, thus *mingling* with every interest of *your own,* and not be *moved* by such a spectacle?— not be *attracted, fixed,* filled with grateful astonishment and devotion,— crucified, as it were, on the cross of Christ, to the flesh, and to the world?

What mark, then, of our possessing no love of *God* can equal this, that we are without love to *Jesus Christ?*— that neither the *visibility* of his divine excellence, nor his *participation* of all our human sufferings, can reach our hearts, and command our affections?

6. In examining whether you love God, examine how you are affected by his *benefits. These* are so numerous and so distinguished, that they ought to excite our most ardent gratitude: night and day they are experienced by us; they pervade every moment of our being. We know that favors from an *enemy* derive a *taint* from the hands through which they are received, and excite alienation rather than attachment: but the kindness of a *friend,* by constantly reminding us of himself, endears that friend more and more to our hearts; and thus, he that has no love to God receives all his favors without the least attraction toward their Author, whom he regards rather as his enemy than his friend. But the Christian feels his love of God excited by every fresh instance of his goodness. The mercies of God have accompanied you through every stage of your journey; and they are exhibited to you in his word as stretching through a vast eternity. Are *these* the *only* benefits you can receive without gratitude, and suffer to pass unregarded? *How,* then, can any love of God dwell in your bosom?

7. Consider, in the next place, in what manner you are impressed by the sense of your *sins.* The question is *not* whether you *have* any sins,— none can admit a doubt on this point; the only inquiry is, how you are affected by those sins? Are they remembered by you with a sentiment of *tender regret, of deep confusion and humiliation,* that you should ever have *so* requited such infinite goodness? And is this sentiment combined with a *sacred resolution to go and sin no more,*— to *devote* yourself to the service of your Divine Benefactor? If you can live without an habitual sense of penitential tenderness and reverential fear, be assured you cannot love God; you have no experience of those scripture declarations: " They shall FEAR the Lord and his goodness in the latter days;" " There is forgiveness with thee, that thou mayest be FEARED;" you know not yet that " the goodness of God leadeth to repentance." If the mind is softened by the love of God, all his favors serve to inflame its gratitude, and confirm its devotion to his will: but he who has no love of God in his soul, thinks of nothing but how he may *escape* from God's hand, and selfishly devours all his favors without an emotion of gratitude to the Giver.

8. Finally, let me remind you to consider how you are affected to

the *present world*. If you could only be exempt from its afflictions, would you wish it to be your *lasting* home? If you could surround yourself with all its advantages and enjoyments, would you be content to dwell in it for ever? Yet you know that it is a place of separation and exile from the Divine Majesty;— that it is a scene of darkness, in comparison with heaven, very faintly illuminated with the beams of his distant glory;— that its inhabitant is constrained to say, "I have heard of thee by the hearing of the ear, but mine eye hath *not* yet *seen* thee;" — while *heaven* is the proper dwelling-place of God and his people! Could you then consent to remain here always, without ever *seeing as you are seen,— seeing light in his light,*— without ever *beholding his glory;* without ever drinking at the fountain, and basking in *that presence which is fullness of joy, and life for evermore!* always to remain *immersed* in the shadows of time — entombed in its corruptible possessions! *never* to ascend up on high to God and Christ and the glories of the eternal world! If such is the state of your spirit, you want the essential principle of a Christian — you want the love of God. The genuine Christian, the lover of God, is certain to feel himself a *"stranger on the earth."* No splendor, no emolument of this world,— not all the fascinations of sensual pleasure,— can detain his heart below the skies, or keep him from sympathizing with the sentiment of the Psalmist: "As for me I shall behold thy face in righteousness; I shall be satisfied when I wake in thy likeness." I do not ask whether you have, at present, *"a desire to depart:"* perhaps you may not be as yet sufficiently prepared and established to entertain so exalted a desire; but still, if you have received a *new* heart, you will deprecate nothing so much as having your portion in *this* life,— as having your eternal abode on *earth*. It is the character of faith to dwell much in eternity: the apostle says, in the name of all real believers, "We look not at the things that are seen, but the things that are not seen; for the things that are seen are temporal, but the things that are not seen are eternal."

II. And now, my brethren, supposing the preceding remarks to have produced in any of you the conviction *that you have not the love of God in you,* permit me very briefly to point out the proper *improvement* of such a conviction.

1. First, it should be accompanied with deep *humiliation*. If you labored under the privation of some bodily organ, requisite to the discharge of an animal function, you would feel it as in some degree a

humiliating circumstance; but what would be any defect of this kind, however serious, in comparison with that *great want* under which you labor — the want of piety, the calamity of *a soul estranged from the love of God!* What are all other subjects of humiliation, compared with *this* — a *moral fall,* a *spiritual death in sin:* and this, unless it be removed, the sure precursor of the *second death — eternal ruin!* "This is a lamentation indeed, and it shall be for a lamentation."

Suppose the children of a family, reared and provided for by the most affectionate of parents, to rise up in rebellion against their father, and cast off all the feelings of filial tenderness and respect; would any qualities those children might possess, any *appearance* of virtue they might exhibit in other respects, compensate for such an unnatural, such an awful deformity of character? Transfer this representation to your conduct in relation to God: "If I," says he, "am a *father,* where is my fear? if I am a *master,* where is my honor?" "Hear, O heavens, and give ear, O earth! I have nourished and brought up children, and they have rebelled against me: the ox knoweth his owner, and the ass his master's crib: but Israel doth not know, my people doth not consider."

2. And let your humiliation be accompanied with *concern and alarm.* To be alienated from the Great Origin of being; to be severed, or to sever yourself from the essential Author and element of all felicity, must be a calamity which none can understand, an infinite woe which none can measure or conceive! If the stream is cut off from the fountain, it soon ceases to flow, and its waters are dissipated in the air: and if the soul is cut off from *God,* it *dies!* Its *vital contact* with God,— its spiritual union with the Father of Spirits through the blessed Mediator, is the only life and beauty of the immortal soul. All, without this, are *dead* — "*dead in trespasses and sins!*" A living death — a state of restless wanderings, and unsatisfied desires! What a condition theirs! And, oh! what a prospect for such, when they look beyond this world! who will give them a welcome when they enter an eternal state? What reception will they meet with, and where? What consolation amidst their loss and their sufferings, but that of the fellow-sufferers plunged in the same abyss of ruin? Impenitent sinners are *allied* to evil spirits; they have an *affinity* with the kingdom of darkness; and when they die, they are emphatically said to "*go to* THEIR OWN *place!*"

3. This is an *awful* state for any to be in at present; but, blessed

be God, it is not yet a *hopeless* situation. Let no person say, " I find by
what I have heard, that I do not love God, and therefore I can entertain
no hope." There is a way of return and recovery open to all. Jesus
Christ, my dear brethren, proclaims to you all, " I am the way. No
man can come to the Father but by me :"— but every one that will may
come by this new and living way ; and, if you lose life eternal, you lose
it because,— according to his words just before the text,— because " you
will not come to Christ that you may have life." If you feel the misery,
deformity, and danger of your state, then listen to his invitation, and
embrace his promise. See the whole weight of your guilt transferred
to his cross! See how God can be at once the just and the justifier!
Take of the blood of sprinkling, and be at peace! *His blood cleanseth
from all sin:* He will send that Spirit into your heart, which will manifest him to you ; and where that Spirit is, *there* is *liberty* and holy love.
He is the *mystical* ladder, let down from heaven to earth, on which angels
are continually ascending and descending, in token of an alliance established between God and man. United by faith to Jesus Christ, you shall
become *a habitation of God through the Spirit;* the Father will make
you a partaker of his *love,* the Son of his *grace,* angels of their *friendship;* and you shall be preserved, and progressively sanctified ; until, by
the last change, all remains of the grand epidemic source of evils shall be
forever removed from your soul ; and the *love of God shall constitute
your eternal felicity.*

XVII

CHRISTMAS EVANS

1766–1838

NO collection of representative sermons would be complete without an example of the style of Christmas Evans, the most celebrated of all Welsh preachers, whom Robert Hall declared to be " one of the first men of his age." His native place was the village of Ysgarwen, Cardiganshire, South Wales, and he received his baptismal name because born on Christmas Day, 1766. His condition in life was humble, and after his father's death, when he was nine years old, he became a servant in a farmer's family. At the age of seventeen, he could not read, but when powerfully converted to Christ a year later, he learned in a surprisingly short time to read his Bible in Welsh. Soon after, without any education in a school, and without waiting for ordination, he began to preach in his native tongue. Realizing his lack of knowledge, he studied for a time under the direction of his pastor. In 1790, he entered upon a regular ministry as a missionary in charge of several small churches of the Baptist faith near Lëyn; but after two years left his field for evangelistic labor in South Wales. Here he was remarkably successful; crowds came to hear him everywhere, churches were awakened, and many souls were won to Christ. He was forty-six years old when he was settled over his first church at Anglesea, where he remained fourteen years; afterwards was pastor at Cærphilly and Cardiff. He wrote for publication about two hundred sermons in his own inimitable style; all in the Welsh language. When we consider that we read his discourses only in a translation, we wonder at the richness of their language, the height of their imagination, and the fervor of their spirit. His death took place in 1838 at Swansea, in his seventy-third year.

THE FALL AND RECOVERY OF MAN.

"For if, through the offence of one, many be dead; much more the grace of God, and the gift by grace, which is by one man, Jesus Christ, hath abounded unto many."— Romans v. 15.

MAN was created in the image of God. Knowledge and perfect holiness were impressed upon the very nature and faculties of his soul. He had constant access to his Maker, and enjoyed free communion with Him, on the ground of his spotless, moral rectitude. But alas! the glorious diadem is broken; the crown of righteousness is fallen. Man's purity is gone, and his happiness is forfeited. "There is none righteous; no, not one." "All have sinned, and come short of the glory of God." But the ruin is not hopeless. What was lost in Adam, is restored in Christ. His blood redeems us from bondage, and His Gospel gives us back the forfeited inheritance. "For if, through the offense of one, many be dead; much more the grace of God, and the gift by grace, which is by one man, Jesus Christ, hath abounded unto many." Let us consider ;— *First,* The corruption and condemnation of man; and *Secondly,* his gracious restoration to the favor of his offended God.

I. To find the cause of man's corruption and condemnation, we must go back to Eden. The eating of the "forbidden tree" was "the offense of one," in consequence of which "many are dead." This was the "sin," the act of "disobedience," which "brought death into the world, and all our woe." It was the greatest ingratitude to the Divine bounty, and the boldest rebellion against the Divine sovereignty. The royalty of God was contemned; the riches of His goodness slighted; and His most desperate enemy preferred before Him, as if He were a wiser counselor than Infinite Wisdom. Thus man joined in league with hell, against heaven; with demons of the bottomless pit, against the Almighty Maker and Benefactor; robbing God of the obedience due to His command, and the glory due to His name; worshipping the creature, instead of the Creator; and opening the door to pride, unbelief, enmity, and all wicked and abominable passions. How is the "noble vine," which was planted "wholly a right seed," turned into the degenerate plant of a strange vine!"

Who can look for pure water from such a fountain? "That which is born of the flesh is flesh." All the faculties of the soul are corrupted by sin; the understanding dark; the will perverse; the affections carnal; the conscience full of shame, remorse, confusion, and mortal fear. Man is a hard-hearted and stiff-necked sinner; loving darkness rather than light, because his deeds are evil; eating sin like bread, and drinking iniquity like water; holding fast deceit, and refusing to let it go. His heart is desperately wicked; full of pride, vanity, hypocrisy, covetousness, hatred of truth, and hostility to all that is good.

This depravity is universal. Among the natural children of Adam, there is no exemption from the original taint. "The whole world lieth in wickedness." "We are all as an unclean thing, and all our righteousness is as filthy rags." The corruption may vary in the degrees of development, in different persons; but the elements are in all, and their nature is everywhere the same; the same in the blooming youth, and the withered sire; in the haughty prince, and the humble peasant; in the strongest giant, and the feeblest invalid. The enemy has "come in like a flood." The deluge of sin has swept the world. From the highest to the lowest, there is no health or moral soundness. From the crown of the head to the soles of the feet, there is nothing but wound and bruises, and putrefying sores. The laws, and their violation, and the punishments everywhere invented for the suppression of vice, prove the universality of the evil. The bloody sacrifices, and various purifications, of the pagans, show the handwriting of remorse upon their consciences; proclaim their sense of guilt, and their dread of punishment. None of them are free from the fear which hath torment, whatever their efforts to overcome it, and however great their boldness in the service of sin and Satan. "Mene! Tekel!" is written on every human heart. "Wanting! Wanting!" is inscribed on heathen fanes and altars; on the laws, customs, and institutions of every nation; and on the universal consciousness of mankind.

This inward corruption manifests itself in outward actions. "The tree is known by its fruit." As the smoke and sparks of the chimney show that there is fire within; so all the "filthy conversation" of men, and all "the unfruitful works of darkness" in which they delight, evidently indicate the pollution of the source whence they proceed. "Out of the abundance of the heart the mouth speaketh." The sinner's speech betrayeth him. "Evil speaking" proceeds from malice and envy. "Foolish talking and jesting," are evidence of impure and trifling thoughts. The mouth full of cursing and bitterness, the throat an open sepulchre, the poison of asps under the tongue, the feet swift to shed blood, destruction and misery in their paths, and the way of peace un-known to them, are the clearest and amplest demonstration that men "have gone out of the way," "have together become unprofitable." We see the bitter fruit of the same corruption in robbery, adultery, gluttony, drunkenness, extortion, intolerance, persecution, apostasy, and every evil work — in all false religions; the Jew, obstinately adhering to the carnal ceremonies of an abrogated law; the Mohammedan, honoring an impostor, and receiving a lie for a revelation from God; the Papist, worshiping images and relics, praying to departed saints, seeking absolution from sinful men, and trusting in the most absurd mummeries for salvation; the Pagan, attributing divinity to the works of his own hands, adoring idols of wood and stone, sacrificing to malignant demons, casting his children into the fire or the flood as an offering to imaginary deities, and changing the glory of the incorruptible God into the likeness of the beast and the worm.

"For these things' sake the wrath of God cometh upon the children of disobedience." They are under the sentence of the broken law; the malediction of Eternal Justice. "By the offense of one, judgment came upon all men unto condemnation." "He that believeth not is condemned already." "The wrath of God abideth on him." "Cursed is every one that continueth not in all things written in the book of the law, to do them." "Wo unto the wicked; it shall be ill with him, for the reward of his hands shall be given him." "They that plow iniquity, and sow wickedness, shall reap the same." "Upon the wicked the Lord shall rain fire and snares, and a horrible tempest; this shall be the portion of their cup." "God is angry with the wicked every day; if He turn not, He will whet His sword; He hath bent His bow, and made it ready."

Who shall describe the misery of fallen man! His days, though few, are full of evil. Trouble and sorrow press him forward to the tomb. All the world, except Noah and his family, are drowning in the deluge. A storm of fire and brimstone is fallen from heaven upon Sodom and Gomorrah. The earth is opening her mouth to swallow up alive Korah, Dathan, and Abiram. Wrath is coming upon "the Beloved City," even wrath unto the uttermost." The tender and delicate mother is devouring her darling infant. The sword of men is executing the vengeance of God. The earth is emptying its inhabitants into the bottomless pit. On every hand are "confused noises, and garments rolled in blood." Fire and sword fill the land with consternation and dismay.

Amid the universal devastation, wild shrieks and despairing groans fill the air. God of mercy! is Thy ear heavy, that Thou canst not hear? or Thy arm shortened, that Thou canst not save? The heavens above are brass, and the earth beneath is iron; for Jehovah is pouring His indignation upon His adversaries, and He will not pity or spare.

Verily, "the misery of man is great upon him!" Behold the wretched fallen creature! The pestilence pursues him. The leprosy cleaves to him. Consumption is wasting him. Inflammation is devouring his vitals. Burning fever has seized upon the very springs of life. The destroying angel has overtaken the sinner in his sins. The hand of God is upon him. The fires of wrath are kindling about him, drying up every well of comfort, and scorching all his hopes to ashes. Conscience is chastising him with scorpions. See how he writhes! Hear how he shrieks for help! Mark what agony and terror are in his soul, and on his brow! Death stares him in the face, and shakes at him his iron spear. He trembles, he turns pale, as a culprit at the bar, as a convict on the scaffold. He is condemned already. Conscience has pronounced the sentence. Anguish has taken hold upon him. Terrors gather in battle array about him. He looks back, and the storms of Sinai pursue him; forward, and hell is moved to meet him; above, and the heavens are on fire; beneath, and the world is burning. He listens, and the judgment trump is calling; again, and the brazen chariots of vengeance are thundering from afar; yet again, and the sentence penetrates his soul with anguish unspeakable — "Depart! ye accursed! into everlasting fire, prepared for the devil and his angels!"

Thus, "by one man, sin entered into the world, and death by sin; and so death passed upon all men, for that all have sinned." They are "dead in trespasses and sins;" spiritually dead, and legally dead; dead by the mortal power of sin, and dead by the condemnatory sentence of the law; and helpless as sheep to the slaughter, they are driven fiercely on by the ministers of wrath to the all-devouring grave, and the lake of fire!

But is there no mercy? Is there no means of salvation? Hark! amidst all this prelude of wrath and ruin, comes a still small voice, saying: "much more the grace of God, and the gift by grace, which is by one man, Jesus Christ, hath abounded unto many."

II. This brings us to our second topic, man's gracious recovery to the favor of his offended God.

I know not how to represent to you this glorious work, better than by the following figure. Suppose a vast graveyard, surrounded by a lofty wall, with only one entrance, which is by a massive iron gate, and that is fast bolted. Within are thousands and millions of human beings, of all ages and classes, by one epidemic disease bending to the grave. The graves yawn to swallow them, and they must all perish. There is no balm to relieve, no physician there. Such is the condition of man as a sinner. All have sinned; and it is written, " The soul that sinneth shall die." But while the unhappy race lay in that dismal prison, Mercy came and stood at the gate, and wept over the melancholy scene, exclaiming—" O that I might enter! I would bind up their wounds; I would relieve their sorrows; I would save their souls!" An embassy of angels, commissioned from the court of heaven to some other world, paused at the sight, and heaven forgave that pause. Seeing Mercy standing there, they cried:—" Mercy! canst thou not enter? Canst thou look upon that scene and not pity? Canst thou pity, and not relieve?" Mercy replied: " I can see," and in her tears she added, " I can pity, but I cannot relieve!" " Why canst thou not enter?" inquired the heavenly host. " Oh!" said Mercy, " Justice has barred the gate against me, and I must not — can not unbar it!" At this moment, Justice appeared, as if to watch the gate. The angels asked, " Why wilt thou not suffer Mercy to enter?" He sternly replied: " The law is broken, and it must be honored! Die they or Justice must!" Then appeared a form among the angelic band like unto the Son of God. Addressing Himself to Justice, He said: " What are thy demands?" Justice replied: " My demands are rigid; I must have ignominy for their honor, sickness for their health, death for their life. Without the shedding of blood there is no remission!" " Justice," said the Son of God, " I accept thy terms! On Me be this wrong! Let Mercy enter, and stay the carnival of death!" " What pledge dost Thou give for the performance of these conditions?" " My word; My oath!" " When wilt Thou perform them?" " Four thousand years hence, on the hill of Calvary, without the walls of Jerusalem!" The bond was prepared, and signed and sealed in the presence of attendant angels. Justice was satisfied, the gate was opened, and Mercy entered, preaching salvation in the name of Jesus. The bond was committed to patriarchs and prophets. A long series of rites and ceremonies, sacrifices and oblations, was instituted to perpetuate the memory of that solemn deed. At the close of the four thousandth year, when Daniel's " seventy weeks " were accomplished, Justice and Mercy appeared on the hill of Calvary

"Where," said Justice, "is the Son of God?" "Behold Him," answered Mercy, "at the foot of the hill!" And there He came, bearing His own cross, and followed by His weeping church. Mercy retired, and stood aloof from the scene. Jesus ascended the hill, like a lamb for the sacrifice. Justice presented the dreadful bond, saying, "This is the day on which this article must be cancelled." The Redeemer took it. What did He do with it? Tear it in pieces, and scatter it to the winds? No! He nailed it to His cross, crying, "It is finished!" The Victim ascended the altar. Justice called on holy fire to come down and consume the sacrifice. Holy fire replied: "I come! I will consume the sacrifice, and then I will burn up the world!" It fell upon the Son of God, and rapidly consumed His humanity; but when it touched His Deity, it expired. Then was there Darkness over the whole land, and an earthquake shook the mountain; but the heavenly host broke forth in rapturous song —"Glory to God in the highest! on earth peace! good will to man!"

Thus grace has abounded, and the free gift has come upon all, and the Gospel has gone forth proclaiming redemption to every creature. "By grace ye are saved, through faith; and that not of yourselves; it is the gift of God; not of works, lest any man should boast." By grace ye are loved, redeemed, and justified. By grace ye are called, converted, reconciled and sanctified. Salvation is wholly of grace. The plan, the process, the consummation are all of grace.

> "Grace all the work shall crown,
>   Through everlasting days;
>   It lies in heaven the topmost stone,
>   And well deserves the praise!"

"Where sin abounded, grace hath much more abounded." "Through the offense of one, many were dead." And as men multiplied, the offense abounded. The waters deluged the world, but could not wash away the dreadful stain. The fire fell from heaven, but could not burn out the accursed plague. The earth opened her mouth, but could not swallow up the monster sin. The law thundered forth its threat from the thick darkness on Sinai; but could not restrain, by all its terrors, the children of disobedience. Still the offense abounded, and multiplied as the sands on the sea-shore. It waxed bold, and pitched its tents on Calvary, and nailed the Lawgiver to a tree. But in that conflict sin received its mortal wound. The Victim was the Victor. He fell, but in His fall, He crushed the foe. He died unto sin, but sin and death were crucified upon His cross. Where sin abounded to condemn, grace hath much more abounded to justify. Where sin abounded to corrupt, grace hath much more abounded to soften and subdue. Where sin abounded to imprison men, grace hath much more abounded to proclaim liberty to the captives. Where sin abounded to break the law and dishonor the Lawgiver, grace hath much more abounded to repair the breach and efface the stain. Where sin abounded to consume the soul as with unquenchable fire and a gnawing worm, grace hath much more abounded to extinguish the flame and heal the wound. Grace hath abounded! It hath established its throne on the merit of the Redeemer's sufferings. It hath put on the crown, and laid hold of the golden scepter, and spoiled the dominion of the prince of darkness, and the gates of the great cemetery are thrown open, and there is the beating of a new life-pulse throughout its wretched population, and Immortality is walking among the tombs!

This abounding grace is manifested in the gift of Jesus Christ, by whose mediation our reconciliation and salvation are effected. With Him, believers are dead unto sin, and alive unto God. Our sins were slain at His cross, and buried in His tomb. His resurrection hath opened our graves, and given us an assurance of immortality. "God commendeth His love toward us, in that, while we were yet sinners, Christ died for us; much more, then, being now justified by His blood, we shall be saved from wrath through Him; for if, when we were enemies, we were reconciled to God by the death of His Son, much more, being reconciled, we shall be saved by His life."

"The carnal mind is enmity against God; it is not subject to the law of God, neither indeed can be." Glory to God, for the death of His Son, by which this enmity is slain, and reconciliation is effected between the rebel and the law! This was the unspeakable gift that saved us from ruin; that wrestled with the storm, and turned it away from the devoted head of the sinner. Had all the angels of God attempted to stand between these two conflicting seas, they would have been swept to the gulf of destruction. "The blood of bulls and goats, on Jewish altars slain," could not take away sin, could not pacify the conscience. But Christ, the gift of Divine Grace, "Paschal Lamb by God appointed," a "sacrifice of nobler name and richer blood than they," bore our sins and carried our sorrows, and obtained for us the boon of eternal redemption. He met the fury of the tempest, and the floods went over His head; but His offering was an offering of peace, calming the storms and the waves, magnifying the law, glorifying its Author, and rescuing its violator from wrath and ruin. Justice hath laid down His sword at the foot of the cross, and amity is restored between heaven and earth.

Hither, O ye guilty! come and cast away your weapons of rebellion! Come with your bad principles and wicked actions; your unbelief, and enmity, and pride; and throw them off at the Redeemer's feet! God is here, waiting to be gracious. He will receive you; He will cast all your sins behind His back, into the depths of the sea; and they shall be remembered against you no more forever. By Heaven's "Unspeakable gift," by Christ's invaluable atonement, by the free and infinite grace of the Father and the Son, we persuade you, we beseech you, we entreat you, "be ye reconciled to God!"

It is by the work of the Holy Spirit within us, that we obtain a personal interest in the work wrought on Calvary for us. If our sins are cancelled, they are also crucified. If we are reconciled in Christ, we fight against our God no more. This is the fruit of faith. "With the heart man believeth unto righteousness." May the Lord inspire in every one of us that saving principle!

But those who have been restored to the Divine favor may sometimes be cast down and dejected. They have passed through the sea, and sung praises on the shore of deliverance; but there is yet between them and Canaan "a waste howling wilderness," a long and weary pilgrimage, hostile nations, fiery serpents, scarcity of food, and the river Jordan. Fears within and fightings without, they may grow discouraged, and yield to temptation and murmur against God, and desire to return to Egypt. But fear not, thou worm Jacob! Reconciled by the death of Christ; much more, being reconciled, thou shalt be saved by His life. His death was the price of our redemption; His life ensures liberty to the believer. If by His death He brought you through the Red Sea in the night, by His life He can lead you through the river Jordan in the day. If by His death He delivered you from the iron furnace in Egypt, by His life He can save you from all the perils of the wilderness. If by His death he conquered Pharaoh, the chief foe, by His life He can subdue Sihon, king of the Amorites, and Og, the king of Bashan. "We shall be saved by His life." "Because He liveth, we shall live also." "Be of good cheer!" The work is finished; the ransom is effected; the kingdom of heaven is opened to all believers. "Lift up your heads and rejoice," "ye prisoners of hope!" There is no debt unpaid, no devil unconquered, no enemy within your own hearts that has not received a mortal wound! "Thanks be unto God, who giveth us the victory, through our Lord Jesus Christ!"

16

XVIII

JOHN FOSTER

1770–1843

JOHN FOSTER, a profound, liberal, and eloquent English essayist on morals, was born in Halifax, Yorkshire, September 17th, 1770. He graduated for the ministry from the Baptist College at Bristol, and spent several years in pastoral duties. The larger part of his life, however, was devoted to literature, and mainly to contributions to the Eclectic Review. He died at Stapleton, in 1843. Of his writings the most famous are: " Essays on Decision of Character," " On the Evils of Popular Ignorance," and this sermon on " Access to God." The latter was republished by the Religious Tract Society, and is also contained in volume second of " Lectures Delivered at Broadmead Chapel, Bristol," shortly before his death. It has a depth and grasp of thought that especially commend it to the honest inquirer and searcher after religious truth.

ACCESS TO GOD.

" He that cometh to God must believe that he is, and that he is a rewarder of them that diligently seek him."— Hebrews xi. 6.

No saying is more common among us, or perhaps leaves a more transient impression, than that to approach to God, while enjoined as a duty, is also an eminent privilege. As no one thinks of questioning it, we easily let it pass, as if there needed no more but to assent to it.

That it can thus be an unmeaning sentence, a lifeless notion, indistinctly presented to the apprehension, and holding no communication with the affections, betrays that the soul is taking little account of its best resources for happiness. But such it will be, unless we can be serious enough for an exercise of thought, to apprehend as a great and interesting reality what we have so often allowed ourselves to hear, or to utter, as little more than an insignificant common-place of religious discourse. Can we be content it should be so? When it is understood that, among the things possible to man, is the very extraordinary one of " Coming to God," shall we not make a faithful, earnest effort, that the thing so affirmed and believed may have to us all the effect of a reality, in being brought with clearness to our apprehension, and with power over our feelings?

It is a wonderful idea, even as apprehended at once, in a single act of thought, without intermediate process of advancing from less to greater, in ascent towards the greatest — the idea of the infinite, almighty, eternal Being, as to be approached, and spoken to, and communicated with, by *man*. But a gradation of thought, a progressive rising toward the transcendent and supreme, might contribute to magnify the wonderfulness of the fact, of man daring and permitted to enter into a direct communication with God.— But by what order and train of ideas might we seek to advance towards the magnificence of the contemplation?

If we might allow ourselves in such an imagination, as that the selected portion of all humanity, the very best and wisest persons on earth, were brought and combined into a permanent assembly, and invested with a sovereign authority — the highest wisdom, virtue, science, and power thus united — would not a perfectly free access for the humblest, poorest, most distressed, and otherwise friendless, to such an assemblage, with a certainty of their most kind and sedulous attention being given — of their constant *will* to render aid — of their wisdom and power being promptly exercised — would not this be deemed an inestimable privilege to all within the compass of such an empire? Indeed, if such a thing might be (an extravagantly wild imagination, we confess), it would take the place of Providence in the minds of the multitude, and be idolized.

But take a higher position, and suppose that there were such an economy that the most illustrious of the *departed saints* held the office of being practically, though unseen, patrons, protectors, assistants, guides, to men on earth; that the spirits of patriarchs, prophets, and apostles, could be drawn, by those who desired it, to a direct personal attention, and to an exercise of their benignity and interference — would not this appear a resource of incalculable value? It is because it naturally would be so, that the Romish church was so successful in imposing on the people the fiction of such an economy as an undoubted reality (and, indeed, paganism had before done something of a similar kind). So gratifying, so consoling, so animating, has this imaginary privilege been felt by millions of that church, that their devotion has seemed actually to stop at this level of invisible existence; the Almighty Father, and the Redeemer, comparatively forgotten.

But there is *another* far loftier ascension. We are informed of a glorious order of intelligences that have never dwelt in flesh; many of whom may have enjoyed their existence from a remoteness of time surpassing what we can conceive of eternity; with an immense expansion of being and powers; with a perpetual augmentation of the goodness inspired by their Creator; and exercising their virtues and unknown powers in appointed offices of beneficence throughout the system of unnumbered worlds. Would it not seem a pre-eminent privilege, if the children of the dust might obtain a direct communication with them; might invoke them, accost them, draw them to a fixed attention, and with a sensible evidence of their indulgent patience and celestial benignity? Would not this seem an exaltation of felicity, throwing into shade everything that could be imagined to be derived to us from the benevolence and power of mortal or glorified humanity?

Now, here we are at the summit of created existence; and up to this sublime elevation we have none of these supposed privileges. No! there is no such conjunction of the greatest virtue, wisdom, and power on earth. Departed saints have no appointment to hear our petitions; and when we perceive, as it were, the distant radiance of an inconceivably nobler order of beings, it is with the consciousness that we cannot come into their sensible presence and recognition, cannot invoke their express attention, cannot lay hold on their power, cannot commit to them the momentous charge of our interests.

Thus we have ascended by degrees to the most illustrious of created beings, for the transient luxury of imagining what it would be to engage in our favor the intelligence, goodness, and power of those glorious spirits; but to find ourselves hopelessly far off from such access. In the capacity of receiving our petitions, they exist not for us; as to *that* object, these mighty agents are strangers to us.

What, then, to do next? Next, our spirits have to raise their thoughts to an awful elevation above all subordinate existence in earth and heaven, in order to approach a presence where they *may* implore a beneficent attention, and enter into a communication with Him who is uncreated and infinite; a transition compared to which the distance from the inferior to the nobler, and then to the noblest of created beings, is reduced to nothing; as one lofty eminence on an elevated mountain — and a higher,— and the highest — but thence to the starry heavens!

But think, who is it that is thus to *"come to God!"* Man! little, feeble, mortal, fallen, sinful man! He is, if we may speak in such language, to venture an act expressly to arrest the attention of that stupendous Being; to signify, in the most direct manner, that he is by choice and design in that presence intentionally to draw on himself the notice, the aspect of the Almighty. The purpose is, to speak to Him in a *personal manner;* to detain Him in communication. The approaching petitioner is to utter thoughts, for God to admit them into *His* thoughts! He would cause himself to be distinctly and individually listened to by a Being who is receiving the adoration of the most exalted spirits, and of all the holy intelligences in the universe; by Him whose power is sustaining and governing all its regions and inhabitants. He seeks to cause *his words* to be listened to by Him whose *own words* may be, at the very time, commanding new creations into existence.

But reflect, also, that it is an act to call the special attention of Him whose purity has a perfect perception of all that is evil, that is unholy, in the creature that approaches Him; of Him whom the applicant is conscious he has not, to the utmost of his faculties, adored or loved: alas! the very contrary.

What a striking, what an amazing view is thus presented of the situation the unworthy mortal is placed in, the position which he presumes to take, in *"coming to God."* How surprising then it is, how alarming it well may be, to reflect on the manner in which, too often, we use this privilege! What a miserably faint conception of the Sovereign Majesty! A reverence so defective in solemnity, that it admits the intrusion of every trivial suggestion. Thoughts easily diverted away by the slightest casual association. An inanimate state of feeling, indifference almost, in petitioning the greatest blessings, and deprecating the most fearful evils. So that, on serious reflection, the consciousness would be forced upon us, of its being too much to hope that such devotions can be accepted, such petitions granted.

To rebuke this irreligion, infesting and spoiling the very acts of religion, think again of the situation of such a creature as man coming into the immediate presence of the Divine Majesty. The very extremes of spiritual existence — the infinitely Most Glorious, and the lowest, meanest of all, brought into communication; the absolutely holy, and the miserably depraved — the guilty. We may conceive that a creature of even such humble rank as man, if he were but perfectly innocent, might approach to a communication with the Eternal and Infinite Essence, though not without inexpressible awe, yet without terror; but since he is impure and guilty, the idea of his *" coming to God"* would be no other than the image of a perishable thing brought within the action of *" a consuming fire;"* the moral quality of the Divine Nature being in direct antipathy to that of such a creature approaching. Let a man, really and deeply affected with the debasement of his nature and his individual guilt, stand consciously before the all-perfect holiness of God; let him think what it must be to come in immediate *contact* (shall we say?) with that holiness; every look at his sinfulness, every secret accusation of his conscience, would fix and determine his attention to the Divine holiness — irresistibly so — rather than to any other attribute: for in all comparisons, even with our fellow-men, our attention fixes the most strongly on that in which we are the most in contrast and antipathy with them, especially when the contrast presents something for us to fear. So with a creature consciously full of sin in immediate approach to Him who is *" glorious in holiness;"* the attention would be arrested by that, as an opposite, a hostile, and a terrible quality; and the longer it were beheld, the more it would appear kindling and glowing into a consuming flame.

A sinful being immediately under the burning rays of Omnipotent Holiness! The idea is so fearful, that one might think it should be the most earnest, the most passionate desire of a human soul, that there should be some intervention to save it from the fatal predicament. No wonder, then, that the most devout men of every age of the Christian dispensation have welcomed with joy and gratitude the doctrine of a Mediator, manifested in the person of the Son of God, by whom the holiness of God and the sinfulness of man are, as it were, *kept asunder;* and a happy communication can take place through the medium of One who stands before the Divine Majesty of Justice, in man's behalf, with a propitiation and a perfect righteousness.

Thus far, and too long, we have dwelt on the wonderfulness of the fact and the greatness of the privilege of *" coming to God."* We have to consider, a little, with *what faith* this is to be done. " Must believe that he is, and that he is the rewarder of them that diligently seek him."

The fact of the Divine existence must be assumed by the seeker for permanent good. What a condition it were to be looking round and afar into boundless inanity in quest of it! uttering the importunate and plaintive cry, " Who will show us any good? "— directed first to poor fellow-mortals, who can only respond in the same words; and then to the fantastic, shadowy creatures of imagination — nature, fortune, chance, good genii.

" Must believe that he is." Must have a most absolute conviction that there is one Being infinitely unlike and superior to all others; the sole Self-existent, All-comprehending, and All-powerful; a reality in such a sense that all other things are but precarious modes of being, subsisting simply in virtue of his will; — must pass through and beyond the sphere of sense, to have a spiritual sight of " Him that is invisible;" and, more than merely a principle held in the understanding, must verify the solemn reality in a vitally pervading sentiment of the soul.

And what a glory of intellect and faith thus to possess a truth which is the sun in our mental sphere, the supreme itself of all lights, and whence radiate all the illuminations and felicities that can bless the rational creation! And what a casting down from heaven, as it may well be named,— what a spectacle of debasement and desolation is presented to us, when we behold the frightful phenomenon of a rational creature *disbelieving* a God! There are such men, who can look abroad on this amazing universe, and deny there is a supreme intelligent Cause and Director; and if some of these are possessed of extraordinary talent and knowledge, the fact may show what human reason is capable of, when rejecting, and rejected by, Divine influence; and we may presage the horrible amazement, when that truth respecting which the lights of science and the splendors of the sky have left them in the dark, shall at length suddenly burst on them!

" He that cometh to God must believe that he is." But how easily it may be said, " We have that faith; we never denied or doubted that there is such a Being." Well; but reflect, and ascertain in what degree the general tenor of your feelings, and your habits of life, have been different from what they might have been if you *had* disbelieved or doubted. The expression *" coming to "* him, seems to tell something of a previous *distance;* see, then, what may have been, in a spiritual sense, the distance at which you have lived from him. Has it been the smallest at which a feeble, sinful creature must still necessarily be left, notwithstanding an earnest, persisting effort to approach him; or rather the greatest that a mere notional acknowledgment of his existence would allow? What a wide allowance is that! and what a melancholy condition to have only such a faith concerning the most glorious and beneficent Object, as shall leave us contented to be so far off from him!

'This belief cannot bring the soul in effectual approach to God, unless it be a penetrating conviction that the truth so believed is a truth of mightiest import; that, there being a God, we have to do with him every moment; that all will be wrong with us unless this awful reality command and occupy our spirits; that this faith must be the predominating authority over our course through the world, the determining consideration in our volitions and actions. When we say then, that we have this belief, the grave question is, What does it do for us? Are we at a loss to tell what? Can we not verify to ourselves that we have this belief, in any other way than by repeating that we believe?

The effectual faith in the Divine existence always looks to consequences. In acknowledging each glorious attribute, it regards the aspect which it bears on the worshipper, inferring what will *therefore be* because *that is*. It is not a valid faith in the Divinity, as regarded in any of his attributes, till it excite the solicitous thought, " And what then? " *He is,* as supreme in goodness; and what then? Then, how precious is every assurance from himself that he is accessible to us! Then, is it not the truest insanity in the creation to be careless of his favor? Then, happy they, for ever happy, who obtain that favor, by devoting themselves to seek it. Then, let us instantly and ardently proceed to act on the conviction that he is the " rewarder of them that diligently seek him."

This actuating conviction must be decided and absolute in him that *"cometh to God."* He must feel positively assured it will not be just the same to him, in the event of things, whether he diligently seek God or not. Without this, there cannot be a motive of force enough to draw or impel him to the spiritual enterprise. His soul will stagnate in a comfortless, hopeless, and almost atheistical inaction; or, with a painful activity of imagination, he may picture forth forms of the good which such a being as the Almighty *could* do for him, and then see those visions depart as some vain creations of poetry; or he may try to give to what keeps him afar from God a character of reason and philosophy, by perverted inferences from the unchangeableness of the Divine purposes, or the necessary course of things; or he may pretend a pious dread of presuming to prescribe to the Sovereign Wisdom: all, in effect, terminating in the profane question, " What profit shall we have if we pray to him? "

Without the assured belief that something of immense importance is depending on the alternative of rendering or withholding the homage of devout application, all aspiration is repressed, and we are left, as it were, prone on the earth. We are to hold it for certain, that, even though divers events, simply as facts, may be the same in either case, yet something involved in them, and in the effect of the whole series of events, will be infinitely different. In each opportune season for coming to God by supplication, at each repetition of the gracious invitations to do so, at each admonition of conscience, there is a voice which tells him that something most invaluable would, *really would,* be gained by sincere, earnest, and constant application. He should say to himself, I am not to remain inactive, as if just waiting to see what will come to pass, like a man expecting the rain or sunshine which he can do nothing to bring on his meadow or garden. If God be true, there is something to be granted to such application, that *will not* be granted without it. As to the particular order of providential dispensation, I can know nothing of the Divine purposes; but, as to the general scope, I do know perfectly that one thing is in God's determination, namely, *to fulfil his promises.* By a humble, faithful persevering importunity of prayer in the name of Christ, I have an assured hold upon,— or, by a neglect of it, I let loose from my grasp and hope,— all those things which he has promised to such prayer. I am, then, assured he is the *"rewarder,"* inasmuch as I know *it will not be all the same to me whether I seek him or not.* And here we may instantly break through all speculative sophistry, by appealing to any man who believes anything of revelation: "Do you really believe that it will not, in the final result, and even in this world too, make a vast difference whether you shall or shall not be habitually, through life, an earnest applicant for the Divine blessing? Answer this question; answer it to yourself, from your inmost conviction."

Let it be observed here, that, God having indicated by his precepts the way in which, conditionally, he will manifest his goodness to men, that way, as so set forth, must be the best. It is not, therefore, a mere dictate of sovereign authority, but a wise adjustment of the means for men's happiness. His goodness is not greater in his willingness to confer his favors, than in the appointment *how* they shall be conferred; that is, the preceptive rule according to which we are to expect them.

That preceptive rule is conspicuous throughout the Bible. That we should *"seek God,"* in the way of unceasing application for his mercies, is inculcated and reiterated in every form of cogent expression. Then we are justly required to believe, confidently, that as this is the very best and only expedient, God will combine the happiness of his servants with their faithful observance of an injunction *intended* for their happiness; that it will be attended by tokens of the Divine complacency; that in keeping the precept there will be *"great reward."* Like Enoch, they will have "this testimony, that they pleased God."

"Must believe that he is the rewarder." This faith is required in consideration of the intention (might we presume to say, reverently, the sincerity?) of the heavenly Father in calling men to come to him. "I have not said, 'Seek ye me in vain.'" To what purpose are they thus required to make his favor the object of their eternal aspiration; to forego all things rather than this; to renounce, for this, everything which it is the perverted tendency of the human soul to prefer; to say, "Whom have I in heaven but thee? and there is none upon earth that I desire beside thee?" Why invited to give their affections, devote their life, and their very existence, to acknowledge their dependence, and testify their confidence by unceasing petitions, and to strive fervently to obtain a more intimate access to him? Why thus summoned, and trained, and exercised, to a lofty ambition far above the world? Not to frustrate all this labor, not to disappoint them of the felicity to which they continually aspire! They "must believe that he is a rewarder;" that he is not thus calling and constraining them up a long, laborious ascent, only that they may behold his glorious throne, come near to his blissful paradise, do him homage at its gate, and then be shut out.

Consider again: it is because there is a Mediator, that sinful men presume, and are authorized, to approach to God, seeking that — no more than that — which the mysterious appointment was made, in Divine justice and mercy, for the purpose of conferring on them. Then they *must* believe, that this glorious office cannot but be availing to their success. There is a peculiar virtue in such a special, remedial interposition to secure its own infallible efficacy, since it was expressly because the original constitution of our nature had failed, and must remain powerless and hopeless for happiness, that this special and extraordinary one was brought into existence; and an expedient which has been adopted, in the Divine government, to accomplish an end for which all else has been proved incompetent, must have a special and peculiar sufficiency for that end. What has been appointed, in the last resort, in substitution and in remedy of an antecedent economy, because that has failed, must be, by eminence, of a nature not *itself* to fail. It rises up conspicuous and impregnable when all around has sunk in ruin; like some mighty rock brought up into the light, and standing high in immovable stability, in the rending and subsidence of the ground by earthquake.

They that *" come to God "* in confidence on this new Divine consti-tution, will find that he, in justice to his appointment of a Mediator, will grant what is promised and sought in *virtue of it;* in other words, will be a *" rewarder "* for Christ's sake. And what is that in which it will be verified to them *" that he is a rewarder? "* For *what* will they have to adore and bless him as such? For the grandest benefits which even He can impart — can impart in doing full justice to the infinite merits of the appointed Redeemer.— An inestimable privilege! that those greatest blessings may be asked for, positively and specifically; whereas the minor benefits are to be requested conditionally, and it is better that the appli-cants should *not* be certain of obtaining them. It is enough for their faith as to these, that an infinitely wiser judgment than theirs will be exercised in selecting, giving, withholding, adjusting.

But the important admonition, to be repeated here in concluding, is, that all this is for them *" that diligently seek;"* so habitually, importu-nately, perseveringly, that it shall really, and in good faith, be made the primary concern of our life; so that, while wishes and impulses to *obtain* are incessantly springing and darting from the busy soul in divers directions, there shall still be one predominant impulse directed towards heaven. And, if such representations as we have been looking at be true, think — (it is truly a most striking reflection),— think what *might* be obtained by all of us, who have them at this hour soliciting our at-tention, on the supposition that we all should henceforward be earnest applicants to the Sovereign Rewarder. Think of the mighty amount of good, in time and eternity, as our collective wealth; and of the value of every individual share.

We said, " on the supposition;" but why are we to admit a word so ominous? for while, on the one side, it points to a grand sum of good, with an averment of Him who has it to give that it may be ours, it darkly intimates, on the other, that possibly it *may not,* may never be ours; that we may practically *consent that it shall not.* But *may* we, believing such things all the while, may we really so consent? With such treasure held forth in our view, and for our attainment, by the munificent Benefactor, and seeing some of our companions actually at-taining it, can we consent to a melancholy destitution by foregoing it? Consent to forego! And to what is it that such consent would be yielded? Could it be to anything else than a malignant, dire, accursed perversity of our nature? No terms of execration are too intense for the noxious thing, within our own selves, that stupefies our affections and our will to the madness of telling our God, in effect, that we can do without his rewards, that he may confer them where they are more desired; while we will look on and see others take them all away, content to retain and cherish in their stead that deadly enemy within, which compels us to let them go.

Can we *not* be so content? Then, finally, what we have the most urgent cause to seek Him for is, that He will deliver us from that which keeps us from Him. We have to implore, " O merciful Power! abolish whatever it is that would detain us at a fatal distance from thee. Let the breath of thy Spirit consume the unbelief, the reluctance, the indifference, the world's enchantments, that would fix us under the doom to '*behold thee, but not nigh.*' Apply to these averse or heedless spirits such a blessed compulsion as shall not leave it even possible for us to be within reach of the sovereign good, and yet linger till all be lost."

And if, by unwearied seeking, we obtain this, it will emphatically be a "*reward,*" for which all under the sun might be gladly given away.

XIX

THOMAS CHALMERS

1780–1847

A PHILOSOPHER, theologian, pulpit orator, and pastor — gifted, earnest, and faithful to a tender conscience in each of these responsible spheres — such was the life-character of Thomas Chalmers, D. D., LL. D., D. C. L. His career was full of godly labors for the good of humanity. Born at Anstruther, in Fifeshire, Scotland, March 17th, 1780, and educated at St. Andrew's, he was licensed a minister of the Church of Scotland in his nineteenth year. His true conversion to God, however, he himself assigns to the year 1810. An excellent article on the " Evidences of Christianity," prepared for the Edinburgh Encyclopedia, and a series of glowing " Astronomical Discourses," are the most popular of his writings, which extend to thirty volumes. As pastor over a parish of two thousand poor families in Glasgow, he organized it into twenty-five districts with supervisors, established week-day and Sunday schools, and faithfully toiled for their spiritual and bodily necessities. Five years were given to the professorship of Moral Philosophy, and fifteen to that of Theology, in the University of Edinburgh. In 1843 Dr. Chalmers was a leader of the Evangelical party which, for conscience' sake, seceded to found the Free Church, and did much for its rapid establishment. He died in Edinburgh, May 30th, 1847. Four volumes of his Sermons are published. One is illustrative of different stages of his ministry; and from that is selected the following masterpiece — a favorite of Dr. Chalmers, and last preached a year before his death.

FURY NOT IN GOD.

" *Fury is not in me: who would set the briers and thorns against me in battle? I would go through them, I would burn them together. Or*

let him take hold of my strength, that he may make peace with me; and
he shall make peace with me." — Isaiah xxvii. 4–5.

THERE are three distinct lessons in this text. The first, that fury
is not in God: the second, that He does not want to glorify Himself by
the death of sinners —" Who would set the thorns and briers against me
in battle? " the third, the invitation —" Take hold of my strength, that
you may make peace with me; and you shall make peace with me."

I. First, then, Fury is not in God. But how can this be? is not
fury one manifestation of His essential attributes? do we not repeatedly
read of His fury — of Jerusalem being full of the fury of the Lord —
of God casting the fury of His wrath upon the world — of Him rendering His anger upon His enemies with fury — of Him accomplishing his
fury upon Zion — of Him causing His fury to rest on the bloody and
devoted city? We are not therefore to think that fury is banished altogether from God's administration. There are times and occasions when
this fury is discharged upon the objects of it; and there must be other
times and other occasions when there is no fury in Him. Now, what is
the occasion upon which He disclaims all fury in our text? He is inviting men to reconciliation; He is calling upon them to make peace;
and He is assuring them, that if they will only take hold of His strength,
they shall make peace with Him. In the preceding verses He speaks
of a vineyard; and in the act of inviting people to lay hold of His
strength, He is in fact inviting those who are without the limits of the
vineyard to enter in. Fury will be discharged on those who reject the
invitation. But we cannot say that there is any exercise of fury in God
at the time of giving the invitation. There is the most visible and direct
contrary. There is a longing desire after you. There is a wish to save
you from that day in which the fury of a rejected Saviour will be spread
abroad over all who have despised Him. The tone of invitation is not
a tone of anger — it is a tone of tenderness. The look which accom-
panies the invitation is not a look of wrath — it is a look of affection.
There may be a time, there may be an occasion, when the fury of God
will be put forth on the men who have held out against Him, and
turned them away in infidelity and contempt from His beseeching voice;
but at the time that He is lifting this voice — at the time that He is
sending messengers over the face of the earth to circulate it among
the habitations of men — at the time particularly among ourselves, when
in our own place and our own day Bibles are within the reach of every

family, and ministers in every pulpit are sounding forth the overtures of the gospel throughout the land — surely at such a time and upon such an occasion, it may well be said of God to all who are now seeking His face and favor, that there is no fury in Him.

It is just as in the parable of the marriage feast: many rejected the invitation which the king gave to it — for which he was wroth with them, and sent forth his armies and destroyed them, and burned up their city. On that occasion there was fury in the king, and on the like occasion will there be fury in God. But well can He say at the time when He is now giving the invitation — there is no fury in Me. There is kindness — a desire for peace and friendship — a longing earnestness to make up the quarrel which now subsists between the Lawgiver in heaven, and His yet impenitent and unreconciled creatures.

This very process was all gone through at and before the destruction of Jerusalem. It rejected the warnings and invitations of the Saviour, and at length experienced His fury. But there was no fury at the time of His giving the invitations. The tone of our Saviour's voice when He uttered — "O Jerusalem, Jerusalem," was not the tone of a vindictive and irritated fury. There was compassion in it — a warning and pleading earnestness that they would mind the things which belong to their peace; and at that time when He would willingly have gathered them as a hen gathereth her chickens under her wings — then may it well be said that there was no fury in the Son of God, no fury in God.

Let us make the application to ourselves in the present day. On the last day there will be a tremendous discharge of fury. That wrath which sinners are now doing so much to treasure up will all be poured forth on them. The season of God's mercy will then have come to an end; and after the sound of the last trumpet, there will never more be heard the sounding call of reconciliation. Oh, my brethren, that God who is grieved and who is angry with sinners every day, will in the last day pour it all forth in one mighty torrent on the heads of the impenitent. It is now gathering and accumulating in a storehouse of vengeance; and at the awful point in the successive history of nature and providence, when time shall be no more, will the door of this storehouse be opened, that the fury of the Lord may break loose upon the guilty and accomplish upon them the weight and the terror of all His threatenings. You misunderstand the text, then, my brethren, if you infer from it that fury has no place in the history or methods of God's administration. It has its time and its occasion — and the very greatest display of it is yet to come, when the earth shall be burned up, and the heavens shall be dissolved, and the elements shall melt with fervent heat, and the Lord Jesus shall be revealed from heaven with His mighty angels, in flaming fire, taking vengeance on those who know not God, and obey not the gospel of our Lord Jesus Christ; and they shall be punished with everlasting destruction from the presence of the Lord, and from the glory of His power. It makes one shudder seriously to think that there may be some here present whom this devouring torrent of wrath shall sweep away; some here present who will be drawn into the whirl of destruction, and forced to take their descending way through the mouth of that pit where the worm dieth not, and the fire is not quenched; some here present who so far from experiencing in their own persons that there is no fury in God, will find that throughout the dreary extent of one hopeless and endless and unmitigated eternity, it is the only attribute of His they have to do with. But hear me, hear me ere you have taken your bed in hell; hear me, ere that prison door be shut upon you which is never, never again to be opened! hear me, hear me, ere the great day of the revelation of God's wrath comes round, and there shall be a total breaking up of that system of things which looks at present so stable and so unalterable! On that awful day I might not be able to take up the text and say — that there is no fury in God. But, oh! hear me, for your lives hear me — on this day I can say it. From the place where I now stand I can throw abroad amongst you the wide announcement — that there is no fury in God; and there is not one of you into whose heart this announcement may not enter, and welcome will you be to strike with your beseeching God a league of peace and of friendship that shall never be broken asunder. Surely when I am busy at my delegated employment of holding out the language of entreaty, and of sounding in your ears the tidings of gladness, and of inviting you to enter into the vineyard of God — surely at the time when the messenger of the gospel is thus executing the commission wherewith he is charged and warranted, he may well say — that there is no fury in God. Surely at the time when the Son of God is inviting you to kiss Him and to enter into reconciliation, there is neither the feeling nor the exercise of fury. It is only if you refuse, and if you persist in refusing, and if you suffer all these calls and entreaties to be lost upon you — it is only then that God will execute His fury, and put forth the power of His anger. And therefore He says to us, " Kiss the Son, lest He be angry, and ye perish from the way, when His wrath is kindled but a little." Such, then, is the interesting point of time at which you stand. There is no fury in God at the very time that He is inviting you to flee from it. He is sending forth no blasting influence upon the fig-tree, even though hitherto it had borne no fruit, and been a mere cumberer of the ground, when He says, we shall let it alone for another year, and dig it, and dress it, and if it bear fruit, well; and if not, then let it be afterwards cut down. Now, my brethren, you are all in the situation of this fig-tree; you are for the present let alone; God has purposes of kindness towards every one of you; and as one of His ministers I can now say to you all — that there is no fury in Him. Now when the spiritual husbandman is trying to soften your hearts, he is warranted to make a full use of the argument of my text — that there is no fury in God. Now that the ambassador of Christ is plying you with the offers of grace and of strength to renew and to make you fruitful, he is surely charged with matter of far different import from wrath and threatening and vengeance. Oh! let not all this spiritual husbandry turn out to be unavailing; let not the offer be made now, and no fruit appear afterwards; let not yours be the fate of the barren and unfruitful fig-tree. The day of the fury of the Lord is approaching. The burning up of this earth and the passing away of these heavens is an event in the history of God's administration to which we are continually drawing nearer; and on that day when the whole of universal nature shall be turned into a heap of ruins, and we shall see the gleam of a mighty conflagration, and shall hear the noise of the framework of creation rending into fragments, and a cry shall be raised from a despairing multitude out of the men of all generations, who have just awoke from their resting-places — and amid all the bustle and consternation that is going on below, such a sight shall be witnessed from the canopy of heaven as will spread silence over the face of the world, and fix and solemnize every individual of its incumbent population. Oh, my brethren, let us not think that on that day when the Judge is to appear charged with the mighty object of vindicating before men and angels the truth and the majesty of God — that the fury of God will not then appear in bright and burning manifestation. But what I have to tell you on this day is, that fury is not in God — that now is the time of those things which belong to the peace of our eternity; and that if you will only hear on this the day of your merciful visitation, you will be

17

borne off in safety from all those horrors of dissolving nature, and amid the wild war and frenzy of its reeling elements, will be carried by the arms of love to a place of security and everlasting triumph.

II. This brings us to the second head of discourse — God is not wanting to glorify Himself by the death of sinners — "Who would set the thorns and the briers against me in battle?" The wicked and the righteous are often represented in Scripture by figures taken from the vegetable world. The saved and sanctified are called trees of righteousness, the planting of the Lord that He might be glorified. The godly man is said to be like a tree planted by the rivers of water, which bringeth forth its fruit in its season. The judgment which cometh upon a man is compared to an axe laid to the root of a tree. A tree is said to be known by its fruit; and as a proof that the kind of character of men is specified by the kind of tree in the woods, we read that of thorns men do not gather figs, nor of the bramble-bush gather they grapes. You will observe that the thorn is one of the kinds instanced in the text, and when God says, I would go through them, I would burn them together, He speaks of the destruction which cometh on all who remain in the state of thorns and briers; and this agrees with what we read in the Epistle to the Hebrews, "That which beareth thorns and briers is rejected, and is nigh unto cursing, whose end is to be burned."

Thorns and briers are in other places still more directly employed to signify the enemies of God. "And the light of Israel shall be for a fire," says one of the prophets, "and his Holy One for a flame, and it shall burn and devour His thorns and His briers in one day." Therefore, when God says in the text, "Who would set the thorns and the briers against me in battle? I would go through them, I would burn them together," He speaks of the ease wherewith He could accomplish His wrath upon His enemies. They would perish before Him like the moth. They could not stand the lifting up of the red right arm of the displeasure of Almighty God. Why set up, then, a contest so unequal as this? Why put the wicked in battle array against Him who could go through them and devour them in an instant by the breath of His fury? God is saying in the text that this is not what He is wanting. He does not want to set Himself forth as an enemy, or as a strong man armed against them for the battle — it is a battle He is not at all disposed to enter into. The glory He would achieve by a victory over a host so feeble, is not a glory that His heart is at all set upon. Oh, no! ye children of men, He has no pleasure in your death; He is not seeking to magnify himself by the destruction of so paltry a foe; He could devour you in a moment; He could burn you up like stubble; and you mistake it if you think that renown on so poor a field of contest is a renown that He is at all aspiring after. Who would set the grasshoppers in battle array against the giants? Who would set thorns and briers in battle array against God? This is not what He wants: He would rather something else. Be assured, He would rather you were to turn, and to live, and to come into His vineyard, and submit to the regenerating power of His spiritual husbandry, and be changed from the nature of an accursed plant to a tree of righteousness. In the language of the next verse, He would rather that this enemy of His, not yet at peace with Him, and who may therefore be likened to a brier or a thorn — He would rather than he remained so that he should take hold of God's strength, that he may make peace with Him — and as the fruit of his so doing, he shall make peace with Him.

Now tell me if this do not open up a most wonderful and a most inviting view of God? It is the real attitude in which He puts himself forth to us in the gospel of His Son. He there says, in the hearing of all to whom the word of this salvation is sent, "Why will ye die?" It is true that by your death He could manifest the dignity of His Godhead; He could make known the power of His wrath; He could spread the awe of His truth and His majesty over the whole territory of His government, and send forth to its uttermost limits the glories of His strength and His immutable sovereignty. But He does not want to magnify Himself over you in this way; He has no ambition whatever after the renown of such a victory, over such weak and insignificant enemies. Their resistance were no trial whatever to His strength or to His greatness. There is nothing in the destruction of creatures so weak that can at all bring Him any distinction, or throw any aggrandizement around Him. And so in Scripture everywhere do we see Him pleading and protesting with you that He does not want to signalize himself upon the ruin of any, but would rather that they should turn and be saved.

And now, my brethren, what remains for you to do? God is willing to save you: are you willing to be saved? The way is set before you most patiently and clearly in the Bible — nay, the very text, brief as it is, points out to you the way, as I shall endeavor to explain and set before you in the third head of discourse. But meanwhile, and all the better to secure a hearing from you, let me ask you to lay it upon your consciences, whether you are in a state that will do for you to die in. If not, then I beseech you to think how certainly death will, and how speedily it may, come upon the likeliest of you all. The very youngest among you know very well, that if not cut off previously — which is. a very possible thing — then manhood will come, and old age will come, and the dying bed will come, and the very last look you shall ever cast on your acquaintances will come, and the agony of the parting breath will come, and the time when you are stretched a lifeless corpse before the eyes of weeping relatives will come, and the coffin that is to enclose you will come, and that hour when the company assemble to carry you to the churchyard will come, and that minute when you are put into the grave will come, and the throwing in of the loose earth into the narrow house where you are laid, and the spreading of the green sod over it — all, all will come on every living creature who now hears me; and in a few little years the minister who now speaks, and the people who now listen, will be carried to their long homes, and make room for another generation. Now, all this, you know, must and will happen — your common sense and common experience.serve to convince you of it. Perhaps it may have been little thought of in the days of careless and thoughtless and thankless unconcern which you have spent hitherto; but I call upon you to think of it now, to lay it seriously to heart, and no longer to trifle and delay, when the high matters of death and judgment and eternity are thus set so evidently before you. And the tidings wherewith I am charged — and the blood lieth upon your own head and not upon mine, if you will not listen to them — the object of my coming amongst you, is to let you know what more things are to come; it is to carry you beyond the regions of sight and of sense to the regions of faith, and to assure you, in the name of Him who cannot lie, that as sure as the hour of laying the body in the grave comes, so surely will also come the hour of the spirit returning to the God who gave it. Yes, and the day of final reckoning will come, and the appearance of the Son of God in heaven, and His mighty angels around Him, will come, and the opening of the books will come, and the standing of the men of all generations before the judgment-seat will come, and the solemn passing of that sentence which is to fix you for eternity will come. Yes, and if you refuse to be reconciled in the name of Christ, now that He is beseeching you to be so, and if you refuse to turn from the evil of your ways, and to do and to be what your Saviour would have you, I must tell you what that sentence is to be —" Depart from me, ye cursed, into everlasting fire, prepared for the devil and his angels."

There is a way of escape from the fury of this tremendous storm. There is a pathway of egress from the state of condemnation to the state of acceptance. There is a method pointed out in Scripture by which we, who by nature are the children of wrath, may come to be at peace with God. Let all ears be open then to our explanation of this way, as we bid you in the language of our text take hold of God's strength, that you may make peace with Him, and which if you do, you shall make peace with Him.

III. Read now the fifth verse:—" Or let him take hold of my strength, that he may make peace with me; and he shall make peace with me." *Or* here is the same with *rather*. Rather than that what is spoken of in the fourth verse should fall upon you — rather than that I should engage in battle with mine enemies — rather than that a result so melancholy to them should take place, as my going through them and burning them together — rather than that all this should happen, I would greatly prefer that they took hold of my strength in order to make peace with me; and I promise, as the sure effect of this proceeding, that they shall make peace with me. We have not far to seek for what is meant by this strength, for Isaiah himself speaks (ch. xxxiii. 6) of the strength of salvation. It is not your destruction but your salvation that God wants to put forth His strength in. There has strength been already put forth in the deliverance of a guilty world — the very strength which He wants you to lay hold of. He will be glorified in the destruction of the sinner, but He would like better to be glorified by his salvation. To destroy you is to do no more than to set fire to briers and thorns, and to consume them; but to save you — this is indeed the power of God and the wisdom of God — this is the mighty achievement which angels desire to look into — this is the enterprise upon which a mighty Captain embarked all the energy that belonged to Him, and travelled in the greatness of His strength until that He accomplished it; and now that it is accomplished, God would much rather be glorified in the salvation of His saints, than glorified in the destruction of sinners. (2 Thess. i. 7, 10). God will show His wrath, and make His power known in the destruction of the sinner. But it is a more glorious work of power to redeem that sinner, and this He engages to do for you, if you will take hold of His strength. He would greatly prefer this way of making His power known. He does not want to enter into battle with you, or to consume you like stubble by the breath of His indignation. No; He wants to transform sinners into saints: He wants to transform vessels of wrath into vessels of mercy, and to make known the riches of His glory on those whom He had afore prepared unto glory. There is a strength put forth in the destruction of the sinner, but there is also a strength put forth in the salvation of a sinner, and this is the strength which He wants you to lay hold of in my text — this is the strength by the display of which He would prefer being glorified. He would rather decline entering into a contest with you sinners; for to gain a victory over you would be no more to him than to fight with the briers and the thorns, and to consume them. But from enemies to make friends of you; from the children of wrath to transform you into the children of adoption; from the state of guilt to accomplish such a mighty and a wonderful change upon you, as to put you into the state of justification; from the servants of sin to make you in the day of His power the willing servants of God; to chase away from your faculties the darkness of nature, and to make all light and comfort around you; to turn you from a slave of sense, and to invest with all their rightful ascendency over your affections the things of eternity; to pull down the strongholds of corruption within you, and raise him who was spiritually dead to a life of new obedience; — this is the victory over you which God aspires after. It is not your destruction or your death that He delights in, or that He wants to be glorified by — it is your thorough and complete salvation from the punishment of sin, and the power of sin, on which He is desirous of exalting the glory of His strength, and this is the strength which He calls you to take hold upon.

Let me now, in what remains, first say a few things more upon this strength — the strength of salvation which is spoken of in the text — and then state very briefly what it is to lay hold of it.

And first we read of a mighty strength that had to be put forth in the work of a sinner's justification. You know that all men are sinners, and so all are under the righteous condemnation of God. How, in the name of all that is difficult and wonderful, can these sinners ever get this condemnation removed from them? By what new and unheard of process can the guilty before God ever again become justified in His sight? How from that throne, of which it is said that judgment and justice are the habitation, can the sentence of acquittal ever be heard on the children of iniquity? How can God's honor be kept entire in the sight of angels, if we men who have repeatedly mocked Him and insulted Him, and made our own wish and our own way take the precedency of His high and solemn requirements — if we, with all this con-

tempt of the Lawgiver expressed in our lives, and all this character of
rebellion against Him written upon our foreheads, shall be admitted to
a place of distinction in heaven — and that too after God has committed
Himself in the hearing of angels — after he had given us a law by the
disposition of angels, and we had not kept it — and after He had said
how the wicked shall not go unpunished, but that cursed is every one
who continueth not in all the words of the book of God's law to do them?
But what is more, it was not merely the good and the obedient angels
who knew our rebellion — the malignant and fallen angels not only
knew it, but they devised and they prompted it. And how, I would
ask, can God keep the awful majesty of His truth and justice entire in
the sight of His adversaries, if Satan and the angels of wickedness
along with him shall have it in their power to say — we prevailed on
man to insult Him by sin, and have compelled God to put up with the
affront, and to connive at it?

Now, just in proportion to the weight and magnitude of the obstacle
was the greatness of that strength which the Saviour put forth in the
mighty work of moving it away. We have no adequate conception upon
this matter, and must just take our lesson from revelation about it; —
and whether we take the prophecies which foretold the work of our
Redeemer, or the history which relates it, or the doctrine which ex-
patiates on its worth and its efficacy — all go to establish that there was
the operation of a power — that there was the severity of a conflict —
that there was the high emprise of an arduous and mighty warfare — that
there were all the throes and all the exertions of a struggling, and at
length a prevailing energy in the execution of that work which our
Saviour had to do — that He had a barrier to surmount, and that, too,
with the cries and the pains and the sorrows of heavy suffering and
labor — that a mighty obstacle lay before Him, and He, in the business
of removing it, had to travel in all the greatness of the faculties which
belonged to Him — that there was a burden laid upon His shoulders,
which by no one else but the Prince of Peace could have been borne —
that there was a task put into His hand which none but He could fulfil.
And had the question ever been reasoned throughout the hosts of paradise, Who can so bend the unchangeable attributes of God, who can
give them a shift so wonderful, that the sinners who have insulted Him
may be taken into forgiveness, and His honor be kept untainted and
entire? — there is not one of the mighty throng who would not have
shrunk from an enterprise so lofty. There is not one of them who

could at once magnify the law and release man from its violated sanctions. There is not one of them who could turn its threatening away from us, and at the same time give to the truth and the justice of God their brightest manifestation. There is not one of them who could unravel the mystery of our redemption through all the difficulties which beset and which surround it. There is not one of them who, by the strength of his arm, could have obtained the conquest over these difficulties. And however little we may enter into the elements of this weighty speculation, let us forget not that the question was not merely between God and man — it was between God and all the creatures He had formed. They saw the dilemma; they felt how deeply it involved the character of the Deity; they perceived its every bearing on the majesty of His attributes, and on the stability of the government that was upheld by Him. With them it was a matter of deep and most substantial interest; and when the Eternal Son stepped forward to carry the undertaking to its end, the feeling amongst them all was that a battle behoved to be fought, and that the strength of this mighty Captain of our salvation was alone equal to the achievement of the victory.

"Who is this that cometh from Edom, with dyed garments from Bozrah? this that is glorious in His apparel, travelling in the greatness of His strength? I that speak in righteousness, mighty to save. Wherefore art thou red in thine apparel, and thy garments like him that treadeth in the wine-fat? I have trodden the wine-press alone; and of the people there was none with me; for I will tread them in mine anger, and trample them in my fury; and their blood shall be sprinkled upon my garments, and I will stain all my raiment. For the day of vengeance is in mine heart, and the year of my redeemed is come. And I looked, and there was none to help; and I wondered that there was none to uphold; therefore mine own arm brought salvation unto me; and my fury, it upheld me."

A way of redemption has been found out in the unsearchable riches of divine wisdom, and Christ is called the wisdom of God. But the same Christ is also called the power of God. In the mighty work of redemption He put forth a strength, and it is that strength that we are called to take hold upon. There was a wonderful strength in bearing the wrath which would have fallen on the millions and millions more of a guilty world. There was a strength which bore Him up under the agonies of the garden. There was a strength which supported Him under the hidings of His Father's countenance. There was a strength which upheld Him in the dark hour of the travail of His soul, and which one might think had well-nigh given way when He called out, "My God, my God, why hast Thou forsaken me?" There was a strength which carried Him in triumph through the contest over Satan, when he buffeted Him with his temptations; and a strength far greater than we know of in that mysterious struggle which He held with the powers of darkness, when Satan fell like lightning from heaven, and the Captain of our salvation spoiled principalities and powers, and made a show of them openly, and triumphed over them. There was a strength in overcoming all the mighty difficulties which lay in the way between the sinner and God, in unbarring the gates of acceptance to a guilty world, in bringing truth and mercy to meet, and righteousness and peace to enter into fellowship — so that God might be just, while He is the justifier of him who believeth in Jesus.

So much for the strength which is put forth in the work of man's redemption. But there is also strength put forth in the work of man's regeneration. Christ hath not only done a great work for us in making good our reconciliation with God — He further does a great work in us when He makes us like unto God. But I have not time to dwell upon this last topic, and must content myself with referring you to the following Scriptures — Eph. i. 19; ii. 10; Phil. iv. 13; 2 Cor. xii. 9, 10; John xv. 5. The power which raised Jesus from the dead is the power which raises us from our death in trespasses and sins. The power that was put forth on creation is the power that makes us new creatures in Jesus Christ our Lord.

Neither have I time to make out a full demonstration of what is meant by laying hold of that strength. When you apply to a friend for some service, some relief from distress or difficulty, you may be said to lay hold of him; and when you place firm reliance both on his ability and willingness to do you the service, you may well say that your hold is upon your friend — an expression which becomes all the more appropriate should he promise to do the needful good office, in which case your hold is not upon his power only, but upon his faithfulness. And it is even so with the promises of God in Christ Jesus — you have both a power and a promise to take hold of. If you believe that Christ is able to save to the uttermost all who come unto God through Him, and if you believe the honesty of His invitation to all who are weary and heavy-laden, that they might come unto Him and have rest unto their souls, thus judging Him to be faithful who has promised, then indeed will you lay hold of Christ as the power of God unto salvation, and according to the faith which has thus led you to fix upon the Saviour so will it be done unto you. To continue in this faith is in the language of Scripture to hold fast your confidence and the rejoicing of your hope firm unto the end. Cast not away this confidence which hath great recompense of reward; or if you have not yet begun to place this confidence in the assurances of the gospel, lay hold of them now — they are addressed to each and to all of you. It is not a vague generality of which I am speaking. Let every man amongst you take up with Christ, and trust in Him for yourself.

I am well aware that unless the Spirit reveal to you, all I have said about Him will fall fruitless upon your ears, and your hearts will remain as cold and as heavy and as alienated as ever. Faith is His gift, and it is not of ourselves. But the minister is at his post when he puts the truth before you; and you are at your posts when you hearken diligently, and have a prayerful spirit of dependence on the Giver of all wisdom — that He will bless the word spoken, and make it reach your souls in the form of a salutary and convincing application. And it is indeed wonderful — it is passing wonderful, that there should be about us such an ungenerous suspicion of our Father who is in heaven. It cannot be sufficiently wondered at that all the ways in which He sets Himself forth to us should have so feeble an influence in the way of cheering us on to a more delighted confidence. How shall we account for it — that the barrier of unbelief should stand so obstinately firm in spite of every attempt and every remonstrance — that the straitening should still continue — not the straitening of God towards us, for He has said everything to woo us to put our trust in Him — but the straitening of us towards God, whereby in the face of His every kind and exhilarating declaration we persist in being cold and distant and afraid of Him?

I know not, my brethren, in how far I may have succeeded, as an humble and unworthy instrument, in drawing aside the veil which darkens the face of Him who sitteth on the throne. But oh, how imposing is the attitude, and how altogether affecting is the argument with which He comes forward to us in the text of this day! It is not so much His saying that there is no fury in Him — this He often tells us in other passages of Scripture; but the striking peculiarity of the words now submitted to us is the way in which He would convince us how little interest He can have in our destruction, and how far it is from His thoughts to aspire after the glory of such an achievement, as if He had said — it would be nothing to me to consume you all by the breath of my indignation — it would throw no illustration over me to sweep away the whole strength of that rebellion which you have mustered up against me — it would make no more to my glory than if I went through the thorns and briers and burned them before me. This is not the battle I want to engage in — this is not the victory by which I seek to signalize myself; and you mistake me — you mistake me, ye feeble children of men, if you think that I aspire after anything else with any one of you than that you should be prevailed on to come into my vineyard, and lay hold of my strength, and seek to make peace with me, and you shall make peace with me. The victory that my heart is set upon is not a victory over your persons — that is a victory that will easily be gotten in the great, day of final reckoning over all who have refused my overtures, and would none of my reproof, and have turned them away from my beseeching offers of reconciliation. In that great day of the power of mine anger it will be seen how easy it is to accomplish such a victory as this — how rapidly the fire of my conflagration will involve the rebels who have opposed me in that devouring flame from which they never, never can be extricated — how speedily the execution of the condemning sentence will run through the multitude who stand at the left hand of the Avenging Judge; and rest assured, ye men who are now hearing me, and whom I freely invite all to enter into the vineyard of God, that this is not the triumph that God is longing after. It is not a victory over your persons then of which He is at all ambitious — it is a victory over your wills now — it is that you do honor to His testimony by placing your reliance on it — it is that you accept of His kind and free assurances that He has no ill-will to you — it is that you cast the whole burden of sullen fear and suspicion away from your hearts, and that now, even now, you enter into a fellowship of peace with the God whom you have offended. Oh! be prevailed upon. I know that terror will not subdue you; I know that all the threatenings of the law will not reclaim you; I know that no direct process of pressing home the claims of God upon your obedience will ever compel you to the only obedience that is of any value in His estimation — even the willing obedience of the affections to a father whom you love. But surely when He puts on in your sight the countenance of a Father — when he speaks to you with the tenderness of a Father — when He tries to woo you back to that house of His from which you have wandered, and, to persuade you of His goodwill, descends so far as to reason the matter, and to tell you that He is no more seeking any glory from your destruction than He would seek glory from lighting into a blaze the thorns and the briers, and burning them together — ah! my brethren, should it not look plain to the eye of faith how honest and sincere the God of your redemption is, who is thus bowing Himself down to the mention of such an argument! Do lay hold of it, and be impressed by it, and cherish no longer any doubt of the good-will of the Lord God, merciful and gracious; and let your faith work by love to Him who hath done so much and said so much to engage it, and let this love evince all the power of a commanding principle within you, by urging your every footstep to the new obedience of new creatures in Jesus Christ your Lord.

Thus the twofold benefit of the gospel will be realized by all who believe and obey that gospel. Reconciled to God by the death of His Son, regenerated by the power of that mighty and all-subduing Spirit who is at the giving of the Son, your salvation will be complete — washed, and sanctified, and justified in the name of the Lord Jesus, and by the Spirit of our God.

XX

WILLIAM ELLERY CHANNING

1780–1842

WILLIAM ELLERY CHANNING, D. D., was the grandson of William Ellery, a signer of the Declaration of Independence. He was born April 7, 1780, in Newport, Rhode Island; entered Harvard College at the age of fifteen, and was graduated with honor at eighteen. In 1803 he was ordained as pastor of the Federal Street Church (Congregational) in Boston. Although Channing possessed a deeply spiritual nature, and had no liking for controversy, it was a sermon preached by him in 1819, at the ordination of Jared Sparks, which formed the occasion for the great division of the Congregational body of New England into Trinitarian and Unitarian churches. While Channing followed his conscience into the Unitarian camp, he retained the sweetness of his temper, a strong sympathy with truth as held by both sides, a devout love of the Scriptures, and a high reverence for the person of Jesus Christ. In 1841 he wrote " I am little of a Unitarian, have little sympathy with the system of Priestly and Belsham, and stand aloof from all but those who strive and pray for clearer light." He was a strong advocate of reforms,— notably of the temperance and anti-slavery movements; — was active in philanthropic endeavors, and even amid the sharp antagonisms of theological controversy, which were rife in his time, was greatly beloved by people of all churches and all creeds. Samuel Taylor Coleridge, whom he met in 1822, said of him, " He has the love of wisdom and the wisdom of love." He died October 2, 1842 at Bennington, Vermont.

THE CHARACTER OF CHRIST.

" This is my beloved Son, in whom I am well pleased."— Matthew xvii. 5.

THE character of Christ may be studied for various, purposes. It is singularly fitted to call forth the heart, to awaken love, admiration,

and moral delight. As an example, it has no rival. As an evidence of
his religion, perhaps it yields to no other proof; perhaps no other has
so often conquered unbelief. It is chiefly to this last view of it, that I
now ask your attention. The character of Christ is a strong confirma-
tion of the truth of his religion. As such, I would now place it before
you. I shall not, however, think only of confirming your faith; the very
illustrations, which I shall adduce for this purpose, will show the claims
of Jesus to our reverence, obedience, imitation, and fervent love.

The more we contemplate Christ's character, as exhibited in the
Gospel, the more we shall be impressed with its genuineness and reality.
It was plainly drawn from the life. The narratives of the Evangelists
bear the marks of truth, perhaps beyond all other histories. They set before us the most extraordinary being who ever appeared on earth, and
yet they are as artless as the stories of childhood. The authors do not
think of themselves. They have plainly but one aim, to show us their
Master; and they manifest the deep veneration which he inspired, by
leaving him to reveal himself, by giving us his actions and sayings without comment, explanation, or eulogy. You see in these narratives no
varnishing, no high coloring, no attempts to make his actions striking,
or to bring out the beauties of his character. We are never pointed to
any circumstance as illustrative of his greatness. The Evangelists write
with a calm trust in his character, with a feeling that it needed no aid
from their hands, and with a deep veneration, as if comment or praise of
their own were not worthy to mingle with the recital of such a life.

It is the effect of our familiarity with the history of Jesus, that we
are not struck by it as we ought to be. We read it before we are capable
of understanding its excellence. His stupendous works become as familiar to us as the events of ordinary life, and his high offices seem as
much matters of course as the common relations which men bear to each
other. On this account, it is fit for the ministers of religion to do what
the Evangelists did not attempt, to offer comments on Christ's character,
to bring out its features, to point men to its higher beauties, to awaken
their awe by unfolding its wonderful majesty. Indeed, one of our most
important functions, as teachers, is to give freshness and vividness to
truths which have become worn, I had almost said tarnished, by long
and familiar handling. We have to fight with the power of habit.
Through habit men look on this glorious creation with insensibility, and
are less moved by the all-enlightening sun than by a show of fire-works.

It is the duty of a moral and religious teacher almost to create a new sense in man, that they may learn in what a world of beauty and magnificence they live. And so in regard to Christ's character; men become used to it, until they imagine that there is something more admirable in a great man of their own day, a statesman or a conqueror, than in Him, the latchet of whose shoes statesmen and conquerors are not worthy to unloose.

In this discourse, I wish to show that the character of Christ, taken as a whole, is one which could not have entered the thoughts of man, could not have been imagined or feigned; that it bears every mark of genuineness and truth; that it ought therefore to be acknowledged as real and of divine original.

It is all-important, my friends, if we would feel the force of this argument, to transport ourselves to the times when Jesus lived. We are very apt to think that he was moving about in such a city as this, or among a people agreeing with ourselves in modes of thinking and habits of life. But the truth is, he lived in a state of society singularly remote from our own. Of all nations, the Jewish was the most strongly marked. The Jew hardly felt himself to belong to the human family. He was accustomed to speak of himself as chosen by God, holy, clean; whilst the Gentiles were sinners, dogs, polluted, unclean. His common dress, the phylactery on his brow or arm, the hem of his garment, his food, the ordinary circumstances of his life, as well as his temple, his sacrifices, his ablutions, all held him up to himself as a peculiar favorite of God, and all separated him from the rest of the world. With other nations he could not eat or marry. They were unworthy of his communion. Still, with all these notions of superiority, he saw himself conquered by those whom he despised. He was obliged to wear the shackles of Rome, to see Roman legions in his territory, a Roman guard near his temple, and a Roman tax-gatherer extorting, for the support of an idolatrous government and an idolatrous worship, what he regarded as due only to God. The hatred which burned in the breast of the Jew towards his foreign oppressor perhaps never glowed with equal intenseness in any other conquered state. He had, however, his secret consolation. The time was near, the prophetic age was at hand, when Judea was to break her chains and rise from the dust. Her long-promised king and deliverer was near, and was coming to wear the crown of universal empire. From Jerusalem was to go forth his law, and all nations were to serve the chosen people of God. To this conqueror the Jews indeed ascribed the office of promoting religion; but the religion of Moses, corrupted into an outward service, was to them the perfection of human nature. They clung to its forms with the whole energy of their souls. To the Mosaic institution they ascribed their distinction from all other nations. It lay at the foundation of their hopes of dominion. I believe no strength of prejudice ever equalled the intense attachment of the Jew to his peculiar national religion. You may judge of its power by the fact of its having been transmitted through so many ages, amidst persecution and sufferings which would have subdued any spirit but that of a Jew. You must bring these things to your mind. You must place yourselves in the midst of this singular people.

Among this singular people, burning with impatient expectation, appeared Jesus of Nazareth. His first words were, "Repent, for the kingdom of heaven is at hand." These words we hear with little emotion; but to the Jews, who had been watching for this kingdom for ages, and who were looking for its immediate manifestation, there must have been awakening as an earthquake. Accordingly we find Jesus thronged by multitudes which no building could contain. He repairs to a mountain, as affording him advantages for addressing the crowd. I see them surrounding him with eager looks, and ready to drink in every word from his lips. And what do I hear? Not one word of Judea, of Rome, of freedom, of conquest, of the glories of God's chosen people, and of the thronging of all nations to the temple on Mount Zion. Almost every word was a death-blow to the hopes and feelings which glowed through the whole people, and were consecrated under the name of religion. He speaks of the long-expected Kingdom of Heaven; but speaks of it as a felicity promised to, and only to be partaken by, the humble and pure in heart. The righteousness of the Pharisees, that which was deemed the perfection of religion, and which the new deliverer was expected to spread far and wide, he pronounces worthless, and declares the Kingdom of Heaven, or of the Messiah, to be shut against all who do not cultivate a new, spiritual, and disinterested virtue. Instead of war and victory, he commands his impatient hearers to love, to forgive, to bless their enemies; and holds forth this spirit of benignity, mercy, peace, as the special badge of the people of the true Messiah. Instead of national interests and glories, he commands them to seek first a spirit of impartial charity and love, unconfined by the bounds of tribe or nation, and proclaims this to be the happiness and honor of the reign for which they hoped. Instead of this world's riches, which they expected to flow from all lands into their own, he commands them to lay up treasures in heaven, and directs them to an incorruptible, immortal life, as the true end of their being. Nor is this all. He does not merely offer himself as a spiritual deliverer, as the founder of a new empire of inward piety and universal charity; he closes with language announcing a more mysterious office. "Many will say unto me in that day, Lord, Lord, have we not prophesied in thy name? and in thy name done many wonderful works? And then will I profess unto them, I never knew you; depart from me, ye that work iniquity." Here I meet the annunciation of a character as august as it must have been startling. I hear him foretelling a dominion to be exercised in the future world. He begins to announce, what entered largely into his future teaching, that his power was not bounded to this earth. These words I better understand when I hear him subsequently declaring that, after a painful death, he was to rise again and ascend to heaven, and there, in a state of pre-eminent power and glory, was to be the advocate and judge of the human race.

Such are some of the views given by Jesus, of his character and reign, in the Sermon on the Mount. Immediately afterwards I hear another lesson from him, bringing out some of these truths still more strongly. A Roman centurion makes application to him for the cure of a servant, whom he particularly valued; and on expressing, in a strong manner, his conviction of the power of Jesus to heal at a distance, Jesus, according to the historian, "marvelled, and said to those that followed, Verily I say unto you, I have not found so great faith in Israel; and I say unto you, that many shall come from the east and west, and shall sit down with Abraham, and Isaac, and Jacob in the kingdom of heaven; but the children of the kingdom" (that is, the Jews) "shall be cast out." Here all the hopes which the Jews had cherished of an exclusive or peculiar possession of the Messiah's kingdom, were crushed; and the reception of the despised Gentile world to all his blessings, or, in other words, the extension of his pure religion to the ends of the earth, began to be proclaimed.

Here I pause for the present, and I ask you, whether the character of Jesus be not the most extraordinary in history, and wholly inexplicable on human principles. Review the ground over which we have gone. Recollect that he was born and grew up a Jew, in the midst of Jews, a people burning with one passion, and throwing their whole souls into

18

the expectation of a national and earthly deliverer. He grew up among them in poverty, seclusion, and labors fitted to contract his thoughts, purposes, and hopes; and yet we find him escaping every influence of education and society. We find him as untouched by the feelings which prevailed universally around him, which religion and patriotism concurred to consecrate, which the mother breathed into the ear of the child, and which the teacher in the synagogue strengthened in the adult, as if he had been brought up in another world. We find him conceiving a sublime purpose, such as had never dawned on sage or hero, and see him possessed with a consciousness of sustaining a relation to God and mankind, and of being invested with powers in this world and the world to come, such as had never entered the human mind. Whence now, I ask, came the conception of this character?

Will any say it had its origin in imposture; that it was a fabrication of a deceiver? I answer, the character claimed by Christ excludes this supposition, by its very nature. It was so remote from all the ideas and anticipations of the times, so unfit to awaken sympathy, so unattractive to the heathen, so exasperating to the Jew, that it was the last to enter the mind of an impostor. A deceiver of the dullest vision must have foreseen, that it would expose him to bitter scorn, abhorrence, and persecution, and that he would be left to carry on his work alone, just as Jesus always stood alone, and could find not an individual to enter into his spirit and design. What allurements an unprincipled, self-seeking man could find to such an enterprise, no common ingenuity can discover.

I affirm next, that the sublimity of the character claimed by Christ forbids us to trace it to imposture. That a selfish, designing, depraved mind could have formed the idea and purpose of a work unparalleled in beneficence, in vastness, and in moral grandeur, would certainly be a strange departure from the laws of the human mind. I add, that if an impostor could have lighted on the conception of so sublime and wonderful a work as that claimed by Jesus, he could not, I say, he *could* not have thrown into his personation of it the air of truth and reality. The part would have been too high for him. He would have overacted it or fallen short of it perpetually. His true character would have rebelled against his assumed one. We should have seen something strained, forced, artificial, awkward, showing that he was not in his true sphere. To act up to a character so singular and grand, and one for which no precedent could be found, seems to me utterly impossible for a man who had not the true spirit of it, or who was only wearing it as a mask.

Now, how stands the case with Jesus? Bred a Jewish peasant or carpenter, he issues from obscurity, and claims for himself a divine office, a superhuman dignity, such as had not been imagined; and in no instance does he fall below the character. The peasant, and still more the Jew, wholly disappears. We feel that a new being, of a new order of mind, is taking a part in human affairs. There is a native tone of grandeur and authority in his teaching. He speaks as a being related to the whole human race. His mind never shrinks within the ordinary limits of human agency. A narrower sphere than the world never enters his thoughts. He speaks in a natural, spontaneous style, of accomplishing the most arduous and important change in human affairs. This unlabored manner of expressing great thoughts is particularly worthy of attention. You never hear from Jesus that swelling, pompous, ostentatious language, which almost necessarily springs from an attempt to sustain a character above our powers. He talks of his glories as one to whom they were familiar, and of his intimacy and oneness with God, as simply as a child speaks of his connection with his parents. He speaks of saving and judging the world, of drawing all men to himself, and of giving everlasting life, as we speak of the ordinary powers which we exert. He makes no set harangues about the grandeur of his office and character. His consciousness of it gives a hue to his whole language, breaks out in indirect, undesigned expressions, showing that it was the deepest and most familiar of his convictions. This argument is only to be understood by reading the Gospels with a wakeful mind and heart. It does not lie on their surface, and it is the stronger for lying beneath it. When I read these books with care, when I trace the unaffected majesty which runs through the life of Jesus, and see him never falling below his sublime claims amidst poverty, and scorn, and in his last agony, I have a feeling of the reality of his character which I cannot express. I feel that the Jewish carpenter could no more have conceived and sustained this character under motives of imposture, than an infant's arm could repeat the deeds of Hercules, or his unawakened intellect comprehend and rival the matchless works of genius.

Am I told that the claims of Jesus had their origin not in imposture, but in enthusiasm; that the imagination, kindled by strong feeling, overpowered the judgment so far as to give him the notion of being destined to some strange and unparalleled work? I know that enthusiasm, or a kindled imagination, has great power; and we are never to lose sight of it, in judging of the claims of religious teachers. But I say first, that, except in cases where it amounts to insanity, enthusiasm works, in a greater or less degree, according to a man's previous conceptions and modes of thought. In Judea, where the minds of men were burning with feverish expectation of a Messiah, I can easily conceive of a Jew imagining that in himself this ardent conception, this ideal of glory, was to be realized. I can conceive of his seating himself in fancy on the throne of David, and secretly pondering the means of his appointed triumphs. But that a Jew should fancy himself the Messiah, and at the same time should strip that character of all the attributes which had fired his youthful imagination and heart — that he should start aside from all the feelings and hopes of his age, and should acquire a consciousness of being destined to a wholly new career, and one as unbounded as it was new, this is exceedingly improbable; and one thing is certain, that an imagination so erratic, so ungoverned, and able to generate the conviction of being destined to a work so immeasurably disproportioned to the power of the individual, must have partaken of insanity. Now, is it conceivable that an individual, mastered by so wild and fervid an imagination, should have sustained the dignity claimed by Christ, should have acted worthily the highest part ever assumed on earth? Would not his enthusiasm have broken out amidst the peculiar excitements of the life of Jesus, and have left a touch of madness on his teaching and conduct? Is it to such a man that we should look for the inculcation of a new and perfect form of virtue, and for the exemplification of humanity in its fairest form?

The charge of an extravagant, self-deluding enthusiasm is the last to be fastened on Jesus. Where can we find the traces of it in his history? Do we detect them in the calm authority of his precepts; in the mild, practical, and beneficent spirit of his religion; in the unlabored simplicity of the language with which he unfolds his high powers, and the sublime truths of religion; or in the good sense, the knowledge of human nature, which he always discovers in his estimate and treatment of the different classes of men with whom he acted? Do we discover this enthusiasm in the singular fact that, whilst he claimed power in the future world, and always turned men's minds to Heaven, he never indulged his own imagination or stimulated that of his disciples by giving vivid pictures, or any minute description of that unseen state? The truth is, that, remarkable as was the character of Jesus, it was distinguished by nothing more than by calmness and self-possession. This trait pervades his other excellences. How calm was his piety! Point me, if you can, to one vehement, passionate expression of his religious feelings. Does the Lord's prayer breathe a feverish enthusiasm? The habitual style of Jesus on the subject of religion, if introduced into many churches of his followers at the present day, would be charged with coldness. The calm and the rational character of his piety is particularly seen in the doctrine which he so earnestly inculcates, that disinterested love and self-denying service to our fellow-creatures are the most acceptable worship we can offer to our Creator. His benevolence, too, though singularly earnest and deep, was composed and serene. He never lost the possession of himself in his sympathy with others; was never hurried into the impatient and rash enterprises of an enthusiastic philanthropy; but did good with the tranquillity and constancy which mark the providence of God. The depth of his calmness may best be understood by considering the opposition made to his claims. His labors were everywhere insidiously watched and industriously thwarted by vindictive foes, who had even conspired to compass, through his death, the ruin of his cause. Now, a feverish enthusiasm which fancies itself to be intrusted with a great work of God, is singularly liable to impatient indignation under furious and malignant opposition. Obstacles increase its vehemence; it becomes more eager and hurried in the accomplishment of its purposes, in proportion as they are withstood. Be it therefore remembered that the malignity of Christ's foes, though never surpassed, and for the time triumphant, never robbed him of self-possession, roused no passion, and threw no vehemence or precipitation into his exertions. He did not disguise from himself or his followers the impression made on the multitude by his adversaries. He distinctly foresaw the violent death towards which he was fast approaching. Yet, confiding in God and in the silent progress of his truth, he possessed his soul in peace. Not only was he calm, but his calmness rises into sublimity when we consider the storms which raged around him, and the vastness of the prospects in which his spirit found repose. I say then that serenity and self-possession were peculiarly the attributes of Jesus. I affirm that the singular and sublime character claimed by Jesus can be traced neither to imposture nor to an ungoverned, insane imagination. It can only be accounted for by its truth, its reality.

I began with observing how our long familiarity with Jesus blunts our minds to his singular excellence. We probably have often read of the character which he claimed, without a thought of its extraordinary nature. But I know nothing so sublime. The plans and labors of statesmen sink into the sports of children when compared with the work which Jesus announced, and to which he devoted himself in life and death with a thorough consciousness of its reality. The idea of changing the moral aspect of the whole earth, of recovering all nations to the pure and inward worship of one God, and to a spirit of divine and fraternal love, was one of which we meet not a trace in philosopher or legislator before him. The human mind had given no promise of this extent of view. The conception of this enterprise, and the calm, unshaken expectation of success in one who had no station and no wealth, who cast from him the sword with abhorrence, and who forbade his disciples to use any weapons but those of love, discover a wonderful trust in the power of God and the power of love; and when to this we add that Jesus looked not only to the triumph of his pure faith in the present world, but to a mighty and beneficent power in Heaven, we witness a vastness of purpose, a grandeur of thought and feeling so original, so superior to the workings of all other minds, that nothing but our familiarity can prevent our contemplation of it with wonder and profound awe. I confess, when I can escape the deadening power of habit, and can receive the full import of such passages as the following: — " Come unto me, all ye that labor and are heavy laden, and I will give you rest,"—" I am come to seek and to save that which was lost,"—" He that confesseth me before men, him will I confess before my Father in Heaven,"—" Whosoever shall be ashamed of me before men, of him shall the Son of Man be ashamed when he cometh in the glory of the Father with the holy angels,"—" In my Father's house are many mansions; I go to prepare a place for you:"— I say, when I can succeed in realizing the import of such passages, I feel myself listening to a being, such as never before and never since spoke in human language. I am awed by the consciousness of greatness which these simple words express; and when I connect this greatness with the proofs of Christ's miracles which I gave you in a former discourse, I am compelled to exclaim with the centurion, " Truly, this was the Son of God."

I have thus, my friends, set before you one view of Jesus Christ, which shows him to have been the most extraordinary being who ever lived. I invite your attention to another, and I am not sure but that it is still more striking. You have seen the consciousness of greatness which Jesus possessed; I now ask you to consider how, with this consciousness, he lived among men. To convey my meaning more distinctly, let me avail myself of an imaginary case. Suppose you had never heard the particulars of Christ's history, but were told in general that, ages ago, an extraordinary man appeared in the world, whose mind was wholly possessed with the idea of having come from God, who regarded himself as clothed with divine power and charged with the sublimest work in the universe, who had the consciousness of sustaining a relation of unexampled authority and beneficence, not to one nation or age, but to all nations and all times, and who anticipated a spiritual kingdom and everlasting power beyond the grave. Suppose you should be told that, on entering the world, he found not one mind able to comprehend his views, and felt himself immeasurably exalted in thought and purpose above all around him, and suppose you should then be asked what appearance, what mode of life, what tone, what air, what deportment, what intercourse with the multitude seemed to you to suit such a character, and were probably adopted by him; how would you represent him to your minds? Would you not suppose that, with this peculiar character, he adopted some peculiar mode of life, expressive of his superiority to, and separation from all other men? Would you not expect something distinctive in his appearance? Would you not expect him to assume some badge, and to exact some homage? Would you not expect that, with a mind revolving such vast thoughts, and raised above the earth, he would look coldly on the ordinary gratifications of men? that, with a mind spreading itself over the world, and meditating its subjection to his truth, he would take little interest in ordinary individuals? and that possessing, in his own doctrine and character, a standard of sublime virtue, he would attach little importance to the low attainments of the ignorant and superstitious around him? Would you not make him a public character, and expect to see him laboring to establish his ascendancy among public men? Would you not expect to see his natural affections absorbed in his universal philanthropy; and would not private attachments seem to you quite inconsistent with his vast superiority and the immensity of his purposes? Would you not expect him to avail himself of the best accommodations the world could afford? Would you not expect the great Teacher to select the most sacred spots for his teaching, and the Lord of all to erect some conspicuous seat from which should go forth the laws which were to reach the ends of the earth? Would you not, in a word, expect this extraordinary personage to surround himself with extraordinary circumstances, and to maintain a separation from the degraded multitude around him?

Such, I believe, would be the expectation of us all; and what was the case with Jesus? Read his history: He comes with the consciousness of more than human greatness, to accomplish an infinite work, and where do you find him? What is his look? what his manner? How does he converse, how live with men? His appearance, mode of life, and intercourse are directly the reverse of what we should have supposed. He comes in the ordinary dress of the class of society in which he had grown up. He retreats to no solitude, like John, to strike awe, nor seeks any spot which had been consecrated in Jewish history. Would you find him? Go to the house of Peter, the fisherman. Go to the well of Samaria, where he rests after the fatigues of his journey. Would you hear him teach? You may find him, indeed, sometimes in the temple, for that was a place of general resort; but commonly you may find him instructing in the open air, now from a boat on the Galilean lake, now on a mount, and now in the streets of the crowded city. He has no place wherein to lay his head, nor will he have one. A rich ruler comes and falls at his feet. He says, "Go, sell what thou hast and give to the poor, and then come and follow me." Nor was this all. Something more striking remains to be told. He did not merely live in the streets and in the houses of fishermen. In these places, had he pleased, he might have cleared a space around him, and raised a barrier between himself and others. But in these places and everywhere, he lived with men as a man, a brother, a friend, sometimes a servant; and entered, with a deep, unexampled sympathy, into the feelings, interests, wants, sorrows of individuals, of ordinary men, and even of the most depressed, despised, and forsaken of the race. Here is the most striking view of Jesus. This combination of the spirit of humanity, in its lowliest, tenderest form, with the consciousness of unrivalled and divine glories, is the most wonderful distinction of this wonderful character. Here we learn the chief reason why he chose poverty, and refused every peculiarity of manner and appearance. He did this because he desired to come near to the multitude of men, to make himself accessible to all, to pour out the fullness of his sympathy upon all, to know and weep over their sorrows and sins, and to manifest his interest in their affections and joys.

I can offer but a few instances of this sympathy of Christ with human nature in all its varieties of character and condition. But how beautiful are they! At the very opening of his ministry we find him present at a marriage, to which he and his disciples had been called. Among the Jews this was an occasion of peculiar exhilaration and festivity; but Jesus did not therefore decline it. He knew what affections, joys, sorrows, and moral influences, are bound up in this institution, and he went to the celebration, not as an ascetic, to frown on its bright hopes and warm congratulations, but to sanction it by his presence, and to heighten its enjoyments. How little does this comport with the solitary dignity which we should have pronounced most accordant with his character, and what a spirit of humanity does it breathe! But this event stands almost alone in his history. His chief sympathy was not with them that rejoice, but with the ignorant, sinful, sorrowful; and with these we find him cultivating an habitual intimacy. Though so exalted in thought and purpose, he chose uneducated men to be his chief disciples; and he lived with them, not as a superior, giving occasional and formal instruction, but became their companion, travelled with them on foot, slept in their dwellings, sat at their tables, partook their plain fare, communicated to them his truth in the simplest form; and though they constantly misunderstood him, and never received his full meaning, he was never wearied with teaching them. So familiar was his intercourse, that we find Peter reproving him with an affectionate zeal for announcing his approaching death, and we find John leaning on his bosom. Of his last discourse to these disciples I need not speak. It stands alone among all writings for the union of tenderness and majesty. His own sorrows are forgotten in his solicitude to speak peace and comfort to his humble followers.

The depth of his human sympathies was beautifully manifested when children were brought to him. His disciples, judging as all men would judge, thought that he who was sent to wear the crown of universal empire, had too great a work before him to give his time and attention to children, and reproved the parents who brought them; but Jesus, rebuking his disciples, called to him the children. Never, I believe, did childhood awaken such deep love as at that moment. He took them in his arms and blessed them, and not only said that "of such was the kingdom of heaven," but added, "He that receiveth a little child in my name, receiveth me;" so entirely did he identify himself with this primitive, innocent, beautiful form of human nature.

There was no class of human beings so low as to be beneath his sympathy. He not merely taught the publican and sinner, but with all his consciousness of purity, sat down and dined with them, and, when reproved by the malignant Pharisee for such companionship, answered by the touching parables of the Lost Sheep and the Prodigal Son, and said, "I am come to seek and to save that which was lost."

No personal suffering dried up this fountain of love in his breast. On his way to the cross he heard some women of Jerusalem bewailing him, and at the sound, forgetting his own grief, he turned to them and said, "Women of Jerusalem, weep not for me, but weep for yourselves and your children." On the cross, whilst his mind was divided between intense suffering and the contemplation of the infinite blessings in which his sufferings were to issue, his eye lighted on his mother and John, and the sensibilities of a son and a friend mingled with the sublime consciousness of the universal Lord and Saviour. Never before did natural affection find so tender and beautiful an utterance. To his mother he said, directing her to John, "*Behold thy son;* I leave my beloved disciple to take my place, to perform my filial offices, and to enjoy a share of that affection with which you have followed me through life;" and to John he said, "*Behold thy mother;* I bequeath to you the happiness of ministering to my dearest earthly friend." Nor is this all. The spirit of humanity had one higher triumph. Whilst his enemies surrounded him with a malignity unsoftened by his last agonies, and, to give the keenest edge to insult, reminded him scoffingly of the high character and office which he had claimed, his only notice of them was the prayer, "Father, forgive them, they know not what they do."

Thus Jesus lived with men; with the consciousness of unutterable majesty he joined a lowliness, gentleness, humanity, and sympathy, which have no example in human history. I ask you to contemplate this wonderful union. In proportion to the superiority of Jesus to all around him, was the intimacy, the brotherly love, with which he bound himself to them. I maintain that this is a character wholly remote from human conception. To imagine it to be the production of imposture or enthusiasm, shows a strange unsoundness of mind. I contemplate it with a veneration second only to the profound awe with which I look up to God. It bears no mark of human invention. It was real. It belonged to and it manifested the beloved Son of God.

But I have not done. May I ask your attention a few moments more? We have not yet reached the depth of Christ's character. We have not touched the great principle on which his wonderful sympathy was founded, and which endeared to him his office of universal Saviour. Do you ask what this deep principle was? I answer, it was his conviction of the greatness of the human soul. He saw in man the impress and image of the divinity, and therefore thirsted for his redemption, and took the tenderest interest in him, whatever might be the rank, character, or condition in which he was found. This spiritual view of man pervades and distinguishes the teaching of Christ. Jesus looked on men with an eye which pierced beneath the material frame. The body vanished before him. The trappings of the rich, the rags of the poor, were nothing to him. He looked through them, as though they did not exist, to the soul; and there, amidst clouds of ignorance and plague-spots of sin, he recognised a spiritual and immortal nature, and the germs of power and perfection which might be unfolded for ever. In the most fallen and depraved man, he saw a being who might become an angel of light. Still more, he felt that there was nothing in himself to which men might not ascend. His own lofty consciousness did not sever him from the multitude; for he saw in his own greatness the model of what men might become. So deeply was he thus impressed that, again and again, in speaking of his future glories, he announced that in these his true followers were to share. They were to sit on his throne and partake of his beneficent power.

Here I pause, and indeed I know not what can be added to heighten the wonder, reverence, and love, which are due to Jesus. When I consider him, not only as possessed with the consciousness of an unexampled and unbounded majesty, but as recognising a kindred nature in human beings, and living and dying to raise them to a participation of his divine glories; and when I see him under these views allying himself to men by the tenderest ties, embracing them with a spirit of humanity which no insult, injury, or pain could for a moment repel or overpower, I am filled with wonder as well as reverence and love. I feel that this character is not of human invention, that it was not assumed through fraud, or struck out by enthusiasm; for it is infinitely above their reach. When I add this character of Jesus to the other evidences of his religion, it gives to what before seemed so strong, a new and a vast accession of strength; I feel as if I could not be deceived. The Gospels must be true; they were drawn from a living original; they were founded on reality. The character of Jesus is not a fiction; he was what he claimed to be, and what his followers attested. Nor is this all. Jesus not only *was,* he is still the Son of God, the Saviour of the world. He exists now; he has entered that Heaven to which he always looked forward on earth. There he lives and reigns. With a clear, calm faith I see him in that state of glory; and I confidently expect, at no distant period, to see him face to face. We have indeed no absent friend whom we shall so surely meet. Let us then, my hearers, by imitation of his virtues and obedience to his word, prepare ourselves to join him in those pure mansions, where he is surrounding himself with the good and pure of our race, and will communicate to them for ever his own spirit, power, and joy.

XXI

EDWARD IRVING

1792–1834

IN power of originality and eloquence as in stature, Edward Irving towered amidst English preachers in the third decade of the nineteenth century. In De Quincey's words, he was "unquestionably, by many degrees, the greatest orator of our times." His sincerity and piety are evident; yet the latter years of his ministry were embittered by indiscreet acts arising, perhaps, from partial insanity. He was born at Annan, Scotland, in 1792, and was educated at the University of Edinburgh. For three years he was an assistant to Dr. Chalmers, in Glasgow, and in 1822 was installed in the Scottish Presbyterian Church, London. Here he enjoyed unbounded popularity, till his encouragement in his congregation of unintelligible rhapsodies as utterances of the Spirit, and alleged misstatements of doctrine, led to his ejection by the Presbytery on the charge of heresy, in 1832. Thence arose the Catholic Apostolic Church, called in Great Britain "Irvingites," with whose beliefs and methods he had little to do. He died in Glasgow of consumption, December 8th, 1834.

THE LORD JESUS CHRIST.

"And from the Lord Jesus Christ."— Eph. i. 2.

THE grace and peace with which Paul the apostle of Jesus Christ doth bless the saints at Ephesus and the faithful in Christ Jesus, proceedeth not from God the Father only, but equally and alike from the Lord Jesus Christ; and this same conjunction of the Father and the Son as the source and origin of all spiritual benefits, our apostle maketh not in one, but in all his epistles, and not he only but also the other apostles. We may never doubt, therefore, from this the constant style of Holy Scripture, that the two Divine Persons thus advanced into equal honor as the fountain of grace and peace, are to be equally acknowledged by the Church, and witnessed to by the saints; that they may not and cannot be separated or contemplated apart: "No man knoweth the Son but the Father; neither knoweth any man the Father save the Son, and he to whom the Son shall reveal him." Therefore the gospel is by our apostle called "the mystery of God, and [both] of the Father, and of Christ," (Col. ii. 2). And by the apostle John it is declared, "If that which ye have heard from the beginning shall remain in you, ye shall also continue in the Son, and in the Father." (1 John ii. 24). And again, "Truly our fellowship is with the Father, and with his Son Jesus Christ." (Chap. i. 3). Into that part and office in the mystery which the Father hath we have inquired diligently in several discourses, and we do now propose, by the help of the Spirit to testify unto the office of the Son, according as it is contained under His name, Jesus Christ the Lord. Into the mystery of His name, Jesus, we would then with all reverence first inquire.

The name Jesus being written at full length is Jehoshua, which consisteth of two parts — Hoshea, which was the original name of the son of Nun; and Jah, which was added by Moses when he sent him to spy out the land of Canaan. Hoshea is "saviour," or "salvation;" on which account it is said, "Thou shalt call his name JESUS, for he shall save his people from their sins." (Matt. i. 21). And Jah is a contraction of Jehovah, used singly to denote the whole force of that name in Ps. lxviii. 4, "Extol him that rideth upon the heavens by his name Jah;" used along with it to give it force and intensity, in two passages of Isaiah. The first is: "Behold, God is my salvation (Hoshea); I will trust, and not be afraid: for the Lord (Jah) Jehovah is my strength and my song; he also is become my salvation (Hoshea)." (Chap. xii. 2). This is a very remarkable passage, both as containing the two parts of the name Jesus, Jah and Hoshea, and as declaring that the Jewish people in the day of their restoration shall say that Jah Jehovah hath become Jah Hoshea, or Jesus their Saviour; and in consequence of this, their confession of the name of Christ, it is added, "Therefore with joy shall ye draw water out of the wells of salvation;" which I understand to signify their abundant and joyful partaking of the Holy Ghost. The other passage in which Jah occurs is to the same effect, and spoken of the same people against the same time,—"We have a strong city: salvation (Hoshea) will God appoint for walls and bulwarks. . . . Trust ye in the Lord (Jehovah) for ever: for in the Lord (Jah) is everlasting strength." (Chap. xxvi.

i, 4). This separation of Jah, a part of the name Jehovah, from the rest, and this use of it in the separate form always in connection with the idea of salvation, and hence with the very word Hoshea, I cannot but regard as a preparation for that combination and composition of the word into the one name Jehoshua, which in the type had been already done by an act of God's minister, and in the antitype was about to be done by the act of God himself. Observe further, that Hoshea had his name changed when he went to spy out the land of Canaan, the inheritance which God had by the covenant of Sinai set apart unto the seed of Abraham. The Son of Nun had already, so to speak, won his name of " saviour," by the various battles wherein God had given him to smite the enemies of Israel; but the name of Jehoshua he had to win for himself, by going into the enemy's land and bringing out of it a faithful and good report, which was to signify that the Son of God upon coming into this world, which God hath intended for an inheritance of His saints, should have the name of Jesus given to Him, and should earn the like, not by reporting it able to be taken, but by purchasing it to himself out of the hands of the enemy, and acquiring the right to it for His people, against the dispensation of the fullness of the times, when the purchased possession shall be redeemed. These being the component parts of the name Jesus, let us now inquire into the meaning of each of them; for it is by understanding the name of the Son that we shall understand His person and His offices in the blessed Trinity.

The name Jah or Jehovah is sufficiently explained to us in that which the Lord spake unto Moses from the midst of the bush,—" And God said unto Moses, I AM THAT I AM : and he said, Thus shalt thou say unto the children of Israel, I AM hath sent me unto you," (Exod. iii. 14) ; which teacheth us that self-existent, underived, unchangeable, self-sufficient being is that which is contained under the name Jehovah : self-existent in himself, underived from any higher origin, and unchangeable by any cause ; all-sufficient in himself, and therefore the origin, the changer, and the sufficiency of every other existing person and thing. This incommunicable name the Jews held to be unutterably sacred, and would by no means name it, but retained it in the mysterious holiness of impenetrable silence ; and whenever it occurred in the text they pronounced in its stead some of the appellations of God,— a fond conceit, which degenerated at length into a base superstition, yet worthy to be mentioned as teaching us the opinion of the nation that in this name lay folded up, as it were, the very essence and substance of that Divine Being, of whom all the other names expressed only the attributes. There might also perhaps be concealed under this rabbinical conceit another act of worship done unto Moses and the Mosaic economy, with a view to which this name was assumed: as it is written in Exod. vi. 3,—" I appeared unto Abraham, unto Isaac, and unto Jacob, by the name of God Almighty; but by my name Jehovah was I not known to them." This name Almighty, or Elohim, is proper to God as the maker of all the creatures, ere yet He had revealed himself as the chooser out and redeemer of a part of the fallen creatures, and was most proper to preserve men from running into the worship of the creature, by continually declaring that it was made by another than itself; but when God began to manifest His purpose according to election by the calling out of Abraham, and His salvation of a Church from the wrecks of fallen nature by the imputation of a righteousness not inherent in it, but derived from Him, then He added to the name of God, the Creator of all, the special and peculiar propriety which He had in His chosen ones, saying, " I am the God of Abraham, and Isaac, and Jacob," and appointing the same for a memorial unto all generations; because this Church portion, the saved portion of the fallen creatures, shall endure unto all ages, and constitute God's most excellent and glorious inheritance. But, at the call of Moses, being about to institute a covenant wherein He was to pledge Himself to ten thousand things, whereof not one was to be perfectly accomplished until after a hundred ages of sore contradiction and oppression, He thinketh it good to take unto Himself a name which shall be expressive of constancy and faithfulness in the highest possible sense, — a name which every one that knew it might trust; a name which should signify the same yesterday, to-day, and for ever. And this name is Je-hovah, of which Jah, the essence, hath been compounded into Jesus. By which component part, therefore, it is signified that the Jehovah of the covenant was no other than the Son, the same Divine Person who ani-mated the child of the virgin; and that all things which were spoken by Jehovah, Jesus undertaketh to fulfil. That word Jah, incorporated with Hoshea in the name of our blessed Lord, is to me a pledge that all things which are written in the law and the prophets the Son of Man hath come not to destroy but to fulfil. And accordingly we do find that Jesus hath applied to Him the essential meaning of Jehovah, which is independence on all outward causes, and unalterable by time, as in Rev. xiii. 8,—" Jesus Christ, the same yesterday, to-day, and for ever." And again (Heb. i. 10), quoting from Psalm cii., " Thou, Lord, in the beginning hast laid the foundation of the earth; and the heavens are the works of thine hands; they shall perish, but thou remainest; and they all shall wax old as doth a garment; and as a vesture shalt thou fold them up, and they shall be changed: but thou art the same, and thy years shall not fail." And, not to enumerate more instances, it is said of Christ (Rev. i. 8), what had just been said of the Father,—" I am Alpha and Omega, the beginning and the ending, saith the Lord, which is, and which was, and which is to come, the Almighty,—an expression which some have thought to be no more than a translation into Greek of the Hebrew words Jehovah Elohim, or the Lord God. Unto this much have we attained, therefore, that all the might and holiness, all the magnificence of power and splendor of operation, all the faithfulness and immovableness of purpose, together with all words whatsoever written of Jehovah and the old dispensation, are the property of Him who hath revealed himself under the new as a man of sorrows and acquainted with grief, the meek, the humble, and the lowly Jesus.

The second part of this blessed name Jehoshua is Hoshea, which signifies salvation, and was added to the name Jah when the person of the Son united itself to the substance of the fallen creature for the end of redeeming and saving it; wherefore in this form of the God-man, while yet only conceived but not born, He is called Jesus, " for He shall save His people from their sins." Though Jehovah had been known under the law as a great deliverer of His people from manifold oppressions, these deliverances had all been frustrated by their persevering disobedience, and they were now sold under the sorest bondage of all which they had ever proved, a bondage which endureth unto this day. He was known to them as yet, therefore, not as their Saviour but as their Judge, and the avenger of their wickedness. Nevertheless, in the mouth of all the prophets He had upon all occasions, and especially upon the eve of each new trial, assured them with the promise of a new and everlasting covenant, under which He would be merciful to their unrighteousness, and would remember their iniquities no more, when the sin of Judah and of Israel should be sought for and should not be found; and when, together with all sin, all suffering and oppression should pass away. To execute these promises and to bring in this dispensation of eternal salvation, the virgin's Son had been promised both by Isaiah and Jeremiah; and now that the virgin's Child is conceived He receiveth the name of Jah Hoshea, Jehovah the Saviour, to assure the faithful that He, and none but He, would accomplish all these things; and accordingly Zecharias, when his tongue was loosed, did prophesy of Him in these words, " Blessed be the

19

Lord God of Israel, for he hath visited and redeemed his people : and hath raised up an horn of salvation for us in the house of his servant David : as he spake by the mouth of all his holy prophets which have been since the world began." To this deliverance not yet accomplished unto the Jewish people, to this salvation from their sins under the penalty of which they are still suffering, there can be no doubt that the name Jesus hath a primary reference, and that it was thus understood both by the blessed virgin and by the prophet Zecharias. It would not have been proper to the Jewish economy, still in existence, to have spoken otherwise of Messiah than as He had been spoken of by all the prophets; and if He had been spoken of to them in the higher sense in which we are now to contemplate His salvation, it would have been to them unintelligible. The sense I mean is that in which all believers look upon Him as their Saviour in taking away their guilt and their judgment, and regenerating their natures, and raising them from the dead to the inheritance of eternal life and blessedness. In this higher sense of the Redeemer of the fallen creatures whom God hath chosen unto life eternal, the Jewish people were not privileged to perceive Him otherwise than through the emblems of their state and nature, and by these emblems it shall yet be taught them against the day of their glory; but to us, taught by the Spirit, it is given to understand how Jehovah became the Saviour that instant He united Himself to the seed of the woman. In taking a part of the fallen creature into union with himself and saving that part from the pollution of sin, the corruption of the grave, and the power of Satan, He gave assurance that God was with Him, and in Him wrought this same thing for His own glory; gave assurance that He was both purposed and able to redeem and restore with greater glory the fallen creature, to save it from sin and death, to bless it with holiness and eternal life. When the Son of God took flesh, He entered upon the travail of salvation; when He carried that flesh triumphant to the right hand of God, he finished the work. By saving His own human nature, by preserving it from the taint of sin, by delivering it from the power of Satan, by carrying it into the region of glory, He did obtain eternal redemption for us, He did receive power to destroy him that had the power of death, and to deliver all them who through the fear of death were subject to bondage. This power of saving others proceedeth from His saving of himself. He voluntarily brought himself into peril by taking to himself our nature; by being incarnate He became the champion of our salvation, by enduring the incarnation and overcoming all the creature's fallen condition, He accomplished our salvation; and from thenceforth He standeth alone the head of salvation, as He had been the head of creation,— not only Jehovah Elohim, the Lord God, but Jehovah Hoshea, the Lord the Saviour. Now this voluntary peril which the Son of God undertook was for the greatest ends of the creature's glory and of the creature's well-being,— seeing God's glory as the Creator had been obscured, and the creature's goodly condition subverted by the fall; and therefore Jehovah is not fully manifested as the Saviour until all the effects of the fall shall have been clean wrought out of creation, and the handiwork of God shall stand sinless and glorious for ever. The name Jesus, therefore, carries us far beyond anything which we behold as yet accomplished, into the future everlasting condition of God's works, when everything that defileth and maketh a lie shall be purged off into the second death of the lake which burneth with fire and brimstone for ever, and the heavens and earth which now are defiled and obscure shall with all their inhabitants, in the estate of infallible blessedness, acknowledge Jehovah their Creator to be also Jehovah their Saviour. Save upon that human nature which He assumed, I may say that the virtue and power of the name Jesus hath not yet been exhibited. In this kind the whole work has been finished by the wonderful act of taking our nature, and going down with it into the region, first, of all temptation, and next of the grave or all corruption, and thence fetching it up and seating it in the place of all honor and all blessedness. This exaltation which will yet be done upon all the chosen ones of God, and upon all that dependeth from them in their several degrees, hath as yet been only partially done upon any one of the saints, whose souls, though they be in glory, have left their bodies under the corruption of the grave — sad memorial of their sinfulness! And we who being now in the body have the first fruits of the Spirit, do nevertheless groan within ourselves, waiting for the adoption, to wit, the redemption of the body: and all the creatures groan and travail together under bondage, waiting for that same glorious manifestation of the sons of God. And if so be that the name Jesus implies salvation from that curse and thraldom of sin under which the creation is now fallen, who will say that the name will be acquitted of its full blessedness until the bodies of the saints be brought up from their graves, and the world delivered from the headship of Satan and the power of death? Now as His being born of the virgin, and manifested as the seed of David, gave the beginning to the great work of our salvation, considered as shut up and represented in His human nature; and as the resurrection of His body from the dead gave

the beginning to the work of conveying and communicating the same
salvation to an elect few individuals in the gift of the Holy Ghost; even
so His work of saving the Jewish nation from the hand of all their
enemies will be the beginning of the work of delivering mankind from
the dominion of Satan, and His being brought again into the world shall
be the signal for delivering the bodies of His Church from the power of
the grave. After which it only remaineth that by the judgment He
should deliver all things created from the power of death; and then is
the glorious name of Jesus, or Jah the Saviour, acquitted of its most
precious burden.

Thus have I endeavored, dear brethren, to set forth unto you the
meaning of the name Jesus, which the Godhead assumed in the act of taking unto itself the substance of the fallen creature, in order to save what
of the fallen creatures it pleased Him to save. And now I would, by the
grace of God, endeavor to draw out from what hath been said certain
conclusions of doctrine and practical inferences, which the Lord may be
pleased to bless unto your edification in knowledge, in faith, and in new
obedience.

First, then, it is manifest from God's revealing himself as Jesus, or
the Saviour, that the creatures are in a state of condemnation and of perdition; otherwise what meaning were there in revealing himself as their
Saviour? As the name Elohim, or God the Almighty One, implies that
every other one is not almighty, but of a limited power and subordinate
place; and as the name Jehovah, or the Unchangeable One, implieth that
all other beings are to undergo change and alteration according to His
will; so doth the name Jesus, or Saviour, imply that all other beings
whatsoever are in a state of condemnation and misery, from under which
they need to be saved. And whence cometh this state of misery and perdition is distinctly and directly revealed in the act of giving unto Him the
name,—" Thou shalt call his name Jesus, for he shall save his people
from their sins." Be it known unto you, therefore, brethren, and of this
be ye steadfastly assured, that our sins have divided between us and God,
and brought us under the dominion of death and the grave, and the resurrection unto judgment, and the sentence of the second death, which
nothing can avert, from which nothing can deliver and save us, but trust
upon the name of Jesus, and believing in God as the only Saviour from
our sins. Put away, therefore, from amongst you all confidence which
is elsewhere rested than upon the name of Jesus, and otherwise proceedeth
than through faith in the incarnation, and obedience, and death, and

burial of the Lord Jesus Christ. Be ye assured, that if God spared not His own Son when He had assumed our fallen nature, and become a partaker of flesh and blood with the rest of the brethren, that He will not spare us who have no divine community of substance with the Father, who have no eternal generation by the Father, who have no inhabitation of the Father's bosom, and participation of his counsel, to interest the Father for our sakes; and if these being present in Jesus did not avert the sword of God from smiting the Shepherd, oh, how think you that we rebellious creatures can ever escape if we should neglect such great salvation! If over Him the law laid its line of righteousness, and its plumbline of judgment, exacting obedience unto every jot and tittle of its holy, just, and good commandments, shall it, oh, can it, be relaxed unto such as we are! If the holiness of God was not prevented from its action and infliction upon Him who was the manifestation of His love, and grace, and glory, how shall it, how can it be silent, be inactive, be changed towards us, who are manifestations of rebellion, ingratitude, unfruitfulness, and sin! Say then, believe then, know then, and be assured that in the way of God's holiness and justice, in the way of His law and our obedience thereto, there is nothing but condemnation and perdition for ever and for ever. Acknowledge this, and have no confidence in the flesh, or in the powers of the natural man. Say, "I am indeed a sinner, and the chief of sinners; my righteousnesses are as filthy rags; in all things I come short of the glory of God; in my best estate I am but vanity. I have been feeding upon the east wind while I trusted in my own works; and I shall continue to feed on the east wind, be parched, be blighted, be shrivelled up like the tree of the wilderness over which the east wind bloweth, so long as I shall look for any righteousness or hope for any salvation through anything which I can do for myself, or which others can do for me. I am a condemned man; I can ask no second trial; my mouth is shut, my doom is written, my fate is sealed." This, even this, no less, is what I require of you to believe, and to feel as the just conclusion from the name of Jesus, which the eternal revealer of God, even the Son, hath taken unto Himself under the gospel dispensation.

And now, in the second place, I call upon you to believe and to feel, that unto a world thus sealed and set apart unto condemnation God hath revealed himself as a Saviour. As He did reveal himself its Creator, so now revealeth He himself its Saviour; and this message of reconciliation hath He committed unto me His minister to make known unto you all, that albeit ye are guilty before Him, and have no plea in your mouth, He is of such wondrous grace, and hath for the creatures of His hand such pitiful love and tender compassion being a Sovereign withal whom no one can question, saying, " What doest Thou? " that He hath given His only-begotten Son, that whosoever believeth in him might not perish, but have everlasting life; that He is in Jesus Christ reconciling the world unto himself, not imputing unto men their trespasses. Believe, then, though all have sinned and come short of the glory of God, you are justified " freely by His grace through the redemption that is in Christ Jesus; whom God hath set forth to be a propitiation through faith in His blood, to declare His righteousness for the remission of sins that are past, through the forbearance of God; to declare, I say, at this time His righteousness, that He might be just, and the justifier of him that believeth in Jesus." As in my former conclusion of doctrine and practice I did entreat you to be separate from all creature trust, and to regard the whole creation of God as under the bondage of sin and death, lying in the wicked one; so now do I entreat and invoke you to look unto Jesus, the Author and the Finisher of your faith. Receive the grace of God by Him preached, and from Him proceeding forth. Receive the pardon of your guilt written in His blood and sealed with the key of David, which openeth and no man shutteth, which shutteth and no man openeth. As the prisoner no more doubteth when the reprieve of his sovereign cometh under the great seal of the kingdom by the hands of the king's proper messenger; so doubt ye no more, let the world doubt no more after it hath received the good news of salvation by the Son of God, to this very end appointed by His name Jesus, and for the assurance of this very thing constituted by His union, His inseparable and indivisible union with the nature of the creatures which had been imprisoned under the sentence of the law of the Jehovah King, the Unchangeable One. Ah! is it not as if to some poor, doubting, disbelieving woman under sentence of death, the king's son, that he might give her fast assurance and chase away her despair, should wed himself to her, join himself as one, that her poor fainting heart might be reassured? So did Christ, in order to convince the children of mother Eve, who in their mother's transgression had transgressed, and in their mother's sentence had been doomed, come and wed himself, His eternal divinity, unto the seed of mother Eve, that the family, all the family, might truly know and feel assured that they had found grace in the sight of God, and were beloved because He is Love, and can love what in itself is all unlovely.

And now I ask you to believe that you are saved in Christ; to rejoice and hold up your heads, because you are redeemed; to go on and rejoice, and prosper, and do exploits under that banner of salvation which He hath displayed because of the truth.

And now, finally, with respect to the manner of conveying this salvation which He wrought out by His obedience unto death, we have to observe that it is not by giving out of himself unto another, but by bringing that other into himself that the communication of the blessedness proceedeth. To give unto us an existence out of himself is the work of creation. To bring the thing created into union, into oneness with himself, is the work of redemption, which therefore proceeded by joining unto himself, by taking up into hypostatical union with himself the nature of man. And every one who is redeemed is in like manner taken up into union with His human nature, so as to be one with Him as He is one with the Father. But this union of the redeemed ones unto Christ is not of the same kind as the union of His human nature unto His divine. The human nature of Christ is a part of His personal, and shall continue so for ever; but not so is it with His saved ones, who are separate persons from Christ, though of the same substance with His human nature unto which they are consubstantiated by the Holy Ghost proceeding from Him to this very end of bringing them into union with Him, just as the seed of plants hath power to assimilate unto itself the elemental substances on which it feeds, and so to produce many seeds and many plants of the like kind. Or to preserve our similitude still more correct, as the one stem of the vine hath power through the appropriation unto itself of elemental matters to put forth many branches, whereon grow the clusters of ripe fruit; so doth Christ the true vine of the Father's planting, of the Father's dressing, by operation of the Holy Spirit upon the creature produce many separate persons in His own likeness, many branches growing out of and unto himself. In their union with Him standeth their fertility, and being separated from Him they are good for nothing but to be cast out and trodden under the foot of men. The Holy Spirit, therefore, which proceedeth from Christ doth unite us unto Christ, and enable us to abide in Him,— doth not unite us unto the Godhead of the Son, but doth unite us to the manhood of Christ. And the completeness of the saved ones will be accomplished at His coming; after which, if I err not, the manner of this salvation will somewhat change. For I reckon there is a dignity and a closeness in the union between Christ and His elect or bridal Church which now is suffering with Him and for Him, that there is not between Him and the numerous hosts which shall come and be joined unto Him in the age to come, of which He is declared to be the Father; whereas of the Church that now is, He is the husband. But still as the children are of the same substance with their parents, so shall the innumerable company of the saints in the age to come be taken out of the stock of an evil nature subject unto death, and brought into the stock of a redeemed nature which hath triumphed over death; and so all the saved ones are saved by being taken out of the sinful mass and consubstantiated with that atom, so to speak, of redeemed substance which the Son joined unto himself, and which the Father gave to have life in itself. And as Christ the great quickener, the eternal life manifested, doth thus draw unto himself those whom the Father giveth Him out of that separateness and wickedness in which they are by nature, and so doth save them in himself, not out of himself; even in like manner do these same saved ones draw along with them this world which was made for man, with its sun, and moon, and stars, and fish and flying fowl, and living creatures, to the utter exclusion of death and extinction of sin and misery; and then the work of creation will appear to have been but the rudiments of and preparation for the work of redemption by the manifestation of Jehovah under the name of Jesus.

And now, brethren, before I close, allow me to express, in a few words, the heartfelt satisfaction with which I return to my charge over your souls, and to the labors of the ministry in this city. The tidings which I received from time to time of your love and fellowship· in the Lord, of your constancy in the duties of public worship, did afford me great consolation in my absence; and a good report concerning you is, I may say, spread abroad amongst the churches. In which let us rejoice together. Let us remark with gratitude the hand of God in sending amongst us ministers of good and honorable report, in whose mouth the substance of the doctrine which I teach hath been confirmed. And now let us proceed with renewed confidence in the great Head of the Church, to hold up in this city a banner for the truth. Let us go on unto perfection, and not stop until we reach the stature of a perfect man in Christ. You may desire naturally to know what reception the word which I preached met with in our native land and in our mother Church. Everywhere, I may truly say, the people heard me gladly, and from the ministers of the gospel I received much brotherly kindness; for all which I return thanks this day to the great Head of the Church. I preached unto them the coming of the Lord in judgment, little thinking that I should witness any act of His judgment; but so it was, the Lord did lift up His hand and make a breach in the midst of the congregation. It is a fearful thing, let me tell you, brethren, to witness such an awful sight; but oh, if those days of judgment and of visitation be so near at hand, what sights more awful await our eyes! If those days be at hand concerning which it is said, that unless they were shortened no flesh should be saved, oh, then, what death, what destruction, what ruin, may we not be prepared to see! Enter, oh enter, then, into your chambers, ye people of the Lord, and shut your doors and hide yourselves as it were for a little moment until the indignation be overpast. Have I not preached unto you this day the name of Jesus, that Rock of refuge and high tower of salvation? Flee unto Him speedily, speedily, who hath been the dwelling-place of His people in all generations. Everything shall change but Jehovah, everything shall perish which is not united unto Jehovah the Saviour. There is no other name given under heaven whereby men must be saved but the name of Jesus; and every one who knoweth His name will put his trust in Him. Trust ye in the Lord for ever, for in the Lord Jehovah is everlasting strength. Amen and amen.

XXII

THOMAS ARNOLD

1795-1842

THOMAS ARNOLD, D.D., from his high abilities, his personal character, and his influential position as an educator, exercised a strong influence upon English religious thought in the middle period of the nineteenth century. He was born at Cowes, in the isle of Wight, June 13, 1795, and was educated at Oxford, where he won distinction as a scholar. Although a clergyman of the Church of England, his work was mainly in educational lines. In 1828 he became Head-Master of Rugby School. It was predicted on his appointment, that he would change the force of public-school education throughout England; and although he lived but fourteen years afterward, the forecast was realized. Yet it was not by new methods of teaching that his influence was felt, so much as by his commanding personality and the earnestness of his nature. One of his successors at Rugby (Dr. Percival) has said of Arnold, " I should describe him as a great prophet among school-masters, rather than an instructor or educator in the ordinary sense of the term." Every boy who came under his influence at Rugby received the impress of his character and carried it through life. He was liberal in his views, but strong in loyalty to the Church of England. His death was sudden on June 12, 1842. One of his sons, Matthew Arnold, became eminent as an author and a poet. Nearly all his published sermons, which appear in five volumes, were preached in the chapel of the Rugby School.

ALIVE IN GOD.

" God is not the God of the dead, but of the living."—Matt. xxii. 32.

WE hear these words as a part of our Lord's answer to the Sadducees; and, as their question was put in evident profaneness, and the

THOMAS ARNOLD.
1795-1842.
The celebrated Doctor Arnold, for fourteen
years headmaster of Rugby School, in England,
frequently referred to by those who came under
his influence, as in "Tom Brown's School Days."

EDWARD IRVING.
1792-1834.
One of the leading orators of the Presbyterian
Church in Scotland and England. His later years
were involved in controversy and charges of
heresy, which are not reflected in his finest sermons.

answer to it is one which to our minds is quite obvious and natural, so we are apt to think that in this particular story there is less than usual that particularly concerns us. But it so happens, that our Lord, in answering the Sadducees, has brought in one of the most universal and most solemn of all truths,— which is indeed implied in many parts of the Old Testament, but which the Gospel has revealed to us in all its fullness,— the truth contained in the words of the text, that " God is not the God of the dead, but of the living."

I would wish to unfold a little what is contained in these words, which we often hear even, perhaps, without quite understanding them; and many times oftener without fully entering into them. And we may take them, first, in their first part, where they say that " God is not the God of the dead."

The word " dead," we know, is constantly used in Scripture in a double sense, as meaning those who are dead spiritually, as well as those who are dead naturally. And, in either sense, the words are alike applicable: " God is not the God of the dead."

God's not being the God of the dead signifies two things: that they who are without him are dead, as well as that they who are dead are also without him. So far as our knowledge goes respecting inferior animals, they appear to be examples of this truth. They appear to us to have no knowledge of God; and we are not told that they have any other life than the short one of which our senses inform us. I am well aware that our ignorance of their condition is so great that we may not dare to say anything of them positively; there may be a hundred things true respecting them which we neither know nor imagine. I would only say that, according to that most imperfect light in which we see them, the two points of which I have been speaking appear to meet in them: we believe that they have no consciousness of God, and we believe that they will die. And so far, therefore, they afford an example of the agreement, if I may so speak, between these two points; and were intended, perhaps, to be to our view a continual image of it. But we had far better speak of ourselves. And here, too, it is the case that " God is not the God of the dead." If we are without him we are dead; and if we are dead we are without him: in other words, the two ideas of death and absence from God are in fact synonymous.

Thus, in the account given of the fall of man, the sentence of death and of being cast out of Eden go together; and if any one compares the description of the second Eden in the Revelation, and recollects how especially it is there said, that God dwells in the midst of it, and is its light by day and night, he will see that the banishment from the first Eden means a banishment from the presence of God. And thus, in the day that Adam sinned, he died; for he was cast out of Eden immediately, however long he may have moved about afterwards upon the earth where God was not. And how very strong to the same point are the words of Hezekiah's prayer, " The grave cannot praise thee, Death cannot celebrate thee; they that go down into the pit cannot hope for thy truth;" words which express completely the feeling that God is not the God of the dead. This, too, appears to be the sense generally of the expression used in various parts of the Old Testament, " Thou shalt surely die." It is, no doubt, left purposely obscure; nor are we ever told, in so many words, all that is meant by death; but, surely, it always implies a separation from God, and the being — whatever the notion may extend to — the being dead to him. Thus, when David had committed his great sin, and had expressed his repentance for it, Nathan tells him, " The Lord also hath put away thy sin; thou shalt not die:" which means, most expressively, thou shalt not die to God. In one sense, David died, as all men die; nor was he, by any means, freed from the punishment of his sin: he was not, in that sense, forgiven; but he was allowed still to regard God as his God; and, therefore, his punishments were but fatherly chastisements from God's hand, designed for his profit, that he might be partaker of God's holiness. And thus although Saul was sentenced to lose his kingdom, and although he was killed with his sons on Mount Gilboa, yet I do not think that we find the sentence passed upon him, " Thou shalt surely die;" and, therefore, we have no right to say that God had ceased to be his God, although he visited him with severe chastisements, and would not allow him to hand down to his sons the crown of Israel. Observe, also, the language of the eighteenth chapter of Ezekiel, where the expressions occur so often, " He shall surely live," and " He shall surely die." We have no right to refer these to a mere extension, on the one hand, or a cutting short, on the other, of the term of earthly existence. The promise of living long in the land, or, as in Hezekiah's case, of adding to his days fifteen years, is very different from the full and unreserved blessing, " Thou shalt surely live." And we know, undoubtedly, that both the good and the bad to whom Ezekiel spoke, died alike the natural death of the body. But the peculiar force of the promise, and of the threat, was, in the one case, Thou shalt belong to God; in the other, Thou shalt cease to belong to him; although the veil was not yet drawn up which concealed the full import of those terms, "belonging to God," and "ceasing to belong to him:" nay, can we venture to affirm that it is fully drawn aside even now?

I have dwelt on this at some length, because it really seems to place the common state of the minds of too many amongst us in a light which is exceedingly awful; for if it be true, as I think the Scripture implies, that to be dead, and to be without God, are precisely the same thing, then can it be denied, that the symptoms of death are strongly marked upon many of us? Are there not many who never think of God, or care about his service? Are there not many who live, to all appearance, as unconscious of his existence as we fancy the inferior animals to be? And is it not quite clear, that to such persons, God cannot be said to be their God? He may be the God of heaven and earth, the God of the universe, the God of Christ's church; but he is not their God, for they feel to have nothing at all to do with him; and, therefore, as he is not their God, they are, and must be, according to the Scripture, reckoned among the dead.

But God is the God " of the living." That is, as before, all who are alive, live unto him; all who live unto him, are alive. " God said, I am the God of Abraham, and the God of Isaac, and the God of Jacob;" and, therefore, says our Lord, " Abraham, and Isaac, and Jacob, are not and cannot be dead." They cannot be dead, because God owns them: he is not ashamed to be called their God; therefore, they are not cast out from him; therefore, by necessity, they live. Wonderful, indeed, is the truth here implied, in exact agreement, as we have seen, with the general language of Scripture; that, as she who but touched the hem of Christ's garment was, in a moment, relieved from her infirmity, so great was the virtue which went out from him; so they who are not cast out from God, but have anything whatever to do with him, feel the virtue of his gracious presence penetrating their whole nature; because he lives, they must live also.

Behold, then, life and death set before us; not remote (if a few years be, indeed, to be called remote), but even now present before us; even now suffered or enjoyed. Even now, we are alive unto God, or dead unto God; and, as we are either the one or the other, so we are, in the highest possible sense of the terms, alive or dead. In the highest possible sense of the terms; but who can tell what that highest possible sense of the terms is? So much has, indeed, been revealed to us, that we know now that death means a conscious and perpetual death, as life means a

conscious and perpetual life. But greatly, indeed, do we deceive ourselves, if we fancy that, by having thus much told us, we have also risen
to the infinite heights, or descended to the infinite depths, contained in
those little words, life and death. They are far higher, and far deeper,
than ever thought or fancy of man has reached to. But, even on the
first edge of either, at the visible beginnings of that infinite ascent or
descent, there is surely something which may give us a foretaste of what
is beyond. Even to us in this mortal state, even to you advanced but
so short a way on your very earthly journey, life and death have a
meaning: to be dead unto God, or to be alive to him, are things perceptibly different.

For, let me ask of those who think least of God, who are most
separate from him, and most without him, whether there is not now
actually, perceptibly, in their state, something of the coldness, the loneliness, the fearfulness of death? I do not ask them whether they are
made unhappy by the fear of God's anger; of course they are not:
for they who fear God are not dead to him, nor he to them. The thought
of him gives them no disquiet at all; this is the very point we start
from. But I would ask them whether they know what is to feel God's
blessing. For instance: we all of us have our troubles of some sort or
other, our disappointments, if not our sorrows. In these troubles, in
these disappointments,— I care not how small they may be,— have they
known what it is to feel that God's hand is over them; that these little
annoyances are but his fatherly correction; that he is all the time loving
us, and supporting us? In seasons of joy, such as they taste very often,
have they known what it is to feel that they are tasting the kindness of
their heavenly Father, that their good things come from his hand, and
are but an infinitely slight foretaste of his love? Sickness, danger,— I
know that they come to many of us but rarely; but if we have known
them, or at least sickness, even in its lighter form, if not in its graver,—
have we felt what it is to know that we are in our Father's hands, that
he is with us, and will be with us to the end; that nothing can hurt those
whom he loves? Surely, then, if we have never tasted anything of this: if
in trouble, or in joy, or in sickness, we are left wholly to ourselves, to
bear as we can, and enjoy as we can; if there is no voice that ever speaks
out of the heights and the depths around us, to give any answer to our
own; if we are thus left to ourselves in this vast world,— there is in this
a coldness and a loneliness; and whenever we come to be, of necessity,
driven to be with our own hearts alone, the coldness and the loneliness
must be felt. But consider that the things which we see around us can-

not remain with us, nor we with them. The coldness and loneliness of the world, without God, must be felt more and more as life wears on: in every change of our own state, in every separation from or loss of a friend, in every more sensible weakness of our own bodies, in every additional experience of the uncertainty of our own counsels,— the death-like feeling will come upon us more and more strongly: we shall gain more of that fearful knowledge which tells us that " God is not the God of the dead."

And so, also, the blessed knowledge that he is the God " of the living " grows upon those who are truly alive. Surely he " is not far from every one of us." No occasion of life fails to remind those who live unto him, that he is their God, and that they are his children. On light occasions or on grave ones, in sorrow and in joy, still the warmth of his love is spread, as it were, all through the atmosphere of their lives: they for ever feel his blessing. And if it fills them with joy unspeakable even now, when they so often feel how little they deserve it; if they delight still in being with God, and in living to him, let them be sure that they have in themselves the unerring witness of life eternal:— God is the God of the living, and all who are with him must live.

Hard it is, I well know, to bring this home, in any degree, to the minds of those who are dead: for it is of the very nature of the dead that they can hear no words of life. But it has happened that, even whilst writing what I have just been uttering to you, the news reached me that one, who two months ago was one of your number, who this very half-year has shared in all the business and amusements of this place, is passed already into that state where the meanings of the terms life and death are become fully revealed. He knows what it is to live unto God, and what it is to die to him. Those things which are to us unfathomable mysteries, are to him all plain: and yet but two months ago he might have thought himself as far from attaining this knowledge as any of us can do. Wherefore it is clear, that these things, life and death, may hurry their lesson upon us sooner than we deem of, sooner than we are prepared to receive it. And that were indeed awful, if, being dead to God, and yet little feeling it, because of the enjoyments of our worldly life, those enjoyments were on a sudden to be struck away from us, and we should find then that to be dead to God was death indeed, a death from which there is no waking, and in which there is no sleeping for ever.

XXIII.

FRANCIS WAYLAND

1796–1865

FRANCIS WAYLAND, D.D., LL. D., as eminent a philosopher as divine, was born in New York, March 11th, 1796. He studied at Union College and Andover Theological Seminary. After a five years' pastorate in the First Baptist Church, Boston, he was appointed in 1827 president of Brown University, Providence, Rhode Island, and retained that office twenty-eight years. From 1857–9 he was pastor of the First Baptist Church, Providence. He died September 30th, 1865. The Sermon entitled " The Moral Dignity of Missions," preached by him in early manhood, wonderfully strengthened the missionary cause at home and abroad. His " Elements of Moral Science," and " Elements of Political Economy," have wisely trained thousands of American students of the older generation. His Christian liberality was ceaseless; for many years he gave away more than half his income. These words of his to a few students —" Do not young gentlemen, throw away your souls without trying to save them. Make *one honest effort* for their salvation. Even if you are lost, it will be something to have tried,"— led to the conversion of one who became a minister, and the writing of a tract, " One Honest Effort," which has awakened many. His sons have written an appreciative " Memoir." By permission, this discourse is extracted from his " University Sermons."

A DAY IN THE LIFE OF JESUS OF NAZARETH.

" And the apostles, when they were returned, told him all that they had done. And he took them, and went aside privately into a desert place, belonging to the city called Bethsaida. And the people

when they knew it, followed him: and he received them, and spake unto them of the kingdom of God, and healed them that had need of healing. And when the day began to wear away, then came the twelve, and said unto him, Send the multitude away, that they may go into the towns and country round about, and lodge, and get victuals: for we are here in a desert place. But he said unto them, Give ye them to eat. And they said, We have no more but five loaves and two fishes; except we should go and buy meat for all this people. For they were about five thousand men. And he said to his disciples, Make them sit down by fifties in a company. And·they did so, and made them all sit down. Then he took the five loaves and the two fishes and looking up to heaven, he blessed them and brake, and gave to the disciples to set before the multitude. And they did eat, and were all filled: and there was taken up of fragments that remained to them twelve baskets."—Luke ix. 10–17.

It was the sagacious opinion of, I think, the late Professor Porson, that he would rather see a single copy of a daily newspaper of ancient Athens, than read all the commentaries upon the Grecian tragedies that have ever been written. The reason for this preference is obvious. A single sheet, similar to our daily newspapers, published in the time of Pericles, would admit us at once to a knowledge of the habits, manners, modes of opinion, political relations, social condition, and moral attainments of the people, such as we never could gain from the study of all the writers that have ever attempted to illustrate the nature of Grecian civilization.

The same remark is true in respect to our knowledge of the character of individuals who have lived in a former age. What would we not, at the present day, give for a few pages of the private diary of Julius Cæsar, or Cicero, or Brutus, or Augustus; or for the minute reminiscences of any one who had spent a few days in the company of either of these distinguished men? What a flood of light would the discovery of such a manuscript throw upon Roman life, but especially upon the private opinions, the motives, the aspirations, the moral estimates, of the men whose names have become household words throughout the world! A few such pages might, perchance, dissipate the authority of many a bulky folio on which we now rely with implicit confidence. Not only would the characters of these heroes of antiquity stand out in bolder relief than they have ever done before, but the individuals themselves would be brought within the range of our personal sympathy; and we

20

should seem to commune with them as we do with an intimate acquaintance.

It is worthy of remark, that we are favored with a larger portion of this kind of information, respecting Jesus of Nazareth, than almost any other distinguished person that has ever lived. He left no writings himself; hence all that we know of him has been written by others. The narrators, however, were the personal attendants, and not the mere auditors or pupils of their Master. The apostles were members of the family of Jesus; they travelled with him, on foot, throughout the length and breadth of Palestine; they partook with him of his frugal meals, and bore with him the trial of hunger, weariness, and want of shelter; they followed him through the lonely wilderness and the crowded street; they saw his miracles in every variety of form, and listened to his discourses in public as well as to his explanations in private. Hence their whole narrative is instinct with life; a vivid picture of Jewish manners and customs, rendered more definite and characteristic by the moral light which then, for the first time, shone upon it. Hence it is that these few pages are replete with moral lessons that never weary us in the perusal, and which have been the source of unfailing illumination to all succeeding ages.

The verses which I have read, as the text of this discourse, may well be taken as an illustration of all that I have here said. They may, without impropriety, be styled a day in the life of Jesus of Nazareth. By observing the manner in which our blessed Lord spent a single day, we may form some conception of the kind of life which he ordinarily led; and we may, perchance, treasure up some lessons which it were well if we should exemplify in our daily practice.

The place at which these events occurred was near the head of the Sea of Galilee, where it receives the waters of the upper Jordan. This was one of the Saviour's favorite places of resort. Capernaum, Chorazin, and Bethsaida, all in this immediate vicinity, are always spoken of in the Gospels as towns which enjoyed the largest share of his ministerial labors, and were distinguished most frequently with the honor of his personal presence. The scenery of the neighborhood is wild and romantic. To the north and west, the eye rests on the lofty summits of Lebanon and Hermon. To the south, there opens upon the view the blue expanse of the lake, enclosed by frowning rocks, which here and there jut over far into the waters, and then again retire towards the land, leaving a level beach to invite the labors of the fishermen. The people, removed at a considerable distance from the metropolis of Judea, culti-vated those rural habits with which the simple tastes of the Saviour would most readily harmonize.   Near this spot was also one of the most fre-quented fords of the Jordan, on the road from Damascus to Jerusalem; and thus, while residing here, he enjoyed unusual facilities for disseminat-ing throughout this whole region a knowledge of those truths which he came on earth to promulgate.

Some weeks previous to the time in which the events spoken of in the text occurred, our Lord had sent his disciples to announce the ap-proach of the kingdom of heaven, in all the cities and villages which he himself proposed to visit.   He conferred on them the power to work miracles, in attestation of their authority, and of the divine character of him by whom they were sent.   He imposed upon them strict rules of conduct, and directed them, to make known to every one who would hear them the good news of the coming dispensation.   As soon as he sent them forth, he himself went immediately abroad to teach and to preach in their cities.   As their Master and Lord, he might reasonably have claimed exemption from the personal toil and the rigid self-denials to which they were by necessity subjected.   But he laid claim to no such exemption.   He commenced without delay the performance of the very same duties which he had imposed upon them.   He felt himself under obligation to set an example of obedience to his own rules.   " The Son of man," said he, " came not to be ministered unto, but to minister, and to give his life a ransom for many."   " Which," said he, " is greater, he that sitteth at meat, or he that serveth? but I am among you as he that serveth."   Would it not be well, if, in this respect, we copied more mi-nutely the example of our Lord, and held ourselves responsible for the per-formance of the very same duties which we so willingly impose upon our brethren?   We best prove that we believe an act obligatory, when we commence the performance of it ourselves.   Many zealous Christians employ themselves in no other labor than that of urging their brethren to effort.   Our Saviour acted otherwise.   In this respect, his example is specially to be imitated by his ministers.   When they urge upon others a moral duty, they must be the first to perform it.   When they inculcate an act of self-denial, they themselves must make the noblest sacrifice. Can we conceive of anything which could so much increase the moral power of the ministry, and rouse to a flame the dormant energy of the churches, as obedience to this teaching of Christ by the preachers of his gospel?

It seems that the Saviour had selected a well-known spot, at the head of the lake, for the place of meeting for his apostles, after this their first missionary tour had been completed. " The apostles gathered themselves unto Jesus, and told him all things, both what they had done, and what they had taught." There is something delightful in this filial confidence which these simple-hearted men reposed in their Almighty Redeemer. They told him of their success and their failure, of their wisdom and their folly, of their reliance and their unbelief. We can almost imagine ourselves spectators of this meeting between Christ and them, after this their first separation from each other. The place appointed was most probably some well-known locality on the shore of the lake, under the shadow of its overhanging rocks, where the cool air from the bosom of the water refreshed each returning laborer, as he came back beaten out with the fatigues of travel, under the burning sun of Syria. You can imagine the joy with which each drew near to the Master, after this temporary absence; and the honest greetings with which every new comer was welcomed by those who had chanced to arrive before him. We can seem to perceive the Saviour of men listening with affectionate earnestness to the recital of their various adventures; and interposing, from time to time, a word either of encouragement or of caution, as the character and circumstances of each narrator required it. The bosom of each was unveiled before the Searcher of hearts, and the consolation which each one needed was bestowed upon him abundantly. The toilsomeness of their journey was no longer remembered, as each one received from the Son of God the smile of his approbation. That was truly a joyful meeting. Of all that company there is not one who has forgotten that day; nor will he forget it ever. With unreserved frankness they told Jesus of all that they had done, and what they had taught; of all their acts, and all their conversations. Would it not be better for us, if we cultivated more assiduously this habit of intimate intercourse with the Saviour? Were we every day to tell Jesus of all that we have done and said; did we spread before him our joys and our sorrows, our faults and our infirmities, our successes and our failures, we should be saved from many an error and many a sin. Setting " the Lord always before us, he would be on our right hand, and we should not be moved." " He that dwelleth in the secret place of the Most High shall abide under the shadow of the Almighty."

The Saviour perceived that the apostles needed much instruction which could not be communicated in a place where both he and they were so well known. They had committed many errors, which he preferred to correct in private. By doing his will, they had learned to repose greater confidence in his wisdom, and were prepared to receive from him more important instruction. But these lessons could not be delivered in the hearing of a promiscuous audience. Nor was this all. He perceived that the apostles were worn out with their labors, and needed repose. Surrounded as they were by the multitude, which had already begun to collect about them, rest and retirement were equally impossible. " There were many coming and going, and they had no leisure, even so much as to eat." He therefore said to them, " Come ye yourselves apart into a desert place, and rest a while." For this purpose, he " took ship, and crossed over with his disciples alone, and went into a desert place belonging to Bethsaida."

The religion of Christ imposes upon us duties of retirement, as well as duties of publicity. The apostles had been for some time past before the eyes of all men, preaching and working miracles. Their souls needed retirement. " Solitude," said Cecil, " is my great ordinance." They would be greatly improved by private communion both with him and with each other. It was for the purpose of affording them such a season of moral recreation, that our Lord withdrew them from the public gaze into a desert place. Nor was this all. Their labor for some weeks past had been severe. They had travelled on foot under a tropical sun, reasoning with unbelievers, instructing the ignorant, and comforting the cast-down. Called upon, at all hours, both of the day and night, to work cures on those that were oppressed with diseases, their bodies, no less than their spirits, needed rest. Our Lord saw this, and he made provision for it. He withdrew them from labor, that they might find, though it were but for a day, the repose which their exhausted natures demanded. The religion of Christ is ever merciful, and ever consistent in its benevolence. It is thoughtful of the benefactor as well as the recipient. It requires of us all, labor and self-sacrifice, but to these it affixes a limit. It never commands us to ruin our health and enfeeble our minds by unnatural exhaustion. It teaches us to obey the laws of our physical organization, and to prepare ourselves for the labors of to-morrow by the judiciously conducted labors of to-day. It was on this principle that our Lord conducted in his intercourse with his disciples. " He knew their frame, and remembered that they were dust."

May we not from this incident derive a lesson of practical instruction? I well know that there are persons who are always sparing themselves, who, while it is difficult to tell what they do, are always complaining of the crushing weight of their labors, and who are rather exhausted with the dread of what they shall do, than with the experience of what they have actually done. It is not of these that we speak. Those who do not labor have no need of rest. It is to the honest, the painstaking, the laborious, that we address the example in the text. We sometimes meet with the industrious, self-denying servant of Christ, in feeble health, and with an exhausted nature, bemoaning his condition, and condemning himself because he can accomplish no more, while so much yet remains to be done. To such a one we may safely present the example of the blessed Saviour. When his apostles had done to the utmost of their strength, although the harvest was great, and the laborers few, he did not urge upon them additional labor, nor tell them that because there was so much to be done they must never cease from doing. No : he tells them to turn aside and rest for a while. It is as though he had said, " Your strength is exhausted ; you cannot be qualified for subsequent duty until you be refreshed. Economize, then, your power, that you may accomplish the more." The Saviour addresses the same language to us now. When we are worn down in his service, as in any other, he would have us rest, not for the sake of self-indulgence, but that we may be the better prepared for future effort. We do nothing at variance with his will, when we, with a good conscience, use the liberty which he has thus conceded to us.

Jesus, with his disciples, crossed the water, and entered the desert; that is, the sparsely inhabited country of Bethsaida. Desert, or wilderness, in the New Testament, does not mean an arid waste, but pasture land, forest, or any district to which one could retire for seclusion. Here, in the cool and tranquil neighborhood of the lake, he began to instruct his disciples, and, without interruption, make known to them the mysteries of the kingdom. It was one of those seasons that the Saviour himself rarely enjoyed. Everything tended to repose : the rustling leaves, the rippling waves, the song of the birds, heard more distinctly in this rural solitude, all served to calm the spirit ruffled by the agitations of the world, and prepare it to listen to the truths which unveil to us eternity. Here our Lord could unbosom himself, without reserve, to his chosen few, and hold with them that communion which he was rarely permitted to enjoy during his ministry on earth.

Soon, however, the whole scene is changed. The multitude, whom he had so recently left, having observed the direction in which he had gone, have discovered the place of his retreat. An immense crowd approaches, and the little company is surrounded by a dense mass of human beings pressing upon them on every side. These are, however, only the pioneers. At last, five thousand men, besides women and children, are beheld thronging around them.

Some of these suitors present most importunate claims. They are in search of cure for diseases which have baffled the skill of the medical profession, and, as a last resort, they have come to the Messiah for aid. Here was a parent bringing a consumptive child. There were children bearing on a couch a paralytic parent. Here was a sister leading a brother blind from his birth, while her supplications were drowned by the shout of a frenzied lunatic who was standing by her side. Every one, believing his own claim to be the most urgent, pressed forward with selfish importunity. Each one, caring for no other than himself, was striving to attain the front rank, while those behind, disappointed, and fearing to lose this important opportunity, were eager to occupy the places of those more fortunate than themselves. The necessary tumult and disorder of such a scene you can better imagine than I can describe.

This was, doubtless, by no means a welcome interruption. The apostles needed the time for rest; for they were worn out in the public service. They wanted it for instruction; for such opportunities of intercourse with Christ were rare. But what did they do? Did our Lord inform the multitude that this day was set apart for their own refreshment and improvement, and that they could not be interrupted? As he beheld them approaching, did he quietly take to his boat, and leave them to go home disappointed? Did he plead his own convenience, or his need of repose, as any reason for not attending to the pressing necessities of his fellow-men?

No, my brethren, very far from it. The providence of God had brought these multitudes before him, and that same providence forbade him to send them away unblessed. He at once broke up the conference with his disciples, and addressed himself to the work before him. His instructions were of inestimable importance; but I doubt if even they were as important as the example of deep humility, exhaustless kindness, and affecting compassion which he here exhibited. When the Master places work before us which can be done at no other time, our convenience must yield to other men's necessities. "The Son of man came not to be ministered unto, but to minister." You can imagine to yourself the Saviour rising from his seat, in the midst of his disciples, and presenting himself to the approaching multitudes. His calm dignity awes into silence this tumultuous gathering of the people. Those who came out to witness the tricks of an empiric, or listen to the ravings of a fanatic, find themselves, unexpectedly, in a presence that repels every emotion but that of profound veneration. The light-hearted and frivolous are awe-struck by the unearthly majesty that seems to clothe the Messiah as with a garment. And yet it was a majesty that shone forth conspicuous, most of all, by the manifestation of unparalleled goodness. Every eye that met the eye of the Saviour quailed before him; for it looked into a soul that had never sinned; and the spirit of the sinner felt, for the first time, the full power of immaculate virtue.

Thus the Saviour passed among the crowd, and " healed all that had need of healing." The lame walked, the lepers were cleansed, the blind received their sight, the paralytic were restored to soundness, and the bloom of health revisited the cheeks of those that but just now were sick unto death.

The work to be done for the bodies of men was accomplished, and there yet remained some hours of the summer's day unconsumed. The power and goodness displayed in this miraculous healing, would naturally predispose the people to listen to the instructions of the Saviour. This was too valuable an opportunity to be lost. Our Lord therefore proceeded to speak to them of the things concerning the kingdom of God. We can seem to perceive the Saviour seeking an eminence from whence he could the more conveniently address this vast assembly. You hear him unfold the laws of God's moral government. He unmasks the hypocrisy of the Pharisees; he rebukes the infidelity of the Sadducees; he exposes the folly of the frivolous, as well as of the selfish worldling; he speaks peaceably to the humble penitent; he encourages the meek, and comforts those that be cast down. The intellect and the conscience of this vast assembly are swayed at his will. The soul of man bows down in reverence in the presence of its Creator. " He stilleth the noise of the seas, the noise of their waves, and the tumult of the people." As he closes his address, every eye is moistened with compunction for sin. Every soul cherishes the hope of amendment. Every one is conscious that a new moral light has dawned upon his soul, and that a new moral universe has been unveiled to his spiritual vision. As the closing words of the Saviour fell upon their ears, the whole multitude stood for a while unmoved, as though transfixed to the earth by some mighty spell; until, at last, the murmur is heard from thousands of voices, " Never man spake like this man."

But the shades of evening are gathering around them. The multitude have nothing to eat. To send them away fasting would be inhuman, for divers of them came from far, and many were women and children, who could not perform their journey homeward without previous refreshment. To purchase food in the surrounding towns and villages would be difficult; but even were this possible, whence could the necessary funds be provided? A famishing multitude was thus unexpectedly cast upon the bounty of our Lord. He had not tempted God by leading them into the wilderness. They came to him of themselves, to hear his words and to be healed of their infirmities. He could not " send them away fasting, lest they should faint by the way." In this dilemma, what was to be done? He puts this question to his disciples, and they can suggest no means of relief. The little stock of provisions which they had brought with them was barely sufficient for themselves. They can perceive no means whatever by which the multitude can be fed, and they at once confess it.

The Saviour, however, commands the twelve to give them to eat. They produce their slender store of provisions, amounting to five loaves and two small fishes. He commands the multitude to sit down by companies on the grass. As soon as silence is obtained, he lifts up his eyes to heaven, and supplicates the blessing of God upon their scanty meal. He begins to break the loaves and fishes, and distribute them to his disciples, and his disciples distribute them to the multitude. He continues to break and distribute. Basket after basket is filled and emptied, yet the supply is undiminished. Food is carried in abundance to the famishing thousands. Company after company is supplied with food, but the five loaves and the two fishes remain unexhausted. At last, the baskets are returned full, and it is announced that the wants of the multitudes are supplied. The miracle then ceases, and the multiplication of food is at an end.

But even here the provident care of the Saviour is manifested. Although this food has been so easily provided, it is not right that it be lightly suffered to perish. Christ wrought no miracles for the sake of teaching men wastefulness. That food, by what means soever provided, was a creature of God, and it were sin to allow it to decay without accomplishing the purposes for which it was created. " Gather up the fragments," said the Master of the feast, "that nothing be lost." "And they gathered up the fragments that remained, twelve baskets full."

Dissimilar as are our circumstances to those of our Lord, we may learn from this latter incident a lesson of instruction.

In the first place, as I have remarked, the Saviour did not lead the multitude into the wilderness without making provision for their sustenance. This would have been presumption. They followed him without his command, and he found himself with them in this necessity. He had provided for his own wants, but they had not provided for theirs. The providence of God had, however, placed him in his present circumstances, and he might therefore properly look to Providence for deliverance. This event, then, furnishes the rule by which we are to be governed. When we plunge ourselves into difficulty, by a neglect of the means or by a misuse of the faculties which God has bestowed upon us, it is to be expected that he will leave us to our own devices. But when, in the honest discharge of our duties, we find ourselves in circumstances beyond the reach of human aid, we then may confidently look up to God for deliverance. He will always take care of us while we are in the spot where he has placed us. When he appoints for us trials, he also appoints for us the means of escape. The path of duty, though it may seem arduous, is ever the path of safety. We can more easily maintain ourselves in the most difficult position, God being our helper, than in apparent security relying on our own strength.

The Saviour, in full reliance upon God, with only five loaves and two fishes, commenced the distribution of food amongst this vast multitude. Though his whole store was barely sufficient to supply the wants of his immediate family, he began to share it with the thousands who surrounded him. Small as was his provision at the commencement, it remained unconsumed until the deed of mercy was done, and the wants of the famishing host were supplied. Nor were the disciples losers by this act of charity. After the multitude had eaten and were satisfied, twelve baskets full of fragments remained, a reward for their deed of benevolence.

From this portion of the narrative, we may, I think, learn that if we act in faith, and in the spirit of Christian love, we may frequently be justified in commencing the most important good work, even when in possession of apparently inadequate means. If the work be of God, he will furnish us with helpers as fast as they are needed. In all ages, God has rewarded abundantly simple trust in him, and has bestowed upon it the highest honor. We must, however, remember the conditions upon which alone we may expect his aid, lest we be led into fanaticism. The service which we undertake must be such as God has commanded, and his providence must either designate us for the work, or, at least, open the door by which we shall enter upon it. It must be God's work, and not our own; for the good of others, and not for the gratification of our own passions; and, in the doing of it, we must, first of all, make sacrifice of ourselves, and not of others. Under such circumstances, there is hardly a good design which we may not undertake with cheerful hopes of success, for God has promised us his assistance. "If God be for us, who can be against us?" The calculations of the men of this world are of small account in such a matter. It would have provoked the smile of an infidel to behold the Saviour commencing the work of feeding five thousand men with a handful of provisions. But the supply increased as fast as it was needed, and it ceased not until all that he had prayed for was accomplished.

Perhaps, also, we may learn from this incident another lesson. If I mistake not, it suggests to us that in works of benevolence we are accustomed to rely too much on human, and too little on divine, aid. When we attempt to do good, we commence by forming large associations, and suppose that our success depends upon the number of men whom we can unite in the promotion of our undertaking. Every one is apt thus to forget his own personal duty, and rely upon the labor of others, and it is well if he does not put his organization in the place of God himself. Would it not be better if we made benevolence much more a matter between God and our own souls, each one doing with his own hands, in firm reliance on divine aid, the work which Providence has placed directly before him? Our Lord did not send to the villages round about to organize a general effort to relieve the famishing. In reliance upon God, he set about to work himself, with just such means as God had afforded him. All the miracles of benevolence have, if I mistake not, been wrought in the same manner. The little band of disciples in Jerusalem accomplished more for the conversion of the world than all the Christians of the present day united. And why? Because every individual Christian felt that the conversion of the world was a work for which he himself, and not an abstraction that he called the church, was responsible. Instead of relying on man for aid, every one looked up directly to God, and went forth to the work. God was thus exalted, the power was confessed to be his own, and, in a few years, the standard of the cross was carried to the remotest extremities of the then known world.

Such has, I think, been the case ever since. Every great moral reformation has proceeded upon principles analogous to these. It was Luther, standing up alone in simple reliance upon God, that smote the Papal hierarchy; and the effects of that blow are now agitating the nations of Europe. Roger Williams, amid persecution and banishment, held forth that doctrine of soul-liberty which, in its onward march, is disenthralling a world. Howard, alone, undertook the work of showing mercy to the prisoner, and his example is now enlisting the choicest minds in Christendom in this labor of benevolence. Clarkson, unaided, a young man, and without influence, consecrated himself to the work of abolishing the slave trade; and, before he rested from his labors, his country had repented of and forsaken this atrocious sin. Raikes saw the children of Gloucester profaning the Sabbath day; he set on foot a Sabbath school on his own account, and now millions of children are reaping the benefit of his labors, and his example has turned the attention of the whole world to the religious instruction of the young. With such facts before us, we surely should be encouraged to attempt individually the accomplishment of some good design, relying in humility and faith upon Him who is able to grant prosperity to the feeblest effort put forth in earnest reliance on his almightiness.

Such were the occupations that filled up a day in the life of Jesus of Nazareth. There was not an act done for himself; all was done for others. Every hour was employed in the labor which that hour set before him. Private kindness, the relief of distress, public teaching, and ministration to the wants of the famishing, filled up the entire day. Let his disciples learn to follow his example. Let us, like him, forget ourselves, our own wants, and our own weariness, that we may, as he did, scatter blessings on every side, as we move onward in the pathway of our daily life. If such were the occupations of the Son of God, can we do more wisely than to imitate his example? Every disciple would then be as a city set upon a hill, and men, seeing our good works, would glorify our Father who is in heaven. "Then would our righteousness go forth as brightness, and our salvation as a lamp that burneth."

XXIV

CHARLES HODGE

1797–1878

THE last, and one of the greatest of the " old-school theologians " in America was Dr. Charles Hodge, of Princeton. He was born in Philadelphia, of Scotch-Irish ancestry, December 28, 1797. His education was mainly at Princeton College and Theological Seminary, from which respectively, he graduated in 1815 and 1819. In 1820 he became an assistant professor in his *alma mater* and held various professorships in the College and Seminary until his death in 1878. He was also editor during forty years of *The Biblical Repository and Princeton Review,* the champion in those days of old-time orthodox Calvinism. His great work was his " Systematic Theology " in three large volumes, long regarded as a standard exposition.

CATHOLICITY OF THE GOSPEL.

" Is he God of the Jews only, and not of the Gentiles also? "— Romans iii. 29.

WE are so familiar with the truth contained in these words that we do not appreciate its importance. Accustomed to the varied beauties of the earth, we behold its manifold wonders without emotion; we seldom even raise our eyes to look at the beauteous canopy of heaven, which every night is spread over our heads. The blind, however, when suddenly restored to sight, behold with ecstasy what we regard with indifference. Thus the truth that God is not a national God, not the God of any one tribe or people, but the God and Father of all men, and that the Gospel is designed and adapted to all mankind, however little it may affect us, filled the apostles with astonishment and delight. They were slow in arriving at the knowledge of this truth; they had no clear

317

perception of it until after the day of Pentecost; the effusion of the Spirit which they then received produced a most remarkable change in their views and feelings. Before that event, they were Jews; afterwards, they were Christians; before, they applied all the promises to their own nation; the only Jerusalem of which they had any idea was the city where David dwelt; the only temple of which they could form a conception was that in which they were accustomed to worship. But when they received the anointing of the Holy Ghost, the scales fell from their eyes; their nation sank and the Church rose on their renovated sight; the Jerusalem that now is, disappeared when they beheld the New Jerusalem descending out of heaven; the temple on Mount Zion was no longer glorious, by reason of the excelling glory of that temple which is the habitation of God by his Spirit; old things passed away, all things became new; what they had mistaken for the building proved to be the scaffolding; the sacrifices, the incense, the pompous ritual of the old economy, which they had so long regarded as the substance and the end, were found to be but shadows. What was the blood of bulls and of goats to men who had looked upon the blood of Him who, with an eternal Spirit, offered himself unto God? What were priests and Levites to the great High Priest, Jesus, the Son of God? What was the purifying of the flesh secured by the sprinkling the ashes of a heifer, to the eternal redemption secured by Him who is a priest for ever after the order of Melchizedec? What was access to the outer court of a temple, in which even the symbol of the Divine presence was concealed by a veil, to access to God himself by the Spirit? What were the tribes of Israel coming up to Jerasalem, to the long procession of nations coming to the new Jerusalem, and kings to the brightness of her rising; the multitudes from Midian and Epha; they too from Sheba, bringing their gifts with them; the flocks of Kedar and the rams of Nebaioth; the sons of strangers and the forces of the Gentiles, hastening to that city whose walls are salvation, and whose gates are praise?

This change in the views of the apostles seems to have been almost instantaneous. While Christ was upon earth, they were constantly misapprehending his doctrines; even in the night in which he was betrayed, there was a contention among them who should be the greatest in his kingdom. But as soon as they received the baptism of the Holy Ghost they ceased to speak and act like Jews, and announced a religion for the whole world.

I. In the general proposition, that the Gospel is designed and adapted for all mankind, there are several important truths involved. The most comprehensive is that contained in the text: God is the God of the Gentiles as well as of the Jews. It is obvious that the Jews generally, and the apostles as Jews, entertained very erroneous views on this until they were enlightened by the Holy Ghost; they mistook even the spirit of the old dispensation. It is true that Jehovah chose their nation for a peculiar people, and that he was their God in a sense in which he was not the God of the heathen. He revealed himself to them as he did not unto the world; he instituted for them a system of religious observances; sent them his prophets to declare his will; exercised over them a special providence, and constituted them, in the strictest sense, a theocracy. There was nothing, however, in the Old Testament which justified the proud and self-righteous spirit which the Jews manifested towards the heathen; they were not authorized to look upon them as reprobates shut out from the hope of salvation, as unworthy of having even the offer of the true religion made to them. The surprise expressed by the apostles that God had granted unto the Gentiles repentance unto life, that the gate of heaven was wide enough to admit more than the descendants of Abraham, shows how much they had misconceived the spirit of their own religion.

Their great mistake, however, was in supposing that the exclusive spirit, as far as it did in fact belong to the old economy, was meant to be perpetual. They mistook a temporary for a permanent arrangement, and supposed that the glory of the theocracy under the Messiah involved nothing beyond the exaltation and extended dominion of their own nation. They were blind to the plainest declarations of their own Scriptures, which foretold that God would pour out his Spirit upon all flesh; that the Messiah was to be a light to the Gentiles, to make known the salvation of God to the ends of the earth; and that the sons of the stranger were to have in his kingdom a name and a place, better than those of sons and daughters. Even the affecting parables of our Lord, designed to rebuke the narrow spirit of his disciples, failed to make any adequate impression on their minds. Though they were told that the prodigal son was to be restored to his father's house, clothed with the best robe, and rejoiced over with peculiar joy, they understood it not.

It is not to be supposed that the ancient Jews conceived of Jehovah as a local Deity, confined in his essence to any one place, or restricted in his authority to any one people. From the beginning they had been

taught that he was the Creator of all things; that he filled heaven and
earth; that he was almighty, doing his pleasure among the armies of
heaven and the inhabitants of the earth; but they believed him to be
indifferent to the welfare of other nations; they did not know that he
had purposes of mercy for the Gentiles, as well as for themselves. When
they called Jehovah their God, they meant not only that he was the God
whom they acknowledged, but that he belonged exclusively to them, that
they monopolized his favor, and were the sole heirs of his kingdom.
What Christ taught them by his Word and Spirit was, that God was as
favorably inclined to the Gentiles as to the Jews; that the same Lord
was rich toward all who called upon him; that there existed no reason
in the Divine mind, why the heathen should not be fellow-heirs and partakers of the grace of the Gospel, why they might not be fellow-citizens
of the saints and of the household of God. This is what is meant, when
it is said he is the God of the Gentiles as well as of the Jews; he stands
in the same general relation to both; he is as favorable to the one as to
the other; as ready to receive one as the other; as willing to receive
and save the one as the other. Christ came not as the minister of the
circumcision only, but that the Gentiles might glorify God for his
mercy, as it is written: Rejoice, ye Gentiles, with his people; praise the
Lord all ye Gentiles, laud him all ye people. This is the ground, brethren, on which we stand. We are in the Church, not by courtesy of
man; not by toleration or sufferance; not as strangers or proselytes,
but as fellow-citizens and fellow-heirs. We that were not beloved, are
now beloved; we that were not his people, are now the people of God,
though Abraham be ignorant of us, and though Israel acknowledge us
not. It is this glorious truth, that God is the God of the Gentiles, that
expands the Gospel and makes it a religion suited for the whole world.
It is no longer the sluggish Jordan flowing through its narrow channel:
it is a sea of glory which spreads from pole to pole. The mercy and love
of God are commensurate with his ubiquity; whenever he looks down on
man and says, My children, they may look up to him and say, Our
Father! Praise him, therefore, O ye Gentiles, laud him, O ye people,
for Israel's God is our God and our Redeemer.

II. Again, the proposition that the Gospel is designed and adapted
for all mankind, supposes the spiritual nature of Christ's kingdom, that
is, that the service which is now required is a spiritual, in opposition to
a ritual and ceremonial service; that the government of that kingdom
is a spiritual government, and that its blessings are spiritual blessings.

The old economy was, from its ritual and ceremonial character, incapable of including all nations. Without the shedding of blood there was no remission, but sacrifices could be offered only at Jerusalem; there was the temple, the priest, and the altar; there was the symbol of the Divine presence; thither the tribes were required to repair three times every year. Innumerable cases were constantly occurring, which rendered attendance at the place where God had recorded his name absolutely necessary. As the Jewish ritual could not be observed out of Jerusalem, it was impossible that the whole world should be subjected to that form of worship. Those who were afar off were without an offering, without a priest, without access to God. The lamentations of David, when absent from the court of God, his earnest longings after liberty of access to the place where God revealed his glory, show how intimately the happiness of the people of God was connected with the services of the sanctuary. Our Lord announced a radical change in the whole economy of religion, and one which disenthralled it from all these trammels, when he said to the woman of Samaria, " Woman, believe me, the hour cometh and now is, when ye neither in this mountain, nor yet at Jerusalem, shall worship the Father; the true worshippers shall worship the Father in Spirit and in truth, for the Father seeketh such to worship him. God is a Spirit, and they that worship him must worship in Spirit and in truth." It was here taught, not only that the worship of God was no longer to be confined to any one place, but also that it was no longer to be ceremonial but spiritual. It is no longer necessary to go up to Jerusalem, in order to draw near to God, but wherever two or three are met together in his name, there is he in the midst of them. The temple, in which his people now worship, is no longer a temple made with hands, but that spiritual temple made without hands. Its pillars rest on the four corners of the earth, and it surmounts the heavens; the southern African, the northern Greenlander, the innumerable company of angels, and the general Assembly and Church of the first born, and all included in its ample courts. The sacrifice which is now offered is not the blood of bulls and of goats, but the precious blood of Christ, as a lamb slain from the foundation of the world. The incense which now ascends before the throne of God, comes not from brazen censers, but from living hearts.

Again, under the old economy the Church had a visible head, who dwelt at Jerusalem, by whom the annual atonement was made for the sins of the people. He was their intercessor before God; the medium

21

of communication between God and his people; the arbiter and director of the whole congregation. Those, therefore, who were at a distance from the High Priest were necessarily cut off from many of the most important advantages of the theocracy. Under the Gospel all this is changed. The head of the Church, the High Priest of our profession, is no longer a man dwelling in any one city, but Jesus, the Son of God, who by the one offering up of himself hath for ever perfected them that are sanctified; who is everywhere accessible, everywhere present to guide and comfort his people, and who ever lives to make intercession for them. The believer cannot be where Christ is not. At any time and in every place he may approach his throne, he may embrace his knees or wash his feet with tears, and hear him say, Son, or daughter, be of good cheer, thy sins are forgiven thee.

Once more, as to this point: the blessings which the Gospel offers being spiritual are adapted to all mankind. The benefits connected with the old economy were in a great measure external and temporal. This idea the apostle expresses by saying its rites could avail only to the purifying of the flesh. Considered in themselves, they could do no more than secure for those who observed them the benefits of the external theocracy. Those who were circumcised became members of the Hebrew commonwealth; those who kept the law, had the promise of fruitful seasons; those who had forfeited their right of access to the sanctuary, had it restored by offering a sacrifice; those who were defiled by any ceremonial uncleanness, might be purified within the temple by the officiating priest. Apart, therefore, from its reference to the Gospel, the blessings secured by that dispensation were exclusively of this external character; for it was impossible that its rites should take away sin. These benefits were not only of little value, but they were necessarily confined to a limited sphere; they were incapable of being extended to all mankind. How low must have been the expectations of those who considered the Messiah's kingdom as nothing but an enlargement of this system! How complete a revolution must it have produced in all their views and feelings to discover that Christ's kingdom was not of this world; that the blessings which it promised were not worldly prosperity, not a pompous ritual or splendid temple, not dominion over other nations, but the forgiveness of sin, the renewal of the heart, reconciliation with God and eternal life! These are blessings, not only of infinite value, but such as are confined to no one locality. They are not more needed by one set of men than another; they are incapable of being monopolized, for they constitute an inheritance which is rather increased than lessened by the number of the heirs. We say then that the Gospel dispensation is Catholic, or designed for the whole world, because it is a spiritual dispensation; the worship which it requires may be as acceptably offered in one place as another; the head of this new covenant is everywhere present and everywhere accessible, and the blessings which he confers are suited to the necessities of all mankind.

III. Another point of no less importance, is, that the righteousness of Christ, by which these blessings of pardon, regeneration, and eternal life are secured, is such as to lay an ample foundation for the offer of salvation to all men. This is a point with regard to which the minds of the apostles underwent a great change. Under the old dispensation, the High Priest, as the representative of the people, made a confession of their sins, imposing them on the head of the victim, and made reconciliation by sprinkling the blood upon the mercy seat. By that atonement the sins of the people, considered as committed against the external theocracy, were forgiven, and the blessings of that dispensation were actually secured. It is obvious that this was an atonement limited in design to that people, having no reference to any other nation. It was limited also in its value, having no intrinsic worth, but deriving all its efficacy from the sovereign appointment. It was also limited in its very nature; being attached to a national covenant, it was in its nature available to none who were not included in that covenant; it was a Jewish sacrifice, designed for Jews, belonging to a covenant made with Jews, and securing blessings in which other nations had no concern.

In complete contrast with all this, we know, in the first place, that the work of Christ was not limited in design to any one nation. Christ himself said, he laid down his life for his sheep, and other sheep he had which were not of that fold; in this sense it is said he is the propitiation for our sins, and not for our sins only, but for the sins of the whole world; or, as the same apostle expresses the same truth in another place, Jesus died not for that nation only, but that he should gather together in one the children of God that were scattered abroad.

In the second place, there is no limit to be placed to the value of Christ's righteousness; its worth is not to be measured by the duration or intensity of the Saviour's sufferings, but by the dignity of his person. In contrasting the sacrifices of the Old Testament with that of the New, the apostle says the former were inefficacious because mere animals were offered; that of Christ was effectual, once for all, because he offered up himself. It is the nature of the offering that determines its value; and as the dignity of Christ's person is infinite, so is the value of his sacrifice; if it suffices for the salvation of one man, it is sufficient for the salvation of all; it is incapable of increase or diminution. The light of the sun is not measured by the number of those who enjoy its brightness; millions can see by it as well as a single individual; it is not the less because many are affected by it, nor would it be the greater though only one enjoyed it. So also the righteousness of Christ is in value infinite and inexhaustible, because it is the righteousness of God.

In the third place, the righteousness of Christ is in its nature suited to all men. As the annual propitiation under the old dispensation belonged to the covenant formed with the whole people of Israel, and was in its nature suited to all included within that covenant; so the righteousness of Christ fulfils the conditions of that covenant under which all mankind are placed. He perfectly obeyed the precepts and endured the penalty of that law by which all mankind are bound; hence his righteousness, being what was due from every man, is in its nature suited to each and every man. As the work of Christ, as connected with the covenant of grace, has special reference to all included in that covenant, and effectually secures their salvation; but as in performing the stipulations of that covenant, he fulfilled the conditions of the covenant of works which all mankind had broken, his work is, in its nature, applicable to all who are under the covenant made with Adam.

Inasmuch, then, as the righteousness of Christ is not limited in the design of God to any one nation; as it is of infinite value; and as it is, in its nature, equally applicable to all men, we are authorized to go to Jew and Gentile, to barbarians, Scythians, bond and free, yea, to every creature, with the offer of salvation. If any man refuses the offer, his blood will be upon his own head; he perishes not for want of a righteousness, but because he rejects that which is of infinite value and suited to all his necessities. The gospel, therefore, is not trammelled; we can go with it round the world, and announce to every creature that Christ has died, the just for the unjust; that he has wrought out an everlasting righteousness, which any man may accept and plead before the throne of God.

IV. Again, the catholic character of the gospel is apparent from its offering salvation on conditions suited to all men. It does not require us to ascend into heaven, or to go down to the abyss; its demands are simple, intelligible, and reasonable; it requires nothing peculiar to any sex, age, or class of men; it is not a religion for the rich in distinction from the poor, or for the poor in distinction from the rich; it is not a system of philosophy intelligible only to the learned, nor is it a superstition which none but the ignorant can embrace. It is truth simple and transcendent; in all that is essential, intelligible to a child, and yet the object of admiration and wonder to angels. It does not suspend our salvation on any particular ecclesiastical connection; it does not require us to decide between conflicting churches which has the true succession; nor does it make grace and salvation to depend on the ministration or will of man; it is not the religion of any one sect or church, and nothing but the wickedness can equal the folly of the attempt to confine the grace of God to the shallow channel of a particular ecclesiastical organization. What the gospel demands "is nigh thee, in thy heart and in thy mouth;" that is, the word of faith which we preach, "that if thou shalt confess with thy mouth the Lord Jesus, and believe in thy heart that God hath raised him from the dead, thou shalt be saved. For with the heart man believeth unto righteousness, and with the mouth confession is made unto salvation." Here, then, are terms of salvation which are suited equally to all men, the Jew and the Greek, the wise and the unwise, the bond and the free.

V. Again, the rule of life prescribed by the Gospel is adapted to all men, in every age and in every part of the world; it is the great law of love, which commends itself to every man's conscience, and is suited to all the relations of domestic, social, and political life. It is a principle which disturbs nothing that is good, which can amalgamate with nothing that is wrong, which admits of being acted out under all circumstances, and of accommodating itself to all states of society, and to all forms of government.

How free, how catholic, how pure, how elevated is the spirit of the Gospel, which reveals God as a universal Father; which makes known a religion confined to no locality, burdened with no expensive ritual, conferring on those who embrace it, not worldly distinctions, but the spiritual blessings of pardon and holiness; which reveals a righteousness sufficient for all, and suited for all; which offers that righteousness to all on the simplest of all conditions, that of sincerely accepting it; whose moral precepts and principles of religious duty and of ecclesiastical organization, admit of being carried out with equal purity and power, in all ages and in all parts of the world!

1. The catholic character of the Gospel, which we have now been

considering, affords one of the strongest arguments for its divine origin. No religion can be true which is not suited to God as its author, and to man for whom it is intended. The Gospel is suited to God because it supposes him to be, as he in fact is, not a national God, but the God and Father of all men; and it is suited to men because it meets not the wants of any one class, nor any one class of wants, but all the wants of every class, tribe, or nation. But besides this, this catholicity is the very characteristic which it would be most difficult to account for on the supposition of its human origin. The apostles were Jews, the very name for all that is narrow, national, and exclusive; how could the most enlarged and comprehensive system of religion owe its origin to such men? We know that the apostles retained much of the narrow and exclusive spirit of their countrymen, as long as their Master was upon earth. When he died they were ready to despair, saying, We trusted it had been He who would have redeemed Israel. Even after his resurrection their eyes were still but half opened, for the last question which they put to him was, " Lord, wilt thou at this time restore the kingdom unto Israel? " Yet, a few days afterward, these same men began to preach that the kingdom of Christ was a spiritual kingdom, not designed specially for Israel, but for all mankind. This fact admits of no other solution than that recorded in the Acts: after the apostles had received the promised effusion of the Spirit, they spake as they were moved by the Holy Ghost, making it apparent that the Gospel is not the product of Jewish minds, but of men divinely instructed and inspired.

This argument may be viewed in another light. The revélations of God, as contained in the Scriptures, admit of being divided into three portions: those written before the advent of Christ; those referring to his personal ministry on earth; and those written after the effusion of the Spirit, on the day of Pentecost. In the first portion, all, at first view, is national and exclusive; the prosperity of Jerusalem and the exaltation of the Jews would seem to be the great subject of prophecy and promise; still there is a constant gleaming through of the imprisoned glory; constantly recurring intimations of a spiritual Jerusalem and of a spiritual Israel, in whom the glorious things spoken of Zion were to meet their accomplishment.

The personal instructions of our Saviour were conveyed mostly in parables, designed to correct the misapprehension and to repress the false expectations of his countrymen, but rather intimating than fully disclosing the nature of his kingdom and the design of his mission.

The descent of the Holy Spirit shed a flood of light on the whole series of divine revelations, back even to the first promise made to our first parents; it is the clear exhibition of the economy of redemption, made in the books written after the day of Pentecost, that enables us to read the outlines of the gospel in the law and the prophets; the relation of these several portions of the Scriptures to each other, written at intervals during the course of fifteen hundred years, shows that the whole is the work of one omniscient Spirit; and the fact that the catholic spirit of the gospel, as unfolded in the later books of the New Testament, is in apparent contradiction, though real agreement with the earlier portions of the Word of God, is a decisive proof that the Bible is indeed the word of God and not the word of man.

2. If the gospel, as has been represented, is designed and suited for all men, it is suited to us. We need the salvation which it reveals; we, being destitute of any righteousness of our own, must accept the righteousness which the gospel offers, or perish in our sins. That righteousness being all that any sinner needs, and being freely and sincerely offered to all who hear the Gospel, we are entirely without excuse if we refuse or neglect the invitations of mercy.

3. If the gospel is suited to all men, it should be maintained wherever it is known, and sent wherever it has not yet been preached. This is the inference which the apostle draws from this subject. If there is no difference between the Jew and Greek; if the same Lord is rich towards all who call upon him, then it is the will of God that all should call upon him. But how shall they call on him on whom they have not believed? And how shall they believe on him of whom they have not heard? And how shall they hear without a preacher? And how shall they preach except they be sent? The Gospel being suited to all men, and being needed by all, not for their temporal well-being, but for their eternal salvation, woe is us if we do not make it known; it is an inheritance in which we are but joint heirs with all mankind, and we cannot keep the knowledge of this inheritance to ourselves without manifest injustice and cruelty.

Let us, then, endeavor to enter more fully into the catholic spirit of the gospel; let us remember that the unsearchable riches that are in Christ Jesus are an inheritance for all the poor and perishing; and while we thankfully apprehend those riches for ourselves, let us labor that they may be made accessible to all mankind.

XXV

HENRY MELVILLE

1798–1871

HENRY MELVILLE, B. D., for many years " the most popular preacher in London," was born in Cornwall, September 14th, 1798. He was educated at St. Peter's College, Cambridge, and ministered in Camden Chapel, London, from 1829 to 1843. Queen Victoria appointed him her chaplain-in-ordinary ten years later, and subsequently canon-residentiary of St. Paul's. Within his frail body were abilities of a high order. His Sermons attest deep thought and skilful elaboration. He had the rare power of developing to its full the spiritual meaning of his text, and of stamping its teachings lastingly upon the hearts and minds of his hearers. He died in London, February 9th, 1871.

THE FIRST PROPHECY.

" *And I will put enmity between thee and the woman, and between thy seed and her seed: it shall bruise thy head, and thou shalt bruise his heel.*"—Genesis iii. 15.

SUCH is the first prophecy which occurs in Scripture. Adam and Eve had transgressed the simple command of their Maker; they had hearkened to the suggestions of the tempter, and eaten of the forbidden fruit. Summoned into the presence of God, each of the three parties is successively addressed; but the serpent, as having originated evil, receives first his sentence.

We have, of course, no power of ascertaining the external change which the curse brought upon the serpent. The terms, however, of the sentence, " Upon thy belly shalt thou go, and dust shalt thou eat all the days of thy life," (Gen. iii. 14), seem to imply that the serpent had not been created a reptile, but became classed with creeping things, as a consequence of the curse. It is probable that heretofore the serpent had been remarkable for beauty and splendor, and that on this account the tempter chose it as the vehicle of his approaches. Eve, in all likelihood, was attracted towards the creature by its loveliness: and when she found it endowed, like herself, with the power of speech, she possibly concluded that it had itself eaten of the fruit, and acquired thereby a gift which she thought confined to herself and her husband.

But we may be sure that, although, to mark his hatred of sin, God pronounced a curse on the serpent, it was against the devil, who had actuated the serpent, that the curse was chiefly directed. It may be said that the serpent itself must have been innocent in the matter, and that the curse should have fallen on none but the tempter. But you are to remember that the serpent suffered not alone: every living thing had share in the consequences of disobedience. And although the effect of man's apostasy on the serpent may have been more signal and marked than on other creatures, we have no right to conclude that there was entailed so much greater suffering on this reptile as to distinguish it in misery from the rest of animal creation.

But undoubtedly it was the devil, more emphatically than the serpent, that God cursed for the seduction of man. The words, indeed, of our text have a primary application to the serpent. It is most strictly true, that, ever since the fall, there has been enmity between man and the serpent. Every man will instinctively recoil at the sight of a serpent. We have a natural and unconquerable aversion from this tribe of living things, which we feel not in respect to others, even fiercer and more noxious. Men, if they find a serpent, will always strive to destroy it, bruising the head in which the poison lies; whilst the serpent will often avenge itself, wounding its assailant, if not mortally, yet so as to make it true that it bruises his heel.

But whilst the words have thus, undoubtedly, a fulfilment in respect of the serpent, we cannot question that their reference is chiefly to the devil. It was the devil, and not the serpent, which had beguiled the woman; and it is only in a very limited sense that it could be said to the serpent, " Because thou hast done this." We are indeed so unacquainted with transactions in the world of spirits, that we cannot pretend to determine what, or whether any, immediate change passed on the condition of Satan and his associates. If the curse upon the serpent took effect upon the devil, it would seem probable, that, ever since the fall, the power of Satan has been specially limited to this earth and its inhabitants. We may gather from the denunciation, "Upon thy belly shalt thou go, and dust shalt thou eat all the days of thy life," that, in place of being allowed, as he might beforetime have been, to range through the universe, machinating against the peace of many orders of intelligence, he was confined to the arena of humanity, and forced to concentrate his energies on the destruction of a solitary race. It would seem altogether possible, that, after his ejectment from heaven, Satan had liberty to traverse the vast area of creation; and that far-off stars and planets were accessible to his wanderings. It is to the full as possible, that, as soon as man apostatized, God confirmed in their allegiance other orders of beings, and shielded them from the assaults of the evil one, by chaining him to the earth on which he had just won a victory. And if, as the result of his having seduced our first parents, Satan were thus sentenced to confinement to this globe, we may readily understand how words addressed to the serpent, dooming it to trail itself along the ground, had distinct reference to the tempter by whom that serpent had been actuated.

But, whatever be our opinion concerning this part of the curse, there can be no doubt that our text must be explained of the devil, though, as we have shown you, it has a partial fulfilment in respect of the serpent. We must here consider God as speaking to the tempter, and announcing war between Satan and man. We have called the words a prophecy; and, when considered as addressed to the devil, such is properly their designation. But when we remember that they were spoken in the hearing of Adam and Eve, we must regard them also in the light of a promise. And it is well worth remark, that, before God told the woman of her sorrow and her trouble, and before he told the man of the thorn, and the thistle, and the dust to which he should return, he caused them to hear words which must have inspired them with hope. Vanquished they were; and they might have thought that, with an undisputed supremacy, he who had prevailed to their overthrow would ever after hold them in vassalage. Must it not then have been cheering to them, whilst they stood as criminals before their God, expecting the sentence which disobedience had provoked, to hear that their conqueror should not enjoy unassaulted his conquest, but that there were yet undeveloped arrangements which would insure to humanity final mastery over the oppressor? And though, when God turned and spake to themselves, he gave no word of encouragement, but dwelt only on the toil and the death which they had wrought into their portion, still the prophecy to which they had listened must have sunk into their hearts as a promise; and when, with lingering steps, and the first tears ever wept, they departed from the glorious precincts of Eden, we may believe that one sustained the other by whispering the words, Though "thou shalt bruise his heel, it shall bruise thy head."

There can be no doubt that intimations of redemption were given to our guilty parents, and that they were instructed by God to offer sacrifices which should shadow out the method of atonement. And though it does not of course follow that we are in possession of all the notices mercifully afforded, it seems fair to conclude, as well from the time of delivery as from the nature of the announcement, that our text was designed to convey comfort to the desponding; and that it was received as a message breathing deliverance by those who expected utter condemnation.

We are not, however, much concerned with the degree in which the prophecy was at first understood. It cannot justly be called an obscure prophecy: for it is quite clear on the fact, that, by some means or another man should gain advantage over Satan. And though, if considered as referring to Christ, there be a mystery about it, which could only be cleared up by after events, yet, as a general prediction of victory, it must have commended itself, we think, to the understanding and the heart of those of our race by whom it was first heard.

But whether or no the prophecy were intelligible to Adam and Eve, unto ourselves it is a wonderful passage, spreading itself over the whole of time, and giving outlines of the history of this world from the beginning to the final consummation. We caution you at once against an idea which many have entertained, that the prediction before us refers only, or even chiefly, to the Redeemer. We shall indeed find, as we proceed, that Christ, who was specially the seed of the woman, specially bruised the head of the serpent. But the prophecy is to be interpreted in a much larger sense. It is nothing less than a delineation of an unwearied conflict, of which this earth shall be the theatre, and which shall issue, though not without partial disaster to man, in the complete discomfiture of Satan and his associates. And no man who is familiar with other predictions of Scripture, can fail to find, in this brief and solitary verse, the announcement of those very struggles and conquests which occupy the gorgeous poetry of Isaiah, and crowd the mystic canvas of Daniel and St. John.

We wish you, therefore, to dismiss, if you have ever entertained, contracted views of the meaning of our text. It must strike you at the first glance, that though Christ was in a peculiar sense the seed of the woman, the phrase applies to others as well as the Redeemer. We are therefore bound, by all fair laws of interpretation to consider that the prophecy must be fulfilled in more than one individual; especially as it declares that the woman, as well as her seed, should entertain the enmity, and thus marks out more than a single party as engaging in the conflict.

Now there are one or two preliminary observations which require all your attention, if you hope to enter into the full meaning of the prediction.

We wish you, first of all, to remark particularly the expression, " I will put enmity." The enmity, you observe, had no natural existence: God declares his intention of putting enmity. As soon as man transgressed, his nature became evil, and therefore he was at peace, and not at war, with the devil. And thus, had there been no interference on the part of the Almighty, Satan and man would have formed alliance against heaven, and, in place of a contest between themselves, have carried on nothing but battle with God. There is not, and cannot be, a native enmity between fallen angels and fallen men. Both are evil, and both became evil through apostasy. But evil, wheresoever it exists, will always league against good; so that fallen angels and fallen men were sure to join in a desperate companionship. Hence the declaration, that enmity should be put, must have been to Satan the first notice of redemption. This lofty spirit must have calculated, that, if he could induce men, as he had induced angels, to join in rebellion, he should have them for allies in his every enterprise against heaven. There was nothing of enmity between himself and the spirits who had joined in the effort to dethrone the Omnipotent. At least whatever the feuds and jarrings which might disturb the rebels, they were linked, as with an iron band, in the one great object of opposing good. So that when he heard that there should be enmity between himself and the woman, he must have felt that some apparatus would be brought to bear upon man; and that, though he had succeeded in depraving human nature, and thus assimilating it to his own, it should be renewed by some mysterious process, and wrought up to the lost power of resisting its conqueror.

'And accordingly it has come to pass, that there is enmity on the earth between man and Satan; but an enmity supernaturally put, and not naturally entertained. Unless God pour his converting grace into the soul, there will be no attempt to oppose Satan, but we shall continue to the end of our days his willing captives and servants. And therefore it is God who puts the enmity. Introducing a new principle into the heart, he causes conflict where there had heretofore been peace, inclining and enabling man to rise against his tyrant. So that, in these first words of the prophecy, you have the clearest intimation that God designed to visit the depraved nature with a renovating energy. And now, whensoever you see an individual delivered from the love, and endowed with a hatred, of sin, resisting those passions which held naturally sway within his breast, and thus grappling with the fallen spirit which claims dominion upon earth, you are surveying the workings of a principle which is wholly from above; and you are to consider that you have before you the fulfilment of the declaration, " I will put enmity between thee and the woman."

We go on to observe that the enmity, being thus a superhuman thing, implanted by God and not generated by man, will not subsist universally, but only in particular cases. You will have seen, from our foregoing showings, that a man must be renewed in order to his fighting with Satan; so that God's putting the enmity is God's giving saving grace. The prophecy cannot be interpreted as declaring that the whole human race should be at war with the devil: the undoubted matter-of-fact being that only a portion of the race resumes its loyalty to Jehovah. And we are bound, therefore, before proceeding further with our interpretation, to examine whether this limitation is marked out by the prediction — whether, that is, we might infer, from the terms of the prophecy, that the placed enmity would be partial, not universal.

Now we think that the expression, " Thy seed and her seed," shows at once that the enmity would be felt by only a part of mankind. The enmity is to subsist, not merely between Satan and the woman, but between his seed and her seed. But the seed of Satan can only be interpreted of wicked men. Thus Christ said to the Jews, " Ye are of your father the devil; and the lust of your father ye will do." (John viii. 44.) Thus also, in expounding the parable of the tares and the wheat, he said, " The tares are the children of the wicked one." (Matt. xiii. 38.) There is probably, the same reference in the expression, " O generation of vipers." And, in like manner, you find St. John declaring, " He that committeth sin is of the devil." (1 John iii. 8.) Thus, then, by the seed of Satan we understand wicked men, those who resist God's Spirit, and obstinately adhere to the service of the devil. And if we must interpret the seed of Satan of a portion of mankind, it is evident that the prophecy marks not out the enmity as general, but indicates just that limitation which has been supposed in our preceding remarks.

But then the question occurs, How are we to interpret the woman and her seed? Such expression seems to denote the whole human race. What right have we to limit it to a part of that race? We reply, that it certainly does not denote the whole human race: for if you interpret it literally of Eve and her descendants, Adam, at least, is left out, who was neither the woman nor her seed. But without insisting on the objection under this form, fatal as it is to the proposed interpretation, we should not be warranted, though we have no distinct account of the faith and repentance of Adam, in so explaining a passage as to exclude our common forefather from final salvation. You must see, that, if we take literally the woman and her seed, no enmity was put between Adam and Satan; for Adam was neither the woman nor the seed of the woman. And if Adam continued in friendship with Satan, it must be certain that he perished in his sins: a conclusion to which we dare not advance without scriptural testimony the most clear and explicit.

We cannot, then, understand the woman and her seed as Eve and her natural descendants. We must rather believe, that as the seed of the serpent is to be interpreted spiritually and symbolically, so also is the seed of the woman. And when you remember that Eve was a signal type of the church, there is an end of the difficulties by which we seem met. You know, from the statement of St. Paul to the Romans, that Adam was the figure of Christ. (Rom. v. 14.) Now it was his standing to Eve in the very same relationship in which Christ stands to the church, which specially made Adam the figure of Christ. The side of Adam had been opened, when a deep sleep fell on him, in order that Eve might be formed, an extract from himself. And thus, as Hooker said, " God frameth the church out of the very flesh, the very wounded and bleeding side of the Son of Man. His body crucified, and his blood shed for the life of the world, are the true elements of that heavenly being which maketh us such as himself is, of whom we come. For which cause the words of Adam may be fitly the words of Christ concerning his church, ' Flesh of my flesh, and bone of my bones.' " We cannot go at length into the particulars of the typical resemblance between Eve and the church. It is sufficient to observe, that since Adam, the husband of Eve, was the figure of Christ, and since Christ is the husband of the church, it seems naturally to follow that Eve was the figure or type of the church. And when we have established this typical character of Eve, it is easy to understand who are meant by the woman and her seed. The true church of God in every age — whether you consider it as represented by its head, which is Christ; whether you survey it collectively as a body, or resolve it into its separate members — this true church of God must be regarded as denoted by the woman and her seed. And though you may think — for we wish, as we proceed, to anticipate objections — that, if Eve be the church, it is strange that her seed should be also the church, yet it is the common usage of Scripture to represent the church as the mother, and every new convert as a child. Thus, in addressing the Jewish church, and describing her glory and her greatness in the latter days, Isaiah saith, " Thy sons shall come from far, and thy daughters shall be nursed at thy side." And again — contrasting the Jewish and Gentile churches —" More are the children of the desolate than the children of the married wife, saith the Lord." So that although the church can be nothing more than the aggregate of individual believers, the inspired writers commonly describe the church as a parent, and believers as the offspring; and in understanding, therefore, the church and its members by the woman and her seed, we cannot be advocating a forced interpretation.

And now we have made a long advance towards the thorough elucidation of the prophecy. We have shown you, that, inasmuch as the enmity is supernaturally put, it can only exist in a portion of mankind. We then endeavored to ascertain this portion and we found that the true church of God, in every age, comprehends all those who war with Satan and his seed. So that the representation of the prediction — a representation whose justice we have yet to examine — is simply that of a perpetual conflict, on this earth, between wicked angels and wicked men on the one side, and the church of God, or the company of true believers, on the other; such conflict, though occasioning partial injury to the church, always issuing in the discomfiture of the wicked.

We now set ourselves to demonstrate the accuracy of this representation. We have already said that there are three points of view in which the church may be regarded. We may consider it, as represented by its head, which is Christ; secondly, collectively as a body; thirdly, as resolved into its separate members. We shall endeavor to show you briefly, in each of these cases, the fidelity of the description, " It shall bruise thy head, and thou shalt bruise his heel."

Now the enmity was never put in such overpowering measure, as when the man Christ Jesus was its residence. It was in Christ Jesus in one sense naturally, and in another supernaturally. He was born pure, and with a native hatred of sin ; but then he had been miraculously generated, in order that his nature might be thus hostile to evil. And never did there move the being on this earth who hated sin with as perfect a hatred, or who was as odious in return to all the emissaries of darkness. It was just the holiness of the Mediator which stirred up against him all the passions of a profligate world, and provoked that fury of assault which rushed in from the hosts of reprobate spirits. There was thrown a perpetual reproach on a proud and sensual generation, by the spotlessness of that righteous individual, " who did no sin, neither was guile found in his mouth." (1 Pet. ii. 22.) And if he had not been so far separated, by the purities of life and conversation, from all others of his nature ; or if vice had received a somewhat less tremendous rebuke from the blamelessness of his every action we may be sure that his might and benevolence would have gathered the nation to his disciple-ship, and that the multitude would never have been worked up to demand his crucifixion.

The great secret of the opposition to Christ lay in the fact, that he he was not such an one as ourselves. We are accustomed to think that the lowliness of his condition, and the want of external majesty and pomp, moved the Jews to reject their Messiah : yet it is by no means clear that these were, in the main, the producing causes of rejection. If Christ came not with the purple and circumstance of human sovereignty, he displayed the possession of a supernatural power, which, even on the most carnal calculation, was more valuable, because more effective, than the staunchest apparatus of earthly supremacy. The peasant, who could work the miracles which Christ worked, would be admitted, on all hands, to have mightier engines at his disposal than the prince who is clothed with the ermine and followed by the warriors. And if the Jews looked for a Messiah who would lead them to mastery over enemies, then, we contend, there was everything in Christ to induce them to give him their allegiance. The power which could vanquish death by a word might cause hosts to fall, as fell the hosts of Sennacherib ; and where then was the foe who could have resisted the leader?

We cannot, therefore, think that it was merely the absence of human pageantry which moved the great ones of Judea to throw scorn upon Jesus. It is true, they were expecting an earthly deliverer. But Christ displayed precisely those powers which, wielded by Moses, had prevailed to deliver their nation from Egypt; and assuredly then, if that strength dwelt in Jesus which had discomfited Pharaoh, and broken the thraldom of centuries, it could not have been the proved incapacity of effecting temporal deliverance which induced pharisees and scribes to reject their Messiah. They could have tolerated the meanness of his parentage; for that was more than compensated by the majesty of his power. They could have endured the lowliness of his appearance; for they could set against it his evident communion with divinity.

But the righteous fervor with which Christ denounced every abomination in the land; the untainted purity by which he shamed the " whited sepulchres " who deceived the people by the appearance of sanctity; the rich loveliness of a character in which zeal for God's glory was unceasingly uppermost; the beautiful lustre which encompassed a being who could hate only one thing, but that one thing sin; these were the producing causes of bitter hostility; and they who would have hailed the wonderworker with the shout and the plaudit, had he allowed some license to the evil passions of our nature, gave him nothing but the sneer and the execration, when he waged open war with lust and hypocrisy.

And thus it was that enmity, the fiercest and most inveterate, was put between the seed of the woman and the seed of the serpent. The serpent himself came to the assistance of his seed; evil angels conspired with evil men; and the whole energies of apostasy gathered themselves, to the effort of destroying the champion of God and of truth. Yea, and for awhile success seemed to attend the endeavor. There was a bruising of the heel of the seed of the woman. " He came unto his own, and his own received him not." (John i. 11.) Charged only with an embassage of mercy; sent by the Father — not to condemn the world, though rebellion had overspread its provinces, and there was done the foulest despite to God, in its every section, and by its every tenant — but that the world through him might have life; he was, nevertheless, scorned as a deceiver, and hunted down as a malefactor. And if it were a bruising of the heel, that he should be " a man of sorrows and acquainted with grief " (Isaiah liii. 3); that a nation should despise him, and friends deny and forsake and betray him; that he should be buffeted with temptation, convulsed by agony, lacerated by stripes, pierced by nails, crowned with thorns; then was the heel of the Redeemer bruised by Satan, for

22

to all this injury the fallen angel instigated and nerved his seed. But though the heel was bruised, this was the whole extent of effected damage. There was no real advantage gained over the Mediator: on the contrary, whilst Satan was in the act of bruising Christ's heel, Christ was in the act of bruising Satan's head. The Saviour, indeed, exposed himself to every kind of insult and wrong. Whilst enduring "the contradiction of sinners against himself" (Heb. xii. 3), it is not to be denied that a strange result was brought round by the machinations of the evil ones; for suffering, which is the attendant on sinfulness, was made to empty all its pangs into the bosom of innocence. And seeing that his holiness should have exempted his humanity from all kinsmanship with sorrow and anguish, we are free to allow that the heel was bruised, when pain found entrance into his humanity, and grief, heavier than had oppressed any being of our race, weighed down his over-wrought spirit.

But, then, there was not an iota of his sufferings which went not towards liquidating the vast debt which man owed to God, and which, therefore, contributed not to our redemption from bondage. There was not a pang by which the Mediator was torn, and not a grief by which his soul was disquieted, which helped not on the achievement of human deliverance, and which, therefore, dealt not out a blow to the despotism of Satan. So that, from the beginning, the bruising of Christ's heel was the bruising of Satan's head. In prevailing, so far as he did prevail, against Christ, Satan was only effecting his own discomfiture and downfall. He touched the heel, he could not touch the head of the Mediator. If he could have seduced him into the commission of evil; if he could have profaned, by a solitary thought, the sanctuary of his soul; then it would have been the head which he had bruised; and, rising triumphant over man's surety, he would have shouted, "Victory!" and this creation have become for ever his own. But whilst he could only cause pain, and not pollution; whilst he could dislocate by agony, but not defile by impurity; he reached indeed the heel, but came not near the head; and, making the Saviour's lifetime one dark series of afflictions, weakened, at every step, his own hold upon humanity.

And when, at last, he so bruised the heel as to nail Christ to the cross, amid the loathings and revilings of the multitude, then it was that his own head was bruised, even to the being crushed. "Through death," we are told, "Christ Jesus destroyed him that had the power of death, that is, the devil." (Heb. ii. 14.) He fell indeed; and evil angels, and evil men, might have thought him for ever defeated. But in grasping this mighty prey, death paralyzed itself; in breaking down the temple, Satan demolished his own throne. It was, as ye all know, by dying, that Christ finished the achievement which, from all eternity, he had covenanted to undertake. By dying, he reinstated fallen man in the position from which he had been hurled. Death came against the Mediator but, in submitting to it, Christ, if we may use such image, seized on the destroyer, and, waving the skeleton-form as a sceptre over this creation, broke the spell of a thousand generations, dashing away the chains, and opening the graves, of an oppressed and rifled population. And when he had died, and descended into the grave, and returned without seeing corruption, then was it made possible that every child of Adam might be emancipated from the dominion of evil; and, in place of the woe and the shame which transgression had won as the heritage of man, there was the beautiful brightness of a purchased immortality wooing the acceptance of the sons and daughters of our race. The strong man armed had kept his goods in peace; and Satan, having seduced men to be his companions in rebellion, might have felt secure of having them as his companions in torment. But the stronger than he drew nigh, and, measuring weapons with him in the garden, and on the cross, received wounds which were but trophies of victory, and dealt wounds which annihilated power. And when, bruised indeed, yet only marked with honorable scars which told out his triumph-to the loftiest orders of intelligent being, the Redeemer of mankind soared on high, and sent proclamation through the universe, that death was abolished, and the ruined redeemed, and the gates of heaven thrown open to the rebel and the outcast, was there not an accomplishment, the most literal and the most energetic, of that prediction which declared to Satan concerning the seed of the woman, " it shall bruise thy head, and thou shalt bruise his heel? "

Such is the first and great fulfilment of the prophecy. The church, represented by its head who was specially the seed of the woman, overthrew the devil in one decisive and desperate struggle, and, though not itself unwounded, received no blow which rebounded not to the crushing its opponent.

We proceed, secondly, to consider the church collectively as a body. We need scarcely observe that, from the first the righteous amongst men have been objects of the combined assault of their evil fellows and evil angels. The enmity has been put and strikingly developed. On the one hand, it has been the endeavor of the church to vindicate God's honor, and arrest the workings of wickedness: on the other, it has been the effort of the serpent and his seed to sweep from the earth these upholders of piety. And though the promise has all along been verified, that the gates of hell shall not prevail against the church, it cannot be denied that a great measure of success has attended the strivings of the adversary. If you only call to mind what fierce persecution has rushed against the righteous; how by one engine or another there has been, oftentimes, almost a thorough extinction of the very name of Christianity; and how, when outwardly there has been peace, tares, sown by the enemy, have sent up a harvest of perilous heresies; you cannot withhold your acknowledgment that Satan has bruised the heel of the church. But he has done nothing more. If he have hewn down thousands by the sword, and consumed thousands at the stake, thousands have sprung forward to fill up the breach; and if he have succeeded in pouring forth a flood of pestilential doctrine, there have arisen staunch advocates of truth who have stemmed the torrent, and snatched the articles of faith, uninjured, from the deluge. There has never been the time when God has been left without a witness upon earth. And though the church has often been sickly and weak; though the best blood has been drained from her veins, and a languor, like that of moral palsy, has settled on her limbs; still life hath never been wholly extinguished; but after awhile the sinking energies have been marvellously recruited and the worn and wasted body has risen up more athletic than before and displayed to the nations all the vigor of renovated youth.

So that only the heel has been bruised. And since, up to the second advent of the Lord, the church shall be battered with heresy, and persecution, and infidelity, we look not, under the present dispensation, for discontinuance of this bruising of the heel. Yet, while Satan is bruising the church's heel, the church, by God's help, is bruising Satan's head. The church may be compelled to prophesy in sack-cloth. Affliction may be her portion, as it was that of her glorified head. But the church is, throughout, God's witness upon earth. The church is God's instrument for carrying on those purposes which shall terminate in the final setting up of the Mediator's kingdom. And, oh, there is not won over a single soul to Christ, and the Gospel message makes not its way to a single heart, without an attendant effect as of a stamping on the head of the temper: for a captive is delivered from the oppressor and to deliver the slave is to defeat the tyrant. Thus the seed of the woman is continually bruising the head of the serpent. And whensoever the church, as an engine in God's hands, makes a successful stand for piety and truth; whensoever, sending out her missionaries to the broad waste of heathenism, she demolishes an altar of superstition, and teaches the pagan to cast his idols to the mole and the bat; or whensoever, assaulting mere nominal Christianity, she fastens men to practice as the alone test of profession; then does she strike a blow which is felt at the very centre of the kingdom of darkness, and then is she experiencing a partial fulfilment of the promise, "God shall bruise Satan under your feet shortly." (Rom. xvi. 20.)

And when the fierce and on-going conflict shall be brought to a close; when this burdened creation shall have shaken off the slaves and the objects of concupiscence, and the church of the living God shall reign, with its head, over the tribes and provinces of an evangelized earth; then in the completeness of the triumph of righteousness shall be the completeness of the serpent's discomfiture. And as the angel and the archangel contrast the slight injury which Satan could ever cause to the church, with that overwhelming ruin which the church has, at last, hurled down upon Satan; as they compare the brief struggle and the everlasting glory of the one, with the shadowy success and the never-ending torments of the other; will they not decide, and tell out their decision in language of rapture and admiration, that, if ever prediction were fulfilled to the very letter, it is that which, addressed to the serpent, and describing the church as the seed of the woman, declared, "It shall bruise thy head, and thou shalt bruise his heel?"

Such is the second fulfilment of the prophecy of our text. The church, considered collectively as a body, is so assaulted by the serpent and his seed that its heel is bruised: but even now it offers such resistance to evil, and hereafter it shall triumph so signally over every opponent, that the prediction, "it shall bruise thy head," must be received as destined to a literal accomplishment.

We have yet to notice the third fulfilment. We may resolve the church into its separate members, and, taking each individual believer as the seed of the woman, show you how our text is realized in his experience.

Now if there be enmity between the serpent and the church generally, of course there is also between the serpent and each member of that church. We have already given it as the description of a converted man, that he has been supernaturally excited to a war with the devil. Whilst left in the darkness and alienation of nature, he submits willingly to the dominion of evil: evil is his element, and he neither strives nor wishs for emancipation. But when the grace of God is introduced into his heart, he will discern quickly the danger and hatefulness of sin, and will yield himself, in a higher strength than his own, to the work of resisting the serpent. Thus enmity is put between the believer and the serpent and his seed. Let a man give himself to the concerns of eternity; let him, in good earnest, set about the business of the soul's salvation; and he will, assuredly, draw upon himself the dislike and opposition of a whole circle of worldly acquaintance, so that this over-preciseness and austerity will become subject of ridicule in his village or neighborhood. We quite mistake the nature both of Christianity and of man, if we suppose that opposition to religion can be limited to an age or a country. Persecution, in its most terrible forms, is only the development of a principle which must unavoidably exist until either Christianity or human nature be altered. There is a necessary repugnance between Christianity and human nature. The two cannot be amalgamated: one must be changed before it will combine with the other. And we fear that this is, in a degree, an overlooked truth, and that men are disposed to assign persecution to local or temporary causes. But we wish you to be clear on the fact, that " the offence of the cross " (Gal. v. 11) has not ceased, and cannot cease. We readily allow that the form, under which the hatred manifests itself, will be sensibly affected by the civilization and intelligence of the age. In days of an imperfect refinement and a scanty literature, you will find this hatred unsheathing the sword, and lighting the pile: but when human society is at a high point of polish and knowledge, and the principles of religious toleration are well understood, there is, perhaps, comparatively small likelihood that savage violence will be the engine employed against godliness. Yet there are a hundred batteries which may and will be opened upon the righteous. The follower of Christ must calculate on many sneers, and much reviling. He must look to meet often with coldness and contempt, harder of endurance than many forms of martyrdom; for the courage which could march to the stake may be daunted by a laugh. And, frequently, the opposition assumes a more decided shape. The parent will act harshly towards the child; the superior withdraw his countenance from the dependent; and all because of a giving heed to the directions of Scripture. Religion, as though it were rebellion, alienates the affections, and alters the wills, of fathers and guardians. So that we tell an individual that he blinds himself to plain matters of fact, if he espouse the opinion that the apostle's words applied only to the first ages of Christianity, " all that will live godly in Christ Jesus shall suffer persecution." (2 Tim. iii. 12.) To "live godly in Christ Jesus" is to have enmity put between yourselves and the seed of the serpent; and you may be assured, that, unless this enmity be merely nominal on your side, it will manifest itself by acts on the other.

Thus the prophecy of our text announces, what has been verified by the history of all ages, that no man can serve God without uniting against himself evil men and evil angels. Evil angels will assault him, alarmed that their prey is escaping from their grasp. Evil men, rebuked by his example, will become agents of the serpent, and strive to wrench him from his righteousness.

But what, after all, is the amount of injury which the serpent and his seed can cause to God's children? Is it not a truth, which can only then be denied when you have cashiered the authority of every page of the Bible, that he who believes upon Christ, and who, therefore, has been adopted through faith into God's family, is certain to be made more than conqueror, and to trample under foot every enemy of salvation? The conflict between a believer and his foes may be long and painful. The Christian may be often forced to exclaim with Paul, "O wretched man that I am, who shall deliver me from the body of this death?" (Rom. vii. 24.) Engaged with the triple band of the world, the flesh, and the devil, he will experience many partial defeats, and, surprised off his guard, or wearied out with watchings, will yield to temptation, and so fall into sin. But it is certain, certain as that God is omnipotent and faithful, that the once justified man shall be enabled to persevere to the end; to persevere, not in an idle dependence on privileges, but in a struggle which, if for an instant interrupted, is sure to be vehemently renewed. And, therefore, the bruising of the heel is the sum total of the mischief. Thus much, undoubtedly, the serpent can effect. He can harass with temptation, and occasionally prevail. But he cannot undo the radical work of conversion. He cannot eject the principle of grace; and he cannot, therefore, bring back the man into the condition of his slave or his subject. Thus he cannot wound the head of the new man. He may diminish his comforts. He may impede his growth in holiness. He may inject doubts and suspicions, and thus keep him disquieted, when, if he would live up to his privileges, he might rejoice and be peaceful. But all this, and we show you here the full sweep of the serpent's power, still leaves the man a believer; and, therefore, all this, though it bruise the heel, touches not the head.

And though the believer, like the unbeliever, must submit to the power of death, and tread the dark valley of that curse which still rests on our nature, is there experienced more than a bruising of the heel in the undergoing this dissolution of humanity? It is an injury — for we go not with those who would idolize, or soften down, death — that the soul must be detached from the body, and sent out, a widowed thing, on the broad journeyings of eternity. It is an injury, that this curious framework of matter, as much redeemed by Christ as the giant-guest which it encases, must be taken down, joint by joint, and rafter by rafter, and, resolved into its original elements, lose every trace of having been human. But what, we again say, is the extent of this injury? The foot of the destroyer shall be set upon the body; and he shall stamp till he have ground it into powder, and dispersed it to the winds. But he cannot annihilate a lonely particle. He can put no arrest on that germinating process which shall yet cause the valleys and mountains of this globe to stand thick with a harvest of flesh. He cannot hinder my resurrection. And when the soul, over which he hath had no power, rushes into the body which he shall be forced to resign, and the child of God stands forth a man, yet immortal, compound of flesh and spirit, but each pure, each indestructible; — oh, though Satan may have battered at his peace during a long earthly pilgrimage; though he may have marred his happiness by successful temptation; though he may have detained for centuries his body in corruption: will not the inflicted injury appear to have been so trivial and insignificant, that a bruising of the heel, in place of falling short of the matter-of-fact, shall itself seem almost an overwrought description?

And, all the while, though Satan can only bruise the believer's heel, the believer is bruising Satan's head. If the believer be one who fights the serpent, and finally conquers, by that final conquest the serpent's head is bruised. If he be naturally the slave of the serpent; if he rebel against the tyrant, throw off his chains, and vanquish him, fighting inch by inch the ground to freedom and glory; then he bruises the serpent's head. If two beings are antagonists, he who decisively overcomes bruises the head of his opponent. But the believer and the serpent are antagonists. The believer gains completely the mastery over the serpent. And, therefore, the result of the contest is the fulfilment of the prediction that the seed of the woman shall bruise the head of the serpent. Oh, if, as we well know, the repentance of a single sinner send a new and exquisite delight down the ranks of the hosts of heaven, and cause the sweeping of a rich and glorious anthem from the countless harps of the sky, can we doubt that the same event spreads consternation through the legions of fallen spirits, and strikes, like a death-blow, on their haughty and malignant leader? Ay, and we believe that never is Satan so taught his subjugated estate, as when a soul, which he had counted as his own, escapes " as a bird out of the snare of the fowlers " (Psalm cxxiv. 7), and seeks and finds protection in Jesus. If it be then that Christ sees " of the travail of his soul " (Isaiah liii. 11), it must be then that the serpent tastes all the bitterness of defeat. And when the warfare is over, and the spirit, which he hath longed to destroy, soars away, convoyed by the angels which wait on the heirs of salvation, must it not be then that the consciousness of lost mastery seizes, with crushing force, on the proud foe of our race; and does not that fierce cry of disappointment which seems to follow the ascending soul, causing her to feel herself only " scarcely saved " (1 Pet. iv. 18), testify that, in thus winning a heritage of glory, the believer hath bruised the head of the serpent?

We shall not examine further this third fulfilment of the prophecy of our text. But we think that when you contrast the slight injury which Satan, at the worst, can cause to a believer, with the mighty blow which the deliverance of a believer deals out to Satan; the nothing-ingness, at last, of the harm done to God's people, with that fearful discomfiture which their individual rescue fastens on the devil; you will confess, that, considering the church as resolved into its separate members, just as when you survey it collectively as a body, or as represented by its head, there is a literal accomplishment of this prediction to the serpent concerning the seed of the woman, " it shall bruise thy head, and thou shalt bruise his heel."

We have thus, as we trust, shown you that the prophecy of our text extends itself over the whole surface of time, so that, from the fall of Adam, it has been receiving accomplishment, and will continue being fulfilled until " death and hell are cast into the lake of fire." (Rev. xx. 14.) It was a wonderful announcement, and, if even but imperfectly understood, must have confounded the serpent, and cheered Adam and Eve. Dust shalt thou eat, foe of humankind, when this long-oppressed creation is delivered from thy despotism. As though to mark to us that there shall be no suspension of the doom of our destroyer, whilst this earth rejoices in the restitution of all things, Isaiah, in describing millennial harmony, still leaves the serpent under the sentence of our text. " The wolf and the lamb shall feed together; and the lion shall eat straw

like the bullock; and *dust shall be the serpent's meat."* (Isa. lxv. 25.)
There comes a day of deliverance to every other creature, but none to
the serpent. Oh, mysterious dealing of our God! that for fallen angels
there hath been no atonement, for fallen men a full, perfect, and sufficient. They were far nobler than we, of a loftier intelligence and more
splendid endowment; yet ("how unsearchable are his judgments") we
are taken and they are left. "For verily he taketh not hold of angels,
but of the seed of Abraham he taketh hold." (Heb. ii. 16, marginal
reading.)

And shall we, thus singled out and made objects of marvellous mercy,
refuse to be delivered, and take our portion with those who are both fallen
and unredeemed? Shall we eat the dust, when we may eat of "the bread
which cometh down from heaven?" (John vi. 50.) Covetous man!
thy money is the dust; thou art eating the serpent's meat. Sensual man!
thy gratifications are of the dust; thou art eating the serpent's meat.
Ambitious man! thine honors are of the dust; thou art eating the serpent's meat. O God put enmity between us and the serpent! Will ye,
every one of you, use that short prayer ere ye lie down to rest this night,
O God, put enmity between us and the serpent? If ye are not at
enmity, his folds are round your limbs. If ye are not at enmity,
his sting is at your heart. But if ye will, henceforward, count him a
foe, oppose him in God's strength, and attack him with the "sword of
the Spirit" (Eph. vi. 17); then, though ye may have your seasons of
disaster and depression, the promise stands sure that ye shall finally
overcome; and it shall be proved by each one in this assembly, that,
though the serpent may bruise the heel of the seed of the woman, yet, at
last, the seed of the woman always bruises the head of the serpent.

XXVI.

JOHN HENRY NEWMAN

1801–1890.

IN that brilliant group of scholars and churchmen who led in "the Oxford Movement" from 1833 to 1845, unquestionably the greatest personality was that of John Henry Newman, the author of the famous Tract No. 90, in the tractarian series. He was born in London, February 21, 1801; received high honors at Trinity College, Oxford, and in 1828 became the vicar of St. Mary's, the University Church. The nine volumes of his sermons were gathered from his preaching in this church; and they show the depth of his insight, the marvellous clearness of his style, and the warmth of his spirit. In the Oxford Movement, toward making the church of England no longer protestant, but catholic — though in no sense *Roman Catholic* — Newman was the recognized leader. Twenty-nine of the "Tracts for the Times," including No. 90, the last of the series, came from his pen. He wrote also a volume of poems, among which may be named the one beginning "Lead, Kindly Light," found in all the hymnals. In 1845, he took the step toward which his logic had been leading him for many years, and left the Church of England for that of Rome. For years he was head of the Congregation of the Oratory. He was made a Cardinal in 1879, and died in 1890. This sermon was preached while he was still a member of the Anglican Church.

COMMUNION WITH GOD.

"One thing have I desired of the Lord, which I will require: even that I may dwell in the house of the Lord all the days of my life, to behold the fair beauty of the Lord, and to visit his temple."—Psalm xxvii. 4.

WHAT the Psalmist desired, we Christians enjoy to the full,— the liberty of holding communion with God in His Temple all through our

347

life. Under the Law, the presence of God was but in one place; and
therefore could be approached and enjoyed only at set times. For far the
greater part of their lives, the chosen people were in one sense " cast out
of the sight of His eyes;" and the periodical return to it which they were
allowed, was a privilege highly coveted and earnestly expected. Much
more precious was the privilege of continually dwelling in His sight,
which is spoken of in the text. " One thing," says the Psalmist, " have
I desired of the Lord . . . that I may dwell in the house of the Lord
all the days of my life, to behold the fair beauty of the Lord, and to
visit His temple." He desired to have continually that communion with
God in prayer, praise, and meditation, to which His presence admits the
soul; and this, I say, is the portion of Christians. Faith opens upon us
Christians the Temple of God wherever we are; for that Temple is a
spiritual one, and so is everywhere present. " We have access," says
the Apostle,— that is, we have admission or introduction, " by faith
into this grace wherein we stand, and rejoice in hope of the glory of
God." And hence, he says elsewhere, " Rejoice in the Lord alway, and
again I say, Rejoice." " Rejoice evermore, pray without ceasing; in
everything give thanks." And St. James, " Is any afflicted? let him
pray: is any merry? let him sing Psalms." Prayer, praise, thanksgiving, contemplation, are the peculiar privilege and duty of a Christian,
and that for their own sakes, from the exceeding comfort and satisfaction
they afford him, and without reference to any definite results to which
prayer tends, without reference to the answers which are promised to it,
from a general sense of the blessedness of being under the shadow of
God's throne.

I propose, then, in what follows, to make some remarks on communion with God, or prayer in a large sense of the word; not as regards
its external consequences, but as it may be considered to affect our own
minds and hearts.

What, then, is prayer? It is (if it may be said reverently) *convers-
ing* with God. We converse with our fellow-men, and then we use
familiar language, because they *are* our fellows. We converse with
God, and then we use the lowliest, awfullest, calmest, concisest language
we can, because He *is* God. Prayer, then, is *divine* converse, differing
from human as God differs from man. Thus St. Paul says, " Our conversation is in heaven,"— not indeed thereby meaning converse of words
only, but intercourse and manner of living generally; yet still in an

especial way converse of words or prayer, because language is the special means of all intercourse. Our intercourse with our fellow-men goes on, not by sight, but by sound, not by eyes, but by ears. Hearing is the social sense, and language is the social bond. In like manner, as the Christian's conversation is in heaven, as it is his duty, with Enoch and other Saints, *to walk with God,* so his voice is in heaven, his heart " inditing of a good matter," of prayers and praises. Prayers and praises are the mode of his intercourse with the next world, as the converse of business or recreation is the mode in which this world is carried on in all its separate courses. He who does not pray, does not claim his citizenship with heaven, but lives, though an heir of the kingdom, as if he were a child of earth.

Now, it is not surprising if that duty or privilege, which is the characteristic token of our heavenly inheritance, should also have an especial influence upon our fitness for claiming it. He who does not use a gift, loses it ; the man who does not use his voice or limbs, loses power over them, and becomes disqualified for the state of life to which he is called. In like manner, he who neglects to pray, not only suspends the enjoyment, but is in a way to lose the possession, of his divine citizenship. We are members of another world ; we have been severed from the companionship of devils, and brought into that invisible kingdom of Christ which faith alone discerns,— that mysterious Presence of God which encompasses us, which is in us, and around us, which is in our heart, which enfolds us as though with a robe of light, hiding our scarred and discolored souls from the sight of Divine Purity, and making them shining as the Angels ; and which flows in upon us too by means of all forms of beauty and grace which this visible world contains, in a starry host or (if I may so say) a milky way of divine companions, the inhabitants of Mount Zion, where we dwell. Faith, I say, alone apprehends all this ; but yet there *is* something which is not left to faith,— our own tastes, likings, motives, and habits. Of these we are conscious in our degree, and we can make ourselves more and more conscious ; and as consciousness tells us what they are, reason tells us whether they are such as become, as correspond with, that heavenly world into which we have been translated.

I say then, it is plain to common sense that the man who has not accustomed himself to the language of heaven will be no fit inhabitant of it when, in the Last Day, it is perceptibly revealed. The case is like that of a language or style of speaking of this world; we know well a foreigner from a native. Again, we know those who have been used to kings' courts or educated society from others. By their voice, accent, and language, and not only so, by their gestures and gait, by their usages, by their mode of conducting themselves and their principles of conduct, we know well what a vast difference there is between those who have lived in good society and those who have not. What indeed is called " *good* society " is often very worthless society. I am not speaking of it to praise it; I only mean, that, as the manners which men call refined or courtly are gained only by intercourse with courts and polished circles, and as the influence of the words there used (that is, of the ideas which those words, striking again and again on the ear, convey to the mind), extends in a most subtle way over all that men do, over the turn of their sentences, and the tone of their questions and replies, and their general bearing, and the spontaneous flow of their thoughts, and their mode of viewing things, and the general maxims or heads to which they refer them, and the motives which determine them, and their likings and dislikings, hopes and fears, and their relative estimate of persons, and the intensity of their perceptions towards particular objects; so a habit of prayer, the practice of turning to God and the unseen world, in every season, in every place, in every emergency (let alone its supernatural effect of prevailing with God),— prayer, I say, has what may be called a *natural* effect, in spiritualizing and elevating the soul. A man is no longer what he was before; gradually, imperceptibly to himself, he has imbibed a new set of ideas, and become imbued with fresh principles. He is as one coming from kings' courts, with a grace, a delicacy, a dignity, a propriety, a justness of thought and taste, a clearness and firmness of principle, all his own. Such is the power of God's secret grace acting through those ordinances which He has enjoined us; such the evident fitness of those ordinances to produce the results which they set before us. As speech is the organ of human society, and the means of human civilization, so is prayer the instrument of divine fellowship and divine training.

I will give, for the sake of illustration, some instances in detail of one particular fault of mind, which among others a habit of prayer is calculated to cure.

For instance; many a man seems to have no grasp at all of doctrinal truth. He cannot get himself to think it of importance what a man believes, and what not. He tries to do so; for a time he does; he does for a time think that a certain faith is necessary for salvation, that certain doctrines are to be put forth and maintained in charity to the souls of men. Yet though he thinks so one day, he changes the next; he holds the truth, and then lets it go again. He is filled with doubts; suddenly the question crosses him, "Is it possible that such and such a doctrine *is* necessary?" and he relapses into an uncomfortable sceptical state, out of which there is no outlet. Reasonings do not convince him; he *cannot* be convinced; he has no grasp of truth. Why? Because the next world is not a reality to him; it only exists in his mind in the form of certain conclusions from certain reasonings. It is but an inference; and never can be more, never can be present to his mind, until he acts, instead of arguing. Let him but act as if the next world were before him; let him but give himself to such devotional exercises as we ought to observe in the presence of an Almighty, All-holy, and All-merciful God, and it will be a rare case indeed if his difficulties do not vanish.

Or again: a man may have a natural disposition towards caprice and change; he may be apt to take up first one fancy, then another, from novelty or other reason; he may take sudden likings or dislikings, or be tempted to form a scheme of religion for himself, of what he thinks best or most beautiful out of all the systems which divide the world.

Again: he is troubled perhaps with a variety of unbecoming thoughts, which he would fain keep out of his mind if he could. He finds himself unsettled and uneasy, dissatisfied with his condition, easily excited, sorry at sin one moment, forgetting it the next, feeble-minded, unable to rule himself, tempted to dote upon trifles, apt to be caught and influenced by vanities, and to abandon himself to languor or indolence.

Once more: he has not a clear perception of the path of truth and duty. This is an especial fault among us now-a-days: men are actuated perhaps by the best feelings and the most amiable motives, and are not fairly chargeable with insincerity; and yet there is a want of straightforwardness in their conduct. They allow themselves to be guided by expediency, and defend themselves, and perhaps so plausibly, that though you are not convinced, you are silenced. They attend to what others think, more than to what God says; they look at Scripture more as a gift to man than as a gift from God; they consider themselves at liberty to modify its plain precepts by a certain discretionary rule; they listen to the voice of great men, and allow themselves to be swayed by them; they make comparisons and strike the balance between the impracticability of the whole that God commands, and the practicability of effecting a part, and think they may consent to give up something, if they can secure the rest. They shift about in opinion, going first a little this way, then a little that, according to the loudness and positiveness with which others speak; they are at the mercy of the last speaker, and they think they observe a safe, judicious, and middle course, by always keeping a certain distance behind those who go farthest. Or they are rash in their religious projects and undertakings, and forget that they may be violating the lines and fences of God's law, while they move about freely at their pleasure. Now, I will not judge another; I will not say that in this or that given case the fault of mind in question (for any how it is a fault), does certainly arise from some certain cause which I choose to guess at: but at least there *are* cases where this wavering of mind *does* arise from scantiness of prayer; and if so, it is worth a man's considering, who is thus unsteady, timid, and dimsighted, whether this scantiness be not perchance the true reason of such infirmities in his own case, and whether a " continuing instant in prayer,"— by which I mean, not merely prayer morning and evening, but something suitable to his disease, something extraordinary as medicine is extraordinary, a " redeeming of time " from society and recreation in order to pray more,— whether such a change in his habits would not remove them?

For what is the very promise of the New Covenant but stability? what is it, but a clear insight into the truth, such as will enable us to know how to walk, how to profess, how to meet the circumstances of life, how to withstand gainsayers? Are we built upon a rock, or upon the sand? are we after all tossed about on the sea of opinion, when Christ has stretched out His hand to us, to help and encourage us? " Thou wilt keep him in perfect peace whose mind is stayed on Thee, because he trusteth in Thee." Such is the word of promise. Can we possibly have apprehensions about what man will do to us or say of us, can we flatter the great ones of earth, or timidly yield to the many, or be dazzled by talent, or drawn aside by interest, who are in the habit of divine conversations? " Ye have an unction from the Holy One," says St. John, " and ye know all things. I have not written unto you because ye know not the truth, but because ye know it, and that no lie is of the truth. . . . The anointing which we have received of Him abideth in you, and ye need not that any man teach you. . . . Whosoever is born of God, doth not commit sin, for his seed remaineth in him; and he cannot sin, because he is born of God." This is that birth, by which the baptized soul not only enters, but actually embraces and realizes the kingdom of God. This is the true and effectual regeneration, when the seed of life takes root in man and thrives. Such men have accustomed themselves to speak to God, and God has ever spoken to them; and they feel "the powers of the world to come" as truly as they feel the presence of this world, because they have been accustomed to speak and act as if it were real. All of us must rely on something; all must look up, to admire, court, make themselves one with something. Most men cast in their lot with the visible world; but true Christians with Saints and Angels.

Such men are little understood by the world because they are not of the world; and hence it sometimes happens that even the better sort of men are often disconcerted and vexed by them. It cannot be otherwise; they move forward on principles so different from what are commonly assumed as true. They take for granted, as first principles, what the world wishes to have proved in detail. They have become familiar with the sights of the next world, till they talk of them as if all men admitted them. The immortality of truth, its oneness, the impossibility of falsehood coalescing with it, what truth is, what it should lead one to do in particular cases, how it lies in the details of life,— all these points are mere matters of debate in the world, and men go through long processes of argument, and pride themselves on their subtleness in defending or attacking, in making probable or improbable, ideas which are assumed without a word by those who have lived in heaven, as the very ground to start from. In consequence, such men are called bad disputants, inconsecutive reasoners, strange, eccentric, or perverse thinkers, merely because they do not take for granted, nor go to prove, what others do,— because they do not go about to define and determine the sights (as it were), the mountains and rivers and plains, and sun, moon, and stars, of the next world. And hence, in turn, they are commonly unable to enter into the ways of thought or feelings of other men, having been engrossed with God's thoughts and God's ways. Hence, perhaps, they seem abrupt in what they say and do; nay, even make others feel constrained and uneasy in their presence. Perhaps they appear reserved too, because they take so much for granted which might be drawn out, and because they cannot bring themselves to tell all their thoughts from their sacredness, and because they are drawn off from free conversation to the thought of heaven, on which their

23

minds rest. Nay, perchance, they appear severe, because their motives are not understood, nor their sensitive jealousy for the honor of God and their charitable concern for the good of their fellow-Christians duly appreciated. In short, to the world they seem like *foreigners*. We know how foreigners strike us; they are often to *our* notions strange and unpleasing in their manners; why is this? merely *because* they are of a different country. Each country has its own manners,— one may not be better than other; but we naturally like our own ways, and we do not understand other. We do not see their meaning. We misconstrue them; we think they mean something unpleasant, something rude, or overfree, or haughty, or unrefined, when they do not. And in like manner, the world at large, not only is not Christian, but cannot discern or understand the Christian. Thus our Blessed Lord Himself was not recognised or honored by His relatives, and (as is plain to every reader of Scripture) He often seems to speak abruptly and severely. So too St. Paul was considered by the Corinthians as contemptible in speech. And hence St. John, speaking of " what manner of love the Father hath bestowed upon us that we should be called the sons of God," adds, " therefore the world *knoweth* us not, because it knew Him not." Such is the effect of divine meditations: admitting us into the next world, and withdrawing us from this; making us children of God, but withal " strangers unto our brethren, even aliens unto our mother's children." Yea, though the true servants of God increase in meekness and love day by day, and to those who know them will seem what they really are; and though their good works are evident to all men, and cannot be denied, yet such is the eternal law which goes between the Church and the world — we cannot be friends of both; and they who take their portion with the Church, will seem, except in some remarkable cases, unamiable to the world, for the " world knoweth them not," and does not like them though it can hardly tell why; yet (as St. John proceeds) they have this blessing, that " when He shall appear, they shall be like Him, for they shall see Him as He is."

And if, as it would seem, we must choose between the two, surely the world's friendship may be better parted with than our fellowship with our Lord and Saviour. What indeed have we to do with courting men, whose faces are turned towards God? We know how men feel and act when they come to die; they discharge their worldly affairs from their minds, and try to realize the unseen state. Then this world is nothing to them. It may praise, it may blame; but they feel it not.

They are leaving their goods, their deeds, their sayings, their writings, their names, behind them; and they care not for it, for they wait for Christ. To one thing alone they are alive, His coming; they watch against it, if so be they may then be found without shame. Such is the conduct of dying men; and what all but the very hardened do at the last, if their senses fail not and their powers hold, that does the true Christian all life long. He is ever dying while he lives; he is on his bier, and the prayers for the sick are saying over him. He has no work but that of making his peace with God, and preparing for the judgment. He has no aim but that of being found worthy to escape the things that shall come to pass and to stand before the Son of Man. And therefore day by day he unlearns the love of this world, and the desire of its praise; he can bear to belong to the nameless family of God, and to seem to the world strange in it and out of place, for so he is.

And when Christ comes at last, blessed indeed will be his lot. He has joined himself from the first to the conquering side; he has risked the present against the future, preferring the chance of eternity to the certainty of time; and then his reward will be but beginning, when that of the children of this world is to come to an end. In the words of the wise man, "Then shall the righteous man stand in great boldness before the face of such as have afflicted him, and made no account of his labors. When they see it they shall be troubled with terrible fear, and shall be amazed at the strangeness of His salvation, so far beyond all that they looked for. And they, repenting and groaning for anguish of spirit, shall say within themselves, This is he whom we had sometimes in derision and a proverb of reproach; we fools counted his life madness, and his end to be without honor. How is he numbered among the children of God, and his lot is among the saints!"

XXVII

HORACE BUSHNELL

1802–1876

IN the middle period of the nineteenth century lived two preachers whose influence was most influential upon preaching, Robertson in England, and Bushnell in America. Yet neither of these was a " popular " preacher as Beecher and Spurgeon at the same epoch were popular. Neither of these two great men spoke to a large congregation from his own pulpit, and neither won fame during his pastoral ministry. Horace Bushnell was born April 14, 1802, in Litchfield, Connecticut, was graduated from Yale College in 1827, and became pastor of the North Congregational Church, Hartford, Connecticut, in 1833. He wrote much on theological subjects, and many of his views, unpopular in his own time, have gradually come to practical acceptance. His book on " Christian Nurture " (1847) is now regarded as an authority as well as a classic. " Nature and the Supernatural " (1858), and " The Vicarious Sacrifice " (1865) were widely read, and being out of accord with the Calvinistic views of the time, led to considerable discussion. But Bushnell's widest and deepest influence began with his first volume of discourses, " Sermons for the New Life," published in 1858, only a year before he resigned his pastorate. These were followed by " Christ and His Salvation " (1864), and " Sermons on Living Subjects " (1872). The three volumes of his sermons were read by preachers everywhere for their peculiar style, their deep spiritual insight, their brilliant thought, their intense earnestness, and their suggestiveness. No other preacher ever saw such sermons in such texts, but the sermon when read seemed to be the only one that fitted that particular sentence of Scripture. The minister who reads only the texts and titles of

Bushnell's sermons will learn much, but far more as he reads and studies the sermons themselves. This sermon has been taken from the volume " Sermons for the New Life " by permission of the publishers, Charles Scribner's Sons, of New York.

UNCONSCIOUS INFLUENCE.

" Then went in also that other disciple."— John xx. 8.

IN this slight touch or turn of history, is opened to us, if we scan it closely, one of the most serious and fruitful chapters of Christian doctrine. Thus it is that men are ever touching unconsciously the springs of motion in each other; thus it is that one man, without thought or intention, or even a consciousness of the fact, is ever leading some other after him. Little does Peter think, as he comes up where his doubting brother is looking into the sepulchre, and goes straight in, after his peculiar manner, that he is drawing in his brother apostle after him. As little does John think, when he loses his misgivings, and goes into the sepulchre after Peter, that he is following his brother. And just so, unawares to himself, is every man, the whole race through, laying hold of his fellow-man, to lead him where otherwise he would not go. We overrun the boundaries of our personality — we flow together. A Peter leads a John, a John goes after a Peter, both of them unconscious of any influence exerted or received. And thus our life and conduct are ever propagating themselves, by a law of social contagion, throughout the circles and times in which we live.

There are, then, you will perceive, two sorts of influence belonging to man; that which is active or voluntary, and that which is unconscious; — that which we exert purposely or in the endeavor to sway another, as by teaching, by argument, by persuasion, by threatenings, by offers and promises,— and that which flows out from us, unawares to ourselves, that same which Peter had over John when he led him into the sepulchre. The importance of our efforts to do good, that is of our voluntary influence, and the sacred obligations we are under to exert ourselves in this way, are often and seriously insisted on. It is thus that Christianity has become, in the present age, a principle of so much greater activity than it has been for many centuries before; and we fervently hope that it will yet become far more active than it now is, nor cease to

multiply its industry, till it is seen by all mankind to embody the beneficence and the living energy of Christ himself.

But there needs to be produced, at the same time, and partly for
this object, a more thorough appreciation of the relative importance of
that kind of influence, or beneficence which is insensibly exerted. The
tremendous weight and efficacy of this, compared with the other, and
the sacred responsibility laid upon us in regard to this, are felt in no
such degree or proportion as they should be; and the consequent loss
we suffer in character, as well as that which the Church suffers in
beauty and strength, is incalculable. The more stress, too, needs to be
laid on this subject of insensible influence, because it is insensible; because it is out of mind, and, when we seek to trace it, beyond a full discovery.

If the doubt occur to any of you, in the announcement of this subject, whether we are properly responsible for an influence which we
exert insensibly; we are not, I reply, except so far as this influence flows
directly from our character and conduct. And this it does, even much
more uniformly than our active influence. In the latter we may fail of
our end by a want of wisdom or skill in which case we are still as meri-
torius, in God's sight, as if we succeeded. So, again, we may really
succeed, and do great good by our active endeavors, from motives altogether base and hypocritical, in which case we are as evil, in God's
sight, as if we had failed. But the influences we exert unconsciously
will almost never disagree with our real character. They are honest influences, following our character, as the shadow follows the sun. And,
therefore, we are much more certainly responsible for them, and their
effects on the world. They go streaming from us in all directions, though
in channels that we do not see, poisoning or healing around the roots
of society, and among the hidden wells of character. If good ourselves,
they are good; if bad, they are bad. And, since they reflect so exactly
our character, it is impossible to doubt our responsibility for their effects
on the world. We must answer not only for what we do with a purpose, but for the influence we exert insensibly. To give you any just
impressions of the breadth and seriousness of such a reckoning I know to
be impossible. No mind can trace it. But it will be something gained
if I am able to awaken only a suspicion of the vast extent and power
of those influences, which are ever flowing out unbidden upon society,
from your life and character.

In the prosecution of my design, let me ask of you, first of all, to expel the common prejudice that there can be nothing of consequence in unconscious influences, because they make no report, and fall on the world unobserved. Histories and biographies make little account of the power men exert insensibly over each other. They tell how men have led armies, established empires, enacted laws, gained causes, sung, reasoned, and taught;—always occupied in setting forth what they do with a purpose. But what they do without a purpose, the streams of influence that flow out from their persons unbidden on the world, they can not trace or compute, and seldom even mention. So also the public laws make men responsible only for what they do with a positive purpose, and take no account of the mischiefs or benefits that are communicated, by their noxious or healthful example. The same is true in the discipline of families, churches, and schools; they make no account of the things we do, except we will them. What we do insensibly passes for nothing, because no human government can trace such influences with sufficient certainty to make their authors responsible.

But you must not conclude that influences of this kind are insignificant, because they are unnoticed and noiseless. How is it in the natural world? Behind the mere show, the outward noise and stir of the world, nature always conceals her hand of control, and the laws by which she rules. Who ever saw with the eye, for example, or heard with the ear, the exertions of that tremendous astronomic force, which every moment holds the compact of the physical universe together? The lightning is, in fact, but a mere fire-fly spark in comparison; but, because it glares on the clouds, and thunders so terribly in the ear, and rives the tree or the rock where it falls, many will be ready to think that it is a vastly more potent agent than gravity.

The Bible calls the good man's life a light, and it is the nature of light to flow out spontaneously in all directions, and fill the world unconsciously with its beams. So the Christian shines, it would say, not so much because he will, as because he is a luminous object. Not that the active influence of Christians is made of no account in the figure, but only that this symbol of light has its propriety in the fact that their unconscious influence is the chief influence, and has the precedence in its power over the world. And yet, there are many who will be ready to think that light is a very tame and feeble instrument, because it is noiseless. An earthquake, for example, is to them a much more vigorous and effective agency. Hear how it comes thundering through the solid foundations of nature. It rocks a whole continent. The noblest works of man,—cities, monuments, and temples,—are in a moment levelled to the ground, or swallowed down the opening gulfs of fire. Little do they think that the light of every morning, the soft, and genial, and silent light, is an agent many times more powerful. But let the light of morning cease and return no more, let the hour of morning come, and bring with it no dawn: the outcries of a horror-stricken world fill the air, and make, as it were, the darkness audible. The beasts go wild and frantic at the loss of the sun. The vegetable growths turn pale and die. A chill creeps on, and frosty winds begin to howl across the freezing earth. Colder, and yet colder, is the night. The vital blood, at length, of all creatures, stops congealed. Down goes the frost toward the earth's center. The heart of the sea is frozen; nay, the earthquakes are themselves frozen in, under their fiery caverns. The very globe itself, too, and all the fellow planets that have lost their sun, are become mere balls of ice, swinging silent in the darkness. Such is the light, which revisits us in the silence of the morning. It makes no shock or scar. It would not wake an infant in his cradle. And yet it perpetually new creates the world, rescuing it, each morning as a prey, from night and chaos. So the Christian is a light, even "the light of the world," and we must not think that, because he shines insensibly or silently, as a mere luminous object, he is therefore powerless. The greatest powers are ever those which lie back of the little stirs and commotions of nature; and I verily believe that the insensible influences of good men are as much more potent than what I have called their voluntary or active, as the great silent powers of nature are of greater consequence than her little disturbances and tumults. The law of human influence is deeper than many suspect, and they lose sight of it altogether. The outward endeavors made by good men or bad to sway others, they call their influence; whereas it is, in fact, but a fraction, and, in most cases, but a very small fraction, of the good or evil that flows out of their lives. Nay, I will even go further. How many persons do you meet, the insensible influence of whose manners and character is so decided as often to thwart their voluntary influence; so that, whatever they attempt to do, in the way of controlling others, they are sure to carry the exact opposite of what they intend! And it will generally be found that, where men undertake by argument or persuasion to exert a power, in the face of qualities that make them odious or detestable, or only not entitled to respect, their insensible influence will be too strong for them. The total effect of the life is then of a kind directly opposite to the voluntary endeavor; which, of course, does not add so much as a fraction to it.

I call your attention, next, to the twofold powers of effect and expression by which man connects with his fellow man. If we distinguish man as a creature of language, and thus qualified to communicate himself to others, there are in him two sets or kinds of language, one which is voluntary in the use, and one that is involuntary; that of speech in the literal sense, and that expression of the eye, the face, the look, the gait, the motion the tone or cadence which is sometimes called the natural language of the sentiments. This natural language too, is greatly enlarged by the conduct of life, that which, in business and society, reveals the principles and spirit of men. Speech, or voluntary language, is a door to the soul, that we may open or shut at will; the other is a door that stands open evermore, and reveals to others constantly and often very clearly, the tempers, tastes, and motives of their hearts. Within, as we may represent, is character, charging the common reservoir of influence and through these twofold gates of the soul, pouring itself out on the world. Out of one it flows at choice, and whensoever we purpose to do good or evil to men. Out of the other it flows each moment, as light from the sun, and propagates itself in all beholders.

Then if we go over to others, that is, to the subjects of influence, we find every man endowed with two inlets of impression; the ear and the understanding for the reception of speech, and the sympathetic powers, the sensibilities or affections, for tinder to those sparks of emotion revealed by looks, tones, manners, and general conduct. And these sympathetic powers, though not immediately rational are yet inlets, open on all sides, to the understanding and character. They have a certain wonderful capacity to receive impressions, and catch the meaning of signs, and propagate in us whatsoever falls into their passive molds, from others. The impressions they receive do not come through verbal propositions, and are never received into verbal proposition, it may be, in the mind, and therefore may think nothing of them. But precisely on this account are they the more powerful, because it is as if one heart were thus going directly into another, and carrying in its feelings with it. Beholding, as in a glass, the feelings of our neighbor, we are changed into the same image, by the assimilating power of sensibility and fellow-feeling. Many have gone so far, and not without show, at least, or reason, as to maintain that the look or expression, and even the very features of children, are often changed, by exclusive intercourse with nurses and attendants. Furthermore, if we carefully consider, we shall find it scarcely possible to doubt, that simply to look on bad and malignant faces, or those whose expressions have become infected by vice, to be with them and become familiarized to them, is enough permanently to affect the character of persons of mature age. I do not say that it must of necessity subvert their character, for the evil looked upon may never be loved or welcomed in practice but it is something to have these bad images in the soul, giving out their expressions there, and diffusing their odor among the thoughts, as long as we live. How dangerous a thing is it, for example, for a man to become accustomed to sights of cruelty? What man, valuing the honor of his soul, would. not shrink from yielding himself to such an influence? No more is it a thing of indifference to become accustomed to look on the manners, and receive the bad expression of any kind of sin.

The door of involuntary communication, I have said, is always open. Of course we are communicating ourselves in this way, to others at every moment of our intercourse or presence with them. But how very seldom, in comparison, do we undertake by means of speech to influence others! Even the best Christian, one who most improves his opportunities to do good, attempts but seldom to sway another by voluntary influence, whereas he is all the while shining as a luminous object unawares, and communicating of his heart to the world.

But there is yet another view of this double line of communication which man has with his fellow-men, which is more general, and displays the import of the truth yet more convincingly. It is by one of these modes of communication that we are constituted members of voluntary society, and by the other, parts of a general mass, or members of involuntary society. You are all, in a certain view, individuals, and separate as persons from each other: you are also, in a certain other view, parts of a common body, as truly as the parts of a stone. Thus if you ask how it is that you and all men came, without your consent to exist in society, to be within its power, to be under its laws, the answer is that while you are a man, you are also a fractional element of a larger and more comprehensive being called society — be it the family, the church, the state. In a certain department of your nature, it is open; its sympathies and feelings are open. On this open side you all adhere together, as parts of a larger nature, in which there is a common circulation of want, impulse, and law. Being thus made common to each other voluntarily, you become one mass, one consolidated social body, animated by one life. And observe how far this involuntary communication and sympathy between the members of a state or family is sovereign over their character. It always results in what we call the national or family spirit; for there is a spirit peculiar to every state and family in the world. Sometimes, too, this national or family spirit takes a religious or an irreligious character, and appears almost to absorb the religious self-government of individuals. What was the national spirit of France, for example, at a certain time, but a spirit of infidelity? What is the religious spirit of Spain at this moment, but a spirit of bigotry, quite as wide of Christianity and destructive to character as the spirit of falsehood? What is the family spirit in many a house, but the spirit of gain, or pleasure, or appetite, in which everything that is warm, dignified, genial, and good in religion, is visibly absent? Sometimes you will almost fancy that you see the shapes of money in the eyes of the children. So it is that we are led on by nations as it were, to a good or bad immortality. Far down in the secret foundations of life and society, there lie concealed great laws and channels of influence, which make the race common to each other in all the main departments or divisions of the social mass — laws which often escape our notice altogether, but which are to society as gravity to the general system of God's works.

But these are general considerations, and more fit, perhaps, to give you a rational conception of the modes of influence and their relative power, than to verify that conception, or establish its truth. I now proceed to add, therefore, some miscellaneous proofs of a more particular nature.

And I mention, first of all, the instinct of imitation in children. We begin our mortal experience, not with acts grounded in judgment or reason, or with ideas received through language, but by simple imitation, and, under the guidance of this, we lay our foundations. The child looks and listens, and whatsoever tone of feeling or manner of conduct is displayed around him, sinks into his plastic, passive soul, and becomes a mold of his being ever after. The very handling of the nursery is significant, and the petulance, the passion, the gentleness, the tranquillity indicated by it, are all reproduced in the child. His soul is a purely receptive nature, and that, for a considerable period, without choice or selection. A little further on, he begins voluntarily to copy everything he sees. Voice, manner, gait, everything which the eye

sees, the mimic instinct delights to act over. And thus we have a whole
generation of future men, receiving from us their very beginnings, and
the deepest impulses of their life and immortality. They watch us every
moment, in the family, before the hearth, and at the table; and when
we are meaning them no good or evil, when we are conscious of
exerting no influence over them, they are drawing from us impressions
and molds of habit, which, if wrong, no heavenly discipline can wholly
remove; or, if right, no bad associations utterly dissipate. Now it may
be doubted, I think, whether, in all the active influence of our lives, we do
as much to shape the destiny of our fellow-men, as we do in this single
article of unconscious influence over children.

Still further on, respect for others takes the place of imitation.
We naturally desire the approbation or good opinion of others. You
see the strength of this feeling in the article of fashion. How few
persons have the nerve to resist a fashion! We have fashions, too, in
literature, and in worship, and in moral and religious doctrine, almost
equally powerful. How many will violate the best rules of society, because it is the practice of their circle! How many reject Christ because
of friends or acquaintance, who have no suspicion of the influence they
exert, and will not have, till the last day shows them what they have
done! Every good man has thus a power in his person, more mighty
than his words and arguments, and which others feel when he little sus-
pects it. Every bad man, too, has a fund of poison in his character,
which is tainting those around him, when it is not in his thoughts to do
them an injury. He is read and understood. His sensual tastes and
habits, his unbelieving spirit, his suppressed leer at religion, have all
a power, and take hold of the hearts of others, whether he will have
it so or not.

Again, how well understood is it, that the most active feelings and
impulses of mankind are contagious. How quick enthusiasm of any
sort is to kindle. and how rapidly it catches from one to another, till
a nation blazes in the flame! In the case of the crusades, you have an
example where the personal enthusiasm of one man put all the states of
Europe in motion. Fanaticism is almost equally contagious. Fear
and superstition always infect the mind of the circle in which they are
manifested. The spirit of war generally becomes an epidemic of madness, when once it has got possession of a few minds. The spirit of
party is propagated in a similar manner. How any slight operation in
the market may spread, like a fire, if successful, till trade runs wild

in a general infatuation, is well known. Now, in all these examples, the effect is produced, not by active endeavor to carry influence, but mostly by that insensible propagation which follows, when a flame of any kind is once kindled.

Is it also true, you may ask, that the religious spirit propagates itself or tends to propagate itself in the same way? I see no reason to question that it does. Nor does anything in the doctrine of spiritual influences, when rightly understood, forbid the supposition. For spiritual influences are never separated from the laws of thought in the individual, and the laws of feeling and influence in society. If, too, every disciple is to be an "epistle known and read of all men," what shall we expect, but that all men will be somehow affected by the reading? Or, if he is to be a light in the world, what shall we look for, but that others, seeing his good works, shall glorify God on his account? How often is it seen too as a fact of observation, that one, or a few good men kindle at length a holy fire in the community in which they live, and become the leaven of a general reformation! Such men give a more vivid proof in their persons of the reality of religious faith, than any words or arguments could yield. They are active; they endeavor, of course, to exert a good voluntary influence; but still their chief power lies in their holiness, and the sense they produce in others of their close relation to God.

It now remains to exhibit the very important fact, that where the direct or active influence of men is supposed to be great, even this is due, in a principal degree, to that insensible influence by which their arguments, reproofs, and persuasions are secretly invigorated. It is not mere words which turn men; it is the heart mounting, uncalled, into the expression of the features; it is the eye illuminated by reason, the look beaming with goodness; it is the tone of the voice, that instrument of the soul, which changes quality with such amazing facility, and gives out in the soft, the tender, the tremulous, the firm, every shade of emotion and character. And so much is there in this, that the moral stature and character of the man that speaks are likely to be well represented in his manner. If he is a stranger, his way will inspire confidence and attract good will. His virtues will be seen, as it were, gathering round him to minister words and forms of thought, and their voices will be heard in the fall of his cadences. And the same is true of bad men, or men, who have nothing in their character corresponding to what they attempt to do. If without heart or interest you attempt to move another, the involuntary man tells you what you are doing in a hundred ways at once. A hypocrite, endeavoring to exert a good influence, only tries to convey by words what the lying look, and the faithless affectation, or dry exaggeration of his manner, perpetually resists. We have it for a fashion to attribute great or even prodigious results to the voluntary efforts and labors of men. Whatever they effect is commonly referred to nothing but the immediate power of what they do. Let us take an example, like that of Paul, and analyze it. Paul was a man of great fervor and enthusiasm. He combined, withal, more of what is lofty and morally commanding in his character, than most of the very distinguished men of the world. Having this for his natural character, and his natural character exalted and made luminous by Christian faith, and the manifest indwelling of God, he had of course an almost superhuman sway over others. Doubtless he was intelligent, strong in argument, eloquent, active, to the utmost of his powers, but still he moved the world more by what he was than by what he did. The grandeur and spiritual splendor of his character were ever adding to his active efforts an element of silent power, which was the real and chief cause of their efficacy. He convinced, subdued, inspired, and led, because of the half divine authority which appeared in his conduct, and his glowing spirit. He fought the good fight, because he kept the faith, and filled is powerful nature with influences drawn from higher worlds.

And here I must conduct you to a yet higher example, even that of the Son of God, the light of the world. Men dislike to be swayed by direct, voluntary influence. They are jealous of such control, and are therefore best approached by conduct and feeling, and the authority of simple worth, which seems to make no purposed onset. If goodness appears, they welcome its celestial smile; if heaven descends to encircle them, they yield to its sweetness; if truth appears in the life, they honor it with a secret homage; if personal majesty and glory appear, they bow with reverence, and acknowledge with shame, their own vileness. Now it is on this side of human nature that Christ visits us, preparing just that kind of influence which the spirit of truth may wield with the most persuasive and subduing effect. It is the grandeur of his character which constitutes the chief power of his ministry, not his miracles or teachings apart from his character. Miracles were useful, at the time to arrest the attention, and his doctrine is useful at all times as the highest revelation of truth possible in speech; but the greatest truth of the gospel, notwithstanding, is Christ himself — a hu-

man body become the organ of the divine nature, and revealing, under
the conditions of an earthly life, the glory of God! The Scripture
writers have much to say, in this connection, of the image of God: and
an image, you know, is that which simply represents, not that which acts,
or reasons, or persuades. Now it is this image of God which makes
the center, the sun itself, of the gospel. The journeyings, teachings,
miracles, and sufferings of Christ, all had their use in bringing out
this image, or what is the same, in making conspicuous the character
and feelings of God, both toward sinners and toward sin. And here is
the power of Christ — it is what of God's beauty love, truth, and justice
shines through him. It is the influence which flows unconsciously and
spontaneously out of Christ, as the friend of man, the light of the world,
the glory of the Father, made visible. And some have gone so far as to
conjecture that God made the human person, originally, with a view to
its becoming the organ or vehicle, by which he might reveal his com-
municable attributes to other worlds. Christ, they believe, came to
inhabit this organ, that he might execute a purpose so sublime. The
human person is constituted, they say, to be a mirror of God; and God,
being imaged in that mirror, as in Christ, is held up to the view of this
and other worlds. It certainly is to the view of this; and if the Divine
nature can use this organ so effectively to express itself unto us, if it
can bring itself, through the looks, tones, motions, and conduct of a
human person, more close to our sympathies than by any other means,
how can we think that an organ so communicative, inhabited by us, is
not always breathing our spirit and transferring our image insensibly
to others?

I have protracted the argument on this subject beyond what I could
have wished, but I can not dismiss it without suggesting a few thoughts
necessary to its complete practical effect.

One very obvious and serious inference from it, and the first which
I will name, is, that it is impossible to live in this world, and escape
responsibility. It is not they alone, as you have seen, who are trying
purposely to convert or corrupt others, who exert an influence; you
can not live without exerting influence. The doors of your soul are
open on others, and theirs on you. You inhabit a house which is well
nigh transparent; and what you are within, you are ever showing yourself to be without, by signs that have no ambiguous expression. If you
had the seeds of a pestilence in your body, you would not have a more

active contagion, than you have in your tempers, tastes, and principles. Simply to be in this world, whatever you are, is to exert an influence — an influence, too, compared with which mere language and persuasion are feeble. You say that you mean well; at least, you think you mean to injure no one. Do you injure no one? Is your example harmless? Is it ever on the side of God and duty? You can not reasonably doubt that others are continually receiving impressions from your character. As little can you doubt that you must answer for these impressions. If the influence you exert is unconsciously exerted, then it is only the most sincere, the truest expression of your character. And for what can you be held responsible, if not for this? Do not deceive yourselves in the thought that you are, at least, doing no injury, and are, therefore, living without responsibility; first make it sure that you are not every hour infusing moral death insensibly into your children, wives, husbands, friends, and acquaintances. By a mere look or glance, not unlikely, you are conveying the influence that shall turn the scale of some one's immortality. Dismiss, therefore, the thought that you are living without responsibility, that is impossible. Better is it frankly to admit the truth; and if you will risk the influence of a character unsanctified by duty and religion, prepare to meet your reckoning manfully, and receive the just recompense of reward.

The true philosophy or method of doing good is also here explained. It is, first of all and principally, to be good — to have a character that will of itself communicate good. There must and will be active effort where there is goodness of principle; but the latter we should hold to be the principal thing, the root and life of all. Whether it is a mistake more sad or ridiculous, to make mere stir synonymous with doing good, we need not inquire; enough, to be sure that one who has taken up such a notion of doing good, is for that reason a nuisance to the church. The Christian is called a light, not lightning. In order to act with effect on others, he must walk in the Spirit, and thus become the image of goodness; he must be so akin to God, and so filled with His dispositions, that he shall seem to surround himself with a hallowed atmosphere. It is folly to endeavor to make ourselves shine before we are luminous. If the sun without his beams should talk to the planets, and argue with them till the final day, it would not make them shine; there must be light in the sun itself, and then they will shine, of course. And this, my brethren, is what God intends for you all. It is the great idea of his gospel, and the work of his spirit, to make you lights in the world. His greatest joy is to give you character, to beautify your example, to exalt your principles, and make you each the depository of his own almighty grace. But in order to this, some thing is necessary on your part — a full surrender of your mind to duty and to God, and a perpetual desire of this spiritual intimacy; having this, having a participation thus of the goodness of God, you will as naturally communicate good as the sun communicates his beams.

Our doctrine of unconscious and undesigning influence shows how it is, also, that the preaching of Christ is often so unfruitful, and especially in times of spiritual coldness. It is not because truth ceases to be truth, nor, of necessity, because it is preached in a less vivid manner, but because there are so many influences, preaching against the preacher. He is one, the people are many; his attempt to convince and persuade is a voluntary influence; their lives, on the other hand, and especially the lives of those who profess what is better, are so many unconscious influences, ever streaming forth upon the people, and back and forth between each other. He preaches the truth, and they, with one consent, are preaching the truth down; and how can he prevail against so many, and by a kind of influence so unequal? When the people of God are glowing with spiritual devotion to Him, and love to men, the case is different; then they are all preaching with the preacher, and making an atmosphere of warmth for his words to fall in; great is the company of them that publish the truth, and proportionally great its power. Shall I say more? Have you not already felt, my brethren, the application to which I would bring you? We do not exonerate ourselves; we do not claim to be nearer to God or holier than you; but ah! you know not how easy it is to make a winter about us, or how cold it feels! Our endeavor is to preach the truth of Christ and his cross as clearly and as forcibly as we can. Sometimes it has a visible effect, and we are filled with joy; sometimes it has no effect, and then we struggle on, as we must, but under great oppression. Have we none among you that preach against us in your lives? If we show you the light of God's truth, does it never fall on banks of ice; which if the light shines through, the crystal masses are yet as cold as before? We do not accuse you; that we leave to God, and to those who may rise up in the last day to testify against you. If they shall come out of your own families; if they are the children that wear your names, the husband or wife of your affections; if they declare that you, by your example, kept them away from Christ's truth and mercy, we may have accusations to meet of our own and we leave you to acquit yourselves as best you may. I only warn you, here, of the guilt which our Lord Jesus Christ will impute to them that hinder his gospel.

24

XXVIII

THOMAS GUTHRIE

1803–1873

IT was said of Thomas Guthrie, D.D., during his lifetime, that "he has a sturdiness of judgment wonderfully tempered by a passionateness of imagination, which, as the lightning-flash in a dark sky lights up into visible being the obscurest recesses of thought." He was born July 12, 1803, at Brechin, Forfarshire, Scotland, where his father was a merchant and banker. He studied for the ministry at the University of Edinburgh, but afterward engaged in banking. In 1830 he took a pastoral charge at Arbirlot, not far from his birthplace; and in 1837 became one of the ministers of the Old Grey Friar's Parish in Edinburgh, a district of poor people, where his labors in philanthropic enterprises were incessant. Dr. Guthrie joined with Chalmers and others in the establishment of the Free Church of Scotland in 1843, and for many years afterward was pastor of the Free St. John's Church in Edinburgh. As a preacher, he ranked next to Dr. Chalmers, and among many was even more popular than Chalmers, because of the fertility and power of the illustrations which flashed out everywhere in his sermons. "The Gospel in Ezekiel," from which this discourse on "Man Converted" is taken, has been a very treasure-house of illustrations to many young preachers. In 1864 the state of his health compelled him to retire from the pulpit; but as editor of "The Sunday Magazine," he still wielded a great influence, until his death on February 24, 1873.

MAN CONVERTED.

"A new heart also will I give you, and a new spirit will I put within you; and I will take away the stony heart out of your flesh, and I will give you an heart of flesh."—Ezekiel xxxvi. 26.

IT is a happy thing that baptism is not the door of heaven; — happy for millions who, dying in earliest infancy, never pass that way. Dying unbaptized, we hold that they die not on that account unsaved; for who-ever dare hang God's mercy on any outward rite, we do not, and although we believe that this interesting ordinance is also, when engaged in with faith, an eminently blessed one, we dare not. Thousands go to heaven without baptism. Thousands, alas! perish with it. Heaven is greatly made up of little children — sweet buds that have never blown, or which death has plucked from a mother's bosom to lay on his own cold breast, just when they were expanding, flower-like, from the sheath, and opening their engaging beauties in the budding time and spring of life. " Of such is the kingdom of heaven." How sweet these words by the cradle of a dying infant! They fall like balm drops on our bleeding heart, when we watch the ebbing of that young life, as wave after wave breaks feebler, and the sinking breath gets lower and lower, till with a gentle sigh, and a passing quiver of the lip, our child now leaves its body, lying like an angel asleep, and ascends to the beatitudes of heaven and the bosom of God. Indeed, it may be that God does with his heavenly garden as we do with our own gardens. He may chiefly stock it from nurseries, and select for transplanting what is yet in its young and tender age — flowers before they have bloomed, and trees ere they begin to bear.

In the words of the Westminster Catechism, " Baptism is a sacra-ment, wherein the washing with water in the name of the Father, and the Son, and the Holy Ghost, doth signify and seal our ingrafting into Christ, and partaking of the benefits of the covenant of grace, and our engage-ment to be the Lord's." Baptism attaches us to the visible church; admits to *that,* and is its door of entrance; but, while it unites to the body of professing believers, it does not of necessity form any living attachment between us and the Saviour. Let us see what is done in these ordinances.

Years ago a man stood up in the house of God, and in his arms there lay a sleeping child. Dipping his hand into a laver, the minister sprinkled some drops on the infant's face, and over the unconscious creature pro-nounced the names of Father, Son, and Holy Ghost. That child was you. By hands now mouldering in the grave, your father then tied you — so to speak — to Christ. Well, time rolls on, and infants grow into children, children shoot up into youths, and youths change into bearded men; and then there comes another day. A table is spread in the house of God. Like the shroud in which kind women swathed his sacred body, a linen cloth covers the memorials of Christ's death. The broken body is uncovered, the commemoration begins; and, amid the stillness of that solemn scene, with thoughtful countenance, a man leaves his seat, and taking the bread, and raising the wine-cup in his hand, he dedicates himself to the Saviour. That man again is you. And now awake, not asleep, conscious of what is done, not passive but active now, with your own hands you cast another knot upon the cord by which your father years ago bound you to Jesus. You are now tied — doubly tied — yet it does not follow that you are yet engrafted into him.

I have seen a branch tied to the bleeding **tree,** for the purpose of being ingrafted into its wounded body, and that thus both might be one. Yet no incorporation had followed; there was no living union. Spring came singing, and with her fingers opened all the buds; and summer came, with her dewy nights and sunny days, and brought out all the flowers; and brown autumn came to shake the trees and reap the fields, and with dances and mirth to hold " harvest home;" but that unhappy branch bore no fruit, nor flower, nor even leaf. Just held on by dead clay and rotting cords, it stuck to the living tree — a withered and unsightly thing. So alas! is it with many; " having a name to live they are dead." They have no faith; they want that bond of living union between the graft and what it is grafted on —between the sinner and the Saviour. And, therefore, in quitting this part of our subject for another, let me ask, " believest thou?" and if thou dost not, O, let me urge you to pray with the man in the Gospel, " Lord, help mine unbelief!"

Do you say I cannot believe? In one sense, that is true; in another it is not. It is not true in the same sense as it is true that a man who has no eyes in his head — nothing but empty sockets — cannot see. All men are born with faith. Faith is as natural to a man as grief, or love, or anger. One of the earliest flowers that springs up in the soul — it smiles on a mother from her infant's cradle; and living on through the rudest storms of life, it never dies till the hour of death. On the face of a child which has been left for a little time with strangers, and may be caressed with their kisses, and courted with their smiles, and fondled and dandled in their arms, I have seen a cloud gathering and growing darker, till at length it burst in cries of terror and a shower of tears. The mother returns; and when the babe holds out its little arms to her, I see in these the arms of faith; and when, like a believer restored to the bosom of his God, it is nestling in a mother's embrace, and the cloud passes from its brow, and its tears are changed into smiles, and its terror into calm serenity, we behold the principle of faith in play. This is one of its earliest, and — so far as nature is concerned — one of its most beautiful developments. So natural, indeed, is it for us to confide, and trust, and believe, that a child believes whatever it is told, until experience shakes its confidence in human veracity. Its eye is caught by the beauty of some flower, or it gazes up with wonder on the starry heavens; — with that inquisitiveness which in childhood, active as a bee, is ever on the wing, it is curious to know who made them, and would believe you if you said you made them yourself. Such is the faith which nature gives it in a father, that it never doubts his word. It believes all he says, and is content to believe where it is not able to comprehend. For this, as well as other reasons, our Lord presented, in a child, the living model of a Christian. He left Abraham, father of the faithful to his repose in heaven; he left Samuel, undisturbed, to enjoy the quiet rest of his grave; he allowed Moses and Elias, after their brief visit, to return to the skies, and wing their way back to glory. For a pattern of faith, he took a boy fom his mother's side, and setting him up in his gentle, blushing, shrinking modesty, before the great assembly, he said, "Whosoever shall not receive the kingdom of God as a little child, shall in no wise enter therein."

Paul said, "When I was a child I spake as a child, I thought as a child; but when I became a man, I put away childish things;" but no man ever thought of leaving the faith of childhood with its rattle and its toys. Faith is, in fact, the soul and life of friendship. What is a friend, but one whom I can trust, one who, I believe, will mingle his tears with mine, and whose support I reckon on when my back is at the wall? Without faith in each other's friendship, kindness, and honesty, this world would be turned into a Bedouin desert; men would become Ishmaelites; — my hand against every man, and every man's hand against me. Faith is the marriage tie; the guardian angel of conjugal felicity; the jewelled zone that binds society together; the power, mightier than steam, or wind, or water, that moves all the wheels of commerce. Unless man could trust his fellow-man, business would come to a dead stand; the whole machinery of the world would stop; our busy streets would bear crops of grass; and, though winds blew and tides flowed as before, rotting ships would fall to pieces in our silent and deserted harbors.

Leaving the busy city for rural scenes, or setting your foot on board ship, and pushing out upon the heaving ocean, you find faith ploughing the fields of both — faith in the laws of nature, in the ordinances of Providence. When the air has still a frosty breath, and, although cleared of winter snow, the earth is cold and — looks dead as a corpse disrobed of its shroud — it shows neither flower nor leaf, nor sign of life, the husbandman, notwithstanding, yokes his team and drives the ploughshare through its breasts. With confidence in his step, liberality in his hand, and hope in his eye, he scatters the seed far and wide on the bosom of the ground. He is a believer; a believer in Providence — in the laws and procession of the seasons. He has faith; not saving faith indeed, but still true faith. He believes that out of these frosty skies gentle zephyrs shall blow, and soft showers shall fall, and summer beams shall shine; and, looking along the vista of time, he sees golden corn waving thick upon these empty fields, and hears in this silent scene the joy of light hearts ringing in the laugh and song of the reapers. His ploughing and his sowing are acts of genuine faith; and, as he strides across the field with his sowing sheet around him, he is an example of one who, with his eye as well as his foot on earth, " Walks by faith, not by sight."

Then again, sailing as much as sowing is an act of faith. In this rough and weather-beaten mariner, on board whose ship we are dashing through the thick gloom of a starless night, and over the waves of a pathless ocean, I see faith standing at the helm. That man has faith in the needle; and believing that the heart of an angel is not more true to God than this needle to the north, he presses forward over the watery waste in a voyage that may with perfect truth be called a voyage of faith. Would to God we had as strong faith in our Bible! Would to God that our trembling hearts pointed as true to Jesus as this needle, in all weathers and on all seas, to the distant pole! What we want divine grace to do, is not so much to give us faith as to give to the principle or faculty of faith, which we have by nature, a right, holy, heavenward direction; to convert it into faith in things eternal. The faith that sees an unseen world — a faith just as strong in the revelations of the Bible as in the ordinary laws of nature, this is what we need. Let it be sought in earnest, persevering prayer. It is " the gift of God." Saving faith has God for its author, the Spirit for its agent, Christ for its object, grace for its root, holiness for its fruit, heaven for its reward. Accepting the righteousness of Christ, it makes us just; and seeing every sin pardoned, all guilt removed, God smiling, and heaven opening to receive us, it is the spring of a peace of mind which is worth more than the wealth of worlds, which passeth all understanding. May

THOMAS GUTHRIE.
1803-1873.
One of the founders of the Free Church of Scotland and widely known as a popular preacher and editor.

HORACE BUSHNELL.
1802-1876.
As a Congregationalist preacher Bushnell obtained a very strong influence upon a wide audience of ministers, molding theological thought by
the depth of his spiritual insight.

God help us to the confession and the prayer, "Lord I believe, help thou mine unbelief."

We have already stated that while salvation was the one thing needful, there were two things needful for salvation. Having considered the first of these, namely, the remission of sin and justification of the sinner, we now enter on the second, namely, the renovation of the soul as enunciated in the words, "A new heart also will I give you, and a new spirit will I put within you, and I will take away the stony heart out of your flesh, and I will give you a heart of flesh." And we remark —

I. This is a great change. Not that all men think so. Once on a time, for instance, we wandered into a church in this city. The preacher read these words for his text, "Except a man be born again, he cannot see the kingdom of God." And just as at the fords of Jordan, they knew a man's country by the way he sounded Shibboleth, so you will never fail to know a man's creed by the way in which he handles such a passage as that. The preacher read his text; and then, as it were, sat down by the cradle, where his charge was sleeping to rock them over into a deeper slumber. The text, forsooth, was an oriental figure! a hyperbole! pointing to an outward change. No more was needed. In the strong and highly figurative language which eastern nations indulge in, it described the change undergone by the man who abandons a wild and wicked life for habits of decency, honesty, and temperance. Far be it from me to speak lightly of temperance societies, or of any scheme, indeed, that aims at the dignity and elevation of man; yet, according to the preacher, our Lord's language meant nothing more than the change which these institutions are of themselves able to accomplish — a change of habits without any gracious change of heart. Did a drunkard become sober? he was born again; a libertine pure? or thief honest? or liar true? he was born again! In short, such was the style and character of the discourse, that if a poor, hungry soul had gone there for bread, he could have got nothing — carried away nothing — but a stone; and instead of a fish, we saw the serpent's coil, and heard her hiss. The preacher taught that these words were applicable only to the scum and offscourings of the city — the dregs of society — those poor, depraved, degraded creatures who, weighed down by a load of poverty, and ignorance, and guilt, have sunk to the bottom, and to our shame, are left to lie there in distressing and dreadful pollution. So far as any congregation of decent, well-dressed, sober, honest, reputable professors of religion were concerned, that truth had no bearing on them; our Lord —

although he assuredly found in Nicodemus one of this class — did not speak of them; they, happy mortals! had no need to be born again.

You cannot fancy any two things more opposed to each other than that doctrine and ours. We believe that the purest, gentlest, loveliest, most amiable creature that blesses fond parents, and adorns earth's happiest home — one of nature's fairest flowers — stands as much in need of a new birth as the vilest outcast who walks these streets — the lost one, whose name is never mentioned but by broken hearts and in wrestling prayers to God. The best of mankind are so bad that all have need to be born again; so bad that the change promised in the text, and insisted on by our Saviour, cannot be a surface or superficial matter,— any mere defilement of the skin which nitre and soap may remove. Words have no meaning unless this change is a radical reform — a change great in its character, and lasting in its consequences — a change which, affecting not the habits only but the heart, both reaches downward into the deepest recesses of the soul, and stretches forward into the ages of eternity.

Now, I am afraid that some — dreaming, as they slumber, that they have been born again, and so are safe because their conduct is changed, and because, so far as their mere habits are concerned, they are better than once they were — have gone to sleep before this work is even begun. Beware of rash conclusions of such momentous importance. Have we not seen passions, like the fire upon the hearth, burn out and die for want of fuel? Have we not seen the course of vice, like a worn-out machine, stop from the decays of nature — from the mere wear and tear of its materials? Virtue is cheap; vice is costly; and, proving a heavy tax upon the purse, destructive of health and damaging to character, we have seen self-interest turn a man from the indulgence of his strongest vices. Old age cools hot blood. Successive bereavements will in a way break the heart, and some deep disappointment may wean those who have the keenest appetite for its pleasures, from the gayeties and vanities of the world. And, as in Roman Catholic countries, many a cowled monk, and many a veiled nun, enters convent or monastery more from feelings of disappointment than devotion; so, when hopes are blasted, and pride is mortified, and ambition has missed her mark, you may get sick of the world. Alas! all who bid adieu to the ball-room and theatre, and giddy round of fashion, do not leave the circle of their enchantments for the closet, for the sanctuary, for fields of Christian benevolence. As by sleight of hand and necromantic trick, Egypt's ma-

gicians produced a set of mimic miracles that were clever counterfeits
of those which God wrought by the hand of Moses, may not other causes
than true love of holiness or godly hatred of sin work such an outward,
as bears some considerable likeness to a saving change? In matters of
religion, beware of confounding an *almost* with an *altogether* Christian.
So far as it goes, any change for the better is good. We hail it with
hope. It is good, so far as it goes, and good so long as it lasts; but
Oh, let us not fall into the fatal mistake of confounding an outward
reformation with that divine, inward, eternal transformation which is
wrought by the Spirit, and promised in the words, " A new heart also
will I give you."

Leaving the nature of this change to be afterwards considered, let
me attempt meanwhile to show that this is a great change. In illustration of the truth, look, I pray you, to the symbols under which it is presented in the Word of God.

It is a birth.

When an infant leaves the womb — that darksome dwelling, where
it has passed the first stage of existence,— although the same creature,
it may be said to be a new creature, and to enter on a new being. How
great the change from that living sepulchre, where it lay entombed,
nor saw, nor heard, nor breathed, nor loved, nor feared, nor took any
more interest than the dead in all that was happening around it! Alive,
yet how like death its state has been! Having eyes, it saw not, and ears
it heard not, and feet it walked not, and hands it handled not, and affections it felt not. Its state was a strange and mysterious mingling of
the characters of life and death. When the windows of its senses are
thrown open, and streams of knowledge come rushing in on its young
and wondering soul, and its eyes follow the light, and with its restless
hands it is acquainting itself with matter, and sounds are entering its
ears, amid whose mingled din it soon learns to distinguish the sweet
tones of one tender voice — its mother's, and it loves and is loved, and
lies nestling in dreamy slumbers on her bosom, or sweetly smiles in her
smiling face — how great the change! Now, just because the change
wrought on the soul in conversion is also great, and introduces its subject
into a new and delightful existence, it borrows a name from that change.
That is the first, this is the second birth; ay, and infinitely the better of
the two. Better! because in that a son of man is born but for the
grave, whereas in this a son of God is born for glory. Better! because
the march of these little feet is along a rough path between a cradle and

a coffin; whereas, the way of grace, however full of trials, toil, and battle, is from the pangs of birth onward and upward to a crown in heaven. Happy for you if you are heaven-born and heaven-bound. It may be that a stormy life lies before you; but let storms rage and tempests roar — however rude the gale or high the rolling billows — a heaven-born passenger in a heaven-bound bark, you cannot miss the haven. "There remaineth a rest to the people of God."

This change is a resurrection. A resurrection is a great change. Go to the churchyard. Go where death shall one day carry you, whether you will or not. "Come," said the angels, "see the place where the Lord lay." Come, let us see the place where we ourselves shall lie, and look at man as we ourselves shall be. Take him in any of his stages of decay. Look at this compressed line of mould, that by its color marks itself out as different from the neighboring clay; it is black earth, and retains no apparent vestige of organization. What resemblance does it bear to a man? None. Yet gather it together and give it to the chemist; he analyzes it, and pronounces this unctious dust to have been once a human creature. It may have been a beauty, who with alarm saw the roses fading on her cheek, and age tracing wrinkles on her ivory brow, and mixing in gray hairs with her raven locks. It may have been a beggar who, tired of his cold and hungry pilgrimage, laid his head gladly in the lap of mother earth, and ended his weary wanderings here. It may have been a king, who was dragged from amid his guards to the tomb, and sullenly yielded to the sway of a monarch mightier than himself. Or, look here at these yellow relics of mortality which the grave-digger — familiar with his trade — treats with such irreverent contempt. Look at these preachers of humility — at this mouldering skull, the deserted palace of a soul, within which high intellect once sat enthroned — at those fleshless cheeks, once blooming with smiles and roses — at that skeleton hand, which may once have grasped the helm of public affairs, or swayed the passions of capricious multitudes, or held up the cross from sacred pulpits to the eyes of dying men — at those mouldering limbs, which piety may have bent to God — and at these hollow sockets — now the nest of slimy worms — where glances of love have melted, and looks of fire have flashed.

Turning away your head with horror and humiliation, to think that you shall lie where they are — and be as they are — you say, Alas! what a change is there! Ah! but Faith steps forward, plants a triumphant foot on the black grave's edge, and silencing my fears, dispelling my gloom, and reconciling me to that lowly bed, she lifts her cheerful voice, and exclaims, True! but what a change shall be there! Looking through her eyes, I see the spell broken. I see that dust once more animate. And when the blast of the trumpet — penetrating the caves of the rocks, and felt down in the depths of ocean — pierces the ear of death in this dark, and cold, and lonely bed, where I have lowered a coffin, and left the dear form and sweet face of some loved one, mortality shall rise in form immortal, more beautiful than love ever fancied or poet sang. How great the change, when these mouldering bones, which children look at with fear, and grown men with solemn sadness, shall rise instinct with life! Think of this handful of brown dust springing up into a form like that on which Adam gazed with mute astonishment, when for the first time he caught the image of himself mirrored in a glassy pool of Paradise; or better still, in a form such as, when awakening from his slumber, he saw with wondering, admiring eyes, in the lovely woman that lay by his side on their bed of love and flowers. And now, because the change which conversion works on the soul is also inexpressibly great, it borrows a name from that mighty change; that, a resurrection of the body from the grave, this, a resurrection of the soul from sin. In this " we pass from death to life "— in this we are " created anew in Jesus Christ." " We rise with Him," says the Apostle, " to newness of life."

The greatness of the change is set forth in the symbolical representation of it in the next chapter. Seized by the hand of the Spirit, Ezekiel is born aloft, carried away through the air, and set down in a lonely valley among the hills of a distant land. This valley seems to have been, at some former period, the scene of a great battle. There hosts had sustained the charge of hosts, and crowns were perhaps staked and won. The peace of these solitudes had been rudely broken by the shrieks of the wounded, the wild shouts of the victors, the clash of arms, and the savage roar of battle. It was silent now. The tide that swept over it had left it strewed with wrecks; the dead had mouldered unburied where they fell: the skull rattled in the cloven helmet; the sword of the warrior lay rusting beside his skeleton, and the handle was still in the relaxed grasp of the bony fingers. On these unburied corpses the " birds of the air had summered," and " the wild beasts of the field had wintered." The rain had washed, and the sun had bleached them; — they were white and dry. In these grim and ghastly skeletons a doleful picture of death lay stretched out before the prophet; and while

he surveyed the scene, there was neither sign nor sound of life, but, it
may be, the croak of the raven, or the howl of the famished wolf, or the
echo of his own solitary footfall. Such was the scene Ezekiel was con-
templating when a voice made him start. It came from the skies,
charged with this strange question, "Son of man, can these bones
live?"

We stay not to relate all that happened and was done. It serves
our purpose to say, that after the prophet had preached to the bones, he
prayed to Him who — to dead bones, dead bodies, dead hearts, dead
souls, dead families, and dead churches — is "the Resurrection and the
Life." Ezekiel's was the prayer of faith — and it had its answer. How
encouraging to us, when on our knees, that answer! We feel as if
Aaron and Hur sat at our side, and held up our weary arms. Ezekiel,
after preaching, prayed; and there came from heaven a living and life-
giving breath. It blows down the valley; and as it kisses the icy lips
of the dead, and stirs their hair, and fans their faces, man after man
springs to his feet, till the field which Ezekiel found covered with ghastly
skeletons is crowded with a mighty army — all armed for battle and war
— the marshalled host of God.

That was a great change, and not less great the work of grace in
conversion. While the prophet is gazing with astonished eye on this
martial array, where, amid trumpet echoes, spears are gleaming and
plumes are dancing, as, bold in aspect and stout for war, the serried ranks
march on, mark what the Lord said: —"Son of man, these bones are the
whole house of Israel; behold they say, Our bones are dried, and our
hope is lost." Now, is not this the very judgment — the very sentence
— which the sinner often pronounces on his own case when his eyes are
first opened and he sees himself lost and undone? What is the house of
Israel here but a type of God's chosen people? In Israel we see our
state by nature; a state of death; a state in which we are "dead in trespasses and sins." On this account Satan would have us yield to despair.
He says that for such sinners there is no help — no hope. It is he who
speaks in the complaint, "Our bones are dried, and our hope is lost."
Yes, it is he, the father of lies, the enemy of souls. Yield not even to a
doubt, for here "he that doubteth is damned;" but mark God's gracious
answer to that unbelieving, dark, desponding complaint —"Thus saith
the Lord God; behold, O my people, I will open your graves, and I will
put my spirit within you, and ye shall live."

Hereafter, we will enter particularly into the nature of this great change; meanwhile, let me ask, Have you any experience of it? I neither ask when, nor where, nor how you felt its first impressions. On these subjects the experience of saints is very different. Some can tell the time of it — giving day and date, the hour, the providence, the place, the text, the preacher, and all the circumstances associated with their conversion. They can show the arrow which, shot from some bow drawn at a venture, pierced the joints of their armor, and quivered in their heart. They can show the pebble from the brook, that, slung, it may be, by a youthful hand, but directed of God, was buried in the forehead of their giant sin. They can show the word that penetrated their soul, and — in some truths of Scripture — the salve that healed the sore, the balm that stanched the blood, and the bandage that Christ's own kind hand wrapped on the bleeding wound. Able to trace the steps and whole progress of their conversion — its most minute and interesting details — they can say with David, " Come and hear, all ye that fear God, and I will declare what he hath done for my soul."

It is not so, however, with all, or perhaps, with most. Some, so to speak, are still-born; they were unconscious of their change; they did not know when or how it happened; for a while at least, they gave hardly a sign of life. With many the dawn of grace is, in more respects than one, like the dawn of day. We turn our face to the east, and our back to the setting stars, to note the very moment of the birth of morning; yet how hard it is to tell when and where the first faint, cold, steel-gray gleam appears! It is so with many in regard to their spiritual dawn,— with the breaking of an eternal day,— with their first emotions of desire and of alarm, as with that faint and feeble streak, which brightened, and widened, and spread, till it blazed into a brilliant sky.

The great matter, about which to be anxious, is not the time, nor place, nor mode of the change, but the fact itself. Has this change taken place in you? Are you other than once you were? Rather than be what once you were, would you prefer not being at all? Would you prefer annihilation to your old corruption? Some, alas! change to the worse, giving themselves up to sins, which once they would have blushed to mention. Dead to all sense of shame, breaking loose from the innocence of their childhood, casting off the comely habits and pious practices of a paternal home, they plunge into excess of riot; and, borne on by the impetus they have acquired in the descent, like one running down hill who cannot stop although he would, when they reach the mouth of the pit they are borne over into perdition. They change, but, like " Seducers," they " wax worse and worse." The night grows darker and darker; the edge of conscience duller and duller; the process of petrifaction goes on in their heart till it acquires the hardness of stone; and wallowing in the mire of the lowest sensuality, they can make a boast of sins — sins, in regard to which, on the day when they left their father's roof, with his blessing on their head, and a mother's warm tears on their cheek, they would have said with feelings of indignant abhorrence —" Is thy servant a dog that he should do such a thing." What a melancholy change!

In blessed and beautiful contrast to a metamorphosis so sad, has the change in you taken an opposite direction? Can you say, I am not what once I was,— but better, godlier, holier! Happy are you! Happy, although afraid of presumption, and in the blushing modesty of a spiritual childhood, you can venture no further than one who was urged to say whether she had been converted? How modest, yet how satisfactory her reply! That, she answered, I cannot — that I dare not say; but there is a change somewhere; either I am changed or the world is changed. If you can say so, it is well. Such an answer leaves no room for painful doubts. Our little child — watching with curious eye the apparent motion of objects — calls out in ecstasy, and bids us see how hedge and house are flying past our carriage. It is not these that move, nor is it the fixed and firm shore, with its trees and fields, and boats at anchor, and harbors and headlands, that is gliding by the cabin windows. That is an illusion of the eye. The motion is not in them but us. And if the world is growing less in your eye, it shows that you are retreating from it, rising above it, and ascending in the arms of grace to higher regions; and if the fashion of this world, to our eye, seems passing away, it is because we ourselves are passing — passing and pressing on in the way to heaven. Sin never changes. And if what was once lovely looks loathsome now — if what was once desired is detested now, if what was once sought we now shun and shrink from, it is not because sin is changed, but — blessed be God, and praise be to his grace — we are changed. Our eyes are opened; the scales have dropped from them; and the solution of the problem may be found in the blind man's answer — " Whereas I was blind, now I see."

XXIX

EDWARDS AMASA PARK

1808–1900

IN the middle period of the nineteenth century, the foremost exponent of the New England theology was Edwards Amasa Park, of the Andover Theological Seminary. Some have called him the last of the great American theologians, as Jonathan Edwards was the first. He was born in Providence, Rhode Island, December 29, 1808; was graduated from Brown University in 1826. After a few years in the pastorate, he entered upon educational work; and in 1836 was called to the professorship of sacred rhetoric at Andover, and nine years later was transferred to the chair of systematic theology, in which position he remained until 1881. As a teacher of preachers Dr. Park exercised a greater influence than any other man of his time in America. The nineteenth century was a period of theological unrest and change; and it was Dr. Park's mission to adapt the old theology to the modern philosophy,— no easy task. Dr. Park was a great preacher; but few of the sermons which swayed audiences of ministers and thinking people, have been preserved. The discourse here given was taken by permission from the memorial volume of his sermons and addresses, published in 1902. He lived to the age of ninety-two years, dying in 1900.

PETER'S DENIALS OF HIS LORD.

"But he began to curse and to swear, saying, I know not this man of whom ye speak." Mark xiv. 71.

IT was on a Thursday evening in the beginning of May, about eighteen hundred years ago, that Jesus sat down with his disciples at his last sad supper. "'Twas on that dark, that doleful night," says Watts, but in reality it was a bright, moonlight evening. On the next morning Christ was to be crucified, but the disciples did not dream of such a catastrophe. "Whither I go, ye cannot come," he says to them, but conveys no idea save that of a terrestrial journey. "Lord, where are you going," says Peter. "Whither I go, ye cannot follow me now; but ye shall hereafter." "But why not *now?*" rejoins Peter; "I am sure I am willing to lay down my life for you." "Willing to lay down your life! All my disciples shall this very night desert me." "Though all men," Peter replies, "shall commit this sin, yet will not I." "Simon! Simon!" Here, observe, Christ does not call him Peter, Peter the rock, as he does elsewhere. "Behold, Satan hath desired to torment you with great trials; but I have prayed for you that you may not irreclaimably apostatize." "I am ready to go with you *anywhere*," exclaims the bold man, "*Anywhere*, to prison, to death." "Verily, I say unto you, Simon, before three o'clock to-night you shall deny me three times." "That I never will do! *Never* will I deny you! My steadfastness may cost me my *life,* but *steadfast I* will be."

The same profession made all the eleven, but in less than three hours they all disgraced it. No sooner was their Friend seized and bound by the police of the Sanhedrin than they all forsook him and fled. At the very hour when he most needed their sympathy, they demonstrated the hollowness of their pretensions. The stout-hearted Peter ran like a panic-stricken boy. But he could not run far. The remembrance of his confident professions worked upon his spirit, and checked his flight. He turned about and followed the temple guard and their sacred prisoner. He took care, however to keep at a safe distance from the police, lest himself, his *bold self*, should be taken to prison and to death. This resolute, sturdy disciple followed Jesus *afar off!*

It is dangerous for a man, even if he follow the Saviour, to follow him *afar off*. Evil results ensued in the case of Peter, and they will in our case, from walking even in a right way *afar* off from Him who only can hold us up.

This fear-stricken disciple did not go farther than to the court of Caiaphas. He dared not enter that court. Not three hours ago he had exposed himself in the garden of Gethsemane by cutting off an ear of one of the police, and that severed ear was still haunting his imagination, and he was afraid to be seen inside the illuminated palace. Still he dared not *go away* more than he dared to *go in*. He remembered his boasts.

" Though I should die with thee, I am ready to follow thee to prison and to death; I, of all men;" and in face of such expressions, he could not abscond.

How, then, does he dispose of himself? He stands out by the door in front of the palace, at dead of night, shivering in the cold, all alone! and that is Simon Peter. " And upon this rock I will build my church; and the gates of hell shall not prevail against it." " Behold that rock," says Calvin; " behold that specimen of human stoutness! It is all smoke, whatever of strength and courage appears in the best of men."

It is probable that Peter would have found some difficulty in gaining admittance into the court had he attempted it, for the Jews were careful to admit to such a trial no spectators who would in any way obstruct their proceedings. They therefore fastened the front entrance into the palace, and appointed a female doorkeeper to guard it. John, however, by his acquaintance with the high priest, having obtained admission into the palace, felt desirous of Peter's admission. He therefore went *out* of the court, *through* the porch to the *door;* interceded successfully with the janitress in behalf of his brother disciple; and then assured his trembling friend that he might without jeopardy hear the trial. " John meant," says Thomas Fuller, " to let him (Peter) out of the cold and not to let him into a temptation; but his (John's) courtesy in intention proved a mischief in event." Under the auspices of John, Peter comes into the court. John was very young, the youngest of the Twelve; Peter was old, one of the oldest of the Twelve. Think now of that stern and hardy laborer, in all the strength and manliness of mature life, hiding under the wings of the mild, amiable and modest young man and daring to move only as that youth moved. First, the impetuous man is apt to be inconsiderate; even the bold man pleads when death stares at him suddenly; the positive man is often an inconsistent one. Who would have thought that *Peter,* who had just pretended to such constancy of adherence, would have been willing to be a *hanger-on* at the door, and at last fall into the arms of that younger, feebler, disciple who had just now been leaning on Jesus' breast! Why did not Peter take the precedence? Why not try to rush into the palace, as he once tried to walk on the sea? When this same Peter and this same John on the following Sunday visited the sepulchre, the other disciple, we are told, did outrun Peter. And why? Because he was so much younger and sprightlier; and he arrived first at the grave; but the sensitive youth stooped down, and looked in, yet went he not in. And why? Because he was too mod-

25

est, and delicate, and refined. "*Then cometh Simon Peter* following him, and went into the sepulchre," without stooping or looking, for he was all boldness and fire, *and in! — in! — he must* go! In *he went;* caring not what men might say or think. Why on this night is the scene reversed? Why was Peter so childlike and fickle? Why not pursue some straightforward course? Why not either take a stand for Christ, or else take care of his own life? — act for his Master or else for himself.

> "The man that fears to drown, will break through flames;
> Or, in his dread of flames, will plunge in waves.
> When eagles are in view, the screaming doves
> Will cower beneath the feet of man for safety."
>
>   — CIBBER.

At the upper end of the court was a platform elevated above the common floor, distinguished by the insignia of authority. On this elevation, like the elevation around this pulpit, were the priests and elders, wrapped about in their venerable, flowing robes, and sitting or reclining on carpets or splendid cushions. In front of them was their meek prisoner. In that part of the court nearest the porch, where there was no platform, on the common floor of the area, corresponding with that part of this church nearest the porch, stood the guard, and the servants of the Sanhedrin. In that distant part of the court was a vessel of burning coals, around which stood the police, who had chilled themselves in their midnight search for Jesus. Peter, with a hesitating heart, placed himself in that circle around the fire. He loved the prisoner at the bar, and was hearkening with anxiety lest he should hear the judges pronounce a verdict against him. At the same time, he was mortified at the pitiable prospects of the Messiah's kingdom, and trembling lest some one should recognize him as a member of that kingdom. He was well-nigh distracted with these conflicting passions. He seems to have been too uneasy for remaining still, and to have been *constantly changing his posture* — one minute standing up, the next sitting down, the next walking about. His countenance doubtless betrayed his feelings; for such a man as Peter, if we may use the common phrase, carried his heart in his face. He was unfortunately constituted to be a spy in an enemy's enclosure. It was a very suspicious circumstance that a man looking as Peter looked, should have entered the palace under the patronage of a known friend of Jesus. All cannot be right, thought the doorkeeper, and she now comes into the court and gazes steadfastly at Peter's countenance. There can be no mistake. Those quivering muscles, that quick-moving eye, and agonized expression, and nervous restlessness of the whole system had a meaning not to be misunderstood. "Are you not one of the disciples who were with this impostor?" There it is out — out, the whole of it! The officers are near him; he is afraid their attention will be roused; he will be imprisoned as an accomplice; will be doomed to die. And the question comes suddenly; no time to guard himself. And yet he must say something, and say it in an instant. To remain speechless is to plead guilty. "I, woman, I one of them with Jesus! *That* I am not. I do not know what you mean by saying ' them with Jesus;' I am not acquainted with this Jesus." O Peter, who art by name rock-like, why didst thou shrink back from this question of the doorkeeper? The question did not come from the band of soldiers, but from one of the maid-servants. Was there indeed no way for a full-grown man to hold his ground against this woman? Simon Peter, what an omen is this for thy future career! If thou hast run with the footmen and they have wearied thee, then how canst thou contend with horses? If in the land of peace, wherein thou trustedst, they wearied thee, then how wilt thou do in the swellings of Jordan?

In an instant after Peter's falsehood, he went in trouble from the court into the porch. Here he hoped to be alone. No sooner had he entered the porch than the cock crew. It was the signal for midnight. His retirement, however, from the court did not relieve him from his remorse. Nearly two hours, certainly more than one hour, he remained in the porch, the prey of his own corroding thoughts. Must there not be some peculiar reason for his withdrawing with a wan countenance from so interesting a trial? This question forced itself upon one of the priest's servants, and she says to some of the bystanders, "I verily believe that this man was with Jesus of Nazareth after all." Not wishing to utter another falsehood if he could help it, Peter made her no reply, and to aid the evasions, turned his face and went back to the court. The door-keeper who first accused him was confident that unless the accusation were true, he would not be so shy. Therefore she followed him into the hall, and said in an undertone (probably the undertone must have been used lest the trial should be disturbed) to the group around the fire: "This man *was indeed* a disciple!" The men heard her; one of them joined with her, "Yes, 't is true, you did belong to the company." "*Certainly*," they all cry out, "*you are* one of his disciples." What now can the terrified man do? Can he silently steal back to the porch, as he had just now evaded the woman? It is not so easy to rid himself of a company of men. Shall he confess the truth? But he has once denied it, and if he now confesses it he will prove himself to be not only a disciple but also a deceiver. He has committed himself, you see. One lie requires ten more to make it good, and if the lie is doubted it must be confirmed by an oath, and the bold man must not only persist in his falsehood, but also swear that it is the truth. Into a *deep ditch,* indeed, had Peter fallen. But silence will not answer — something must be said outright. "It is false; I am not one of his disciples. I do not know the man whom you call Jesus of Nazareth. I will take my oath upon it — I appeal to God. The direst ends I call down upon myself if I know anything about this prisoner."

The officers and servants noticing the violence of Peter's gestures, and the boldness of his asseveration, could not believe that he was swearing to a falsehood, and they seem to have remained in quietness a little more than an hour. But could Peter be quiet? Was he not all this time straining painfully to overhear what was said, and tossed about with anxiety lest suspicion should again rise against him? Did not the occasional glances at the meek prisoner and at the pitiful countenance of John, work up his sensibilities to painful excitement? Indeed — indeed *this must have been* a long hour of dismal foreboding. It must have seemed to him as if the time would *never* pass away. His conscience made an hour a symbol of eternity. Every person whom he saw seemed an informer against him. The merest whisper agitated him. But though his heart was fluttering, he put on as much of an air of courage as he could, and appears to have been so imprudent as to have taken some part in the conversation around the fire.

But here presented itself a new difficulty. As he was a native of Bethsaida, in Galilee, he spoke in a provincial style, as different from the style at Jerusalem as the brogue of Yorkshire is from the accent of the Londoner. "The Bethsaidans pronounced the Aramean vowels," says Michaelis, "confusedly, and accented the penultimate of their words." They were also distinguished from the natives of the capital by their inability to sound at all three letters of their alphabet, and also, according to Tholuck, by a flat enunciation.

One of the bystanders, recognizing Peter's provincialisms, exclaimed with an air of confidence, "Truly you *are* a disciple of the impostor; for you are Galilean, and nearly all the disciples are Galileans." "Your speech shows you to be a Galilean," cried others; "there is no such thing as concealing it; you must be guilty." "*Did I not see you in the garden with him?*" asked a relative of Malchus, whose ear Peter had cut off in the garden of Gethsemane. "Did I not see you in the garden with him?" This allusion to the garden where Peter had so unfortunately signalized himself, seemed to intimate that the smiting of Malchus was to be a means of identifying the smiter. A cousin of the wounded man was present; and, what is worse, the police were present also! *He knows not what to say.* But he has gone too far to retrace his steps. Irritated at the importunity of the bystanders, he is quiet in his reply. "*On my oath, I tell you the truth. I am not acquainted with Christ Jesus. I do not know what you mean by your questions about him.*" Then began he not only to swear but also to curse. He probably raised his voice louder than usual. He certainly spoke in a rage, and in the midst of his tumultuous asseverations the cock crew. It was a signal for the hour of three. In fear he now turns his eye up to Jesus. The persecuted prisoner had been standing with his back to the disciple, but the uncommon loudness of the third denial reached his ear. The most fearful denial of the three; the one which, with its oaths and blasphemies, would have been most gladly concealed, was heard by him more distinctly than any other; perhaps was the only one which was heard at all. Peter sees what he has done, and with the most harrowing solicitude keeps his streaming eyes fixed on the man whom he "did not know." The poor sinner has suddenly forgotten that he did not know Jesus of Nazareth. He has forgotten to remember that he never saw the Man of sorrows. He has become all at once most unfortunately honest. With a witness he is now detected. Murder will out. Truth will out. Here stands the prisoner, mild, solemn, unruffled. There stands the profane disciple, trembling, restless, terrified, his eye fixed upon Christ, as the eye of a servant upon the master's uplifted rod. What a contrast in the countenance of these two men! As much difference as between innocence and guilt; between the sufferer and the doer of wrong; between an afflicted spirit, comforted from above, and a sinning one goaded on by influences from beneath. This handcuffed prisoner was by his virtue free as the mountain air, but that disciple, free though he seemed, was yet the only prisoner, manacled and fettered by his crime, and thrust through and through by the spear of conscience. Conscience had given to the bound man the liberty of the angels, and had made the unbound man the very slave of himself, of sin, of torture. Just so it is. Conscience is the master of a man after all. This, this makes the difference between the placid and the wretched — this the difference between a heaven and a hell.

It is touchingly recorded that at this moment Jesus turned round and looked after Peter. The most cunning artists have, tried to express on canvas the effect of this look of Christ; but they have laid down their pencil in despair. The sacred historians dared not attempt to describe the look, but simply said that Jesus turned and looked upon Peter. That simple look darted into Peter's memory the scorned prediction, "Before the cock crow, thou shalt deny me thrice." The look was beyond the endurance of the vociferous sinner. Though the hands of Christ were tied, and he could make no rebuking gesture, yet that eye which had once disconcerted the whole company of the Nazarenes on the brow of the hill; that eye which had once unmanned and confounded the money-changers and marketmen of the temple-porch; that eye, which had, a few hours ago, disheartened and prostrated the constables in Gethsemane; that eye which we have reason to believe was at times more energetic than any other human eye, wilts down all the apostle's hope. He goes out of the court with quick and violent steps, in despair. He wept; was softened; he wept bitterly, with penitence proportioned to his sin. He went out and wept; for he chose a secret place, aloof from his evil company, where he might mourn and pray alone. As the doves of the valleys fly to the mountains, all of them mourning, it was the language of his heart, "Oh that I had wings like a dove! that I might fly away, and bewail my transgression." From three o'clock until sunrise, he probably spent in astonishment at his guilt. The stillness of the night and the dark shadows of the morn tended only to excite his conscience the more. "Not six hours ago" (such must have been the substance of his soliloquy), "not six hours ago, I partook of Christ's body and his blood from his own hand. I have committed my sin fresh, fresh from the communion table. My words spoken can never be recalled. I have made a ruinous impression on immortal souls. I have wounded the heart of Jesus. I have pierced his side. It is done. It cannot be undone. I have done it." Turn which way the apostle would he could not make his escape from that eye which had just flung its glance upon him. Like the eye of a good portrait it followed him, and, if he does turn away his head, it still follows him, and lives and burns before him. The eye was constantly speaking to him. "Simon, son of Jonas, you who would never forsake me, much less deny me, when you ought to be with the judges as a witness in my favor, are you afraid to acknowledge me before the servants? Do you not know me, Simon? Did you never know me? Alas, unhappy disciple, Satan has desired to have you that he may sift you as wheat! I knew it long ago. I wished you to know your danger. I told you of it again and again. You insisted that I was in the wrong and you in the right, and yet, Peter, I will pray for you. In all my present troubles, I will intercede for you. On my cross I will make entreaty for you, and when I am dead and you are converted, strengthen the brethren by the experience of this hour."

Oh, that eye, that speaking eye of the Redeemer! No wonder that it will one day cause the kingdom of the earth to wail by its glance. Oh, that, whenever we sin, the same eye may turn upon us, in the same way as it turned upon our brother in guilt! In the hour of Christ's dismal gloom he retained his erring disciple, and will he not much more in the days of his triumphant reign restore the modern backslider? Will he not move toward us while we, as Peter, remain unmoved, and persuade our reluctant hearts to love him, because he *first* loved us? Behold the goodness and the severity of God! Severity how kind! Behold how awful goodness is!

The sin of Peter suggests a few remarks: —

First, it teaches us the necessity of avoiding temptation. It is probable that Peter had never believed until the event occurred that our Lord would be imprisoned, and his mind became confused by the sudden dissipation of his hopes. He was expecting his own imprisonment and death, and resorted to his falsehood on the principle of self-preservation. Some have supposed that we have a right to utter falsehood in self-defense, and have justified Peter's crime because the meddlesome persons who asked him about his discipleship had no right to ply him with such queries. But no man is justified in any circumstances in order to secure any good, to violate the law of veracity. And yet we can see at once how strong must have been Peter's inducement, while in the splendid palace of the hierarch, and surrounded by the proud enemies of the Messiah, to fawn for their favor and to struggle against their resentment. Just so certainly as he went among the officers he would fall. He ought to have remembered that he had been a sailor, and that sailors are apt to use profane language, and that his old habit of hearing, and perhaps of uttering oaths would predispose him to swear if he became excited; to swear without thinking, as familiar words will spring out before we know they are coming. He ought, therefore, to have anticipated the mysterious influence of temptation, especially to wonted sins, to have said with

David, "I have hated the congregation of evil doers; and will not sit with the wicked." How appropriate was our Lord's repeated injunction to Peter, "Watch ye and pray, lest ye enter into temptation." We are not only forbidden to commit sin, but forbidden to expose ourselves to it. Evil companions are more dangerous in the high priest's palace than in the debauchee's hovel. Wealth, splendor and power lend attractions to wickedness, and it is no more safe to associate for pleasure with ungodly men in high places than to put fire into our bosoms. Not at all uncommon is it for pretended friends of Christ when in converse with fascinating sinners, especially when in prospect of obtaining from them some selfish good, to say by their actions as loud as Peter said by his words, " We do not know Jesus of Nazareth; neither his doctrine nor his spirit." They fear to press his commands, to stand upright for his truth. They even blush when their religious calling is alluded to by such men as Caiaphas the judge and Pilate the governor. The sin of denying Christ before men whom we respect or fear is the prevailing sin of the present day; and yet we are lavish in our condemnation of Peter, who denied not for popularity alone but for safety, for life — not deliberately, as we, but under a pressure of strong temptation. Beware of such temptation. Repress your love of popular applause. Is there any fascinating sinner among you? Shun him except to do him good. Go not into his society for the pleasure of it. That pleasure allures unto devious ways. Put a mill stone around your neck, and go down into the bottom of the sea, rather than seek your repose and comfort among men who may tempt you to a selfish and unfaithful life.

Secondly, the denial of Peter illustrates the folly and danger of self-confidence. When this apostle, speaking of his beloved brother Paul, says that in his epistle are some things hard to be understood, he probably had no reference to what Paul said about him that thinketh he standeth, that he should take heed lest he fall. This was all plain to Simon Peter. If the erring disciple had not felt, at first, that he was a rock, and could never be moved, he would not have ventured without precautionary thought into the circle of dignified sinners, nor hazarded his life without imploring help to sacrifice it for his duty. Says Dr. Young:

> "Temptations seize when fear is laid asleep,
> And ill, foreboded, is our strongest guard."

Point to any man who feels that he is in no danger of sinning, and he is in so much the greater peril for the very thought. He is walking on the utmost verge of a precipice, and dreams that he is walking on a wide plain. He is less guarded than if he were afraid; *uses fewer means of security, falls the sooner. He has never disciplined himself to encounter perils by bringing them into clear view. He is bold in regard to distant evils, but yields to them as they approach.* Are we stronger men than David and Peter? Have they not been held up to us as monuments of human frailty, as beacons to guard us against trusting in ourselves? Why may we not lapse as they did? Why not the most conscientious of us be left to falsehood, to perjury and blasphemy and murder? Do you think, my hearers, that you could ever reach a depth of sin equal to that of the tempted disciple? No, you say, and Peter said No before you, just as decisively as you. Is thy servant a dog that he should do this great thing? Yes, yes, my friend. In yourself nothing better, with all your talents, with all your strength, with all your accomplishments, whosoever you may be, your character is written on your forehead, a worm and no man. So far as you and I are concerned, there is no faith to be reposed in us, bereft of the grace of God, but that this day we shall commit a sin which will bring reproach upon ourselves and disgrace upon the church. God alone must be exalted and every man abased in that day.

Thirdly, we may learn from Peter's denial the importance of preserving a habitual sensitiveness to the turpitude of sin. Our danger arises from the sudden onset of temptation. Almost every disciple who lapses into gross transgression, says: "If there had been a longer time for me to reflect, I should not have been beguiled." His conscience was asleep; then temptation surprised him. His resolution was unnerved; he had but few, too few moments to nerve it up. Ere his fleeting, unstable piety could be summoned to resistance, the deed was done.

If he had reflected habitually on the baseness of sin, he would have been prepared for the sudden emergency. He would have had less temptation, and more power to resist what he had. As the enemy, intent on sacking a city, fly with the greatest eagerness to the open gate, the forsaken tower, the weak breastwork, rather than to the places strongly barred, fortified and manned, so our arch enemy chooses to assail us in our most defenceless state, and to finish his work upon us before we collect our scattered armor, and mend our broken shields. The first denial of Peter, that one unpremeditated sin, led him into a labyrinth of other crimes, from which he was not relieved until Jesus turned and looked upon him. Had he thought, had he at first taken into view the evil of falsehood, he would not have lifted up the floodgate; in one moment he lifted it, and then for hours the torrents poured through.

A nice regard to truth, especially in little things, will save us from ten thousand little deviations, which will wind up into inextricable mazes. No sin is so prolific as that of the tongue. One falsehood is the precursor of crimes which seem to have no connection with it. More than any other sin, falsehood should be resisted in its beginnings. Those little falsehoods, those unmeaning, complimentary lies, they deaden the sensibility, they benumb the conscience, they sink the soul into the meanest obliquities. The parent should make his child vow against the smallest equivocation, what Amilcar made young Hannibal swear against the Romans, perpetual hatred. This is the lesson which Simon Peter should have learned before his fall, and he did learn after it, and therefore in the lapse of a few weeks he asked a mendacious man, " Why hath Satan filled thine heart to lie to the Holy Ghost?" and then three hours afterward he said to the woman, " Behold the feet of them which have buried thy husband are at the door."

Fourthly, the sin of one who pretends to be a disciple of Christ brings an especial dishonor upon Christ himself. In the estimation of the world, Peter was identified with his Master. His actions were representative of the deeds of Christ. His words were a specimen of the sayings of Christ. His example was the best means men had of determining the Saviour's merits. When he rushed out to weep, he let all the bystanders know that it was the mention of the truth alone which had made him blaspheme. If then the scholar be so passionate, how must the teacher be regarded? This was the most eminent of the disciples. Is not that a demoralizing school where the most forward pupil is so profane? Reasoning thus, it may be that some around the palace fire that night were permanently influenced against Christianity by the angry look of the blasphemer, and while he is in heaven their souls may be enduring the consequences of his blasphemy. Doubtless Christ was in some respects more grieved at the baseness of Peter's denials than at all the impudence and cruelty of Caiaphas. And he is, in some respects, more affected now by the inconsistencies of those who pretend to represent him than by the scandals of those who know him not. It is our unfaithfulness, my brethren, that creates for the impenitent their most specious excuses and gives them the opiate that lulls them into a spiritual sleep, which may never know a waking. Should we expect that He would be wounded in the house of his friends? Could we suppose that after having eaten of the bread and drunk of the cup, we should so soon crucify him afresh? For this, for nothing more than this, does Christ utter the inviting words, My body, eat ye of it; my blood, drink of it; yea, eat and drink, without money and without price. Is this repeated denial of him all the reward which is due for his amazing love?

Fifthly, the sin of Peter, like that of every other man, was conformed to his constitutional temperament. His temperament, like that of every other man, had its peculiar advantages and its peculiar evils. It allured him to a particular class of sins, and aided him in a particular class of duties. Whenever he is mentioned in the Gospels, it is in connection with somewhat marked and unique. All his acts were those of Simon Peter, son of Jonas. Is Jesus walking on the sea? Peter must walk in the same way, while his comrades remain in the boat. Is Jesus on the shore? Peter must gird his fisher's coat about him, and cast himself into the water. When Christ is transfigured on the mountain, all the disciples are amazed, but Peter must needs cry out, " Lord, . . . let us make three tabernacles; one for thee, and one for Moses, and one for Elias." What did the man mean by this strange request? What did he mean? " Not knowing," saith the historian, " what he said," " for he wist not," said another, " what to say; because he was sore afraid." But he is Simon Peter; he must be forward; he must say something. When Christ is assaulted in the garden, all the other disciples are affrighted, but Peter draws a sword and attempts to pierce the head itself of a soldier, but in his haste, he only smites off an ear. Rash man! It is to be expected that he will be rash also in his sins; that he will do something startling; something unique, something altogether his own. Not one of the converted eleven was so boastful as he, that he never would forsake his Lord; and in six hours afterwards, he was the only one of the converted eleven bold enough to venture on so singular a denial. The truth is that his energetic soul, always full of some one subject, was now full of a curiosity to see the end of the trial. The passion for seeing the end absorbed all his attention, and prevented him from seeing his own danger. And when this danger had at last engulfed him, the violence of his desire to see the end gave way to an equal violence of remorse, as a few moments before he was blinded to all things but that of seeing the end. So, now, he can think of nothing but his crime! his crime! He weeps, not as other men weep, but bitterly. In a few minutes and he could see the end, but he has now lost his desire, and he rushes out from the palace, enveloped in sorrow for his sin, not a persevering sin, but one which in six hours after its commission he forsakes and abhors.

> "The needle which in the shaken compass flew hither and thither,
>   At last, long quivering, poises to the north."

So the heart of the disciple, after its trembling and oscillating turned promptly to his Lord. No one can tell the distress, the aching of the heart, the pain of the bones, the wringing of the whole system in anguish which the penitent endured. He then felt as a humble preacher has since declared of himself, that his very repentance needed to be repented of, and his very tears needed to be washed in some sacrificial blood. He had no excuse to plead. He did not say, as would some modern transgressors, " It was foretold that I should deny Christ; therefore it was certain, therefore it was decreed, and therefore I am not blamable for having accomplished a decree." Neither did he palliate his crime by pointing to the good results, the admonitory lessons coming from it to himself and to the Church — lessons that may come to us this day, and to all men in all time. He thinks of only one thing, the exceeding sinfulness of his sin. We can almost hear him use the strong phraseology of his epistle, which some suppose was suggested to him by the perils of that night: " I am a dog, returned again to my vomit; like a swine that was washed, I have gone back again to my wallowing in the mire." It is reported by some of the ancients that from this evening until his dying day, Peter never heard the crowing of a cock without bursting into tears. True or false, it is a good representation of the strength of his agony.

And yet, after he had sunk as low as possible into the dust, he rose again with his native elasticity. In less than forty days we hear the question, " Simon, son of Jonas, lovest thou me? " " I trust that I do; it is very hard to know one's own heart. I hope, I have a humble hope that I do." This is not his blushing reply as he hangs his head before the man whom he did not know. He is grieved that the question should be asked him. " Lovest thou me? " " Yes! yes! Lord, thou knowest all things, and of course thou knowest that I love thee." Nor was he afraid of publicly defending the man whom he did not know, and did not know whom men meant when they spake of him. Instead of slinking back into a corner — I have now brought such a reproach upon the cause of Christ that it is imprudent for me to preach — he bated not a jot or tittle of heart or hope. He went forward straightway and uttered the anathemas of the gospel against all gainsayers. In less than two months we find him in Jerusalem lifting up his voice to men out of every nation under the heaven, and proclaiming to them intrepidly; "Ye men of Israel, hear these words. (Hear them from me; I have indeed been unfaithful; but that is no reason why you should remain rebellious.) Jesus of Nazareth, being delivered up (but the fact that he was delivered up is no reason why you should take him sinfully, and do to him what your malice prompted,) being delivered up by the determinate counsel . . . of God (but such a determinate counsel as left you free to avoid the sin, if you chose to avoid it), (you with wicked hands), I have done a shameful wrong with my tongue, and you with wicked hands have crucified and slain the Holy One. Say not to me, Physician, heal thyself, for I am going to heal myself, and I charge you in the name of the Highest to make yourselves pure from the blood of this righteous man. Say not to me, Cast the beam out of thine own eye. I have cast it out through grace; and because my vision has been disordered, that were a miserable reason why your vision should continue to be disordered. True, I have done one grievous wrong, but that were a wretched apology for my doing a second grievous wrong, in refusing to exhort you to do right."

And when they were pricked in their heart, and asked, "What shall we do?" the bold man answered as if he had never exposed himself to the least suspicion of a fault, "Save yourselves from this untoward generation. What if I have been untoward, save yourselves from this untoward generation." Soon after this, we find him before the whole Jewish council, and though he once cowered and quailed before their maid-servants, he now, in severe rebuke, cuts the whole Sanhedrin to the heart. Do his former comrades write epistles? He writes also and fills them with denunciation against sin and incitement to fidelity. His crime he did not hesitate to confess and publish to the world. It is the testimony of some of the ancients that Mark wrote his Gospel from the things which had been rehearsed by Peter; that he submitted his Gospel before it was published to Peter's revisal, secured the apostle's approbation of it, and thereby made Peter endorse the Gospel so as to warrant some in calling it "The Gospel according to Peter." Yet Mark is more circumstantial than any in recording the apostle's disgrace. The guilty man himself employed Mark as an amanuensis to make this mournful story known to all men, to the latest age. And yet this same transgressor, in his epistles which he knew would go bound up with his gospel to the future times, hesitates not to exclaim, These men, natural brute beast-spots and blemishes — wells without water, clouds carried with a tempest — that speak great swelling words of vanity — if they are entangled and overcome — better for them not to have known the way of righteousness.

And Peter, Abdias relates, approaching the cross on which he was to be martyred, asked that he might be fixed upon it with his feet turned upward. St. Chrysostom is in ecstacy when he records this fact. "Re- joice," he cries out, "rejoice, O Peter, for you have now tasted the cross, and you could not aspire to the honor of doing it as your Saviour did, in an erect posture, but rather turned upon your head, with your feet aloft, as if you were to walk from earth up to the skies. Behold the man, Simon Peter, the bold sinner, the bolder saint!"

Behold him, as the great painters have shown him, with his head inverted, surcharged with blood, his feet nailed to the top of the cross, his hands to the base. He is just entering heaven. Behold the man!— forward to the last in duty, peculiar to the last in self-denial — that is the man; nobody else; his individuality secure; Simon Peter, son of Jonas, going into heaven as none ever went before, and none, save his own imitators, ever went after him. And when that sufferer passed through the door of Paradise, turning as it did on golden hinges, was he not received, think you, by his fellow saints with an enthusiasm al- together novel? He was the rock on which the Church had been built. He had held the keys of life and death. He had been a leader of the brave band of Christians on earth; had been a valiant, a victorious soldier of the cross; a pioneer in Christian martrydom; had given up his all, the mighty energies of his body, the restless untamable vigor of his feelings, all for the despised Nazarene.

On the Sabbath morning when that Nazarene was raised from his tomb one of the angels said. "Go . . . tell his disciples *and* Peter, that he goeth before you into Galilee." Peter was one of his disciples, but it is the disciples *and* Peter who are reunited in Paradise. There he is, this morning, a bright spirit, his eyes beaming with celestial luster, unwonted even in that brilliant circle; his voice swelling in a melody (and a loudness even) above the other voices which are all a choral symphony, harmonious numbers sweet. He presses up round the throne nearer than others, for he is Simon Peter. He leaps in ecstacy more joyous than others, for he is Simon Peter. He no longer wraps his fisher's coat about him, for he has exchanged it for a white robe. No more does he sit, mending his ragged net, for he was long ago made a fisher of men, women and children. No longer does he sail on a terrestrial sea, but walks as a king and a priest by the crystal river, that floweth hard by the throne of God. No more disputes now with his brother apostles. He was once at variance with some of them, but now he has done with his disputation. " I withstood him to the face," says Paul of him, " because he was to be blamed." But Paul no longer withstands him — Peter is no longer to be blamed. The reprover and the reproved now face to face smile on each other as two yokefellows, different in disposition and yet one, who have passed through great tribulation and their souls escaped as a bird out of the snare of the fowler.

Simon, son of Jonas, lovest thou Christ? No more of these suspicions! No more grief in that ardent soul. We love, we love that noble apostle! Interesting even in his foibles; majestic, sublime in his virtues! God grant that his mantle may fall on us, and that we may strike hands with him in the home of the redeemed! Whenever we are weeping biterly for our sins, then may Jesus turn and look upon us in his mild, forgiving love, and at last may he join us to that glorious company of his apostles, the noble army of his martyrs, and crown both us and them with everlasting crowns!

XXX

MATTHEW SIMPSON

1810–1884

MATTHEW SIMPSON, D.D., LL. D., one of the Bishops and the incomparable orator, of the Methodist Episcopal Church, was born at Cadiz, Ohio, June 21st, 1810. From childhood a diligent student, he mastered the German language, so as to read Luther's version of the Bible in his ninth year. He graduated from Alleghany College, Meadville, Pennsylvania, and in 1833 received a medical diploma. His heart, however, was given to Christ's work, and the following year he became a minister in the Pittsburgh Conference. In 1839 he was elected president of Asbury (now De Pauw) University, Greencastle, Indiana. Nine years later the General Conference appointed him editor of the " Western Christian Advocate," and in 1852 he was called to the episcopate. His residence for the rest of his life was in Philadelphia. Throughout the Civil War, Bishop Simpson did much to strengthen the hands of President Lincoln, and to nerve the spirit of the nation to endure any sacrifice for the cause of the Union. His zeal and executive abilities enabled him to perform herculean labors; but his overtaxed constitution demanded a rest from all work from time to time during the later years of his life. He died in 1884. A magnetic power of personal sympathy, exhaustless stores of illustration from nature and literature, picturesqueness of expression, are elements of his almost undefinable eloquence. No printed page can do justice to his preaching, which derived a part of his power from his peculiar tenor voice and his warmth of feeling. The following is an unedited discourse, reported as delivered on Easter Sunday, 1866.

THE RESURRECTION OF OUR LORD.

"But now is Christ risen from the dead, and become the first fruits of them that slept."— 1 Cor. xv. 20.

A LITTLE more than eighteen hundred years ago, as the light of the morning was breaking around the walls of Jerusalem, there was a guard placed about a sepulchre in a small garden near the walls of the city. They were guarding a grave. Some strange scenes had occurred on the Friday before. While a man whom they had taken from the hills of Galilee and around the little lake of Capernaum had been hanging on the cross crucified as a malefactor, strange signs appeared in the heavens, and on the earth, and in the temple. It was rumored that he had said he would rise the third morning. The third morning was coming, and, as the light began to break in the East, there came two women silently and sadly wending their way among the tents that were pitched all around the city of Jerusalem; they had sojourned all night in the tents, for as yet the gates of the city had not been opened. They came to see the sepulchre, and were bringing spices in their hands. They loved the man who had been crucified as a malefactor, because of his goodness, his purity, and his compassion. They seemed to be almost the only hearts on earth that did love him deeply, save the small circle of friends who had gathered around him. There had been curses upon his head as he hung on the cross — curses from the bystanders, curses from the soldiers, curses from the people. They cried: "Away with him; his blood be on us and on our children!" and on that morning there were none but a few feeble, obscure, heart-broken friends that dared to come near his grave.

A little more than eighteen hundred years have passed away, and on the anniversary of that day, the morning of the first day of the week, the first Sabbath after the full moon and the vernal equinox, at the same season, the whole world comes to visit that grave. The eyes of princes and of statesmen, the eyes of the poor and the humble, in all parts of the earth, are turned toward that sepulchre. All through Europe, men and women are thinking of that grave, and of him who lay in it. All over Western lands, from ocean to ocean, on mountain top and in valley, over broad prairies and deep ravines, the eyes and hearts of people are gathered round that grave. In the darkness of Africa, here and there, we see them stretching out their hands towards it.

Along from the coasts of India and the heights of the Himalayas, they
have heard of that grave, and are bending toward it. The Chinese, laying
aside their prejudices, have turned their eyes westward, and are looking
toward that sepulchre. Along the shores of the seas, over the mountain
tops and in the valleys, the hearts of the people have not only been
gathering around the grave, but they have caught a glimpse of the rising
inmate, who ascended in his glory toward heaven. The song of jubilee
has gone forth, and the old men are saying, "The Lord is risen from
the dead." The young men and matrons catch up the glowing theme,
and the little children around our festive boards, scarcely comprehending
the source of their joy, with glad hearts are now joyful, because Jesus
has risen from the dead. All over the earth tidings of joy have gone
forth, and as the valleys have been ringing out their praises on this bright
Sabbath morning how many hearts have been singing,

> "Our Jesus is gone up on high."

Why this change? What hath produced such a wonderful difference in public feeling? The malefactor once cursed, now honored; the
obscure and despised, now sought for; the rising Redeemer, not then regarded by men, now universally worshipped. What is the cause of this
great change? — how brought about? The subject of this morning,
taken from the associations of this day, call us to consider, as briefly as
we may, the fact of the resurrection of Christ from the dead, and some
of the consequences which flow to us from that resurrection.

It is important for us to fix clearly in our mind the fact that this
is one reason why such days are remembered in the annals of the church,
as well as in the annals of nations; for our faith rests on facts, and the
mind should clearly embrace the facts that we may feel that we are
standing on firm ground. This fact of the resurrection of Christ is the
foundation of the Christian system; for the Apostle says: "And if
Christ be not raised, your faith is vain, ye are yet in your sins; then
they also which are fallen asleep in Christ will perish." If Christ be
not risen, we shall never see the fathers and the mothers who have fallen
•asleep in Jesus; we shall never see the little ones which have gone up to
be, as we believe, angels before the throne of God. If Christ be not
raised, we are of all men the most miserable, because we are fancying
future enjoyment which never can be realized; but if Christ be raised,
then shall we also rise, and them that sleep in Jesus will God bring with
him. And that our minds may rest as to the fact of Christ's resurrec-

tion, let us notice how God hath arranged the evidences to secure the knowledge of this fact clearly to man.

The first point to which our attention is invited is the fact of Christ's death. Were not this fact clearly established, it would be in vain to try to prove his resurrection from the dead. Christ might have suffered for man in some obscure place; he might have laid down his life as a ransom, and yet there would have been no legal evidence of it. God allowed the wrath of man to become the instrument of praising him, in that he suffered Christ to be taken under what was then the legal process — arrested first by the great council of the Jews, and then by the authority of the Roman governor, so that the matter became a matter of public record — a legal transaction. The highest power, both of the Jewish and Roman governments, united in this fact of his arrest, his trial, and his condemnation to death. Not only was this permitted, but the time of the occurrence was wisely arranged. It was at the feast of the Jews, the Passover, when all the Jews came up to keep the Passover. They came, not only from Egypt, but from all the country through which they were scattered. Jerusalem could not hold the people that came together; they pitched their tents all around the city, on the hills and in the valleys. It was the time of full moon, when there was brightness all night, and they came together with safety and security. The multitude, then, was there to witness the scene, so that it might be attested by people from all parts of Judea, and from all countries round about Judea.

Then, again, the form of the death was such as to be not a sudden one, but one of torture, passing through many hours. Had the execution been a very sudden one, as it might have been, the death would have been equally efficacious, yet it would not have been witnessed by so many; but as he hung those dreadful hours, from nine until three, the sun being darkened, what an opportunity was given to the people passing by to be impressed with the scene! The crucifixion was near the city; the crowd was there; the temple worship was in process; the strangers were there; and as one great stream passes on some festive day through the great thoroughfare of your city, so passed the stream of men, women, and children by that cross on which the Saviour hung. They wagged their heads and reviled as they passed by. The very ones whom Jesus had healed, whose fathers had been cured of leprosy or fever, whose mothers' eyes had been opened; the ones who had been raised up from beds of sickness by the touch of that Saviour, passed by and reviled, and said: "He saved others, himself he cannot save." The multitude saw him as he hung suffering on the cross.

Then, again, the circumstances attending his death were such as to invite universal attention. It was not designed that the death should be a private one; not merely a legal transaction, a matter soon over, but a protracted and agonizing spectacle — one to be seen and known by the multitude; but, in addition, that man's attention should be drawn to something to be connected with that wonderful scene; hence God called upon the heavens and the earth, the air and the graves, and the temple itself for testimony. It is said that before the coronation of a Prince in olden times in Europe, and in some kingdoms the custom is still observed, there is sent forth a herald, sometimes three days in advance, at different periods according to the custom, to issue a challenge to any one that dares to claim the kingdom to come and prove his right, and to announce that the coronation of his Prince is to take place. Methinks it was such a challenge God gave to all the powers of humanity and to all the powers of darkness. There hung suffering on the cross he who died for human woe, and as he hung God was about to crown him King of kings and Lord of lords on the morning of the third day. He sends forth his voice of challenge, and as he speaks the earth rocks to its centre; that ground, shaking and convulsing, was a call to man to witness what was about to occur. Not only is there a voice of earth. Yonder the sun clothed himself in sackcloth for three hours, as much as to say: "There may be gloom for three days; the great source of light hath veiled himself, as in a mantle of night, for three days. As, for three hours, this darkness hangs, but as out of the darkness the light shines forth, so, at the end of the three days, shall the Sun of Righteousness shine out again, the great centre of glory, with that glory which he had with the Father from the foundation of the world." It was the herald's voice that passed through the heavens, and that spoke through all the orbs of light, "Give attention, ye created beings, to what is to happen!" But it was not alone in the earth, which is the great centre, nor in the heavens, which is the great source of light, that the tidings were proclaimed.

Look in yonder valley. The tombs are there; the prophets have been buried there. Yon hill-side is full of the resting-places of the dead; generations on generations have been buried there; friends are walking in it, and they are saying, "Yonder is a mighty judge in Israel; there is the tomb of a prophet." They were passing to and fro through that valley of death, when the earthquake's tread was heard, and behold! the tombs were opened, the graves displayed the dead within, and there was a voice that seemed to call from the very depths of the graves, "Hear, O sons of men!" What feelings must have thrilled through the hearts of those who stood by those monuments, and bended over those graves, when, thrown wide open, the doors bursting and the rocks giving way, they saw the forms of death come forth, and recognised friends that once they had known. What was to occur? What could all this mean? Then the great sacrifice was offered. It was at three o'clock in the afternoon when Christ was to give up the ghost. Yonder the multitude of pious people were gathered toward the temple. The outer court was full; the doors and gates which led into the sanctuary were crowded; the lamb was before the altar; the priest in his vestments had taken the sacrificial knife; the blood was to be shed at the hour of three; the multitude were looking. Yonder hangs a veil; it hides that inner sanctuary; there are cherubim in yonder, with their wings spread over the mercy-seat; the shekinah once dwelt there; God himself in his glory was there, and the people are bending to look in. No one enters into that veil save the high priest, and he, with blood and in the midst of incense, but once a year; but it was the mercy-seat, and the eye of every pious Jew was directed toward that veil, thinking of the greater glory which lay beyond it. As the hour of three came, and as the priest was taking the sacrificial knife from the altar and was about to slay the lamb, behold! an unseen hand takes hold of that veil and tears it apart from top to bottom, and has thrown open the mercy-seat, not before seen by men. The cherubim are there; the altar, with its covering of blood, is there; the resting-place of the ark is there; it is the holiest of holies. Methinks the priest drops the knife, the lamb goes free, for the Lamb that was slain from the foundation of the world is suffering for man. The way to the holy of holies is open — a new and a living way, which man may not close, which priest alone cannot enter; but a way is open whereby humanity, oppressed and downtrodden, from all parts of the earth, may find its way to the mercy-seat of God. There was a call to the pious worshipper by voices which seemed to say: "An end to all the sacrifices, an end to all the suffering victims, an end to all the sprinkled hyssop that is used in purification, for One has come to do the will of God on whom the burden of man had been laid."

Now here were all these calls to humanity from all parts, as if to announce the great transaction. While all this was occurring, Christ was on the cross suffering the agony of crucifixion. How deep that agony, we need not attempt to tell you; it was fearful; and yet no complaint escaped his lips, no murmuring was there. He bore the sins of many in his own flesh on the tree. He heard the multitudes revile him; he saw them wag their heads; he remembered that the disciples had fled from him — one followed afar off, but the rest had gone; and yet he complained not. Friends and kindred had all left him, and he trod the wine-press alone. He drank the cup in all its bitterness, and no complaint escaped from him. One left him that had never forsaken him before. " The world is gone, the disciples I have fed and taught have fled and passed away — all have forsaken me." But there was no time until that moment of fearful darkness came, when all the load of guilt was upon him and for our sins he was smitten, that his spirit was crushed, and he called out, " My God, my God, why hast Thou forsaken me? " All else might go — it were little; " Why hast *Thou* forsaken me? " But it is over; the darkness is past; the load is borne; and I hear him say, " It is finished;" he bows his head and dies.

Now there is publicity for the transaction. It demanded public investigation, it received it. There was not only the mental agony united with the agony of crucifixion, but there was the voluntary giving up of his life; yet, lest there might be some suspicion, to all this was added the proof of the fact of his death. When the limbs of the others were broken, and he was perceived to be dead, the soldier thrust the spear into his side, and there came out of that side both water and blood. There is a peculiarity in the sacred writings. A little incident, that seems to be mentioned without care, becomes the strongest possible proof, not only of the fact of Christ's death, but of the nature of his death. When that sentence was written, the human frame was not understood, the circulation of the blood was not understood. Anatomists had not then, as they have now, unveiled the human system; the great science of pathology had not yet been clearly taught to man; and yet, in that sentence we have almost a world of meaning. For it is well attested now that where persons die from violent mental emotion, by what is termed a broken heart, a crushed spirit, there is always formed a watery secretion around the heart. It was not known then to the soldier who lifted up that spear and pierced the body; but so much of that water had secreted around the heart that he saw it issuing forth from the pierced side, unstained by blood, which showed that that great heart had been crushed by agony within.

When taken from the cross he was put in the sepulchre. His

friends had given him up, his disciples had forsaken him; some of them saw him die; they knew that he was crucified, and they abandoned him. They were returning to their former employments; but his enemies remembered he had said he would rise the third day, and they put a guard around him. The Roman soldiers were there; the king's seal was on the stone rolled over the mouth of the sepulchre; they made everything secure. Here again God ordered that we should have abundant proof of Christ's crucifixion. He was crucified on Friday, which was to them the last day of the week, resting in the grave on our Saturday, which is their Sabbath, and then comes the first day of the week, our Sabbath morning, made our Sabbath because of Christ's resurrection from the dead. There came an humble visitant to the tomb, Mary Magdalene; she had been healed of much, forgiven much, and she loved much. Mary, the mother of James, came also and beheld the scenes that occurred; but there had been strange commotions elsewhere. Heaven had been gathering around that grave. Angels had been watching there; they had seen the Roman guard; they had seen the shining spear and the polished shield; they had seen that Christ was held as a prisoner by the greatest powers on earth. Methinks I see the angelic host as they gathered around the throne of God and looked up into the face of Omnipotence, and if ever there was a time when there was silence in heaven for half an hour, it was before the morning light of the third day dawned. I hear them say, " How long shall man triumph? How long shall human power exalt itself? How long shall the powers of darkness hold jubilee? Let us away and roll away the stone; let us away and frighten yonder Roman guard and drive them from the sepulchre." They waited until permission was given. I see the angel coming down from the opening doors of glory; he hastens outside the walls of Jerusalem and down to the sepulchre; when they saw him coming the keepers shook, they became like dead men; he rolls away the stone and sets himself by the mouth of the sepulchre. Christ, girding himself with all the power of his divinity, rises from the grave. He leads captivity captive, tears the crown from the head of death, and makes light the darkness of the grave. Behold him as he rises just preparatory to his rising up to glory. Oh, what a moment was that! Hell was preparing for its jubilee; the powers of earth were preparing for a triumph; but as the grave yields its prey, Christ, charged with being an impostor, is proved to be the son of God with power; it is the power of his resurrection from the dead.

There was Christ's resurrection from the dead. He became the first fruits of them that slept. But to give the amplest proofs of his resurrection he lingered on earth to be seen of men, and to be seen in such a manner as to show that he was still the Saviour Christ. In my younger days I used often to wonder why was it that Mary Magdalene came first to the sepulchre, and the mother of James that stood there — why he should appear to them; but in later days I have said it was to show that he was the Saviour still; that the same nature was there which had made him stoop to the lowliest of the low — the power that enabled him to heal the guiltiest of the guilty; that that power, that compassion, were with him still. Though now raised beyond death and triumphing over hell, he still had within him the Saviour's heart. Methinks I see when Peter had run in anxiety to tell the news, Mary remained there; she could not fully comprehend it; the grave was open, the napkins were there; it was said he was not there, but he was risen. And yet, there was a darkness upon her; she could not fully conceive, it seems to me, the resurrection of the dead. She stood wondering, when she heard a voice behind her which said, " Woman, why weepest thou?" Bathed in tears as she was, she turned round and saw the man standing, and taking him to be the gardener, and supposing that he had taken the body and carried it away as not fit to lie in that tomb or be in that garden, she said: " If thou hast taken him away, tell me where thou hast laid him, and I will take him away. If he must not lie in this tomb, if he cannot lie in the garden, if as a malefactor he must be cast out from man, tell me where the body is, and I will take it away." It was a proof of her affection. A voice said, " Mary, Mary." Oh, she recognised it, and her heart cried out: " Rabboni, my Lord and my God!" and then she would have thrown herself at his feet and bathed those feet again with her tears, but he said: " Touch me not, I am not ascended to my Father; go and tell the disciples and Peter that I am risen from the dead." See the compassion of the Saviour! and then that message! " Tell the disciples, and Peter." Why send a message to him? Because he cursed and swore and denied the Master. The other disciples might have said, if Christ is risen, he may receive and bless us all, but Peter is gone, hopelessly and irretrievably gone; he that forsook his Master and denied him, there is no hope for him. And yet, said Jesus, " Go and tell the disciples and Peter "— poor blackslidden Peter. Jesus knew his sorrow and anguish, and almost felt the throbbings of his broken heart, and he sent a message to Peter. He may be a disciple still — may come back and be saved through the boundless love of Christ. Oh, the compassion of the Son of God! Thank God that Peter's Saviour is on the throne this morning. Not only was he seen by these, but he met with the disciples journeying by the way and explained the Scriptures to them; and as they met in the upper room he was there. When the doors were unopened he came in their midst and said, "Peace!" breathed on them and said, "Receive ye the Holy Ghost." Thus he met with them, and said to Thomas, "Reach hither thy fingers, and be not faithless but believing." Then afterward he was seen by five hundred, and from the Mount of Olives, while the disciples were gathered around him, he was received up into glory. They saw him, and as he went he blessed them. The last vision that ever humanity had of the Son of God ere he ascended to heaven was that of spreading out his hands in blessing. Oh, my Saviour hath thus gone up, and he dropped from those outstretched hands a blessing which falls to-day like the gentle dew all over the earth; it reaches heart after heart. It hath reached patriarchs, apostles, martyrs, fathers and mothers and little children, and, thank God, the heavenly dew, as from those outstretched hands, is coming down on our assembly this very morning. On this glad day blessings are dropping from the throne of God upon us from this risen Saviour. He hath ascended up on high, the gates have opened for him, and he hath gone to his throne in glory.

Let us look at a few of the results that flow to us from these facts thus sustained of his death and resurrection from the dead!

In the first place, it establishes all Bible declarations. It had been predicted that he should not stay in the grave, and when he arose it put the seal to the Old Testament as the Word of God. The prophecy in him fulfilled gave glorious proof that the other parts of it should be also fulfilled as the word of an unchanging God.

Again, in his resurrection we see a proof of his divine power. No man hath been raised from the dead by his own power. All died, from Adam to Moses, with the exception of Enoch and Elijah, who, because of their devotion and acknowledgment of the divine head, themselves became prophets of a coming Saviour. He rose by his own power. He conquered death itself, the grave, and the whole powers of humanity.

Jupiter is represented by an old classic writer as saying to the lesser gods that if all of them combined together and should endeavor to throw down his throne — if all power was arrayed against him — he, by his own might, would be able to overcome them all. What was fiction with the ancients becomes gloriously realized in Christ. Take all the powers of humanity — the Jewish power, the Roman power; the power of learning, of art, of public opinion; take all the powers of earth and hell, death and the grave, and combine them all against the Saviour, and, without one effort, without one single apparent movement — the sleeper lies in death, his eyes are sealed, and, as if all unconscious, for the warning had not been given before — in an instant those eyes were opened, that frame rises, the grave yields up its prey, death retires conquered, and Christ demonstrates himself to be the ruler of the whole universe. He made the earth to tremble, the sun to put on sackcloth, the very air to grow dark, the graves to open, the dead to come forth, and proclaimed himself to be the conqueror of death and hell. So we have proof of his being the Son of God with power.

In that resurrection from the dead we have a pledge of our own resurrection. Christ has become the first fruits of them that slept. You know the figure of the first fruits as understood by the Jews. Their religion was connected with the seasons of the year — with the harvest crops; one of their feasts was called the feast of the first fruits, and was on this wise: When the first heads of grain began to ripen in the field, and there was thus a pledge of harvest, they cut off those first ripened heads and went up to Jerusalem. Before that the grain was not crushed, no bread was baked out of it, and nothing was done to appropriate that crop to man's use until first those ripened heads of grain were brought up to Jerusalem and presented to the Lord as a thank offering. He was acknowledged as Lord of the harvest, and they were laid up as a kind of thank offering before God. They were the first fruits. Then they went away to the fields, and all through Judea the sickle was thrust in, the grain was reaped and gathered into sheaves, and when the harvest was secured they baked the bread for their children out of this first grain. They came up to the temple, where the first fruits had been laid, and they held a feast of thanksgiving, and shouted harvest home. The old harvest feast seems to be descended from this ancient custom. Christ rose as the first fruits, and there is to be a glorious resurrection. Christ came, the first man to rise in this respect, by his own power, from the grave, having snatched the crown from death, having thrown light into the grave, having himself ascended up toward glory. He goes up in the midst of the shouts of angels; the heavens open before him; yonder is the altar; there is the throne, and around it stand the seraphim and the cherubim; and Christ enters the victor and sits down upon the throne, from henceforth expecting until his enemies be made his footstool. He is the first fruits of the harvest, but the angels are to be sent out like the reapers, and by and by humanity is coming. As Christ, the first fruits, passed through the grave and went up to glory, so there shall come from their sleeping dust in Asia, in Africa, in Europe and in America, from every mountain top, from the depths of the sea, from deep ravines, and from plains outspread — Oh there shall come, in the time of the glorious harvest — the uprising of humanity, when all the nations, waking from their long sleep, shall rise and shall shout the harvest home! Thank God! at that time none shall be wanting. Oh, they come, they come, from the nations of the past and from the generations yet unborn! I see the crowd gathering there. Behold, the angels are waiting, and, as the hosts rise from the dead, they gather round the throne. Christ invites his followers to overcome and sit down with him on his throne, as he overcame and sat down with the Father on his throne. In that is the pledge of our resurrection from the dead. Can I not suffer, since Christ suffered? Can I not die, since Christ died? Let the grave be my resting-place, for Christ rested there. Is it cold? The warmth of his animation is in it. Is it lonely? He shall be beside me in all his spirit's power. Does the load of earth above me, and beneath which I am placed, press upon me? Christ hath power to burst the tomb; he shall burst the tomb, though deep it be, and I shall rise through his almighty power. Yes, let the malice of men be directed against me; let me be taken, if it must be, as a martyr, and be bound to the stake; let the faggots be kindled, let the flame ascend, let my body be burned; gather my ashes, grind my bones to powder, scatter them on the ocean's surface; or carry those ashes to the top of yonder volcano and throw them within its consuming fire — let them be given to the dust — and yet I can sing:

> " God, my Redeemer, lives,
>   And ever from the skies
> Looks down and watches all my dust,
>   Till he shall bid it rise."

Thank God! it may be scattered on the wings of the wind — Christ is everywhere present; he has marked every particle, and it shall rise again by his own almighty power. And what is it to sleep awhile, if I am Christ's? To die, if I am like Christ in dying? and be buried, if I am like Christ in being buried? I trust I shall be like him when he comes forth in his glory. I shall be like him, for the Apostle says, We shall be like him, for we shall see him as he is; we shall be changed from glory into glory, into the same image as by the Spirit of God. It would be a great change to be changed from glory to glory, from saints to angels, from angels to cherubim, from cherubim to seraphim, from glory to glory; but, thank God! we shall not stop being changed; for the change shall go on from glory to glory until we shall be transformed into the likeness of the Son of God, brighter than angels ever shone, more glorious than were ever cherubim. We shall be near the throne; we shall sit beside him, for he hath made room for us there. Then if we can calmly look at death and face him, because his strength has been overcome, it reconciles us to parting a little while with friends. A father or a mother may be taken from us, but we shall see them again; they shall not sleep for ever. The little ones that drop from our arms, we can almost see them this morning; some of us can almost feel them in our arms — can see the glance of that beautiful eye, and hear the sound of that little prattling lip; they seem to be with us now, as a little while ago they dropped from out of our arms. We followed them to the grave, and we left them there, where the winter's storm has been howling around them. Sometimes loneliness like that terrible storm has swept over our hearts and left them almost in despair; but through Christ's resurrection we see our children yonder in glory, safe in the Saviour's arms. Their little forms shall rise all-glorious from the tomb in the morning of the resurrection; we shall find them, for Jesus is the resurrection and the life. All this comes to us from the resurrection of Christ from the dead. He died once; he dies no more; the condemnation of death is for ever gone; he sits on the throne of everlasting dominion; his kingdom is an eternal kingdom; and as he died once and has risen to die no more, so when we have died once and gone to the grave, and entered the dark valley and shadow of death, and we come up safely on the other side, thank God! death is passed for ever; we shall then put our feet on the neck of the monster, and shall be able to say:

> "Oh death, where is thy sting?
> Oh, grave, where is thy victory?"

Looking at the resurrection of Christ we exclaim, Thanks be unto God, who hath given us the victory! Such is the eternity of glory and blessedness that awaits us. Thank God for a spiritual body! Here some of us long to triumph over nature. We would grasp, if we could, angelic wisdom; but our brows will ache with pain, our frames decay, our eyes grow dim, our hearing fail. This flesh of ours will not stand hours of painful study and seasons of protracted labor; but, thank God! when the body that now oppresses us is laid in the grave, a spiritual body will be given to us, pure, ethereal, and holy. Oh, what an extent of knowledge shall flash upon us! what light and glory! what spirituality and power! Then we shall not need to ask an angel anything. We shall know as we are known. Jesus will be our teacher; the Everlasting God, the Man whose name is Wonderful, the Counsellor, the Prince of Peace. He himself shall be our Leader. We shall know then as also we are known.

Then rejoice in God. Dry up those tears. Cast away that downcast look. Child of the dust, you are an heir of glory. There is a crown all burnished for you; there is a mansion all ready for you; there is a white robe prepared for you; there is eternal glory for you; angels are to be your servants, and you are to reign with the King of kings for ever. But while you wait on earth, be witnesses for God; attest the glory of your Master; rise in the greatness of His strength; bind sin captive to your chariot wheels; go onward in your heavenly career, and be as pure as your ascended Head is pure. Be active in works of mercy; be angels of light, be flames of fire; go on your mission of mercy, and convert the world unto God before you go up higher. When you go, not only go forward to present yourselves, but may every one of you be able to say: " Here am I, and those which thou hast given me."

XXXI

HENRY WARD BEECHER

1813–1887

A T the head of the American pulpit in the nineteenth century must be placed the name of Henry Ward Beecher,— preacher lecturer, reformer and philanthropist. He belonged to a famous family. His father, Lyman Beecher, was one of the great theologians and religious leaders of his age; three of his brothers were ministers of eminence; one of his sisters, Catherine Beecher, was a forerunner in the education of young women; and another sister, Mrs. Harriet Beecher Stowe, was one of the foremost authors of her time, and wrote the famous story "Uncle Tom's Cabin," which is said to have been read by more people than any other book ever written by an American, and became one of the forces leading to the great Civil War. Henry Ward was the eighth child in the family; was born in Litchfield, Connecticut, June 24, 1813, and was graduated from Amherst College in 1834. He studied theology with his father in Lane Seminary, and was pastor of a Presbyterian church in Lawrenceburg, Indiana, then of a Congregational church in Indianapolis. In 1847 he became pastor of Plymouth Congregational church in Brooklyn, New York, and at once became prominent, not only as a preacher, but as an advocate of reforms. The anti-slavery agitation was at white heat throughout the north, and Mr. Beecher was one of its most eloquent advocates. For nearly forty years his church, seating nearly 3,000 people, was thronged both morning and evening. His sermons were never written in advance, but were generally shaped on the day of delivery; and were taken from his lips by a stenographer. Many volumes of them were published during his lifetime, and were widely read. Two volumes of selected sermons were prepared by Dr. Lyman Abbott, who was closely associated with him, and may be regarded as representative of his discourses. His fame on the lecture platform was as great as in the pulpit; and his voice was heard almost everywhere in the northern section of the United States. In 1863, during the Civil War, he visited England, and by a series of addresses aided in shaping British sentiment in favor of the Union. At the close of the war he was appointed by President Lincoln to deliver the address at Fort Sumter in South Carolina, in April 1865. His popularity as a preacher continued until his death on March 8, 1887.

THE PROBLEM OF JOY AND SUFFERING IN LIFE.

"Her ways are ways of pleasantness, and all her paths are peace."— Prov. iii. 3.

"In the world ye shall have tribulation; but be of good cheer: I have overcome the world."— John xvi. 33.

THE Old Testament is a bright and sunny book, and represents virtue and obedience as bringing forth the most pleasant fruits; and one, in reading it, would be apt to get the idea that a moral and God-fearing man must be supremely happy. The promises abound, to the one side, of obedience; and the threats abound, to the other side, of disobedience. But if one turn to the New Testament, another style of teaching seems to prevail. There is a ministration of sorrow; and it is declared that if a man will live righteously, he shall suffer tribulation. "He shall be happy," says the Old Testament; "He shall be unhappy," says the New Testament. "All his ways shall be ways of peace," says the Old Testament. "He shall take my cross," says the New Testament. "Obedience, virtue, prudence, piety, are a crown of riches," says the Old Testament; "A crown of thorns they are," says the New Testament.

What shall we do between these two differing representations? This seeming conflict of statement runs through the Bible. There are in the New Testament intimations of the same doctrine that breaks out in such power in the Old. There are echoes in the New Testament of those very promises of earthly joy in obedience which so superabound in the Old Testament. Religion is joyful; and yet, crucifixion is its symbol. The way of piety is called *peace;* and yet, we are commanded to put on the whole armour, and be ready, as warriors, to fight at any hour. Are these the symbols of peace? We are to rejoice; and yet we are to deny ourselves, and take up our cross and follow Christ. We are to inherit the world; and yet we are to forsake the world, and not be conformed to it. The Old Testament seems to exclude suffering from its ideal saint; and yet the New Testament sets forth the divine man as " a man of sorrows, and acquainted with grief."

One class of minds goes to these diverse representations, and by elective affinity takes the joyous side, and simply does not meddle with the other. There are men who go through the Bible taking out its promises, its joyous, hopeful, cheering, comforting passages, and elect these things to themselves. They do not see that there is any controversy or conflict, simply because they do not consider the other side at all. They let it alone. As the disciples, when they walked through the fields eating corn, *rubbed the ears in their hands,* to get rid of the chaff; so there are a great many people who take the Scripture and rub it in their hands, and cut out the part that they like, and throw the rest away. Therefore there are many persons who talk about religion as being a life of supreme and continuing joy, and for ever appeal to persons to become Christians because it is so joyful. Well, it is joyful — in spots.

These persons are fairly matched by the ascetic spirits, who see the suffering element in the New Testament and in the Old, and make it the very prime experience of life. They believe in joy: but it is that which is to be found hereafter. The true ascetic throws forward his joy, and he has it only by expectation. Here he has to wear the girdle and the sackcloth. Here he has to play the martyr, in order that he may play the saint and the conqueror hereafter.

But the greater number of men vibrate in perplexity between these two representations. They have a notion that true religion confers supreme happiness; but they are far from being fully happy. They are far from being very happy. And when they look round about them in the church, they see there all gradations, from sleepy good nature and indolent content, at the top of the scale, along down to the utmost disquiet and aspiration made unhappy. But then, they account for it, without any very close reasoning or examination, on the theory that persons are not happy who are religious, because they have not enough religion. This, as a mere matter of fact, is very true; but really, it does not seem to be an adequate philosophical statement to cover the whole meaning and harmonize these two elements of joy and sorrow that the Bible abounds in. This class are nearer the truth than either of the former extremes; but they hold it in an empirical form.

Now, cannot we get a larger view? Cannot we throw light upon this problem of the mingling of joy and sorrow in this world? I propose it, not so much for the gratification of curiosity, or for the sake of exercising the philosophical ingenuity; but because it has become indispensable to discuss such themes. Every age has to make a new statement of moral facts in the light of the consciousness of that age. The old statements held good for their time. They satisfied the yearnings, they met the moral necessities of the aspiring souls of their day. But the world goes on, and new statements become indispensable. If any age gains anything it lifts the next one up to a higher plane; and you must take new observations from that higher plane, and not change the truth, but recast the statements of it, and newly form the theories which cover all the voluminous facts of moral consciousness among men. Besides, it is out of this large view of the mingling of joy and sorrow in life that we shall derive, as I trust, in the sequel, some of the most potent motives for right living, and some of the most comforting views for our weakness, infirmities, and afflictions.

If the race of men were ideally perfect, they would be perfectly happy. The ultimate divine idea in man is that he should be a creature organized to produce happiness in every one of his multiform faculties. Although happiness is not the end and aim of being, it is yet the invariable concomitant of moral perfection. Happiness may be said to be one of the signs, therefore, of ripeness in any faculty. In other words, if the mind of man is imagined as standing in the complete condition for which it was designed, it would be in harmony with universal law, with universal being, with its own self; and it would, under the divine purpose, ring out true and perfect happiness. It is an agent complex, but made to be happy.

Religion, then, regarded as a theory of a perfect state, is right in pronouncing itself a *way of pleasantness,* and a *path of peace.* If a man could but walk perfectly in the way of religion, he would be perfectly happy. The way *is* pleasant, and all the paths *are* peace; and yet, along that pleasant way there are groans and sorrows innumerable; and along that way of peace there is struggle, turmoil, combat, and confusion. But the divine plan and intent, the ultimate state, is a state of supreme blessedness. It is the *teleological* condition — if you have read modern

27

books, and accepted their terminology. The nature of man is one which, when brought fully up to its divine ideal, will produce constant happiness.

But man is not born into an ideal state — into a perfect state, even. On the contrary, he is born farther from his nature than any other creature on earth. Some creatures are born right up to their nature. They have their whole nature at birth. The fly never grows a particle. It never takes on a faculty, nor augments a faculty. It is a complete fly, it is a patriarch, the minute it is hatched. There is no expansion to it. As you go down on the scale to the lowest form of animated creation, you shall observe that, there, all the faculties a creature is to have, he has in their full, plenary power the moment he starts; but you will observe, as you go up in the scale, that there is this distinguishing peculiarity: that as animal nature rises in structure and in scope of being, the space between the birth-point and the full possession of itself is augmented and widened. And how long it takes an animal to come to its maturity, measures somewhat the place on the scale of animal creation where it stands. The lower down you go, the nearer the creation is to perfection when it starts; and the higher up you go, the farther it is from perfection when it starts. And nothing is so far from it as a man. There is nothing so far from the perfection of even his physical powers as a man. Born as a babe, what is a man that neither sees nor hears; that distinguishes nothing; that knows nothing; that is as near to pulp as anything can be? And yet that child is a son of God, and is destined yet, through evolution and education, and sanctifying grace or inspiration, to rise and be but little lower than the angels. But oh! how long the journey from the cradle to the crown! Man is not born into his perfect state. He is born just as far from it, it would seem, as God could put him. It is not an accident, either, I take it. It is a characteristic fact, not to be lost sight of in any moral theory of facts respecting the human family in this mortal state.

Regarding man historically — that is, through the whole race, and the periods of it — he was born at the point at which the animal stops, and moral intelligence begins. To be unfolded from this seminal point, and grow up to the full spiritual manhood in Christ Jesus, is the real problem of historic times. Races of men, savage, uncivilized, animal, began at the very lowest conceivable point. There is no revelation that gives us anything to the contrary. There is no true knowledge that does not point in that direction, namely, that the race originated in conditions just a little above the animal, but with the capacity to go on immeas-

urably beyond them. On the whole, but slowly, with wide intermissions and many retrocessions, and with a vast waste, the race has
steadily grown away from its animal conditions, and is surely reaching
upward toward its ideal spiritual state. As a race, it is going to give
evidence of a far higher condition than might be suspected from anything we can see by looking backward; and you should remember, when
you speak of the human race, that nature does not lie backward. Nature to us lies forward, always. That is our nature to which we come
when we are unfolded and developed by the education of God's spirit —
not that with which we started. For God put us as far from himself as
his arm could reach, when he started us.

Each generation in this race is set back, as it were, and has to do
for itself what the whole race had to do — namely, find its way up
from nothing to something; and from something to the highest form of
development. Every child is born an animal. It is that and nothing
else, literally, at the beginning. Every child has to learn how to control
itself as an animal. The lamb does not. Dropped in the morning, by
night it sports over all the pasture, nimbler, if possible, than its own
dam. But the child that is born awaits its year before it even knows
how to walk. It does not know how to find its foot or its hand except
through slow feeling and rude gropings after it, through months, and
months, and months. A child has to learn from the beginning everything. It knows absolutely nothing. And that which the race is doing
on the great scale, each individual of it is doing in his generation.

It becomes easier, every age, to do it. That is to say, every single
individual man has to learn how to use his physical organization; how
to use his intellectual faculties; how to use his social capacity; how to
employ his moral nature. These things are not made known to him.
They are not set into him like machinery, to work themselves. They
are things which belong to that great process of education which is going
on in the world, in regard to the whole race, and in regard just as much
to every individual of that race. At first it was slow and operose;
but it becomes easier in every age, because each man now born has the
accumulated wisdom and experience of all that went before him. Books
are only another form of giving immortality to the best part of men
that lived hitherto. They are the resultant of men's lives in their
highest forms. All that past races knew, thought, felt, found out,
invented, they passed on down, so that when men are born now they do
not have to find everything out by such tedious methods as men did in

earlier times. A child born in the wilderness is born into a condition where roads are to be made, and bridges are to be constructed, and churches and school-houses and dwellings are to be built, and furniture is to be made, and everything has to be done; but a child born in a civilized community finds thousands of things ready for his use, and is spared the trouble of discovering them, so that he can go on to higher ones. In earlier periods men had to go on, part by part, finding out intellectual, moral, and social problems. As far down as the time of the patriarchs, men did not know any difference between their children and their oxen. Both were their property. It used to be the case that a man wooed his wife with his pocket. He bought her. If anything had been said about *courting* a wife, men would have looked upon it as an invasion of their prerogatives. They were so low down in the scale of development that they did not know the difference between intellectual, and moral, and physical qualities — between an organized intellectual and moral being, and a lower organization of mere material things. Therefore men bought and sold their servants; bought and sold children; bought and sold wives; bought and sold everything. It was a low and undeveloped condition of things. But we have been born into a state of the world, thank God, that is advanced far beyond that — though I can remember when men read the Bible and preached those old doctrines; as though six thousand years' experience had not taught the race anything, and the world had not learned anything. It has, however, learned a great deal; and now, when men are born into the world, there is a vast accumulation of science and art. Vast treasures in every direction meet us. And this abbreviates the work that we have to do. Each individual has to go over the same path that the race has gone over. But the race, having gone on before, has broken roads, and set up sign-boards, so that every individual that follows after goes faster and surer than those who preceded him. And the world is better fitted to receive and educate its children than it was once. Children are not born into such desolate conditions as they used to be — in civilized nations, at any rate.

Then the force of great laws in hereditariness is increasing. For God has brought the most powerful motive to bear on the parental heart — namely, the law that we roll over on our children the qualities that are dominant in ourselves. Where a man lives in virtue, the presumption is that his children will take on virtue easier than if he had not. If you live for intelligence, the presumption is that your children will be educated easier than if you had not. And if a whole generation of men are brought successively through periods of education, their posterity will begin with a hereditary educating impulse which will avail them immensely. It is a law which was revealed as far back as the Old Testament, that *God will visit the sins of the parents upon the children to the third and fourth generation.* And this law is making it easier and easier, in every condition, for men to grow away from their animal conditions.

But whatever progress has been made, it is still true, just as really of the very best as of the most neglected, that men are born empty of holiness. They are at the farthest extreme and remove from perfection. There is not one single man born virtuous and good. We are born negative. Every single person born has the necessity of growing up into Christ in all things. There is no more universal proposition than this: "Except a man be born again, he cannot see the kingdom of God."

This is the truth which I suppose men were feeling after, and which they really, to their own inward thoughts, did embody in their phrases, when they described men as being depraved, and doubly depraved. They were feeling after fundamental facts, which are all-important in any ministration. I should prefer to dismiss that term "depraved," as not according to our later views, and as not best expressing the facts as they exist. I reject it because it is on one side covered with prejudices, and on the other side with misconceptions; yet that which was meant by the term is unquestionably a truth of fundamental importance. It is true that by nature all men are without God. All men are in this sense alienate from God. It is thus also, and in the same way, that men are without knowledge; alienate from skill; ignorant of wealth, of self-government, of everything. They do not know how to think, nor to discriminate, nor how to love, nor how to have moral inspiration. When men are born, in the earlier stages of their lives all the preparations are with them for these experiences; but not only are they born without holiness, but this is only a partial statement: they are born without knowledge, without refinement, without skill, without anything but a pack, packed up tight, which they are to unpack and learn how to use. For a man is a great bundle of tools. He is born into this life without the knowledge of how to use them; but he may learn how to use them, and how to use himself according to the laws of his nature, according to the world in which he lives, and according to the society to which he belongs.

The problem of human life is, how to unfold what God has put into you; how to make it more and more; how to co-ordinate it, so that the faculties shall rank themselves together, and march in organizations; so that it may go away from the animal toward the spiritual, and live more by the power of the spiritual world than by the power of the senses in the material world. This is man's business here on earth. And when you say that a man is born depraved, if you mean that he has no holiness, I believe so, too. He is without God. But then, he is without any knowledge of his own father and mother. He does not know his brothers and sisters. He is ignorant of his neighbors. He has no consciousness of his own nation. Spread before the child the country's flag, the sight of which thrills us with such patriotic emotions, and what does he see in it but a plaything? It has no associations to him. He has no knowledge concerning it. Everything is to be learned. This is the organic decree. God did not make men perfect. He made them pilgrims after perfection.

As I have said, men are born with all the faculties of reason; but not with knowledge. That they are to find. Men are born with social natures; but not with social loves and refinements of experience. These they are to work out. Men are born with moral sense; but not with knowledge of its fruits, its inspirations, its various experiences. It is the business of their life to find out these things.

To teach all this vast lore of experience, God has established what I may call five schools. The first school into which a man is born is the school of the family, where parental love is the schoolmaster. But he is just as much born into a school of the material world. And it is a part of the teaching of the family to induct the child into a knowledge of his physical organization, and into a knowledge of physical actions, so that he shall learn what is good and bad; what is sharp and blunt; what is high and low; what is water and fire. It is a part of our early experience to learn how to live according to the law of the material globe.

Then comes the school of civil society — or, organized social life on a large scale. Men have to learn that. And in learning that, they learn what are civil laws; what are the rights of their fellow-men; and what are the modes of getting along with men. In learning it, they are still further to develop the faculties, and still further to bring them into subjection to the laws of organization.

Then comes the school of business, or creative industry, which some men seem to think is a necessary evil, which a man has to run into in order to get a mouthful of bread, and then run out of in order to be pious! But the great kingdom of work is a part of God's church on earth. It is there that God teaches us moral ideas. We learn a part of our lesson in the family; a part of it in the material world, dealing with matter; a part of it in civil society, dealing with the laws and the interests of men; and a part of it from the creative force exerted upon matter, which is industry. But all this is not something exceptional, and a necessary evil in this life. It is a department of that one great school in which men are to find themselves.

Then comes the school of the church, which is the last, and in which men learn moral and spiritual truths. Some of these things men have learned, if they have been brought up rightly, before the church reaches them; but here is the culminating influence in God's grace working through the truth as it is in Christ Jesus, and sent home by the inspiration of the Holy Ghost. This is the highest department of the great university of life. Beginning in the family, and going through the physical world, through the civil world, and through the industrial world, up into the moral or spiritual world — this is the unity of that preparation which God has made by which men, born at nothing, shall learn how to take out the store and treasure of their faculties, and educate them, develop them, co-ordinate them, control them, carry them up from step to step, until they are made perfect men in Christ Jesus.

These are simple facts that I have been stating — not theories. Men are born just as I have said they were. They are educated just as I have said they were. I believe they are facts that are not accidental, but that indicate the divine mind. At any rate, it is the best light I can get at present, in my age. Looking at the difficulties which men have to contend with; looking at the evils which beset them on every side, I see no other theory on which you can explain these unquestionable facts in respect to the way in which men come into this world, and in respect to the way in which the world takes care of them, develops them, and prepares them.

It is in the light of such a development that we see the relation between sorrow and joy in the Christian scheme. Joy is an attribute of man's nature drawn out and perfected. It abides with him. Its perfect form will be the fruit of his highest state. He is living toward joy, if he is living toward development. If he is rising higher and higher, he is becoming what God meant every nature should become — a perfect enginery for the production of manifold joys in sublime harmonies. This is that which we are all seeking. This is that which the race will ultimately reach.

But sorrow, on the other hand, is that conflict which every person experiences as he is endeavoring to learn. Sorrow is the non-observance of laws, whether it be through ignorance or momentary wilfulness. Sorrow is the conflict of men on the way to themselves. It is the conflict of men with their lower nature, when they are attempting to take possession of it and control it by their higher faculties. It is the participation of each individual with something of the sadness which belongs to the whole economy in which he lives. In other words, it is a part of his social liability. It is the incident of growth from a lower to a higher state. When men are seeking themselves, and do not know how to walk, and fall down, that is *hurt,* if it is bodily; and if it is moral, it is *suffering*. If a child puts its hand in the fire, it is *pain;* and it is pain that will keep the child from ever putting its hand there again. He has learned something. If a man, being selfish, and having once suffered from the results of selfishness, were as wise as the child that puts its hand in the fire, he would avoid selfishness in the future; but that is not the way of the world. A man, walking along a path at night, as long as it is smooth feels that he is in the path; but by and by, falling into some quag, he says, " What! quags in good roads?" And then he says, " Oh! no, I am not in the road. The road is pleasant and easy; and if I get my feet into the mud, it is because I am not in the road."

What, then, is the fact but this: that if a man only knows the right path, he goes on without suffering, and that if he suffers, it is because he is not in the right path. Suffering is God's regent of the universe, saying, " The way is a way of pleasantness, and all its paths are peace; and therefore when you suffer it is because you are out of the way." So there is something to be learned in this direction. When the boys whisper and laugh, instead of studying their lessons, there comes a gentle rap, not hurting them much, which says, " The teacher is behind you, and you are not doing your duty;" and they gather up. And so there are inconveniences in life rapping us men, and saying, You are not doing your duty. But when boys are ugly and malicious and quarrelsome, and they are hitting each other, and pinching each other, and pinning each other, the schoolmaster comes behind them with a most vehement souvenir, that teaches them more — namely, that they are wicked, and are doing wrong, first, in neglecting their lessons; and, secondly, in inflicting pain unnecessarily upon each other. And in life the things that men suffer are testimonies of the ever-watchful Master that is behind you, and saying, " You are neglecting your duty, and you are doing wrong." The way in which you should walk is a pleasant way, and suffering, in this world, is nothing but that necessary chastisement and pain which God has infixed throughout the whole divine scheme, in order to keep men from wrong paths, and keep them going toward that higher state where they are to emerge into immortality and glory.

Therefore it is that the two ideas are perfectly harmonious and consistent. You might call suffering the labor-pain of virtue, being born into a higher state out of a lower. It is not a thing desirable in itself; but instrumentally it is desirable, as a motive, as a spur, as an incitement, as an inducement, in men, to rise to a higher state.

If this be so, I remark,

1. The search for the origin of evil, about which so much has been thought and said, is a mistaken search, in the direction in which men are looking for it. When men have squared the circle, and found the philosopher's stone, and discovered perpetual motion, then they will find this too. But they will not find any of them. They are, all four of them, mistakes. The reason why God made seeds instead of perfected fruit is the only question. Why did God make men at the bottom, and then say to them, " Climb clear up to the top? " Evil is nothing in the world but a part of the divine system by which we are to be unfolded. And if men were made to find their way up from nothing to something, through various gradations, and pain and suffering are but incitements and pressures to help them on, the question is not, " What is the origin of evil? " for the origin of evil is but another name for the origin of suffering. And suffering is not evil. You might as well ask what is the origin of a man's suffering when he is learning to drive nails, and he hits his thumb instead of the nail, as to ask what is the origin of evil. He does not know how to strike straight: that is the origin of it. What men call " evil " originates from their not knowing to carry their faculties. They were born without knowing it.

Here is a man with forty plenary powers in him, every one of which is a prince, every one of which is seeking development, and every one of which is left to find out, by experiment, its own nature, and capacity, and design. He was born without knowledge, for the most part of himself. And, do you ask, what was the origin of his mistakes? Simply the fact that he did not know, and was born not to know. What is the reason that a man who is lost in the woods travels, in finding his way out, ten miles, when he might get out by travelling one mile? Because he did not know the road, and he kept wandering about here and there to find it. And so men are wandering about in life to find themselves. And what are called sins are to be limited to those wrong things which men do on purpose. The rest are infirmities which God looks compassionately upon, and sorrows over. He punishes sins which are in the nature of purposed wrong-doing, and pities the infirmities which men fall into, not knowing how to do any better, or only partially knowing how to do better.

Let us not, therefore, look about and say, "How does evil get into the world?" for that question will only be answered when you can tell why God preferred to make men as he did make them, the sum of nothing, with the capacity to develop into infinite power in infinite directions. It pleased him to do it.

2. We see, from the statements that have been made, if they be accepted, what is the true and proper meaning of *self-denial*. One of the earliest lessons that a man learns is to be an animal. He learns the animal functions first. He learns the faintest animal relations of truth. Matter is the thing that first addresses itself to him. A child learns the physical globe before it even learns its mother. The mother is learned through the child's material wants. The first education of every human being in this world is to teach him to be a little animal. But very soon there begin to be conflicting claims in the child. And now comes the question of priority. And every once in a while there will come a time when there will arise a little conflict in the child's mind as to which shall rule, those faculties that represent the affections, or those that represent the appetites, and when one or the other must prevail. And if the child triumphs, and the affections prevail, that is self-denial. It is affection saying to passion, "You are lower than I, and you must step down there and wait for me." That is self-denial. It is a higher faculty making a lower one keep down, and know its place.

Then, the moment the affections begin to get strong, there are moral sentiments which rise up and assert their authority over the affections. Questions present themselves where persons are called to decide whether they will follow their affections or their duty. Duty rises in every soul, and says, " I am higher than affection." And if there is a question as to which shall govern, duty must govern, and not affection. And affection experiences suffering. And this is self-denial. It is self-denial of a lower feeling for the sake of giving liberty and power and influence to a higher one.

Every time a true act of self-denial takes place, two things happen: first, a lower feeling suffers, because it cannot have its own way: and, secondly, a higher feeling rejoices, because it has its own way. There are two feelings that enter into every act of self-denial: one of sorrow, because a lower faculty is brought into subjection; and the other of joy, because a higher faculty is brought into the ascendancy.

Now see how this clears away all the absurd notions that have prevailed in this world about the mission of pain and suffering. Many persons say, " I ought to deny myself." They are going along in life very happily, and do not perceive any particular reason for changing their course, but they have read that a man must deny himself, and they say to themselves, " What shall I deny myself in? I wish I knew how I could deny myself." And they go to work and invent modes of self-denial. One person says, " I will not eat any butter." So he denies himself. Another person says, " I enjoy a good coat as well as anybody else; but, being a Christian, my duty is to deny myself; so I will get linsey-woolsey and let the broadcloth go." That is his self-denial. Men have no idea of what self-denial is. They are floundering after something, they do not know what. They are searching for an opportunity for self-denial, not understanding that to deny one's self is simply to put down a lower feeling, in order to give a higher feeling ascendancy. You have an opportunity for self-denial every time you see a man. If you meet a man that you dislike, put down that hateful enmity of soul. That will be self-denial. Every time you see a person in misery, and you shrink from relieving him, then relieve him. That will be self-denial. Do not say, " I am so busy I cannot stop to see that little curmudgeon in the street;" but stop. God says, " You are all brethren;" and, ragged and dirty as that child is, it is related to you in the larger relationship of the eternal world; and you must not be so busy as not to have time to care for him. If your selfishness says, " I cannot stop; I do not want to be plagued with these little ruffians of the street," and a diviner element in the soul says, " Stop! neither business nor pleasure has any right here: religion and humanity and duty must rule here:" and if you obey the dictates of that divine element, then you deny yourself. You put down mean indifferences and pestiferous selfishness for the sake of giving a royal tone of joy to your upper nature, do you not?

"In honor preferring one another." This injunction suggests an ample field for self-denial. You that invent sack-cloth and hair-mittens to rub yourselves with, so as to get up self-denial and suffering; when you sit and hear your brother in the law, of the office next to yours, praised, what is it that makes you hold your breath? "Oh!" you say, "that is envy. I ought not to feel so." There is a blessed struggle. What is born out of it? If you rise superior to that comparison between yourself and him, and say, "I thank God that he is esteemed more than I am; I love and honor him, and I am glad to see his name go up, and it does not hurt me to have his name go above mine," then there is a glorious self-denial. What are the elements of it? Why, putting down your own selfishness, and putting up the brotherhood feeling.

No man, then, need hunt among hair-shirts; no man need seek for blankets too short at the bottom and too short at the top; no man need resort to iron seats or cushionless chairs; no man need shut himself up in grim cells; no man need stand on the tops of towers or columns, in order to deny himself. There are abundant opportunities for self-denial. If a man is going to place the higher part of his nature uppermost, he will have business enough on hand. He will not need to go into the wilderness to deny himself. And, by the way, to go alone into the wilderness is no safeguard against evil. A man never went into the wilderness in this world that the devil did not go with him. In the city, the devil has so much to do that he cannot pay much attention to any one man; but in the wilderness he has you! It is a bad plan to keep by yourself too much. When you are under wholesome excitements in life, when you are made to vibrate and respond to genial influences, these things help you on toward self-denial.

It is not meant that a man should suffer because there is any good in suffering, in and of itself. Suffering is merely incidental. The good lies in the struggle in you between a higher and a lower feeling; and self-denial is the triumph of the higher feeling over the lower. Therefore, every man that suffers when he denies himself shows that the upper feeling is yet faint.

A man takes a musical instrument and undertakes to bring up one part of it, so that it shall sound louder than any other part. The moment he brings it up so that it sounds a little louder than the others, people say, "Yes, I think I do hear that upper note;" but it is so faint that a person has to put his hand to his ear to hear it. But by and by the man works the instrument so that out rolls this upper note so clearly that, although the under notes are there, everybody says, "Ah! now it has come out; now I hear it; it is all right now." And a man that denies himself in the truest Christian way, does it so that the joy of the upper feelings rolls clear over the pain and suffering of the lower feelings. Where this does not take place, the self-denial is very imperfect,

3. In the line of this discussion we see, too, the foreshadowings of the cross in human life. In the whole line of development we see, in this world, the great principle of love, which is divine, because it did not spring from anything that we can see, but from the original creative decree. The principle of love and the nature of love were certainly as directly from God, when it was infixed in the human composition, as anything that we can imagine. If you will watch the development of love as it takes place between the parent and the child, even in the savage state, you will see that there is infixed in the nature of human love a tendency to bear, not for one's self, but for others; to bear their troubles and cares.

The first experience we have of self-abnegation, joyful and beautiful, is where the mother bears for her child. It is not merely the love of recipiency. The love that men mostly know in their adult life is the susceptibility of being played upon by others; of being made happy by the intercourse of other natures. That is a poor love. The nature of the truer love is to exercise the parental instinct. We see *substitution* in it. If the child does wrong, the parent takes the smart, and lets the child learn a lesson — that is, to some extent, for this cannot go to all lengths. Love attempts to substitute the experience of older hands and bodies and minds for the inexperience of younger ones, so that the child shall not suffer so much as it would if it had none to take care of it. Nay, we see *imputation* in parental love; so that the parent is all the time accounting with the child as if it had virtues that it has not. The parent, for instance, persuades the child to do things which the child would not do of its own accord, and gives it large credit and large praise for that which the parent incited and fixed in the child.

4. We see love suffering in life. Although the various developments of love are imperfect, yet we see the sphere of these qualities widening and widening, until we see love in all the organisms of

society, as existing in the intimate relationships of friend and friend, of parent and child, and of brothers and sisters. We see in love the over-shadowings of that sublime disclosure which was made on the cross, of divine love. God so loved the world that he gave his Son to die for it. And what is revealed by that fact? That God had learned to do it? No; but that the faint snatches which we see of such a nature of love as is manifested in the family, are parts of the revelation of divine truth in nature, which was more gloriously revealed in the person of Jesus Christ. Parental love is John Baptist to the atoning love of Christ Jesus. And though it is very imperfect, a mere scratch, simply an out-line, shorthand, as it were, yet it is sufficient to prepare us to under-stand, and assist us in understanding, when the disclosure is made of it, that greater love in Christ Jesus, who gave himself, not only that he might redeem the world, but that he might redeem every individual in the world, making all men at last pure and spotless, when he shall present them before the throne of his Father in eternal glory.

This power, therefore, of perfectness to take on suffering, for the sake of shielding from suffering those that are in a lower sphere, is the secret of the Cross. The hidden mystery of Christ's sacrifice and death is not alone taught us in the New Testament. The expectation for it is created when we look out into nature and society. And when, afterward, we go back to the word of God, it is susceptible of no other interpretation but this — that God does bear the sins of men, and carry their sorrows; and that when he puts men into a world where there are pain and sorrow, and shortcomings, and infirmities, and sufferings, he does not leave them alone. He himself dwells in the household. And as a parent that is bringing up a child inflicts suffering and permits suffering to be inflicted upon the child, for his good, watching his prog-ress and studying to meet his wants all the way up through his educa-tion; so God is the educator of time and the world, and by suffering he develops men to that perfectness which at last shall be without suffering in the eternal sphere.

5. In the light of these disquisitions, they that are in trouble or in sorrow must learn the true way out of it. There is but one way out of suffering, and that way is upward. All other ways are adjourning it, or preparing for its recurrence in even greater measure. When men suffer in any of the vicissitudes of life, and go down toward their pas-sions as a refuge, or go out laterally, as it were, to hide themselves in amusements, their sufferings are like the blossoms of an apple-tree that

fall without fruit, multitudes of them. No lesson is learned, no victory is gained, no strength is attained. But when a man suffers, and accepts the suffering, and says, "It is a messenger of God sent to teach me to rise higher in that part of my being in which I am living; to strengthen that which is good over against that which is bad: I must think higher; I must live better; I must be nobler; I must commune more with God; I must come nearer to the invisible and eternal world; the farther I go down toward the animal, the more I must suffer; and the higher I rise toward the spiritual, the less shall I suffer"— when a man does this, he has learned the lesson that every one should learn. If God has sent afflictions upon you, whether they come from yourself or from your social liabilities — from your connection one with another — the golden gate that leads into the way which is pleasant, and into the paths which are peace, is an upward gate. And the nearer a man can get to God, the less anything on earth can afflict him. That is one reason why prayer, even when men in their own consciousness are not Christians, is so soothing and quieting. In the act of lifting the soul up above its passions into the conscious presence of the Eternal, though it be blind, though it be the pleading of a child with an unknown Father, there is something that lifts a man in the right direction. But how much more when God is dearer to the soul than all the contents of earth; when the soul can say, "There is none on earth like thee, and there is none upon the earth that I desire beside thee!" Communion with God is prayer — oh! what a refuge out of trouble! Oh! what a pavilion in which God does hide men, according to his promise, until the storm be overpast! Out of sorrow by going down? Ah! that is bad comfort. Out of sorrow by resorting to stoical philosophy? It only hardens and toughens the fibre of feeling. Out of the mere erosion of suffering? That is not a manly comfort. Oh! lift up your head. Find peace and comfort by giving flight to the higher elements of your highest nature: love, and faith, and hope, and joy in the Holy Ghost. There is the divine prescription. And there never was a trouble so grievous that there was not, in this joy in the Holy Ghost, assuagement and peace. There never was a heart so smitten that there was not restoration in true Christian faith.

When the rude ox or the fierce wind has broken off the shrub, and laid it down on the ground lacerated and torn, it lies there but a few hours before the force of nature in the stem and in the root begins to work; and soon new buds shoot out; and before the summer shall have gone round, the restorative effort of nature will bring out on that shrub other branches. And shall the heart of a man be crushed, and God send sweet influences of comfort from above to inspire it, and that heart not be able to rise above its desolateness?

What sorrow is there that has God's liberty to ride you as a despot? What bereavements did God ever give liberty to be your tyrant? What laws did God ever give leave to come to you and say, "I own you?" You are God's, and no one else's. And there is no suffering, no sorrow, no human experience, that you have not the power to rise above, to subdue — nay, to harness to you, and make carry you. For sufferings rightly understood are, as it were, God's courses harnessed to your chariot to bear you up. Horses and a chariot of fire did the prophet have to take him to heaven; but he is not the only one that went to heaven in a chariot of fire. Thousands are riding in chariots of fire. Sorrow is the fire; and troubles are those coursers by which myriads of men are being drawn, in that flaming chariot, heavenward.

Do not understand, then, that suffering or sorrow are incidental or accidental. They are all of them divine. Rightly understood and rightly used, sorrow is to the man what the whetstone is to the razor. You are made sharper by it. Without it you very soon lose your edge, and cut dull. With sorrow men never forget. Sorrow is the trumpet that sounds through the camp when the enemy is near, that you may be aroused and ready to meet your adversary. Sorrow is that friendly blow by which you, sleeping in the midst of suffocating fumes, are aroused. For God does not mean that you shall perish. He loves you too well. Ah! is there not comfort in the declaration, "Whom I love I chasten, and scourge every son whom I receive"? "You had children," says God, "and you chastised them for your own pleasure; but I, that they may be partakers of my holiness." There is the Gospel; the whole of it.

Blessed are they that have sorrow. Sad are they that are without it. He must be a very good man that has lived in this world and has not had any trouble. Steamships do not care whether the wind blows or not, because they have internal motive forces; but we are not steamships, and we need troubles as winds to bear us on. We make no voyages without troubles, unless we are very good indeed.

Blessed be God, then, that gives us sorrow upon sorrow, trouble upon trouble, stroke upon stroke. These things are so many knockings at the gate of heaven, saying, "Open, Lord." Let heaven's gate fly open when they fall on you.   See to it that they take you to God.   See to it that they take you to higher manliness and to God.   Never in sorrow be sorry for anything which you have done that was right, and pure, and true.   Never in sorrow say, "Oh! that I had the leeks and onions of Egypt, and were not obliged to eat this food of the desert which I so much loathe."   When God is taking you through the wilderness toward the promised land, never look back, nor shrink.   Bear your trouble, and say, "Strike, God, and strike again, and as often as needful; do anything to me and take anything from me; but let me have thee, and life, and life eternal."

28

XXXII

EDWIN HUBBELL CHAPIN

1814–1880.

IN years when denominational lines were drawn far more strictly than they are now, when " orthodox " belief was regarded as all important, one minister in New York was able to make an unpopular church popular, and to win admiration and honor from members of all the churches. That minister was Edwin Hubbell Chapin, D.D., pastor of the Fourth Universalist church, which was named " The Church of the Divine Paternity." Dr. Chapin was born in Union Village, Washington County, New York, in 1814. His education was only in the grammar school; but nature and study made him one of the most finished orators of his age. His ministry began in 1837 at Richmond, Va., over a church of mingled Unitarians and Universalists. Afterward he preached in Charlestown, Mass. In 1848, he came to New York, and soon made his church famous. He was the orator in the pulpit, but his oratory was not merely that of rhetorical language or of a rich voice,— both of which he possessed in a remarkable degree,— but also the eloquence of strong, persuasive thought and warm sympathy. While his pulpit was in New York, his voice was heard on the lecture platform almost everywhere, for those were the halcyon days of the lecture-course, when even villagers could hear John B. Gough, Wendell Phillips, Henry Ward Beecher, and Edward H. Chapin, the four most popular lecturers of the generation. Chapin was a man of massive frame, corpulent in his later years, but to the last vigorous in his manner, and a tireless worker. He became the editor of " The Christian Leader," the most widely-circulated Universalist paper, in 1872; issued volume after volume of sermons and lectures, and was active in the reforms and philanthropies

EDWIN HUBBELL CHAPIN.
1814-1880.
Chapin was one of the finest orators of his
time, and while he occupied the pulpit so devoted
himself to the lecture platform as to become very
popular as a public speaker.

HENRY WARD BEECHER.
1813-1887.
The most celebrated preacher of the nineteenth
century in America, one of the strongest anti-
slavery factors in the United States before the
Civil War.

of his day. He died in 1880. This sermon is taken from a series
entitled " Characters in the Gospels."

NICODEMUS: THE SEEKER AFTER RELIGION.

*" There was a man of the Pharisees, named Nicodemus, a ruler of the
Jews: The same came to Jesus by night."*— John iii. 1, 2.

ALTHOUGH we have but few glimpses of Nicodemus in the Gospels,
he is a personage of peculiar interest. A Pharisee, and a member of the
great Jewish Senate, or Sanhedrin, he shows us that the influence of
Christ was not limited to the poor and the obscure; but that, while his
Words and Works awoke enmity and fear among the higher classes,
they struck, in the breasts of some of these, a holier chord.

It may not be certain that Nicodemus ever openly confessed Christ;
yet, in this chapter, he appears in the attitude of a disciple, and we find
him defending Jesus before the Sanhedrin, and assisting at his burial.
Still, unless the last-mentioned act be considered as such, we do not
discover, in his conduct, that public and decisive acknowledgment which
the Saviour required; we do not behold the frank avowal of Peter, or
the intrepidity of Paul. There is an air of caution and of timidity about
him. He carefully feels the ground of innovation, before he lets go
the establishment; and, indeed, he appears to have taken no step by
which he forfeited his caste or his office. It is difficult, too, to discover
the precise purpose of this visit to Jesus. Perhaps he sought the inter-.
view from mixed motives. A religious earnestness, kindled by the
teachings and the character of Christ, may have blended with speculative curiosity, and even with the throbbings of political ambition. His
coming by night, too, may have indicated timidity, or he may have chosen
that season as the best time for quiet and uninterrupted discourse. But,
whatever may have been his motives, the position in which we find him
shows, I repeat, that the power of Christ's ministry was felt, not only
by the excitable multitude, but by the more thoughtful and devout of the
Jewish people.

Nicodemus, however, presents a peculiar interest, not only because
he exhibits the influence of Jesus upon the higher orders of his nation,
but because he appears as a *Seeker after Religion,* and as one personally
interested in its vital truths. His interview with the Saviour, gives
occasion for one of the most important passages in the New Testament.

The conversation of Christ, in this instance, is not uttered in general principles and accommodated to the multitude, but it is directed to an intelligent and inquiring spirit, in the calm privacy of the night-time, laying bare its very depths, and craving the application of religion to its own peculiar wants. To be sure, Nicodemus did not profess this want, but commenced the conversation with the language of respect and with suggestion of more general inquiry. But he who " knew what was in man," had already penetrated the folds of the Ruler's breast, and saw the real need that had sent him; so, putting by all compliments, and all secondary issues, he struck at once the conscious chord that throbbed there, and exclaimed: " Verily, verily, I say unto thee, except a man be born again, he cannot see the Kingdom of God!" These words must have filled Nicodemus with surprise, both from their sudden *heart-searchingness,* and as addressing to him a term which was usually applied to men of very different condition. For the phrase, " *new birth,"* was a customary one to express the change through which the Gentile passed in becoming a Jew. But it was indeed a strange doctrine that he, a son of Abraham, a Pharisee, a Ruler, must be born again, before he could be fit for the Messiah's kingdom. Therefore, really or affectedly, he misunderstood the Saviour's words, and gave to a phrase, plain enough when applied to a heathen, the most gross and literal interpretation. But Christ reiterated the solemn truth, assuring him that an *inward change,* and an *outward profession,* a regeneration of the affections and the will, and a renunciation of pride and fear, by the symbol of baptism — a new birth of water and of the Spirit — was essential to true discipleship. And thus, stripping away all the reliances of formal righteousness, and all the supports of birth and position, in reply to the earnest question of Nicodemus: " How can these things be? " the great Teacher proceeded to utter some of the sublimest doctrines of the Gospel. As I have already said, whether Nicodemus became an avowed follower of Jesus, or not, is uncertain; but we know that the truths which he then heard are of everlasting importance, have a personal application to every man, and appeal to wants in our own souls, which are as real and as deep as those of the Ruler of old.

But while thus Nicodemus exhibits a need of our common humanity, he especially represents a class who may be called " Seekers after Religion," either as being unsettled and inquiring in their spirits, or as resting upon something which is not Religion, but only, perhaps, a tendency toward it — they are seekers after it, as not having actually found it. In other words, for this class, Religion has its meaning and its pressure; they think about it, and they feel its claims, yet they do not thoroughly and mentally know it; or, like Nicodemus, they rest upon some substitute. Some of these positions I propose now to illustrate.

I observe, then, in the first place, that some seek Religion in *Rituals* and *Sacraments*. The tendency of the human mind, as to matters of faith and devotion, has always been to complicate rather than to simplify, and to associate these with set forms and symbols. In all ages, men have shrunk from naked communion with God, from the solitude of an intense spirituality, and have conducted transactions with the Invisible, through the mediation of ceremony. But that which, at first, was an expression of the individual soul, has grown into a fixed and consecrated Rite. Gestures and modes of worship, suggested by the occasion, have been repeated in usage, and grown venerable with age, until they have become identified with Religion itself. They have been exalted into mystic vehicles of Grace, have been considered as possessing virtue in themselves, and as constituting an awful paraphernalia, through which, alone, God will deign to communicate with man, and through which man may even propitiate and move God. Christianity has not escaped this tendency; and, even now, there are many with whom the Sacraments are something more than expressive signs and holy suggestions, and with whom the position of an altar, the shape of a vestment, and the form of a church are among the *essentials* of Religion. With such, Baptism speaks, not merely to the eye of an inward washing, but it is of itself a regenerative process. In their view, the Communion Bread is not simply a representation of the broken body of the Redeemer; but is itself so sacred, so identical with that body, that they must receive it by a special posture, and upon a particular part of the hand. As a matter of course, to such, Religion must appear eminently conservative and retrospective; the genius of the established and the past, rather than of the reformatory and the future. Cherishing the minutest fibres of these ancient rites, they chiefly venerate the men who authenticate them, and the soil out of which they grow. With them, the fluent spirit of Religion became organized and fixed into a form, with fast-days and feast-days, with mitre and cassock, and a lineal priesthood, ages ago.

It cannot be said that this method is entirely unfounded. It has its justification in human nature, if not elsewhere. There are those who can find peace only in the arms of an hereditary Faith: who can feel the inspiration of worship only among forms that have kindled worship in others for a thousand years: with whose earliest thoughts and dearest memories is entwined a Ritual and an Established Church, so that personal affection and household sanctity, as well as religious feeling, demand that every great act of life — of joy or sorrow — should be consecrated by the familiar sacrament. For that church, too, their fathers have died in darker times, and beneath its chancels, sainted mothers moulder into dust. All, too, that can exalt the ideal, or wake the pulses of eloquent emotion, is connected with such a church. To them it opens a traditional perspective, the grandest in all history. Behind its altars, sweep the vestments of centuries of priests, and rises the incense of centuries of prayer. In its stony niches, stand rows of saints, who have made human life sublime, and who, through all the passing ages, look down upon the turmoil of that life with the calm beatitude of heaven; while its flushed windows still keep the blood-stain of its own martyrs, plashed against it ere yet it had become an anchored fact, and while it tossed upon the stormy waves of persecution. I can understand, then, how an imaginative and reverential mind can find the truest religious life only in connection with Ritual and Sacrament.

I can understand, moreover, the reaction in this direction, which is taking place at the present day. It is the retreat of the Religious sentiments from the despotism of an imperious reason. It is the counter-protest of loyal affections against what is deemed an anarchical tendency. It is the clinging of men's sympathies to the concrete, alarmed by the irreverent and analytic methods of science. It is the retirement of faith and devotion to those cloistered sanctities that shut out the noise of the populace, and the diversions of the street. It is the reluctance of taste and imagination at our new and varnished Protestantism, with its bare walls, its cold services, and its angular churches, of which one wing, perchance, rests upon a market, and the other upon a dram-shop. Especially would I not deny the profound spiritual life, the self-sacrifice, and the beautiful charities which have consisted at all times, and which consist in the present time, with this Ritual and Sacramental form of Religion.

But when men claim that this alone is the genuine form — that these are essentials of the only true Church — then I deny that claim. If it fills some wants of our nature, it repudiates others equally authentic. If one class of minds find peace only under its consecrated shadows, others find no satisfaction but in the discipline of a spontaneous devotion, and the exercise of an individual reason. If it suffices for men like Borromeo or Newman, it does not suffice for men like George Fox or Channing; and the religion of these is as evident, in their simple spirituality, as of those in their mystic symbolism. When it sneers at the Puritan, then I must vindicate that rugged independence of soul, that faithfulness to the individual conscience, that sense of the Divine Sovereignty, which could kneel at no man's altar, and to God alone; which sacrificed all things for the right, but yielded not a hair to the wrong; which could find no medicine for the spirit in Sacraments, but only in the solitude of the inner life; and which has, under God, wrought out this noble consummation of modern times, whereby others may plant their vine of ritual under the broad heaven of toleration, and have liberty to sneer. When the Ritualist deprecates the ultraism and irreverence of the Anti-formalist, I must urge the tendency of his own principles to mummery and absolutism. And, finally, when he falls back upon Tradition, I must fall back upon the Bible. The spirit of the New Testament is not that of Rituals or Sacraments; and the universal sentiments of the Old are not. The prophet Isaiah, who exclaims: "Bring no more vain oblations; incense is an abomination unto me; your new moons, and your appointed feasts, my soul hateth . . . Wash you, make you clean . . . cease to do evil, learn to do well!" joins with the Apostle, who says that Christ "blotted out the handwriting of ordinances . . . nailing it to his cross," and that no man should judge us in meat or drink, or times, or seasons. And, surely, there is no argument for forms or places in those Divine Words, which declare that "God is a Spirit, and they who worship Him, must worship Him in spirit and in truth."

We cannot deny, then, that pure religion may consist with Rituals and Sacraments; we cannot deny that it may exist without these. But I insist upon this point: that the Sacrament, the Ritual, is not, itself, Religion. It may be a beautiful sign — it may be a quick suggestion — it may be a medium of spiritual influence; but, alone, it cannot take the place of inward, personal piety, of right affections, and an obedient will. No punctilious form can stand substitute for a vigilant conscience; no posture of devotion can supply the place of living deeds; no ascetic mortification can atone for guilt; no auricular confession can speak, instead of the breathings of repentance, in the ear of God, and out from the depths of the solitary soul. He who relies upon these forms, and finds sanctity *only in them,* may be sincere, may be serious about religion, but as yet he is only a *Seeker;* and, speaking to his heart with all-penetrating meaning, comes to him the decree: "Ye must be born again."

Again; there is a class who seek Religion in *Philosophy*. They believe in God by a course of reasoning. They believe in immortality, because it is a conclusion riveted in their minds by the iron links of induction. They pray, or not, according as it seems logical to do so. They would be good, because goodness is useful. But every proposition upon which they act, must first be strained through the alembic of the intellect, and must stand out in the clear definition of science. They verify and build up their religion with callipers and dissecting-knife. It is a system of digestion and pneumatology. They find an organ for veneration, and another for conscientiousness, and therefore conclude that religion has a legitimate place in the harmony of human character. But all must be calm and balanced. They dare not trust the feelings, and give but little scope to enthusiasm. Sometimes, indeed, they rise to eloquence in expatiating upon the truths of natural theology, and of "the elder scripture;" though they believe in Christ also, because he seems well authenticated as an historical Fact. In short, such men are religious like Cicero, or Seneca, with some modifications from modern science, and from the Sermon on the Mount.

Now there is a close alliance between true Philosophy and true Religion. That the New Testament is eminently free from fanaticism, and makes no appeal to mere credulity, any one will see who examines. That it is rational and sober, constitutes one of its great internal evidences. A Christian Philosopher is no anomaly, but a beautiful expression of the essential harmony of all truth. Knowledge and Piety burn and brighten with an undivided flame. Revelation and Science are continually interpreting one another, while every day the material universe is unfolding a more spiritual significance, and indicating its subservience to a spiritual end. But, after all, in order to be religious, it is not necessary that a man should be a philosopher, and it is certain that often he is a philosopher without being religious. Religion and Philosophy may coalesce, but they are two different spheres. Philosophy is out-looking and speculative; Religion is inner and vital. In the scheme of Philosophy, Religion is reasoned out as a consequence, and adopted as an appendage to character. In the true scheme, it is the central germ of our being, the controlling force of life. The religion of Philosophy consists of right *views* of things, and a prudential schooling of the passions. True Religion consists in a right state of the affections, and a renunciation of self. In the one case, Religion may "play round the head, but come not near the heart;" in the other, it breaks up the great deep of conscience, and pours an intense light upon the springs of motive. Philosophy contains the idea of intellectual rectitude; Religion, of moral obedience. Philosophy speaks of virtue; Religion, of holiness. Philosophy rests upon development; Religion requires regeneration. In short, we make an every-day distinction between the two, which is far more significant than any verbal contrast. It is the one, rather than the other, that we apply, in the profounder experiences of our moral nature, in the consciousness of sin, and in the overwhelming calamities of life. The one pours a purifying, healing, up-lifting power into the homes of human suffering, and into the hearts of the ignorant and the poor, that the other has not to bestow. Philosophy is well, under all circumstances; but it is not the most inner element of our humanity. Religion, in its humility, penitence, and faith — at the foot of the cross, and by the open sepulchre — rejoices in a direct and practical vision, to which Philosophy, with its encyclopædia and telescope, cannot attain.

Under this head, too, may be ranked a class of men who, though they may not be exactly philosophers, fall into the same conception of Religion, as a matter of the intellect — as the possession of correct views — rather than a profound moral life. They estimate men according to what they believe, and attribute the same sanctity to the Creed that others attribute to the Ritual. And as Religion, in their conception of it, consists in a series of correct opinions, the great work should be an endeavor to make men think right. So the pulpit should be an arsenal of controversial forces, incessantly playing upon the ramparts of dogmatic error, with the artillery of dogmatic truth, and for ever hammering the same doctrinal monotony upon the anvils of logic and of textual interpretation. They are satisfied if some favorite tenet is proved to a demonstration, and go forth rejoicing in the superiority of their " views," without asking if Saving Love has melted and transfigured their own hearts, or whether personal sin may not canker in their souls, if hereditary guilt is not there. Now, it is true that great principles lie at the foundation of all practical life, and the more elevated and clear our views, the more effectual are the motives to holiness and love. But it matters little to what pole of doctrine the intellect swings, if the heart hangs unpenetrated and untouched. It matters little to what opinions in Theology the pulpit has made converts, if all its mighty truths have not heaved the moral nature of the hearer — if it has not shot into the individual soul, like an arrow, the keen conviction: " I must be born again! "

Once more: there are those who seek Religion in a routine of outward and commendable deeds — in mere *morality*. With such, the great sum of life is to be sober, chaste, humane; laying particular stress upon the business-virtues, honesty, industry, and prudence. In their idea, that man is a religious man who is an upright dealer, an orderly citizen, a good neighbor, and a charitable giver. To be religious, means to do good, to keep your promises, and mind your own business. They tell us that benevolence is the richest offering, and that the truest worship is in the workshop and the field — that a man prays when he drives a nail or ploughs a furrow, and that he expresses the best thanksgiving when he enjoys what he has got, and is content if he gets no more.

Now, the world is not so bad that there is not a good deal of this kind of religion in it. It would be unjust to deny that many golden threads of integrity wind through the fabric of labor; that there is a strong nerve of rectitude holding together the transactions of daily life, and a wealth of spontaneous kindness enriching its darker and more terrible scenes.

But, after all, these easy sympathies and these prudential virtues, lack the *radicalness* of true Religion. Religion cannot exist without morality; but there is a formal morality which exists without religion. I say, a *formal* morality; for essential morality and essential Religion are as inseparable as the sap and the fruit. Nor is morality a mere segment of religion. It is one-half of it. Nay, when we get at absolute definitions, the two terms may be used interchangeably; for then we consider religion presenting its earthly and social phase, and we consider morality with its axis turned heavenward. But, in the case of these outside virtues, which are so common, we behold only one-half of religion, and that is its earthly and social form; and even this lacks the root and sanction of true morality. For the difference between the morality of a religious man and that of another, consists in this: with the one, morality bears the sanctions of an absolute law, and God is at its centre. It is wrought out by discipline, and maintained at all cost. With the other, it is an affair of temperament, and education, and social position. He has received it as a custom, and adopted it as a policy; or he acts upon it as an impulse. With the one, it is a matter of profit and loss, or a fitful whim of sentiment. With the other, it is the voice of a divine oracle within, that must be obeyed; it is the consecrated method of duty, and the inspiration of prayer. Now, to say that it makes no difference about the motive of an act, so long as the act itself is good, indicates that very lack of right feeling, and right perception, which confounds the formal morality of the world with religion. For, in the distinctions of the Christian System, the *motive* makes the deed good or bad; makes the two mites richer than all the rest of the money in the treasury; makes the man who *hates* his brother a murderer. The good action may bless others, but if I do not perform it from a right motive, it does not bless me; and the essential peculiarity of religion is, that it regards inward development, individual purity, personal holiness — so that one essential excellence of the good deed consists in its effect upon the agent — consists in the sinews which it lends to his moral power, and the quantity it adds to his spiritual life. When, from a right motive, with effort and sacrifice, I help a weak and poor man, I enrich my individual and spiritual being. If I bestow from a mere gush of feeling, I receive no permanent spiritual benefit; if from a bad motive, I impoverish my own heart. Acts, then, which appear the same thing in form, differ widely, considered in their *religious* bearings. There is the morality of impulse, the morality of selfishness, and the morality of principle, or religious morality. The motive of the first-named, we obey instantaneously, and it may do good, just as we draw our hands from the flame, and thereby obey a law of our physical nature, though we act without any consideration of that law. A great deal of the morality in the world is of this kind. It may do good, but has no reference to the law of rectitude. It is impulsive, and, therefore, does not indicate a steadfast virtue, or a deep religious life. For the very impulsiveness that leads to the gratification of the sympathies, leads to the gratification of the appetites, and thus we often find generous and benevolent characteristics mixed with vicious conduct. Then, as I have said, there is the morality of selfishness. In this instance, I may perform many good actions from sheer calculation of material profit. I may be benevolent, because it will increase my reputation for philanthropy. I may be honest, because, " honesty is the best policy." But is this the highest, the religious sanction of morality? No: the morality of the religious man is the morality of *principle*. The motive in his case is not " I will," or " I had better," but " I ought." He recognises morality as a law, impersonal, overmastering the dictates of mere self, and holding all impulses in subservience to the highest good. The morality of impulse is uncertain. The morality of policy is mean and selfish. The morality of religion is loyal, disinterested, self-sacrificing. It acts from faith in God, and with reference to God.

But another trait separates the religious from the merely formal moralist. It consists in the fact that with him, " *morality,*" as we commonly employ the term, is not all. Piety has its place. His affections not only flow earthward, but turn heavenward. He not only loves his neighbor as himself, but he loves the Lord his God. He not only visits the widows and the fatherless in their affliction, but he keeps himself unspotted from the world. With him, toil *is* prayer, and contentment *is* thanksgiving, but because he infuses into them a spirit of devotion, which he has cultivated by more solitary and special acts. With him it *is* a good thing to live honestly, industriously, soberly; but all life is not outward, is not in traffic and labor, and meat and drink. There is an inward world, to which his eyes are often introverted — a world of spiritual experience, of great realities, and everlasting sanctions — a world behind the veil — a holy of holies in his soul, where rests the Shechinah of God's more immediate presence; yea, where he meets God face to face. And it is this that directs his public conduct. The orderly and beautiful method of his life is not the huddled chance-work of good impulses, it is not the arithmetic of selfishness; but it is a serene and steady plan of being projected from the communion of the oratory, and the meditation of the closet.

Again, I say, let us not depreciate morality. Let us condemn that ostentatious piety which lifts up holy hands to God, but never stretches them out to help man — which anoints its head with the oil of sanctity, but will not defile its robes with the blood of the abused, or the contact of the guilty — which is loud in profession and poor in performance — which makes long prayers, but devours widows' houses. Let us condemn this, but remember that this is not real religion, only its form; as often, the kind deed, the honest method, is not true morality, only its form. Of both these departments of action, let it be said: that these we have done, and not left the other undone. Let us recognise the perfect harmony, nay, the identity of religion and morality, in that One who came from the solitary conflict of the desert, to go about doing good, and who descended, from the night-prayer on the mountain, to walk and calm the troubled waves of the sea.

But those who rest in a mere routine of kind and prudential deeds, need the deeper life and the inner perception which detects the meaning.

and gives the sanction to those deeds. Such need the vital germ of morality — the changed heart, the new birth.

And as I have spoken of a subordinate yet somewhat distinct class who may be ranked under the general head of seekers after religion in philosophy, let me here briefly allude to some with whom religion is a matter of mere sentiment and good feeling. Such are easily moved by the great doctrines of the New Testament. They are affected by the sermon; they have gushes of devout emotions during the prayer. But with them, religion is not a deep and steady pulse of divine life. Prayer is not a protracted aspiration — is not a habit. They feel well towards God, because they consider him a good-natured, complacent Being; but they do not meditate upon the majesty of His Nature, upon His Justice, and His Holiness. From the doctrine of immortality they draw consolation, but not sanctity. They regard it as a good time coming, but it furnishes them with no personal and stringent applications for the present. They need a more solemn and penetrating vision; a profounder experience in the soul. They need to be born again.

Then, again, there are those who may be called *amateurs* in religion. That is, they are curious about religious things. They like to speculate about it, to argue upon its doctrines, and to broach or examine new theories. They go about from sect to sect, and from church to church, tasting what is novel in the reasoning, or pleasing in the manner of the preacher; in one place to-day to hear an orator; in another to-morrow to hear a latter-day saint; it is all the same thing to them. All they want with religion is entertainment and excitement. They are Athenians, ever seeking some new thing. They smack at a fresh heresy as if they were opening a box of figs, and are as delighted with a controversy, as a boy with a sham-fight. They have no fixed place in the Church universal. They are liberalists, without any serious convictions, and cosmopolites without any home affections. In fact, to them religion *is* a sham-fight — a matter of spectacle and zest — not a personal interest, or an inward life. They would seek Jesus by night, because they hope to learn something wonderful or new, and would be startled to hear his solemn words tingling in their hearts: " Ye must be born again! "

Nay, my friends, would not these solemn words startle many of us? It may be, we have never made any inquiry concerning religion — have never even come to Jesus, as it were, by night. Such, with their barks of being drifting down the stream of time, have never asked the meaning of their voyage, or reckoned their course; nay, perhaps they live as though religion were a fable, as though earth were our permanent abiding-place, and heaven a dream. If such there are, they have not even listened to the Saviour's words. But there are others among us, perhaps, who are interested in the subject of religion, who are in some way or another engaged in it; but who are restless seekers after it, rather than actual possessors of it; who are resting upon insufficient substitutes for it. And I ask, would not these words, breaking forth from the lips of Jesus, startle us in our ritualism, our philosophy, our outside morality, our sentimentalism, or our mere curiosity? And do they not speak to *us?* Are they not as true now as when they struck upon the shivering ear of Nicodemus? Do they not make us feel as intensely our obligation and our religious want, as he might have felt there, with the wind flitting by him as though the Holy Spirit were touching him with its appeal, and with the calm gaze of the Saviour looking into his heart? Do they not demand of us, resting here awhile from the cares and labors of the world, something more than mere conformity, or intellectual belief, or formal deeds? Do they not demand a new and better spirit, a *personal apprehension* of the religious life, a breaking up and regeneration of our moral nature, a change of heart?

XXXIII

ARTHUR PENRHYN STANLEY

1815–1881

ARTHUR PENRHYN STANLEY, D.D., son of the Bishop of Norwich, was born at Alderley, England, December 13th, 1815. A pupil of Dr. Arnold at Rugby, he paused, after winning the highest honors at Oxford, to write a worthy biography of that lamented school-master. While regius professor of ecclesiastical history, Oxford, and honorary chaplain in ordinary to the Queen, he was made Dean of Westminster in 1864, having declined the honorary appointment of Archbishop of Dublin. As Dean he made Westminster Abbey the center, not only of the Anglican, but of the Christian world. His position was among the group of great men known as " the Broad Church " scholars. In 1878 he visited the United States and was received heartily among all denominations. He died in 1881. The Holy Land was visited by him in 1852, and again ten years later as chaplain to the Prince of Wales. This sermon was preached on Good Friday, 1862, in the encampment by the Spring of Nazareth. Dean Stanley adorned every subject he wrote upon by his deep scholarship and his clear style. His " Sinai and Palestine " is the most vivid and best portraiture of those sacred scenes. Chief among his works are: " Sermons and Essays on the Apostolic Age;" " The Epistle to the Corinthians;" " Lectures on the Eastern Church;" " Lectures on the Jewish Church." Our extract is from " Sermons in the East."

JESUS OF NAZARETH

" Pilate wrote a title, and put it on the cross. And the writing was, 'Jesus of Nazareth, the King of the Jews.' "— John xix. 19.

WHAT are the lessons of Good Friday? especially of Good Friday in Palestine and in this place? In the words of the text, in the title written on the Cross, the name of Jesus Christ is at that supreme moment of His Last Passion brought together with the recollection of His early years at Nazareth. What are the lessons which they both teach in common?

I. Everywhere the event of Good Friday speaks to us of the universal love of God to His Creatures. That is why it is so truly called *Good* Friday. It has its good news as much as Christmas Day or Easter Day. It tells us not only that God is Love, but that He bears love to every one on earth, however far they may seem to be removed from Him. It was for this that He sent His Son into the world,— it was for this that Christ died. It was by His death, more even than by His life, that He showed how His sympathy extended far beyond His own nation, His own friends, His own family. "I, if I be lifted up" on the Cross, "will draw all men unto me." It is this which the Collects of this day bring before us. They speak, in fact, of hardly anything else. They tell us how He died that "all estates," not one estate only, but "*all* estates in His Holy Church,"— that "*every* member of the Church" in its widest sense, not the clergy or the religious only, but every one, in his "several vocation and ministry," might "truly and godly serve Him." They pray for God's mercy to visit not Christians merely, but all religions, however separate from ours,—"Jews, Turks, Heretics, and Infidels,"— in the hope that they may all at last, here or hereafter, be "one fold under one shepherd," the One Good Shepherd who laid down His life not for the flock of one single fold only, but for the countless sheep scattered on the hills, not of the fold of the Jewish people, or of the Christian Church only, but of all mankind.

This is a truth which comes home to us with peculiar force in Palestine. What is it that has made this small country so famous? What is it that has carried the names of Jerusalem and of Nazareth to the uttermost parts of the earth? It is in one word, "the death of Christ." Had He not died as He did, His religion,— His name,— His country,— the places of His birth and education and life,— would never have broken through all the bonds of time and place as they have. That we are here at all on this day, is a proof of the effect which His death has had even on the outward fortunes of the world.

This universal love of God in Christ's death is specially impressed upon us in Nazareth. What Christ was in His death, He was in His life. What He was in His life, He was in His death. And if we wish to know the spirit which pervades both, we cannot do so better than by seeing what we may call the text of His first sermon at Nazareth. He was in the synagogue. The roll of the Hebrew Scriptures was handed to Him. He unrolled it. His former friends and acquaintance fixed their eyes upon Him to see what He would say. And what were the words which he chose? They were these:— The Spirit of the Lord is upon me, because he hath anointed me to preach the Gospel to the poor; he hath sent me to heal the broken-hearted, to preach deliverance to the captives, and recovering of sight to the blind, to set at liberty them that are bruised, to preach the acceptable year of the Lord." What He said on this text is not described; we are only told that they "marvelled at the gracious words that proceeded out of his mouth." But what those gracious words were we can well see from the words of the passage itself. "The Spirit of the Lord was upon Him," first, "to preach the gospel to the poor," the glad tidings of God's love to the poor, the humble classes, the neglected classes, the dangerous classes, the friendless, the oppressed, the unthought-for, the uncared-for. The Spirit of God was upon Him, secondly, "to heal the broken-hearted;"— to heal, as a good physician heals, not with one medicine, but with all the various medicines and remedies which Infinite Wisdom possesses, all the fractures and diseases and infirmities of our poor human hearts. There is not a weakness, there is not a sorrow, there is not a grievance, for which the love of God, as seen in the life and death of Christ, does not offer some remedy. He has not overlooked us. He is with us. He remembers us. The Spirit of God was upon Him, thirdly, "to preach deliverance to the captive." Whatever be the evil habit, or the inveterate prejudice, or the master passion, or the long indulgence, which weighs upon us like a bondage, He feels for us, and will do His utmost to set us free,— to set at liberty those that are cramped and bruised and confined by the chain of their sins, their weakness, their misfortunes, their condition in life, their difficulties, their responsibilities, their want of responsibilities, their employments, their want of employments. And, fourthly, "The Spirit of God was upon Him," to "give sight to the blind." How few of us there are who know our own failings, who see into our own hearts, who know what is really good for us! That is the knowledge which the thought of Christ's death is likely to give us. That is the truth, which, above all other truths, is likely to set us free. "Lord, that I may receive my sight," is the prayer which each of us may offer

29

up for our spiritual state, as the poor man whom He met at Jericho did for his bodily eyesight.

For every one of these conditions he died. Not for those only who are professedly religious, but for those who are the least so,— to them the message of Good Friday and of Nazareth is especially addressed. Christianity is, one may almost say, the only religion, of which the Teacher addressed Himself, not to the religious, not to the ecclesiastical, not to the learned world, but to the irreligious, or the non-religious, to those who thought little of themselves and were thought little of by others, to the careless, to the thoughtless, to the rough publican, to the wild prodigal, to the heretical Samaritan, to the heathen soldier, to the thankless peasants of Nazareth, to the swarming populations of Galilee. He addresses Himself now, to each of us, however lowly we may be in our own eyes, however little we think that we have a religious call, however encompassed we are with infirmities; His love is ready to receive, to encourage, to cherish, to save us.

II. I pass to the other lesson which Good Friday teaches us here. It is that, whatever good is to be done in the world, even though it is God Himself who does it, cannot be done without an effort,— a preparation,— a Sacrifice. So it was especially in the death of Christ,— so it was in His whole life. His whole life from the time when He grew up, " as a tender plant " in the seclusion of this valley, to the hour when He died at Jerusalem, was one long effort,— one long struggle against misunderstanding, opposition, scorn, hatred, hardship, pain. He had doubtless His happier and gentler hours, we must not forget them: His friends at Bethany, His apostles who hung upon His lips, His mother who followed Him in thought and mind wherever He went. But here, amongst His own people, He met with angry opposition and jealousy. He had to bear the hardships of toil and labor, like any other Nazarene artisan. He had here, by a silent preparation of thirty years, to make Himself ready for the work which lay before Him. He had to endure the heat and the cold, the burning sun and the stormy rain, of these hills and valleys. " The foxes " of the plain of Esdraelon " have holes," " the birds " of the Galilean forests " have their nests," but " He had " often " not where to lay his head." And in Jerusalem, though there were momentary bursts of enthusiasm in His behalf, yet He came so directly across the interests, the fears, the pleasures, and the prejudices of those who there ruled and taught, that at last it cost Him His life.

By no less a sacrifice could the world be redeemed, by no less a struggle could His work be finished.

In that work, in one sense, none but He can take part. " He trod the winepress alone." But in another sense, often urged upon us in the Bible, we must all take part in it, if we would wish to do good to ourselves or to others. We cannot improve ourselves, we cannot assist others, we cannot do our duty in the world, except by exertion, except by unpopularity, except with annoyance, except with care and difficulty. We must, each of us, bear our Cross with Him. When we bear it, it is lightened by thinking of Him. When we bear it, each day makes it easier to us. Once the name of " Christian," of " Nazarene," was an offence in the eyes of the world; now, it is a glory. But we cannot have the glory without the labor which it involves. To " hear His words, and to *do* them," to hear of His death, and to *follow* in the path of His sufferings, this, and this only, as He himself has told us, is to build our house, the house of our life, of our faith, of our happiness, upon a *rock;* a rock which will grow firmer and stronger the more we build upon it, and the more we have to bear. " The rains may descend, and the floods may come, and the winds may blow and may beat upon that house;" but the house will not fall, " for it will have been founded upon the rock."

XXXIV

FREDERICK WILLIAM ROBERTSON

1816–1853

N O printed sermons in the nineteenth century were circulated as widely among thoughtful preachers, and none exercised so great an influence in shaping the methods of preaching, as those by Frederick William Robertson. Yet his life was a short one, his church was small, he lived almost unnoticed, and not until after his death did he become influential or famous. As the grandson and son of English military officers, his aspirations, life, and character were naturally permeated with the spirit of fearlessness, manliness, and ardor. He was emphatically a Christian Soldier — brave, impulsive, chivalrous, and wholly unselfish. To these characteristics were added the gifts of great grasp of thought, keen intellectual incisiveness, rare independence of character, acute sensibility to the beautiful, child-like purity of soul, and a tongue nerved with spiritual fire. Born in London, February 3d, 1816; educated at Oxford; at first seeking, but afterwards declining, an army commission; repeatedly battling against a keenly sensitive, overwrought nervous temperament; a curate for four years in Cheltenham; a six years' incumbency in Trinity Chapel, Brighton, ending with his death at the early age of thirty-seven, August 15th, 1853: such is his biography, in brief.

THE LONELINESS OF CHRIST.

"Jesus answered them, Do ye now believe? Behold, the hour cometh, yea, is now come, that ye shall be scattered every man to his own, and shall leave me alone; and yet I am not alone, because the Father is with me."— John xvi. 31, 32.

THERE are two kinds of solitude: the first consisting of insulation in space; the other, of isolation of the spirit. The first is simply sepa-

FREDERICK WILLIAM ROBERTSON.
1816-1853.
Through his printed sermons Robertson achieved
a fame which his early death prevented him from
realizing. His writings have wielded a powerful influence on clergymen and the intellectuals
of all churches.

ARTHUR PENRHYN STANLEY.
1815-1881.
Dean Stanley, of Westminster Abbey, was one
of the great men of England in the time of Queen
Victoria. He was a favorite with all denominations for the broadness of his faith.

ration by distance. When we are seen, touched, heard by none, we are said to be alone. And all hearts respond to the truth of that saying, This is not solitude; for sympathy can people our solitude with a crowd. The fisherman on the ocean alone at night is not alone, when he remembers the earnest longings which are arising up to heaven at home for his safety. The traveller is not alone, when the faces which will greet him on his arrival seem to beam upon him as he trudges on. The solitary student is not alone, when he feels that human hearts will respond to the truths which he is preparing to address to them.

The other is loneliness of soul. There are times when hands touch ours, but only send an icy chill of unsympathizing indifference to the heart; when eyes gaze into ours, but with a glazed look which cannot read into the bottom of our souls; when words pass from our lips, but only come back as an echo reverberated without reply through a dreary solitude; when the multitude throng and press us, and we cannot say, as Christ said, " Somebody hath *touched* me:" for the contact has been not between soul and soul, but only between form and form.

And there are two kinds of men, who feel this last solitude in different ways. The first are the men of self-reliance,— self-dependent: who ask no counsel, and crave no sympathy; who act and resolve alone, — who can go sternly through duty, and scarcely shrink, let what will be crushed in them. Such men command respect: for whoever respects himself constrains the respect of others. They are invaluable in all those professions of life in which sensitive feeling would be a superfluity: they make iron commanders, surgeons who do not shrink, and statesmen who do not flinch from their purpose for the dread of unpopularity. But mere self-dependence is weakness; and the conflict is terrible when a human sense of weakness is felt by such men. Jacob was alone when he slept in his way to Padan Aram, the first night that he was away from his father's roof, with the world before him, and all the old broken up; and Elijah was alone in the wilderness when the court had deserted him, and he said, " They have digged down thine altars, and slain thy prophets with the sword: and I, even I, only am left, and they seek my life to take it away." But the loneliness of the tender Jacob was very different from that of the stern Elijah. To Jacob the sympathy he yearned for was realized in the form of a gentle dream. A ladder raised from earth to heaven figured the possibility of communion between the spirit of man and the Spirit of God. In Elijah's case, the storm, and the earthquake, and the fire, did their convulsing work in the soul, before a still, small voice told him that he was not alone. In such a spirit the sense of weakness comes with a burst of agony, and the dreadful conviction of being alone manifests itself with a rending of the heart of rock. It is only so that such souls can be taught that the Father is with them, and that they are not alone.

There is another class of men, who live in sympathy. These are affectionate minds, which tremble at the thought of being alone: not from want of courage nor from weakness of intellect comes their dependence upon others, but from the intensity of their affections. It is the trembling spirit of humanity in them. They want not aid, nor even countenance, but only sympathy. And the trial comes to them not in the shape of fierce struggle, but of chill and utter loneliness, when they are called upon to perform a duty on which the world looks coldly, or to embrace a truth which has not found lodgment yet in the breasts of others.

It is to this latter and not to the former class that we must look, if we would understand the spirit in which the words of the text were pronounced. The deep Humanity of the Soul of Christ was gifted with those finer sensibilities of affectionate nature which stand in need of sympathy. He not only gave sympathy, but wanted it, too, from others. He who selected the gentle John to be his friend,— who found solace in female sympathy, attended by the women who ministered to Him out of their substance,— who in the Trial hour could not bear even to pray without the human presence, which is the pledge and reminder of God's presence, had nothing in Him of the hard, merely self-dependent character. Even this verse testifies to the same fact. A stern spirit never could have said, " I am not alone: the Father is with me;" never would have felt the loneliness which needed the balancing truth. These words tell of a struggle, an inward reasoning, a difficulty and a reply, a sense of solitude,—" I shall be alone;" and an immediate correction of that: " Not alone: the Father is with Me."

There is no thought connected with the Life of Christ more touching, none that seems so peculiarly to characterize His Spirit, as the solitariness in which he lived. Those who understood Him best only understood him half. Those who knew Him best scarcely could be said to know Him. On this occasion the disciples thought, Now we do understand, now we do believe. The lonely Spirit answered, " Do ye now believe? Behold the hour cometh that ye shall be scattered, every man to his own, and shall leave me alone."

Very impressive is that trait in His history. He was in this world alone.

I. First, then, we meditate on the loneliness of Christ.

II. On the temper of His solitude.

1. The loneliness of Christ was caused by the Divine elevation of His character. His infinite superiority severed Him from sympathy; His exquisite affectionateness made that want of sympathy a keen trial.

There is a second-rate greatness which the world can comprehend. If we take two who are brought into direct contrast by Christ Himself, the one the type of human, the other that of Divine excellence, the Son of Man and John the Baptist, this becomes clearly manifest. John's life had a certain rude, rugged goodness, on which was written, in characters which required no magnifying-glass to read, spiritual excellence. The world, on the whole, accepted him. Pharisees and Sadducees went to his baptism. The people idolized him as a prophet; and, if he had not chanced to cross the path of a weak prince and a revengeful woman, we can see no reason why John might not have finished his course with joy, recognised as irreproachable. If we inquire why it was that the world accepted John and rejected Christ, one reply appears to be, that the life of the one was finitely simple and one-sided, that of the Other divinely complex. In physical nature, the naturalist finds no difficulty in comprehending the simple structure of the lowest organizations of animal life, where one uniform texture, and one organ performing the office of brain and heart and lungs, at once, leave little to perplex. But when he comes to study the complex anatomy of man, he has the labor of a lifetime before him. It is not difficult to master the constitution of a single country; but when you try to understand the universe, you find infinite appearances of contradiction: law opposed by law; motion balanced by motion; happiness blended with misery; and the power to elicit a divine order and unity out of this complex variety is given to only a few of the gifted of the race. That which the structure of man is to the structure of the limpet, that which the universe is to a single country, the complex and boundless soul of Christ was to the souls of other men. Therefore, to the superficial observer, His life was a mass of inconsistencies and contradictions. All thought themselves qualified to point out the discrepancies. The Pharisees could not comprehend how a holy Teacher could eat with publicans and sinners. His own brethren could not reconcile His assumption of a public office with the privacy which He aimed at keeping. "If thou doest these things, show thyself to the world." Some thought He was "a good man;" others said, "Nay, but He deceiveth the people." And hence it was that He lived to see all that acceptance which had marked the earlier stage of His career — as, for instance, at Capernaum — melt away. First, the Pharisees took the alarm; then the Sadducees; then the political party of the Herodians; then the people. That was the most terrible of all: for the enmity of the upper classes is impotent; but when that cry of brute force is stirred from the deeps of society, as deaf to the voice of reason as the ocean in its strength churned into raving foam by the winds, the heart of mere earthly oak quails before that. The apostles, at all events, did quail. One denied; another betrayed; all deserted. They "were scattered, each to his own:" and the Truth Himself was left alone in Pilate's judgment-hall.

Now learn from this a very important distinction. To feel solitary is no uncommon thing. To complain of being alone, without sympathy, and misunderstood, is general enough. In every place, in many a family, these victims of diseased sensibility are to be found, and they might find a weakening satisfaction in observing a parallel between their own feelings and those of Jesus. But before that parallel is assumed, be very sure that it is, as in His case, the elevation of your character which severs you from your species. The world has small sympathy for Divine goodness; but it also has little for a great many other qualities which are disagreeable to it. You meet with no response; you are passed by; find yourself unpopular; meet with little communion. Well! Is that because you are above the world,— nobler, devising and executing grand plans, which they cannot comprehend; vindicating the wronged; proclaiming and living on great principles; offending it by the saintliness of your purity, and the unworldliness of your aspirations? Then yours is the loneliness of Christ. Or is it that you are wrapped up in self,— cold, disobliging, sentimental, indifferent about the welfare of others, and very much astonished that they are not deeply interested in you? *You* must not use these words of Christ. They have nothing to do with you.

Let us look at one or two of the occasions on which this loneliness was felt.

The first time was when He was but twelve years old, when His parents found Him in the temple, hearing the Doctors and asking them questions. High thoughts were in the Child's soul: expanding views of life; larger views of duty, and His own destiny.

There is a moment in every true life — to some it comes very early — when the old routine of duty is not large enough; when the parental roof seems too low, because the Infinite above is arching over the soul; when the old formulas, in creeds, catechisms, and articles, seem to be narrow, and they must either be thrown aside, or else transformed into living and breathing realities; when the earthly father's authority is being superseded by the claims of a Father in heaven.

That is a lonely, lonely moment, when the young soul first feels God — when this earth is recognised as an " awful place, yea, the very gate of heaven;" when the dream-ladder is seen planted against the skies, and we wake, and the dream haunts us as a sublime reality.

You may detect the approach of that moment in the young man or the young woman by the awakened spirit of inquiry; by a certain restlessness of look, and an eager earnestness of tone; by the devouring study of all kinds of books; by the waning of your own influence, while the inquirer is asking the truth of the Doctors and Teachers in the vast Temple of the world; by a certain opinionativeness, which is austere and disagreeable enough; but the austerest moment of the fruit's taste is that in which it is passing from greenness into ripeness. If you wait in patience, the sour will become sweet. Rightly looked at, that opinionativeness is more truly anguish; the fearful solitude of feeling the insecurity of all that is human; the discovery that life is real, and forms of social religious existence hollow. The old moorings are torn away, and the soul is drifting, drifting, drifting, very often without compass, except the guidance of an unseen hand, into the vast infinite of God. Then come the lonely words, and no wonder, " How is it that ye sought me? Wist ye not that I must be about my Father's business? "

2. That solitude was felt by Christ in trial. In the desert, in Pilate's judgment-hall, in the garden, He was alone; and alone must every son of man meet his trial-hour. The individuality of the soul necessitates that. Each man is a new soul in this world: untried, with a boundless Possible before him. No one can predict what he may become, prescribe his duties, or mark out his obligations. Each man's own nature has its own peculiar rules; and he must take up his life-plan alone, and persevere in it in a perfect privacy with which no stranger intermeddleth. Each man's temptations are made up of a host of peculiarities, internal and external, which no other mind can measure. You are tried alone; alone you pass into the desert; alone you must bear and conquer in the Agony; alone you must be sifted by the world. There are moments

known only to a man's own self, when he sits by the poisoned springs of existence, "yearning for a morrow which shall free him from the strife." And there are trials more terrible than that. Not when vicious inclinations are opposed to holy, but when virtue conflicts with virtue, is the real rending of the soul in twain. A temptation, in which the lower nature struggles for mastery, can be met by the whole united force of the spirit. But it is when obedience to a heavenly Father can be only paid by disobedience to an earthly one; or fidelity to duty can be only kept by infidelity to some entangling engagement; or the straight path must be taken over the misery of others; or the counsel of the affectionate friend must be met with a " Get thee behind me, Satan :"— O! it is then, when human advice is unavailable, that the soul feels what it is to be alone.

Once more :— the Redeemer's soul was alone in dying. The hour had come,— they were all gone, and He was, as He predicted, left alone. All that is human drops from us in that hour. Human faces flit and fade, and the sounds of the world become confused. " I shall die alone,"— yes, and alone you live. The philosopher tells us that no atom in creation touches another atom,— they only approach within a certain distance; then the attraction ceases, and an invisible something repels,— they only *seem* to touch. No soul touches another soul except at one or two points, and those chiefly external,— a fearful and a lonely thought, but one of the truest of life. Death only realizes that which has been fact all along. In the central deeps of our being we are alone.

II. The spirit or temper of that solitude.

1. Observe its grandeur. I am alone, yet not alone. There is a feeble and sentimental way in which we speak of the Man of sorrows. We turn to the Cross, and the Agony, and the Loneliness, to touch the softer feelings — to arouse compassion. You degrade *that* loneliness by your compassion. Compassion! compassion for Him! Adore if you will,— respect and reverence that sublime solitariness with which none but the Father was,— but no pity; let it draw out the firmer and manlier graces of the soul. Even tender sympathy seems out of place.

For even in human things, the strength that is in a man can be only learnt when he is thrown upon his own resources and left alone. What a man can do in conjunction with others does not test the man. Tell us what he can do alone. It is one thing to defend the truth when you know that your audience are already prepossessed, and that every argument will meet a willing response; and it is another thing to hold the truth when truth must be supported, if at all, alone,— met by cold looks and unsympathizing suspicion. It is one thing to rush on to danger with the shouts and the sympathy of numbers; it is another thing when the lonely chieftain of the sinking ship sees the last boat-full disengage itself, and folds his arms to go down into the majesty of darkness, crushed, but not subdued.

Such and greater far was the strength and majesty of the Saviour's solitariness. It was not the trial of the lonely hermit. There is a certain gentle and pleasing melancholy in the life which is lived alone. But there are the forms of nature to speak to him; and he has not the positive opposition of mankind, if he has the absence of actual sympathy. It is a solemn thing, doubtless, to be apart from men, and to feel eternity rushing by like an arrowy river. But the solitude of Christ was the solitude of a crowd. In that single Human bosom dwelt the Thought which was to be the germ of the world's life — a thought unshared, misunderstood, or rejected. Can you not feel the grandeur of those words, when the Man, reposing on His solitary strength, felt the last shadow of perfect isolation pass across His soul:—" My God, my God, why hast *Thou* forsaken me?"

Next, learn from these words self-reliance. " Ye shall leave me alone." Alone, then, the Son of Man was content to be. He threw Himself on His own solitary thought: did not go down to meet the world; but waited, though it might be for ages, till the world should come round to Him. He appealed to the Future, did not aim at seeming consistent, left His contradictions unexplained:— I came from the Father,— I leave the world, and go to the Father. " Now," said they, "thou speakest no proverb:" that is, enigma. But many a hard and enigmatical saying before He had spoken, and He left them all. A thread runs through all true acts, stringing them together into one harmonious chain: but it is not for the Son of God to be anxious to prove their consistency with each other.

This is self-reliance — to repose calmly on the thought which is deepest in our bosoms, and be unmoved if the world will not accept it yet. To live on your own convictions against the world, is to overcome the world — to believe that what is truest in you is true for all: to abide by that, and not be over-anxious to be heard or understood, or sympathized with, certain that at last all must acknowledge the same, and that, while you stand firm, the world will come round to you — that is independence. It is not difficult to get away into retirement, and there live upon your own convictions; nor is it difficult to mix with men, and follow their convictions; but to enter into the world, and there live out firmly and fearlessly according to your own conscience — that is Christian greatness.

There is a cowardice in this age which is not Christian. We shrink from the consequences of truth. We look round and cling dependently. We ask what men will think; what others will say; whether they will not stare in astonishment. Perhaps they will; but he who is calculating that will accomplish nothing in this life. The Father — the Father which is with us and in us — what does He think? God's work cannot be done without a spirit of independence. A man is got some way in the Christian life when he has learned to say humbly, and yet majestically, " I dare to be alone."

Lastly, remark the humility of this loneliness. Had the Son of Man simply said, I can be alone, He would have said no more than any proud, self-relying man can say; but when He added, " because the Father is with me," that independence assumed another character, and self-reliance became only another form of reliance upon God. Distinguish between genuine and spurious humility. There is a false humility which says, " It is my own poor thought, and I must not trust it. I must distrust my own reason and judgment, because they are my own. I must not accept the dictates of my own conscience; for it is not my own, and is not trust in self the great fault of our fallen nature?"

Very well. Now, remember something else. There is a Spirit which beareth witness with our spirits; there is a God who " is not far from any one of us;" there is a " Light which lighteth every man which cometh into the world." Do not be unnaturally humble. The thought of your own mind perchance is the Thought of God. To refuse to follow that may be to disown God. To take the judgment and conscience of other men to live by, where is the humility of that? From whence did their conscience and judgment come? Was the fountain from which they drew exhausted for you? If they refused like you to rely on their own conscience, and you rely upon it, how are you sure that it is more the Mind of God than your own which you have refused to hear?

Look at it in another way. The charm of the words of great men — those grand sayings which are recognised as true as soon as heard — is this, that you recognise them as wisdom which passed across your own mind. You feel that they are your own thoughts come back to you, else you would not at once admit them: " All that floated across me before, only I could not say it, and did not feel confident enough to assert it, or had not conviction enough to put into words. Yes, God spoke to you what He did to them: only they believed it, said it, trusted the Word within them, and you did not. Be sure that often when you say, "It is only my own poor thought, and I am alone," the real correcting thought is this, "Alone, but the Father is with me,"—therefore I can live by that lonely conviction.

There is no danger in this, whatever timid minds may think — no danger of mistake, if the character be a true one. For we are not in uncertainty in this matter. It has been given us to know our base from our noble hours: to distinguish between the voice which is from above, and that which speaks from below, out of the abyss of our animal and selfish nature. Samuel could distinguish between the impulse — quite a human one — which would have made him select Eliab out of Jesse's sons, and the deeper judgment by which "the *Lord* said, Look not on his countenance, nor on the height of his stature, for I have refused him." Doubtless deep truth of character is required for this: for the whispering voices get mixed together, and we dare not abide by our own thoughts, because we think them our own, and not God's: and this because we only now and then endeavor to know in earnest. It is only given to the habitually true to know the difference. He knew it, because all His blessed life long He could say, "My judgment is just, *because* I seek not my own will, but the will of Him which sent me."

The practical result and inference of all this is a very simple, but a very deep one: the deepest of existence. Let life be a life of faith. Do not go timorously about, inquiring what others think, and what others believe, and what others say. It seems the easiest, it is the most difficult thing in life to do this — believe in God. God is near you. Throw yourself fearlessly upon Him. Trembling mortal, there is an unknown might within your soul, which will wake when you command it. The day may come when all that is human — man and woman — will fall off from you, as they did from Him. Let His strength be yours. Be independent of them all now. The Father is with you. Look to Him, and He will save you.

XXXV

CHARLES KINGSLEY

1819–1875

CHARLES KINGSLEY, D.D., professor of modern history at Cambridge, chaplain in ordinary to the Queen, and Dean of Rochester, was born at Holne Vicarage, Devonshire, June 12th, 1819. He gained honors at Magdalen College, Cambridge, and became rector of Eversley, Hampshire, about 1844. His writings are various and able — Village, and National, Sermons, novels, and poems. "Hypatia, or, New Foes with Old Faces," his greatest work, vividly outlines the struggles of Christianity at Alexandria with the neo-platonic philosophers of Greece, and the paganism of the barbarous Goths. It is designed to show that the sophisms of spiritualists are mere revampings of worn-out theories. "Alton Locke" shows the working classes, their wrongs, and his opinions regarding their betterment. "Yeast" and "Westward, Ho!" are also novels with a purpose. Dean Kingsley labored faithfully to improve the condition of the English working classes, and aided in the formation of co-operative associations. In 1864 his health failed, as the result of his intense labors in mind and body, and in 1875 he died. He was a leader in social reform, and the influence of his life remains in a deepening interest of the various classes in one another. The following is taken from "Village Sermons," characterized as "downright, honest wisdom, conveyed in a plain and simple style."

THE TRANSFIGURATION.

"Jesus taketh Peter, and James, and John, and leadeth them up into a high mountain apart, and was transfigured before them."—Mark ix. 2.

THE second lesson for this morning service brings us to one of the most wonderful passages in our blessed Saviour's whole stay on earth, namely, His transfiguration. The story, as told by the different Evangelists, is this,— That our Lord took Peter, and John, and James his brother, and led them up into a high mountain apart, which mountain may be seen to this very day. It is a high peaked hill, standing apart from all the hills around it, with a small smooth space of ground upon the top, very fit, from its height and its loneliness, for a transaction like the transfiguration, which our Lord wished no one but these three to behold. There the apostles fell asleep; while our blessed Lord, who had deeper thoughts in His heart than they had, knelt down and prayed to *His* Father and *our* Father, which is in heaven. And as he prayed, the form of His countenance was changed, and His raiment became shining, white as the light; and there appeared Moses and Elijah talking with Him. They talked of matters which the angels desire to look into, of the greatest matters that ever happened in this earth since it was made; of the redemption of the world, and of the death which Christ was to undergo at Jerusalem. And as they were talking, the apostles awoke, and found into what glorious company they had fallen while they slept. What they felt no mortal man can tell — that moment was worth to them all the years they had lived before. When they had gone up with Jesus into the mount, He was but the poor carpenter's son, wonderful enough to *them,* no doubt, with His wise, searching words, and His gentle, loving looks, that drew to Him all men who had hearts left in them, and wonderful enough, too, from all the mighty miracles which they had seen Him do; but still he was merely a man like themselves, poor, and young, and homeless, who felt the heat, and the cold, and the rough roads as much as they did. They could feel that he spake as never man spake — they could see that God's Spirit and power was on Him as it had never been on any man in their time. God had even enlightened their reason by His Spirit, to know that he was the Christ, the Son of the living God. But still it does seem they did not fully understand who and what He was; they could not understand how the Son of God should come in the form of a despised and humble man; they did not understand that His glory was to be a spiritual glory. They expected His kingdom to be a kingdom of this world — they expected His glory to consist in palaces, and armies, and riches, and jewels, and all the magnificence with which Solomon and the old Jewish kings were adorned; they thought that he was to conquer back again from the Roman emperor all the inestimable treasures of which the Romans had robbed the Jews, and that He was to make the Jewish nation, like the Roman, the conquerors and masters of all the nations of the earth. So that it was a puzzling thing to their minds why he should be King of the Jews at the very time that he was but a poor tradesman's son, living on charity. It was to show them that His kingdom was the kingdom of heaven that He was transfigured before them.

They saw His glory — the glory as of the only begotten of the Father, full of grace and truth. The form of His countenance was changed; all the majesty, and courage, and wisdom, and love, and resignation, and pity, that lay in His noble heart, shone out through His face, while He spoke of His death which he should accomplish at Jerusalem — the Holy Ghost that was upon Him, the Spirit of wisdom, and love, and beauty — the Spirit which produces everything that is lovely in heaven and earth, in soul and body, blazed out through His eyes, and all His glorious countenance, and made Him look like what He was — a God. My friends, what a sight! Would it not be worth while to journey thousands of miles — to go through all difficulties, dangers, that man ever heard of, for one sight of that glorious face, that we might fall down upon our knees before it, and, if it were but for a moment, give way to the delight of finding something that we could utterly love and utterly adore? I say, the delight of finding something to worship; for if there is a noble, if there is a holy, if there is a spiritual feeling in man, it is the feeling which bows him down before those who are greater, and wiser, and holier than himself. I say, that feeling of respect for what is noble is a heavenly feeling. The man who has lost it — the man who feels no respect for those who are above him in age, above him in knowledge, above him in wisdom, above him in goodness,— *that* man shall in no wise enter into the kingdom of heaven. It is only the man who is like a little child, and feels the delight of having some one to look up to, who will ever feel delight in looking up to Jesus Christ, who is the Lord of lords and King of kings. It was the want of respect, it was the dislike of feeling any one superior to himself, which made the devil rebel against God, and fall from heaven. It will be the feeling of complete respect — the feeling of kneeling at the feet of one who is immeasurably superior to ourselves in everything, that will make up the greatest happiness of heaven. This is a hard saying, and no man can understand it, save he to whom it is given by the Spirit of God.

That the apostles *had* this feeling of immeasurable respect for Christ there is no doubt, else they would never have been apostles. But they felt more than this. There were other wonders in that glorious vision besides the countenance of our Lord. His raiment, too, was changed, and became all brilliant, white as the light itself. Was not *that* a lesson to them? Was it not as if our Lord had said to them, " I am a king, and have put on glorious apparel; but whence does the glory of my raiment come? *I* have no need of fine linen, and purple, and embroidery, the work of men's hands; *I* have no need to send my subjects to mines and caves to dig gold and jewels to adorn my crown: the earth is mine and the fullness thereof. All this glorious earth, with its trees and its flowers, its sunbeams and its storms, is *mine*. *I* made it — *I* can do what I will with it. All the mysterious laws by which the light and the heat flow out for ever from God's throne, to lighten the sun, and the moon, and the stars of heaven — they are mine. *I* am the light of the world — the light of men's bodies as well as of their souls; and here is my proof of it. Look at Me. I am He that ' decketh Himself with light as it were with a garment, who layeth the beams of His chambers in the waters, and walketh upon the wings of the wind.' " This was the message which Christ's glory brought the apostles — a message which they could never forget. The spiritual glory of His countenance had shown them that he was a spiritual king — that His strength lay in the spirit of power, and wisdom, and beauty, and love, which God had given Him without measure; and it showed them, too, that there was such a thing as a spiritual body, and a body as each of us some day shall have if we be found in Christ at the resurrection of the just — a body which shall not hide a man's spirit when it becomes subject to the wear and tear of life, and disease, and decay; but a spiritual body — a body which shall be filled with our spirits, which shall be perfectly obedient to our spirits — a body through which the glory of our spirits shall shine out, as the glory of Christ's spirit shone out through His body at the tranfiguration. Brethren, we know not yet what we shall be, but this we do know, that when He shall appear, " we shall be *like him,* for we shall see Him as He is." (1 John iii. 2.)

Thus our Lord taught them by His appearance that there is such a thing as a spiritual body, while, by the glory of His raiment in addition to His other miracles, He taught them that He had power over the laws of nature, and could, in His own good time, " change the bodies of their humiliation, that they might be made like unto His glorious body, according to the mighty working by which He is able to subdue all things to Himself."

But there was yet another lesson which the apostles learned from the transfiguration of our Lord. They beheld Moses and Elijah talking with Him:— Moses the great lawgiver of their nation, Elijah the chief of all the Jewish prophets. We must consider this a little to find out the whole depth of its meaning. You remember how Christ had spoken of himself as having come, not to destroy the Law and the Prophets, but to fulfil them. You remember, too, how He had always said that He was the person of whom the Law and the Prophets had spoken.

Here was an actual sign and witness that His words were true — here was Moses, the giver of the Law and Elijah, the chief of the Prophets, talking with Him, bearing witness to Him in their own persons, and showing, too, that it was His death and His perfect sacrifice that they had been shadowing forth in the sacrifices of the law and in the dark speeches of prophecy. For they talked with Him of His death, which He was to accomplish at Jerusalem. What more perfect testimony could the apostles have had to show them that Jesus of Nazareth, their Master, was He of whom the Law and the Prophets spoke — that He was indeed the Christ for whom Moses and Elijah, and all the saints of old, had looked; and that He was come, not to destroy the Law and the Prophets, but to fulfil them? We can hardly understand the awe and the delight with which the disciples must have beheld those blessed three — Moses, and Elias, and Jesus Christ, their Lord, talking together before their very eyes. For of all men in the world, Moses and Elias were to them the greatest. All true-hearted Israelites, who knew the history of their nation, and understood the promises of God, must have felt that Moses and Elias were the two greatest heroes and saviours of their nation, whom God had ever yet raised up. And the joy and the honor of thus seeing them face to face, the very men whom they had loved and reverenced in their thoughts, whom they had heard and read of from their childhood, as the greatest ornaments and glories of their nation — the joy and the honor, I say, of that unexpected sight, added to the wonderful majesty which was suddenly revealed to their transfigured Lord, seemed to have been too much for them — they knew not what to say. Such company seemed to them for the moment heaven enough; and St. Peter, first finding words, exclaimed, " Lord, it is good for us to be here. If thou wilt, let us build three tabernacles, one for Thee, and one for Moses, and one for Elias." Not, I fancy, that they intended to worship Moses and Elias, but that they felt that Moses and Elias, as well as Christ, had each a divine message, which must be listened to; and therefore, they wished that each of them might have his own tabernacle, and dwell among men, and each teach his own particular doctrine and wisdom in his own school. It may seem strange that they should put Moses and Elias so on an equality with Christ, but the truth was, that as yet they understood Moses and Elias better than they did Christ. They had heard and read of Moses and Elijah all their lives — they were acquainted with all their actions and words — they knew thoroughly what great and noble men the Spirit of God had made them, but they did *not* understand Christ in like manner. They did not yet *feel* that God had given Him the Spirit without measure — they did not understand that He was not only to be a lawgiver and a prophet, but a sacrifice for sin, the conqueror of death and hell, who was to lead captivity captive, and receive inestimable gifts for men. Much less did they think that Moses and Elijah were but His servants — that all *their* spirit and *their* power had been given by Him. But this also they were taught a moment afterwards; for a bright cloud overshadowed them, hiding from them the glory of God the Father, whom no man hath seen or can see, who dwells in the light which no man can approach unto; and out of that cloud a voice, saying, " This is my beloved Son; hear ye Him;" and then, hiding their faces in fear and wonder, they fell to the ground; and when they looked up, the vision and the voice had alike passed away, and they saw no man but Christ alone. Was not that enough for them? Must not the meaning of the vision have been plain to them? They surely understood from it that Moses and Elijah were, as they had ever believed them to be, great and good, true messengers of the living God; but that their message and their work was done — that Christ, whom they had looked for, was come — that all the types of the law were realized, and all the prophecies fulfilled, and that henceforward Christ, and Christ alone, was to their Prophet and their Lawgiver. Was not this plainly the meaning of the Divine voice? For when they wished to build three tabernacles, and to honor Moses and Elijah, the Law and the Prophets, as separate from Christ, that moment the heavenly voice warned them: " *This — this* is my beloved Son — hear ye *Him,* and Him only, henceforward." And Moses and Elijah, their work being done, forthwith vanished away, leaving Christ alone to fulfil the Law and the Prophets, and all other wisdom and righteousness that ever was or shall be. This is another lesson which Christ's transfiguration was meant to teach them and us, that Christ alone is to be henceforward our guide; that no philosophies or doctrines of any sort which are not founded on a true faith in Jesus Christ, and His life and death, are worth listening to; that God had manifested forth His beloved Son, and that Him, and Him only, we are.to hear. I do not mean to say that Christ came into the world to put down human learning. I do not mean that we are to despise human learning, as so many are apt to do now-a-days; for Christ came into the world not to destroy human learning, but to fulfil it — to sanctify it — to make human learning true, and strong, and useful, by giving it a sure foundation to stand upon, which is the belief and knowledge of His blessed self. Just as Christ came not to destroy the Law and the Prophets; but to fulfil them — to give them a spirit and a depth in men's eyes which they never had before — just so He came to fulfil all true philosophies, all the deep thoughts which men had ever thought about this wonderful world and their own souls, by giving *them* a spirit and a depth which *they* never had before. Therefore let no man tempt you to despise learning, for it is holy to the Lord.

There is one more lesson which we may learn from our Lord's transfiguration: when St. Peter said, Lord! it is good for us to be here," he spoke a truth. It *was* good for him to be there; nevertheless, Christ did not listen to his prayer. He and his two companions were not allowed to *stay* in that glorious company. And why? Because they had a work to do. They had glad tidings of great joy to proclaim to every creature, and it was, after all, but a selfish prayer, to wish to be allowed to stay in ease and glory on the mount while the whole world was struggling in sin and wickedness below them; for there is no meaning in a man's calling himself a Christian, or saying that he loved God, unless he is ready to hate what God hates, and to fight against that which Christ fought against, that is, sin. No one has any right to call himself a servant of God, who is not trying to do away with some of the evil in the world around him. And, therefore, Christ was merciful when, instead of listening to St. Peter's prayer, He led the apostles down again from the mount, and sent them forth, as He did afterwards, to preach the Gospel of the kingdom to all nations. For Christ put a higher honor on St. Peter by that than if he had let him stay on the mount all his life, to behold His glory, and worship and adore. And He made St. Peter more like Himself by doing so. For what was Christ's life? Not one of deep speculations, quiet thoughts, and bright visions, such as St. Peter wished to lead, but a life of fighting against evil; earnest, awful prayers and struggles within, continual labor of body and mind without, insult and danger, and confusion, and violent exertion, and bitter sorrow.

This was Christ's life — this is the life of almost every good man I ever heard of ;— this was St. Peter's, and St. James's, and St. John's life afterwards. This was Christ's cup, which they were to drink of as well as He ;— this was the baptism of fire with which they were to be baptized as well as He ;— this was to be their fight of faith ;— this was the tribulation through which they, like all other great saints, were to enter into the kingdom of heaven; for it is certain that the harder a man fights against evil, the harder evil will fight against him in return: but it is certain, too, that the harder a man fights against evil, the more he is like his Saviour Christ, and the more glorious will be his reward in heaven. It is certain, too, that what was good for St. Peter is good for us. It is good for a man to have holy and quiet thoughts, and at moments to see into the very deepest meaning of God's word and God's earth, and to have, as it were, heaven opened before his eyes; and it is good for a man sometimes actually to *feel* his heart overpowered with the glorious majesty of God, and to *feel* it gushing out with love to his blessed Saviour; but it is not good for him to stop there, any more than it was for the apostles; they had to leave that glorious vision and come down from the mount, and do Christ's work; and *so have we;* for, believe me, one word of warning spoken to keep a little child out of sin,— one crust of bread given to a beggar-man, because he is your brother, for whom Christ died,— one angry word checked, when it is on your lips, for the sake of Him who was meek and lowly in heart; in short, any, the smallest, endeavor of this kind to lessen the quantity of evil which is in yourselves, and in those around you, is worth all the speculations and raptures, and visions, and frames, and feelings in the world; for those are the good *fruits* of faith, whereby alone the tree shall be known, whether it be good or evil.

XXXVI

WILLIAM MORLEY PUNSHON

1824–1881

A GENERATION ago, the foremost pulpit orator in the Wesleyan Methodist Church of Great Britain was William Morley Punshon. He was born at Dorcester, in Yorkshire, May 29, 1824. His youth was spent as clerk in a countinghouse; but at eighteen he was an effective and popular local-preacher, in such demand that in 1844, after only a few months in a theological institution, he entered the regular ministry among the Wesleyans. In accordance with the itinerant system of Methodism, he was pastor over various churches of England and before many years was everywhere regarded as the leading preacher in his denomination. His sermons were always written out with the greatest care and committed to memory; although his delivery was so impressive as to make them appear spontaneous. In 1868 he was sent to Canada, and for five years served as President of the Conference, and also of the College in Toronto. He returned to England in 1873, and in 1875 was made Secretary of the Wesleyan Missionary Society. He died in 1881. This sermon was preached in St. Paul's Methodist Episcopal Church, New York, in 1869.

THE HEALING WATERS.

"And it shall come to pass, that everything that liveth, which moveth, whithersoever the rivers shall come, shall live: and there shall be a very great multitude of fish, because these waters shall come thither: for they shall be healed; and everything shall live whither the river cometh."
— Ezekiel xlvii. 9.

THE last clause of the verse is that to which I especially direct your attention: "And everything shall live whither the river cometh."

I have somewhere seen a picture which, in brief words and from dim memories only, I will endeavor to describe. The scene is in the far East, the hour just when the earth is lighted up with that rare Oriental sunrise which we Westerns love to see; the time, the sultry August, when the fierce sun has it all his own way, and when the earth has a sickly cast upon it, as if it fainted almost beneath the intensity of the glare; the plain is scorched and arid, the river pressing within its sedgy banks seems to have hardly strength enough to propel its sluggish stream. There, on an eminence, beneath a group of ancestral palms, is a knot of Egyptian peasants, swarthy and muscular, their eyes strained wildly towards the south, in which quarter there seems to be an indescribable haze, forecasting the shadow of some atmospheric or other change. Why wait they there so eagerly? Why is their gaze fastened distinctly upon the point where the river glimmers faintly on the horizon's dusky forehead? Because they are conscious from the experience of years, that the time has come for the inundation of the Nile. They do not know how it will be swelled: they are not able to tell the source from which the tribute is distilled, how in the far Abyssinia it gathers its volume of waters; but as certainly as if their knowledge was profound and scientific, they calculate upon the coming flood. And they know, too, that when the flood does come, that arid plain shall wave with ripening grain; there shall be corn in Egypt, and those blackened pastures will be gay with such fertile plenty that the whole land shall eat and be satisfied, "for everything shall live whither the river cometh." So marvellous shall be the transformation that the Turkish description of the Egyptian climate shall almost hold good: that for three months it is white like pearl, for three months brown like musk, for three months green like emerald, for three months yellow like gold.

This picture has struck me as furnishing us with a very graphic representation of Ezekiel's vision embodied in the experience of Eastern life. Nothing certainly can better image the moral barrenness of the world and the wilderness of sin than that plain upon which the consuming heat has alighted, withering the green herb and inducing the dread of famine. Nothing can better set forth the life and healing of the Gospel of Christ than the flow of that blessed life-giving river; and nothing can better show the attitude befitting all earnest Christian men than the attitude of these peasants, eager and earnest, watching the first murmurings of the quiescent waters that they might catch and spread the joy.

There is, of course, a spiritual application of the vision, which appears to have been intended in the glowing language of Ezekiel, and that spiritual application is in the Gospel of Jesus Christ, made effectual by the Holy Ghost for the healing and for the salvation of men.   You remember that, under the same similitude, the Gospel is frequently presented to us in the pages of the Word.   After the similitude of living water, its blessings were promised to the Samaritan woman; the stranger who lifted up his voice in the feast said that in the heart of each believer there should be a fountain springing up into everlasting life; and in identity between the seer of the Old Testament and the evangelist of the New, John saw a river of water of life, clear as crystal, proceeding from the throne of God and of the Lamb.   We do not err, therefore, if we present to you these holy waters as emblematic of the scheme of perfected atonement, made vital by the Spirit of God, and adapted for the salvation of men. In this aspect of it, meditation for a few moments upon the source, the progress, and the efficacy of the healing waters, will not be out of place to-day.

There is said to have been a copious fountain upon the west side of the city of Jerusalem.   At this fountain, which was called Gihon, Zadok and Abiathar, priests of the Lord, stood by the side of the youthful Solomon, and, with many holy solemnities, proclaimed him king. The prudent Hezekiah, foreseeing that in time of war its waters might be cut off by an enemy, conducted them by a secret aqueduct into the city.   David found in the purifying virtues of the fountain one of his choicest inspirations when he struck his harp and sang, " There is a river the streams whereof make glad the city of God, the holy place, the tabernacle of the Most High."   Now, it may be that there was some subtle connection of thought between this fountain and the vision which floated before the senses of Ezekiel, as the stream was from the foundations of the temple, and from the foundations of the holy house in the vision the prophet saw the healing waters spring.   Be this at it may, the truth is significant to us that through the temple come to us the tidings of blessing, that the tidings do not originate in the temple, but have their source and origin that is invisible and afar.

In God's provision for the restoration of the fallen race there are both instrumentalities and efficient agencies.   He has appointed means, and although there is no innate power in means as God's appointed channels of blessing, they are not to be despised.   There is not now, as in the Jewish dispensation, any central spot where the holy oracles exclusively speak and where religion preserves its most precious and hallowed memories; the prestige and the sacredness of the old Jerusalem have passed away for ever, but the means of grace are invested with a sacredness that is peculiarly their own. There are special promises of favor yet for those who wait upon God and for those who call upon his name. They deprive themselves of a large inheritance of blessing, and are deeply criminal withal, who forsake the assembling of themselves together in the place where the ordinance of preaching is celebrated, where the sacraments are duly administered, and where prayer is wont to be made. The ordinances of religion may be, and very often are, observed only with external decorum. The song may be the formal verse, the prayer may be lip-service merely, and the whole service may be a Sabbath compromise with conscience and for a week's indulgence in sin, but to the true-hearted and to the contrite, it is from the temple that the healing waters flow.

The heart, ignorant of God and of its own duty, dimly conscious that the reconciliation for which it pants must come to it through the merits of another, hears of him in the temple, and is glad. The contrite one, loathing his former practices of iniquity, bows tearfully in the temple as he says, " The foolish shall not stand in thy sight, and thou hatest all the workers of iniquity; but as for me, I will worship toward thy holy temple." Here, as in a spiritual laver sea, the polluted soul is cleansed by the washing of water and the word. Here the poor children of sin smile through their tears as they are satisfied with the goodness of his house, and the lame halts no longer as he emerges from this Bethesda of the paralyzed whose waters have been sent from on high. It is between the cherubim that God especially shines; it is among the golden candlesticks that God walks to bless his people. Here, as in a gorgeous and well-furnished hall of banqueting, believers eat of the fatness of his house and drink of the river of his pleasure; in the temple is at once the highest instruction, the sweetest comfort, the closest fellowship with God, and the amplest preparation for heaven.

Brethren, your presence in the temple this morning proves that the way to it is a familiar road to you — but do you love its courts? are they homes to you — homes of endearment and of blessing? " The Lord loveth the gates of Zion more than all the dwellings of Jacob." A gate more than a house — that is the Lord's arithmetic in reference to the temples of his presence. " The Lord loveth the gates of Zion more than all the dwellings of Jacob." Are your likes like his? or like his servant's — the holy psalmist —" that you may dwell in the house of the Lord, to behold the beauty of the Lord, and to inquire in his temple," as the oracle where your eager minds may discover the perfection of truth, as a shrine where your enamored hearts may behold the perfection of beauty? Oh! they who love the temple are the likeliest, standing on its banks, to trace the source of it as it issues from the throne. So much for the instrumental agency.

While we appreciate the advantages of the temple, while we rejoice in the flow of the healing waters, we must remember always that they issue from the foundations of the house, and that their springs are in the everlasting hills. In other words, that God is the only source of life, and that means, unless he vitalizes them, are but the letter that killeth — the shadow of good things to come. You are sufficiently instructed in the things of God to know that he has confided the great work of human redemption to no agency that is less powerful than his own; for, while the atheist cannot find God, while the deist is deaf to his revelation, and while the pantheist reduces him to an abstraction, the heart of a good woman leaps up within her at remembering that all around her there is God — a living, personal, omnipotent, gracious God.

One of the glorious beliefs which fence round our own individual faith, as with a rampart of impregnable strength, is this: that ever since the revelation of Christianity, this tear-stricken world of ours has been not many days orphaned of a present God. In olden time, God spake to the world in symbol, in vision, by thunder and by fire; but even amid the comparative dimness of the Mosaic economy, the Son of God, as if impatient to begin his great work of redemption, paid preliminary visits to the scene of his future incarnation, and took upon him the form of an angel, while yet the fullness of time had not come for him to take upon him the form of a man. In the days of his flesh, he perfected the work of atonement by one offering for sins for ever, needing no repetition, losing none of its rich crimson through the lapse of years. By one offering for ever, he gave the world at once its sublimest morality and its most spotless example; vanquished death by dying, and gave the proof of the victory by the resurrection out of a baffled tomb, and then, having furnished the instrument of propagation, and having promised the agent of propagation, he ascended up on high.

Through the interval, heavy and trying to the expectant twelve, but not many days according to the calendar, the promise of the Father bridged over the chasm between the ascent of the Son and the descent of the Spirit. It was a solemn hush, like the stern silence that reigns

along the line of battle between the hoarse word of command and the
fierce onslaught upon the foe. The Saviour had said upon the cross,
" It is finished," and, as a token that it was finished — a token that
neither men nor devils could gainsay — he snatched up the thief by his
side, and took him with him as the first fruits of the Pentecost; and then,
when he had chosen his disciples, and furnished them with every qualifi-
cation for their great work, what was his language? Strange scene!
" Go! but tarry. Do not march undisciplined and without a leader.
Wait until, like the mysterious stranger that appeared before the camp
of Gideon, the Captain of the Lord's host shall come. Tarry ye in the
city of Jerusalem until ye be endued with power from on high." And
suddenly and richly that baptism of fire came — fell upon the anointed
ones in the upper room, was kindled by their instrumentality in many
hearts in Jerusalem, and has gone burning on until now. Oh! do you
not see the fullness and the richness of the provision? The world could
not be trusted without a God in it, and so, not many days after, God
the Son went up, and God the Spirit came down. The issues pending
were so solemn, the results of failure would have been so appalling to
the universe of God, that there must be a present Deity in order to carry
on the great work in the world; and so, while the atheist cannot find
God, while the deist is deaf to his revelation, and while the pantheist
deprives him of his personality, here is God, the Holy Ghost, as the
Christian's living representative of God, as the great Inspirer, not of
the ancient seers only, but of the modern truth, and as the great, constant, living Agent in the conviction and in the conversion of souls.

Brethren, so soon as Christ had ascended up on high, the fullness of
the Spirit came down. Is it not a comforting truth " We believe in the
Holy Ghost?" Is there any one who would wish us to blot that article
out of our creed? Was there ever a time when it was more necessary
for us to affirm it to the teeth of men, and in the face of hostile con-
federacies of error and of scorn? " We believe in the Holy Ghost."
What else would assure our confidence amid the insolence of error and
the haughtiness of scorn, amid the craft of demon hate and hostile con-
spiracies of evil, amid the audacious wickedness of our own hearts, amid
earth's fickle people and earth's banded kings? What else would fortify
our trust in the word, which has within it every element of opposition
to ungodliness, but no element of triumph over evil?

Men say that truth is power. It is not: alone, it is as feeble as the
pliant osier or as the bruised reed against the banded malignity of men;

but let the Spirit come into it, and then it overcomes speedily, is brave, and is mighty to prevail. Brethren, that Spirit is in the truth which I preach in your hearing to-day. He has promised to apply the truth to every conscience and to every heart. Let us honor him by asking for his presence. Prayer will be a profitless litany, praise will be a foolish tinkling of cymbals, and our whole devotional service will be a bootless trouble unless he come down in the midst of us with his inspiration and with his blessing. We shall still dishonor God, we shall still be greedy to do evil, we shall still follow in the trail of the serpent, we shall still fall into a recompense of doom, unless the Holy Spirit inspire us. The prayer of the stammerer will be eloquent, the most tuneless strain a doxology, and the meanest offering an acceptable sacrifice, if only he inspire them; the darkness of the ignorant shall be enlightened, the distress of the contrite shall be soothed, the way of the perplexed shall be straitened, the wound of the apostate shall be healed, and visions of brightness shall break upon the dulled eyes of the dying, if only the Divine Spirit — God the Holy Ghost — be there. Here, then, are the instrumental and efficient agencies for the propagation of the Gospel of Christ — the flowing river, and the source of the river. "Everything shall live whither the river cometh." It issues out of the temple; but its springs are away from the foundation of the house, far off in the everlasting hills.

Let us notice, secondly, for a moment or two, the progress of the healing waters. You notice that in the vision the progress of it is presented to us as gradual and constant. The prophet saw the waters flowing first to the ankles, then to the knees, then to the loins, and then it was a river that could not be passed over; even a river for a man to swim in. The progress was gradual and constant. There was no ceasing of the flow; there was no ebbing of the waters; they gradually and constantly flowed in an ever-deepening stream. This is a description of the Gospel of Christ, small and feeble in its beginnings. Trembling but earnest fishermen were its first preachers; wealth, rank, patronage, and power were all arrayed against it; Cæsars conspired to strangle it, and armies marched out against its fugitive sons.

How marvellous was its triumph! Think of the rapidity of its original spread! Jerusalem filled with the doctrine; Antioch, Corinth, Ephesus, Thessalonica, Athens, Rome, all trembling beneath its denunciations of their vices within a century of its Founder's death. "We are but of yesterday," says Tertullian in his apology, "and we have filled your cities, islands, towns, and boroughs; the camp, the senate, and the forum." Writers of the second century speak of the whole world of the Roman Empire as filled with the doctrine of Christ, and it is known that Constantine placed the cross upon the imperial banners, establishing Christianity as the religion of the state, and at the close of the fourth century, when Julian gasped out his celebrated dying cry, it was not the apostate only, it was the world that the Galilean had overcome: and although after the establishment of Christianity, there came an eclipse of faith, and blemishes disfigured somewhat the comeliness of the bride of Christ, yet its gradual progress among the nations did not cease. One after another they heard its tidings and submitted to its sway; insensibly it moulded the institutions of society and stamped upon them its own beauteous image; sanguinary codes were relaxed, unholy traffic was terminated, cruelty had its arm paralyzed and its sword blunted; fraud, lust, and drunkenness became no longer things of glorying, but things of shame; and there was a gradual uplifting in the moral health, as if men felt the bracing air-waves of a new atmosphere, and they wondered whence the healing came.

Oh! it was the river that did it all, flowing on, now in the gurgling brook, and now on the open plain, now fertilizing the swards upon its banks, and now rejoicing in the depths of its own channel, imperceptible almost in the increasing volume of its waters to those who gazed upon it every day, but to those who gazed upon it only at intervals, seeming to be widening and deepening every hour that it has rolled. And it is rolling still. Perhaps there never was an age of such quickened activity and privilege as the age in which we live. Here and there and yonder there have been manifestations of the healing power of the Gospel. You see the cloud rising and bursting over this and over that hill of Zion, in plenteous showers of blessing. Is it not so? Churches that for years have been languid have been quickened into a warmth of life which has astonished them, and the heart of old formalities has been smitten like the rock of Horeb, and the crystal waters have flowed forth even in the wilderness to rejoice the hearts of men. Ministers who have toiled disheartened, for years and years sowing the seed, as they fancied, upon the rock where it baffled the skill of the husbandman, have been bringing their sheaves with the reaper's bursting gladness, and everything has told that the moral summer of the world has been coming. And what is it all? Oh! just the flowing of the ancient river coming past our homesteads, its waters sparkling in the healing sun, and the melody of the daughters of music on its banks, making glad the city of our God.

Now, brethren, if this be so, there are two solemn thoughts here. Do not rejoice in the progress and forget the application: the one encourages our trust, the other reminds us of our responsibility. If it be really so that God has appointed that this Gospel should spread and progress in the world, and if we get fastened into our spirits a conviction that this Gospel shall and must triumph, the only thing for us to mind is that we are in the partnership, in order that, as workers together with God, we may be sure and have our share in the recompense when the sowers and the reapers shall rejoice together. Oh! if we could only get this thought fastened into our spirits, we should be preserved from unusual elation in the time of apparent prosperity, and from unusual depression in times of apparent languor. Opposition may crumble into dust, or, like mountains of ice, may melt before the warmth of the sun, while public opinion, changeful ever and always, may applaud the heroism or laugh at the fanaticism of the Church; legislation may benefit or may brand godliness (it has done both, and it will do both again with equal heartiness and with equal facility); the choicest of the Church's youth may press into the ranks of the ministry, with a holy emulation to be baptized for the dead, or it may leave the ministry to be recruited from the ranks of the comparatively mean and unlettered, themselves preferring opulence and lettered ease; the spirit of revival may spread like a beacon blaze from hill to hill, or it may be thwarted by indifference, or thwarted equally by the excesses or fanaticism of its votaries; good men may fall in quick succession out of Zion — but the Gospel goes on through all vicissitudes; it wins its widening way; it is never languid, although its advocates fail; it marches with the ages, or they wonder at finding it ahead of them in the great course of civilization, progress, freedom, and heavenly endeavor. Its doctrines never became antiquated, its face never shrivels up, and just as it was in the beginning, it is to-day. Time writes no wrinkle on its azure brow; there is immortal youth about it, and a fitness for the world of the nineteenth, as for the third, century. There is no modern error that can set itself up insolently without meeting the fate of Dagon before the ancient Ark.

Christianity can be trusted by the world to-day as by the world of the early apostolic age; there is nothing can master it; there is nothing can retard or overcome it. It can gather its triumphs still, just as it was wont to do, from the very dregs and refuse of society; and if it wants its choicest apostle, it can take hold of the blasphemer, the persecutor, and the injurious man, and lift him up into an apostleship, higher than they all. It saves sinners still; it comforts believers now; it shines with sweetest lustre in the chamber of affliction, and its praises are gasped from pale beds of death. Oh! you can trust the Gospel! If you believe that it is destined to prevail, and that the power of the Holy Ghost within it shall never suffer it to die, then, calm and free from tumult, catch somewhat of the spirit of the Master. All the troubles of the world do not affect him. " This man, after he had offered one sacrifice for sins, for ever sat down." Men do not sit when their work is going on; they are standing as long as there is anxiety about that. But " this man, after he had offered one sacrifice for sins, for ever sat down, expecting."

O the sublimity of that imperial quiet! " The heathen rage " down below; it does not move him. He sits " expecting." " The kings of the earth take counsel together against the Lord and against his anointed." Not a muscle of his face moves; he sits " expecting." " The people " (worse than all external opposition), the people themselves, " imagine a vain thing." He that sits in the heaven still sits expecting until his enemies be made his footstool. He knows that the end will come; he has done his work, and he is satisfied; already he sees before him of the travail of his soul, and the duty of imperial quiet which the Master has assumed should be the attitude so far as the anticipation of the future triumph of the Gospel is concerned, of the Master's people too. You will not be discouraged if your faith is strong, and if, with a living personality of consciousness, you believe in the Holy Ghost.

Well, then, the second thought reminds you of your responsibility. How impressively it comes upon you! Being heirs of such a heritage as this, born in such a day of privilege, around which so many solemn associations and beliefs gather, surely there must be responsibility devolving upon us; for it is a law of God's government that wherever there is power, there is a use and a mission for that power. Oh! it is a great thing to live in times like these, but it is a greater thing to be fit to live in times like these. It is impossible to live in such an age, an age when no ordinary privileges are enjoyed, when there is a special unction attending the ministration of the word, where there are large and manifest workings of the Holy Ghost, without entailing an added responsibility to do anything which our fathers have done. We are the Chorazins and the Bethsaidas of the present in whom all God's mighty works are done, and if the ancient Capernaum has a successor at all, it will be surely in the nations where the light of Gospel truth has long been shining, and where the country spreads her ægis over the worshippers, that none may dare to make them afraid.

The question, then, presses itself upon all: Am I holier, am I more spiritually-minded, do I get heavenlier by my privilege day by day? The waters have been flowing past my homestead for years and years; am I perishing or thirsting by their side? Have I never stooped to drink them yet? Brethren, the waters wear the stones (that is a wonderful passage); but they are stones still, although worn. The waters do not change their nature, and what water cannot change it petrifies. Have you never heard of the dropping wells that have been outpouring continually for years, converting the mosses upon the shelvy rock into the richest emerald that your eyes ever gazed upon? But what is the ground underneath? Cold, hard stone. And there are some consciences that have sat so long under the sound of the Gospel, that they shall never be broken, not even by the hammer of the Word. May God save us from such a doom! These thoughts have come, almost when I did not reck of them, in reference to the efficacy of these healing waters. It is not necessary, therefore, for me at any length to enlarge. It has been almost impossible to avoid allusion to them in a former part of the discourse. The places, however, into which the waters flowed are very striking. They did not direct their course into spots that were very slightly defective, and, therefore, very readily healed; they did not impart a partial and temporary life under very favorable circumstances. They flowed into the desert and into the sea; into the desert where no stream had flowed before; into the Dead Sea in whose sad, sluggish waters nothing which had breath could live. Thus their mission was to supply all that was lacking, and to purify all that was impure.

How complete and effectual the healing! "Everything shall live whither the river cometh." And this is true of the Gospel of Christ. There is no desert of worldliness anywhere which the Gospel cannot turn into a garden; there is no Dead Sea of error which the Gospel cannot purge from its pollution and transform into a receptacle of life. The completeness of the healing is one of the most agreeable of its characteristics, and furnishes to those who rejoice in it their loftiest materials of praise. The world is a vast valley — a valley of the dead, without motion, without strength, without hope; but there is not one of those

unburied corpses that may not be quickened into life. "Everything"—
am I bold to affirm it?—"everything may live whither the river cometh!" The Gospel has life in it for all. Its voice can reach to the
farthest wards of the sepulchre, and there is no catacomb that is too
remote, too crowded, or too loathsome to be visited and to be emptied;
however long death may have had sway, the Gospel can chase it from
the heart—ay, though time may have resolved the dust into dust
again, and though the soul, like a mummy of the Pharaohs, may be
swathed in its embalmment for many centuries of years, everything shall
live whither the river cometh.

Not only may each man be brought under the influence, but each
part of each man may be redeemed: light for the understanding, that it
may no longer be darkened by the clouds of speculative error; light for
the imagination, that it may quench its strange fires in the blood of the
Lamb and snatch from the altar of his cross a brighter and more hallowed flame; light for the memory, that it may be haunted no longer
by the ghostly scenes and spectral thoughts of evil, but that it may
hoard with miser's care every fraction of knowledge and transform it
into an argument for God; life for the affections, that they may spend
the bloom of their intensity of love on an object upon which they can
expatiate without fear of idolatry, and without fear either of treachery
or change; life for the whole nature, that it may rise from the
death of sin into the better life of God; life for the soul, that it
may not be sullied even by the shadow of death, but that, in the pure
white light of the Redeemer's presence, it may go upward and upward
into the sacred, high, eternal noon of heaven. "Everything shall live
whither the river cometh." It shall flow into the desert, the life of
God shall be implanted in the wilderness, and the whole nature shall
be so turned about, that the barrenness shall become a bloom. "Instead of the thorn shall come up the fir-tree, and instead of the brier
shall come up the myrtle-tree, and it shall be to the Lord for a name,
for an everlasting sign which shall not be cut off." It shall flow into
the sea, and though the proud waters resist its influence, it shall overcome their frantic billows, and in spite of them shall heal it of its
plague.

Some of you may have seen what I conceive to be an illustration
of this, as I have seen, in nature's bounteous kingdom. I stood some
years ago, on a bright summer's day, at the meeting of the waters near the
city of Geneva, where two rivers meet, but do not mingle, the Aar and

the Rhone. One with its beautiful water of heavenly blue, which it is almost worth a pilgrimage to see, and the other muddy, partly from the glaciers, of which it is largely composed, and partly from the clay soil which it upheaves, come meeting together from two several points. For miles and miles they go, with no barrier between them except their own innate repulsions; they meet, but do not mingle. Now and then one makes a slight encroachment into the province of the other, but is speedily beaten back again; like mighty rival forces of good and evil do they seem, and for a long while the struggle is doubtful; but if you will look far down the valley, into a quiet little nook, you find the Rhone has mastered, and covered the whole surface of the river with its own emblematic and beautiful blue. I thought, as I stood there and gazed, that there was a grand illustration of the ultimate triumph of truth over error; and in meditating upon this vision of Ezekiel, and reading that those healing waters shall flow into the sea and heal it, the scene rose up before me fresh and vivid, as if I had seen it yesterday, and as my own faith was confirmed, and my own apprehension quickened by the memory, I have sought in these few words to impart some of the vividness of the apprehension to you. "Everything!"— oh! it is a beautiful thought, and I can rest in it because God has spoken it, otherwise the plague of my own heart would weigh me down; otherwise the great, the giant temptations that impart to my soul a struggling bitterness which no stranger may know, might well cause me to despond —"everything shall live whither the river cometh." No impurity, no leprosy, no death which cannot be healed by the flowing of this lifegiving river.

There is hope for every one of you. Perhaps there has straggled into this room this morning some one whose life has been a treason and an outrage upon all the traits of humanity; some one who is looked upon even by society around him as a very Pariah, whom a high-caste Brahmin would hardly stoop to look upon, and would gather up the fringes of his robes as he passed him by, but to whom, as I speak this morning, the Holy Spirit has come, and has impressed upon him a strange, strong agony of desire to repent and reform. My brother, there is hope for thee, though thou hast far gone in evil; though thou hast blasphemed thy Maker, and trampled under foot the blood of the covenant, counting it an unholy thing; though thou hast gone so far that thou art almost standing upon the verge of the bottomless pit; though the ground is unsteady as if an earthquake slumbered beneath it; though the yell of demon voices sounds hoarsely in the distance, and the tramp of demon feet appears to be coming nearer and nearer, exultingly to claim thee as their prey — now in this crisis of your fate, one cry, one upward glance of penitence and faith, the silent whisper of prayer, and He who gives that penitence and imparts that faith will lift thee up out of the horrible pit, and out of the miry clay; he will set thy feet upon the rock of ages; will lift thee up higher that thou mayest sit in heavenly places in Christ, so that all the world, looking at thee and at the Saviour who has delivered thee, may say: "Is not this a brand plucked from the burning?" Who of you will accept of this salvation now? "Everything shall live whither the river cometh."

Some of you have already rejoiced in the life and healing of the waters. You know that they issue from the foundation of the house, and that it is in the temple you are to find some of their channels. By God's blessing, those of you who love the Lord, and have taken upon you the vows of discipleship, are here this morning to receive the tokens of a Father's love, in the Father's house, at the Father's table. He blesses and sustains you at home; he consecrates the frugal board, and makes it often a banquet; and what is there that he will refuse to you in his own house, and on his own day, and at his own table? You are coming into his house now — his banqueting hall — and his banner over you is love.

The communion that you are to celebrate this morning is not a test of membership in the Church; it is the feast of the faithful, when the Father spreads the board, and all the sons and daughters come round, and feel the pleasure of his countenance. "They joy before thee according to the joy of harvest, as men rejoice when they divide the spoil." Come and renew your faith again; come and pay your vows again! When David, in the olden time, was bewildered with the multitude of God's mercies, and said, "What shall I render unto the Lord for all his benefits toward me?" how soon he came to the answer: "I will take the cup of salvation, and call upon the name of the Lord. I will pay my vows unto the Lord now in the presence of all his people." May he descend in the fulness of his real presence, and let us all feel that the world is not to-day orphaned of a God! Amen.

XXXVII

ALEXANDER MACLAREN

1826–

"THE Prince of expositors" is the title given to Alexander Maclaren, and no man in the last two generations has deserved it more. He was the son of a merchant in Glasgow, born February 11, 1826; and was brought up in the thorough manner befitting a Scottish Presbyterian household. His education was in the schools and university of his own city. In 1846 he entered the Presbyterian ministry and became minister of Portland Chapel, Southampton, England; but in 1858 was called to Union Chapel, Manchester, and has stood in that pulpit as preacher during all the years since. He will attain a fifty years' pastorate in one church in 1908, if another year is given to his life. Dr. Maclaren has always been recognized as a Biblical preacher, searching the Scriptures rather than the newspapers for his themes. His views with respect to the Bible are more nearly allied to the scholarship of the past, than that of the present; as he has seemed to pay little attention to what is known as "the higher criticism." But no man has studied the Bible more closely, or has brought forth from it richer treasures of thought. The results of his sixty years of Bible searching are now being published in a series of expository sermons, which it is said will include thirty volumes.

WHAT CROUCHES AT THE DOOR.

"If thou doest not well, sin croucheth at the door: and unto thee shall be his desire, and thou shalt rule over him."— Genesis iv. 7 (R. V.).

These early narratives clothe great moral and spiritual truths in picturesque forms, through which it is difficult for us to pierce. In the

484

world's childhood God spoke to men as to children, because there were
no words then framed which would express what we call abstract conceptions. They had to be shown by pictures. But these early men,
simple and childlike as they were, had consciences; and one abstraction
they did understand, and that was sin. They knew the difference between good and evil.

So we have here God speaking to Cain, who was wroth because
of the rejection of his sacrifice; and in dim, enigmatical words setting
forth the reason of that rejection. "If thou doest well, shalt thou not be
accepted?" Then clearly his sacrifice was rejected because it was the
sacrifice of an evil-doer. His description as such is given in the words
of my text, which are hard for us to translate into our modern, less
vivid and picturesque language. "If thou doest not well, sin lieth at
the door; and unto thee shall be his desire, and thou shalt rule over
him." Strange as the words sound, if I mistake not, they convey some
very solemn lessons, and if well considered, become pregnant with meaning.

The key to the whole interpretation of them is to remember that
they describe what happens after, and because of, wrong-doing. They
are all suspended on "If thou doest not well." Then, in that case, for
the first thing —"sin lieth at the door." Now the word translated here
"lieth" is employed only to express the *crouching* of an animal, and
frequently of a wild animal. The picture, then, is of the wrong-doer's
sin lying at his door there like a crouching tiger ready to spring, and if
it springs, fatal. "If thou doest not well, a wild beast crouches at thy
door."

Then there follow, with a singular swift transition of the metaphor,
other words still harder to interpret, and which have been, as a matter of
fact, interpreted in very diverse fashions. "And unto thee shall be *its*"
(I make that slight alteration upon our version) "desire, and thou shalt
rule over it." Where did we hear these words before? They were
spoken to Eve, in the declaration of her punishment. They contain the
blessing that was embedded in the curse. "Thy desire shall be to thy
husband, and he shall rule over thee." The longing of the pure womanly
heart to the husband of her love, and the authority of the husband over
the loving wife — the source of the deepest joy and purity of earth, is
transferred, by a singularly bold metaphor, to this other relationship, and,
in horrible parody of the wedded union and love, we have the picture of
the sin, that was thought of as crouching at the sinner's door like a

wild beast, now, as it were, wedded to him. He is mated to it now, and it has a kind of tigerish, murderous desire after him, while he on his part is to subdue and control it.

The reference of these clauses to the sin which has just been spoken of involves, no doubt, a very bold figure, which has seemed to many readers too bold to be admissible, and the words have therefore been supposed to refer to Abel, who, as the younger brother, would be subordinate to Cain. But such a reference breaks the connection of the sentence, introduces a thought which is not a consequence of Cain's not doing well, has no moral bearing to warrant its appearance here, and compels us to travel an inconveniently long distance back in the context to find an antecedent to the " his " and " him " of our text. It seems to be more in consonance, therefore, with the archaic style of the whole narrative, and to yield a profounder and worthier meaning, if we recognize the boldness of the metaphor, and take " sin " as the subject of the whole. Now all this puts in concrete, metaphorical shape, suited to the stature of the hearers, great and solemn truths. Let us try to translate them into more modern speech.

1. First think, then, of that wild beast which we tether to our doors by our wrong-doing.

We talk about " responsibility " and " guilt," and " consequences that never can be effaced," and the like. And all these abstract and quasi-philosophical terms are implied in the grim, tremendous metaphor of my text. " If thou doest not well, a tiger, a wild beast, is crouching at thy door." We are all apt to be deceived by the imagination that when an evil deed is done, it passes away and leaves no permanent results. The lesson taught the childlike primitive man here, at the beginning, before experience had accumulated instances which might demonstrate the solemn truth, was that every human deed is immortal, and that the transitory evil thought, or word, or act, which seems to fleet by like a cloud, has a permanent being, and hereafter haunts the life of the doer, as a real presence. If thou doest not well, thou dost create a horrible something which nestles beside thee henceforward. The momentary act is incarnated, as it were, and sits there at the doer's doorpost waiting for him; which being turned into less forcible but more modern language, is just this: every sin that a man does has perennial consequences, which abide with the doer for evermore.

I need not dwell upon illustrations of that to any length. Let me just run over two or three ways in which it is true. First of all, there is that solemn fact which we put into a long word that comes glibly off people's lips, and impresses them very little — the solemn fact of responsibility. We speak in common talk of such and such a thing lying at some one's door. Whether the phrase has come from this text I do not know. But it helps to illustrate the force of these words, and to suggest that they mean this, among other things, that we have to answer for every deed, however, evanescent, however long forgotten. Its guilt is on our heads. Its consequences have to be experienced by us. We drink as we have brewed. As we make our beds, so we lie on them. There is no escape from the law of consequences. " If 'twere done, when 'tis done, then 'twere well it were done quickly." But seeing that it is not done when 'tis done, then perhaps it would be better that it were not done at all. Your deed of a moment, forgotten almost as soon as done, lies there at your door; or to take a more modern and commercial figure, it is debited to your account, and stands inscribed against you for ever.

Think how you would like it, if all your deeds from your childhood, all your follies, your vices, your evil thoughts, your evil impulses, and your evil actions, were all made visible and embodied there before you. They are there, though you do not see them yet. All round your door they sit, ready to meet you and to bay out condemnation as you go forth. They are there, and one day you will find out that they are. For this is the law, certain as the revolution of the stars and fixed as the pillars of the firmament : " Whatsoever a man soweth, that shall he also reap." There is no seed which does not sprout, in the harvest of the moral life. Every deed germinates according to its kind. For all that a man does he has to carry the consequences, and every one shall bear his own burden. " If thou doest not well," it is not, as we fondly conceive it sometimes to be, a mere passing deflection from the rule of right, which is done and done with, but we have created, as out of our very own substance, a witness against ourselves whose voice can never be stifled. " If thou doest not well," thy sin takes permanent form and is fastened to thy door.

And let me remind you, too, how the metaphor of our text is confirmed by other obvious facts, on which I need but briefly dwell. Putting aside all the remoter bearings of that thought of responsibility, I suppose we all admit that we have consciences; I suppose that we all know that we have memories; I suppose we all of us have seen, in the case of others, and have experienced for ourselves, how deeds long done and long forgotten have an awful power of rising again after many long years.

Be sure that your memory has in it everything that you ever did. A landscape may be hidden by mists, but a puff of wind will clear them away, and it will all lie there, visible to the farthest horizon. There is no fact more certain than the extraordinary swiftness and completeness with which, in certain circumstances of life, and often very near the close of it, the whole panorama of the past may rise again before a man, as if one lightning flash showed all the dreary desolation that lay behind him. There have been men recovered from drowning and the like, who have told us that, as in an instant, there seemed unrolled before their startled eyes the whole scroll of their earthly career.

The records of memory are like those pages on which you write with sympathetic ink, which disappears when dry, and seems to leave the page blank. You have only to hold it before the fire, or subject it to the proper chemical process, and at once it stands out legible. You are writing your biography upon the fleshly tables of your heart, my brother; and one day it will all be spread out before you, and you will be bid to read it, and to say what you think of it. The stings of a nettle will burn for days, if they are touched with water. The sting and inflammation of your evil deeds, though it has died down, is capable of being resuscitated, and it will be.

What an awful menagerie of unclean beasts some of us have at our doors! What sort of creatures have you tethered at yours? Crawling serpents, ugly and venomous; wild creatures, fierce and bloody, obscene and foul; tigers and bears; lustful and mischievous apes and monkeys? or such as are lovely and of good report,— doves and lambs, creatures pure and peaceable, patient to serve and gentle of spirit? Remember, remember, that what a man soweth — be it hemlock or be it wheat — that, and nothing else, " shall he reap."

2. Now, let us look for a moment at the next thought that is here; which is put into a strong, and, to our modern notions, somewhat violent metaphor; — the horrible longing, as it were, of sin toward the sinner: " Unto thee shall be its desire."

As I explained, these words are drawn from the previous chapter, where they refer to the holy union of heart and affection in husband and wife. Here they are transferred with tremendous force, to set forth that which is a kind of horrible parody of that conjugal relation. A man is married to his wickedness, is mated to his evil, and it has, as it were, a tigerish longing for him, unhallowed and murderous. That is to say — our sins act towards us as if they desired to draw our love to themselves. This is just another form of the statement, that when once a man has done a wrong thing, it has an awful power of attracting him and making him hunger to do it again. Every evil that I do may, indeed, for a moment create in me a revulsion of conscience; but it also exercises a fascination over me which it is hard to resist. It is a great deal easier to find a man who has never done a wrong thing than to find a man who has only done it once. If the wall of the dyke is sound it will keep the water out, but if there is the tiniest hole in it, the flood will come in. So the evil that you do asserts its power over you, or, in the vigorous metaphor of my text, it has a fierce, longing desire after you, and it gets you into its clutches.

" The foolish woman sitteth in the high places of the city, and saith, Whoso is simple let him turn in hither." And foolish men go after her, and —" know not that her guests are in the depth of hell." Ah! my brother! beware of that siren voice that draws you away from all the sweet and simple and pure food which Wisdom spreads upon her table, to tempt the beast that is in you with the words, " Stolen waters are sweet, and bread eaten in secret is pleasant." Beware of the first step, for as sure as you are living, the first step taken will make the second seem to become necessary. The first drop will be followed by a bigger second, and the second, at a shorter interval, by a more copious third, until the drops become a shower, and the shower becomes a deluge. The river of evil is ever wider and deeper, and more tumultuous. The little sins get in at the window, and open the front door for the full-grown house-breakers. One smooths the path for the other. All sin has an awful power of perpetuating and increasing itself. As the prophet says in his vision of the doleful creatures that make their sport in the desolate city, " None of them shall want her mate. The wild beasts of the desert shall meet with the wild beasts of the island." Every sin tells upon character, and makes the repetition of itself more and more easy. " None is barren among them." And all sin is linked together in a slimy tangle, like a field of seaweed, so that the man once caught in its oozy fingers is almost sure to be drowned.

3. And now, lastly, one word about the command, which is also a promise: " To thee shall be its desire, and thou shalt rule over it."

Man's primitive charter, according to the earlier chapters of Genesis, was to have dominion over the beasts of the field. Cain knew what it was to war against the wild creatures which contested the possession of the earth with man, and to tame some of them for his uses. And, says the divine voice, just as you war against the beasts of prey, just as you subdue to your purposes and yoke to your implements the tamable animals over which you have dominion, so rule over *this* wild beast that is threatening you. It is needful for all men, if they do not mean to be torn to pieces, to master the animal that is in them, and the wild thing that has been created out of them. It is bone of your bone and flesh of your flesh. It is your own evil that is thus incarnated there, as it were, before you; and you have to subdue it, if it is not to tyrannise over you. We all admit that in theory, but how terribly hard the practice! The words of our text seem to carry but little hope or comfort in them, to the man who has tried — as, no doubt, many of us have tried — to flee the lusts that war against the soul, and to bridle the animal that is in him. Those who have done so most honestly know best how hard it is, and may fairly ask, Is this useless repetition of the threadbare injunction all that you have to say to us? If so, you may as well hold your tongue. A wild beast sits at my door, you say, and then you bid me, "Rule thou over it!" Tell me to tame the tiger! Canst thou draw out Leviathan with a hook? Wilt thou take him a servant for ever?

I do not undervalue the earnest and sometimes partially successful efforts at moral reformation which some men of more than usual force of character are able to make, emancipating themselves from the outward practice of gross sin, and achieving for themselves much that is admirable. But if we rightly understand what sin is — namely, the taking self for our law and centre instead of God — and how deep its working and all-pervading its poison, we shall learn the tragic significance of the prophet's question, "Can the leopard change his spots?" Then may a man cast out sin from his nature by his own resolve, when the body can eliminate poison from the veins by its own energy. If there is nothing more to be said to the world than this message, "Sin lieth at thy door — rule thou over it," we have no gospel to preach, and sin's dominion is secure. For there is nothing in all this world of empty, windy words, more empty and windy than to come to a poor soul that is all bespattered and stained with sin, and say to him: "Get up, and make thyself clean, and keep thyself so!" It cannot be done.

So my text, though it keeps itself within the limits of the law and only proclaims duty, must have hidden, in its very hardness, a sweet kernel of promise. For what God commands God enables us to do.

Therefore these words, " Rule thou over it," do really point onwards through all the ages to that one fact in which every man's sin is conquered and neutralized, and every man's struggles may be made hopeful and successful, the great fact that Jesus Christ, God's own Son, came down from heaven, like an athlete descending into the arena, to fight with and to overcome the grim wild beasts, our passions and our sins, and to lead them, transformed, in the silken leash of His love.

My brother! your sin is mightier than you. The old word of the Psalm is true about every one of us, " Our iniquities are stronger than we." And, blessed be His name! the hope of the Psalmist is the experience of the Christian: " As for my transgressions, Thou wilt purge them away." Christ will strengthen you to conquer; Christ will take away your guilt; Christ will bear, has borne your burden; Christ will cleanse your memory; Christ will purge your conscience. Trusting to Him, and by His power and life within us, we may conquer our evil. Trusting to Him, and for the sake of His blood shed for us all upon the cross, we are delivered from the burden, guilt, and power of our sins and of our sin. With thy hand in His, and thy will submitted to Him, " thou shalt tread on the lion and the adder; the young lion and the dragon thou shalt trample under foot."

XXXVIII

JOHN A. BROADUS

1827–1895

A LEADER in religious thought, not only of the Baptist denomination, and in the South, but of the American church in general, was the Rev. John A. Broadus, LL. D., of Louisville, Kentucky. He was born in Culpeper County, Virginia, in 1827, and was graduated from that great fountain of Southern education, the University of Virginia, in 1850. For several years he combined the two vocations of a professor in the University and of the pastor over the Baptist church in Charlottesville. In 1859 a Baptist Theological Seminary was established at Greenville, South Carolina, and Dr. Broadus was chosen as its professor of New Testament interpretation, and of homiletics, or the principles of preaching. The Civil War broke out, and Dr. Broadus with the people of his section espoused the cause of the Southern Confederacy. Although he held no public office, either in military or civil life, he was employed upon several important missions in behalf of the Confederate Government, and his services were regarded as of high value. After some years the Theological Seminary, with which he was connected, was removed to Louisville, Kentucky, and Dr. Broadus became its president. Here his broad and strong scholarship, his ability in administration, his kindness of character, and his interest in young men, gave him a great influence over the lives of many ministers. He died in 1895, at the height of his intellectual powers.

SOME LAWS OF SPIRITUAL WORK.

" But he said unto them, I have meat to eat that ye know not. The disciples therefore said unto one another, Hath any man brought him

JOHN A. BROADUS.
1827-1895.
Born in Virginia, Dr. Broadus was an adherent
of the Confederate cause during the Civil War.
Later he moved to Louisville, and as President
of a Theological Seminary widely indulged his interest in young men.

ALEXANDER MACLAREN.

1826-

Alexander Maclaren is noted for the clearness and literalness of his Biblical expositions. He was born in Glasgow, but occupied a pulpit in Manchester for the greater part of his life.

aught to eat? Jesus saith unto them, My meat is to do the will of him that sent me, and to accomplish his work. Say not ye, There are yet four months, and then cometh the harvest? Behold, I say unto you, Lift up your eyes and look on the fields, that they are white already unto harvest. He that reapeth receiveth wages, and gathereth fruit unto life eternal; that he that soweth and he that reapeth may rejoice together. For herein is the saying true, One soweth, and another reapeth. I sent ye to reap that wheron ye have not labored: others have labored, and ye are entered into their labor."— John iv. 32-38.

THE disciples must have been very much astonished at the change which they observed in the Master's appearance. They left him, when they went away to a neighboring city to buy food, reclining beside Jacob's well, quite worn out with the fatigue of their journey, following upon the fatigues of long spiritual labors. And here now he is sitting up, his face is animated, his eyes kindled. He has been at work again. Presently they ask him to partake of the food which they had brought, and his answer surprised them: " I have food to eat that ye know not." They looked around, and saw nobody; the woman to whom he had been speaking was gone, and they said: " Has any one brought him something to eat?" Jesus answered: " My food is to do the will of him that sent me, and to accomplish his work." And then, with this thought of work, he changes the image to sowing and reaping, and bids them go forth to work.

Now, from this passage with its images, I have wished to discourse upon *some laws of spiritual work,* as here set forth. For we are beginning to see, in our time, that there are laws in the spiritual sphere as truly as in the mental and in the physical spheres. What are the laws of spiritual work which the Saviour here indicates? I name four:

I. Spiritual work is *refreshing* to soul and body. " My food is," said the tired, hungry one, who had aroused himself, " to do the will of him that sent me, and to accomplish his work." We all know the power of the body over the mind, and we all know, I trust, the power of the mind over the body; how any animating theme can kindle the mind until the wearied body will be stirred to new activities; until the man will forget that he was tired, because of that in which he is interested. But it must be something that does deeply interest the mind. And so there is suggested to us the thought that we ought to learn to love spiritual work. If we love spiritual work it will kindle our souls; it will even give health and vigor to our bodies. There are some well-meaning, but good-for-nothing, professed Christians in our time, who would have better health of mind and even better health of body, if they would do more religious work and be good for something in their day and generation.

How shall we learn to love religious work so that it may kindle and refresh us? Old Daniel Sharp, who was a famous Baptist minister in Boston years ago, used to be very fond of repeating, " The only way to learn to preach is to preach." Certainly, the only way to learn to do anything is to *do* the thing. The only way to learn to do spiritual work is to do spiritual work, the only way to learn to love spiritual work is to keep doing it until we gain pleasure from the doing; until we discern rewards in connection with the doing; and to cherish all the sentiments which will awaken in us that "enthusiasm of humanity" which it was Jesus that introduced among men; and to love the souls of our fellow-men, to love the wandering, misguided lives, to love the suffering and sinning all around us with such an impassioned love that it shall be a delight to us to do them good and to try to save them from death. Then that will refresh both mind and body.

II. There are *seasons* in the spiritual sphere — sowing seasons and reaping seasons, just as there are in farming. "Say not ye," said Jesus, "there are yet four months and then cometh the harvest?"— that is to say, it was four months from that time till the harvest. They sowed their wheat in December; they began to reap it in April. "Say not ye, there are four months, and then cometh the harvest? behold, I say unto you, lift up your eyes and look on the fields; for they are white already to harvest." In the spiritual sphere it was a harvest time then, and they were bidden to go forth and reap the harvest that waved white and perishing. We can see, as we look back, that the ends of all the ages had now come to that time; that the long course of providential preparation, dimly outlined in the Old Testament, had led to the state of things that then prevailed; that the fulness of the times had come, when God sent forth his Son to teach men and to atone for men, and to rise again and come forth as their Saviour, and that his servants should go forth in his name. And the like has been true in many other seasons of Christianity; there have been great reaping times, when men have harvested the fruits which come from the seed scattered by others long before.

I persuade myself that such a time will be seen ere long in the world again. I think that the young who are here present to-day — though they may forget the preacher and his prediction — will live to see the time when there will be a great season of harvest that will astonish mankind. In the great heathen world I think it will be true that the labors of our missionaries are preparing the way, and that in the course of divine providence — the same providence that overruled the history of Egypt and Assyria and Greece and Rome — the greatest nations of Asia are now becoming rapidly prepared to receive a new faith. They say, who live there and ought to know, that there is a wonderful breaking up of religious opinion in all Hindostan, with its two hundred and fifty millions of people — five times as many, almost, as in our great country — that they are learning to let go their old faiths, and that the time must soon come when, in sheer bewilderment and blindness, as it were, men will search round for something else to look upon, something else to lay hold upon. It is a sad thing to see great nations of mankind surrendered to utter unbelief, but it has often proved the preparation for their accepting a true and mighty and blessed faith. I think one can see, in the marvellous changes which are going on in Japan, a preparation for like effects there; and as Japan is, for the civilized world, the gateway into China, and our missionaries are already at work there and great changes are taking place there, so it is quite possible that even in one or two generations there will be a wide-spread of Christianity in that wonderful nation of mankind. God grant that it may be so!

I think the same thing is going to happen in our own country. We have been living in a time of eclipse, so to speak, of late years, but I think another reaction will come. Some of us can remember that thirty or forty years ago there was almost no avowed infidelity in this country. There was not a publisher in New York, who had any respect for himself and any large hope of success, that would have had a book with one page of avowed unbelief in it on his shelves. How different it is now!

We have been passing, as I said, through a reaction. In the early part of this century our whole country was honeycombed with infidelity. It was ten times worse than it is to-day. But in 1825, 1830, 1840, 1850, there were wide-spread changes, revivals; and a great many men were brought into our churches who had not the root of the matter in them, and a lax discipline and a low state of religious living became, alas! too common, and we have been reaping the bitter fruits. Alas! how often it has happened that some man has become notorious in the newspapers as a defaulter or a criminal in some other way, and we have been compelled to read the added statement, that he was a member of such and such a church, was a Sunday-school superintendent, teacher, or what not. How often it has happened! This has been one of many causes — I cannot stop now to analyze and point out, but they can be analyzed and pointed out — of such wide-spread unbelief of late years. But it cannot last. There never was such activity in the Christian world; and if our earnest Christian people stand firm, if they practice in all directions that earnestness of Christian purpose, if they try to maintain the truth of the gospel and live up to it in their own lives, and lift up their prayer to God for his blessing, there will come another great sweeping reaction. It is as sure to come as there is logic in history or in human nature. It is as sure to come as there is truth in the promises of God's word. O, may many of you live to see that day and rejoice at its coming!

The same thing is true in individual churches, that there are seasons of sowing and reaping. It has to be so. We sometimes say we do not believe in the revival idea; we think there ought to be revival in the church all the time. If you mean that we ought always to be seeking for spiritual advancement, it is true. But if you mean that you expect that piety will go on with even current in the church, that there will be just as much sowing and reaping at any one time as at any other, then you will certainly be disappointed. That is not the law of human nature. That is not possible in the world. Periodicity pervades the universe. Periodicity controls the life of all individuals, shows itself in the operations of our minds. Periodicity necessarily appears in the spiritual sphere also. People have their ups and downs. They ought to strive against falling low. They ought not to be content with growing cold. They ought to seek to maintain good health of body all the while, but it will not be always equally good; and good health of mind and soul all the time, but it will not be always equally good. They ought to be seeking to reap a harvest of spiritual good among those around them all the while; but they will have seasons which are rather of sowing, and other seasons which will be rather of reaping. O! do you want to see a great season of harvest among your own congregation? And do you not know, brethren, as well as the preacher can tell you, what is necessary in order that you may see it? What are the conditions but deepened spiritual life in your own individual souls, stronger spiritual examples set forth in your lives, more earnest spirituality in your homes, a truer standard in your business and social relations to mankind, more of heartfelt prayer for God's blessing, and more untiring and patient and persevering effort, in season and out of season, to bring others to seek their salvation?

III. Spiritual work *links the workers in unity.* "Herein is the saying true," said Jesus; "one soweth, and another reapeth. Other men have labored, and ye are entered into their labors." The prophets, centuries before, had been preparing for that day, and the labors of Jesus himself in his early ministry had been preparing the way, and now the disciples could look around them upon the fields where, from the sowing of others, there were opportunities for them to reap. "Other men have labored, and ye are entered into their labors. One soweth and another reapeth." That is the law everywhere; it is true of all the higher work of humanity,—"One soweth, and another reapeth;" and our labors link us into unity. It is true of human knowledge. How little has any one individual of mankind been able to find out beyond what the world has known before! Even the great minds that stand like mountain peaks as we look back over the history of human thought, when we come to look into it, do really but uplift the thought that is all around them; else they themselves could not have risen. It is true in practical inventions. We pride ourselves on the fact that ours is an age of such wonderful practical inventions; we sometimes persuade ourselves that we must be the most intelligent generation of mankind that ever lived, past all comparison; that no other race, no other century, has such wonderful things to boast of. How much of it do we owe to the men of the past? Every practical invention of to-day has been rendered possible by what seemed to us the feeble attainments of other centuries, by the patient investigation of the men who, in many cases, have passed away and been forgotten. We stand upon the shoulders of the past, and rejoice in our possessions, and boast; and when we grow conceited and proud of it, we are like a little boy lifted by his father's supporting arms, and standing on his father's shoulders, and clapping his hands above his father's head, and saying, in childish glee, "I am taller than papa!" A childish conclusion, to be sure. We stand upon the shoulders of the past, and thereby we are lifted up in all the higher work of mankind; and we ought to be grateful to the past, and mindful of our duty to the future; for the time will come when men will look back upon our inventions, our slow travel, our wonderful ignorance of the power of physical forces and the adaptations of them to physical advancement, and smile at the childishness with which, in the fag end of the nineteenth century, we boasted of ourselves and our time.

And now it is not strange that this same thing should be true of spiritual work. When you undertake to do some good in a great city like this, you might sit down and say, "What can I do with all this

32

mass of vice and sin?" But you do not have to work alone. You can associate yourselves with other workers, in a church, with various organizations of workers, and thereby re-enforce your own exertions; you can feel that you are a working force, and you can feel that you are a part of a mighty force of workers, of your own name and other Christian names. Grace be with all them that love our Lord Jesus Christ in sincerity, and are trying to do good in his name! And it will cheer our hearts to remember that wide over the land and over the world are unnumbered millions of workers of the army to which we belong. They tell us that the International Sunday-school lessons which most of us study every Sunday, are actually studied now every Lord's Day by at least ten millions of people, all studying on the same day the same portion of the Bible. That is but one fact to remind us that we are members of a great spiritual host, doing a great work in the world.

And not merely are there many cotemporaries with whom we are linked in unity, but we are in unity with the past; other men have labored and we have entered into their labors. All the good that all the devout women and all the zealous men of past ages have been doing have come down to us, opening the way for us to do good. And not merely with the past, but we are linked with the laborers of the future. They may hear our names or they may hear them not. We may perish from all memory of mankind, but our work will not perish, for he that doeth the will of God abideth forever, and if we are engaged in his work, we link ourselves to his permanency and his almightiness, and our work will go down to help the men who are to come after.

The same thing is true here, also, in the individual church; one soweth and another reapeth. A pastor seldom gathers half as much fruit from the seed that others have sown. And there will come some man here — God grant it may be soon, and wisely, and well — who will gather seed from the sowing of the venerable pastor so well and worthily beloved in years ago, seed from the sowing of the energetic pastor of recent years, and O my soul, he may gather some harvest, even from the seed scattered in the brief fleeting interim of this summer. We put all our work together. We sink our work in the one great common work. We scatter seed for God and for souls, and we leave it to God's own care and blessing. One soweth, and another reapeth.

My brethren, there is nothing like Christianity to individualize mankind. It was Christianity that taught us to appreciate the individuality of men: "Every man must give account of himself unto God." Men were no longer to lose themselves in the state, as classical antiquity taught them to do, but to stand out in their separate personality and individual responsibility and individual rights and duties. But at the same time much of what we can do that is best in the world we must do by close connection and interaction with one another. Let us rejoice to act through others. Priscilla and Aquila! what a power they were for early Christianity when they took that eloquent young Alexandrian Apollos and taught him in private the way of God more perfectly! Priscilla, that devout woman, stood, in fact, before delighted assemblies in Corinth and spoke to them the perfect way of God through the eloquent man whom she had taught. And how often does the Sunday-school teacher, who labored long and, as the world might have thought, fruitlessly, with her little naughty boys and girls, become in future times a great power for good in the world through one or other of them! The teacher has to sink himself in his pupils: never mind if he sinks all out of the world's sight, provided he can make his mark upon *them* and prepare them for greater usefulness, and put into them some good spirit, and send them forth to do the work which to him personally is denied. Here lies the great power of Christian women. There is much they can do personally, with their own voice and their own action, but there is more they can do by that wondrous influence which men vainly strive to depict, that influence over son and brother and husband and friend whereby all the strength and power of the man is softened and guided and sobered and made wiser through the blessed influence of the woman. God be thanked that we can not only do good in our individual efforts, but we can do good through others! Let us cultivate this, let us delight in this, that we can labor through others. Whenever your pastor may stand before the gathered assembly he can speak with more power because of you, if you do your duty to him and through him.

May I mention some of the ways in which we may help our pastor? I speak as one who at home sits for the most part, a private member of the church in the pew, toiling all the week, and often unable to preach on Sunday, and yet as one whose heart is all in sympathy with the pastor's heart, and perhaps a little better able than common to sympathize with both sides. We can help him to draw a congregation. You know we always say now-a-days, that it is very important to get a man who can draw a congregation. So it is, though it is very important to consider what he draws them there for, and what he does with them after he gets them there; and sometimes it does seem to me that it would be better for

some people to remain not drawn than to be drawn merely to hear and to
witness that which does them harm rather than good. But we do want a
man who can draw a congregation; and we can help our pastor to draw a
congregation. How? Well, by taking care that we are always drawn
ourselves, by occupying our own place, sometimes when we do not feel like
it, on Sunday evening; because it is our duty to our pastor, our duty to the
congregation, and our duty to the world. And we can do something to
bring others. I recall a story, that a few years after the war (which is the
great chronological epoch in a large part of our country), at the White
Sulphur Springs, in Virginia, was a venerable man at whom all the people
looked with profound admiration, whose name was Robert E. Lee. He
was a devout Episcopalian. One day a Presbyterian minister came to
preach in the ball-room, according to custom, and he told me this story.
He noticed that General Lee, who was a very particular man about all
the proprieties of life, came in late, and he thought it was rather strange.
He learned afterwards that the General had waited until all the people
who were likely to attend the service had entered the room, and then he
walked very quietly around in the corridors and parlors, and out under the
trees, and wherever he saw a man or two standing he would go up and
say gently: "We are going to have divine service this morning in the
ball-room; won't you come?" And they all went. To me it was very
touching that that grand old man, whose name was known all over the
world and before whom all the people wanted to bow, should so quietly
go around, and for a minister of another denomination also, and persuade them to go. Should not we take means to help our pastor to draw
a congregation? And when he begins to preach, cannot we help him to
preach? Demosthenes is reported to have said (and he ought to have
known something about it), that eloquence lies as much in the ear as in
the tongue. Everybody who can speak effectively knows that the power
of speaking depends very largely upon the way it is heard, upon the sympathy which one succeeds in gaining from those he addresses. If I were
asked what is the first thing in effective preaching, I should say, sympathy; and what is the second thing, I should say sympathy, and what
is the third thing, sympathy. We should give our pastor *sympathy* when
he preaches. Sometimes one good listener can make a good sermon; but
ah! sometimes one listener who does not care much about the gospel can
put the sermon all out of harmony. The soul of a man who can speak
effectively is a very sensitive soul, easily repelled and chilled by what is

unfavorable, and easily helped by the manifestation of simple and unpretentious sympathy.

How can we help our pastor? We can help him by talking about what he says; not talking about the performance and about the performer, and all that, which, if it is appropriate anywhere, is surely all inappropriate when we turn away from the solemn worship of God, and from listening to sermons intended to do us good — but talking about the thoughts that he has given us, recalling them sometimes to one who has heard them like ourselves, repeating them sometimes to one who has not had the opportunity of hearing them. Thus may we multiply whatever good thoughts the preacher is able to present, and keep them alive in our own minds and the minds of fellow-Christians. Will you pardon an illustration here, even if it be a personal one? Last year in a city in Texas, I was told of the desire on the part of a lady for conversation, and when we met by arrangement she came in widow's weeds, with a little boy, ten or twelve years old, and began to tell this story: Her husband was once a student at the University of Virginia, when the person she was talking to was the chaplain there, more than twenty-five years ago. He was of a Presbyterian family from Alabama, and said he never got acquainted with the chaplain, for the students were numerous, but that he heard the preaching a great deal, and in consequence of it, by God's blessing upon it, he was led to take hold as a Christian, and went home and joined the church of his parents. After the war he married this lady, and a few years ago he passed away. She said he was in the habit, before she knew him, she learned, of talking often in the family about things he used to hear the preacher say; the preacher's words had gotten to be household words in the family. And then when they were married he taught some of them to her, and was often repeating things he used to hear the preacher say. Since he died she had been teaching them to the little boy — the preacher's word. The heart of the preacher might well melt in his bosom at the story. To think that your poor words, which you yourself had wholly forgotten, which you could never have imagined had vitality enough for that, had been repeated among strangers, had been repeated by the young man to his mother, repeated by the young widow to the child — your poor words, thus mighty because they were God's truth you were trying to speak and because you had humbly sought God's blessing! And through all the years it went on, and the man knew not, for more than a quarter of a century, of all that story. Ah, we never know when we are doing good. Sometimes when we think we are going to do great things, and so far as can ever be ascertained, we do nothing; and sometimes when we think we have done nothing, yet, by the blessing of God, some truth has been lodged in a mind here and there, to bear fruit after many days.

How can we help our pastor? We can furnish him illustrations. Mr. Spurgeon tells us that he requests his teachers, and his wife, and various other friends to hunt up illustrations for him. He asks them, whenever they have come across anything in reading or in conversation that strikes them as good, to write it down and let him have it, and whenever he sees a fit opportunity he makes a point of it. We can all furnish our pastors with illustrations. In that very way, perhaps, we might give a preacher many things that would be useful to him. In other ways we can all do so. Ah, when the preacher tells how it ought to be, if you can sometimes humbly testify, in the next meeting on Tuesday or Friday evening, how it has been in your experience, you are illustrating for the preacher. When the preacher tells what Christianity can do for people, if your life illustrates it for all around, there is a power that no speech can ever have. There remains a fourth law of spiritual work.

IV. Spiritual work has rich rewards: "And he that reapeth receiveth wages," saith Jesus, "and gathereth fruit unto life eternal." Spiritual work has rich rewards. It has the reward of success. It is not in vain to try to do good to the souls of men through the truth of God and seeking his grace. Sometimes you may feel as if you were standing at the foot of a precipice a thousand feet high and trying to spring to its summit, and were all powerless. Sometimes you may feel as if you had flung your words against a stone wall and made no impression at all. Sometimes you may go away ashamed of what you have said in public or in private. But there was never a word spoken that uttered God's truth and sought God's blessing, that was spoken in vain. Somehow it does good to somebody, it does good at some time or other; it shall be known in earth or in heaven that it did do good. Comfort your hearts with these words: It is not in vain to try to do good. You may say, " I have not the lips of the eloquent, the tongue of the learned, how can I talk? There is many a minister who is eloquent and has preached to gathered congregations, who could tell you that he knows of many more instances in which his private words have been blest to individuals than he knows of such instances in public. I knew of a girl who had been so afflicted that she could not leave her couch for years, who had to be lifted constantly — poor, helpless creature! — but who would talk to those who came into her room about her joy in God, and would persuade them to seek the consolations of the gospel, and many were benefited and would bring their friends to her, till after a while they brought them from adjoining counties, that she, the poor, helpless girl, might influence them; at length she even began to write letters to people far away, and that girl's sick-bed became a centre of blessing to people throughout a whole region. We talk about doing nothing in the world. Ah, if our hearts were in it! we do not know what we can do. That tiger in the cage has been there since he was a baby tiger, and does not know that he could burst those bars if he were but to exert his strength. O the untried strength in all our churches, and the good that the people could do if we would only try, and keep trying, and pray for God's blessing. My friends, you cannot save your soul as a solitary, and you ought not to dare to try to go alone into the paradise of God. We shall best promote our own piety when we are trying to save others. We shall be most helpful to ourselves when we are most helpful to those around us. Many of you have found it so; and all of you may find it so, again and again, with repetitions that shall pass all human telling. " For he that watereth shall be watered also again!"

Spiritual work shall also be rewarded in the Lord of the harvest's commendation and welcome. Ah, he will know which was the sowing and which was the reaping. The world may not know; *we* may never hear; but *he* will know which was the sowing and which was the reaping, and who tried to do good and thought he had not done it, and who was sad and bowed down with the thought of being utterly unable to be useful, and yet *was* useful. He will know, he will reward even the desire of the heart, which there was no opportunity to carry out. He will reward the emotion that trembled on the lip and could find no utterance. He will reward David for wanting to build the temple as well as Solomon for building it. He will reward all that we do, and all that we try to do, and all that we wish to do. O blessed God! he will be your reward and mine, forever and forever.

XXXIX

JOHN HEYL VINCENT

1832–

JOHN HEYL VINCENT, D.D., LL. D., needs no introduction to our readers, for he has been a prominent personality as minister, educator, and Bishop, for more than a generation. He was born in Tuscaloosa, Alabama, February 23, 1832, but grew up in Pennsylvania, where he began to preach at the age of eighteen. He studied for a time in the Wesleyan Academy, Newark, N. J., but was not able to accomplish his desire of a course in College. Perhaps this loss to the young preacher was the cause of a greater gain to multitudes; for it gave him a deep and abiding interest in education for those who, like himself, felt their need of it, and led him to establish later " the Chautauqua system " of instruction for men and women out of school. In 1853, he entered the ministry of the Methodist Episcopal church in New Jersey; but after preaching in two churches near Newark, N. J., was transferred to Illinois. In his little congregation at Galena, he had at the opening of the war a quiet business man, afterwards known as General Grant. He was also pastor of Trinity church in Chicago, but in 1865 gave up his church to become a worker for the awakening and rapidly developing Sunday School movement. In 1868 he was called to the editorship of Sunday School literature for the Methodist Episcopal Church: and for twenty years was the recognized leader of the Sunday School world. In 1874, in conjunction with Lewis Miller of Ohio, he organized and conducted the first Chautauqua Assembly, the mother of assemblies, having children in every state of the Union. In 1878, he established the Chautauqua Literary and Scientific Circle, a system of home-study, which has opened the door to culture for untold thousands of people.

His church made him one of its bishops in 1888; and he was engaged in the work of administration until 1904, when he retired from active service as Bishop, while still retaining his interest in Chautauqua and its varied departments. His preaching has always been a rare combination of the intellectual, the ethical, and the spiritual qualities, with the charm of a wide and flexible voice, and that indefinable gift which everybody calls "magnetism." Bishop Vincent has been frequently called to deliver sermons and lectures at Cornell, Harvard, and other great Universities. He received the degree of LL. D. from Harvard University. The sermon here given was delivered as the baccalaureate discourse at Chautauqua, before the C. L. S. C. class of 1899. Not less than six thousand people listened to it in the Chautauqua Amphitheater, on August 16, 1899.

THE REVELATION OF GOD.

" He made known His ways unto Moses, His acts (in the new version, "His doings") unto the children of Israel."— Psa. ciii. 7.

THE psalmist here says that God has revealed Himself to man. Nothing can be more reasonable. Can it be that a Supreme Intelligence would create intelligent subjects of his government and children of his family, and have no further communication with them? Intelligence creating intelligence, revelation is inevitable. But how did God reveal Himself to man? When I was a very little child I supposed that He had revealed himself in a Book, and that the self-revelation was limited to the Book. If I had been told that He wrote it Himself, and by a supernatural process transmitted it to the earth, I should not have been surprised. If some day I had stolen into the room where the family Bible lay, and it should suddenly have flashed with supernal light, it would have caused me no surprise. Was it not God's book? Did He not make it? Is it not a revelation from heaven to man? And must I not go to that Book for all that I know about God? And there are to this day persons who so revere the edition of the Holy Scriptures, which they have been accustomed to read from their childhood, and to regard it as a book of God, that they shrink from the very idea of any revision.

I wish this morning to insist that God, in revealing himself to humanity, does not limit himself to a book; that he did not write a complete and perfect book in heaven and hand it down to humanity; but that God "made known his ways" unto individuals, "his doings" unto nations, and that his revelation was a revelation chiefly by action, a revelation on the plane of human activity, in vast historic unfoldings, through long centuries, on a colossal scale and with deep incisions. He did not write, he wrought. And man wrote. God wrought deeds to make words possible, to give significance to words; but his revelation was primarily a revelation in action.

"He made known His ways unto Moses." Let us glance for a moment at that wonderful scene recorded in the book of Exodus, where Moses and Aaron appear before Pharaoh. Let us not hesitate to accept the historic record. If any one does hesitate, let him not at this time dwell on his doubt, but let us look at the principle hidden within this impressive scene. Pharaoh is on his throne. Moses and Aaron, representatives of the Hebrew people, stand before him. How shall those men impress the sovereign and secure the royal mandate that shall set free from Egyptian bondage two and one-half million of people? Words are of little effect here and now. The two Hebrews may talk for hours and for days, and the effect be no more than if snow flakes fell for hours on the sands by the Nile. Remember the five great forces represented that day: the powers of nature; the human government represented by the king; the learning of Egypt represented by the magicians they also being representatives of an ancient and powerful religious faith and worship; and finally, that marvelous personality, Pharaoh himself, whose presence would have inspired a certain awe even though he had not been a king. Here, then are five mighty factors felt in every part of the world to-day: Nature, Government, Learning, Religion, and Personality. How shall these powers be controlled in the Hebrew interest? We may be very sure that it will not be by words which Aaron may speak, even though they are backed by the strong personality of Moses.

In the history that we now report it is written that Pharaoh demanded a sign, and that Aaron in obedience to Moses' command cast his rod upon the ground and it became a living serpent. At Pharaoh's command, his magicians cast their rods to the ground and they became living serpents. But "Aaron's rod swallowed up their rods." And then became a series of marvelous deeds which made the people of Israel and the people of Egypt acknowledge that the finger of God was there. The outcome was that the children of Israel were delivered from bondage and taken into the wilderness, where through many years they were guided by the God who had delivered them. Thus, " God made known His ways unto Moses, His acts unto the children of Israel."

From the Old Testament let us go to the New. Jesus himself never wrote a book, a sermon, an essay. He never wrote anything that we know of except that mysterious sentence on the floor of the synagogue, when the woman brought before him received the scorn of her perse-cutors and the grace of her Lord. What He wrote that day in the sand no one knows. Jesus did not write; " He went about doing good." His words were the explanation of the things He did, and the things that God did in nature and in providence. When John sent his disciples to Jesus, whether to strengthen the faith of his disciples or to confirm his own faith, they asked the question: " Art thou He that should come, or do we look for another? " Here was an opportunity for a condensation of all the arguments in favor of His Messiahship drawn from the law and the prophets. But his first answer was — silence. Then, he touched the eyes of the blind man and he saw; He touched a lame man and he walked; a leper and he was cleansed; a deaf man and he heard; and pointing to the son of the widow of Nain, who the day before had been rescued from his bier and restored to his mother, He said: " Go your way and tell John what things ye have seen and heard; the blind receive their sight, the lame walk, the lepers are cleansed and the deaf hear; the dead are raised up; the poor have good tidings preached to them." Thus He made known His ways, His doings to the children of men.

As in the time of Moses and in the time of Jesus, so in all history has God manifested himself as Lord of nature, who works His will on the material and with the forces He has created. And is He bound to any one mode or order of action, because of the nature He has created? See the fountain breaking loose on the top of the mountain, pouring forth its water! Following the laws of nature, these waters work their way through the yielding soil to the edge of the mountain, and then fall over in a succession of fine cascades to the plain below, where winding their way through the sand they join the river and pass to the sea. We say that this movement is the work of nature. We say this is what nature does. Is there any other.way of doing with the water that springs from the mountain than that which we have observed? Certainly. Even a man can do something other and better with this stream on the mountain. As proprietor of the land he proceeds to dig, regulate, guide and carry for a mile along the brow of the hill the waters that break from the fountain. He then causes the stream to descend in waterfalls down the mountainside, and then in artificial channels, crossed by rustic bridges, here and there expanding into little lakelets, and now confined in narrow limits, he brings the stream to the river and to the sea. Thus, there are two ways of using the same elements in nature. Nature does one thing if left to herself. Man's ingenuity and power can make nature do another thing, without violating the laws of nature. Can God do with his own resources what man can do with God's resources? And should there not be action in the realm of human history that is not simply a product either of nature or of man? And why may we not encounter in the records of human history marvels of which we are compelled to say: "Lo! God hath wrought this." I believe in nature, but I believe in nature as the perpetual expression of divine power and wisdom, and I believe in other manifestations of the same power and wisdom.

I once listened to a rendition of a concerto by Rubenstein, where Rubenstein himself took part. Before the artist himself appeared, Thomas' orchestra delighted the great audience with Rubenstein's music. Although I did not see him I heard his music. After a little while he came in and took his place at the piano, while his own music was going on. After awhile he touched the keys himself, and accompanying his own music rendered by other performers, he swept from the instrument strains of exquisite harmony that held the multitude spell-bound. The same artist produced indirectly the music he had composed through the orchestra that rendered it, and directly through the instrument under his fingers. Can God do such things with His Universe? Through all the ages His purposes have gone rolling on in harmony with His wisdom, in display of His power, in manifestation of His goodness; but there came a time when on the plains of Palestine, One walked the earth, the incarnation of wisdom and love and power, and went about doing good to the children of men.

Thus God has made known His ways unto men, with them and independently of them, on battle fields, in senates, in laboratories, in observatories, in fields, in parlors, in nurseries. In forces of gravitation and electricity and evolution, God makes known His ways unto men, His doings unto nations. The truth is, that the best place to study God's ways and will is in modern civilization, for He was never nearer the planet than He is to-day. I would a thousand times rather live five years in this age than forty in the times of the incarnation and of the apostles. God is not far away, reaching down from remote distances and touching humanity here and there, now and then. He fills the universe with His presence. "In Him we live and move and have our being." These sacred records report what God once did on the earth, but like a clock in a glass case which reveals the process by which all clocks move, they show to us the secret of springs of all historic movements. We who live in these latter days may sing:

> " Mine eyes have seen the glory of the coming of the Lord
> He is tramping out his vintage where the grapes of wrath are stored,
> He has loosed the fateful lightning of his terrible swift sword;
> His truth is marching on.
>
> I have seen him .in the watchfires of an hundred circling camps,
> They have builded Him an altar 'mid the evening dews and damps,
> I can read his righteous sentence by the dim and flaring lamps;
> His day is marching on."

We are now living in the very midst of the divine activity. God has never been nearer to the world or to the human heart than He is at this moment.

1. In the light of this law of revelation by action, let us look at the life of Jesus. He came to reveal God to man that He might reveal man to himself. He did not come to startle our race by the wonders that he wrought. He did not come to depreciate nature as a revelation of God, by simply showing that there were possibilities beyond nature. He did not come to stifle human research or to put a ban on human science and discourage culture. He came to set forth before all the ages God's holiness and love, the worth of man and his destiny and his possibilities. Coming for this, how shall He accomplish His work? By a poem? By an oration? By some matchless picture? By a sculptured group? By some splendid edifice — a miracle in architecture? But He wrote no poem, delivered no oration, painted no picture, carved no statue, built no architectural pile. He wrote no book; he established no library. See Him yonder hanging on that cross between heaven and earth, revealing by action God's loathing of sin, His love of righteousness and His boundless mercy. By His victory over death, as He emerged from the sepulchre, He demonstrated by action the power of the immortal life. By His ascent from the summit of Olivet into the visible heavens, He revealed, as no literary or artistic production could ever have revealed, the fact of a realm of being beyond this. Re-appearing in tongues of fire at Pentecost, He made known to men the fact of his presence and

power on the earth for the ages to come. Thus " He made known His ways " and " doings " to humanity.

2. In the light of this law of revelation by action, let us look at the Holy Scriptures. It is easy to us to fancy what a divine book ought to be — how perfect and flawless, with no syllable in it that is not exact and divine; a book completed in heaven and handed down to humanity. But this is not the Bible which we do have. We can easily see what would happen if the law of revelation by action through gradual processes be the divine way of revelation. First, the Bible would be largely biographical; then, of course, historical; and gradually developed. It must be characterized by an all-pervading unity; there would be progressiveness in the unfolding of truth, and we should expect to get a fuller, larger and worthier idea of God through Paul than through Moses, and through Paul's last writings than through Paul's earliest writings. If it were to be revelation by action, it would take ages to produce it and ages to complete it. Its perpetuity would be guaranteed. It would be a trustworthy book, if rightly interpreted. The human element would be present in it, for if God revealed Himself through men, He would recognize the limitations of the man through whom He reveals Himself, and do the best He could with the material in hand without violating the laws of nature or of man. A book produced in this way would be a book full of wonders; a book requiring great research; a book rewarding at every step the most diligent and painstaking endeavor to arrive at its richest meaning; a book the study of which would depend more on the spirit of the student than on external helps; a book never complete, because having within itself the germs of truth to be unfolded and expanded as its interpretation became possible through growing human interest and deepening human experience.

3. In the light of this law of revelation by action, let us look at the Christian life. There are three versions of the Bible about which we speak; The " old "—the King James version which you and I studied when we were children; the " new version " which we have had for about two decades or more; and the next version which is to come when the crescent wanes from the capital of the Turkish empire, and the powers that favor investigation and research lay hold on that great region, bringing out old manuscripts and records not yet discovered, the study of which will help us still further to revise and interpret this holy Word of God. So, there we have the old and the new and the next version. I look at children in our day and con-

gratulate them in my heart on the fact that they are to live the next twenty-five, thirty and fifty years, and that they shall read this larger, richer revision of the divine Word.

There is a still better version of God's word: When an individual soul receives the divine truth into his own man and lives it out, he makes known to men by action the divine truth he has received. Horace Bushnell has a great sermon entitled "Every Man's Life a Plan of God." Chrysostom says, "The true Shechinah is man." Give me a living man in whom God dwells, whose character is moulded by the divine truth, whose spirit is possessed by the divine spirit, and whose life is under the divine direction, and I will show you a version of the scriptures that will be of immense value to the community in which that man dwells. You have read an essay about the sun. You have seen pictures of the sun, although artists are usually ingenious enough to give a landscape just before the sun rises or just after the sunset. You have seen the sun reflected in a dewdrop as it trembles on the little twig. You have seen the sun embodied in the beauty of the flower. But there is still another embodiment of sunlight. It is when on a cold day I come to your house, and a man puts a huge piece of bituminous coal on the fire. Millions upon millions of years ago the sunlight was stored in that lump of coal, but now in your house it comes out again, and the flashing light with its brightness and its warmth, is the old sunlight millions of years ago hidden, and now giving blessing to your household. So, God by action has put into this Book of divine truth the energies of His grace. These in turn have been transferred by faith to the souls of earnest and obedient students, and they in their turn make known again by action the ways of God to men. The Christian is thus a "living epistle," read and known of all men. He is in this world to reproduce the heroism and purity recorded in the old Book. There is no revelation to humanity so valuable as the simple being and living of the soul that accepts the truth. I often think of Michael Angelo engaged in the study of Moses. After a while, charged with a great thought, he produced that marvel in marble, the statue of Moses in the monument of Pope Julian II.

I long to see the domestic, social and political life in our civilization, the products of the faith we have, in the things that were once wrought, which the Book records and gives to us for our profit. Do I depreciate the Bible because I believe in continued revelation of God to man? I exalt and glorify and build my hope of eternal life upon the Book and the Christ it reveals. The doctrine I teach is, that the best effect of divine revelation is in the personal character and conduct of one who, believing, makes known by conduct and silent influences the truth of God to man.

Members of the Class of 1899: My heart goes out toward you and the large number of earnest souls you represent. My message to you, representatives of this latest Class, is this: Since God still works and has His way, let Him have His way with you. You need not approach Him with pleadings, persuasions and arguments to bring Him near. He is always pressing in upon you, seeking your consent, and when He has that consent, you cannot tell what he will do within you. Let God have His way with you. The best self-revelation of God is the personal inner revelation of His spirit. Let Him have His way, and do you say every minute, until it becomes the habit of your soul to breathe it without words, " Thy will be done."

Often in walking through the palace of Versailles, where those fine historic paintings fill the wall, I have imagined the trembling of the canvas, and then the coming down to the floor of those pictured men and women, no longer dead but living and walking as they did one hundred years ago and more. It is a great thing for people to get the ideas that are in the Book inwrought into personal character, so that ideas, growing into ideas, will become realities, and people whom you meet will seem more and more like the prophets and apostles of old. Thus, may we walk among men, incarnations of the divine truth, and work over again the works of God. Therefore, let Him have His way with you, that He may make known to others through you His ways of grace and power and victory and blessing.

JOHN HEYL VINCENT.

1832-

One of the leading Methodists of the United
States, Bishop Vincent is most popularly known
as the founder of the great Chautauqua movement.

T. DE WITT TALMAGE.
1832-1902.
The great Tabernacle in Brooklyn was crowded
every Sunday by magnetic preaching of this
famous pulpit orator. He was one of the great
public figures of his age.

XL

T. DE WITT TALMAGE

1832–1902

WHETHER Thomas DeWitt Talmage is to be ranked among the great preachers may be questioned, but it must be admitted that in the last thirty years of the nineteenth century he was one of the two or three most popular. His great church in Brooklyn was thronged twice every Sunday. As in earlier decades one might follow the crowd to find Beecher's church, so in later years one might in the same way be led to Talmage's Tabernacle. His sermons were printed every week by 3600 newspapers, reaching every hamlet in the Union, and every English-speaking land on the earth. When he gave lectures at Chautauqua Assemblies or in cities special trains were run from every direction. The minister who can win and hold such popularity must have a place among the famous preachers of all ages. Thomas DeWitt Talmage was born in Bound Brook, New Jersey, January 7, 1832. He studied for a time in the University of the City of New York, but did not complete the course. He was graduated from the New Brunswick, N. J., Theological Seminary in 1856, and in the same year entered the ministry of the Dutch Reformed Church, as pastor at Belleville, New Jersey. He was also a pastor in Syracuse, N. Y., and in Philadelphia. In his early ministry he showed few of the peculiarities or eccentricities of manner which became marked after the opening of his ministry in Brooklyn, N. Y., 1869, in the Central Presbyterian church, afterward known as the Brooklyn Tabernacle. This building was three times burned down during Dr. Talmage's ministry; twice rebuilt, and finally in 1894 abandoned, and the church with an enrolled membership of two thousand was dissolved. Dr. Talmage became co-pastor with an

33

aged Presbyterian minister in Washington, and remained there until his death in 1902. He was a lecturer of fame equal to that of his preaching; and was also the nominal editor of several periodicals. His preaching was simple, clearly outlined, old-time in its theology, practical in its aim, expressed in the language of a prose-poet, (though sometimes extravagant), garnished with abundant illustrations, and delivered in a vehement manner that is indescribable. This discourse is given here by the kind permission of Dr. Louis Klopsch, publisher of the twenty volumes of Dr. Talmage's sermons, an abundant mine of illustrative material.

BEAUTY AND STRENGTH.

" Fair as the moon, clear as the sun, and terrible as an army with banners."— S. of Sol. vi. 10.

THE fragrance of spikenard, the flash of jewels, the fruitfulness of orchards, the luxuriance of gardens, the beauty of Heshbon fish-pools, the dew of the night, and the splendor of the morning — all contribute to the richness of Solomon's style when he comes to speak of the glory of the Church. In contrast with his eulogium of the Church, look at the denunciatory things that are said in our day in regard to it. If one stockholder become a cheat, does that destroy the whole company? If one soldier be a coward, does that condemn the whole army? And yet there are many in this day so unphilosophic, so illogical, so dishonest, and so unfair, as to denounce the entire Church of God because there are here and there bad men belonging to it.

There are those who say that the Church of God is not up to the spirit of the day in which we live; but I have to tell you that, notwithstanding all the swift wheels and the flying shuttles and the lightning communications, the world has never yet been able to keep up with the Church. As high as God is above man, so high is the Church of God higher than all human institutions. From her lamp the best discoveries of the world have been lighted. The best of our inventors have believed in the Christian religion — the Fultons, the Morses, the Whitneys, the Perrys, and the Livingstones. She has owned the best of the telescopes and Leyden jars; and while infidelity and atheism have gone blindfolded among the most startling discoveries that were about to be developed, the earth and the air and the sea have made quick and magnificent responses to Christian philosophers.

The world will not be up to the Church of Christ until the day when all merchandise has become honest and merchandise and all governments have become free governments and all nations evangelized nations, and the last deaf ear of spiritual death shall be broken open by the million-voiced shout of nations born in a day. The Church that Nebuchadnezzar tried to burn in the furnace and Darius to tear to pieces with the lions and Lord Claverhouse to cut with the sword, has gone on, wading the floods and enduring the fire, until the deepest barbarism and the fiercest cruelties, and the blackest superstitions have been compelled to look to the East, crying: "Who is she that looketh forth as the morning, fair as the moon, clear as the sun, and terrible as an army with banners?"

Yet there are people who are ashamed to belong to the Church of Christ; and if you ask them whether they are in such associations, they say: "Yes, I sometimes attend the church;" instead of realizing the fact that there is no honor compared with the honor of being a member of the Church of God. I look back with joy to the most honored moment of my life, when, in the old country meeting-house, the minister of Christ announced my name as a follower of the Lord.

You who are floating about in the world, seeking for better associations, why do you not join yourself to some of the churches? An old sea captain was riding in the cars toward Philadelphia, and a young man sat down beside him. He said: "Young man, where are you going?" "I am going to Philadelphia to live," replied the young man. "Have you letters of introduction?" asked the old captain. "Yes," said the young man, and he pulled some of them out. "Well," said the old sea captain, "haven't you a church certificate?" "Oh, yes," replied the young man; "I didn't suppose you would want to look at that." "Yes," said the sea captain, "I want to see that. As soon as you get to Philadelphia, present that to some Christian church. I am an old sailor, and I have been up and down in the world, and it is my rule, as soon as I get into port, to fasten my ship fore and aft to the wharf, although it may cost a little wharfage, rather than have my ship out in the stream, floating hither and thither with the tide." O men and women, by the tides of frivolity and worldliness, swept this way and swept that way, seeking for associations and for satisfactions for the immortal soul, come into the church of Jesus Christ. Lash fast to her. She is the pillar and the ground of the truth. I propose to speak of the three-fold glory of the Church, as it is described in the text:

First: "Fair as the moon." God, who has determined that everything shall be beautiful in its season, has not left the night without charm. The moon rules the night. The stars are only set as gems in her tiara. Sometimes before the sun has gone down the moon mounts her throne, but it is after nightfall that she sways her undisputed sceptre over island and continent, river and sea. Under her shining the plainest maple leaves become shimmering silver, the lakes from shore to shore look like shining mirrors, and the ocean under her glance with great tides comes up panting upon the beach, mingling, as it were, foam and fire. Under the witchery of the moon the awful steeps lose their ruggedness, and the chasms their terror. The poor man blesses God for throwing so cheap a light through the broken window-pane of his cabin, and to the sick it seems like a light from the other shore that bounds this great deep of human pain and woe. If the sun be like a song, full and loud and poured forth from brazen instruments that fill heaven and earth with harmony, the moon is plaintive and sad, standing beneath the throne of God, sending up her soft, sweet voice of praise, while the stars listen and the sea! No mother ever more lovingly watched a sick cradle than this pale watcher of the sky bends over the weary, heart-sick, slumbering earth; singing to it silvery music, while it is rocked in the cradle of the spheres.

Now, says my text, "Who is she, fair as the moon?" Our answer is, the Church. Like the moon, she is a borrowed light. She gathers up the glory of a Saviour's sufferings, a Saviour's death, a Saviour's resurrection, a Saviour's ascension, and pours that light on palace and dungeon, on squalid heathenism and elaborate skepticism, on widow's tears and martyr's robe of flame, on weeping penitence and loud-mouthed scorn. She is the only institution to-day that gives any light to our world. Into her portal the poor come and get the sympathy of a once pillowless Christ; the bereaved come and see the bottle in which God saves all our tears; and the captives come and on the sharp corners of her altars rend off their chains; and the thirsty come and put their cup under the "Rock of Ages," which pours forth from its smitten side living water, sparkling water, crystalline water, from under the throne of God and the Lamb. Blessed the bell that calls her worshipers to prayer. Blessed the water in which her members are baptized. Blessed the wine that glows in her sacramental cups. Blessed the songs on which her devotions travel up and the angels of God travel down.

As the moon goes through the threatening storm-clouds unflushed and unharmed, and comes out calm and beautiful on the other side; so the Church of God has gone through all the storms of this world's persecution and comes out uninjured, no worse for the fact that Robespierre cursed it, and Voltaire caricatured it and Tom Paine sneered at it and all the forces of darkness have bombarded it. Not like some baleful comet shooting across the sky, scattering terror and dismay among the nations; but above the long howling night of the world's wretchedness the Christian Church has made her mild way, " fair as the moon."

I take a step farther in my subject: " Clear as the sun." After a season of storm or fog, how you are thrilled when the sun comes out at noonday! The mists travel up hill above hill, mountain above mountain, until they are sky-lost. The forests are full of chirp and buzz and song; honey-makers in the log, bird's beak pounding the bark, the chatter of the squirrel on the rail, the call of a hawk out of the clear sky, make you thankful for the sunshine which makes all the world so busy and so glad. The same sun which in the morning kindled conflagrations among the castles of cloud stoops down to paint the lily white and the buttercup yellow and the forget-me-not blue. What can resist the sun? Light for voyager on the deep; light for shepherds guarding the flocks afield; light for the poor who have no lamps to burn; light for the downcast and the weary; light for aching eyes and burning brain and consuming captive; light for the smooth brow of childhood and the dim vision of the octogenarian; light for queen's coronet and sewing-girl's needle. " Let there be light!"

Now, says my text: " Who is she that looketh forth clear as the sun?" Our answer is, the Church. You have been going along a road before daybreak, and on one side you thought you saw a lion, and on the other side you thought you saw a goblin of the darkness; but when the sun came out you found these were harmless apparitions. And it is the great mission of the Church of Jesus Christ to come forth " clear as the sun," to illumine all earthly darkness; to explain, as far as possible, all mystery; and to make the world radiant in its brightness; and that which you thought was an aroused lion is found out to be a slumbering lamb; and the sepulchral gates of your dead turn out to be the opening gates of heaven; and that which you supposed was a flaming sword to keep you out of paradise, is an angel of light to beckon you in. The lamps on her altars will cast their glow on your darkest pathway, and cheer you until, far beyond the need of lantern or light-house, you are safely anchored within the veil. O sun of the Church! shine on until there is no sorrow to soothe, no tears to wipe away, no shackles to break, no more souls to be redeemed. Ten thousand hands of sin have attempted to extinguish the lamps on her altars, but they are quenchless; and to silence her pulpits, but the thunder will leap and the lightning would flame.

The Church of God will yet come to full meridian; and in that day all the mountains of the world will be sacred mountains touched with the glory of Calvary, and all streams will flow by the mount of God like cool Siloam, and all lakes be redolent with Gospel memoirs like Gennesaret, and all islands of the sea be crowned with apocalyptic vision like Patmos, and all cities be sacred as Jerusalem, and all gardens luxuriant as paradise, with God walking in the cool of the day. Then the chorals of grace will overpower all the anthems of earth. Then the throne of Christ will overtop all earthly authority. Then the crown of Jesus will outflame all other coronets. Sin destroyed. Death dead. Hell defeated. The Church triumphant. All the darknesses of sin, all the darknesses of trouble, all the darknesses of earthly mystery, hieing themselves to their dens. " Clear as the sun! clear as the sun!"

I take one more step in this subject, and say that if you were placed for the defense of a feeble town, and a great army were seen coming over the hills with flying ensigns; then you would be able to get some idea of the terror that will strike the hearts of the enemies of God when the Church at last marches on like " an army with banners!" You know there is nothing that excites a soldier's enthusiasm so much as an old flag. Many a man almost dead, catching a glimpse of the national ensign, has sprung to his feet and started again into battle. Now I do not want you to think of the Church of Jesus Christ as a defeated institution, as the victim of infidel sarcasm! something to be kicked and cuffed; and trampled on through all the ages of the world. It is "an army with banners." It has an inscription and colors such as never stirred the hearts of any earthly soldiery. We have our banner of recruit, and on it is inscribed, " Who is on the Lord's side?" Our banner of defiance, and on it is inscribed, " The gates of hell shall not prevail against us." Our banner of triumph, and on it is inscribed, " Victory through our Lord Jesus Christ!" and we mean to plant that

banner on every hill-top and wave it at the gate of heaven. With Christ
to lead us we need not fear. I will not underrate the enemy. They are
a tremendous host. They come on with acutest strategy. Their weapons, by the inhabitants of darkness have been forged in furnaces of everlasting fire. We contend not with flesh and blood, but with principalities and powers and spiritual wickedness in high places; but if God be
with us, who can be against us? Come on, ye troops of the Lord!
Fall into line! Close up the ranks! On, through burning sands and
over frozen mountain-tops, until the whole earth surrenders to God.
He made it; he redeemed it; he shall have it. They shall not be
trampled with hoofs; they shall not be cut with sabres; they shall not
be crushed with wheels; they shall not be cloven with battle-axes; but
the marching and the onset and the victory will be none the less decisive. With Christ to lead us, and heaven to look down upon us, and
angels to guard us, and martyr spirits to bend from their thrones, and
the voice of God to bid us forward into the combat, our enemies shall
fly like chaff in the whirlwind, and all the towers of heaven ring because
the day is ours.

I divide this army with banners into two wings — the American
wing and the European wing. The American wing, starting from these
Gospel latitudes, will march on across the wilds of the West, over the
table-lands, come to the ocean, no more stopped by the Pacific than
the Israelites were stopped by the Red Sea, marching on until the remaining walls of China will fall before this army with banners, and cold
Siberia will be turned to the warm heart of Christ, and over lofty Hima-
layan peaks shall go this army with banners until it halts at Palestine.
The European wing will march out to meet it, and Spanish superstition shall be overcome; and French infidelity shall be conquered; and
over the Alps, with more than Hannibal's courage, shall march that
army with banners; and up through the snows of Russia, vaster in multitude than the hosts that followed Napoleon into the conflict. And Hun-
gary and Poland, by the blood of their patriots and by the blood of
Christ, shall at last be free. And crossing into Asia, the law shall again
be proclaimed on Sinai; and Christ, in the person of his ministers, will
again preach on Olivet, and pray in Gethsemane, and exhibit his love
on Calvary. And then the army will halt in front of the other wing,
the twain having conquered all the earth for God.

History tells that one day the armies of Xerxes shouted all at once,
and the vociferation was so mighty that the birds flying through the air

dropped as though they were dead. Oh, what a shout of .triumph when all the armies of earth and all the armies of heaven shall celebrate the victory of our King — all at once and all together: " Hallelujah! for the Lord God omnipotent reigneth. Hallelujah! for the kingdoms of this world have become the kingdoms of our Lord Jesus Christ."

When the Prussian army came back from their battle they were received in 1866 at the gates of Berlin, and a choir stood above the gates, and as the first regiment advanced and came to the gates, the choir in music asked them what right they had to enter there. And then the first regiment in song replied, telling over the stories of their conflicts and their victories. Then they marched in, and all the city was full of gladness and triumph. But, oh, the greater joy when the army with banners shall come up to the gates of our King! It will be choir to choir, music to music, hosanna to hosanna, hallelujah to hallelujah. Lift up your heads, ye everlasting gates, and let them come in. Then will be spread the banquet of eternal victory, and the unfallen ones of heaven will sit at it, and all the ransomed of earth will come in and celebrate the jubilee. All the walls of that celestial mansion will be a-glitter with shields won in victorious battle, and adorned with the banners of God that were carried in front of the host. Harp shall tell to harp the heroism in which the conquerors won their palm; and the Church that day will sit queen at the banquet. Her wanderings over, her victories gained, Christ will rise up to introduce her to all the nations of heaven; and as she pulls aside her veil and looks up into the face of her Lord the King, Christ shall exclaim: " This is she that looketh forth as the morning, fair as the moon, clear as the sun, and terrible as an army with banners."

XLI

CHARLES HADDON SPURGEON

1834–1892

CHARLES HADDON SPURGEON, the most widely popular of English preachers in the nineteenth century, was the son and grandson of dissenting ministers. He was born at Kelvedon, Essex, June 19th, 1834. After an academic training in the Maidstone Agricultural College, he served as a tutor several years. In 1850 he began to preach, and in his nineteenth year was installed in the New Park Street Chapel, Southwark, London. His great Baptist Tabernacle on the Kensington Road was consecrated in 1861, and its regular audience numbered for many years five thousand. Yearly volumes of his Sermons were published, and their sales rise among the millions. "Morning by Morning" and "Evening by Evening" are attractive guides for religious meditation. Power, fervor of conception, and passionateness of appeal, individualize his Sermons, rather than delicacy and the graces of culture, every thought translucent with Christian earnestness. It has been said of him that "In theology he was a pronounced Calvinist, in biblical science an extreme conservative, in policy an open communion Baptist, in politics a liberal Unionist, in all things independent." In his later years his work was frequently interrupted by ill-health. He died in 1892, at Mentone, in France.

THE CONDESCENSION OF CHRIST.

"For ye know the grace of our Lord Jesus Christ, that, though he was rich, yet for your sakes he became poor, that ye through his poverty might be rich."— 2 Cor. viii. 9.

THE apostle, in this chapter, was endeavoring to stir up the Corinthians to liberality. He desired them to contribute something for those

521

who were the poor of the flock, that he might be able to minister to their necessities. He tells them, that the churches of Macedonia, though very much poorer than the church at Corinth, had done even beyond their means for the relief of the Lord's family, and he exhorts the Corinthians to do the same. But, suddenly recollecting that examples taken from inferiors seldom have a powerful effect, he lays aside his argument drawn from the church of Macedonia, and he holds before them a reason for liberality which the hardest heart can scarcely resist, if once that reason be applied by the spirit. " My brethren," said he, " there is One above, by whom you hope you have been saved, One whom you call Master and Lord: now if you will but imitate him, you cannot be ungenerous or illiberal. For, my brethren, I tell you a thing which is an old thing with you and an undisputed truth —' For ye know the grace of our Lord Jesus Christ, that, though he was rich, yet for your sakes he became poor, that ye through his poverty might be rich.' Let this constrain you to benevolence." O Christian, whenever thou art inclined to an avaricious withholding from the church of God, think of thy Saviour giving up all that he had to serve thee; and canst thou then, when thou beholdest self-denial so noble,— canst thou then be selfish, and regard thyself, when the claims of the poor of the flock are pressed upon thee? Remember Jesus; think thou seest him look thee in the face and say to thee, " I gave myself for thee, and dost thou withhold thyself from me? For if thou dost so, thou knowest not my love in all its heights and depths and lengths and breadths."

And now, dear friends, the argument of the apostle shall be our subject to-day. It divides itself in an extremely simple manner. We have first, *the pristine condition of our Saviour* —" He was rich." We have next, *his condescension* —" He became poor." And then we have *the effect and result of his poverty* —" That we might be made rich." We shall then close by giving you a doctrine, a question, and an exhortation. May God bless all these, and help us to tell them aright.

I. First, then, our text tells us THAT JESUS CHRIST WAS RICH. Think not that our Saviour began to live when he was born of the Virgin Mary; imagine not that he dates his existence from the manger at Bethlehem; remember he is the Eternal, he is before all things, and by him all things consist. There was never a time in which there was not God. And just so, there was never a period in which there was not Christ Jesus our Lord. He is self-existent, hath no beginning of days, neither end of years; he is the immortal, invisible, the only wise God, our

Saviour. Now, in the past eternity which had elapsed before his mission to this world, we are told that Jesus Christ was rich; and to those of us who believe his glories and trust in his divinity, it is not hard to see how he was so. Jesus was rich *in possessions*. Lift up thine eye, believer, and for a moment review the riches of my Lord Jesus, before he condescended to become poor for thee. Behold him, sitting upon his throne and declaring his own all-sufficiency. "If I were hungry, I would not tell thee, for the cattle on a thousand hills are mine. Mine are the hidden treasures of gold; mine are the pearls that the diver can not reach; mine every precious thing that earth hath seen." The Lord Jesus might have said, "I can stretch my sceptre from the east even to the west, and all is mine; the whole of this world, and yon worlds that glitter in far off space, all are mine. The illimitable expanse of unmeasured space, filled as it is with worlds that I have made, all this is mine. Fly upward, and thou canst not reach the summit of the hill of my dominions; dive downward, and thou canst not enter into the innermost depths of my sway. From the highest throne in glory to the lowest pit of hell, all, all is mine without exception. I can put the broad arrow of my kingdom upon everything that I have made."

But he had besides that which makes men richer still. We have heard of kings in olden times who were fabulously rich, and when their riches were summed up, we read in the old romances, "And this man was possessed of the philosopher's stone, whereby he turned all things into gold." Surely all the treasures that he had before were as nothing compared with this precious stone that brought up the rear. Now, whatever might be the wealth of Christ in things created, he had the *power of creation,* and therein lay his boundless wealth. If he had pleased he could have spoken worlds into existence; he had but to lift his finger, and a new universe as boundless as the present would have leaped into existence. At the will of his mind, millions of angels would have stood before him, legions of bright spirits would have flashed into being. He spake, and it was done; he commanded, and it stood fast. He who said, "Light be," and light was, had power to say to all things, "Be," and they should be. Herein, then, lay his riches; this creating power was one of the brightest jewels of his crown.

We call men rich, too, who have *honor,* and though men have never so much wealth, yet if they be in disgrace and shame, they must not reckon themselves among the rich. But our Lord Jesus had honor, honor such as none but a divine being could receive. When he sat upon his throne, before he relinquished the glorious mantle of his sovereignty to become a man, all earth was filled with his glory. He could look both beneath and all around him, and the inscription, " Glory be unto God," was written over all space ; day and night the smoking incense of praise ascended before him from golden viols held by spirits who bowed in reverence ; the harps of myriads of cherubim and seraphim continually. thrilled with his praise, and the voices of all those mighty hosts were ever eloquent in adoration. It may be, that on set days the princes from the far off realms, the kings, the mighty ones of his boundless realms, came to the court of Christ, and brought each his annual revenue. Oh, who can tell but that in the vast eternity, at certain grand eras, the great bell was rung, and all the mighty hosts that were created gathered together in solemn review before his throne ? Who can tell the high holiday that was kept in the court of heaven when these bright spirits bowed before his throne in joy and gladness, and, all united, raised their voices in shouts and hallelujahs such as mortal ear hath never heard ? Oh, can ye tell the depths of the rivers of praise that flowed hard by the city of God ? Can ye imagine to yourselves the sweetness of that harmony that perpetually poured into the ear of Jesus, Messias, King, Eternal, equal with God his Father ? No ; at the thought of the glory of his kingdom, and the riches and majesty of his power, our souls are spent within us, our words fail, we cannot utter the tithe of his glories.

Nor was he poor in any other sense. He that hath wealth on earth, and honor too, is poor if he hath not *love*. I would rather be the pauper, dependent upon charity, and have love, than I would be the prince, despised and hated, whose death is looked for as a boon. Without love, man is poor — give him all the diamonds, and pearls, and gold that mortal hath conceived. But Jesus was not poor in love. When he came to earth, he did not come to get our love because his soul was solitary. Oh no, his Father had a full delight in him from all eternity. The heart of Jehovah, the first person of the Sacred Trinity, was divinely, immutably linked to him ; he was beloved of the Father and of the Holy Spirit ; the three persons took a sacred complacency and delight in each other. And besides that, how was he loved by those bright spirits who had not fallen ! I cannot tell what countless orders and creatures there are created who still stand fast in obedience to God. It is not possible for us to know whether there are, or not, as many races of created beings as we know there are created men on earth. We cannot tell but that in the boundless regions of space, there are worlds inhabited by beings infinitely superior to us; but certain it is, there were the holy angels, and they loved our Saviour; they stood day and night with wings outstretched, waiting for his commands, hearkening to the voice of his word; and when he bade them fly, there was love in their countenance, and joy in their hearts. They loved to serve him, and it is not all fiction that when there was war in heaven, and when God cast out the devil and his legions, then the elect angels showed their love to him, being valiant in fight and strong in power. He wanted not our love to make him happy, he was rich enough in love without us.

Now, though a spirit from the upper world should come to tell you of the riches of Jesus he could not do it. Gabriel, in thy flights thou hast mounted higher than my imagination dares to follow thee, but thou hast never gained the summit of the throne of God.

"Dark with insufferable light thy skirts appear."

Jesus, who is he that could look upon the brow of thy Majesty, who is he that could comprehend the strength of the arm of thy might? Thou art God, thou art infinite, and we poor finite things, are lost in thee. The insect of an hour cannot comprehend thyself. We bow before thee, we adore thee; thou art God over all, blessed for ever. But as for the comprehension of thy boundless riches, as for being able to tell thy treasures, or to reckon up thy wealth, that were impossible. All we know is, that the wealth of God, that the treasures of the infinite, that the riches of eternity, were all thine own: thou wast rich beyond all thought.

II. The Lord Jesus Christ, then, was rich. We all believe that, though none of us can truly speak it forth. Oh, how surprised angels were, when they were first informed that Jesus Christ, the Prince of Light and Majesty, intended to shroud himself in clay and become a babe, and live and die! We know not how it was first mentioned to the angels, but when the rumor first began to get afloat among the sacred hosts, you may imagine what strange wonderment there was. What! was it true that he whose crown was all bedight with stars, would lay that crown aside? What! was it certain that he about whose shoulders was cast the purple of the universe, would become a man dressed in a peasant's garment? Could it be true that he who was everlasting and immortal, would one day be nailed to a cross? Oh, how their wonderment increased! They desired to look into it. And when he descended from on high, they followed him; for Jesus was "seen of angels," and seen in a special sense, for they looked upon him in rapturous amazement, wondering what it all could mean. " He for our sakes became poor." Do you see him as on that day of heaven's eclipse he did ungird his majesty? Oh, can ye conceive the yet increasing wonder of the heavenly hosts when the deed was actually done, when they saw the tiara taken off, when they saw him unbind his girdle of stars, and cast away his sandals of gold? Can ye conceive it, when he said to them, " I do not disdain the womb of the virgin; I am going down to earth to become a man"? Can ye picture them as they declared they would follow him! Yes, they followed him as near as the world would permit them. And when they came to earth they began to sing, " Glory to God in the highest, on earth peace, good will toward men." Nor would they go away till they had made the shepherds wonder, and till heaven had hung out new stars in honor of the new-born King. And now wonder, ye angels, the Infinite has become an infant; he, upon whose shoulders the universe doth hang, hangs at his mother's breast; he who created all things, and bears up the pillars of creation, hath now become so weak that he must be carried by a woman! And oh, wonder, ye that knew him in his riches, whilst ye admire his poverty! Where sleeps the new born King? Had he the best room in Cæsar's palace? hath a cradle of gold been prepared for him, and pillows of down, on which to rest his head? No, where the ox fed, in the dilapidated stable, in the manger, there the Saviour lies, swathed in the swaddling bands of the children of poverty! Nor there doth he rest long; on a sudden his mother must carry him to Egypt; he goeth there, and becometh a stranger in a strange land. When he comes back, see him that made the worlds handle the hammer and the nails, assisting his father in the trade of a carpenter! Mark him who has put the stars on high, and made them glisten in the night; mark him without one star of glory upon his brow — a simple child, as other children. Yet, leave for a while the scenes of his childhood and his earlier life; see him when he becomes a man, and now ye may say, indeed, that for our sakes he did become poor. Never was there a poorer man than Christ; he was the prince of poverty. He was the reverse of Crœsus — *he* might be on the top of the hill of riches, *Christ* stood in the lowest vale of poverty. Look at his dress, it is woven from the top throughout, the garment of the poor! As for his food, he oftentimes did hunger; and always was dependent upon the charity of others for the relief of his wants? He who scattered the harvest o'er the broad acres of the world, had not sometimes wherewithal to stay the pangs of hunger? He who digged the springs of the ocean, sat upon a well and said to a Samaritan woman, " Give me to drink!" He rode in no chariot, he walked his weary way, foot sore, o'er the flints of Galilee! He had not where to lay his head. He looked upon the fox as it hurried to its burrow, and the fowl as it went to its resting-place, and he said, " Foxes have holes, and the birds of the air have nests; but I, the Son of man, have not where to lay my head." He who had once been waited on by angels, becomes the servant of servants, takes a towel, girds himself, and washes his disciples' feet! He who was once honored with the hallelujahs of ages, is now spit upon and despised! He who was loved by his Father, and had abundance of wealth of affection, could say, " He that eateth bread with me hath lifted up his heel against me." Oh, for words to picture the humiliation of Christ! What leagues of distance between him that sat upon the throne, and him that died upon the cross! Oh, who can tell the mighty chasm between yon heights of glory, and the cross of deepest woe! Trace him, Christian, he has left thee his manger to show thee how God came down to man. He hath bequeathed thee his cross, to show thee how man can ascend to God. Follow him, follow him, all his journey through; begin with him in the wilderness of temptation, see him fasting there, and hungering with the wild beasts around him; trace him along his weary way, as the Man of Sorrows, and acquainted with grief. He is the byword of the drunkard, he is the song of the scorner, and he is hooted at by the malicious; see him as they point their finger at him, and call him " drunken man and wine-bibber!" Follow him along his *via dolorosa,* until at last you meet him among the olives of Gethsemane; see him sweating great drops of blood! Follow him to the pavement of Gabbatha; see him pouring out rivers of gore beneath the cruel whips of Roman soldiers! With weeping eye follow him to the cross of Calvary, see him nailed there! Mark his poverty, so poor that they have stripped him naked from head to foot, and exposed him to the face of the sun! So poor, that when he asked them for water they gave him vinegar to drink! So poor that his unpillowed head is girt with thorns in death! Oh, Son of man, I know not which to admire most, thine height of glory, or thy depths of misery! Oh, Man, slain for us, shall we not exalt thee? God over all, blessed for ever, shall we not give thee the loudest song? " He was rich, yet for our sakes he became poor." If I had a tale to tell you this day, of some king, who, out of love to some fair maiden, left his kingdom and became a peasant like herself, ye would stand and wonder, and would listen to the charming tale; but when I tell of God concealing his dignity to become our Saviour, our hearts are scarcely touched. Ah, my friends, we know the tale so well, we have heard it so often; and, alas, some of us tell it so badly that we cannot expect that you would be as interested in it as the subject doth demand. But surely, as it is said of some great works of architecture, that though they be seen every morning, there is always something fresh to wonder at; so we may say of Christ, that though we saw him every day, we should always see fresh reason to love, and wonder, and adore. " He was rich, yet for our sakes he became poor."

I have thought that there is one peculiarity about the poverty of Christ, that ought not to be forgotten by us. Those who were nursed upon the lap of want feel less the woes of their condition. But I have met with others whose poverty I could pity. They were once rich; their very dress which now hangs about them in tatters, tells you that they once stood foremost in the ranks of life. You meet them amongst the poorest of the poor; you pity them more than those who have been born and bred to poverty, because they have known something better. Amongst all those who are poor, I have always found the greatest amount of suffering in those who had seen better days.

I can remember, even now, the look of some who have said to me when they have received assistance — and I have given it as delicately as I could, lest it should look like charity —" Ah, sir, I have known better days." And the tear stood in the eye, and the heart was smitten at bitter recollections. The least slight to such a person, or even too unmasked a kindness, becomes like a knife cutting the heart. " I have known better days," sounds like a knell over their joys. And verily our Lord Jesus might have said in all his sorrows, " I have known better days than these." Methinks when he was tempted of the devil in the wilderness, it must have been hard in him to have restrained himself from dashing the devil into pieces. If I had been the Son of God, methinks, feeling as I do now, if that devil had tempted me, I should have dashed him into the nethermost hell, in the twinkling of an eye! And then conceive the patience our Lord must have had, standing on the pinnacle of the temple, when the devil said, " Fall down and worship me." He would not touch him, the vile deceiver, but let him do what he pleased. Oh! what might of misery and love there must have been in the Saviour's heart when he was spit upon by men he had created; when the eyes he himself had filled with vision looked on him with scorn, and when the tongues, to which he himself had given utterance, hissed and blasphemed him! Oh, my friends, if the Saviour had felt as we do, and I doubt not he did feel in some measure as we do — only by great patience he curbed himself — methinks he might have swept them all away; and, as they said, he might have come down from the cross, and delivered himself, and destroyed them utterly. It was mighty patience that could bear to tread this world beneath his feet, and not to crush it, when it so ill-treated its Redeemer. You marvel at the patience which restrained him; you marvel also at the poverty he must have felt, the poverty of spirit, when they rebuked him and he reviled them not again; when they scoffed him, and yet he said, "Father, forgive them, for they know not what they do." He had seen brighter days; that made his misery more bitter, and his poverty more poor.

III. Well, now we come to the third point — WHY DID THE SAVIOUR COME TO DIE AND BE POOR? Hear this, ye sons of Adam — the Scripture says, "For your sakes he became poor, that ye through his poverty might be made rich." For *your* sakes. Now, when I address you as a great congregation, you will not feel the beauty of this expression, "For *your* sake." Husband and wife, walking in the fear of God, let me take you by the hand and look you in the face, let me repeat those words, "for *your* sakes he became poor." Young man, let a brother of thine own age, look on thee and repeat these words, "Though he was rich, yet for your sake he became poor." Gray-headed believer, let me look on you and say the same, "For *your* sake he became poor." Brethren, take the word home, and see if it does not melt you —"Though he was rich, yet for *my* sake he became poor." Beg for the influences of the Spirit upon that truth, and it will make your heart devout and your spirit loving — "I the chief of sinners am, yet for my sake he died." Come, let me hear you speak; let us bring the sinner here, and let him soliloquize —"I cursed him, I blasphemed, and yet for my sake he was made poor; I scoffed at his ministers, I broke his Sabbath, yet for my sake was he made poor. What! Jesus, couldst thou die for one who was not worth thy having? Couldst thou shed thy blood for one who would have shed thy blood, if it had been in his power? What! couldst thou die for one so worthless, so vile?" "Yes, yes," says Jesus, "I shed that blood for thee." Now let the saint speak: "I," he may say, "have professed to love him, but how cold my love, how little have I served him! How far have I lived from him; I have not had sweet communion with him as I ought to have had. When have I been spending and spent in his service?

34

And yet, my Lord, thou dost say, ' for *thy* sake I was made poor.' "
" Yes," saith Jesus, " see me in my miseries; see me in my agonies; see
me in my death — all these I suffered for *thy* sake." Wilt thou not love
him who loved thee to this great excess, and became poor for thy
sake?

That, however, is not the point to which we wish to bring you, just
now; the point is this, *the reason why Christ died* was, " that we through
his poverty might be rich." He became poor from his riches, that our
poverty might become rich out of his poverty. Brethren, we have now a
joyful theme before us — those who are partakers of the Saviour's
blood are rich. All those for whom the Saviour died, having believed
in his name and given themselves to him, are this day rich. And yet I
have some of you here who cannot call a foot of land your own. You
have nothing to call your own to-day, you know not how you will be
supported through another week; you are poor, and yet if you be a child of
God, I do know that Christ's end is answered in you; *you are rich.* No,
I did not mock you when I said you were rich: I did not taunt you — you
are. You are really rich; you are *rich in possessions;* you have in your
possession now things more costly than gems, more valuable than gold and
silver. " Silver and gold, have I none," thou mayest say; but if thou
canst say afterward, " Christ is all," thou hast outspoken all that the man
can say who had piles of gold and silver. " But," thou sayest, " I have
nothing." Man, thou hast all things. Knowest thou not what Paul
said? He declares that " things present and things to come, and this
world, and life and death, all are yours and ye are Christ's, and Christ is
God's." The great machinery of providence has no wheel which does
not revolve for you. The great economy of grace with all its fullness,
is yours. Remember that adoption, justification, sanctification, are all
yours. Thou hast everything that heart can wish in spiritual things; and
thou hast everything that is necessary for this life; for you know who
hath said, " having food and raiment, let us therewith be content." You
are rich; rich with true riches, and not with the riches of a dream.
There are times when men by night do scrape gold and silver together,
like shells upon the sea shore; but when they wake in the morning they
find themselves penniless. But, yours are everlasting treasures; yours
are solid riches. When the sun of eternity shall have melted the rich
man's gold away, yours shall endure. A rich man has a *cistern* full of
riches, but a poor saint has got a *fountain* of mercy, and he is the richest
who has a fountain. Now, if my neighbor be a rich man, he may have

as much wealth as ever he pleases, it is only a cistern full, it will soon
be exhausted; but a Christian has a fountain that ever flows; and let him
draw, draw on for ever, the fountain will still keep on flowing. However large may be the stagnant pool, if it be stagnant, it is but of little
worth; but the flowing stream, though it seem to be but small, needs
but time, and it will have produced an immense volume of precious water.
Thou art never to have a great pool of riches, they are always to keep
on flowing to thee; " Thy bread shall be given thee, and thy water shall
be sure." As old William Huntingdon says, " The Christian has a
hand-basket portion. Many a man, when his daughter marries, does
not give her much, but he says to her, ' I shall send you a sack of flour
one day, and so-and-so the next day, and now and then a sum of gold;
and as long as I live I will always send you something.' Says he, ' She
will get a great deal more than her sister, who has had a thousand
pounds down.' That is how my God deals with me; he gives to the rich
man all at once, but to me day by day." Ah, Egypt, thou wert rich
when thy granaries were full, but those granaries might be emptied;
Israel was far richer when they could not see their granaries, but only
saw the manna drop from heaven, day by day. Now, Christian, that is
thy portion — the portion of the fountain always flowing, and not of the
cistern-full, and soon to be emptied.

But remember, O saint, that thy wealth does not all lie in thy possession just now; remember thou art rich in *promises*. Let a man be
never so poor as to the metal that he hath, let him have in his possession
promissory notes from rich and true men, and he says, " I have no gold
in my purse, but here is a note for such-and-such a sum — I know the
signature — I can trust the firm — I am rich, though I have no metal in
hand." And so the Christian can say, " If I have no riches in possession,
I have the promise of them; my God hath said, ' No good thing will I
withhold from them that walk uprightly,'— that is a promise that makes
me rich. He has told me, ' My bread shall be given me, and my water
shall be sure.' I cannot doubt his signature, I know his word to be
authentic; and as for his faithfulness, I would not so dishonor him as to
think he would break his promise. No, the promise is as good as the
thing itself. If it be God's promise, it is just as sure that I shall have
it, as if I had it."

But then the Christian is very rich in *reversion*. When a certain
old man dies that I know of, I believe that I shall be so immensely rich
that I shall dwell in a place that is paved with gold, the walls of which

are builded with precious stones. But, my friends, you have all got an old man to die, and when he is dead, if you are followers of Jesus, you will come in for your inheritance. You know who that old man is, he is very often spoken of in Scripture; may the old man in you die daily, and may the new man be strengthened in you. When that old man of corruption, your old nature, shall totter into its grave, then you will come in for your property. Christians are like heirs, they have not much in their minority, and they are minors now; but when they come of age, they shall have the whole of their estate. If I meet a minor, he says, "That is my property." "You cannot sell it, sir; you cannot lay hold of it." "No," says he, "I know I cannot; but it is mine when I am one-and-twenty, I shall then have complete control; but at the same time, it is as really mine now as it ever will be. I have a legal right to it, and though my guardians take care of it for me, it is mine, not theirs." And now, Christian, in heaven there is a crown of gold which is thine to-day; it will be no more thine when thou hast it on thy head than it is now.

I remember to have heard it reported that I once spoke in metaphor, and bade Christians look at all the crowns hanging in rows in heaven — very likely I did say it — but if not, I will say it now. Up, Christian, see the crowns all ready, and mark thine own; stand thou and wonder at it; see with what pearls it is bedight, and how heavy it is with gold! And that is for thy head, thy poor aching head; thy poor tortured brain shall yet have that crown for its arraying! And see that garment, it is stiff with gems, and white like snow; and that is for thee! When thy week-day garment shall be done with, this shall be the raiment of thy everlasting Sabbath. When thou hast worn out this poor body, there remaineth for thee, "A house not made with hands, eternal in the heavens." Up to the summit, Christian, and survey thine inheritance; and when thou hast surveyed it all, when thou hast seen thy present possessions, thy promised possessions, thine entailed possessions, then remember that all these were bought by the poverty of thy Saviour! Look thou upon all thou hast, and say, "Christ bought them for me." Look thou on every promise, and see the bloodstains on it; yea, look too, on the harps and crowns of heaven, and read the bloody purchase! Remember, thou couldst never have been anything but a damned sinner, unless Christ had bought thee! Remember, if he had remained in heaven, thou wouldst for ever have remained in hell; unless he had shrouded and eclipsed his own honor, thou wouldst never have had a ray of light to shine upon thee. Therefore, bless his dear name, extol him, trace every stream to the fountain; and bless him who is the source, and the fountain of everything thou hast. Brethren, "Ye know the grace of our Lord Jesus Christ, that, though he was rich, yet for your sakes he became poor, that ye through his poverty might be rich."

IV. I have not done, I have three things now to say, and I shall say them as briefly as possible.

The first *is a doctrine;* the doctrine is this: If Christ in his poverty made us rich, what will he do now that he is glorified? If the Man of Sorrows saved my soul, will the man now exalted suffer it to perish? If the dying Saviour availed for our salvation, should not the living, interceding Saviour, abundantly secure it?

> "He lived, he lives and sits above,
>   For ever interceding there;
>   What shall divide us from his love,
>   Or what shall sink us in despair?"

If when the nail was in thine hand, O Jesus, thou didst rout all hell, canst thou be defeated now that thou hast grasped the sceptre? If, when the thorn-crown was put about thy brow, thou didst prostrate the dragon, canst thou be overcome and conquered now that the acclamations of angels are ascending to thee? No, my brethren, we can trust the glorified Jesus; we can repose ourselves on his bosom; if he was so strong in poverty, what must he be in riches?

The next thing was *a question,* that question was a simple one. My hearer, hast thou been made rich by Christ's poverty? Thou sayest, "I am good enough without Christ; I want no Saviour." Ah, thou art like her of old, who said, "I am rich and increased in goods, and have need of nothing, whereas, saith the Lord, 'Thou art naked, and poor, and miserable.'" O ye that live by good works, and think that ye shall go to heaven because you are as good as others; all the merits you can ever earn yourselves, are good for nothing. All that human nature ever made, turns to a blot and a curse. If those are your riches, you are no saints. But you can say this morning, my hearers, "I am by nature without anything, and God has by the power of his Spirit taught me my nothingness."

My brother, my sister, hast thou taken Christ to be thine all in all? Canst thou say this day, with an unfaltering tongue, "My Lord, my God, I have nothing! but thou art my all?" Come, I beseech thee, do not shirk the question. Thou art careless, heedless; answer it, then, in the negative. But when thou hast answered it, I beseech thee, beware of what thou hast said. Thou art sinful, thou feelest it. Come, I beseech thee, and lay hold on Jesus. Remember, Christ came to make those rich, that have nothing of their own. My Saviour is a physician; if you can heal yourself, he will have nothing to do with you. Remember, my Saviour came to clothe the naked. He will clothe you, if you have not a rag of your own; but unless you let him do it from head to foot, he will have nothing to do with you. Christ says he will never have a partner; he will do all, or none. Come then, hast thou given up all to Christ? Hast thou no reliance and trust save in the cross of Jesus? Then thou hast answered the question well. Be happy, be joyous; if death should surprise thee the next hour, thou art secure. Go on thy way, and rejoice in the hope of the glory of God.

And now I close with the third thing, which was *an exhortation*. Sinner, dost thou this morning feel thy poverty? Then look to Christ's poverty. O ye that are to-day troubled on account of sin — and there are many such here — God has not let you alone; he has been ploughing your heart with the sharp ploughshare of conviction; you are this day saying, "What must I do to be saved?" You would give all you have, to have an interest in Jesus Christ. Your soul is this day sore broken and tormented. O sinner, if thou would'st find salvation, thou must find it in the veins of Jesus. Now, wipe that tear from thine eye a moment, and look here. Dost thou see him high, where the cross rears its terrible tree? There he is. Dost see him? Mark his head. See the thorn-crown, and the beaded drops still standing on his temples. Mark his eyes; they are just closing in death. Canst see the lines of agony, so desperate in woe? Dost see his hands? See the streamlets of blood flowing down them. Hark, he is about to speak. "My God, my God, why hast thou forsaken me!" Didst hear that, sinner? Pause a moment longer, take another survey of his person; how emaciated his body, and how sick his spirit! Look at him. But hark, he is about to speak again — "It is finished." What means he by that? He means, that he has finished thy salvation. Look thou to him, and find salvation there. Remember, to be saved, all that God wants of a penitent, is to look to Jesus. My life for this — if you will risk your all on Christ, you shall be saved. I will be Christ's bondsman to-day, to be bound for ever if he break his promise. He has said, "Look unto me, and be ye saved, all the ends of the earth." It is not your hands that will save you; it must be your eyes. Look from those works whereby you hope to be saved. No longer strive to weave a garment that will not hide your sin, throw away that shuttle; it is only filled with cobwebs. What garment can you weave with that? Look thou to him, and thou art saved. Never sinner looked, and was lost. Dost mark that eye there? One glance will save thee, one glance will set thee free. Dost thou say, " I am a guilty sinner "? Thy guilt is the reason why I bid thee look. Dost thou say, " I cannot look "? Oh, may God help thee to look now. Remember, Christ will not reject thee; thou mayst reject him. Remember now, there is the cup of mercy put to thy lip by the hand of Jesus. I know, if thou feelest thy need, Satan may tempt thee not to drink, but he will not prevail; thou wilt put thy lip feebly and faintly, perhaps, to it. But oh, do but sip it; and the first draught shall give thee bliss; and the deeper thou shalt drink, the more of heaven shalt thou know. Sinner, believe on Jesus Christ; hear the whole gospel preached to thee. It is written in God's Word, " He that believeth and is baptized shall be saved." Hear me translate it — He that believeth and is *immersed* shall be saved. Believe thou, trust thyself on the Saviour, make a profession of thy faith in baptism, and then thou mayest rejoice in Jesus, that he hath saved thee. But remember not to make a profession till thou hast believed: remember baptism is nothing, until thou hast faith. Remember, it is a farce and a falsehood, until thou hast first believed; and afterwards, it is nothing but the profession of thy faith. Oh, believe that; cast thyself upon Christ, and thou art saved for ever! The Lord add his blessing, for the Saviour's sake. Amen.

XLII

LYMAN ABBOTT

1835–

AMONG the leaders of religious thought in America, at the opening of the Twentieth Century, no man would be placed in advance of Lyman Abbot, who stands as the direct successor of Henry Ward Beecher, with whom he was a close friend and fellow-worker. Dr. Abbott was born in Roxbury, Mass., Dec. 18, 1835. His father was Jacob Abbott, author of the widely read " Rollo Books " and many other stories for children. The family removed to New York while Lyman Abbott was a child; and he was graduated from the College of the City of New York in 1853; studied and practiced law for a few years; was ordained to the ministry in the Congregational Church, and became a pastor at Terre Haute, Indiana, in 1860. In 1865 he came to New York, and for a few years was in charge of a church; but in 1869 resigned his pastorate and entered upon literary work. For some years he was connected with " Harper's Magazine;" then was associated with Mr. Beecher in the editorship of " The Christian Union." After Mr. Beecher's death he became his successor not only in the editorial office, but also, in 1888, as the pastor of Plymouth Church. Under Dr Abbott, the Plymouth pulpit maintained its place at the fore-front of progressive Christianity, while holding firmly to the principles of faith in God and in the Lord Jesus Christ. For ten years, he continued in charge of both his pulpit and his paper (of which the name was changed to " The Outlook "); but in 1898, he was compelled by the state of his health to surrender either one or the other, and gave up his church. No man in our time is more frequently called upon to preach at colleges and on great occasions, and no preacher is listened to by larger con-

LYMAN ABBOTT.

1835-

Lyman Abbott is to be counted among the most
progressive Christian thinkers of the twentieth
century. His sermons are not written before delivery, but are taken by shorthand as they come
from the preacher's lips.

CHARLES HADDON SPURGEON.
1834-1892.
The greatest favorite among English preachers
of the nineteenth century. The power and earnestness of Spurgeon's sermons caused them to
reach an enormous circulation.

gregations of thinking men and women. He has written many books, of which the most characteristic are " The Life of Christ," " Evolution and Christianity," " The Theology of an Evolutionist," and " Christianity and Social Problems." Dr. Abbot never writes his sermons, but thinks out with great care both the thought and the language. This discourse was preached before the students of Vassar College, on March 11, 1900; was reported by a stenographer, revised by the author, and printed in " The Outlook," from which it is here republished by permission.

THE LIBERTY OF GOD'S CHILDREN.

" The liberty of the glory of the children of God."— Rom. viii. 21, Revised Version.

IN speaking on these words I must take a few moments for what I am afraid you will regard as a somewhat academic definition. I shall make this definition as brief as possible, because I am quite as desirous as you can be to get away from the philosophical to the practical and spiritual.

Law is the expression of the will of a superior who has power, or is supposed to have power, to enforce that will on others. If he has no such authority, his will is not law. The doctor visiting a sick child, says: " You have been working too hard and sleeping too little. You ought to go to bed every night at nine o'clock." That is advice, but not law. Then the father says: " My child, you heard what the doctor says; and you must go to bed every night at nine o'clock." That is not advice, that is law. The father is supposed to have authority to enforce it. When Governor Roosevelt says, Franchises ought to be taxed in this State, that is not law, it is counsel. But when the Legislature passes a statute levying such a tax, that is law, because the Legislature expresses the will of the State, and the State has authority, or is supposed to have authority, to levy such a tax. But if the Court of Appeals should decide that by passing such an act the Legislature overstepped its authority, then the statute would cease to be law, because it would have been decided that the Legislature had not power to levy such a tax. Thus you see there are two elements in law: the will of a superior and the power or supposed power to enforce it on others.

I believe that law of every kind comes within that generic definition. The laws of nature are an expression of the Creator respecting the way in which he means the creation shall be carried on, and that expressed will of the Creator is enforced by him through forces which he has stored within nature, or by the force which he exercises himself in nature. The laws of light, of gravitation, of electricity, are all expressions of the will of the Creator respecting the material creation which he has made. The same definition applies to what we call the moral law. The difference between natural laws and moral laws is that physical things cannot violate the law, and moral laws can be violated by the free moral agents over whom the law acts. But by the moral laws the Creator has shown how he would have free moral agents act; and he has power, in the consequences that will come upon them from disobedience, to enforce the law in the one realm as truly as in the other.

Law is everywhere. Nothing is outside of law, for law is God, and God is law. Law is the expression of the Infinite and Eternal Presence. We never can escape law; science shows us that the law of gravitation binds the molecules of the smallest atom together, as well as the planets, and that the chemical laws in the remotest burning sun are the laws we employ in our laboratory. Law is universal; is absolute, uniform, never set aside; sometimes violated, but never overturned, destroyed, truly nullified.

What shall be your relation and mine to this law of the Superior which he has power to enforce? That is the question which I want you to consider with me this morning. There are three possible relations to that law, that is, to the will of our Superior. We may disregard it altogether and act as if it did not exist. We may disregard the laws of heat, and burn our fingers; we may disregard the laws of gravitation, tumble down and be bruised. We may act as if there was no such thing as law. Or we may recognize the law, and live in subjection to it. We may say, Here is a master mind, a master will, which has power to enforce its decree, and since we cannot escape we will submit. Or, we may, by obedience, use the laws for our own equipment in power.

This third relation is the one which I wish more fully to put before you. It is the attitude of mind of one who sees in the forces with which God has stored both the material and the moral realm, instruments of power put into the hands of children, and in law the way in which those instruments of power can be used for their best advantage. The first attitude of mind is lawlessness; the second, subjection; the third is the attitude of mind of one who perceives more or less clearly the liberty of the glory of the children of God. This relation to law is clear in the physical realm. There are laws of nature, heat, light, electricity, gravitation. The savage knows nothing about them, ignores them, acts as though there were none; little by little learns them, one after another; submits to them; and so comes into what we call the idyllic state, in which there is no great advance, no great progress, no great civilization, but exemption from the penalties of absolute lawlessness.

But this is not the end. This is not civilization. There is something better than mere obedience, and that something better our modern life illustrates. We to-day are taking these great forces of nature, studying these laws, and, by our understanding of the laws, making the forces our servants. We are not under the laws. They are under us, because we understand them. The birds understand this. Have you ever seen a sea-gull, its wings outspread, resting on the bosom of the north wind, and have you not wished that you too had wings and could fly? He flies because he sufficiently understands the law of gravitation to be upheld by it. As a kite is held to the ground by a string, so the bird is held in the air by the law of gravitation. Cut the string and the kite falls; break the law and the bird would fall. He uses the law of gravitation, and by it soars above the earth. If he violated the law, he could not fly; if he merely was obedient to the law, he could not fly; like the duck, he would simply waddle. He uses the law, makes it his servant, and it aids him to fly above the earth to which it binds him. We are not content not to be burned by fire; we use its heat, convert it into force, and set that force to do our drudgery for us. We are not merely obedient to electricity and so escape its perils; we acquaint ourselves with it, catch and domesticate it, bring it to the earth, and use it to light our houses and run our trolley cars. The whole process of material civilization is a process which inducts us into the glory of the liberty of the children of God, that is, the glory of the liberty of those who have in some measure the power of their Father to use the forces of the universe in the service of man, and make them subject to man's will.

This principle is equally clear as regards what we call the laws of health. The lawless person says, I do not care for the laws of health; I am going to do what I like. I am going to walk as much as I like one day, another not at all; I am going to sleep now six hours, now ten; I am going to dance in the hot, fetid atmosphere of a ballroom if I choose; I am going to eat what I like. That is lawlessness. The man in subjection to the laws says, I perceive the laws of health, and I suppose that I must obey them. I wish it were not so. I wish I could do as I like, but I dare not, for fear I shall make myself sick. The third man studies the laws of health, rejoices in them, endeavors to understand them, and by understanding them to use the bodily organs to build up the body and make it strong. When I was a boy, they did not know much about the laws of health. They had no gymnasiums, no laws of exercise. My teacher thought that a boy must be allowed to play because he was a boy, but the ideal boy would stay indoors and study all the time. We are wiser now. Pupils are required to go out for play, if they will not go of their own accord. We are learning that laws are not limitations; they are secrets of power. We are coming to understand that there are forces in the body whose secret we have not yet quite learned, and by observing them we will be able to build up the body and the brain, and come into the liberty of the glory of the children of God; by using the laws of health, not by being in subjection to them, certainly not by disregarding them.

This principle is equally true in the moral realm. The great moral laws are not restrictions, they are equipment in power; not a limitation of liberty, but an endowment in liberty. The great social laws recorded in the Ten Commandments, Thou shalt not kill; thou shalt not steal; thou shalt not commit adultery; thou shalt not bear false witness — what are they? Respect the rights of person, respect the rights of property, respect the rights of the household, respect the rights of reputation. These are the great principles of the social order. There are some persons who pay no regard to them. They care nothing for the laws of society. They belong to the criminal class. There is another class who observe the laws of society because they fear to disobey. They will not kill, but they squeeze their neighbor as one would squeeze an orange, and then throw the rind away. They will not rob a man, but they will pick his pocket in lawful ways. They live under the limitations of law, and as near the border line as they dare. But these social laws — respect for person, respect for property, respect for the home, respect for reputation, out of them grows a whole fabric of moral civilization. You write a letter to-night and drop it into the post-box, and, after going through all sorts of strange hands, it will be delivered in San Francisco in six or eight days. Why? Because there is respect for property in the United States, which there is not in lands where a post-office is not possible. You draw your check on a bank; it will pass through a hundred hands, and one after another will pay the money. Why? Because we have built up a great credit system in the United States, and in all the great commercial nations where there is respect for property. There is not a country in the world, and never has been, that has had a banking system or a credit system, or even a post-office system, where first respect for property and respect for person has not been wrought into the heart of the common people. These laws are not mere laws for restraint; that is not their primary object. They are the secret of a great industrial and commercial power. They are equipments for the service of life.

All the great moral reforms rest upon this principle. Up to the year 1776 the European Powers used their colonies for what they could get out of them. England was using India to enrich herself. She was using her American colonies to enrich herself. Our fathers fought, not for the principle that government should rest on the consent of the governed, but for the principle that government should be for the benefit of the governed; and the success of the American Revolution brought about a change in England's colonial policy. She changed her whole aspect toward her colonies. For at least the last half-century she has been administering her colonies in the interest and for the benefit of the colonies themselves, and she has been growing rich by the process. Our forefathers believed in a great principle — government for the benefit of the governed. They declared their belief in it, and appealed to the moral judgment of mankind and the favor of Almighty God in its support; and mankind said, It is right; and the appeal to the sense of right wrought the reformation. This is why "one with God is a majority." The child can move a lever that will set an engine at work which a thousand horse-power could not do. A single moral reformer, with a clear vision of the truth and a deep faith in the dormant truth in the hearts of men, will move a spiritual lever and accomplish work which a thousand angel-power could not do. The power is there, and when we understand the laws we set the power at work. This is one of the secrets of the power of Christianity in the primitive ages. There was a great body of men, slaves, serfs, freedmen, peasants, villeins, herded like beasts. Christianity came to them with this message: "You are children of God, immortal beings; rise up, be men, live as children of God." The appeal awoke within them that which was dormant before. Christianity was the awakening from sleep of a world which answered to the touch of a divine hand.

This principle, true in the natural realm, true in the moral realm, is true in the intellectual realm. There are certain great questions which confront all thoughtful men and women. Are we living in a world of chance, or is there a Governor, a Lawgiver, a God, in this world? If there be a God, has he ever spoken, or is he a silent God, and we dumb? Is there any revelation of God in the hearts of his children? Has he ever spoken to the less sensitive souls through the experience of inspired prophets and teachers? In the life of Christ is there any revelation of God otherwise veiled and unknown? Did anything important to the life of the world occur when Jesus was born at Bethlehem? or was the manger like innumerable other cradles of the children of the poor? Did anything important to the life of the world occur at Calvary? or was the crucified only one more martyr, a victim to the pride, the ambitions, and the passions of mankind? Is there any forgiveness of sins? any truth, any reality, in the invitation, Lift up the hands which hang down, and the feeble knees? Or must the broken arm be always limp, and the lame knee always stiff, and the violator of divine law carry always with him the penalty of God's violated law?

These are as stupendous questions as any man can ask. How shall we treat them? In the first place, we may pass them by; we may say, We do not care, truth is what we think it to be. Many people think free thinking to be the right to think anything they please. You can think what you will as you can do what you will. You can play with fire and burn your fingers. So you can think lawlessly, and never reach a conclusion by your thinking. You can violate law in the physical realm, and you can violate law in the intellectual realm. Lawless thinking is not free thinking; it is free not-thinking. The man who says, I am not going to puzzle myself about the question whether God exists, or Christ is divine, or the Bible is inspired, is not a thinker at all. It is a misuse of terms to call such a man a free thinker; he is a free no-thinker. Thinking is pursuing a question until an answer is reached; and that pseudo-liberalism that looks with scoffing and scorn on creeds is no thinking at all. It is lawlessness in the intellectual world.

The second attitude toward these questions is that of the man who says, You may think as much as you please about these things, but you cannot know anything about them. No one knows anything about them; no one ever can know anything about them. That is agnosticism. And akin to this is the third, the attitude of mind of him who says, There is an intellectual clique who can think, and they did most of their thinking in the seventeenth century; what they thought I will accept. That is dogmatism; dogmatism and agnosticism are close akin. One says, No one can ever know; the other says, Only an elect few can know.

The fourth attitude of mind is that which I am trying to put before you this morning. God has given to all his children power to deal with the problems of life and eternity. " Quench not the spirit. Despise not prophesyings. Prove all things. Hold fast to that which is good." That is Magna Charta of intellectual and spiritual liberty. You have a spiritual nature, a power of faith, a power of dealing with the invisible. Do not quench it. Do not let any one else quench it. Keep it alive. There are prophets and poets who possessed this in large measure. Do not despise them. Take the opinions of scientific men, or rationalistic men, of practical men, of men who possess what I will call power of outsight. But take also the witness of poets, of prophets, of intuitionalists, of men of insight. Ask what Darwin has to tell you, but do not forget to ask what Browning has to tell you. Ask what Herbert Spencer has to tell you, but no not forget to ask what Tennyson has to tell you. These men also have their testimony; they have been caught up into the eternal, and reflect something from the eternal in their prophesyings. Do not forget these men. Do not despise the men of vision. But do not take without question all they say. Test their testimony; prove all things. How? Do you find in their thoughts that which makes you stronger, that which lifts you up and makes you more true, more worthy, more able to live a life that should be lived? Accept it; hold fast to it; for it is beneficent. Hold fast that which is good.

It is true also that the laws of the spiritual life are not limitations, but instruments of power. There are a great many people who believe that in the spiritual realm law is a hindrance to be endured, not a strength to be employed. They imagine that they ought to read a chapter in the Bible every day; that they ought to pray so much every morning and so much every night; that they ought to go to church as a duty which they pay to their God; that they ought to keep the Sunday — but the less of it they can keep and obey the law, the better they are satisfied. Sunday is the Lord's day; week days are men's days. They must not rob the Lord of his day, but all they can get for themselves is gain. No! a thousand times no! Church and Sunday and Bible are not limitations on our liberty; they are endowments, equipments, bestowments, enlargements of power.

The Bible is a library. What is a library? I remember, when I was a young minister in New York, my uncle was moving from his house, and put at my disposal his library of three or four thousand volumes. I had at my church a library-room with rows of empty shelves and no books to put in them, and I welcomed the books with great gratification. When they were piled up on the floor, and I was arranging them on the shelves, and thinking what an addition to my life these books were going to be, the sexton opened the door, looked in, drew a long sigh, and said: " Well! I am glad I haven't got to read all these books!" I think that a great many good people have this idea of the Bible. I have got to read the Bible — a chapter a day. As soon as I get through the morning reading, I shall be free from that duty for that day: that is their attitude.

What is a library? A library is made up of the best thoughts of the best thinkers of the world's history. In a library Plato will talk to you of philosophy, Dante of the spiritual world, Homer of ancient Greece, Thackeray of London, Scott of the world of romance and chivalry, Browning or Tennyson of the world that no man ever sees. Each will talk when you want him to talk, and be silent when you want him to be silent. The Bible is a library of the best thought of the Hebrew nation. In my sorrows I ask Jeremiah to talk to me; discouraged, I ask Isaiah to repeat to me again the message of comfort that he brought to Israel of old; I have sinned, and I ask that unknown writer of the Fifty-first Psalm, who had gone down into the valley of death, to tell me his experience of penitence and forgiveness; I am in temptation, fighting with Apollyon in the valley of humiliation, and I turn to Paul in my struggle, and he gives me strength to win the victory; for he takes me up out of that valley of despair into the hilltop where the birds are singing and the sun is shining, into the atmosphere of the liberty of the glory of the sons of God. These are men who have lived with God, and through them God may talk to me. This it is to read the Bible.

What is prayer? Is it something that I owe to God? Perhaps. But the great and fundamental fact is this: I can go to the All-Father and he will hear me, and I can talk to him, and he will reply to me. If this is true, is it not a great truth? The Creator of the universe, the upbuilder and the destroyer of nations, the guider of each individual destiny — I can talk to him, and he will talk to me. Is this limitation, or is it equipment of power?

What is Sunday? It is preëminently man's day. Christ says so: " The Sabbath was made for man," he says. I am sorry for the man who, when Sunday morning comes, Sunday which God has set apart for rest and recuperation, saying to men, Now you may leave the turmoil and strife of life, and have this day for spiritual upbuilding and the noblest things in life — I am sorry for the man who on such a day has nothing better to do than read the Sunday newspaper. Years ago I paid a visit to the mining regions of Pennsylvania at the time of a threatened strike. I said to one of the miners, " Why don't you go out West and take a farm and work there, and be independent? " He replied, " We don't want to work out-of-doors. We want to work down in the mines, where it is nice and dark, and the sun doesn't shine, and it isn't hot, and when it rains we are dry." When I see the man to whom God has said, You may have one day on the hill-top, where the birds are singing and the sun is shining and the heavens are full of the liberty of the glory of the sons of God — when I see him sit down and read the Sunday paper, full of the news of the factory and the market and the turmoil and strife of politics, I think, " There is another miner who doesn't care to live out-of-doors."

I have taken a much larger field than I can put in one sermon; to cover it I should have to preach four or five sermons on this topic. I am not going to do that; but I want to leave this one thought with you — that the laws of God are not limitations. They are not bonds; they are equipments, they are endowments. The Almighty puts at our disposal the spiritual forces, the moral forces, the physical forces, saying, " When you understand how to use them, you will be sons of God, you can control them as I control them, and rule by means of them as I do." This is what Christ means when he says, " I have come that they might have life, and that they might have it more abundantly." This is what he means when he says, " Ye shall receive power after that the Holy Ghost is come upon you." This is the liberty of the children of God. Lawlessness is not liberty; subjection is not liberty; taking the great forces of God himself, understanding how he uses them, and then using them as he does — for divine ends — that is the liberty of the glory of the children of God.

XLIII

PHILLIPS BROOKS

1835–1893

IF Henry Ward Beecher will appear in history as the representative preacher of America in the middle period of the Nineteenth
Century, Phillips Brooks will rank as the leading light of the pulpit
in the later period, from 1870 to 1893. He was born in Boston from
one of the oldest and best of the New England families, Dec. 13,
1835, was graduated from Harvard College in 1855, and studied
afterward in the Protestant Episcopal Theological Seminary, at Alexandria, Virginia. He became rector of the Church of the Advent
(Protestant Episcopal) in Philadelphia, in 1859, and at once attracted notice through the power of his preaching and the peculiar
magnetism of his personality. He was a giant in physical frame, with
a mind and a spirit befitting such a body. Although loyal to his own
church, he was a lover of all the churches, and beloved in all. No
church-building was large enough to hold the congregations which
were eager to hear him. From his first pastorate he was transferred
in 1862 to Holy Trinity, in the same city of Philadelphia; and in 1869
became rector of Trinity Church, Boston. Here the multitudes
drawn together to listen to him compelled the building of a new church,
which became the architect Richardson's masterpiece, Trinity Church,
Boston, perhaps the finest ecclesiastical building in America. But
large as was the church, it was always too small for its congregation,
as long as Phillips Brooks stood in its pulpit. The breadth of his
views, the richness of his diction, the depth and sincerity of his convictions, and the warmth of his nature gave him a power possessed by
not more than one minister in a generation. In 1891 he was elevated
to the episcopacy as Bishop of Massachusetts, but lived less than two

years afterward, dying in the fullness of his powers on Jan. 23, 1893. He gave the Yale Lectures on Preaching in 1877, which were afterward published, as were also another series of lectures delivered in Philadelphia on " The Influence of Jesus." His biography, by Prof. A. V. G. Allen, was published in 1901. The six volumes of Phillips Brooks' sermons have inspired many, both clergymen and laymen; but inspiring as they are upon the printed page, they fall far below the intense tide of enthusiasm which they bore from the lips of the living preacher.

THE POSITIVENESS OF THE DIVINE LIFE.

" This I say then, Walk in the Spirit, and ye shall not fulfil the lust of the flesh."— Galatians v. 16.

WE very often forget, when we are wondering whether Christianity is really a religion for all men, capable of meeting all kinds of characters in every kind of age, how far that question went towards its settlement even in the times of the New Testament. We forget what a great variety of people became subject to the influences of the Gospel even then. We open one epistle after another, and always it is a different order and kind. Often a wholly different race of men, to whom the new epistle is addressed. These Galatians, for instance, who were they? Years ago a party of Gauls from the Pyrenees had wandered eastward, and after many violent experiences had settled down here among the mountain fastnesses of Asia Minor. There were some Jews living among them, but mainly they were of another race,— a fierce, brave, generous, unnamed nest of barbarians. It is strange always to light on a new company of men, and see how like they are to the men we know. Through the doorway of St. Paul's epistle we enter into the homes of these wild mountaineers; and when we once get over the wildness of their life, how clear their human nature stands before us. No one can read the epistle without feeling sure that St. Paul liked them for the headlong and enthusiastic frankness which made the best part, as it made the worst part, of their character, and with which he had much in common.

What sort of people were they, then? " Walk in the Spirit, and ye shall not fulfil the lust of the flesh." The lusts of the flesh! Here they are at work in Galatia just as they are among us: the same temptations, the same vexatious, exacting, persecuting demands of this fleshly body in which we all live. And here are men who have so had their deeper nature stirred, their deeper ambition aroused, that they are trying not to fulfil the lusts of the flesh. That struggle to be a self-controlling man, and not a self-indulgent brute, which is the glorious thing in all human history, is going on here in Galatia. What multitudes of strugglers there have been in that struggle, in what multitudes of ways! Leave out that struggle in its various forms from the life of man, and what would the life of man be worth? Here are these Galatians fighting the everlasting human fight in their remote corner of the world, trying to be men and not brutes; and here is Paul, their friend, their teacher, trying to tell them how. " Walk in the Spirit, and ye shall not fulfil the lusts of the flesh."

It is hardly possibly to conceive any two human lots more different than that of the wild Galatian reading this epistle in his smoky hut, and that of us quiet Bostonians reading it in our quiet homes. But if our battle is the same as theirs, if the same lusts of the flesh are still here, as well as there, to be met and conquered, it is good for us, as well as for them, to try to see what help we can gather out of the words of St. Paul.

The point that strikes us in this passage, and the point which I want to make my subject of this morning, is the positiveness of Paul's morality. It is so wonderfully bold and strong. There are two ways of dealing with every vice that troubles us, in either ourselves or others. One is to set to work directly to destroy the vice; that is the negative way. The other is to bring in as overwhelmingly as possible the opposite virtue, and so to crowd and stifle and drown out the vice; that is the positive way. Now there can be no doubt about St. Paul. Here comes his poor Galatian fighting with his lust of the flesh. How shall he kill it? St. Paul says not, " Do as few fleshly things as you can," setting him out on a course of repression; but, " Do just as many spiritual things as you can," opening before him the broad gates of a life of positive endeavor. And when we have thoroughly comprehended the difference of those two methods, and seen how distinctly St. Paul chose one instead of the other, we have laid hold on one of the noblest characteristics of his treatment of humanity, one that he had gained most directly from his Lord. I should despair of making any one see the distinction who did not know it in his own experience. Everywhere the negative and the positive methods of treatment stand over against each other, and men choose between them. Here is a man who is beset by doubts, perhaps about the very fundamental truths of Christianity. He may attack all the objections in turn, and at last succeed in proving that Christianity is not false. That is negative. Or he may gather about him the assurance of all that his religion has done and sweep away all his doubts with the complete conviction that Christianity is true. That is positive, and that is better. A man has a grudge against you, inveterate and strong. You may attack his special grievance and try to remove it; or you may try not to show him that you meant him no harm, but by laborious kindness that you mean him every good, and so soften his obstinacy. A church is full of errors and foolish practices. It is possible to attack those follies outright, showing conclusively how foolish they are; or it is possible, and it is surely better, to wake up the true spiritual life in that church, which shall itself shed those follies and cast them out, or at least rob them of their worst harmfulness.

It is strange how far and wide this necessity of choosing between the positive and negative methods of treatment runs. In matters of taste, for instance, there are two distinct ways of trying to perfect the tasteful man. One is by the repression of what is in bad taste; the other is by the earnest fostering of what is good,— the method of repression and the method of stimulus. And everybody knows that no great effect of human genius was ever yet produced except in the latter, larger way. A cold and hard and limited correctness, a work " faultily faultless," weak and petty and timid, is all that the other methods make. For, whether in manners or in art, that which appears at first as coarseness is very often the strength of the whole work. To repress it for its coarseness is to make the whole feeble while we make it fine. To keep its strength and fill its strength with fineness, this is the positive method of the truest taste.

We are witnessing constantly the application of the same principle to the matter of reform, the breaking up of bad habits in an individual or in a community. All prohibitory measures are negative. That they have their use no one can doubt. That they have their limits is just as clear. He who thinks that nothing but the moral methods for the prevention of intemperance and crime can do the work is a mere theorist of the closet and knows very little about the actual state of human nature. But, on the other hand, the man who thinks that any strictest system of prohibition, most strictly kept in force, could permanently keep men from drink, or any other vice, knows little of human nature either. That nature is too active and too live to be kept right by mere negations. You cannot kill any one of its appetites by merely starving it. You must give it its true food, and so only can you draw it off from the poison that it covets. Here comes in the absolute necessity of providing rational and cheap amusements for the people whom our philanthropists are trying to draw off from the tavern and the gambling-house. Pictures, parks, museums, libraries, music, a healthier and happier religion, a brighter, sunnier tone to all our life,— these are the positive powers which must come in with every form of prohibition and restraint before our poorer people can be brought to live a sensible and sober life. Look at the lives that our rich people live. It is not any form of prohibition, legal, or social, that keeps them from disgusting and degrading vice. It is the fulness of their lives, the warmth, glow, comfort, and abundance of their homes, the occupation of their minds, the positive and not the negative, the interest and plenty which the poor man never knows. Before you or I dare blame him, or despise him, we must, in imagination, empty our lives like his, and ask what sort of people we should be in the squalor of his garret, and the comfortlessness and hopelessness of a lot like his.

We see the same principle, the superiority of the positive to the negative, constantly illustrated in matters of opinion. How is it that people change their opinions, give up what they have steadfastly believed, and come to believe something very different, perhaps its very opposite? I think we all have been surprised, if we have thought about it, by the very small number of cases in which men deliberately abandon positions because those positions have been disproved and seem to them no longer tenable. And even when such cases do occur, the effect is apt to be not good, but bad. The man abandons his disproved idea, but takes no other in its stead; until, in spite of their better judgment, many good men have been brought to feel that, rather than use the power of mere negation and turn the believer in an error into a believer in nothing, they would let their friend go on believing his falsehood, since it was better to believe something, however stupidly, than to disbelieve everything, however shrewdly. But what then? How do men change their opinions? Have you not seen? Holding still their old belief, they come somehow into the atmosphere of a clearer and richer faith. That better faith surrounds them, fills them, presses on them with its own convincingness. They learn to love it, long to receive it, try to open their hands and hearts just enough to take it in and hold it along with the old doctrine which they have no idea of giving up. They think that they are holding both. They persuade themselves that they have found a way of reconciling the old and the new, which have been thought unreconcilable. Perhaps they go on thinking so all their lives. But perhaps some day something startles them, and they awake to find that the old is gone, and that the new opinion has become their opinion by its own positive convincing power. There has been no violence in the process, nor any melancholy gap of infidelity between. Dear friends, if you have any friend who believes an error, and whom you want to make believe the truth, for his sake, for your own sake, for the truth's sake, I beg you deal with him positively and not negatively. Do not try only to disprove his error. Perhaps that error, because no error is wholly erroneous, is better for him than no faith at all. But make your truth live and convincing. Through every entrance force its life home on his life. Let him hear it in your voice, see it in your face, feel it in your whole life. Make it claim its true kinship with the truth that is lying somewhere in the midst of all his error. Who would go a hundred miles merely to make a Mohammedan disbelieve Mohammed? Who would not go half round the world to make him believe Christ and know the richness of the Saviour?

It seems to me that there is something so sublimely positive in Nature. She never kills for the mere sake of killing; but every death is but one step in the vast weaving of the web of life. She has no process of destruction which, as you turn it to the other side and look at it in what you know to be its truer light, you do not see to be a process of construction. She gets rid of her wastes by ever new plans of nutrition. This is what gives her such a courageous, hopeful, and enthusiastic look, and makes men love her as a mother and not fear her as a tyrant. They see by small signs, and dimly feel, this positiveness of her workings which it is the glory of natural science to reveal more and more.

And now, if we have illustrated enough, and understand our principle, let us come to St. Paul and his Gospel. In Him, and in all the New Testament, there is nothing more beautiful than the clear, open, broad way in which the positive culture of human character is adopted and employed. If you have ever really entered into sympathy with your New Testament, you know, you certainly have sometimes felt, the thing I mean, We can conceive of a God standing over His moral creatures, and whenever they did anything that was wrong, showed any bad temper or disposition, putting a heavy hand on the malignant manifestation and stifling it; and so at last bringing them to a tight, narrow, timid goodness,— the God of repression. We conceive of such a God, and we know as we read the New Testament that the God of the New Testament is not that. We can conceive of another God who should lavish and pour upon His children the chances and temptations to be good, in every way should make them see the beauty of goodness, should so make life identical with goodness that every moment spent in wickedness should seem a waste, almost a death, should so open His fatherhood and make it real to them that the spontaneousness of the father's holiness should be reëchoed in the child,—not the God of restraint, but the God whose symbols should be the sun, the light, the friend, the fire, everything that is stimulating, everything that fosters and encourages and helps. We conceive of such a God, and when we read in the New Testament, lo, that is the God whose story is written there, the God whose glory we see in the face of Jesus Christ. The distinction is everywhere. Not by merely trying not to sin, but by entering farther and farther into the new life, in which, when it is completed, sin becomes impossible; not by merely weeding out wickedness, but by a new and supernatural cultivation of holiness, does the saint of the New Testament walk on the ever-ascending pathway of growing Christliness and come at last perfectly to Christ. This is the true difference between law and grace; and the New Testament is the book of grace. Oh, that the richest and livest and most personal word in all the language did not sound so meagre, dead and formal.

And this character of the New Testament must be at the bottom in conformity with human nature. The Bible and its Christianity are not in contradiction against the nature of the man they try to save. Let us never believe they are. They are at war with all his corruptions, and, in his own interest, though against his stubborn will, they are forever laboring to assert and reëstablish his true self. And in this fundamental character of the New Testament, by which it is a book not of prohibitions, but of eager inspirations, there comes out a deep harmony between it and the heart of man. For man's heart is always rebelling against repression as a continuous and regular thing. Man is willing to make self-sacrifices for a certain temporary purpose. The merchant will give up his home, the student shut his books, the mother leave her household for a time, to do some certain work. The world is full of self-sacrifice, of the suppression of desires, the forcing of natural inclinations; but all the while under this crust the fire is burning; all the time under this self-sacrifice, there is a restless, hungry sense that it is not right, that it cannot be final; there is a crying out for self-indulgence. All the time there is a great human sense that not suppression but expression is the true life. Every now and then, in the most guarded and self-sacrificing men, that restlessness breaks out, and through the strictest moral prohibitions, which have been growing hard and strong for a whole lifetime of obedience, the imprisoned spontaneity bursts forth; and some wild, flagrant act is the man's assertion that no law or practice of self-sacrifice can kill or has a right to kill the man's live self. This I see everywhere in man's history, and this it seems to me as if the Gospel so exactly met. It comes to a young man who is just becoming aware of what a forced and artificial and arbitrary state of things there is in this world where his work is just beginning. He has just found out that he has a heart full of passions and desires; and he is just growing half indignant and half perplexed as all the moral laws of life, all the decencies of society, all the proverbs and traditions of his fathers gather up about him and give him their good advice. " You will find in yourself," they say, " this passion. It is there simply to be sacrificed and killed." " You will find that appetite. It is never to be gratified." " You will find such and such a desire. Your duty in life is to watch for that desire's rising, and every time it shows its head to smite it and drive it back." " You are full of the lusts of the flesh. They are put into you that you may not fulfil them." He takes this programme for his life and starts out to perform it. It is not very inspiring surely. Its hard negations little suit the eager desire to be doing something strong and positive which belongs to his eager years. It is taking a brave young soldier who wants to be out in the very front scaling the enemy's ramparts, and setting him to guard the baggage in the rear. That is the low and spiritless tone of so much of the negative morality which rules all the way up from the teaching of the nursery to the doctors of moral philosophy in their college chairs. It makes all enthusiasm of virtue impossible, and instead of letting the effort to be good become, as it ought to be, the brightest, keenest, and most interesting search that man can undertake, it makes it the dull, heavy thing which we all see it and all feel it,— the dreary, hopeless trying not to be bad which drags so heavily and fails so constantly.

The young man accepts this theory of life, this negative theory of pure repression for a while; but by and by there comes a great explosion and remonstrance. " It cannot be," he says. " These passions cannot have been given me just to be killed. These strong desires are not in me only to be sacrificed. Why am I living this guarded life of circumspection? Here I am saying No! to all my strongest appetites, and for what? to make this poor, tame, colorless, half-animate conventionality of virtue which is worth nothing after it is made. It is not right. The law of life cannot be endless self-restraint, endless self-disappointment. I must try something freer and more natural. Let me let myself go. Let me give up restraint and try indulgence. Let every passion have its way." And then what comes? Ah, you all know: that wild unbridled life that seems so free and is such a slavery; that endless cheating of one's self to think that he is happy in his dissipation when he knows that he is wretched; that reckless flinging away of health and vitality till they are all gone, and the worn-out young man settles down into a middle age of enforced and dreary decency, and expects an old age of imbecility and pain. And yet at the back of that young man's outbreak there was a certain clutching at what really is a truth. He could not believe that self-mortification was the dreary law of life. He did not believe that the killing of the powers and appetites which He had given them was the education of God intended for His children. And now what has the New Testament, what has Christianity, what has Christ to say to that young, hot, and rebellious soul? Anything? Remember, his is just the soul that is running its career of ruin in our schools, our colleges, our stores, along our grandest and our meanest streets. It seems to me I can see Christ approach that man, that just rebellious boy. I do not hear him use such words of utter and unsparing rebuke as I have many a time heard lavished on youthful dissipation, and yet his face is sadder over that poor boy's wandering than father's or mother's face ever grew. My brother, I can hear him say, you are not wholly wrong. Nay, at the bottom, you are right. Self-mortification, self-sacrifice, is not the first or final law of life. You are right when you think that these appetites and passions were not put into you merely to be killed, and that the virtue which only comes by their restraint is a poor, colorless, and feeble thing. You are right in thinking that not to restrain yourself and to refrain from doing, but to utter yourself, to act, to do, is the purpose of your being in the world. Only, my brother, this is not the self you are to utter, these are not the acts you are to do. There is a part in you made to think deeply, made to feel nobly, made to be charitable and chivalric, made to worship, to pity, and to love. You are not uttering yourself while you keep that better self in chains and only let these lower passions free. Let me renew those nobler powers, and then believe with all your heart and might that to send out those powers into the intensest exercise is the one worthy purpose of your life. Then these passions, which you are indulging because you cannot believe that you were meant to give your whole life up to bridling them, will need no forcible bridling, and yet, owning their masters in the higher powers which come out to act, they will be content to serve them. You will not fulfil your passions any longer, but the reason will not be that you have resumed the weary guard over your passions which you tried to keep of old. It will be that you have given yourself up so utterly to the seeking after holiness that these lower passions have lost their hold upon you. You will not so much have crushed the carnal as embraced the spiritual. I shall have made you free. You will be walking in the spirit, and so will not fulfil the lusts of the flesh.

Is not this Christ's method? Is not this the tone of His encouraging voice? "Whosoever committeth sin is the servant of sin," but " Ye shall know the truth, and the truth shall make you free." It is the positive attainment and not the negative surrender. It is the self-indulgence of the highest and not the self-surrender of the lowest that is the great end of the Gospel. And yet I know that there comes up to you at once very much in the teachings of Christ and in the whole spirit of Christianity which seems to contradict what I am saying. Has not the religion of Jesus always been called the very religion of self-sacrifice? Is not self-surrender exalted into a virtue and crowned with glory as it never was in any other faith? That certainly is true! But we want to read the Gospels far more wisely than we have read them yet unless we see that in Christ's teaching self-sacrifice is always temporary and provisional, merely the clearing the way for the positive culture which alone is creative of those great results of spiritual life which the Lord loved. The right hand is to be cut off, the right eye is to be plucked out, some part, some organ of the body is to be put to death, but it is only that man may "enter into life." The life, and not the death, is the object. And just this is the reason why self-sacrifice in Christianity has acquired a glory that it never had before; because it has looked beyond its own negations, and ministered to, and caught some of the splendor of, the positive culture that was to follow it; as John the Baptist ministered to and caught some of the beauty of the coming Christ. Indeed, the negative discipline, the discipline of prohibitions, is the John the Baptist who merely cries, " Make straight in the desert a highway for our God," and then the positive Christ comes. The negative decreases that the positive may increase. How easily we see the difference. Two young men restrain their passions. You ask one of them, " Why do you deny yourself this dissipation? " and his answer is, " Because it is wrong. I must not do it." And you respect him for his self-control. You ask the other and he says something different, though the course of life to which it brings him is just the same. He says, " I am so busy about other things that I love better. I have greater and more beautiful work to do and cannot come down. It is my doing of duty that helps me to resist temptation." When a man simply, honestly, unaffectedly, without cant or hypocrisy, by lip or life, says something of that sort, then there is something more than respect for him in our hearts,— there is a spontaneous affection and enthusiasm.

The self-sacrifice of the Christian is always an echo of the self-sacrifice of Christ. It is true just in proportion as it copies that perfect pattern. The Christian's self-surrender is called a being " crucified to the world," taking its very name from the crucifixion of our Lord. When, then, we turn to Christ's crucifixion to get there the key to the character of the crucifixion of the Christian we see, I am sure, what I have just been speaking of. How different, how utterly different that sacrifice of Calvary is from all the most heroic sacrifices that heroic men have made under the pressure of hard necessity. How its positive power shines out through it. It is not simply the giving up of something, it is the laying hold of something too. He who suffers is evidently conquering fear by the present power of a confident hope, a triumphant certainty. It is because He is walking in the Spirit that He is able so victoriously not to fulfil the lusts of the flesh. It was because He clung to His Father that He came strong out of Gethsemane.

I think that no one reads the story of the Saviour's crucifixion without feeling underneath it all a certain undertone of triumph, a latent joyousness which is never lost through all its horror. Here are the fearful circumstances, the brutal soldiers, the cowardly governor, the mocking dress, the nails driven through the quivering hands, the groans, the taunts, the weeping women, the darkness,— everything to make it horrible,— and yet, underneath it all there runs a current of confident and expectant joy. What does it mean? No doubt, in part, it is the accumulated sense of joy which has gathered there from the subsequent experience of the multitudes who, in all ages, have found at that cross salvation. But it is not all this. Even those who stood around and witnessed the crucifixion must have felt it. It surely was in the mind of that centurion. It is the clear conviction that we are witnessing there upon the cross, not merely the murder of a body, but the triumph of a soul; not merely the humbling and wounding and lacerating of a flesh, but the exaltation, the coronation of a spirit. Dear friends, the New Testament talks about our being crucified with Christ. Have you never, in your own suffering or in some suffering you watched, had opened to you strange new glimpses of the complete meaning of those words? Have you never been surprised by detecting beneath your sorrow that undertone of triumph, that latent joyousness which makes the wonder of your Lord's " Put to death in the flesh, but quickened in the Spirit," have you never found your cross too a lifting-up, the everlasting parable of the thorns that made a crown repeating itself for you.

Indeed, how through the whole life of Jesus the subject that I am preaching to you about to-day, the positiveness of the Divine Life, found its abundant illustration. He was the sinless man. Yet in Him, just as in you or me, were all these lusts of the flesh, all these passions and appetites, that make our sins. Who can be thankful enough for that story of the Temptation, the story of the Saviour in the wilderness with the Devil, and that other story of Gethsemane, both of which tell us so clearly that the same weaknesses that are in us were in their germs, the self same things, in Him? And yet He never sinned. His sinlessness, even if He had done nothing else for our salvation, would stand out still for the most saving fact for man that the world ever saw. There is something very touching in the way in which the world of men, so full of sin and of the consciousness of sin, has clung about that certainty of the one sinless man. Whatever else they believed or disbelieved about Him, men could not let it go, this assurance that there has been once a man like us who did not sin. And yet a large part of the fascination which has kept men's eyes fastened upon Him certainly comes not from the mere fact of His sinlessness, but from its quality. It is of just the kind that holds men's hearts and kindles their enthusiasm. And its quality is positiveness. If Jesus had lived a guarded, cautious life, forever trying merely not to do wrong, His character might have been described in lectures on moral philosophy from a professor's chair; but it would never have been taken home as it has been taken into the world's very heart of hearts. It was because His sinlessness was holiness that the world seized on it. The reason why He did not serve the Devil was the Godhood of which He was full. Nothing can be more unlike the repressive theories of virtue in their methods and results than the way in which Christ lived His positive life, full of force and salvation.

Think back one moment from the God incarnate to the God revealed, from Jesus to the Father. What shall we say about the dear and lawful life of God our Maker and our King. He does no sin. And why? Is it a blasphemy to ask the question? Is it not good for us to ask it, if in trying to answer it we have to realize the supreme and awful positiveness of the life of God? He does not sin because of the completeness of His infinite goodness, because from end to end of His unmeasured nature holiness and love fill completely His every capacity and thought.

And now how shall we bring all this to our own lives and fix it there? Shall we not say to one another, Let us pray God for a positive life. Not merely a life that is not bad, but a good life, truly and spiritually and deeply good. You are tempted to steal. Do not stand over the object which you covet, making perpetually resolutions not to touch it; but go, throw yourself into some honest, brave, healthy work, that shall establish for you right and fair relations with your fellow-men, and then the mean life of the thief will lose its enticement for you so entirely that you will wonder how you ever could have tolerated the thought of stealing for an hour. If you are tempted to skepticism, do not spend your time in trying not to disbelieve, do not study too many books of answers to objections. Even if they solve your doubts, they keep your religion in a low tone. But set yourself where the manliest faith is living its bravest life. Set what little faith you have to doing its best work, so it will grow into more. Make more of what you do believe than of what you do not believe. I have heard men say, " I believe nothing! " " Well," I ask them, " and what is it that you don't believe? " And then they specify some minor point, some comparative trifle. " But," I say to them, " do you not believe in God and in his help, and Jesus and the Holy Spirit and the everlasting life? " " Oh, yes," the answer is, " I believe all those." And yet the man has been so busy thinking about what he did not believe that all these which he did believe have gone for nothing, and have grown into no earnest faithful life.

So everywhere positives, not negatives. The way to get out of self-love is to love God. Do we not see what Paul was teaching the Galatians when he said, " Walk in the Spirit, and ye shall not fulfil the lust of the flesh? "

And to help us to this positive life we have this positive salvation, these positive things fairly revealed to us, God's will, Christ's love, and the eternal life. It is no hard master that stands over us. It is the King in His beauty. Before Him repentance and faith become but one perfect act. When we really get the scales off our eyes and see Him, the struggle of life will be over. We shall not have to leave our sins to go to Him, as if they were two acts. The going of the soul to Him will be itself the easy casting away of sin, the easy mastery of this world which masters us so now. May God grant it for us all.

XLIV

JAMES MONROE BUCKLEY

1836–

SINCE 1880, when he became editor of " The Christian Advocate," no man has possessed an influence in the Methodist Episcopal Church, with its three millions of members, equal to that of James Monroe Buckley, D.D., LL.D. His power proceeds from a rare combination of qualities in the man :— an interest in the most varied departments of knowledge, a matchless memory and command of his mental resources, a quick and clear understanding of detail, however intricate, an apt and facile expression, a skill and aggressiveness in debate, and an unswerving fidelity to principle. No one who knows Dr. Buckley doubts that if instead of the church he had chosen as his field, the law, or medicine, or politics, he would have made the same success; for in each one of these directions he has shown remarkable ability. He was born of English parentage in Rahway, New Jersey, on Dec. 13, 1836, his father being a Methodist minister. He entered the Wesleyan University, Middletown, Conn., in 1856, and in college was long remembered for his wide reading and powers in debate, but was not graduated, as he left after two years of rather irregular study. He entered the ministry of the Methodist Episcopal church in New Hampshire, in 1858, and soon attracted attention; in 1863 was transferred to the charge of a large church in Detroit; thence to another in Brooklyn in 1866; and was pastor of leading churches in the New York East Conference until 1880, when he was chosen editor of " The Christian Advocate " of New York. He has been a member and leader in many General Conferences of his denomination; has travelled in many lands and written entertainingly about them; has lectured year after year at Chautauqua, and in all

JAMES MONROE BUCKLEY.
1836-
One of the most versatile men the Methodist
Church has produced, Dr. Buckley gained and
held an immense audience of readers, and is regarded as one of the most persistent opponents
of heterodoxy.

PHILLIPS BROOKS.
1835-1893.
Phillips Brooks' churches were always too small
to accommodate the vast numbers who thronged
them. In personality, force and culture, Brooks
was the representative preacher of his time.

parts of the American continent, upon widely diverse subjects, never failing to draw large audiences; and has not hesitated to attack whatever he has regarded as false or perverted doctrine. Of the various books written by Dr. Buckley, the best-known are " Extemporaneous Oratory," " Travels in Three Continents," " Faith Healing, Christian Science, and Kindred Phenomena." He has preached sermons by the thousand, but no volume of his discourses has been published, and they are to be read only in the newspapers for which they have been reported. This sermon was published in 1886, in " The Christian Union," now " The Outlook," and is here given by permission.

THE PROBLEM OF PERSONAL AND SOCIAL INEQUALITIES.

" Let the brother of low degree rejoice in that he is exalted: but the rich, in that he is made low: because as the flower of the grass he shall pass away."— James i. 9, 10.

In all ages and parts of the world, men of high and low degree, according to the standards prevailing where they live, are to be found. There is no society, except that which is but little above the brute development — such as the inhabitants of Patagonia, or some of the more degraded regions of the Dark Continent — in which several general distinctions may not be found.

First, and most numerous, the poor: in which are to be included not only paupers and those who are indigent, but those who live by what they earn which is barely enough to support them, and whom the sickness of a week, or perhaps a day, would transform into objects of charity. In most parts of the world these constitute an immense majority. In the United States, owing to the operation of causes too obvious to need explanation, thus far they are in the minority. It is, however, a serious question whether they are not increasing faster than the population, and whether they are not elements at work which give ground for fear that within a period of time no longer than that which has elapsed since the foundation of the Constitution the poor as thus defined will not become a majority.

Broadly distinguished from these are the rich: those who possess an

amount of property the mere income of which without any further labor
on their part than is necessary to superintend their investments, is sufficient to support them in luxury.   Many of the rich are engaged in business.   The capital that they now have in business, invested at the ruling
rates, low as they are, would maintain them in luxury: these persons may
be said to be rich.   But the man who has not capital enough in his business to support him without increasing his revenues by business would
hardly be defined as rich, but would come under the third general distinction observable in society, which may be called the medium.   A practical philosopher in such a condition is content, and not anxious for
greater accumulations; but if he have not attained this wisdom, recommended alike by ancient and modern teachers, moral and religious, he is
hopeful by the prosecution of business to add such an amount to his
capital as to elevate him to what he regards the highest point of human
achievement — the station of the rich.

Others, yet, in medium position, having " neither riches nor poverty,"
are in a declining state.   This is a very numerous class.   Infirmity, losses,
the rise of new modes of transacting business to which men somewhat
advanced in years cannot adapt themselves, misfortunes of various kinds,
cause a diminution of capital and in the volume of the business.   Such
men sadly realize that they are worth considerably less at sixty than they
were at fifty, and begin to be troubled with gloomy forebodings concerning old age and the proper provision of their families.

I suggest these not as arbitrary distinctions, but as general divisions.
In some instances the poor and those who are declining from a medium
condition approach each other, while the more prosperous of the middle
classes approximate to the lower stratum of the rich.

But learning and intellectual gifts create other distinctions: the wise,
the ignorant, and, between the genuinely wise and the ignorant, a class
of ordinarily educated persons.   That State or Nation is happiest in
which this class is most numerous.   But where is that nation in which the
ignorant is not the most numerous class?   If it is not in this country,
where is it?   But who, with the knowledge of all the facts, will assume
that in this country the numerical majority of the population of all the
States is otherwise than ignorant?

From the other distinctions arise those of honor and obscurity.   The
honored are generally rich or approaching riches, or learned; occasionally they are both.   The obscure are generally poor; only occasionally honored beyond the circle of their personal acquaintance.   But

often the rich, through their parsimony or want of public spirit, are deservedly obscure, receiving only that· notice from the public which is concentrated in the assessor and the collector, and that they try to escape.

THE OPPOSITION OF FEELING ARISING FROM THESE INEQUALITIES.

From these differences of degree, opposition of feeling of the most intense character have arisen, under every form of government that has ever existed. In despotisms they are solidified in institutions. The old Roman world in its vicissitudes passed through the absolute monarchy, the limited monarchy, the republic, and the aristocracy and within all the institution of slavery nestled like a viper; and thus its history is the history of the human race. The Asiatic and the Russian monarchies are mighty structures in which the various degrees support the final despotism; and " caste " is a term that suggests the indestructibility of these distinctions in the most offensive form. Republics, which in theory maintain the equality of man, yet retain distinctions of different kinds, and these, as they increase in wealth and capital, become more and more numerous; the tendency then is to give unrepublican distinctions recognition in the laws. Our own republic in its relation to the institution of slavery was a striking illustration; but many laws enacted since the abolition of slavery contain the germs of arbitrary discrimination without basis in right, which, if logically carried out and universally applied, would transform the institutions of the country into something very different from what its eulogists describe.

Protests, many without and some with reason, have been made by men of low degree against the situation in which they find themselves. When a child is born into the world to-day, unless he is an heir of an owner of real estate, every foot of land in the country in which he lives is preëmpted, belongs to some one else. And, no matter who now owns all the land in the State of New York, exclusive of certain tracts belonging to the State, some one has owned it, and some one else will own it by inheritance, who never directly or indirectly earned it. The signature of a dead man determines the transfer; and socialistic and communistic movements have in them what appears to be (unless one reflect upon the elements which hold society together and make human life tolerable upon the earth) natural justice when they demand, " What right has a dead man to·control anything in the world, and what right has any individual to the solid earth in fee simple? "

CHECKS UPON A TOO HASTY CONCLUSION.

Against a too hasty conclusion, however, from the confessed difficulties of the situation, four facts start up from human history and human nature. First: wherever human society is found, except among the most brutal tribes, the institution of private property exists. Second: such are the differences of human beings in disposition, working power, and judgment, that if all the property in the world were equally divided, in a very few years or months the dissipation, imbecility, and infirmities of many on the one hand, and the energy, industry, and sagacity of many on the other, would produce inequalities of goods, wisdom, power, and social position. Third: for the State to hold all property, and force the people to work, and to compel the support of multitudes who would not or could not work by the involuntary and excessive exertions of those who would be willing to work, would be to oppose the strongest instincts of human nature. This would require a despotism as rigid as that of ancient Persia, though it might be less capricious. Fourth: most communistic experiments, whether based upon religion or secularism have failed in accomplishing the end in view by those who affiliate with them. The few that have attained temporal prosperity have dwindled in numbers, average human beings preferring to take their chances in active competition to entering upon a life so unnatural and circumscribed.

CHRISTIANITY, AND PERSONAL AND SOCIAL INEQUALITIES.

These differences, with the corresponding oppositions of feeling, and with an unjust and oppressive government, existed when Christ came; and Christianity might be expected to solve the problem of the relations of Christian disciples of high and low degree. It did so, and that in two ways.

First, by laying down principles which if universally accepted and practiced, would reduce these inequalities to the smallest possible proportions, and so adjust men to their neighbors that all malevolent feeling would disappear. Christianity condemns idleness. " If any will not work, neither shall he eat," says the Apostle. As the same Apostle gives directions to feed the hungry and help the poor, it is obvious that those who will not work, though able, are meant. The Christian believer is to be not slothful in business; he is to labor, working with his hands that which is good. He is to do this that he may provide things honest in the sight of all men, that he may pay his taxes, and that he may have to give to him that needeth. He is to support all that are dependent upon him; if he will not do so, he denies the faith, and is worse than an infidel that will do these things.

Christianity specifically prohibits vice of all kinds: drunkenness, which is the great cause of human inequalities; gluttony, which is a waster and the precursor of extravagance, which is the gluttony of the eye; licentiousness, which is a waster of the substance in every sense of the word; anger, from which various crimes and impediments arise; avarice, which leads a man to desire to get all that he can from his fellows; it specially and emphatically denounces dishonesty, the essence of which is to try to get anything from a man without giving him a fair equivalent.

It also requires fidelity in every station and under every obligation, universal benevolence and helpfulness. The parable of the good Samaritan is not a fancy sketch, but a model, the work of the Divine Teacher, after which his disciples are to fashion themselves. And instead of struggling for honor, their rule is to be, In honor preferring one another — a passage which does not signify that the competent are to neglect responsibility and push forward the incompetent, but that, while suitable men appear for honor accompanied with responsibility, men are not to seek, but to be sought, for positions of special honor.

Our Lord gave a number of special directions to His disciples. They were not to lay up treasures upon the earth. When he was discoursing upon spiritual things a man hastily interrupted him with, " Lord, speak to my brother, that he divide the inheritance with me." " Man," said Christ, " who made me a ruler and a divider over thee? A man's life consisteth not in the abundance of the things which he possesseth."

The Count Tolstoi, of Moscow, whose work " My Religion," just translated into English, is intensely interesting, exhibiting, as it does, the action of a mind yearning for the truth, unable to accept the preposterous gorgeous pageant of the Russo-Greek Church; but he takes an unequal view of the religion of Jesus, holding it to be opposed to all human governments and to the institution of private property. By isolating texts, and not modifying what Christ says in one place by what he says in another, by ignoring even our Lord's own modifications in the very passages which he gives, he appears to make out a case of exceeding strength. Thus, when our Lord commands his disciples to take no thought for the body and for the things of the morrow, he interprets it literally, as though no effort were to be made to provide for the future; forgetting that the

Apostles, under the very eye of Christ had a treasurer, and carried money, and that he said, " Your Father knoweth that ye have need of all these things," and " All these things shall be added unto you, if ye seek first the kingdom of heaven and its righteousness." The sin of the Gentiles was not in paying some attention to these matters, but in making them the object of their lives. The contrast drawn is, Seek *first* the kingdom of God; then, since your Father knoweth that ye have need of these other things, if you live in obedience to the principles which I inculcate, you will have these things. Again, he said, " Whose image and superscription is this? " " Cæsar's." " Render therefore unto Cæsar the things that are Cæsar's."

The Apostles, who spent three years under the instruction of Christ, and who were inspired of God to expound his precepts, having the promise of the Holy Spirit which was to bring all things whatsoever he said to their remembrance, and especially St. Paul, who, though not under the personal instruction of Christ, was a chosen vessel, clearly place government upon a divine basis; requiring honor to be given to whom it is due — kings, governors, and all that are in authority — and praying for them, and even makes an argument in favor of the payment of taxes based on the ground that governments properly administered are God's ministers, attending continually on this very thing. He also recognizes the distinctions between " masters and servants," and gives directions to each.

In the light of these facts, the original communistic experiment, when they that believed had all things in common, appears to have been a temporary expedient, very important in view of the suspicion and persecution to which Christians were exposed, and the losses in employment and property which they had to undergo, and the necessity of moving from place to place and of protecting each other; but not designed as a permanency, or to be made obligatory upon all. To hold any other view involves the subsequent directions before referred to, as well as the subsequent acts of the Apostles and of Christian believers, in inextricable confusion and irreconcilable contradiction.

Second, Christ and his Apostles well knew that it would be an indefinite period of time before Christian principles existed throughout the earth, and that these distinctions would exist, and therefore they grappled the problem as to the relation of brethren of high and low degree in the world as it now is.

THE BROTHER OF LOW DEGREE.

"Let the brother of low degree," says the Apostle James in the text, "rejoice in that he is exalted." He is of low degree in the world as it is now: poor, or ignorant, or obscure — perhaps all. In Christ he is a member of a new aristocracy, the kingdom of Christ, which kingdom is not of this world, cometh not with observation. While its members are in the world they bear themselves properly at every point of contact with it, walking in wisdom toward them that are without. The brother of low degree in the world is a genuine aristocrat in the kingdom of Christ, for the King is his Father, and Christ his Elder Brother. In that kingdom he is not a servant, but a son; and God hath sent forth his Spirit bearing witness that he is a son of God. He is an heir of God, and a joint heir with Christ. Now, an heir may be under tutors and governors; he may be somewhat restricted in his means, but he expects to enter upon his inheritance, and he is known to be the son of the owner. In South America the owner of a very large undeveloped mine was greatly embarrassed for money. While opening it, his son and himself, together with a number of common workmen, toiled side by side for many months; but how different the feeling of the common workman and the son of the owner! One was the heir; the other received only wages for his daily toil.

The brother of low degree may be, so far as the world is concerned, in a much more doleful condition than many who are not brethren at all. He may be the servant or the slave of a pagan, an infidel, or an entirely corrupt man, but he *expects his inheritance*. He may enter upon it at any time; he is certain to do so comparatively soon.

Fifteen years ago there was a man living in Paris in the depths of poverty. He was separated from an immense fortune by five lives. There was no reasonable probability of his ever getting any portion of the amount; but in the Franco-German War one of the persons was killed; this caused the death from grief of another, and from various causes the remaining three died, and the pauper entered upon the vast estate. But the brother of low degree has only one life between the enjoyment of his inheritance and himself, and that life is his own. Let him rejoice; the inheritance incorruptible, undefiled, and that passeth not away may be his within a year or a day — at most, within a very few years. Meanwhile all things work together for his good. He is saving and adding to his patrimony; for his being of low degree works for him "a far more exceeding and eternal weight of glory." While he looks not at the things that are seen (namely, his low degree, for it is only by comparison with the things that are seen that he appears to be of low degree), for they are temporal, " but at the things which are not seen " (namely, his exaltation in the kingdom of Christ), for they are eternal.

THE BROTHER OF HIGH DEGREE.

" But the rich, in that he is made low." Here is a striking contrast. The brother of low degree in the world is made of high degree in the kingdom of Christ; the brother of high degree in the world is, in a certain definite sense, made of low degree; and each is to rejoice. What, then, is the meaning implied in the injunction to the rich Christian to rejoice in that he is made low? First, that he has been led to see himself a helpless sinner; to discover that all true honor cometh from above; that his riches do not elevate him in the sight of God. If he be a true Christian he has " humbled himself under the mighty hand of God." Here we find St. Peter expressing the same idea. Made low and rejoicing in it is humbling one's self; for the very word humility is derived from *humus,* the ground, and the original conveys the same idea — " that you may be exalted in due time."

Without being made low it would be impossible for the rich Christian to receive the Gospel. Not one of the blessings promised by Christ in his sermon on the Mount could be his. There is a blessing to the poor in spirit — the kingdom of heaven; but the rich man who is not made low is not poor in spirit. There is a blessing to them that mourn; to the meek; to them that hunger and thirst after righteousness; to the pure in heart; to those that lay up treasure in heaven, not to those that lay up treasure for themselves upon earth.

The rich Christian has need for special rejoicing in that he is made low; for so few do humble themselves under the mighty hand of God. Behold the young man in the Gospel, apparently so humble and ingenuous that Christ looked upon him and loved him. He fancied that he had kept all the commandments from his youth up, and with mingled complacency and modesty affirmed it. Jesus knew that as his heart was upon his possessions, he had not kept one of them in spirit, though outwardly correct; hence he commanded, " Sell all thou hast and give it to the poor," which was a special test imposed upon him, and not a universal law. If it were a universal rule, without a constant miracle, all Christian disciples would at once become paupers, and the paupers enriched. The test was effectual: "He went away sorrowful, because he had great possessions."

But if the rich man rejoices that he is made low, his riches become a means of grace to him. He makes unto himself friends of the mammon of unrighteousness, that when he falls they may receive him into everlasting habitations; or, as it is in the Revision, which brings the idea out much more clearly: "And I say unto you, Make to yourselves friends by means of the mammon of unrighteousness; that, when it shall fall, they may receive you into the eternal tabernacles."

Such a rich man is independent of mutations. He may become poor and have to take his place with the brother of low degree, but his spirit cannot be broken, for his heart was not upon his riches. He was not rich toward himself, but toward God. Again, he rejoices because he is prepared to "fade away in his ways," from which there is no escape. Yet it is not to be supposed that this is the bad rich man — the rich man similar to the one in the parable who fared sumptuously every day, and had his good things in this life, but afterward was tormented. It is the Christian rich man; the wicked rich man is described by the same Apostle in other language. "Go to now, ye rich men, weep and howl for your miseries that shall come upon you. Your riches are corrupted and your garments are moth-eaten. Your gold and silver is cankered; and the rust of them shall be a witness against you, and shall eat your flesh as it were fire. Ye have heaped treasure together for the last days. Behold, the hire of the laborers who have reaped down your fields, which is of you kept back by fraud, crieth; and the cries of them which have reaped are entered into the ears of the Lord of Sabaoth. Ye have lived in pleasure on the earth, and have been wanton; ye have nourished your hearts as in a day of slaughter. Ye have condemned and killed the just; and he doth not resist you."

Yet the Christian rich man rejoices because he has been made low, for he must fade away in his ways, and he is prepared, and he only, to relinquish all. It has been said that possessions make a death-bed terrible. Said Jesus the son of Sirac: "O death, how bitter is the remembrance of thee to a man that liveth at rest in his possessions, unto the man that hath nothing to vex him, and that prospers in all things: yea, unto him that is yet able to receive meat!" But the rich man that glories in that he has been made low considers his heavenly inheritance as the culmination of all his hopes, and though daily and hourly thankful for his earthly comforts, counting himself as a steward whose accounts shall be approved when his master calleth for him, when he finds himself passing away can release all without a sigh. And if he be genuinely a disciple, he disposes of his property by will as conscientiously under the laws and institutions of the country in which he lives, in the interest of the kingdom of Christ, as he distributed while living; his uniform rule being, " Freely ye have received, freely give."

Some expositors have strangely misunderstood the meaning of this part of the text. They have fancied that James meant to say to Christians who had lost their property to rejoice on that account; or that he turned aside here to denounce the wicked rich man; but either of these constructions is forced and unnatural. The contrast is plainly between the poor brother and the rich brother.

Stier, in his comments on this passage, beautifully expresses its meaning: Of worldly-minded rich men St. James is not here speaking. He refers assuredly to a brother who is rich; only to such can he attribute a boasting or rejoicing; and what rejoicing? " Let the brother that is rich rejoice that he is made low." Mark that well! Rejoice in this, that thou knowest the Lord, who dealeth in mercy upon earth, and giveth grace to the humble; that thou hast seen the danger and escaped the snare of riches, and art no longer a camel too large for the needle's eye; that thou hast found security against destruction, and a better hope than fleeting riches can afford.

Rejoice that thou hast learned this; rejoice in thy lowliness before God as a spiritually poor man, who is not wanting in his spiritual gifts; so that as a brother of the poor, thou art also an inheriter of the kingdom, and *rich in God.*

CONCLUSION.

The low degree spoken of in the text is, from the Christian point of view, temporary. The highest state of the brother is spiritual and eternal; his exaltation is not like human fame or honor, which is but a breath, but is as everlasting as God and the soul. The high degree is temporary also, and he who is made low so regards it. All are equal at the cross of Christ.

The difference between the true Christian who is rich or honored, and one who is poor and obscure while passing through this world, is like that between two men crossing the sea in equally confident expectation of a fortune. The voyage of one may be in the first cabin and the finest stateroom in it, while that of the other may be in the steerage.

One may be more comfortable than the other, but both are sustained in the various inconveniences of the voyage by hope. Again, the difference may be illustrated by two voyages, one sailing over quiet seas and the other tossed about. Yet such an illustration, though true to human thought and expression, falls short of the measure required; for the very storms that are sent come in mercy and love. Nor is that all; in a beautiful passage in the Old Testament it is said, " And Jacob served seven years for Rachel, and they seemed unto him but a few days, for the love he had for her." So the true Christian believer passes through life, his afflictions " light and but for a moment," because the love of Christ constraineth him. The disagreeable things of poverty are reduced to small proportions, the evils of riches neutralized. The life of the brother of low degree is one of honesty, industry, and temperance, and his condition in all probability improves. If it does he is grateful and humble; if not, he can exclaim, " Nay, in all things we are more than conquerors."

Pride in the rich, and envy in the poor, are equal evidences that the man is in an unregenerate state; and it is absolutely certain that the proud rich man would — without a radical change of character — be envious if poor; and the envious poor man — without a similar change of character — would be arrogant if rich. He who rejoices in that he is made low can never be arrogant; he who glories in that he is exalted can never be envious.

Great transitions often show that the heart has not been upon God; the gloomy discontent of those once rich now poor, and the assumption of those once poor and now rich, in many instances illustrate the statement.

If Christianity were universally received and practiced, all social evils would vanish, and there would be very few rich persons. The majority of mankind would be in that happy condition, having neither riches nor poverty; comparatively few would be poor, and those would be worthy of universal sympathy and help which they would receive. The whole population of the earth, with the exception of those of inferior mental endowment, would possess general education, and a great number attain to true wisdom.

In communities where these principles are practiced to any considerable degree — and always in just such proportion as they are practiced — these results follow. " The fruit of righteousness is sown in peace of them that make peace;" and what the socialistic schemes could never give, because of their failure to purify the heart and prepare it for the works of fidelity and mercy necessary to their consummation, attaining Christian believers enjoy, though the number of them in proportion to that of the nominal Christians is so small as to recall the words of Christ: "Strait is the gate, and narrow is the way, that leadeth unto life eternal and few there be that find it."

The infidel and socialistic lecturer would destroy the institution of private property, overthrow human governments, to destroy inequalities which would speedily return unless human nature were changed by the influence of Christian principles. Ignorant of this fact, they attack Christianity itself — the only system that affords the poor any consolation, or confers upon them any dignity whatsoever, or that threatens the rich with the loss of God's favor if they oppress the poor. The direct consequences of the Gospel are, quietness, peace, hope, love; seeking improvement through industry, virtue, and wisdom, and accepting cheerfully whatever may come. When a rich man who has not been made low before God dies, he enters the other world a pauper; in the heavenly inheritance he has no part, while Lazarus is exalted to the highest place. But the poor man who is not exalted is of low degree in this world and also in the world to come.

Godliness with contentment is great gain, for it is profitable unto all things, having the promise of the life that now is and of that which is to come. Therefore let the brother of low degree (of whom there seem not many present) rejoice in that he is exalted; and the rich, or comfortable, or learned, or honored, in that he is made low.

These principles I understand to be the contribution of Christianity to the problem of personal and social inequalities. Only as they prevail can human inequalities be removed or made tolerable. May we have grace to bear witness to them, in word, spirit, and life.

(A sermon preached in the special Evening Course of the Brick Presbyterian Church, New York City.)

XLV

CHARLES HENRY FOWLER

1837–

CHARLES HENRY FOWLER, D.D., LL. D., one of the Bishops of the Methodist Episcopal Church, was born in Burford, Ontario, Canada, August 11, 1837, of English and Scottish ancestry. His boyhood and youth were passed on a farm in Central Illinois. He was graduated as the first scholar in his class, in 1859, at Genessee College, now Syracuse University; studied law for a time, but renounced a brilliant prospect in that profession, and entered Garrett Biblical Institute, the Methodist Theological school of the west, and completed the course of study in 1861. For eleven years he held pastoral charges in the city of Chicago and as a preacher and lecturer he was soon known throughout the west. In 1872 he became president of the Northwestern University, at Evanston, Illinois. In 1876 he was chosen by the General Conference of the Methodist Episcopal Church as editor of the Christian Advocate, the most important paper of the denomination. But editorial tasks were less attractive to him than the public platform, and in 1880, he was made one of the Missionary Secretaries of the church. The General Conference of 1884 elevated Dr. Fowler to the episcopate; and during the twenty years following, as Bishop, he visited almost every quarter of the globe, and took part in directing the activities of the church everywhere; for the diocese of a Methodist Bishop is continental in dimensions and is changed every year. Since 1904, he has made his home in New York, as Resident Bishop. He has written some books and many articles; but his field of power is in the pulpit and on the platform. His great lecture on " Abraham Lincoln " takes nearly two hours and a half for its delivery, but of the hundreds of thousands who have listened to it, no one was ever heard to say that it was too long. His sermons are carefully prepared, every word fitted to its place, and every illustration beaten out into perfect shape; nevertheless, they do not " smell of the lamp " nor show the droppings of the pen; for they are spoken without notes, in such a fiery fervor as to appear absolutely spontaneous. The discourse here given was preached in 1870 at the dedication of the Arch Street Methodist Episcopal Church in Philadelphia.

DIVINE AND HUMAN COPARTNERSHIP.

"For ye are laborers together with God: ye are God's husbandry: ye are God's building."— 1 Cor. iii. 9.

I LIKE this passage that I have read in your hearing as a text, because there is so much in it — simple and plain, and familiar, yet full, and possibly profound — certainly practical. It is an epitome of the divine economy; it is full of the richest and profoundest human philosophy; it is quivering all over with divine power. Like the nightly pillar in the camp of Israel, it stands in this epistle radiant and glorious with the divine presence. What an inlook it gives us, when we look carefully at it, into the mystery of our living and into the dignity of our fellowships, and into the glory of our destiny!

It is an entire income of divinity into humanity, with its mangers and its wildernesses, with its gardens and its Calvaries; and it is also a transfiguration — an exaltation of humanity under the divine commission, with its inspirations and its resurrections, with its ascensions and its enthronements, for we are " laborers together with God."

I suppose, in the exposition of this text, like the exposition of most other texts of Scripture, that which is best is that which is simplest and most manifest on the surface. The critical putting of the passage is that you and I are workers together of or under God. The general application of the passage is that we are workers together *with* God, supported by the general Scripture teaching. The same truth is put in another passage by the apostle when he says: " We are to work out our salvation with fear and trembling, while God worketh in us to will and to do of his own good pleasure." And he also exhorts these same Corinthians as laborers together with God. So, it seems, we have a right to a joint application of the passage as it stands before us, that God and we are in copartnership.

Notice a moment the exceeding skill almost amounting to a cunning perception of the case — the skill with which the apostle brings out the kind of work to be done by us in the very words used to put it: "Ye are God's husbandry"— God's farm, farm-making, farm-working. This rude Corinthian heart is to be brought in and subdued, so as to bear a gospel harvest. "Ye are God's building"— an edifice erected, constructed — not an outgrowth, but here an erection, here a construction, here something done by an outside power — God's building, a house in which God shall be at home — a house built around the idea of God's presence, characters in which we are to live with God, which shall have all the sacredness of the inner sanctuary, and all the familiarity of the home. "Ye are God's building."

And pause now a moment to see how adroitly the apostle lets down these conceited Corinthians in the putting of the text itself. The text, back of our English version, has this suggestive thing in it. In this short sentence there is no word at all to represent these Corinthians who are contending about men and about their personal advancement, but the name of God is put in full three times, and the Corinthians are only drawn in by the person of the verb; these conceited men are left out, and the Almighty is made the controlling thought of the text, and yet the copartnership is maintained — a copartnership in which all the power is of God, and all the glory belongs to God, and yet the power so adjusted that all — absolutely all — the responsibility rests with us. These are the conditions of our copartnership.

. . *This law of human and divine action — co-labor, laboring together — is a universal law.* You cannot touch humanity anywhere but you strike this truth. It makes up the warp and woof of nature, of our lives, of society; it is everywhere divine power and human agency — it is a combination of these forces. One fact indicating that is this:—

Either element, when left to itself, fails. Men have blundered concerning this subject, as concerning all other subjects, and whenever they have left out the divine element in their calculations, they have failed. Mere humanitarian systems that did not or ought not to pretend to be religions, but only systems of philosophy, built not upon the divine Christ, but upon the human Jesus, have demonstrated that, leaving out the supernatural power, they have failed to accomplish the supernatural work. They move among men doing a kind of human work, but they do not move among men doing the divine work. They some-how demonstrate that their systems are circumscribed by the bounds of their nationalities, and their influence seldom survives the sexton who digs their unwilling graves; that which is born of the flesh proves to be flesh; the fountain not bubbling on the summit, the stream never rises there. Having no power from on high, they necessarily fail to lift up fallen humanity.

And in accordance with this fact of the failure of the elements, when separated, we find this one thing in history: the richest and choicest peoples — the peoples who have most culture and thought and education and intellectual power, are the peoples who have utterly died out of history; so that the perfect languages are the dead languages.

And parallel with this we find another fact as startling, that the low animal peoples who live a kind of sensual or animal life, who have no great outlook of thought, who mount no summits of culture, who sink to no depth of philosophy — these are the peoples who live on and on through centuries. Humanity accepted as a fallen fact persists like an animal instinct through the ages; but whenever she undertakes to rise, she wears herself out by the endeavor. Leaving out the divine power, the elements fail because they are separated.

And the divine element fails as utterly when separated from the human. It seems to inhere in the nature of the case that they cannot believe except they hear, and they cannot hear except one be sent. And here is the human agency. The man who can sit down in a leaky boat and fold his arms, thinking that if it is the Lord's great will that he should be saved he will be saved, will find that God's great will will be done, and that it is his great will that he should go to the bottom, because God has no better use for such a man. And the churches which undertake to let the Lord do all their work are the churches whose work will never — *no, never* be done. The divine element in itself fails in the work. It seems to me conclusive, then, that, as the elements, when separated, fail, there is, in the purpose of God concerning it, this anticipated and necessary union.

Take another fact. *See how God works in things.* It is one vast plan spread out before us in such a way that we may, by chance, avail ourselves of the energies of nature to do our work, to carry our burdens. God turns the great wheels always one way, so that we may see them and catch the secret, find how they move, and throw about them the belts of our creative and inventive thought, and thus, claiming our possible copartnership, cause things to come to pass. He gives us bodies, possible strength, time, opportunity, brain, but these, in themselves, are not enough. Left to themselves, they produce either the sloven or the savage — either the Bushman or the Sioux. Civilization means more than these. It means very much labor in the shop, very much weariness in the study, very much anguish in the closet, and very much patient on-going after the seers and the prophets. God gives soil, sunlight, moisture, nourishment, germs, but these are not enough. Left to themselves, they produce thistles and noxious weeds. There is required also your thought and nerve and plan and skill, and then you and God can produce a loaf of bread.

You wanted this church. God gave the stone and the clay, and the iron and the lumber, but not here. The stone was in the quarry, the clay was in the bank, the iron was in the vein, the lumber was in the forest, and you know what it has cost to put them together.

And this same old law holds as firmly over character as it does over materials. This poor man has fallen into bad habits, and staggered out of the way and gotten down into the street, until the filth is upon his garments. Now, there is no process by which he may come back to respectability that is not based on his individual struggle. Sometimes gold dust thrown into the air may dim or divert the public eye, but soon that is past, and the unfortunate victim is left to hew his way up to respectability at the hardest.

These are but material and social applications of a law that finds its first legitimate and original cause, the reason of its existence, back in our moral nature. If, then, we do actually find that, in the world about us, God does so work in the system of copartnership with us, need we be alarmed, overwhelmed, if he requires us in his spiritual interest, in our spiritual lives, to obey the same rule?

Take another fact that looks to this copartnership — *the fact of destitution,* anywhere — poverty — poverty of purse or of spirits: all poverty is inexplicable except on the supposition of this copartnership. There is a beautiful island — Erin, the island of the heart — and yet her children actually gnaw their bones in famine. No fault of God. He loves Erin; he loves all men. Yonder, in the great valley between the mountains, waves a harvest large enough for all men. It needs the human instrumentalities to take yonder harvest to yonder starving ones. There, in the alley, comes up a boy, dandled on the lap of corruption, fed on vice, graduated in a brothel, trained up a thief, and

37

turned out a cut-throat. He has no fair chance. No fault of God. God loves that little cut-throat as much as he does anybody else in his universe. Not his fault that he has no chance. Look, there are wide zones of fertile land, upon which all the cities may scatter their victims into freedom. God has provided for them. It needs the human intervention to make the right distribution. And then there are vast Christless empires which never heard of him. But it is no fault of God. He loves them; he is no respecter of persons; he willeth not the death of him that dieth, but he would that all men would turn and live. No Christ has touched their shores; no prophet has cried in their ears; yet it is no fault of God. Fault there must be somewhere. It is only a demonstration of the human element in the copartnership. If God could have his way, to-morrow's sun would not rise over an unsaved sinner in all the universe. If God's way could be carried out, every lost profligate would be accepted of God; for "Jesus Christ, by the grace of God, tasted death for every man." Yea, more than that. If God could have his way, the very last prison-pen in all the universe would be open, and the very last mourning and sorrowing one would be lifted up into peace and purity and joy unspeakable. But there is in the way, the human element in the copartnership. There is a human will in the path, and human rebellion in the way. No fault of God.

Take another fact looking to this copartnership. *All our blessings come to us through human instrumentality.* We have some elements — we have air and time and life, a few things from God directly, or apparently directly; and yet when you come back to them you find that we are, after all, related to them through some human instrumentality. How crude they are as they come from the Almighty! — hardly worth having. Indeed, it is not possible for us to have them without human instrumentality. Life itself is such a little, helpless thing; yet little as it is, it comes to us only by the tenderness of maternal love. We receive it through maternal agencies. And what a long journey it is from the helplessness of that little babe, only a lump of possibilities on the lap of its mother, to that stalwart man! It is a long way, and much drilling and wearing along the way to realize the power.

Take this revelation of God, God's truth, his Word, too grand for our invention, and too vital for us to dispense with; and yet *what a human thing it is!* Here you can find full-length portraits of the

prophets and the seers.   Here you can come in contact with living men —
God-anointed, God-appointed, God-smitten men; yet men sent out to be
the light of the world. This book, with the divine element left out of it,
is like the sculptor's studio — full of statues,— stone men; but when
it accepts the divine element, these statues catch the inspiration of
life, and go forth — not gods, but men, speaking to us God's secret
by human lips, and yet with human speech.

The highest and the last demonstration of this is *seen in the incarnation itself*. It seems to me that when God would bring his salvation into the world — what he wanted was salvation — and when
he would bring it into the world, he had to incarnate it in his own
Son; he could come to us only in the Son of Man. It is the only
salvation that could by any chance reach us at all, if you will think
about it. It seems as if somehow the remedial agencies came down
into our weakness and touched them into power, so that these weak
and broken elements rise up apparently instead of being lifted up,
lifted up in fact; yet not by an outside power, but by an inside power,
that has been catalogued with the fallen forces of humanity, so that
Jesus enters into our humanity, is born under the law, is made like
unto his brethren, and is obedient unto death, that he may come even
to us, and give salvation that is in us and of us, yet supernatural.

Look at these terms a little. "Ye are God's husbandry," and the
work there indicated shows a little something of what we are to
do, and how much you need this divine help in the case. The old
nature is to be grubbed out by a kind of clearing-up process. The
old forest that occupies the soil and shuts out the light and prevents
the good seed from getting root or nourishment, is to be taken down
and transformed, through divine agencies, into a protection and defence for the heavenly crop; and this is no small work. This means
earnest endeavor. Try it. Put yourself at the work. Stand against
the flood. Run against the tempest. See how weak and utterly helpless
you are without the divine power. And yet this work is to be done by
you, and through you, God helping.

I think the figure looks, a little farther on, *to building your characters*. And this to me seems the core of this whole question — the
building up of your characters into the likeness of God. Not by a mere
human endeavor, but by the human strengthened and made out by
the divine; not that you can do it alone and unfold from within
you that which shall be pleasing to God, but that, with the divine

power, everyone of you can build up your character so that it shall be acceptable to God in our Lord Jesus Christ. This sweeps out over the whole field of our character and destiny. And just here let me say, we are liable, in touching any of these points and discussing questions of this kind, to go too far, or lose sight too much of the other side of the question. The problem of a religious life is made up of many equations and as many factors. Your religious character is many-sided. The Gospel comes to you many-sided. Here, seen from this standpoint, it is all divine; and seen from another, it is all human. Here it is all devotion; there it is all activity. Here it has the breath and the billow of emotion; there it glistens in the cold serenity of the intellections. Now we see it with the grip of a syllogism holding the convictions of the intellect; then it comes in among the intuitions, warming by the breath of inspiration. Now it stands erect, holding the reins of eternal obligation; next it settles upon the soul with dew like peace of heaven, with the impleadings of divine mercy, and thus wins us to God. It is many-sided. It is — Work out your faith, from your fingers' ends. It is one perfect system.

The foundation of our hope is salvation by faith only. It could not have been otherwise, even if God had not said: " By grace are ye saved through faith, and that not of yourselves; it is the gift of God." Yes, the fact that eternal life is an *infinite gift* puts it outside the possibility of our earning it. What we earn is limited and measured by day or hour; but God's gift, eternal life, is infinite, and so necessarily a gift; and if a gift, necessarily to be taken by faith only, so that when the bond for the ten thousand talents is pressed for collection, then there is no footing at all left for works; it is only, Believe — solely by faith. And this freeness makes it a gospel indeed. It would be no gospel at all but for this. It is necessary that the system that meets us should be capable of delay, that we might put it off and off and off, even till life's latest hour, and then, by divine power, through faith, take life and live.

Aye, if I didn't believe that the very lowest mortal on earth — the vilest and lowest — even though he should stand on the very crumbling verge of time, falling headlong into the pit, if he would but look once toward Christ, and offer believing prayer, might be saved, I would never enter the pulpit again. It is because we need something to repair all our failures that we must have a system that comes only by faith.

Now, then, having *the one point of our pardon settled by faith, it seems to me the power of that faith must come out through works —divine aid, human activity.* Coming through our characters, then, it is not possible for God to save us without our activity. A salvation that would fall upon us from heaven would only crush us, not cure us. God slays not our power, but our sins; he saves us, not the remnants of us; he saves our forces, our humanity, our will, our ability to feel and act and be. He saves us, not slays us, by a system with which we have nothing to do. It seems to me — though it is a startling fact, it is true — that a man, full grown, lost in the solitude of his sin, plunging on in the loneliness of his suffering, a dethroned king, yet a king crowned and enthroned above his own wretchedness and sin — that such a being is worth infinitely more in the universe of God than a whole army of shining puppets, polished by no purpose of their own.

We are sometimes told that God might have sent angels to do this work he has left in our hands; that the work of saving men might have been committed to orders of life above us. I am not prepared to say that it is impossible, yet I am prepared to say that it is not thinkable to me. It is not possible in the light of thought. In the first place, it is not something to be put upon us, but something to be wrought within us; not an outside cloak covering over our old corruptions, but an inside life and power — something that takes the whole being and occupies every part and fibre; and so, to be anything at all, must be worked out through the man himself, and cannot be put upon the man from the outside. Horace Bushnell has made a statement which is liable to be misunderstood, but which contains a substantial truth. When a bush is bent down in a forest, nature does not send another bush, nor yet a tree, to pick up the bush, but puts life and power into the bush itself. So it seems to me God operates upon us by his grace. He comes with his supernatural power into us, and works along the normal lines of our activity, and thus enables us to rise into his likeness.

And then, if there were any possibility that angels could come, and by swarming the whole vault above us into the brightest glory, and crowding in untold millions into the path of each wanderer, could hasten forward the salvation of one single sinner, the infinite love of God, that stops at nothing, would, of necessity, crowd all angels into this world of ours, and put an immediate stop to sin. But it is not in the nature of the case. We misapprehend the nature of sin itself. It is not something that may be put to death by an outside being; it can be killed only when the creature from whose bosom it leaps, and in whose purpose it lives, becomes the executioner. And we mistake the character of the work itself. It is not outside work, done for something else and somebody else; it is an inside work, done in and for use as the end. We do not work like hirelings, we are sons; we work not for wages, but an inheritance — an inheritance not to be received after some grave has been filled, but that is to be received here, and under God, and with God, to be worked out by us for the home yonder.

This outside work, pushing forward the interests of the Church, building edifices, attending prayer-meetings, going after the poor, and other Christian work that comes upon a Christian's heart that seems to be outside, may be, after all, only one field for his development. Yonder is a man who goes into a shop to make an engine. Unwittingly, he develops his arm, fills out his chest. Yonder man goes into a gymnasium, swings dumb-bells, climbs ropes, leaps bars, pounds bags of sand, and the like. Wittingly, he develops his chest and arms. Now, in God's plan, both these systems work in together. Many a thing seems like making the engine, doing some outside thing, yet actually it is the only way by which we can be brought on in this co-operating work with God. And it is just here that the necessity is put upon us to do so much outside work for God; and the man who does it — who carries the burdens, who gets under the tremendous pressure, who agonizes in the darkness — is not the man to be pitied; but the man who does not do it — the man who dodges — he is the man to be pitied; the sick man, whom the Lord has to nurse and lead on to heaven, and whom he stands a great chance of losing before he gets there with him, he is the man to be pitied, because it is in this process of co-operation with God that this poor material is fashioned up into a man, then a saint, then an angel.

There is another thing that is true. If this fact of co-operation is true, *then Christ's kingdom goes forward or is retarded, according as we are active or negligent.* I think that is an inevitable sequence from the proposition that we are co-workers with him. Then, what follows? Just as the falling of an autumn leaf will jar the most distant sun, so the slightest faltering of even the weakest and lowest saint holds back the coming of the kingdom of Christ. Look at the case a little. There is no lack of love on his part. He has come for the sole purpose of saving men. He came into the world at the earliest hour. All through the ages he carried humanity on his heart, crying: "O that there were such an heart in you that you would hear my voice!" longing to come always from the moment of the first transgression, anxious to come to the oppressed and sorrowing and wounded, to comfort the mourning, and bind up their wounds. And this, of necessity, in the nature of infinite love. He could not have infinite love and hold back anywhere. It must press out at the earliest chance. So he waits, and waits, and waits for his people. He waited four thousand years for a virgin to say: "Thy will be done." I doubt not he waited a thousand years for grand old Martin Luther, and that he stood and watched and looked for twelve centuries for the coming of John Wesley; and to-day he waits, and his cause hangs back, and his kingdom is delayed, because we, his children, allow our hands to hang down. He is here for the salvation of all men, coming to establish a kingdom of righteousness, and it delays because we lack faith and devotion and consecration. The thought to me is oppressive. We are so related to God's kingdom that our lack of prayer and faith and sacrifice actually retards the coming of the kingdom.

With this immense responsibility, as we might expect, there comes *also a commensurate dignity.* It could not be otherwise. And yet it is to me incomprehensible. We can only look at it a little. It is amazing to me that such a being as Jesus Christ, full of his infinite love, clothed in light, the first-born of every creature, by whom all things consist, King of kings, and Lord of lords, invisible, immortal, eternal, God over all, blessed for ever more — it is to me inconceivably grand that such a being as Jesus Christ has actually burst into our humanity, and is here ready to work, here for our salvation; but more than this, he takes us, little and weak and frail as we are into copartnership with himself, and we, little as we are, are under his divine commission. And more than this, we are sent out to have his character, to be like him, to repeat his wonderful words, to walk among the sorrowing, and tell of his compassion. This to me is the infinite thing. All else in life is but as dust and ashes, and the chance of standing for him among the dying and sinning, and there crying, "Behold, behold the Lamb!" is more than all else in this life. It seems to me, if we could but see the dignity of the work he has given us, its power, depth, height, glory, irresistible victory, divine radiance, we would go though we starved; we would work though it were a thousand years; we would pray on while we had breath. It seems to me, in this fact, our relationship to Christ is the highest of all possible dignities; and yet we have such a miserably poor way of measuring dignity, getting at the real power in the case, we can, at best, only get little glimpses, and only guess concerning it.

It is something, too, *to be a citizen of this republic;* it means something, though we cannot comprehend it. That poor soldier-boy may not know the day of the republic's birth, nor the number of her commonwealths, nor count the stars of her flag even, and yet he wears the sign of the nation's power; and it is something to be a citizen of this republic, because there is no land on all the earth, no dungeon anywhere under the sun, no island in the sea, where prince or potentate can harm a hair of his head with impunity. Let the despot touch him, and forty millions of citizens rise for his defence! I remember reading awhile ago, how that, yonder in South America, a poor Norwegian sailor, by some transgression of the local laws, was involved in serious trouble. The petty government tried him for conspiracy; they found him guilty, and sentenced him to death. He did not understand his crime, nor his relations to their government; he only knew the horror that was coming upon him. But the ministers of the governments of England and of the United States interfered in his behalf; they protested; the petty authorities insisted; the ministers forbade the execution, but the local government took the victim out, and drew up the line of soldiers for his execution, when the representatives of these two great governments, taking the flags of the two countries, went in before the man and wrapped around him the Stars and Stripes and England's flag, and the soldiers dared not shoot. It meant something to be a citizen of the United States, or Great Britain; but infinitely more than this is it to be a citizen of that country beyond. We are brought into fellowship with God, and permitted to work in copartnership with him; and though little, and ignorant, and unable to count his stars, nor tell his glory, nor know the time of his coming, yet we are in copartnership with him, and his flag is over us, and his angels are about us, and absolutely nothing can, by any chance, harm us. God's infinite love comes in just back of our weakness. He has given his only begotten Son for us, and with him will he not freely give us all things? This tenderness comes to us so that we may know that we are his, and kept by his almighty power.

I remember once standing by the surging billows, all one weary day, and watching for hours a father struggling beyond in the breakers for the life of his son. They came slowly toward the breakers on a piece of wreck, and as they came the waves turned over the piece of float, and they were lost. Presently we saw the father come to the surface and clamber alone to the wreck, and then saw him plunge off into the waves, and thought he was gone; but in a moment he came back again, holding his boy. Presently they struck another wave, and over they went; and again they repeated the process. Again they went over, and again the father rescued his son. By and by, as they swung nearer the shore, they caught on a snag just out beyond where we could reach them, and for a little time the waves went over them there, till we saw the boy in the father's arms hanging down in helplessness, and knew they must be saved soon or be lost; and I shall never forget the gaze of that father. And as we drew him from the devouring waves, still clinging to his son, he said, "That's my boy, that's my boy!" and half frantic, as we dragged them up the bank, he cried all the time: "That's my boy, that's my boy!" And so I have thought, in hours of darkness, when the billows roll over me, the great Father is reaching down to me, and, taking hold of me, crying, "That's my boy!" and I know I am safe.

XLVI

RUSSELL HERMAN CONWELL

1842–

FEW men in the American pulpit have passed through a career as varied as that of Russell Herman Conwell, D. D., pastor of the Baptist Temple in Philadelphia. He was born in the little village of Worthington, in Central Massachusetts, Feb. 15, 1842, and was educated mainly at the Wesleyan Academy, Wilbraham, Mass., not far from his home. He entered the Yale Law School in 1860, but his plans for study, like those of multitudes in that stirring time, were changed by the breaking out of the Civil War. He entered the Union Army as one of its youngest captains of infantry, fought through the war, and near its close was made lieutenant-colonel of his regiment. When peace returned, he began the practice of law in Minneapolis, but gave up his profession for a time to become a newspaper correspondent, in which capacity he went around the world and wrote reports of his journey for the New York Tribune and the Boston Traveler. His observations and experiences in many lands, were storing up, unconsciously to himself, abundant facts and illustrations for the years to come. In 1870, he returned to the law, and established an office in Boston. But while practising he was also occasionally preaching, and in 1879 was ordained to the Baptist ministry. In 1881 he was called to the Grace Baptist Church in Philadelphia, which afterward became the Baptist Temple, the largest church of his denomination in America, with a congregation so great that admission has been for many years by ticket, and the evening audience different from that of the morning; besides a regular " overflow " with an associate pastor, which fills a hall larger than an ordinary church. The energies of Dr. Conwell have never been con-

RUSSELL HERMAN CONWELL.
1842-

As lawyer, soldier and journalist, Dr. Conwell gained distinction before he entered upon the ministry in the Baptist Church. Besides drawing great crowds to hear him preach in the Temple, he founded Temple College, one of the great institutions of the country.

CHARLES HENRY FOWLER.
1837-

Bishop Fowler's sermons are carefully prepared, but delivered with such vigor as to appear extemporaneous. He was born in Canada, and in 1904, after a varied career in the service of the Church, was made Bishop of New York.

fined to his pulpit. In 1888 he organized the Temple College in connection with his church, an institution which now has 3,600 students. In 1890 he founded the Samaritan Hospital, which is mainly supported by his church; and of both college and hospital Dr. Conwell is President. Many men who make lecturing their sole business deliver fewer lectures in a year than does Dr. Conwell. His most famous lecture is " Acres of Diamonds," which he is said to have given more than three thousand times; and the present writer having heard it at least half a dozen times is prepared to believe that it is never delivered twice in the same language and line of illustrative stories. Originality, simplicity, directness, and illustrativeness are the principal traits of Dr. Conwell's preaching. This sermon was delivered in the Chautauqua Amphitheater, on August 10, 1890, before five thousand intensely interested hearers. The little scheme of delaying his text until the close caused every one present to listen all the more intently in order to find out in advance what the text would be. The report is from the Assembly Herald, as the sermon was taken down by a stenographer, and without revision by Dr. Conwell; so that it does not represent his language at its best. It is given as thoroughly characteristic of the man and his preaching.

" THE CHURCH IN THE FUTURE."

I SHALL not tell you where my text is this morning; because I do not need to deal with these circumstances of the Bible until I have finished my discourse of the morning, and then I may, or may not. It depends upon whether I remember to do so, or whether I think of it. I am here to speak the words that I believe that God shall give to me; and to say those things that I hope shall be of help to you, for the Lord hath not sent us here for nought this morning. We are here this morning for a good purpose. God has his lessons for us to learn and his providential purpose to carry out in this gathering; and so, this morning, I will call your attention to the highest type of a church member, taking the Lord Jesus for authority. I will lead you up, if I can, to the text, and close with the text, as I say, if I don't forget it. There is a trend in all the providences of God which shows that the day is soon coming when every denomination of Protestant Christians will be united under one common name. It is not far to that glorious union when the churches shall be one; and the natural question which we ask as sectarians, is, will it be my church, or will it be some other church? As a Baptist I am naturally anxious that it shall be the Baptist Church. I am equally certain that our Methodist friends are of a similar opinion, hoping that it may be their church, and I could go over the list of the denominations in the same way. But I wish to call your attention this morning to the Lord Jesus' testimony, the highest, the only authority, as to what shall be the surviving church. What will be the denomination of that church that will survive, when in the early future, we are united under one common name and in one common cause. Which of our churches is going to survive? Which of our present creeds and Christianity, which of our principles when all are brought to the common test, and the survival of the fittest takes place in the providence of God? So I call your attention to an humble church member which will represent the church membership of the future, of the church which will survive in the future. The Lord Jesus Christ pointed to him, and showed to his friends around, as well as to his enemies, that there was one who in all coming ages should be the standard of the highest type of Christianity and church membership or of church organizations. He is represented to have been one of those characters which shall never die in history. I shall call your attention to this man; and we shall discuss his character, and see if you all find the text before I reach it.

The man of whom I speak was born in the mountains of Judea some thirty to thirty-five miles to the north and west of Jerusalem. He was born in the mountains. I do not know that that had anything to do with Jesus' estimate of the nobility of his character, but I am sure of this, that it is a grand thing to be born in the mountains. There is something in the surroundings with which a man is met as he cometh forth into this beautiful world. The great sailors are born by the sea, and the mighty adventurers are born in the mountains, and the even, calm civilizations are born upon the plains. There is something in the providence of God in the situation where a man first sees the trees, or looks upon the water, or breathes the air. I do not think that Jesus selected this man to be the representative man because he was there born, and yet we find in his character that there were used his surroundings for definite purposes. So I believe it is a grand thing to be born upon the mountains; to be brought up where the waters dash and crash, where they thunder their mighty bass, where they sing their beautiful soprano; to be born where the birds soar to the sky, and the eagle's nest can be seen as well as the sweet robin's retreat; to be born where mighty chasms cause men to think deep, and where lofty peaks raise his mind to the sky.   There is something in that; and if you are born upon the plains, or in the city, let me say that I believe that it is one of the teachings of God that we shall go for our vacations to the mountains, go to the diversified surfaces and the world shall teach God's character through nature.

There is no better place to take your children.   If you would have them grow in everything that is deep and high and broad and — grand, then take them to the mountains.   And this man was born among the mountains.

He was born of a mixed race.   His race was mixed; that is, he could trace his ancestry, on the one side, back to the cave of Machpelah; he could trace it away back to Egypt, away back to the earliest days of history.   On the other side, he could trace his family connections to the old Babylon of Nineveh.   He was of a mixed race, and it may be that through his veins ran the blood of the philosophers of ancient Greece.   It is a grand thing to be of a mixed race.   This is the hope of the United States of America, that is the hope of Canada, that is the hope of these new countries; because in the intermingling of different peoples and different tribes and different nations there is always developed the best features of them all.   And the mighty, leading nation of the future, in all that makes for good, must be the nation in which is intermingled the blood of all the various races of men.   It is grand to be of a mixed race.   I do not care who my great, great grandfather was; whether he wore a crown is of but little consequence; and you need not care whether you are descended from the mighty of all, or whether your nation be ignoble, or whether your blood has run through scoundrels since the flood.   It is of little consequence to you and me who our great grandfathers were.   It is of consequence to us in one sense that we are of mixed race.   I do not care to keep my blood pure in a single line, and to boast that I am English, that that there is no Scotch, or Irish, or French, or German in my constitution.   A man that boasts that he has come in a single line may boast of that which is the highest evidence of his weakness.   And so, while I do not believe that it is the highest proof and evidence of church membership that Jesus selected a man of mixed race to be his highest type of church membership, yet I believe that it is a good thing to be of a mixed race.

Then, in the next place, he was born at a period when he must have been trained in all that was taught in that day. He was trained where he was brought within the influence of the Romans, for near his home was a great Roman camp and that was the headquarters of the Romans of that portion of Palestine. And he must have seen throughout all of his boyhood days, the coming and going of the Roman legions, and he must have been acquainted with the Roman language. Not only that, he lived in a situation where there was a Grecian school, and he must have been acquainted with the philosophy of the Grecian writers. And in his own church and in his own creed, he was compelled to go to school and learn of the ancient prophets. There are people who come here to Chautauqua who think if they attend none of its exercises at all, they will through the atmosphere draw in such inspiration, spiritual and educational, that when they go back home they will be almost the equals of a college graduate! There is something, but not everything in it. No person could stay within these surroundings for the period of four weeks without receiving inspirations from which they can never part. And he being brought up in that neighborhood, and with all those things about him, must have felt the educational influences of that life.

But I approach immediately the discussion of this man's life and character, because that is of greater consequence. It is not so much matter where we were born, or in what nation, as it is that we should have a character which makes the highest type of a Christian. This man whom Jesus selected was a man of good common sense, and that is necessary to the making of church membership; and the great church of the future will be the church in which the chiefest characteristics of its membership will be their broad common sense. It will be such a combination of men and women as will give the largest and best exercise to the individual characteristics along the line of direct and sincere and spiritual worship of God. Jesus Christ told the woman at the well that the time would come when we must worship God in spirit and in truth. We ask, will the ritualism of the old church remain? Will it remain in the church of the future? Or will we swing entirely aside into the complete independence and the same wide liberality of the congregational form of government? What will be the church of the future? It will be this — whether we speak through a liturgy, or whether we speak without preparation, there will be in it the sincerity of the living God, and not one word uttered but it is meant by the lips of those who speak. In the government of the future church we shall find common sense applied everywhere. Local circumstances will have their influence upon the church, and national circumstances, also, will have theirs, and the cause of Christ will be so administered as to influence the greatest possible number of people, and use all the powers, social and educational, for the purpose. The church of the future will be the church of progress, which adapts itself spiritually to the wants and ideas of each individual.

A sailor whom I met the other day was cast away upon an island. He was not a Christian, nor was either of the four who were cast away with him, but they had a Bible. And they said, " Here we are; we have got to turn now to God, if we never did before." And they read the Bible, and prayed to God. They worshipped God. What kind of a church did they have? Was it of the apostolic succession? Was it a church in which they could use the forms of that church? or my own? They did not know anything about that. What kind of a church did they have? You cannot tell? They did not have any name for it at all. And yet those five persons organized a church there upon that desert island. They organized a church, and worshipped God sincerely, and adapted their worship to the needs of the people cast upon that shore. And the great church of the future will be that church so adjusted to the social needs of men and the will of God as to fit the feelings and needs of all people; and if any man wishes to worship by the old forms he can do it, or if he wishes to worship by the new forms he can do that. But it must be a sincere work, one that shall apply entirely to the spiritual side of his nature.

And I say this man described by Jesus Christ was a man of excellent common sense. The great need of every church and denomination is men of common sense. Not men who can merely preach, for some of the brightest preachers on earth, those who will deliver their sermons with impressiveness to the heart and mind, and whose spiritual fervor never seems to cease, make entire shipwrecks of their church life; and the church is divided with difficulties and quarrels arising all the time, because, while these men can preach with genius and emotion, they seem to lack that business common sense which is necessary to the conduct of other organizations, to preserve harmony, peace and prosperity in it. The day is coming when it will be just as necessary for a minister to have a business education as it will be to study theology. The day is coming when every minister must exercise his strong common sense, and rest largely upon his common sense in the interpretation of the word of the living God. We in our different needs find here just what supplies our spiritual necessities. I may be in one circumstance a thousand miles away, and you may be in a different set of circumstances, a thousand miles the other way, and yet this Bible comes into all our needs, wants, wishes — everything. Here is the supply for every man and woman; and what would fit you in Chautauqua would not fit you in New York or in the city of Chicago. The twelfth chapter of Romans, that marvellous chapter read in our hearing this morning, no two of us think alike concerning it, and yet to each one of us, if we listen reverently, there come some lessons, some help from the spirit of God. And each exercising his own common sense, recognizes that which he needs, and uses that which he needs, hence the Holy Spirit applies the Scriptures to every person present. The day is coming when the church shall be at perfect liberty, when it will use all the good things of scriptures, and of the liturgies of the church that are available for the uplifting of men's hearts and minds.

I am glad that Jesus Christ didn't point to a minister of the gospel whose duty and inclination and selfishness combine to make him a good man, outwardly, anyhow. If a man's business and profits combine on the same line of goodness it is easier to serve the Lord. I have found it immensely easier to do what seems to be right outwardly since I have been in the ministry than I did when I was a lawyer. Immensely different. So wide is the difference that I hardly dare stop to reason concerning it. Jesus did not point to a minister of the gospel and say, " Here is your type, here is your example." No, he didn't. He did not even point to a person who prayed a great deal. The Lord Jesus Christ did not say that the man prayed at all, although I believe, am positively sure he was a praying man. Yet Christ did not say that he prayed at all. I know by the record that he was a church-going man. He was a sectarian man. But I don't read that Jesus said he ever prayed. He did not point to that as the most important thing in his life. The most important thing in his life was that he was a careful, good-sensed business man. That will be the type of the church member of the future, and I include woman under the term man. Jesus intended the church to be a reign of practical Christianity, in which men should do the things in which they pretended to believe, and that it should be a condition of action, action, action — as Webster defines oratory. Dear friends, this man possessed excellent common sense. He was a practical business man. I do not believe that that man through all his history, from the day he left his father's stone cottage in his morning of life, picking the pomegranates and apricots, and figs, to go and establish a home for himself, ever dealt with a man so that he was swindled out of five dollars — putting it in modern money. I do not believe that he was ever cheated in his life. I do not believe you could cheat him. I do not believe there was power enough in Judea or skill enough in all Jerusalem to have deceived him and swindled him out of five dollars. He was a careful business man.

In the good old days of my father, one of the things in my good old Methodist father's testimony in the church was, he had tried to be a good man, and he had oftentimes been deceived. I often went home wondering why the Lord let my good father be deceived, when he was trying to be good; and I advanced beyond my father's position. The Bible says, "Be not deceived," and the Bible is good authority. The Bible says, "Be not overcome with evil," don't let the evil overcome you, overcome evil with good, don't let any evil man or woman overcome you.

My good brother in Boston left his overcoat in the front hall, and a man came in and stole it, and pawned it, and took the money and got drunk, and set a house on fire and people were burned. That man was wrong. He would preach most excellent sermons, he was a wonderful power in the pulpit, but he did more harm in leaving that overcoat where a thief could get it than his preaching would do good in many weeks. He had no right to be overcome with evil. Some church member says, "Does not the Bible teach us that we are to give?" Yes, but it teaches us never to give without carefulness, without following it up, without seeing that it does the good he intends.

In the next place, this man whom Jesus pointed out was non-sectarian. He left his home one morning. He laid upon his beast the products of his farm, and went on his way to Jerusalem, where the other people despised him. Up that valley he saw a man dressed in beautiful robes approaching him, and the humble man got down off his beast, and put his face to the ground, although that man was a minister who belonged to the other denomination; he showed respect to this other man who was serving God according to the dictates of his own conscience. The man with his long robes did not see an humble man like him. Then he met another man and he got down from his beast and gave him reverence, but the man did not notice him. As he came up into the defile of the valley he heard sounds, and he found a man who had been robbed and stabbed and was dying. The man belonged to another church, but when he saw him bleeding and dying all questions of sec-

38

tarianism and denominationalism went out of his heart, and he brought out his oil and wine and bound up his wounds and lifted him on his beast, and then hastened to the inn, and lifted the man of the other denomination off of his beast, and secured for him the best of accommodations, and told the landlord to take care of him, and that he would pay the bill as he came again that way. And when he went home he told his boys and girls how that he had found a man belonging to the other denomination in great trouble, and that he had helped him, and he said, " Now I feel better."

And now I am going to give you the closing chapter in the story of the Good Samaritan, a part which for some reason Luke omitted in his narration; that part I will give you this morning.

The sick man arose from his couch and went to his home. Suppose the next day was Sabbath. He said to the children, " Now come with me," and they went up to the temple to worship. As they went into the outer court a man in magnificent costume went by on his way to the altar. And little Johnny says to his father, " Who is that man?" And the father answers, " That is the priest; he is going to the altar to worship." And as he catches a glimpse of his face, he says, " Why, Johnny, that is the man who passed me when I was dying, and did not stop to look at me." " Is that the man?" asks Johnny. " Yes, that is the same man." And the boy says, " Don't stay here; they don't want us here; let us go somewhere else." But the father replies, " This is our church." Presently another man with the dishes in his hands, goes by on his way to the altar, and the little girl asks, " Who is that man?" The father answers, " That man is a Levite, who comes to assist in the services." And as he caught sight of his face, he says, " That is one of the men who passed by me when I was bruised and dying, and he never stopped to look at me." And the little girl says, " Father, what do you worship here for? Is there no other place to worship? Where is the Good Samaritan's church? Oh, find it father, the Good Samaritan's church, and let us go there?" The father says, " He may worship in a cave." " That don't make any difference, beautiful towers, magnificent domes, and gleaming pillars are nothing. Give us the place where the Good Samaritan worships, and we will go, and go, until we die." The place to worship is where the Good Samaritan worships; and the church of the future, and the creed of the future, and the Christianity of the future, will be that where the Good Samaritan lives and shows most of the Good Samaritan's character. And my next text this morning is, " Go thou and do likewise."

XLVII

ALEXANDER HARRISON TUTTLE

1844–

ALTHOUGH this minister may not be famed as widely as many others whose sermons appear in this volume, the circle of churches wherein he has been heard will accord him a place among the great preachers. Alexander Harrison Tuttle, D. D., was born in Bordentown, New Jersey, on February 28, 1844, in a Methodist parsonage, for his father was a minister before him, as well as three of his uncles; so that he grew up in a preaching atmosphere. He was educated in Pennington Seminary, New Jersey; in the Wesleyan University, Middletown, Connecticut, graduating in 1866; and in the Drew Theological Seminary, Madison, New Jersey, receiving his bachelor's degree in divinity in 1869. In the same year he entered the ministry of the Methodist Episcopal Church. In the order of the old-fashioned itinerancy, his earlier ministry was limited to three successive years in one church, so that since 1869 he has been the pastor of many churches, nearly all in northern New Jersey, but by transfer preaching for a term in Wilkes-Barre, Penn., and in the Mount Vernon Place Church, Baltimore. His present charge is in Summit, New Jersey. Wide reading, deep insight into Scripture, remarkable gifts of language, apt and original illustration, and a peculiar fervency of spirit are combined in his preaching. A bishop who listened to him often said, "Tuttle has the spiritual insight of Robertson, infused with the warmth of Spurgeon." He has published only one volume of sermons.

THE SPIRITUAL BODY.

"There is a natural body and there is a spiritual body."— 1 Cor. xv. 44.

PAUL teaches that we have two bodies: not that we have one now and will have another hereafter, but that we have two bodies at one and the same time, a body within a body. "There *is* a natural body and there *is* a spiritual body."

The one with which we are familiar is this physical organism with its flesh, bones, nerves and many organs marvelously adapted to the purposes of our earthly life.

We cannot speak too reverently of this body; for it was fashioned by the Creator in infinite wisdom to tabernacle for awhile His own children. The Eternal Son himself "was made flesh." "I will praise thee, for I am fearfully and wonderfully made. In thy book all my members were written."

But this body is doomed to decay. It was never meant to be immortal. It would have been a curse indeed if the Creator had given us a soul with faculties that aspire for the Infinite, and then shut them up forever in a finite body. That would have been a real Prometheus chained to a barren rock, with the birds coming from out of the measureless spaces to devour his vitals, which would immediately recover only to be devoured again. What an immeasureable affliction it would be for a spirit made for the boundless realms, to be doomed to live forever in this narrow cell. The wail of the Wandering Jew would soon become the universal cry. Having exhausted all that could come to us through the senses the deathless spirit would pant for realms beyond, from which it would be forever debarred by the fact of its physical immortality. Hence its constant prayer would be "Let me die, let me die."

But God did not make this body to live forever. After it had served its purpose, it was to pass away.

Accordingly the New Testament term which is used to designate and distinguish it from other parts of our being, is a term which means all we have in our corporeal being excepting the principle of life which animates and preserves it *(ptoma)*. Eliminate life, and what remains is *ptoma*. I would not hesitate to call it a corpse, only we are not in the habit of calling this body a corpse before the life has gone out. Perhaps we might safely call it the corpse body, meaning by it that part which is destined to become a corpse.

The Apostle nowhere speaks of the resurrection of the *ptoma*. On the contrary Paul distinctly says that it will *not* rise from the dead. Flesh and blood not only *will* not, but "*cannot* inherit the kingdom of God." "The body thou sowest is *not* that body that shall be." The corpse body will no more be recovered than the shroud that enwraps it in the grave.

Within this body Paul says is another which he calls the *soma,* and which he says is to survive the grave.

Though intimately related to the flesh body and permeating every part of it, it is not it. The flesh body has no life of itself, while the *soma* is the very principle of life. Nor is it to be identified with the divine essence in man. That is spiritual, while this body is material, and is really the spirit's form. Just as we think of a soul embodied in mortal flesh, so Paul speaks of the spirit embodied in the soul.

Thus man is a trinity, having a body, a soul and a spirit. By the body *(ptoma)* we mean the perishable flesh. By the spirit (pneuma) we mean the divine principle in us by which we are the sons of God. By the soul we mean that in us which is at once the life of the flesh and the form of the spirit. When speaking of it as the spirit's body, Paul calls it the *soma.* When speaking of it as the life of the flesh, he calls it the *psyche.*

It is this middle nature of our triune being that we are now to study. It is not a theme simply philosophical and speculative, but spiritual and practical. It lays hold of the very springs of our divine being and gives a large and eternal significance to our mortal life.

There are three propositions we will discuss in particular.

First, the soul is not a formless thing, but a substantial entity — the spirit's body.

Secondly, the essential feature of that body is life. Nothing can annihilate it. It survives the grave.

Thirdly, this soul-body is fashioning itself day by day, both in form and quality in exact correspondence to our personal character.

Simple as these statements are, they are as deep as character and as wide reaching as destiny.

I. The first proposition we make is that the spiritual body *is* a body. The soul is not a formless thing but is a being with shape and parts — a body. We are not to think of the soul as floating away in the universe like an unworded idea or as music shaken from the strings of a harp. It is a substantial entity.

But the material of the soul is so subtle and ethereal as not to be recognizable by the physical senses. It eludes the searchings of the crucible and the vision of the microscope.

Had we, however, the quickened vision such as was given for awhile to the timid servant of Elisha at Dothan, we would see in every person we met, a form majestic like the ghost of Banquo, or contemptible in revolting shamefulness.

This is not so difficult for us to conceive. When we see clay transformed into beryls, soot into diamonds and filth into the most lovely flowers, we cannot doubt the possibility of matter taking forms so refined as to approach wonderfully near the spiritual. See that water in the tank of the engine. It is heavy and measurable. Heated, it lifts itself up in fleecy clouds suggesting the immaterial. Heated again, the steam becomes invisible and dry. As the water becomes more and more ethereal, its force increases, but it is still matter.

Above this are other substances such as electricity, magnetism, ether, which are so refined as to seem to pass out of the realm of the material altogether and become immaterial. It is suggested by those who make a specialty of the study of infinitesimals, that there are still other things more remotely removed from these subtle forms of matter as they are removed from the grosser forms, and yet are to be studied as elements of matter.

It is easy for us then to believe that this refinement continues further still till at last it rises into existences absolutely indistinguishable from the spiritual. We can understand how some of our scientists teach that matter is only a spiritual entity in manifestation.

We do not then detract from the dignity nor the spirituality of the soul when we affirm that it is a body. It is not the fact of its having a form that degrades the soul, but its frequent shameful deformity wrought by its self abuse, and which will make the morning of the resurrection, when the real self is exposed in everlasting contempt, a morning of indescribable woe.

But to awake in that great day, restored and fashioned anew in the beauty of God's Eternal Son, which will certainly be the case with all those who are born again by faith in his name, will give no occasion for shame.

We so often see the finer forms of matter freely pervading the grosser forms, that we have no difficulty in believing that the spiritual body may dwell in the earthly body and both unfold their individual character side by side. This is a fact which the latest science is strongly asserting; yet Paul taught it long ago. It is pleasant for us to hear the ripest scholars repeating as if it were a new discovery, what has been a commonplace in the thought of those who have implicitly accepted the teachings of the Bible.

Dr. Luther T. Townsend has at great labor collected numerous testimonies from many schools of thought. From these we quote but three. Julius Mueller, the distinguished professor of Halle, says, " It is not the corpse, the mass of earthly matter, but the *soma* to which the Scriptures promise a resurrection. The organism as the living form which appropriates matter to itself, is the true body which in its glorification becomes the spiritual body." Franz Delitzsch, one of the highest authorities in the field of Biblical and scientific criticism, teaches that the " psychical *soma* is the uniting medium or bond between the soul on the one hand and the physical body on the other." Professor Rauch means essentially the same thing when he says, " The psyche (the psychical *soma*) unfolds itself externally in the life of the body, and internally in the life of the spirit."

II. An intrinsic feature of the soul-body is *life*. " Made a living soul " is the Old Testament description of its origin. It is the life principle in us.

So thoroughly had the Hebrew mind been imbued with this conception, that the same word is used to express both soul and life. Hence we are often perplexed to know just how we ought to translate the word; for we are in doubt whether the writer means what we commonly understand as soul, or whether he means simply life. " What shall a man give in exchange for his soul? " is an instance. Many of our older commentators think that the word here ought to be translated Life. But there is no real need for any confusion, for the two are really one. The soul is the life.

In that fact is a great and practical truth. The life of this earthly body does not depend half so much on the food we eat, the air we breathe or the medicine we take, as upon the streams that flow in upon it from the soul. Food, air, medicine are doubtless needed, and may for awhile keep this body in existence. But its beauty, health, majesty all come from the soul.

Doubt it? See that man dragging his feet along the pavement like ragged skirts, his arms swinging like wet ropes, his jaw fallen and his tongue lying on his slobbering lips. What is the matter? He has air and food enough; but not soul enough. He is an idiot.

See that other man whose brow " is like the front of Jove," whose face beams with intelligence, love, courage, decision. His step is firm and every movement has the stamp of royalty. Whence came it but from the soul?

Our dread of the follies of certain modern cults which profess to have their root in this great truth, should not fright us from the truth itself. The deadliest heresies often lie nearest to the most vital truths, just as the darkest shadows are cast by the brightest lights. It is certainly true that a healthy soul life is a potent factor in our mortal bodies. Thoughts and passions tell as mightily and oftentimes more mightily upon our physical frame than drugs themselves.

An able medical writer says: "Every thought tends to reproduce itself, and ghastly mental pictures of disease, sensuality and vice of all sorts produce scrofula, and leprosy of the soul, which reproduce them in the body." On the other hand, noble thoughts, love, courage, faith pour invigorating streams into the body. "He healeth all our diseases."

Just how far the soul life will tell upon the flesh, I do not know. I think that originally the Creator placed absolutely no limit to it. Its destiny was completely to transmute the mortal without death: to convert the clay into the ruby, the soot into the diamond, to evolve by processes of life the very thing that was accomplished in the person of our Lord, who when on the slope of Hermon, was transfigured and stood clothed in the indescribable splendor of the body spiritual. That I think was the original plan. We were to come into the immortal state by the glorious way of unfolding life rather than by the gate of the sepulcher.

Milton in Paradise Lost makes Raphael sing

> "Time may come when men
> With angels may participate, and find
> No inconvenient diet, nor too light fare;
> And from these corp'ral nutriments, perhaps
> Your bodies may turn all to spirit,
> Improved by tract of time, and winged, ascend
> Etherial as we."

But as it is now, our souls are so impaired by sin, and our bodies are so grossly carnalized, that for the present, we cannot escape death. Yet as in two instances, soul life has triumphed, why may not the time come when all may? May not the saying, "Thou wilt not suffer thine holy One to see corruption," apply not only to Christ, but also to all who are in Him?

III. The spiritual body is fashioning itself even now, and taking its form and quality in exact correspondence with our personal character.

I have sometimes wished that it was so with this mortal body; that every thought, desire and passion would fix itself in the lines and colors and bearings of the earthly frame in such a way as that there would be no mistaking its character. Thus in this world as in the world to come, there would nothing enter that maketh a lie.

In a measure that is actually so. A particular line of character working over a long period and several generations, does actually produce types of physical manhood and womanhood. There is the civilized type and the savage type. There is the degenerate type, the criminal type, the monkish type, the commercial type, the professional type and many another. The law operates right before our eyes. But it is not immediate and direct.

And it is well for us that it is not. If all we are were beaming out in our bodily frame, we would all perhaps be hiding in the shadow " from the voice of the Lord God walking in the garden." Who would not be sewing fig leaves to hide his shame?

Here are many contradictions. An ugly soul may occupy a beautiful body. Many a lovely spirit has carried a decrepit and homely frame. Healthful minds are often conjoined with bodies diseased by their ancestors.

But in the inner realm of the soul there is no such disharmony. There, every feature of the soul is emblazoned in its form. Nothing can be hidden. The soul-body is not a veil, but a crystal, transparent and luminous, showing accurately and fully the innermost character.

And this soul-body is forming all the time in exact form with all we are thinking and feeling and doing. It is Emerson, I think, who says that every man is carving his own statue.

It is a great law of the universe that like attracts like. The thought or passion that is dominant, draws to itself from the world invisible and visible that which is akin to it, which it chrystallizes about itself. No chisel ever wrought so accurately as the soul's inner life cuts and fashions its immortal form.

It is this body with its perfect truthfulness of character, that is to survive the grave. The mortal flesh will melt back into the dust; but the spiritual body is in no particular changed, much less destroyed by death. That is the form in which we will appear in the last great day. Some will come into the resurrection of life, and others into everlasting contempt. The form of every one will be the truthful embodiment and exhibition of his personal character, while in this probationary life.

This is a fact that may well fill the mind of the morally unclean with dread apprehension. In the great and terrible day of the Lord, we cannot robe our gangrened self with velvet and ermine. Not even the rocks can hide us from his presence. Everything will be manifest in unmistakable exactness.

But to those who are in Christ the resurrection body is a glorious hope. Our life may have been wrecked by our sin. But the gospel recovers us from our despair. Christ comes to redeem us from our sin, and all its awful consequences. When received by simple faith, he restores the ruin. He awakens as from the dead, the fullness of the oldtime spirit life, such as was breathed into the nostrils of the first man. He who has experienced this spiritual quickening, has already received into his being, "the power of the resurrection." The apostle identifies the two. " That ye may know what is the exceeding greatness of his power to usward who believe, according to the working of his mighty power which he wrought in Christ when he raised him from the dead."

That is our hope. Because of his renewing power in us, which is the power of the resurrection, we also shall appear with him in glory.

" Whence also we look for the Saviour, the Lord Jesus Christ, who shall change our vile body, that it may be fashioned like unto His glorious body, according to the working whereby He is able to subdue all things unto Himself."

ALEXANDER HARRISON TUTTLE.
1844-
Remarkable talent for language, combined with insight and fervor, give this preacher's discourses great power. He combines the virtues of scholarship with those of popular interest.

DAVID JAMES BURRELL.
1849-
A vigorous opponent of the hypercritical analysis of the Bible, Dr. Burrell stands firmly for the
inspired authority of the Holy Scriptures. He is
practical and helpful in his exhortations.

XLVIII

DAVID JAMES BURRELL

1849–

IT has been said that no minister in New York, on Sunday evening, preaches to as many men, and especially as many young men,
as does Dr. David James Burrell, in the Marble Collegiate Church, on
Fifth avenue. Other congregations have found it necessary to forsake this " down-town " locality for one in a better residential region;
and until 1891, when Dr. Burrell came from Minneapolis to take
charge of this church, its speedy removal up-town was expected. But
while Dr. Burrell stands in its pulpit its success in its present field seems
to be assured. This church, by the way, stands as the oldest religious
organization in the city, having been organized in 1628, when New
York was New Amsterdam. It belongs to the Reformed Protestant
Dutch Church, which had its origin in Holland. For more than a
century after its foundation its services were conducted in the Dutch
language. Dr. Burrell was born at Mount Pleasant, Pennsylvania,
August 1, 1849; was graduated from Yale College in 1867; and
preached in Chicago, Dubuque, and Minneapolis before coming to New
York. In his theology he represents vigorously the views concerning
the inspiration of the Bible held by the scholars of the last generation,
as against the opinions of the so-called advanced " higher criticism."
His sermons are reported stenographically, printed and distributed
weekly in pamphlet form, and collected in annual volumes, generally
named from the first sermon in each book. Their clear expression,
forceful application to practical life, and felicity of illustration make
them interesting not only to the hearers, but to readers as well.

THE DEFINITION OF A CHRISTIAN.

" Then Jesus beholding him, loved him, and said unto him, One thing thou lackest: go thy way, sell whatsover thou hast, and give to the poor, and thou shalt have treasure in heaven: and come, take up the cross, and follow me."— Mark x. 21.

It is not an easy thing to frame a definition of any religious thing in these days. Such simple words as " God," " Truth," " Divinity," " Inspiration," " Incarnation " and " Atonement," words which were formerly clear and definite, have by a sort of quibbling jugglery been rendered so obscure that it is difficult to say whether they have any significance at all. The term " Christian " was once intelligible; but recent developments in some quarters have so broadened it that pretty much everybody who has not been in Sing Sing can rest under its shadow. Is a Jew a Christian? Certainly, if he tells the truth and pays his honest debts. Is a Moslem a Christian? Beyond all peradventure, if he is a moral man. Presto, change! And lo, the word has just reversed itself; so much so that the people of Antioch, its inventors, would not recognize it.

If anybody is competent to pass upon the true meaning of the word it is Christ himself. To the young ruler, who came running to him with the eager question, " What shall I do that I might inherit eternal life? " he replied, " One thing thou lackest." The man was rich, learned, influential and so amiable that " when Jesus looked upon him he loved him." But one thing was lacking to make him a Christian. He was like a foreigner who comes to America, settles down to business, makes a fortune and is regarded as an estimable member of the community, but is not an American, because he fails to take out his papers of naturalization. That is the one thing lacking, it is the *sine qua non.* He may be everything that is praiseworthy otherwise, but he is not an American until he has attended to that particular thing.

The question, now, is as to this one thing needful; the desideratum, without which no man can honestly claim to be a Christian or deserve to be called so. We are left in no uncertainty about it; for Christ after saying, " One thing thou lackest," immediately added, by way of explanation, " Go, part with everything that separates between thee and me, and come and follow me." So, then, it is following Christ that makes a Christian; and nothing else can do it.

No fault was found with the young ruler on the ground of personal probity. On being reminded of the Ten Commandments, he said with honest impulsiveness, " All these have I kept from my youth up! " The claim of mere morality can no further go. Yet, as to the matter in hand,— that is, salvation or the inheritance of life,— the keeping of those Ten Commandments, so long as they are imperfectly kept, leaving any unforgiven sin, was no more efficient for the purpose of salvation than ten ciphers arranged in a row. One thing was lacking. If you can place a unit before those ten ciphers you make the young ruler a multi-millionaire. The unit that thus puts him in possession of life and gives him boundless " treasure in heaven " is indicated in Christ's words, " Come and follow me."

If this means anything, it means that practical Christianity is simply a personal relation with Christ; that *the sum total of being a Christian is to follow him*. This is the etymological meaning of the word. To be a Buddhist is to attach one's faith to Buddha; to be a Mohammedan is to be able to say " There is one God and Mohammed is his prophet "; to be a Confucianist is to adjust one's life to the Confucian analects; and, by the same token, to be a Christian is to be in personal relation with Christ.

And this is the historical meaning of the word. The reason why the disciples were originally called Christians was because the people of Antioch saw them assembling in the fellowship of Christ's service, worshiping in his name and holding themselves in readiness to die on occasion for him. How natural that they should call them Christians.

And this is the popular meaning of the word. Non-Christians know that Christians are expected to be loyal to Christ. If they find a church-member living at odds with Christ's teaching, no matter though he remain " in good and regular standing," they regard him as an impostor and not a Christian at all. In other words, the world's definition of a Christian is one who follows Christ.

So far all is clear. It remains, however, to determine just what is signified by that requirement, " Follow me."

First.— *It suggests faith in Christ.*

And faith is immeasureably more than a mere acceptance of the historic Christ. It would be a difficult matter to find any one who does not believe that nineteen hundred years ago there lived a Man called Jesus who went about doing good, preached wonderful sermons, lived a wonderful life and died ignominiously on an accursed tree. But that is not faith in him.

The minimum of faith required of one who professes to be a Christian is that he believe *that Christ was what he claimed to be.*

He claimed to be *the Messiah,* that is, the promised and long-looked for deliverer, who was to bruise the serpent's head and save the world from the shame and bondage of sin. To the woman of Samaria who said with a sigh, "I know that Messias cometh, which is called the Christ; and when he is come he will tell us all things," he affirmed, " I that speak unto thee am he!"

He claimed, also, to be *the only-begotten Son of God;* not merely one of God's great family of Children by creation or adoption, but the Only-begotten, the One who could speak of pre-existence in the glory of the Father before the world was, and who was able to say, " Before Abraham was, I am!"

And as the Messiah and the only-begotten Son he claimed *Equality with God.* To Philip, who said, " Show us the Father and it sufficeth us," he replied, " Have I been so long time with you, and yet hast thou not known me, Philip? He that hath seen me hath seen the Father; and how sayest thou then, Show us the Father? Believest thou not that I am in the Father and the Father in me?" It was for this claim that he was sentenced to death. The high priest, before whom he was tried, said " I adjure thee by the living God, that thou tell us whether thou be the Christ, the Son of God?" And Jesus answered, " Thou hast said." Whereupon the high priest rent his clothes, saying, " He hath spoken blasphemy! What further need have we of witnesses? What think ye?" They answered and said, " He is guilty of death." There were other charges in the indictment against him; but he was put to death for making himself equal with God.

It should be obvious that an admission of these claims is essential to faith in him. For how can a man be said to be a Christian or to follow Christ who will not go so far as to admit that Christ was an honest man? He who stops short of this may be a moral man, upright in his dealings, a kind father, a good neighbor and a desirable citizen, but he cannot call himself a Christian, because he lacks the one essential thing that would make him so.

Second. To follow Christ means, absolution from sin.

Why do men want religion? In part, because they long to be delivered from the penalty of the mislived past; in part, because they feel the need of a suitable equipment for the discharge of present duty; and in part because they would fain have a title clear to mansions in the skies. But the desire to be delivered from the record of past sins is the Alpha of it. "A certain fearful looking-for of judgment" drives the sin-weary soul to him who alone can say, "Thy sins be forgiven thee." The consciousness of unpardoned sin is a desperate handicap; it is a ball-and-chain hampering all our progress toward life. Christ proposes to remove that handicap. He, having paid a ransom for the imprisoned soul, calls it forth into the glorious liberty of the children of God. This deliverance is made possible by his having tasted death for every man. "As Moses lifted up the serpent in the wilderness, even so," he said, "must the Son of Man be lifted up; that whosoever believeth in him should not perish but have eternal life." His gospel is the gospel of Blood, the fountain opened for uncleanness, the blood that purges the soul from sin.

And the condition affixed to its benefits is faith. It is not enough to regard the cross as an objective fact; it must be appropriated. As the blood of the paschal lamb had no virtue except as it was sprinkled upon the door posts of Israel, so the death of Christ is futile for those who do not receive it. Faith is the hyssop-branch that sprinkles the blood upon the heart. A man may be worthy of the highest esteem in every other way, but he is surely not a Christian so long as he refuses to take a vital interest in the atoning work of Christ. Here and here only lies the Christian's hope of inheriting eternal life.

> "Lift up Thy hand, O bleeding Lord,
> Unseal the cleansing tide;
> I have no refuge from my sin
> But in Thy wounded side!"

Third. To follow Christ means discipleship.

This was the term, "disciples," which he commonly applied to those who followed him. They were his pupils, sitting about his feet and learning of him. A true disciple of Christ is one who takes his teaching at its face value, that is, without any attempt to explain it away or in any wise modify it.

The teachings of Christ were in part *doctrinal*. This is strangely overlooked by certain persons who profess to be Christians and yet cry out against creeds and "dogmas." The greatest dogmatist that ever lived was Christ. He not only set forth in clearest terms every truth which is included in the doctrinal system of Christianity, such as the personality of God, the truth of the Scriptures, the frightful Character of Sin and its sure and Eternal Punishment, the Incarnation, the Atonement, Justification by Faith, Regeneration, Sanctification — he taught these with such an air of absolute authority as was never assumed by any other mortal man. He did not say, " Thus saith the Lord," but sealed his sayings sometimes with a " Verily," sometimes with a " Verily, verily," and sometimes with a " Verily, verily, I say unto you! "

His teachings were, also, *ethical*. He emphasized the importance of the Moral Law. Truth, honesty, the sanctity of wedlock, sabbath observance and every other essential of moral character were included in his far-reaching philosophy of life.

But, more than that, he enjoined that these truths and precepts should be *put into practice*. And here his teaching was singular. In other religions there is little or no vital relation between doctrine and life. A man, for example, may be an exemplary Moslem while living in open and flagrant violation of the common rules of decency and morality. It is enough that he knows the Koran, and repeats the *Deen,* and cries *Allah il Allah* a hundred times a day. But Christ said, " By their fruits ye shall know them." The doctrines which he taught are to be translated into life. His ethics are to be transmuted into character. " By this shall a man know that ye are my disciples, if ye do whatsoever I command you." The man who professes to follow Christ and lives an unworthy life is not a Christian but a mask-wearer. A true life is a replica of his life. As the Light of the World he shines by reflection, through Christians for all. " Ye are the light of the world," he said, " let your light so shine before men that they may see your good works and glorify God."

Fourth. To follow Christ means *service*.

" Ye call me Lord and Master, and ye say well, for so I am." A Christian is one who lives under the regime of Christ, recognizes his jurisdiction, is loyal to his government and bows in unreserved subjection to him.

He is our King. " All power is given unto me," he said, " in heaven and on earth." He is now setting up his kingdom among the children of men. Day by day the royal standards forward go. Optimism is a vital part of our faith. The time is coming when Christ shall reign from the river unto the ends of the earth.

And meanwhile, with a view to this consummation of all things, we are laborers together with him. A Christian is in commission; he is under orders; he is seeking the kingdom of God first of all.

To be a Christian thus is to be abreast of the age. The definition is an unchangeable one, since Christ himself is the same yesterday, to-day and forever. The laws and principles underlying our religion were adjusted at the outset to the progress of the revolving years. The definition of a Christian is no more affected by the vicissitudes of time than is the law of gravitation by the falling of the autumn leaves. The Spirit of the Age, is subservient to the Spirit of God. The Christian of nineteen hundred years ago was called a "living epistle of Christ;" and the Christian of our time, believing in the same eternal laws and principles and following the unchangeable One, is no more nor less than that. On the byssus-bands, unwound from the mummy of the Prime Minister of Rameses II, were found inscriptions from the Book of the Dead and tributes to Osiris and Pharaoh. A dead man doing obeisance to a dead sovereign, a dead religion and dead gods! Our lives as "living epistles" pay tribute to a gospel which is alive and abreast of every age. We speak not in the language of a superannuated book nor bow the knee to memory. We follow a Leader whose influence is the most commanding factor in the progress of Civilization. The name which our fathers received at Antioch, because of their loyalty to Christ, is the name which we also bear because we march in the van of events as we follow him.

This then is the definition: A Christian is one who follows Christ; follows him through evil and through good report, receives his teaching and hews to the line. He calls himself a Christian because he believes in Christ; and up to the full measure of his honesty he swerves not.

It is said that the heathen among whom Judson preached the gospel were wont to call him "Jesus Christ's man." That name is ours; God help us to be worthy of it.

39

XLIX

FRANK WAKELEY GUNSAULUS

1856–

FRANK WAKELEY GUNSAULUS came from the State of Ohio, which during the last half-century has raised an unusually large crop of great men. He was born at Chesterville, on New Year's day, 1856: obtained his early education at the public school; was graduated from Ohio Wesleyan University in 1875, and immediately entered the Methodist ministry. After four years of circuit riding, he changed to the Congregational Church, and preached successively in Columbus, Ohio, in Newtonville, Mass., and in Baltimore. In 1887 he came to Chicago as pastor of Plymouth Church, and remained in that pulpit twenty-two years. When Dr. Hillis was called from the Central Church, Chicago, to Plymouth Church, Brooklyn, Dr. Gunsaulus was invited to succeed him in 1899. His church is independent of all denominations, draws its following from people of all creeds and includes some people of no creed; but is active in efforts for the public good, and its pulpit is ever loyal to the great principles of the Fatherhood of God, the supreme authority of Jesus Christ, and the brotherhood of man. Few preachers possess in equal measure with Dr. Gunsaulus the native attractions of a noble presence, a rich, expressive voice, and a splendid diction. Add to these a mind stored with the best literature, an interest in humanity, and a lofty ideal of character, and it is easy to see what fascination has drawn multitudes in the second city of the continent to listen for twenty years to his message. To his work at the head of a great church he has added that at the head of a college. When in 1892, largely through his influence a member of his congregation founded the Armour Institute of Technology, Dr. Gunsaulus became its first president, and has since continued in that position.   More than one great church in the East has signified its willingness to call him, but he has felt that he still has a mission in Chicago, and has remained at his post as preacher and as president.   Dr. Gunsaulus has written in literature and poetry, in fiction and in history, and some of his writings have received high praise; but he is best known and most highly successful in his own pulpit in Chicago, at college commencements, at Chautauqua assemblies, and on the lecture platform.

THE MESSAGE OF THE MINISTRY OF TO-DAY.

" Rise and stand upon thy feet; for I have appeared unto thee for this purpose, to make thee a minister."— Acts xxvi. 16.

IT is a fortunate moment for us to be in at this trial.   It is fortunate to see Paul now, if it is our first and last chance, especially if we are Christians who desire to find out what is the true method of making a minister and the divine way of endowing a man for that work.   Paul's career is ended; the harvest of the whole enterprise is in evidence; the man has passed by all immaturities and partial views that might cloud or otherwise vitiate his conclusions; he knows what he thinks; years have kindly remanded to forgetfulness the valueless and unimportant events of a lifetime; his perspective is now made right by his nearness to God's City of Rest.   Now let us gladly learn from his experience and words something of the significance and function of the Christian ministry.

The Christian ministry has its power and hope of making this a better world and otherwise serving God and man, in helping toward an erect manhood,— a manhood which is erect because it has first confessed the Lordship of Jesus Christ and then has been uplifted and inspired by a vision of Jesus Christ as the revelation of God and the revelation of man.

The world of men has always been crying out of its divinely imbreathed destiny for that leadership which shall inspire and cultivate a stalwart and self-respectful manhood.   It is useles to deny that we have often been weak, because we have failed to obtain the primary and fundamental energies indispensable for success in our work.

Much of our effort at preaching is weak and unhelpful,— it cannot even be said to stir with promise of life,— because Saul, before or as he stood on the verge of becoming Paul, has never felt his lips moving with even the questioning cry: "Who art Thou, Lord?" The emphasis of Saul's nature is on the word "Lord"— he is surer of his belief than he is of his doubt: "Who art Thou?" Never was a Saul, however brilliant and honest in his cruel devotion, lifted upon his feet and reconstituted into a Paul, the princely preacher, if he missed the experience of this confession forming itself at the centres of his thought and feeling, and uttering itself resistlessly upon his lips by divine logic and by impulse inevitable,— the Lordship of Jesus Christ. "Who art Thou?" Let him be uncertain as to a thousand other points,— yea, let him be only an inquirer as to all other belongings and qualities of Jesus of Galilee; but he must tingle in every drop of his blood with the omnipotent conviction that lies in that word, "Lord." The true minister is the true minstrel of the human soul,— the words minstrel and minister have a common root. He organizes the vagrant and apparently opposing sounds, the devious wafts of melody and the split and recalcitrant currents of tone about a common and regnant centre. That centre is the all-supreme and embracing theme. It alone co-ordinates and compels each aimless shiver of a chord and each stubbornly isolating tonic energy into harmony. Its power is the power of music, hushing discord by completing it or by rescuing it into concord; its energy is the energy of harmony coercing to order, not by mechanical strength, but by inherent beauty and truth; expanding half-tones or allaying them to wedded loveliness of utterance by the might, not of external volume or intensity, but by internal and perfect sweetness. Such is Jesus, and such is His Lordship,— the master-soul and master-theme, first, of the spirit and heart of the preacher, and then, the all-mastering and transforming master-soul and master-theme in the world of men. The human heart, mind, life, go searching for a Lord,— yea, for the Lord,— not for an abstract philosophy, not for a radiant ideal, not even for a noble memory or for a deathless hope; but for all of these it cries, and it expects these, in its living Lord, divine and human, near enough to touch, lofty enough to command. It throngs our churches, until it is sure the preacher has not heard or seen Him,— and then it sadly stays away. It besieges the altars of the faith which has awakened its pristine and fundamental desires, and, never as to-day, it hangs about, lingering yet in hope, asking for a sovereign, a living sovereign whom no death may vanquish or change; and the heart of humanity will never give up the church and the preacher, until, either by its fears or by the facts, it is compelled to say: "They have taken away my Lord, and I know not where they have laid Him."

Believe it, my friends, the race's opposition to Jesus Christ Himself, whatever may be the race's present antagonism to our cheap sensationalism and to our cold ceremonialism, is marshalled behind a wall as thin as was that which divided Saul, the persecutor, with hands of blood, from Jesus his Lord, with hands of blessing. Nothing else will satisfy the demands of man which are feeling through, except the Lordly Christ before whose majesty of moral lovableness the wall is trembling down. The really great minister has experienced all this,— he can get it in no other way; and his experience of it makes his appeal the utterance of a personal affair, warm as his blood, and as full of reality as he himself. I repeat that the moral Lordship, the spiritual supremacy by which Christ chose to be supreme over men, comes only by experiencing it. I cannot unwind the faultless argument for Christ's kingly nature and quality which came into Saul's mind at that unique and sudden moment, though I have no doubt it is as straight and strong as a cable between earth and heaven. I perceive this, however, that at once it carried into him the conviction that the reality he confronted commanded him so completely, flung over him the spell of such an undeniable sovereignty, that, however much he might have to say: "Who art Thou? Who art Thou?" he must also say: "Who art Thou, Lord?" Here was what no teacher of earth could teach him. No theological seminary can ever impart that conviction. Men still call Jesus Lord, only by the might of the Holy Spirit within them. Saul of Tarsus was convinced by a logic swift as lightning; premises and conclusions followed one another by the speed of God rushing in upon him. Here began his deep and thorough preparation for the ministry. It began in that event, not in the process of reasoning, not in the advent of theory,— in that event came and remained his theological position. It placed him. He did not place it. Christ had taken him, as the sovereign harmony takes the wandering tone. He was apprehended, as he said, that he might apprehend. So completely had Christ won him that he said "Lord" with swift inevitableness. Every great truth comes in this way. Its way of coming fixes it in the life-tissue. He never would have to defend the proposition that Jesus is Lord, after that. The fact is that Christ had divinely Lorded it over him. Do we defend that proposition? Do we doubt that men can or will believe in the Lordship of Christ? Do we spin our thread of logic and argument to convince at length? Brothers, it is so only because Paul's experience is not our experience. No preacher ever convinced a man that Jesus is Lord; only Jesus Himself can do that. Christ is His own argument for Himself; — it is too great for you and me to manipulate. No preacher ever had evangelic power who did not know that Christ is Lord by the indubitable fact that He actually has taken his soul by moral majesty and so ruled at the center of his life that while he questions: " Who art Thou? " as to a thousand other things, he says in deepest, unconscious confession, " Who art Thou, Lord? "

Ah, do you say, what then is the business of the church, if the church is not to compel men to acknowledge the power and right of Jesus to rule men, even at the point of the sword, or at the more stinging point of a condemnation as a heretic? Hear ye Him, as He says: " Peter, put up thy sword into its sheath;" " Let us leave My true kingliness to rule from its own throne." He seems to say: " If moral Lordship does not command, it is neither moral nor Lordly. Let me have My cross, instead of the legions who might protect Me. Let men see Me die and live there, and there will I draw all men unto Me." This was His own trust in His spiritual royalty. So did His divinity risk itself. So let the Church and pulpit risk Him. We need only to manifest Him as so much the Lord over us personally that we have become Christlike, and then the pulpit and the church will hear thousands crying out on the Damascus road: " Who art Thou, Lord? "

Now, it is this Lord before whose moral grandeur and right to reign over him, Saul has fallen upon the earth,— this it is who says: " Rise, stand upon thy feet." It seems strange at first that it is the same power,— Jesus. But Jesus were not the soul's true Christ if it had been otherwise. His Lord had other uses for Saul, now that he had confessed Jesus' Lordship, than to leave him there flat and uneffective upon this disordered and needy planet. It is of first importance to note that only the power which commands our admiration can lift us up. " We live by admiration." We are made erect and manly by adoration. Before a merely beautiful character, a profound moralist, a true philosopher, a heroic martyr, we do not fall to earth in obedience, neither do we rise to our full height at his command. Divine enough must be that power which endows the minister of men,— divine enough to make our unhelped humanity lie full length upon the common earth which is our fate and home without that power, and yet divine enough that power must be on the other side, to lift man into the image of God and place him permanently on his feet before the problem of life.

Secondly, the moment Saul is swept into the march of God's energies by the sublime and moral energy of Christ, the very power whom Saul calls Lord must lift him up for other holy ministry. God's economics demand this of God's power; it must put the worshipper on his feet.

Great, indeed, have been the services unto man and God wrought by men prone upon earth in adoration and prayer. There, truly, is found the right to rise and to labor, and there alone is born the power to hear the voice saying: " Stand upon thy feet." Angels bow when most angelic, men refuse to bow when least they are men. Supreme are some of the cables to which captains and law-givers, saints and prophets, psalmists and reformers have hitched their otherwise motionless trains of hope when these souls were prostrate before the Divine Glory. But the ministry of Christ only begins to be powerful there. Matched with the truths which we find there, side by side in importance with the energies there felt and adopted, the completing and enriching powers for those which we know there, are the other sovereign inspirations and forces that promise and guarantee the vaster achievements of righteousness on earth, and the deeper joy of heaven; and these are for man only when a man honors his own conscience and hope, and lifts his head as God's son above the earth and into the free air of heaven.

Christ — the power of God in humanity before whose spiritual sovereignty every Saul must bow,— He alone has the voice, the speech, the right to say: " Rise, stand upon thy feet." The hope for an erect, self-respectful, lofty-souled ministry lies in what Jesus is and does for humanity. It is our business to get Him to humanity or humanity to Him. He alone can fairly say to Saul: " Rise, stand upon thy feet; for I have appeared unto thee for this purpose, to make thee a minister."

Ours, like Saul's age, has been an age of self-conceit and self-abasement. Pompousness has lived with pessimism and kept open house. Intellectual arrogance and groveling discontent have mated. Man has been crying out: " I am nothing ! " and yet he has asserted: " I can do anything." One moment has found an extemporaneous philosopher averring: " Man is the only God," and then shouting, " God is less than man." Man has been self-depreciative largely because of the recoil consequent upon his pretense; his confessedly abject position has often been

the result of his audacity.   Misanthropic he is, because of the collapse of
his impious egotism.   From whatever cause, he has been lying flat upon
the earth, and often has he revelled in what Carlyle called " a dirt philosophy."   Not as Saul of Tarsus, has man in the nineteenth century been
humbled by the spiritual glory of Christ; but he lies there nevertheless.
He is cursed by the sin from which he alone cannot free himself.   He is
also half hopeless of a valid solution for the problem of life as it appears
in himself or in his race.   I have mentioned the fact of sin as one of the
most restless influences which has caused, and still causes, hopelessness.
Sin is only practical faithlessness.   Our age's philosophy does not extinguish or even hide it.   We are enough like Saul to behold in humiliation its disaster and we see it more clearly as it writhes or slidders darkly
against the back-ground of a better day, for ours is the most luminously
Christian age the world has ever seen.   We are not only prostrate on
the earth, but we are tired of it.   The mind of man is not more weary
of the speculative materialism which has failed as a dogma, than the
heart and conscience of men are in revolt against a practical materialism
which has failed as a dogma, than the heart and conscience of men are in
revolt against a practical materialism which fails as a method of life.
Hucksters of our day are advertising enough religious nostrums to demonstrate what a market there is for something to re-inspire the soul of
man.

Here, the Christian minister finds himself and his message.   Who
is he?   What is his message?   How does it appeal to men?

First of all, he is personally an erect and inspired man.   How has he
been made so.   He has felt, in a moment, unspeakably precious and grand,
the actual Lordship of Jesus of Galilee.   He has had a vision — but more,
he is a man of vision.   He has not been persuaded of it by logic.   He has
known of it, yielded to it, gone into partnership with it as a fact in his experience.   The triumphant Christ has entered his life and thinking and
hope, by Christ's triumphing over him and not otherwise.   He has been
going to some Damascus a persecutor of that which seemed to die on Calvary; he has entered Damascus its disciple and champion.   The very power
he antagonized in vain has first humbled him; then has lifted him to his
feet.   He first adored it when he suddenly discovered its splendor in absolute
command of his soul.   But obeisance, however abject, submissive, and
humble, has not been enough for him who has seen the living Christ.
He has felt the fortunate contagion of the aggressive spiritual power of

Jesus. He must get on his feet. The gravitations that held him fast to earth, either because of his unworthiness, or because of the contrasting glory of Jesus, have been caught up, through a larger, higher circle of law, by the other gravitations that pull him upward. The spiritual tallness he gained by his humility has now straightened itself in the light of God, in the hope of God for man that Jesus carries over Him. The whole fact is that he has fallen in love with God as Christ revealed Him; he has also accepted the ideal and reality of man as Christ has revealed man also, and, on that ground, his sin has fallen dead, sloughed away, been forgotten by God and by man. He is a new man in Christ. Can we marvel that he is now an erect, hopeful, aggressive, stalwart man? What else could he be, under the spell of such an uplifting force? Would it not be strange, if he were not on his feet?

I have little hope of valuable service to men from any so-called ministry to which all this is not intensely personal. Let us see how personal it all is with Saul, who is being transformed into Paul. He asks, with an incomplete theology, it is true, but with vivid eagerness, " Who art Thou Lord?" and the answer is as personal as the "who" and "thou" of his query. "I am Jesus, whom thou (Saul) persecutest." Every disguise is torn away. Religious experience under Christ emphasizes " I," " Jesus," and " thou." It is almost fearfully accurate, and it is searchingly true. Ugly facts also emerge, sinister and illumined. There can be no mistake. "I am Jesus,"— not vague goodness, not your individual ideal of truth, but God's own purpose incarnate, the very heartthrob of this whole system of things,—" I am Jesus whom thou persecutest." "Wrong is an attack on Me; sin is a stab in My soul," so Jesus seems to say,— does say. All this enforces the personal element in the fundamental experience of the man who is to be a minister. It is his seal of a divine prerogative. He is to help men get upon their feet. Nothing of this sort is possible unless he is intense in the sense of his own recovered personality, unless by his own right to reverence and to make his own self and life distinct, he can clear away all circumstances and abolish all trivialities from every other man and bring that man personally close up to the burning heart of the personal Christ. Each man must be thus distinguished before God. Jesus erect amidst depravity and doubt; His minister stalwart and full of faith also,— these are the facts that make distinct and sacred every man's soul and life. Then will each man respect himself as God deals with him by His providence and grace.

This is the true call to the ministry. But Jesus makes it yet more personal. Hear His voice again, "I have appeared unto thee." "I" and "thee,"—these are the great words of the Good News unto men; and these are the two supreme facts in all thorough-going religion. Not the creed, not the church, and not society in general, nor even the noble fortune of race,—but "I" and "thee." Christ never had a real minister who was not made self-respectful and powerful because he was thus led to honor his own personality and to lead every other man to honor his, as God Himself honored it. O man, if. thou wouldst be a minister, "rise, stand upon thy feet." Fear not to be personal, for impersonalness is cloud-land, weakness and death.

An erect humanity in the pulpit, speaking to the humanity that honors it, trusts it, and provides support for it,—how sublime it all is!

Secondly, what is his message? His message is really the wine pressed from grapes grown on the soil of this experience. He has the right to believe that what has lifted him and set him upon his feet will exalt and make stalwart other men. In truth, whatever else we may carry, this only is each minister's working faith. If Jesus has truly become Saul's Lord, and lifted Saul up to his full manhood, that, and that only, will He expect and work for in His people. By no magic or miracle can you get out of your minister what he has not to give.

Experience, which is so personal and particular, which is to be crystallized into his message, makes the erect man not less, but more conscious of the facts of sorrow and sin in the world. They lie heavy on the heart of the time, and often they conduce to a conclusion of despair. The true man cannot be erect and have an outlook of hope, unless he appreciates the maddening riddle of life in its most involved snarl. I think every true minister must have in him the making of a pessimist as gloomy as Schopenhauer, and he must know enough of the tragedy of life to shake the courage of a Liebnitz. But this must not be his all. He must have been on the dull earth, and felt its sick heart beat woe; he must also have been lifted up, conscious of it all, yet equally conscious that the very Christ who lifts him up and restores his faith was so much more conscious of it all that it brake His heart. It crowned Him with thorns when He flung upon its hidden night the first promise of a golden day. This is the only way God has of making Paul the minister. God's manifestation of Himself in our humanity is the uplifting fact in a world where, without Him man is on all fours in his animalism, or flat upon the earth,—earth to earth, ashes to ashes, dust to dust,—in his despair.

If our ministry is Christian, it surpasses the keenest-eyed pessimism in perceiving the historical fact that " in Adam all die." But if it is Christian, it surpasses philosophic optimism by its discovery of an outlook through the fact that " in Christ all are made alive." Universal as was, and is, the disaster in Eden, so universal was, and is, the recovery at Calvary. The minister, of all men, is the one who can be erect and free because he is true to both these facts. He knows it is a groaning creation, but he knows also that it is loaded with divine destinies; he is aware that his is a race strained in ignorance and toil, often whelmed in anguish and defeat. But against that fact he puts this, the Son of Man, the very fact whose luminousness lays bare this dolorous reality, has lived to the bottom of its woe, felt in His own heart its blind cruelty, and, after being the victim of its calculating malice and dull-eyed villainy, Jesus emerges the most hopeful and the most powerful of leaders. He who was gibbeted by man, comes assuring us, for He is carrying the fortunes of redeemed humanity in His wounded hands. Surely, he can say: " Rise, stand upon thy feet." Surely, His minister must believe in man.

And this is the central flame that lights and warms the heart of the preacher. Jesus believed in man, because He believed in God. He revealed man in revealing God. No one ever so depended upon God to reinforce man at his best. No one ever so trusted in man at his worst. He would not even save Himself at Calvary from man's fury. He would rather trust man to come again to Calvary, age after age, to find if one drop of His blood still quivered there. But this trust of His in man was fundamentally a trust in God, His Father and man's Father. Jesus knew in Himself what God the Father meant for man. He Himself was that meaning. Human worth, the right and duty of a man to respect himself, the joy of a man ought to find in his privilege of being a man,— all these had their source in the fact that Jesus felt in Himself that the concerns of God and man are one. He illustrated the capacity of humanity to receive God and the willingness of God Himself to come into man and abide with him. In the manger at Christmas, humanity was proven capable of the Incarnation. Other events came in due order. That stable-event glorifies man; Calvary saves man; Easter rebuilds man; Olivet sees him go back to heaven.

This, then, is the meliorism which must be Christ's gift to the man who is his minister. It is far from that pessimism which says that the world is as bad as it can be, and is far from that optimism which says

that the world is as good as it can be. It is meliorism, as it has been
called, and its assurance is in Jesus Christ, when it says that this is not the
worst possible world, nor is this the best possible world, but, by the certain victory of Jesus, it shall be the best possible world.

This hope kindles most as Jesus deals with the perplexing problems
of evil. To Him, the problem was not speculative, but practical. Witness Gethsemane and the heights of Golgotha. There would be nothing
but a deeper discontent and a more bitter cynicism in our bewildered
world if on looking upon the moral beauty of Jesus Himself, we failed to
find that in its very beautifulness, its sovereign power, lies in the fact
that He is not thus divine for His own sake.

A taint of self would undivinize even Him. He is " the Lamb of God
that taketh away the sins of the world." He worked His divinity for all
there was in it in His struggle with the undivine. Let no man presume
to be a minister of Christ unto men; let him not expect to get upon his
own feet; least of all, to get other men to rise and stand upon their feet,
by his vaguely passing over the fact that wrong is in the world, and that
men are down and life is groveling for that very reason, and that men
must be delivered from wrong unto righteousness. The pulpit which
fails here, may succeed in being an arsenal of brilliant rhetoric and a
fortress of valuable learning, but as a pulpit it is a pitiful sham and a
wicked deceit. It will leave man prone on his face, without the vision
Saul had of the real Christ. The Christ whom Saul saw, the Jesus who
spoke to Saul, had been no connoisseur of morals or ingenious exponent
of a new cult which gathered about Him a unanimous coterie of dille-
tantes. No. His face was more marred than any of the sons of man.
He has met sin fatally at Calvary, as before He had met sin and wrestled
with evil in Peter and Judas and Mary Magdalene. He was Lord only
because He had triumphed over sin and iniquity. He had won the heart
of man when sin had its carnival in His crucifixion.

True and almost pathetic is the cry of the race's heart for a self-
respecting ministry,— a ministry whose erect mental and spiritual manhood will lift a discouraged yet proud mob of human beings upon their
feet. Man is conceited enough, but he is not self-respectful. He is
jaunty enough when walking vainly to Damascus, but, if he falls, he
does not worship. He curses. Within his assertiveness and egotism, is
a strain of petulent apology. He blames things. He reads and patron-
izes the literary autobiography of hopelessness rescued from filthy ancient

sepulchres. What shall transform cultivated and skillful Saul? What will transform ignorant, bestial Saul, also? Jesus alone, can do it. Nothing but an erect, self-respectful, divinely-clad Christian ministry will be His true witness and testimony.

Let us be honest with God and conscience and the fact that it is a hopeless world without this Lord of man unfurling His blood-stained banner of hope. The only pulpit that men respect permanently pours forth the music of the redemption. It is tremulous with the minors of Good Friday. Men scorn to squander an otherwise pleasant hour of their Sunday where two things are not believed,— first, the fact that humanity, unhelped from God, is prostrate and despairing; second, the fact that with the Christ there come hope, self-respect, and manhood. People were never as willing,— nay, so desirous to go to church as they are now, if Christ is there to get them on their feet. Without him, they will not stay to hear your dream of a better day; and with Him, they will not tolerate your depreciation of humanity and your defamation of the soul of man. " I have appeared unto thee " makes the minister, and it alone will hold a congregation. Pessimism hears the story of Christ's death and cries out, " There, that is proof that this is a damnable world. Such a thing should not happen." The deeper philosophy of Paul who once was Saul of Tarsus, says: " No. While it is the saddest event of the world's long tragedy and the most disheartening, it is the gladdest and the most encouraging, because evil, at its supreme hour, suicided there in its bold attempt to kill goodness in its supreme hour. Because of this event man stands on his feet in hope." I return to this pulpit with just this point of view and just this outlook. If the vision of Christ has made our church broad enough, let us depend on that vision to make it correspondingly deep and high.

Often, indeed,— not too often, perhaps, do we quote Tennyson's fine lines:

> " Self-reverence, self-knowledge, self-control,
> These three alone lead life to sovereign power,
> Yet not for power (power of herself
> Would come uncalled for) but to live by law
> Acting the law we live by without fear;
> And because right is right, to follow right
> Were wisdom in the scorn of consequence."

I think it only fair to say that to the sincerest of baffled souls these words depart on the air, leaving one to battle hopelessly, while he asks:

"How am I to get this self-reverence and self-control?" As I am, I can never revere myself, and I cannot control myself. Who or what shall speak to me as to bring out any hidden or essential nobleness there may be in me? Who or what shall so attach me lovingly to a noble ideal or to a fair and lofty reality that I may gain something of its grace or beauty or power? Who shall so exalt me morally that I shall believe that right is right? Who shall command me so royally that I will actually rise and stand upon my feet self-respectful and clean-hearted and therefore confident of my worth?" Well, the Christian minister has but one reply to this searching demand of the soul, humiliated by its own sinfulness and defeated of self-respect, and that is, Jesus Christ.

It is a fearful thing to fail to tell men of Christ in an age both as misanthropic and aspiring, as our own. Dr. Roswell Hitchcock mentions a Bedouin on the desert whose piteous condition was this. He had been without food so long that he was starving. His hope was that some other traveler who had already gone that way, might have left, by chance or provision, a packet of food. Away, beyond, near a fountain, he spied what he took to be a traveler's bag, and to his hunger it must contain bread. Slowly and hardly he pulled himself over the hot sand to the little pouch. He took it up and poured out before his vacant eyes a stream of glorious gems. As they wooed the sun by their splendor, his famished body fell over, while he murmured, "Oh, it is only diamonds, only diamonds!" Merciful heaven, that this should be an honest description of so much that is called preaching! "Diamonds, only diamonds!" It is a piteous thing for the preacher and the people. Both are disappointed sadly. Diamonds! And he, the preacher, works so long to find them, and so hard to grind them well, and so unceasingly, perhaps, to set them in a golden paragraph,— and they, the people, want only the bread of life. One mouthful of plain bread, and you may have the polished dogmas, the glittering periods, the flame-like phrases, the splendid sentences. All glowing exordiums, all flashing epigrams, all brilliant perorations, for one taste of the bread of life! When Christ Jesus said to Saul, "I have appeared unto thee to make thee a minister," he gave Paul his theme, his method of appeal to men, his certainty of success. Jesus Himself is the capital on which alone the pulpit is in business. Men have the right to expect their ministers to be experts in manhood, erect, Christlike manhood, fearless, hopeful, free. They have no right to expect their ministers to compete with their fellow-men in anything else except in manifesting

this Christ in His actual Lordship over them, " In our mortal flesh."
Other men have better right to speak with plain authority on a multitude
of other interesting subjects, than has the minister! No man ought to
be able to over-match his mental and moral right to speak on the truth,
the way, the life of manhood. Few of us are worthy to stand here!
None save by God's grace. But we fail only when we vacate our particular throne of power. No ton of diamonds is worth an ounce of
bread to a hungry man. We ought to feed men bread. We have no
responsibility as to creating the food. God does that. Christ is given
to us, and we have no need to strive to induce hunger. Believe it, men
are hungry and are hunting for bread. While I am searching for a
triviality bright enough to attract a crowd, my brothers who have the
right to expect me to give them to eat are begging for plain bread. No
man to whom Jesus has appeared as Lord, who also has been lifted to
his feet by the hopefulness of Christ, ever was solicitous for a subject
to preach on or a text for a discourse. The true minister does not run
his race with the lecturer, essayist, or poet or statesman, foolishly aban-
doning his prerogative, to be beaten in a contest, perhaps, with a magazine article purchasable for a quarter, but sufficient to emphasize the
extemporaneousness of the parson's suddenly-acquired information which
could not be disguised. The minister of Christ has an unfailing theme.
His topic's interest depends not on war or peace, parties or revolutions,—
it is the Lamb of God slain from the foundation of the world. His
sermon is not a bit of pious oratory or unctuous literature, neither is it an
impersonal or sentimental relating of the precious story of Jesus. His
is the argument in favor of bread addressed to hunger. It is an address
by a man in favor of hope and it has the impulse of his hope grounded
in Jesus. It is his experience with One who has said: " Rise, stand
upon thy feet, for I have appeared unto thee," and it is this experience
re-inforced by all the history and prophecy of humanity, glorified by the
love of God, and illumined by the mighty presence of Jesus as a living
Lord — it is this, in the giving of comfort, in the urgency of appeal, in
the defiance of wrong, and in the championship of right,— this, as it
furnishes hope for mankind in Jesus Himself, makes the minister.

I have fifty-two precious Sunday mornings before me. I can waste
not. I can idle not. I will not take these fifty-two hours from you for
any less sublime task or privilege. I do not know enough of politics,
sociology, art, literature, music or science to justify your coming to hear

me speak on these topics. I know here but one thing, and if I am true to it, you will never weary of my use of your time and the expending of my limited strength. My theme has the breadth of God's love and the many-sidedness of His abundant goodness. It is perennially fresh and beautiful. I will not attempt to vie with your other sources of intellectual and spiritual vitality, in furnishing you delightful information or high entertainment. If they are valuable to you, it is because each to whom you give your attention is a specialist. So, also, am I. Any minister may say without hesitation: " No one else has been traveling my path with Christ. No one else has met Him where I have met Him. No man can have another's experience. Others have more of genius, learning, eloquence, health, than I; no man has had my soul and its history with Christ. Many have had greater vision proportionated to greater piety, but no one else's vision of Him do I know. I do know my own." I will preach only what I believe,— the time is short. I will preach only what I know is supremely important in the thought of Jesus — the time is short. I will preach only what I have fallen down upon and found safe and able to bear me up,— the time is short. I will preach only what I found true when lately I went up to the gate of Otherwhere,— the time is short. I will preach these things with absoluteness of conviction that God will bless us and I will look for the fruit of this ministry here, where the time is short, and there, also, where time shall vanish in the morning-glow of Eternity.

FRANK WAKELEY GUNSAULUS.

1856-

In the ministry of the Middle West Dr. Gunsaulus occupies a prominent place. He is also well-known through the United States as educator, lecturer and author.

NEWELL DWIGHT HILLIS.
1858-
The successor of Henry Ward Beecher and
Lyman Abbott in the pulpit of Plymouth Church,
Brooklyn. His sermons have had a great influence in forming public opinion throughout the
country.

L'

NEWELL DWIGHT HILLIS

1858–

NEWELL DWIGHT HILLIS, D. D., the third in the succession of great preachers in Plymouth Church, Brooklyn, New York, was born in Magnolia, Iowa, Sept. 2, 1858. He received his education in Iowa College, Lake Forest University, and McCormick Theological Seminary of Chicago; and entered the ministry of the Presbyterian Church in 1887. He was pastor at Peoria, and at Evanston, Illinois; in 1894 succeeded Dr. David Swing as minister of the Central Church, Chicago, an independent society. After five years of success in Chicago he was called to Plymouth Church, Brooklyn, as successor to Lyman Abbott, who had followed Henry Ward Beecher. Dr. Hillis is broad in his theological views, representing in his teaching the trend of the Twentieth Century in thought. His appeal is at once to the intellect and the conscience of his hearers. The sermon which he preaches on Sunday morning is generally nearly an hour in length; but no one has ever been heard to say that it was too long, for it holds the eager attention of every person in the audience. A number of books by Dr. Hillis have attained to a large circulation, as " Great Books as Life Teachers," and " The Influence of Christ in Modern Life." From the latter work, a series of sermons and addresses, this discourse is taken by the kind permission of the publishers, The MacMillan Company.

THE SIMPLICITY AND BREADTH OF CHRIST AS A RELIGIOUS TEACHER.

" Never man so spake."— John vii. 46.

THE excavators who have uncovered for us the streets and houses of Pompeii have assembled in a museum all the bronzes, marbles, ivories, mosaics they have discovered. Unfortunately, not one single object has escaped some form of injury. The winged Mercury stands forth with broken arms and legs. The white forehead of Venus holds a black stain. All the precious tablets are cracked, while the rolls found in Pliny's father's tomb hold writings faded and dim. The universal damage that has befallen the products of man's arts and industries leads the mind to expect that man's customs and institutions will suffer some grievous accidents. And experience wrings from us the confession, that imperfection does attend all that man achieves. Through some error, man's train leaves the track, his ship strikes the rock, his bridge breaks, his wealth takes wings, his health gives way. Even the wisest book holds some ignorance, the greatest oration includes some error, the sweetest music holds some discord; nor is there any nation whose constitution needs no amendment. These errors that have accompanied man as builder and writer, as scientist and inventor, prepare us for the errors that have accompanied him as a teacher of morals. If the baron and lawyer of the fifteenth century toast over the hot fire the feet of the witness in order to elicit testimony, we may expect that the priests and people of that dark day will rush together in crowds to behold the burning of the witch or the heretic. If, in the fourteenth century, the king and the prince misused their wealth and became drunkards, profligates, and criminals, we must expect that in the reaction from these excesses good men will exalt poverty, live in caves, wear rags, and eat crusts of moldy bread.

If the education of that far-off time must needs wait long for the schoolhouse, if the field must wait long for the steam plough and the reaper, if love and marriage must wait for beautiful homes, it seems natural to expect that religion must wait for the waning of ignorance and superstition, and the waxing of wisdom and character. Fascinating, indeed, is the museum filled with stone hammers, the war clubs, the spears and crude implements of man's early industry and life. But what a museum would be that stored with the symbols of man's religious progress — the astrologer's chart, the diviner's rod, the map with the flight of birds, the hazel rod for detecting hidden veins of water, the charms for warding off danger, the secrets of medicine men, going on at last to the Te Deum, holy aspirations, the songs, with all noble arguments toward worship. The sweet simplicity of the religion of love to-day makes yesterday's religion, with its cumbrous forms and grievous burdens, well-nigh intolerable.

Travellers in India tell us that when pagan mothers are led into the light of education and Christianity, they often weep bitterly, remembering the sweet babes they cast into the Ganges in obedience to the dictates of superstition. Thus, in the light of to-day's toleration and charity, the sufferings of Huss and Cranmer, of Savonarola and Luther, speak eloquently of the bigotry and intolerance of the former days. The dawn, with its sunshine, lends a deeper darkness to the midnight with its owls and bats, its deep black gloom.

How refreshing, therefore, the contrast between the complexity and cumbersomeness of the philosophers and the simplicity of Christ as a religious teacher. He rises like a white shaft, simple, yet sublime. In every realm simplicity is the proof of greatness. Any increase in the number of wheels for engine, press, or loom lessens its utility. Each inventor counts a gain in simplicity as a gain in power. All the immortals, Moses, Paul, and Socrates, are men plain to the verge of harshness. History knows no pretentious hero. All who are " to the manner born " carry with them a certain air of quiet repose, and their simplicity is the finest ornament of their greatness. Nature achieves all her strength and beauty by the avoidance of complexity. The strength of the bee's cell is in the use of the fewest lines and the least wax. How simple the lily's whiteness, shaped by a single curve! The giant of the forest has its strength through the trunk springing a hundred feet into the air without a branch, crowned with a slight tuft of green. All the great artists understand that the line of beauty is the line of economy. Michael Angelo once defined perfection as " the purgation of superfluities." How chaste the lines of the Venus de Milo. In the golden age of art each Parthenon was a very simple temple. But when the fine arts entered upon their decline, the Venetians began to ornament their statues. Each Apollo wore a gilt crown; the marble cheek of Aphrodite was stained red; the legs of the Dying Gladiator flamed with a bright flesh color; soon all beauty fled away before this complexity.

In their garb also the Greek women understood that simplicity was beauty. Outdoor life and perfect health lent each maiden an arm and brow of marble and a cheek of purest rose. With instinctive grace the girl draped herself in one color, white, in a robe falling to the ground in one straight line, a line with one flower at the throat — a red rose. But when art had declined in the fifteenth century the ladies of the French court forsook simplicity and asked Jacquard to weave in each robe of silk a full hundred roses. If in Pericles' day the simple gown was an incident for setting forth the beauty of the Greek maiden, in the age of Voltaire all had changed, and the young girl became only an incident for exhibiting a mass of tulle and silk. In literature also all the great poems, dramas, and orations are simple. The song, " Home, Sweet Home," is influential because it has as few notes as the song of the nightingale. Gray's " Elegy " influences the multitude profoundly because it is the biography of a single emotion. The mind wanders in a complex philosophy like a child in a dense wood. The very simplicity of Newton's principle becomes an argument for its truth. An English professor in Oxford University was quoted as saying that Longfellow had a hundred readers in England where Browning had one. The distinguished lecturer explained this fact by saying that the American poet seems like a single pasture-grown oak, while the Englishman was a tangled forest, where the very richness of the vines hid all the trees.

In the world, therefore, in which complexity injures the drama and the picture, where man admires the single star more than the diffused light of the Milky Way, admires Hamlet or Lear more than Hegel's philosophy in a score of volumes; in a world where complexity injures the oration and the song, and simplicity increases the value of the tool and the mechanism, we naturally expect that the world's greatest religious teacher will present a very simple system of thought. It must not be like the maze in Hampton Court, where one searches long and in vain for some way out of the bewildering growth, but rather a plain way, along which each little child may run heavenward with happy feet. For, be it instantly confessed that if the mariner needs a pilot to guide him in his wanderings o'er the sea; that if each Stanley needs some native to conduct him through the trackless forest; if each caravan journeying across the Arabian sands needs some leader skilful in journeying across the pathless desert, so the soul, moving upward toward the heavenly heights, needs to journey forward under the guidance of some one who has dwelt long midst the solemn beauty of the heavenly mountains, and therefore knows where is the path to each cool spring, and what way will avoid the most of danger and secure the most of safety, happiness and peace.

In words that a child could understand Christ portrayed the simple majesty and beauty of God. No definition was given, no philosophy was fashioned, no articulated dogma wrought out. He simply unveiled before man's admiring vision the Infinite One, Whose solicitude for man was such that none was too great or too small to be loved; Who was so deeply interested in the progress of His earthly child that He could not bear to overlook a single hour in the upward career. History tells us of a traveller who, visiting Athens for a single day, went at once to Phidias to ask him for the secret of his art. To whom the artist replied, that while one day was too short to unfold sculpture as a system, it was long enough for looking upon a single statue that embodied the beautiful. So he unveiled his Minerva before the eye of the enraptured Spartan, who went away to deduce from that lustrous face all the abstract principles of beauty. Thus Christ seems to say that, while man's three score years and ten are too brief for a study of the philosophy of religion, they are long enough for the exhibition of that matchless One, who sits upon the world's throne and counts man His beloved child. It has been said that all the beloved ones of history stand forth in some alluring atmosphere of heroism, truth, and beauty, and without any defilement of meanness or sin. Thus, in simple speech, Christ caused the great God to stand forth clothed with all these alluring qualities that fascinate the intellect, that enrapture and satisfy the heart; portrayed God as one whose garments trailed in the sunset, who whispered upon " the colossal harp of nature," whose frame was made of worlds, whose strings were rays of shining light; a God for whom the universe itself was one vast temple, where storms and winds and cataracts, with songs of birds and men, combined in one vast hymn of adoration and delight.

And this simple story of God's eternal fatherhood and His unfailing love, falls upon the old views, that portrayed God as fear, vengeance; as a black shadow; as an iron fate. Christ smote them as the sun smites the April fields and makes them bloom. In ancient times the Greek general offered his god in exchange for victory as many goats as there were enemies dead upon the battle-field. And Solomon, also, in dedicating his temple, killed one hundred and twenty thousand sheep, never dreaming in his ignorance that herds and flocks were God's already, and that He would be better pleased with the flocks alive and feeding upon the happy hillsides than with their dead carcasses lying in the slaughter pen. In ages when such views of God prevailed the only way to estab· lish an idea was to cut off the heads of all who held to any other system. In such an era the world seems much like a sinking ship, to which God draws near with a small lifeboat to save now and then a drowning wretch. Thus a thousand errors and fallacies entered into and defiled the simple truths of Christ. In the Middle Ages the Crusaders returned from their holy wars laden with spoil. The knight fastened a great piece of carved furniture to the back of his horse, or collected in a huge sack strange objects to satisfy the curiosity of wife and child. Soon the army became impotent for battle as soldiers, and appeared under the aspect of travelling peddlers.

Thus the scholastics of the Middle Ages moved across the years like these ancient soldiers, and swept together all the curiosities of superstition and ignorance until the theologians of that time seem like philosophical beggars and peddlers, laden with all the rubbish of mental ragpickers. The simplicity of Christ was lost. His teachings became sadly belittered. The scholastics took away Christ's beautiful garments and replaced them with rags. Loyola exhibited Him as one who handled flames in which to burn heretics. Torquemada portrayed Him as a smith who forged fetters, instead of one who came to set the prisoners free. Michael Angelo, in his "Last Judgment," exhibited Christ as a sinewy athlete who matched His gianthood against feeble sinners and swept them into the fiery furnace, mid the plaudits of admiring saints. Forgetting that each thirsty pilgrim may take of the water of life freely, a few Augustinians degraded Christ to the level of one who condemned many to hell for His mere good pleasure. In Luther's day scholasticism had so corrupted men's minds from the simplicity of Christ that the great German thought many had mistaken the devil for the great God.

It is a truism with scientists that the simplest explanation is the truest. Doubtless, clouds and darkness will always be about God's throne, nor will the mind ever solve all mysteries. Nevertheless, in contrast with other religious systems Christ's teachings seem simple as a sunbeam. When a philosopher declares that each seed and leaf, each babe and sage, fall back into the clouds or rise into the clouds to the " all in all " God — we have pantheism. When a writer declares that atoms falling through a little space could hardly come together into those forms of beauty called an apple or a lark or a sage, but if these atoms fall through much space they could take on the forms of beauty found in this great world — we have atheistic materialism.

When the excavator in Ephesus uncovers a tomb and finds the bust of an emperor he reasons from the statue to the sculptor who carved it. But when a philosopher beholds the movement of the seed toward the tree, the grain toward the harvest, the adaptation of the eye toward the light, yet denies that these thoughts imply a world thinker and affirms that if such a thinker exists, he cannot be known — then we have agnosticism. When a writer declares that man's destiny is fully determined by his heredity and environment, that the blind force of nature or the iron will of God dooms man to eternal happiness or everlasting woe, then we have fatalism.   But when God is unveiled as a Father whose thought is the gulf stream of history, whose wisdom is equal to each emergency in life, who counts man as His child, who makes darkness not less than light, suffering as well as prosperity, defeat as well as triumph, lead on to ultimate victory — then we have the simplicity of Christ.   In that faith Tennyson whispered to his lifelong friend: "There is One who guides our steps and our individuality survives the grave.   In this let us live and die."   In that simple faith also of Christ lived Paschal and Bunyan. In that simple faith lived Channing and Lincoln and Livingstone.   That simple faith has made slaves free, has lent a new sweetness to music, has given a new beauty to art, has furnished a new motive to all culture.   In that simple faith the falling statesman, the dying mother, the sweet child, have all fallen asleep in perfect peace.

Having portrayed as an Infinite Father that God who holds the earth in His hand and rolls the sun like a golden ball along the pavement of the morning, Christ made God's Fatherhood to cause man to step into the scene, the child of a noble and thrilling destiny.   Had nature, with its forces of the summers and the winters, stood behind man and been his sponsor, a speedy catastrophe might have been expected, and man's future would have been full of blackness and fear.   But because the infinite mind that stands back of the vast earthly scene is made man's sponsor, the full power of this creator stands pledged to share in all the glorious achievements of His Father.   As the sculptor who holds in his mind a dream of ideal beauty can take a square block of marble and shape it into the lines of the lustrous ideal held in his mind, so there is rich hope for man — not because of what he is, but because of what God is in His wealth of mind and heart, that are prophecies of what man shall be when time and the divine resources have accomplished their purpose upon the human soul.   Plato tells us the ancient Greeks were deeply impressed with the beauty of forests and fountains and deep seas.   Indeed, the earthly scene was so rich as to make it seem incredible that the thrilling of the harvests and forests would have been prepared for man alone. The rich banquet spread by the summers and the winters seemed to ask for heavenly guests to sit down to drink at the table spread with these viands fit for the gods.

So men explained this palace beautiful named earth, by peopling the leafy woods and the cool streams with fauns and nymphs and graces.

And in similar vein Christ saw a thrilling beauty and power streaming forth from God's throne and surrounding man with a rich and stimulating atmosphere. With words of matchless eloquence He called about Him the multitudes, the children of poverty and ignorance, the children of sickness and suffering, the publican and the prodigal, and lifted above all alike a banner inscribed, not with those words called wisdom or riches or birth, but with the words, " Made in the image of God." He reminded man that ambassadors who represented a royal court should wear a garb befitting the greatness of the monarch whose power they represented; that those in whose veins ran kingly blood should aspire to kingly garb, refuse to wear rags or eat crusts of bread. With the thrilling pathos of His own life and death, Christ exhibited man as the child of supreme genius, because He is the child of God and carries eternity and immortality in His heart.

It is also a part of the simplicity of Christ as a religious teacher that He grounded duty and responsibility in man's moral constitution and separated them entirely from creeds and churches. The only duties He taught are the duties found in man's nature and constitution. It is the misfortune of our age that to-day men are urged toward right because they have taken unto themselves the vows of the church. But Christ called men unto a life of whiteness and beauty because all bore the image of God. The divine stamp man carried put him under a solemn pledge to avoid the stamp of demonhood. The motive of duty was not fidelity to a church, but fidelity to what man is fundamentally and constitutionally, through his original endowment of mind and heart. The time has come when men may think to escape the obligations of a Christian life by refusing to pledge themselves to a church. But Christ affirmed that man was pledged to a life of integrity by virtue of what he was in birth gifts. No man can escape responsibility by staying outside of a church. No man can increase his responsibilities by entering into a church. Duty antedates the church, and right precedes the Bible.

The laws of right and wrong were organized into man's mind and body. Finding them there, Moses wrote them down for society's help. The Ten Commandments did not begin with the Bible; they began with our father man. The mind existed long before the mental philosophy. The stars existed long before Newton wrote his " Principia." This great continent lay behind the setting sun long before Columbus first thought of a western passage to India. And every principle of the Christian life existed prior to the church and its statements. Duty is binding upon a man, therefore, not at all because he is a church member. He who has never set foot inside of a church and never recognized a single principle of the Bible, is bound to the same law of Christian living as is the man who, each Sunday, renews his fidelity. Nor does any Paul or John add one iota to his duty by recognizing his debt to God and to the community. The laws of brain and nerve and blood are fundamental and constitutional, and whether man denies the laws or whether he accepts them, they work invariably and remorselessly. Christian living, therefore, is binding upon man because of the nature of things and the facts in the case. Fire burns, cold chills, rocks bruise — not because man says they may, but because that is their nature. And the Sermon on the Mount is binding on men, not because they stand up in church and accept it, but because prior to the cradle God organized right into the nature of man and things.

To His sublimely simple statement regarding God and man, Christ added a conception of the church that is beautiful. Without dividing the multitude into church and non-church members, He called the men about Him, and reminding them that they were the children of the same cradle and moving toward a common grave, He bade them all alike swear fidelity to conscience. Passing by all creedal tests of belief, He asked for only one test — personal allegiance to Himself and the universal principles for which He stood. Soon the little group of disciples included all temperaments, all shades of belief,— those who represented much virtue and those who represented little; those who had much faith and those who had little. But His love united them, just as the roof of some splendid mansion unites a hundred rooms of different size and shape; just as the one blue sky overarches and unites mountains and pastures and vineyards. In those days there was only one church, and all the disciples were one, just as the many boughs are one in the same tree; just as the planets are one in the same starry system. The germ, indeed, of every possible denomination was there — John, the seer and mystic; Peter, the man of feeling and impulse; Paul, the philosopher and the theologian; James, who believed in a religion of deeds, and thought a dollar's worth of flour would do more for a hungry orphan than a day of praying. In their oneness of life the disciples were not so much driven together by a creedal necessity from without, as drawn together by a love of their Master from within. Now there are one hundred and forty denominations in our country. The churches threaten to destroy the church.

Our judicial courts recognize but one or two or three grounds for divorce between husband and wife; but the church has found one hundred and forty grounds for divorcing its disciples one from another. If every one of these one hundred and forty differences were rooted out, every important principle would still remain — love to God and man, and love to Him who is the soul's Master and Saviour. To-day some of the most distinguished teachers of our evangelical churches have expressed the belief that the time is drawing near when there is to be a return to the simplicity of Christ's church, when again all shall be one. These scholars give it as their judgment that Christ never intended that there should be a church roll of church membership, or a denomination. Christ's thought does not seem to have been that men should stand up and by a simple verbal statement imagine that they had fulfilled all righteousness. Christ's idea of the church was that men should band themselves together, not as church members but as men and women made in the image of God, and bend their associated energies to the promotion of virtue and knowledge and the defeat of ignorance, of vice, of superstition and sin.

Out of His beautiful ideas of the church grew Christ's beautiful use of symbols. Looking toward the constitution, the state asks the citizen through the ballot to swear fidelity to the laws of the land. Looking toward property, the state uses the symbol of the deed or the promissory note for emphasizing the sanctity of property. Looking toward the court room, society uses that symbol called taking the oath for the purpose of emphasizing the solemnity of the truth. Looking toward the home and marriage, the state uses that symbol called the wedding ring for emphasizing the sanctity of love. And in the realm of conscience, also, Christ made a beautiful use of symbols for emphasizing the importance of a white life, and setting forth man's dependence upon God. How beautiful his use of the water that, bubbling from some cool spring like a little poem out of the earth, falls upon man with a cleansing power for setting forth the cleansing grace of God. If some scientist had searched through all nature for some beautiful symbol of what Christ and God are to the soul, what symbol could he have found comparable to the bread that represents all harvests, all fruits and grains upon which man feeds, or the wine that represents the purple flood of grapes, the dripping juices of the apple and orange, with all rich tropic growths.

But having taught men how to move through these symbols of nature up to nature's God, Christ led men toward a generous toleration and charity. Having left man free to choose what flowers he would plant in his garden, free to choose what grains he would sow upon his fields, free to choose his own profession and his own occupation, Christ also left man free to choose his church government and to make his own creeds. God makes harvests, but not a bill of fare. And God makes truth, but not church polity, not church government. God makes forests, but the furniture is made by man. God makes the symbols, but their use and government is made by men. Therefore, Christ expresses no preference as to whether men should be baptized with much water or little. He leaves each teacher to decide for himself whether he shall wear a long white robe in the pulpit or a short black one. He gives no teaching in regard to millinery. If a man is benefited by fasting Friday and feasting Saturday; if a man is helped by the tinkling of bells and the burning of incense, and finds that the perfumed clouds passing through the open windows and rising heavenward have become chariots that lift his aspirations heavenward, then such an one is free to burn his incense and tinkle his bells. If the wants of one individual are best served by a bishop and another by the presbytery and another by a conference, let each choose with the same freedom with which he chooses to live under a republic or chooses a limited monarchy. The one principle is, toleration and charity for all. Only let not the Pope wipe his golden-bowed spectacles and say, "The truth is with me." And let not the Baptist say, "I have been to the very bottom of the Jordan, therefore the truth is with me." Neither let the Presbyterian say, "Sprinkling is like the rain; it comes down from the heaven, the truth is with me." But for all let there be sympathy, love, and fellowship. God is ever working toward variety and difference, and man is forever trying to rub out the differences. Nature does not turn all flowers into roses, but works toward a thousand varieties of bloom and blossom, a thousand varieties of fruit and grains in field and forest. There is room for all.

To many the new teachings seem revolutionary, destructive, and provocative, indeed, of grave anxiety. For, strangely enough, many Christian teachers have accepted the atheistic motto, "It is safer to trust our fears than our hopes." But God is abroad in the world, and is causing new glowing and glorious truths to break forth out of His word. And these new truths are working great changes in the realm of philosophy and theology. For some these changes mean only terror and alarm. The conditions of these frightened ones is not unlike that of the people of the Arctic region. It is said that the ice in certain interior rivers of the extreme north sometimes does not move out for an entire generation. And because the ice bridge binds the two shores together, the savages are accustomed to fish upon these ice-locked streams. One year the summer came early and stayed long. Slowly the sun bored holes in the ice above, slowly the warm currents gnawed the ice beneath. One July day the huge mass began to move, and its movement threw the people into an agony of terror.

They did not know that the open river with a boat would do a thousand times more for them than ice-locked streams, or that summer with its fruit was worth a thousand times more than the wintry ice with its fish. Thus, unto this winter-clad earth, God is drawing near. Many a great system has been caught like an iceberg by the rich tropic currents. Each new influence is a wind made warm and summery by God's heart. Soon the " systematic " icebergs will dissolve, and lend themselves to the universal ocean that blesses every continent with its dew and rain. God is working. The light is growing. Many, alarmed, are clubbing together to resist it. But the sword and the spear cannot drive back the south winds and the summer. The scholars are too many and too wise. Soon all bats and owls with their scared cries must return to the caves of fear. Already the song of birds is in the air. Once more God's presence makes all the earth radiant. The day for which the fathers prayed and hoped, the promised land which was denied them, has come at length unto their children. Men are opening their eyes to the blue rifts in the sky, they are opening their ears to the voices that call. Once more above us is the multitude of angels, singing, " Peace on earth, good will to man." Already the night is far spent. The day is at hand. Christ is abroad upon His mission of recovery.

LI

J. WILBUR CHAPMAN

1859–

AMONG the preachers of our time must be represented the evangelists; the men who hold no pastoral charge, but preach for a brief period of a week or two weeks in one place, and then in another, visiting sometimes fifty cities in a year; now heard by a multitude in Portland, Maine, and perhaps a month afterward by another multitude in Portland, Oregon. One of the most eminent preachers of this class is the Rev. J. Wilbur Chapman, D. D., LL. D., who at the present date (1907) is Corresponding Secretary of the General Committee on Evangelistic Work for the Presbyterian Church, by appointment of its General Assembly. Dr. Chapman was born at Richmond, Indiana, June 17, 1859; was graduated from Lake Forest University, Illinois, in 1879, and from Lane Theological Seminary in 1882. He began work in the pastorate in Albany, in the Reformed Church, but in 1890 took charge of the great Bethany Presbyterian Church in Philadelphia, world-famous for its Sunday-school, of which the Hon. John Wanamaker is the Superintendent. Dr. Chapman was abundantly successful in his church, but was in such constant demand as an evangelist that after three years he gave up his pulpit and held "revival services" throughout the land. He again took charge of a church in New York, on West End avenue, and it was at once filled with listeners. But at the voice of the General Assembly he again left his pulpit, this time to become not only an evangelist, but a superintendent of evangelism in the Presbyterian Church, frequently organizing campaigns of aggressive work with a staff of helpers, over an entire state at one time. His preaching is practical, strongly Biblical, based on the old-fashioned views of Bible authorship and inspiration, filled with telling illustrations, and aiming for immediate decision on the part of the hearer. This sermon, which Dr. Chapman has furnished us for publication, was preached in the summer of 1906 in the Amphitheater at Chautauqua, New York, before at least five thousand people, among whom was the editor of this volume.

AN OLD-FASHIONED HOME.

"What have they seen in thy house?"— 2 Kings xx. 15.

IF you will tell me what is in your house by your own choice I will tell you the story of your home life and will be able to inform you whether yours is a home in which there is harmony and peace or confusion and despair. Let me read the names of the guests in your guest book, allow me to study the titles of the books in your library in which you have special delight, permit me to scan your magazines which you particularly choose, allow me to listen to your conversation when you do not know that you are being overheard; give me the privilege of talking but for a moment to your servants and make it possible for me to visit with your friends in whom you have particular delight, and I will write a true story of what you have been, of what you are and of what you will be but for the grace of God, even though I may not know you personally at all. In other words whatever may be seen in your home determines what your home is.

I was a man grown before I visited Washington, the capital of the Nation. I was the guest of a member of the President's Cabinet. Riding with him the first evening, when the moon was shining, we suddenly came upon the National Capitol, and I said to my host. "What in the world is that?" He said with a smile as if he pitied me, "That is the Capitol building, and that is the home of the Nation." I am sure he was right in a sense, because the building is magnificent and is in every way the worthy home of such a Nation as ours, but I think I take issue with him after careful thought in his statement that the Capitol building is the home of the Nation. I can recall a visit made to a home which was not in any sense palatial, where the old-fashioned father every morning and evening read his Bible, knelt in prayer with his household about him, commended to God his children each by name, presented the servants at the throne of grace and then sang with them all one of the sweet hymns of the church, and from the morning prayer they went forth to the day of victory, while from the evening prayer they went to sleep the undisturbed sleep of the just with the angels of heaven keeping watch over them.

I recall another home in the State of Ohio where the father and mother were scarcely known outside of their own county. The size of their farm was ten acres, but they reared two boys and two girls whose mission has been world-wide and whose names are known wherever the church of Christ is known and wherever the English language is spoken. These in the truest sense are the homes of the nation and such homes give us men and women as true as steel.

Napoleon was once asked, " What is the greatest want of the French nation? " He hesitated a moment and then said with greatest emphasis, " The greatest want of the French Nation is mothers." If you will ask me the greatest need of America I could wish in my reply that I might speak with the power of a Napoleon and that my words might live as long, for I would say, " The greatest need of the American Nation to-day is homes. Not palatial buildings of necessity, but homes where Christ is honored, where God is loved and where the Bible is studied."

A returned missionary who had been for twenty-five years away from his home because he would not accept his furloughs, was asked after he had been in California for a little season what impressed him the most after his absence of a quarter of a century. The reporter expected him to say that he was impressed with the telephone system which bound houses and cities together, or that he was amazed at the wireless telegraphy by means of which on the wave currents of the air messages were sent from one city to another, but the returned missionary expressed no such surprise. He said, " When I went away from America, almost every home had its family altar, now that I have returned I have watched very carefully and find a family altar in a house is the exception and not the rule." Wherever this is true there is some cause for great alarm, for in proportion as the home fails the nation is in danger.

Hezekiah had been sick unto death. The word of the Lord by the mouth of the prophet came to him saying, " Set thy house in order for thou must die." Then he recovered for a season. The King of Babylon sent messengers to him and when the messengers had gone Isaiah asked him the question of the text, " What have they seen in thy house? "

The dearest and most sacred spot on earth is home. Around it are the most sacred associations, about it cluster the sweetest memories. The buildings are not always palatial, the furnishings are not always of the best, but when the home is worthy of the name ladders are let down from Heaven to those below, the angels of God come down bringing Heaven's blessings and ascend taking earth's crosses. Such a home is the dearest spot on earth because there your father worked and your mother loved. There is no love which surpasses this.

Some years ago when the English soldiers were fighting and a Scotch regiment came to assist, the Scotchmen strangely enough began to die in great numbers. The skill of the surgeons was baffled. They could not tell why it was that there seemed to be such a rapid falling away of the men, but at last they found out. The Scotch pipers were playing the tunes that reminded the Scotchmen of the heather and the hills and they were dying of home-sickness. When the music was changed the deaths in such large numbers almost instantly ceased.

We are drifting away from our old-fashioned homes, fathers have grown too busy, mothers have delegated their God-given work to others. We have lost instead of gained. Wherever the homes are full of weakness the government is in danger. The homes of our country are so many streams pouring themselves into the great current of moral and social life. If the home life is pure then all is pure. I stand with that company of people to-day who believe that we are at the beginning of a great revival of religion and I am persuaded that this revival is to be helped on not so much by preaching, though that is not to be ignored, nor by singing, though that is in itself useful, but which I think is absolutely true to conditions of the homes in our land.

I.

I have a friend who says that when God himself would start a nation he made home life the deciding question. He selected Abraham as the head of the home and in Genesis the 17th chapter and the 19th verse he gives the reason for this in these words, " For I know him that he will command his children and his household after him." There are two great principles which must prevail in every home.

First — AUTHORITY, suggested by the word command.

Second — EXAMPLE, suggested by the expression, " He will command his children and his household after him."

In order that one may rightly command he must himself be controlled or be able to obey an authority higher than his own. It is absolutely impossible for one to be the father he ought to be and not be a

Christian, or to be worthy the name of mother and not yield allegiance to Jesus Christ. If we are to set before those about us a right example we cannot begin too soon. Your children are a reproduction of yourself. Weakness in them is weakness in yourself, strength in them is but the reproduction of your own virtue.

A convention of mothers met some years ago in the city of Cincinnati and was discussing the question as to when one ought properly to train the child for Christ. One mother said, "I began at six;" another suggested seven as the proper age; another said, "I begin when my child takes first step and thus point him to Christ or when they speak their first word I teach them the name of Jesus." Finally an old saint arose and said, "You are all of you wrong; the time to begin to train the child is the generation before the child is born," and this we all know to be true.

But the responsibility does not rest simply upon mothers; fathers cannot ignore their God-given position. Judge Alton B. Parker and his favorite grandson, Alton Parker Hall, five years old, narrowly escaped death by drowning in the Hudson river. For half an hour the two played in the water. Then Judge Parker took the boy for a swim into deep water. Placing the boy on his back, he swam around for a while, and then, deciding to float, turned over, seating the boy astride his chest. In this manner the Judge floated a distance from the wharf before noticing it. Then he attempted to turn over again, intending to swim nearer the shore. In the effort to transfer the boy to his back the little fellow became frightened and tightly clasped the Judge about the neck. Judge Parker called to the boy to let go his hold, but the youth only held on the tighter, and frightened at the evident distress of the Judge began to whimper. In a few moments the grasp of the boy became so tight that Judge Parker could not breathe. He tried to shake the boy loose and then attempted to break his grasp. The boy held on with the desperation of death, however, and every effort of the Judge only plunged them both beneath the choking waves. With his last few remaining breaths Judge Parker gave up the struggle and shouted for assistance.

The mistake that the distinguished man made was that he went too far from shore with the boy. There are too many men to-day who are doing the same thing. They are going out too far in social life, they are too lax in the question of amusements, they are too thoughtless in the subject of dissipation. Some day they will stop but their boys will be gone.

41

Example counts for everything in a home. If there is any blessing in my own life for others, if there has been any helpfulness in my ministry to others, I owe it all to my mother who lived before me a consistent Christian life and died giving me her blessing; and to my father who with his arms about me one day said, " My son, if you go wrong it will kill me." I was at one time under the influence of a boy older than myself and cursed with too much money. I had taken my first questionable step at least and was on my way one night to a place which was at least questionable if not sinful. I had turned the street corner and ahead of me was the very gate to hell, and, suddenly, as I turned, the face of my father came before me, and his words rang in my very soul. If my father had been anything but a consistent Christian man I myself, I am sure, would have been far from the pulpit and might have been in the lost world. There are those who seem to think that the height of one's ambition is to amass a fortune, to build a palace or to acquire a social position. My friend, George Stuart, says you may build your palaces, amass your fortunes, provide for the satisfaction of every desire, but as you sit amid these luxurious surroundings waiting for the staggering steps of a son or as you think of a wayward daughter, all this will be as nothing, for there is nothing that can give happiness to the parents of godless, wayward children. Some one has said: " Every drunkard, every gambler, every lost woman once sat in a mother's lap and the downfall of the most of them may be traced to some defect in home life."

The real purpose of every home is to shape character for time and eternity. The home may be one of poverty, the cross of self-sacrifice may be required, suffering may sometimes be necessary, but wherever a home fulfills this purpose it is overflowing with joy. One of my friends has drawn the following picture which he says is fanciful, but it is to be helped or hindered by the life. Clear back in the country there is a boy who wants to go to a college and get an education. They call him a book-worm. Wherever they find him — in the barn or in the house — he is reading a book. " What a pity it is," they say, " that Ed cannot get an education." His father, work as hard as he will, can no more than support the family by the products of the farm. One night Ed has retired to his room and there is a family conference about him. The sisters say, " Father, I wish you would send Ed to college; if you will we will work harder than we ever did, and we will make our old dresses do." The mother says, " Yes, I will get along without any hired help; although I am not as strong as I used to be, I think I can get along without any hired help." The father says, "Well, I think by husking corn at night in the barn I can get along without any assistance." Sugar is banished from the table, butter is banished from the plate. That family is put down on rigid, yea, suffering economy that the boy may go to college. Time passes on. Commencement day has come. Think not that I mention an imaginary case. God knows it happened. Commencement day has come and the professors walk in on the stage in their long gowns and their classic but absurd hats. The interest of the occasion is passing on, and after a while it comes to a climax of interest as the valedictorian is to be introduced. Ed has studied so hard and worked so well that he has had the honor conferred upon him. There are rounds of applause, sometimes breaking into vociferation. It is a great day for Ed. But away back in the galleries are his sisters in their old plain hats and faded sacks, and the old-fashioned father and mother. Dear me, she has not had a new hat for six years; he has not had a new coat for six years. And they get up and look over on the platform, and they laugh and they cry, and they sit down, and they look pale, and then they are very flushed. Ed gets the garlands and the old-fashioned group in the gallery have their full share of the triumph. They have made that scene possible, and in the day that God shall more fully reward self-sacrifice made for others he will give grand and glorious recognition. " As his his part is that goeth down to battle, so shall his part be that tarrieth by the stuff."

This experience describes a home in the truest sense of the word better than all the palaces the world has ever known where wealth is lacking and the Spirit of God is gone.

II.

There are two great forces in every home. I speak of the father and the mother, not but that the children have their part in either making or breaking a household, but these two are the mightiest of agencies.

The mother stands first. There are certain things which must be true of every mother. She must be a Christian. The father may fail if he must, but let the mother fail and God pity the children. She must be consistent. The children may forget the inconsistencies of the father but when the mother fails the impression is lasting as time and almost as lasting as eternity. She must be prayerful. I do not know of anything that lifts so many burdens, or puts upon the face such a look of beauty as the spirit of prayer. And she must study her Bible. When we pray we talk with God, but when we read the Bible God talks with us; and every mother needs His counsel.

A poor young man stood before a judge in a great court to be sentenced to death. When asked if he had anything to say he bowed his head and said, " Oh, your honor, if only I had had a mother."

A mother's love is unfailing. When I was in Atlanta, Georgia, in October, 1904, a little girl and an old mother came to see the Governor. They had met on the train and the child agreed to take the old lady to see the Governor of the State. They entered the Governor's office and she spoke as follows:

" I want to see the Governor," was the straightforward request of the little lady addressed to Major Irwin, the private secretary to the Governor, as he inquired her errand.

" That is the Governor standing there. He will see you in a moment," replied the Major, indicating Governor Terrell standing in the group. The Governor went over to her. " What can I do for you, dear?" he asked. Throwing back her curls she opened wide her baby eyes and said:

" Governor, it is not for me; it is for this old lady. Her name is Mrs. Hackett and she wants to talk to you about pardoning her boy." This was said by a little lady of eleven, who spoke with all the grace and *savoir faire* of a woman twice her age.

In a voice choked with emotion, Mrs. Hackett began her tearful, scarcely audible story and presented her petition for clemency for her boy.

" Governor, have mercy on me," she began, and threw back her bonnet showing a face wrinkled by age and furrowed and drawn by suffering, " and give me back my boy."

Breaking down under the strain of talking to the Governor, whom she had planned for months to see, the pleading mother gave way to her grief. The Governor was visibly moved and continued to stroke the curly hair of Mrs. Hackett's little Samaritan. " Give me back my boy. I am an old woman going on seventy-nine, and I cannot be here long. I know I am standing with one foot in the grave, and I do want to hear my boy, my baby, say to me, ' Ma, I'm free.' Let me go down on my knees to you and beg that you have mercy on a mother's breaking heart. During the last month I picked five hundred pounds of cotton and made two dollars to get here to see you. I got here without a cent and this little angel gave me a dollar — her all. I don't care if I have to walk home, for I've seen you and told you of my boy."

With unsteady voice the Governor told her the law, and referred ıer gently to the Prison Commission, assuring her that they would give her petition the most considerate attention. I am told that when the books were examined the crime was found to be one of the blackest on the calendar and yet the mother loved him. Her love always stimulates love. It lasts when every thing else fails. A man cannot wander so far from God as to forget his mother or go so deep in sin as to be unmindful of her sweet influence.

The following is a sketch, full of touching interest, of a little ragged newsboy who had lost his mother. In the tenderness of his affection for her he was determined that he would raise a stone to her memory.

His mother and he had kept house together and they had been all to each other, but now she was taken, and the little fellow's loss was irreparable. Getting a stone was no easy task, for his earnings were small; but love is strong. Going to a cutter's yard and finding that even the cheaper class of stones were far too expensive for him, he at length fixed upon a broken shaft of marble, part of the remains of an accident in the yard, and which the proprietor kindly named at such a low figure that it came within his means. There was much yet to be done, but the brave little chap was equal to it.

The next day he conveyed the stone away on a four-wheeled cart, and managed to have it put in position. The narrator, curious to know the last of the stone visited the cemetery one afternoon and he thus describes what he saw and learned:

"Here it is," said the man in charge, and sure enough, there was the monument, at the head of one of the newer graves. I knew it at once. Just as it was when it left our yard, I was going to say, until I got a little nearer to it and saw what the little chap had done. I tell you, boys, when I saw it there was something blurred my eyes, so's I couldn't read it at first. The little man had tried to keep the lines straight, and evidently thought that capitals would make it look better and bigger, for nearly every letter was a capital. I copied it, and here it is; but you want to see it on the stone to appreciate it:

MY mOTHER
SHEE DIED LAST WEAK
SHEE WAS ALL I HAD. SHE
SED SHEAD BEE WAITING FUR

and here, boys, the lettering stopped. After awhile I went back to the man in charge and asked him what further he knew of the little fellow who brought the stone. "Not much," he said, "not much. Didn't you notice a fresh little grave near the one with the stone? Well, that's where he is. He came every afternoon for some time, working away at that stone, and one day I missed him, and then for several days. Then the man came out from the church that had buried the mother, and ordered the grave dug by her side. I asked if it was for the little chap. He said it was. The boy had sold all his papers one day, and was hurrying along the street out this way. There was a runaway team just above the crossing, and — well — he was run over, and lived but a day or two. He had in his hand, when he was picked up, an old file sharpened down to a point, with which he did all the lettering. They said he seemed to be thinking only of that until he died, for he kept saying, 'I didn't get it done, but she'll know I meant to finish it, won't she? I'll tell her so, for she'll be waiting for me,' and he died with those words on his lips." When the men in the cutter's yard heard the story of the boy the next day they clubbed together, got a good stone, inscribed upon it the name of the newsboy (which they succeeded in getting from the superintendent of the Sunday school which the little fellow attended), and underneath it the touching words: "He loved his mother."

God pity the mother with such an influence as this if she is leading in the wrong direction.

It is necessary also to say just a word about the father. There are many pictures of fathers in the Bible. Jacob gives us one when he cries, "Me ye have bereft of my children."

David gives another when he cries, "Oh, Absalom, my son." The father of the prodigal adds a new touch of beauty to the picture when he calls for the best robe to be put upon his boy. I allow no one to go beyond me in paying tribute to a mother's love but I desire in some special way to pay tribute to the devotion and consistency of a father. There are special requisites which must be made without which no father can maintain his God-given position.

He must be a Christian. I rode along a country road with my little boy some time ago. I found that he was speaking to my friends just as I spoke to them. One man called my attention to it and said, "It is amusing, isn't it?" To me it was anything but amusing. If my boy is to speak as I speak, walk as I walk, then God help me to walk as a Christian.

He must be a man of prayer. No man can bear the burdens of life or meet its responsibilities properly if he is a stranger to prayer.

He must be a man of Bible study. One of the most priceless treasures I have is a Bible my father studied, the pages of which he turned over and over and which I never used to read without a great heart throb.

> "I con its pages o'er and o'er,
> Its interlinings mark a score
> Of promises most potent, sweet,
> In verses many of each sheet;
> Albeit the gilding dull of age,
> And yellow-hued its every page,
> No book more precious e'er may be,
> Than father's Bible is to me.

> "Its tear-stained trace fresh stirs my heart
> The corresponding tear to start,
> Of trials, troubles herein brought,
> For comfort never vainly sought,
> For help in sorest hour of need,
> For love to crown the daily deed;
> No book more precious e'er may be,
> Than father's Bible is to me."

He must also erect in his house a family altar. I know that many business men will say this is impossible, but it is not impossible. If your business prevents your praying with your children then there must be something wrong with your business. If your life prevents it then you ought to see to it that your life is made right and that quickly.

I have a friend, George R. Stuart, one of the truest men I know, who gives the following picture of a Christian home. He said: "When I was preaching in Nashville at the conclusion of my sermon a Methodist preacher came up and laid his hand upon my shoulder and said, 'Brother Stuart, how your sermon to-day carried me back to my home. My father was a local preacher, and the best man I ever saw. He is gone to heaven now. We have a large family; mother is still at home, and I should like to see all the children together once more and have you come and dedicate our home to God, while we all re-dedicate ourselves to God before precious old mother leaves. If you will come with me, I will gather all the family together next Friday for that purpose.' I consented to go. The old home was a short distance from the city of Nashville. There were a large number of brothers and sisters. One was a farmer; one was a doctor; one was a real estate man; one was a bookkeeper; one was a preacher; and so on, so that they represented many professions of life. The preacher brother drove me out to the old home, where all the children had gathered. As we drove up to the gate I saw the brothers standing in little groups about in the yard, whittling and talking. Did you never stand in the yard of the old home after an absence of many years, and entertain memories brought up by every beaten path and tree and gate, and building about the old place? I was introduced to these noble-looking men who, as the preacher brother told me, were all members of churches, living consistent Christian lives, save the younger boy, who had wandered away a little, and the real object of this visit was to bring him back to God.

"The old mother was indescribably happy. There was a smile lingering in the wrinkles of her dear old face. We all gathered in the large old-fashioned family room in the old-fashioned semi-circle, with mother in her natural place in the corner. The preacher brother laid the large family Bible in my lap and said, 'Now, Brother Stuart, you are in the home of a Methodist preacher; do what you think best.'

"I replied, 'As I sit to-day in the family of a Methodist preacher, let us begin our service by an old-fashioned experience meeting. I want each child, in the order of your ages, to tell your experience.'

"The oldest arose and pointed his finger at the oil portrait of his father, hanging on the wall, and said in substance about as follows: 'Brother Stuart, there is the picture of the best father God ever gave a family. Many a time he has taken me to his secret place of prayer, put his hand on my head, and prayed for his boy. And at every turn of my life, since he has left me, I have felt the pressure of his hand on my head, and have seen the tears upon his face, and have heard the prayers from his trembling lips. I have not been as good a man since his death as I ought to have been, but I stand up here to-day to tell you and my brothers and sisters and my dear old mother that I am going to live a better life from this hour until I die.' Overcome with emotion he took his seat, and the children in order spoke on the same line. Each one referred to the place of secret prayer and the father's hand upon the head. At last we came to the youngest boy, who with his face buried in his hands was sobbing, and refused to speak. The preacher brother very pathetically said, ' Buddy, say a word; there is no one here but the family, and it will help you.'

" He arose, holding the back of his chair, and looked up at me and said, ' Brother Stuart, they tell me that you have come to dedicate this home to God; but my old mother there has never let it get an inch from God. They tell you that this meeting is called that my brothers and sisters may dedicate their lives to God, but they are good. I know them. I am the only black sheep in this flock. Every step I have wandered away from God and the life of my precious father I have felt his hand upon my head and heard his blessed words of prayer. To-day I come back to God, back to my father's life, and so help me God, I will never wander away again.'

" Following his talk came a burst of sobbing and shouting, and I started that old hymn, ' Amazing grace, how sweet the sound, that saved a wretch like me!' etc., and we had an old-fashioned Methodist class-meeting, winding up with a shout. As I walked away from that old homestead I said in my heart: ' It is the salt of a good life that saves the children.' A boy never gets over the fact that he had a good father."

" What have they seen in thy house?" If we are to help our children for time and eternity our homes must be better, our lives must be truer, our ambition to do God's will must be supreme. When these conditions are met it will be possible for us to answer the question of the text.

LII

S. PARKES CADMAN

1864–

IN the year 1890 a Methodist Bishop from America, passing through London, met a young Wesleyan minister who had recently graduated from Richmond College, affiliated with London University. Perceiving that here was "a lad o' parts," he urged him to go to America; and as a result of the interview, the young man, whose name was Samuel Parkes Cadman, entered the ministry of the Methodist Episcopal Church in the New York Conference. His first charge was at Milbrook, in Dutchess county, fourteen miles east of the Hudson river; but before many months he was known everywhere in a radius of fifty miles by his brilliant addresses and lectures. He was soon called to Central Church in Yonkers, and then to the Metropolitan Temple in New York, a large institutional church under Methodist auspices on the lower west side. Here he speedily took rank among the leading preachers in the city, and was in wide demand as a lecturer and college preacher. In the General Conference of the Methodist Episcopal Church at Chicago, in 1900, he was a prominent member, taking an active part in debate and legislation. Soon afterward he was called out of the Methodist fold to the Central Congregational Church in Brooklyn, the most powerful church in the city of churches and of commanding pulpits. Dr. Cadman is a wide reader, a broad-minded and progressive thinker, the exponent of strong thoughts set in eloquent language, and a man of catholic spirit, still as popular in his old church as in his new one. Many years of power and of usefulness may be hoped for him, as he is still a young man, having been born in Shropshire, England, Dec. 18, 1864, and now (in 1907) forty-two years of age. This discourse was preached by Dr. Cadman as the baccalaureate sermon before Columbia University on June 10, 1906, and was subsequently published in "The Christian Work and Evangelist."

One who has often listened to Dr. Cadman writes of his preaching: "Under other attention-compelling qualities there is utter fearlessness in thought and speech, thorough devotion to the things of the highest spiritual life, and rare power of self-communication through the spoken word. He is one of the most effective preachers now in the American pulpit."

AN AGE OF CONFLICT.

"For God gave us not a spirit of Fearfulness, but of Power and Love and Discipline."— 2 Timothy i. 7.

THESE arresting words, which hold you in their grip of boldness, certitude and wisdom, were written in a day marked by transition and conflict. The Old World was yielding up its life to the New World, that world in which we to-day exist, and which in its turn, is obedient to the pulse of life in continuous change. They indicate the attitude of an authoritative man toward his times, a man whose absorption in the verities of God equipped him as an apostle of Christian civilization. They are a part of the trenchant front he presented in this period of crisis, when the vail was being lifted from off the face of many nations. It is not possible for us to fully understand the strength and importance of these ancient disputes between Græco-Roman culture on the one hand and the beginnings of the Christian Church upon the other. But there is discernible in their stress and confusion the formation of a new watershed in human affairs. Religion, ethics, politics, in fact, the entire social structure, were regenerated and refashioned.

The Christian literature is linked at many turns with these contending forces, while among the writers of the New Testament none knew more comprehensively and thoroughly the strength and the weakness of the controversy than did St. Paul. He reveals at every stage in his mental processes his intimacy with the gains and losses of civilization, as it then existed. He is not an annalist, chronicling the simple histories he desired men to know. He is not a teacher, content to expound his theme and leave you to its application. He is our guide to-day because the text is a solemn annunciation of the spiritual forces which sway all civilized conditions. He deals with these in an ardent and meditative spirit. And he speaks not only as a high officer of the church, but as a representative man whose acquired beliefs had shed new light upon his former heritage. Therefore the writings of St. Paul stand in sacred literature for that for which the cathedral stands in sacred architecture. They are embracive and inspiring, with far-flung reaches of thought and aspiration: the high Gothic of the later Scriptures, every line of them replete with devoutness and insight, and the whole structure one upraised splendor of vital energy, irradiated with the rich hues of " the many-tinted wisdom of God."

This precept is full of the breath of that older world which was the mother of modernity. *Fearlessness, Discipline, Power* — a Roman general's appeal to his legions, a Stoic's discoursing under the porches, a Hebrew's passionate memories of the magistrates of his lineage, could have embodied with recognition, this fruitage of their common experience. And Christianity's sovereign truth is crowned in the exhortation unto Charity, the Charity which ameliorates and adjusts sterner considerations and which is the perfect bond of a true human union.

Again, these forces are not of to-day, nor of yesterday, they are forever; their catholic human extent is created by the divine depth of their intent. It was a wider and a grander age upon which men then entered, its perils by no means a negligible quantity, but its capabilities beyond all former expectation; while underneath the pressure of its problems and its pains, there was a spirit of deliverance, which could make men equal to their tasks and duties. I question if some Christian apologists have always been willing to do justice to the Græco-Roman world. Yet without it we could never have been what we are to-day. The " Orientalism " which flourished in Egypt, Assyria and Crete bred indifference to liberty and nurtured a blind and tyrannical fatalism. For five hundred years before the text was issued, the scepter of civilization had passed from those earlier nations which seemed to have enjoyed so much and accomplished so little. Upon the northern shore of the Mediterranean, mankind founded another center, a center which became the sanctuary of knowledge, the home of culture and the fortress of law. What infinite betterment this transfer brought to us all! It is not exaggeration to say that modern life and history can be dated from those initiators of the classical eras upon whose foundations we gladly build.

For do we conceive of God? So did the Greeks, and they embodied their conception in the " Absolute " of Plato, and the " First Cause " of Aristotle. These were the high confessions of that nation, and supreme as it became in ethical discussion, even the ethical moment was not the sole factor in human destiny. The journeyings of human life went beyond the pale of creaturely consideration and creaturely control, and that which these polite thinkers knew and named as Fate was a dim foreshadowing of the clearer view of the Apostle. He saw that which the Athenian philosophers felt, that human value and human futurity were within the compass of the Being of God. So in one unbroken continuity certain ideals of Grecian religion survived states of elevation ·and depression, and the language which flourished in this loftier atmosphere became a vehicle of the truth for all civilization. If you seek a practical proof of the value of Grecian ideals, consider their attainments in civic virtue. The uplifting duties and the unselfish aims of true citizenship were by them subtly analyzed, eloquently advocated and exemplified with a prompt and sane patriotism whose Courage, Discipline and Power have never been excelled.

Moreover, St. Paul was himself a Roman citizen, writing these words in the Greek language and in the full consciousness of his franchise. The Roman type of social organism is apparent in much he has to say. It took a different direction than did that of Greece, but it was none the less explicit, luminous, open to reason and impervious to dismay. Those lords of the ancient world made their center of civilization in man, in his faculties and his interests, and in his government under legal control. That which the Greek found through the medium of Nature, the Roman found in the individual and in the State.

The qualities of the text were patterned in the glory that once was Rome's. Energy, self-control, valor, fortitude, tenacity of purpose, adherence to pledges, insistence on rights, ability both to obey and to command — these were the prominent traits inherent in Roman morality and stamped on Roman records.

But under and over all which this Scripture has to offer is the enveloping influence of the royal faculty of the Chosen Race, that undisturbed and undisturbable faith in the covenanting Jehovah, which is the all-powerful contribution of Hebraism in every subsequent civilization. It requires no excess in us to portray Abraham leaving Ur of the Chaldees with these words upon his lips. Behind him lay the shining city, a mirror of that age which he then forsook. Before him were the trackless wastes, homeless and sinister. Within him was " the grand instinct " which has since peopled the world with its altars and its temples, its prophecies and its decrees.

Could I sum up in one pregnant phrase the legislative gifts of Moses, and the predictive visions of Isaiah, the text would best serve the purpose.

St. Paul became one of this great fraternity which o'erleaps the bounds of time, the pride of birth, the barriers of creed and blood. Socrates and Marcus Aurelius and Samuel the Prophet and the Apostle were alike incarnations of those spiritual laws and purposes which lie behind all progress. His soul was drawn to their souls as flame is drawn to flame. And we should be compelled to forego ourselves and to be other than we are before we could escape the discipline of God, which these elected ones displayed. Of a certainty we are their debtors beyond discharge, and these garnered results are set before us for our profit withal.

It is the highest pursuit of scholarship to discover in its researches the imperishable elements which alone give significance to outward organizations, and after our employments are thus recompensed to ask the questions no merely intellectual methods can satisfactorily answer — Whence come these elements, and whither do they tend?

St. Paul's reply was simple and, for him at any rate, decisive. He was not heedless of the alarming admixtures of current life. He saw its fierce activities, its diseased and morbid elements, its wide reciprocities, its joy and pain. That ironic medley of good and evil which puzzles us was familiar to him. He knew that the religion for which he must later die was despised and rejected of men. He knew that Rome's might was dissolving, and that the fall would shatter the social fabric of the world. But while Rome tottered, he remained unshaken, and spoke with the calmness and ease of one whose confident eye might have rested upon a golden age. Why was this? Surely it was not the callousness of the careless one, nor the fanaticism of the obscurantist. None who know him can accuse him of either. It was because he was held in the courage of enlightenment, the courage of training, the courage of powers invisible, and the courage of victorious love for God and men. He was assured that God could not be overthrown by his own order, and because of this, that man would continue to move with larger freedom on the earth. Brutality may rage and cynicism imagine a vain thing, but no catastrophe could halt the surging march toward the appointed goal.

For had the world been left to the disposition of Rome's worst emperors, their hand of anarchy would have dropped the curtain and universal darkness would have covered all. But the world was never in their keeping, and the throes of death were also the pangs of regeneration. Had the age no power of flight, Nero would not have essayed to build his monstrous cage; hence out of the eater came the meat and out of the destroyer the sweetness.

The forces of civilization were then, as always, beyond the reach of violence. In ordained tranquillity, they moved majestically forward to shine on Athens as they had never shone on Babylon; to shine in deathless splendor on New York as they had never shone on Rome. And it was because of the war which their light made on all darkness that the woe of Rome's expiring Paganism was a long-drawn agony, which, please God! may we never know again.

Yet whoever suffered and struggled, whether for his own misdeeds or for the sins of others, the suffering was the necessary toll of advancement, and the ruptures of the time were fissures through which incorruptible strength and grace flowed beyond death's congealing into the living order of the modern day.

St. Paul did not know the law of historic science, which has since demonstrated these claims, aided by the light of after events, but his intuitions served him well, and the abiding features of any civilized condition were never more frankly chosen or loyally ensphered.

There was another law which St. Paul enunciated with monotonous sublimity — and that, the law of altruistic sacrifice. It was long held in leash by human selfishness and desire, but unloosed in Christ's supremacies, it has since become the operative force which is content to work among conditions of ruin and loss with the patience of hope and the warmth of benevolence.

Comrades in this common effort, we must never be silent about these principles. They teach us that which we have to learn; how little we are in our own hands, and how much we are in the hands of the Infinite and the Blessed One; how wise are those restraints and limitations which engirdle our province of achievements, and how no gift we have or can acquire is held in freehold, but is ours to be used in larger service than we know; and how the truths we most thoroughly believe can only be made an active reality by personal sacrifice. For sacrificed we must be, and if willingly, so much the better.

This age, like that of St. Paul, is one of restless interrogation. If poise and mastery were ever incumbent upon trained men like yourselves, men to whom civilization, as we know it, has freely given its best, this is the appointed hour. The rapidity of our gain in material wealth and privilege has embarrassed our reflecting nature. Experience has gone beyond the balance of wisdom, and wide as are its circumferences now, to-morrow they will be reduced to the strength of the center. For the kingdom of God is within us, and while our outward apparatus is gigantic, those inward faculties which make man an imperishable soul must be sustained and fed, or our rule will diminish while our curiosity increases.

Seats of learning, such as is this university, churches of all creeds which exalt the spiritual principle, courts of justice, high and low, are only efficient by means of your personal unshrinking resolution to be yourselves the sons of God, without blame, holding forth the torch of truth in all darkness and perversity.

Because we are persuaded of this, let us assume our vocation fearlessly. For God has outlawed the spirit of cowardice which is the chief enemy of both our faith and our effort. When the text, as translated, speaks of " fear," it does not convey the original meaning of the word St. Paul used here.

For fear is a sentiment to which all breasts are liable, and many a brave heart rallies to the call of obligation despite its quakings. But the principle the apostle would describe is that moral hardihood which crucifies fear in the righteous handling of our life's opportunities. It is here emergent, it brooks not little excuses, it sets aside the maxims of prudence, falsely so called, it bids you keep tryst with omnipotence, and it has the self-sufficiency which Medea had, who when her husband was recreant, when her children were murdered, and when all had cast her out, being asked " What remains? " replied, " Myself."

> " So nigh is grandeur to our dust,
>   So near is God to man,
>   When duty whispers low, Thou must,
>   The soul replies, I can."

The traditionalist who mutilates courage and progress by separating faith and knowledge forgets that the worst heresy of which we can be guilty is to be afraid for the truth. The temporal thinker who is captured by the theory of the moment presses upon us certain pet words of his, such as " necessity " and " environment." The pensive doubter can hear nothing in the sounds around him save the low roar of faith's retreating tide down the naked beach to the sighing of the night wind.

The representative types may serve some lesser purposes in the restatement of our social and religious creeds, but their value is derivative and subordinate because it lacks the hold on God and the ages given by unshaken trust in the divine purpose.

Beyond them, and far below them in moral stature, are men and women whose undoing is being fixed by greed and covetousness and vanity and lies. They heap upon the staggering Atlas the burdens of their dishonesty and of their baleful frenzy for gain or adventitious eminence. These children of folly pierce themselves through with many sorrows, and disfigure the fair countenance of our civilization with sullying humors which are palpable to all.

But I shall waste no time in elaborate analysis of the causes which have debilitated the mental and moral tone of present society. We are better employed when we re-assert the right to think freely, to act with independence and to be dissenters from any ruling conventionalities which injure the forces named by the text.

For it is more than a current assumption that men must do right though the heavens fall, the doing of right as we are enabled to know the right is the only law of action which keeps the heavens from falling. Of course, we give assent to this, but it is by no means such a commonplace in action as it is in theory. Yet it should be so, since the moralities alone are eternal. Society is absolutely dependent upon them, and true expediency is never opposed to them.

Wherein then do we abound, save in the restraints of cowardice? And wherein do we lack, save in the executive ability of courage? The shabby output we lament is largely a consequence of impoverished souls which dread categorical propositions in ethics. We accept these propositions in physical science. We should account it a masquerade if men who knew better rejected the axioms of mathematics, and the reasonings of the gravitation hypothesis. No less a sorry spectacle are men who put social convenience first and justice and honor and humanity secondary. However difficult it may be to enforce these and suppress their antagonists, to do otherwise is to destroy self-respect and hamstring civilization.

Mr. John Morley has clearly marked the course in his essay on "Compromise." He warns us against those inglorious predispositions which encourage a lazy accommodation with error, and an ignoble econ-

42

omy of truth. Any temporary gains thus secured are dearly purchased by permanent loss. "Do not regard thoroughness as a blunder, or nailing your flag to the mast a bit of delusive heroics." It is not for you "to think wholly of to-day, and not at all of to-morrow, to beware of the high and hold fast to the safe, to dismiss conviction and study popularity." He who does this is ten thousand times a coward and a traitor, denuded of zeal, perhaps full of low-minded geniality, but one who has sold his birthright and condemned his future.

Apply this ruling to your religious beliefs. They may be somewhat abstract in their nature and crude in their setting-forth. It may be difficult to understand or articulate them, but they are yours, and they are a deposit to guard for yourselves and posterity. They have fascinated the imagination and excited the hope of your fathers, and that they may be realized, millions have suffered and died. Now these sanctions restrain the riot of unadulterated secularism, and when they become pale and weak and numb, the work of destruction always follows; silently, dreadfully follows. The soul unmastered by these implicit assumptions about goodness is tenanted by the seven devils of a fate to which words can add no bitterness.

You will urge that it is hard to believe — sometimes. Yes, and it is harder to disbelieve — always. For in you and in all men there is a greatness which cannot be set aside and which is not beholden to reason's logic.

The truly learned man knows the rights of his own nature and that the instincts which plead for good as opposed to evil are scientifically trustworthy. He looks beyond mere phenomena to the master light which shines more or less in every breast.

Sir Isaac Newton belonged to the first magnitude of intellectual strength, and when he closed his "Principia," which is one of the largest products of mental discipline in existence to-day, he offered a fervent and devout testimony to the living God. La Place, who wrote later, and with less distinction, commented upon Newton's testimony and said, "We have no need for this hypothesis." Now it was really an intellectual difference that separated these two thinkers, and the superior mind the more clearly perceived the spiritual dynamic which lies behind the stars in their courses. When you are tempted to unbelief because our clumsy mental organism does not furnish larger proof of these primary controllings, remember that nothing worth proving can be proven, nor can it be disproven.

> Thou can'st not prove the nameless, oh my son;
> Nor can'st thou prove the world thou livest in;
> Nor can'st thou prove that thou art body alone,
> Nor can'st thou prove that thou art spirit alone,
> Nor can'st thou prove that thou are both in one.

It is a mental achievement in the darkest hours of doubt to grip the worthful and wait and be wise, cleaving to the sunnier side of doubt when doubt must obtain, and ever clinging to faith beyond all forms of faith.

But the second word which I have linked with Courage is the word which seems to me to stand as its keeper. It is rendered in the authorized version of the Scriptures as "A sound mind," and better translated here as "Discipline." For next to the mischief inflicted by those who starve their conclusions to death, or hold them in reserve for the sake of self-interest, is the mischief of ignorance, of the illiterate and the unthinking dispositions. These assume coarse and revolting shapes and recommend remedies almost worse than the disease. The superstitions of the vulgar and their gross formulæ are not so deadly as the soulless cynicism of the worldling or the empty mouthings of the hypocrite; but they have a paralysing poison of their own.

In an age of breadth, and we are found prating about breadth pretty constantly, there is apt to be a lack of depth; it is better to believe a few things with great tenacity than to maintain an extensive system simply for the sake of repetition or as a badge of accepted respectability. The unflinching self-expression and self-repression which created the potent individualism of the earlier Hebrews and the first Christians and the grim Puritans are not given to flourishing in a favored and luxurious atmosphere. The undisciplined man knows not what he sees and unwittingly cultivates illusion, failure and finally chagrin. He expects too much or too little from civilization, and when he is disappointed his criticisms are like himself, without measure and equally without weight. At intervals he cultivates a specious humanism, and then it is hard to restrain him from doing injustice and acting beyond the law, because he is tempted by his pseudo-benevolence. That he may pluck his cluster he will root up the vine, and the lawlessness which self-reverence, self-knowledge and self-control are set to obliterate finds its outlet in reckless speech and reckless conduct. There is no courage shown in marching when we ought to wait, and when waiting is best; and the lurid language which flames in headlines of the press is salient cowardice when the speaker should be silent because silence is best.

In brief, the disciplined man plays no tricks with fundamental righteousness at the call of the wild, for he realizes that such action cripples society and hurts the general weal. It is worth while to spurn delights and live laborious days in order to make as sure as we can of knowing the ways of truth and its application to our circumstances. And if this method has to bide its time and take its chances, do you seek it for yourself and live with it alone and be careless of all that seems to threaten it.

So those men believed who founded here a school of law and of the arts and sciences. In the foundation they made a concrete plea for minds and hearts molded and fashioned by the standards of an ancient discipline — ancient because it has ever been the characteristic of true mastery in the past of man or of his community life in the world. Without it there can be no living air for our civilization to breathe, and when I think of this America of ours upon whose happy shores the gifts of God have been lavished with peerless munificence, I protest to you that my one apprehension is lest we should be smothered beneath the weight of our panoply. The alert and sturdy athleticism of the soul which draws its virtue out of the heavenlies can alone preserve us from this doom, and I believe it will do so. For here is a nation with expansive territories and growing authority and strength at home and abroad, with soil most generous and mines of richest treasure, but best of all with a social and political history whose lawfulness and expediency have never been outdone. Of all societies since the Roman republic, England and America have been stronger and deeper and wider, and more successful than any other; and the one great reservoir of our national increase has been the growth of the power to govern ourselves, to look at actualities with honest eyes, with sobriety and with justice. We are not to be driven away from this capacity by denunciations which seek through exposure of our weakness to gain profit or satisfy ambition, and certainly we are not to yield to that spirit of pride which feeds on flattery and goes before a fall.

We shall reverence civilization's forces before its advantages and meet the issue in honor, in sincerity and in manliness.

A comprehensive view of the records shows that there has been a steady development in the right use of these wonderful resources, and men have come to larger aims and to wider fields of action because the ruling faculties have known justice as justice and have been more apt for common obedience to wise leadership and more given to the spirit of self-sacrifice for mutual welfare.   ,

The power which made the beginnings of our American civilization was not of earth. In that poor and persecuted band which cared so little for the things of time and sense, the Eternal One nourished thoughts of nobleness and types of men foreign to all save himself. His ideal of society was their pillar of cloud by day and of fire by night. They knew it was a reality, and though it baffled them they wrestled for its presence and would not let it go. So step by step America grew and came into greater place and meaning. Causes which were elsewhere flouted or obscured, were here uncovered and displayed. So came our competency, our moral colonization, our service as a race for the race. The fathers were once and you are now vicars of the invisible. You have the treasures of Power and of Love for administration; and just as Courage and Discipline lead to the triumph of civilization so do these two remaining forces support the progress and enhance the joy.

As an organized priesthood, with a knowledge of true expediency, you are asked to administer these forces through the medium of personality.

These words "Power" and "Love" are first and last moral in their significance, and both are spiritual because they are moral, and both are moral and spiritual because in a great nature, they are qualities which count. Any material embodiments of power or of love are a hint of the vast proportions they have in the universe, and what we may expect from them.

When the universe in its present known dimensions was first shown by modern knowledge man was confused by these eternities of space which seemed beyond his understanding; but the larger heavens into which the instruments of astronomy pierce are no longer habitations of dreadful mystery. The writ of the king, as known in laws of light and heat and gravitation, obtains in the Pleiades as it does on the earth. Our powers are reborn in the greatness of the whole of which we form a part, and our affections are reanimated when we consider what manner of love the Father hath toward his children, if such stupendous works are but the creation of his benevolent will.

Again, we are sustained in the vicarage of the Invisible because not only are we in these wonders,— they are in us; and they are infinitely great because our greatness conceives them such and needs them as they are. In the office that you occupy toward creation you have fellowship with its originator, and that fellowship is a privilege granted to none other. To accept this is to act under freedom, and to reject it is to remain under fate, for no man can properly estimate his ability to rule who has not taken into the scope of his research God's ideal for him and God's interest in him. You are significant because you are enfolded in the qualities of the everlasting God, and though you may resist the currents you never escape the sea of the Divine Being and the Divine Purpose.

Your office as a vicar of eternal power is simplified because the tokens of a common purpose which guides all things to " The Goal " are everywhere manifest. No greater discovery has belonged to the scientific religion or the inspired poetry of our age. Bulk and materialism have been subjected to spiritual laws and made obedient to moral ends. The very earth and stars palpitate with ethical purposes; and all power, the fragment you and I possess by our cleaving to the Invisible, as well as the inexpressible and authoritative force and activity beyond us, is building the soul and the habitation of the soul on a scale of proportionate extent.

When the apostle asserts that we are delivered over to this upward motion he would have you know that in your alliance with its proposals you have gained your dynamic. So argued the children of wisdom, and they acted upon the argument, and wisdom has been justified of her children.

Look forward then without undue anxiety to what awaits you beyond this university. You may find your place and work in the Senate or upon the judicial bench; you may live in the cloisters of the church and the academy; you may obtain great possessions in monetary fortune, and again you may know the compensations which enrich poverty, or the blessings which attend neither poverty nor riches. What matters it how these incidentals shape themselves if you are in touch with the Infinite. Rejoice in the all-pervasive truth that you are robed and girt of God for this vicarious office of your soul, and know that he that doeth the will of his heavenly Father abideth forever. Such a bond determines your personal value to all things in time and eternity.

The greatest word comes last, the word to which St. Paul pays tribute in his Corinthian Epistle, where he exalts Charity beyond all other gifts and faculties, and makes it the mother of virtues, the worker of the highest will, and the supreme evidence of the divine nature in men.

If we have known God as the name ineffable, standing for one of whose greatness it seems presumptuous to speak, and in whose presence silence is the truest worship, we have done well. But there is a further step into that knowledge. He who is love hath given us love for ourselves, and in this love we are assured that men are the vital products of his affection and the partakers of his nature.

The despotisms which hitherto harassed men are gone forever. For this is the Love which is possessed of all ethical qualities and is enriched by all social service. "If love," said Thackeray, "lives through all life and survives through all sorrow and remains steadfast to us through all changes, and in all darkness of spirit burns brightly, and if we die, deplores us forever, and exists with the very last gasp and throb of the faithful bosom, whence it passes with the pure soul beyond death," surely the force that interlocks all covenants and sustains all life and fosters all hope in sorrow; surely that force, that passion, that sublime source of our highest good, shall be immortal. If we love still those whom we lose, how can we ever lose those whom we love? For twenty centuries the constraint of this affection has been active and blessed. God's beauty, love, justice and truth have shone through Jesus upon society at large.

Thus Love shines on our path, not because it will, but because it is luminous; and in these latter days we are thinking differently about God and man, and the new thought is inculcating the new helpfulness, the care for others, the aid of the weak, the restoration of the fallen, the redemption of the criminal. The old savageries die hard, the hells we imagine and the hells we make, and which punish for punishment's sake, these linger and wait. But society has gone beyond the primitive half-emancipated man who sought to cure by terror and by the infliction of pain, and in sympathy and sacrifice will give the better self a chance, will stand in with the weakest struggler as a brother and not an outcast.

So I complete my task, a task which is indeed a privilege and a responsibility. For I have greatly desired to say some word here given me from that Holy Father above, so that on this, your day of crisis and decision and outlook, you may have reason for gratitude toward him and strength and resolve to serve him.

None shall persuade me that I have held too high a standard before you, or that the hopes of your professors and better still, the ambitions of your dearest ones, out-distance your resolves and your capacities. I am sanguine, and so are they, that love will yet obtain its own and enthrone you on the seats of the brave and the just. Be less careful for what awaits you than for what you become in yourself, and see in virtue's deathlessness the prophecy of your own immortality.

We do not so much covet those quiet Isles of the Blessed, where rest is the occupation, but we are keen for the strife for the right which makes any rewards a mere camping by the wayside until the fight is won and our nature is complete in the perfection of Courage, of Discipline, of Power and of Love.

INDEX